GROWTH WITHOUT MIRACLES

Growth Without Miracles

Readings on the Chinese Economy in the Era of Reform

Edited by
ROSS GARNAUT
YIPING HUANG

OXFORD
UNIVERSITY PRESS

OXFORD
UNIVERSITY PRESS

Great Clarendon Street, Oxford OX2 6DP

Oxford University Press is a department of the University of Oxford.
It furthers the University's objective of excellence in research, scholarship,
and education by publishing worldwide in

Oxford New York

Athens Auckland Bangkok Bogotá Buenos Aires Cape Town
Chennai Dar es Salaam Delhi Florence Hong Kong Istanbul Karachi
Kolkata Kuala Lumpur Madrid Melbourne Mexico City Mumbai Nairobi
Paris São Paulo Shanghai Singapore Taipei Tokyo Toronto Warsaw

with associated companies in Berlin Ibadan

Oxford is a registered trade mark of Oxford University Press
in the UK and in certain other countries

Published in the United States
by Oxford University Press Inc., New York

Selection and editorial material © R. G. Garnaut and Y. Huang 2001

British Library Cataloguing in Publication Data

Data available

Library of Congress Cataloging in Publication Data

Growth without miracles: readings on the Chinese economy in the era of reform /
edited by Ross Garnaut and Yiping Huang.
p. cm.
Includes bibliographical references.
1. China—Economic conditions—1976– 2. China—Economic policy—1976–
3. Government ownership—China. 4. Capitalism—China. I. Garnaut, Ross.
II. Huang, Yiping, 1964–
HC427.92 .G76 2000   338.951—dc21   00-069295
ISBN 0–19–924060–4 (hbk.)
ISBN 0–19–924059–0 (pbk.)

10 9 8 7 6 5 4 3 2 1

Printed in Great Britain
on acid-free paper by
T.J. International Ltd.,
Padstow, Cornwall

Contents

Agricultural Policy

Rural Industrialisation

Enterprise Reform and Industrial Development

Factor Markets and Income

Contributors

William Byrd
The World Bank, Washington, DC
Fang Cai
China Center for Economic Research, Peking University, Beijing
Chung Chang
Department of Finance, Carlson School of Management, University of Minnesota-Twin Cities, Minneapolis, Minnesota
Gregory C. Chow
Department of Economics, Princeton University, Princeton, New Jersey
Mark Elvin
Division of Pacific and Asian History, Research School of Pacific and Asian Studies, The Australian National University, Canberra
Christopher Findlay
Department of Economics, University of Adelaide, Adelaide
Ross Garnaut
The Australian National University, Canberra
Alan Gelb
The World Bank, Washington, DC
R.G. Gregory
Research School of Social Sciences, The Australian National University, Canberra
Theodore Groves
University of California, San Diego
Yongmiao Hong
Cornell University, New York
Yiping Huang
Research School of Pacific and Asian Studies and Asia Pacific School of Economics and Management, The Australian National University, Canberra
Gary H. Jefferson
Department of Economics, University of Pittsburgh
Hehui Jin
Department of Economics, Stanford University, California
E.L. Jones
Melbourne Business School, University of Melbourne
Nicholas R. Lardy
Foreign Policy Studies, Brookings Institute, Washington, DC
Zhou Li
Rural Development Institute, Chinese Academy of Social Sciences, Beijing
Justin Yifu Lin
China Center for Economic Research, Peking University, Beijing

Guonan Ma
Asia Pacific Economic Research, Salomon Brothers, Hong Kong
Xin Meng
Research School of Pacific and Asian Studies, The Australian National University, Canberra
John McMillan
University of California, San Diego
Barry Naughton
University of California, San Diego
John Knight
Institute of Economics and Statistics, University of Oxford, Oxford
Dwight Perkins
Harvard University, Cambridge, Massachusetts
Yingyi Qian
Department of Economics, Stanford University
Geoff Raby
Department of Foreign Affairs and Trade, Canberra
Thomas G. Rawski
Department of Economics, University of Pittsburgh
Carl Riskin
Columbia University
Jeffrey Sachs
Harvard University
Terry Sicular
Department of Economics, Social Science Centre, University of Western Ontario, London, Ontario
Ligang Song
Research School of Pacific and Asian Studies and Asia Pacific School of Economics and Management, The Australian National University, Canberra
Lina Song
Institute of Economics and Statistics, University of Oxford
Yijang Wang
Industrial Relations Center, Carlson School of Management, University of Minnesota-Twin Cities, Minneapolis
Andrew Watson
University of Adelaide
Lorraine A. West
Bureau of the Census, United States Department of Commerce
Christine P.W. Wong
Asian Development Bank, Manila
Wing Thye Woo
University of California at Davis
Yongzeng Yang
National Centre for Development Studies, The Australian National University, Canberra
Shahid Yusuf
Development Economics Research Group The World Bank, Washington, DC

Acronyms

ABC	Agricultural Bank of China
CASS	Chinese Academy of Social Sciences
CITIC	China International Trust and Investment Company
CMEA	Council for Mutual Economic Assistance (usually abbreviated as COMECON)
CPI	consumer price index
CRS	contract responsibility system
DI	Development Institute
EU	European Union
FOB	free on board
FSU	former Soviet Union
GATS	General Agreement of Trade and Services
GATT	General Agreement of Tariffs and Trade
GDP	gross domestic product
GOV	gross output value
GVA	gross value added
IDA	International Development Association
IE	Institute of Economics
MFA	Multifibre Arrangement
MFN	most-favoured nation
NIE	newly industrialising economy
OECD	Organisation for Economic Cooperation and Development
PC	producer cooperative
RCC	Rural Credit Cooperatives
RCRD	Research Centre for Rural Development
SOE	state-owned enterprise
SSB	State Statistical Bureau
TFP	total factor productivity
TRIM	Trade Related Investment Measure
TVCE	township and village community enterprises
TVE	township and village enterprises
TVG	town and village government
TVP	township, village and private enterprise
UNCTAD	United Nations Conference on Trade and Development
VAD	value-added deflator
WTO	World Trade Organization

Foreword

In December, 1987 the government of China embarked upon a program of economic reform and opening to the outside world. Within two decades, new policies were to transform its economic performance, with total output increasing four times, and the consumption standards of Chinese people rising rapidly. The economic transformation was associated with large changes in the domestic and international political face of China.

China's approach to reform of a centrally planned and inward-looking economy was different from that of any of the other socialist economies within the Marxist-Leninist-Stalinist tradition. The approach favoured gradual economic change, preceding fundamental change in the political superstructure. It was associated with the emergence of new economic institutions, which responded with exceptional strengths to the incentives provided by economic reform.

This book brings together important papers written over the reform period, which sought to explain internationally-oriented reform in China as it unfolded. Together they provide an authoritative perspective on the debates along the path of reform, and on the agenda for reform policy that remained unfinished at the end of the twentieth century.

The Editors are grateful to the authors who have agreed to publication of their work in this volume.

A number of papers are being made accessible to a wide readership for the first time. For the others, the Editors thank the publishers who have agreed to republication. They are especially grateful for the large effort in preparation of the volume from Asia Pacific Press at The Australian National University and to Maree Tait and Debra Grogan.

Ross Garnaut
Canberra
October 2000

Yiping Huang
Hong Kong
October 2000

1 Twenty Years of Economic Reform and Structural Change in the Chinese Economy

Ross Garnaut

On 22 December 1978, the Eleventh Central Committee of the Chinese Communist Party completed its third plenary meeting. There was no contemporary recognition in the West of the significance of the meeting.

The twentieth anniversary of the third plenum received far more attention. In the intervening years, China, and its relations with the international community, have been transformed. China's economy has expanded by five times, and its foreign trade by twelve. It has greatly increased consumption levels of what had been about half of the world's people in poverty. Then an isolated, autarchic economy, China through the mid and late 1980s absorbed about half of the direct foreign investment flows to developing economies. From having no trade or investment ties with Taiwan and the Republic of Korea, it is now the first or second export destination of one and the third of the other.

Even greater has been the transformation of the Chinese mind. Tens of millions of Chinese are now part of an international community of ideas and information. Personal security is provided significantly by the value of people's labour and produce in the market place, in the stead of an intrusive and overwhelming state. With the expanded role of the market has come a substantial widening in the sphere of personal freedom—to travel and communicate with others.

Changes of this dimension and at this extraordinary speed are unsettling, and potentially destabilising. Yet for all the disruption of change, and the many new problems that it has generated, most Chinese welcome the transformation. Certainly the large increase in living standards and the expanded sphere of personal freedom are appreciated enough to provide a base for continuity in political leadership and institutions despite the immense stress and dislocation.

Reform in China has not and could never have been a smooth or a painless process. There have been challenges at every step, some bumps in the road, detours, and dead ends. Reform faced its greatest danger in the traumatic aftermath of the Beijing massacre in May 1989 which compounded the risks of an inflationary boom and a major effort to bring it under control. The financial and economic crisis in neighbouring East Asian economies since 1997 is the great challenge of the late 1990s.

Reprinted with permission. Ross Garnaut, 1999. 'Twenty Years of Economic Reform and Structural Change in the Chinese Economy', in Ross Garnaut and Ligang Song (eds), 1999, *China: twenty years of reform*, Asia Pacific Press at the Australian National University, Canberra:1–26.

I. The Distance Travelled

Ideas and policy

Twenty years ago, Deng Xiaoping and his supporters took decisive control of the Central Committee of the Chinese Communist Party. This ended what Deng himself once described in my presence as two years of indecisive economic strategy and policy after the death of Mao Zedong. During those two years, policies embodying pragmatic acceptance of a large role for domestic and international market exchange were in continual contest with the Maoist commitments to local and national autarchy, central planning, state-owned enterprises in the cities and people's communes in the countryside.

Deng and his key supporters were victims of the Cultural Revolution, and the anarchy of that decade was their political launching pad. They were not in any sense political or economic liberals. Deng and his senior supporters had been the managers of the early periods of Communist Party success, in the 1950s before the Great Leap Forward, and in the brief interlude between the recognition of failure in that first lethal experiment in unworldly application of Maoist theory, and the anarchy of the second. They harked back to earlier success, when markets had been allowed to play substantial roles at least in the countryside, within a system in which central planning was supported by a firm administrative order.

The reformist leaders of December 1978 were aware that the world had changed from the earlier, naive days of partial success. They were aware of China's military vulnerability, as an economically weak and technologically backward society. They were deeply conscious that China shared the world's longest border with an apparently economically successful, technologically advanced and politically expansionist authoritarian state, the world's second military superpower. Some of them were aware as well that their rivals from the Chinese Civil War across the Taiwan Strait, their compatriots in colonial Hong Kong, and their cold war enemies in southern Korea were enjoying sustained economic success that raised deeply challenging questions about China's own continuing backwardness.

It was the strategic vulnerability that had caused and allowed Premier Zhou Enlai to champion the modernisation of industry, agriculture, science and technology and national defence in the early 1970s, after the armed clashes on the Heilongjiang. The intensification of the Sino-Soviet conflict, and the four modernisations, provided the context for diplomatic rapprochement with the United States, and for Deng Xiaoping's temporary rehabilitation as Vice Premier in the early 1970s. China's national policy lurched dangerously as competing ideas and political forces struggled over the tiller of state. The ultimate directions were settled by the People's Liberation Army's arrest of the 'Gang of Four' after the death of Mao, although policy continued to wobble until Deng Xiaoping's ascendancy in 1978.

Important steps were taken to lay a base for future growth in the period of indecisive policy. The awesome denial of formal education during the Cultural Revolution ended, with the return of competitive entry into the great universities in 1978. China's state enterprises experimented with the purchase of exotic new technologies from abroad. But there were cross-currents and counter-currents, continued ideological contests over high policy, and uncertainty as subordinate leaders watched for the emergence of a clear national direction.

Since December 1978 there has been no turning back.

It is not that Deng and his colleagues obtained endorsement for an elaborate, comprehensive new economic policy or plan. There was no blueprint for China's economic reform and internationalisation—even less than there had been in Taiwan and Korea at the beginnings of their sustained, rapid growth one and a half decades earlier.

But after the 1978 Plenum there was acceptance that domestic and international exchange through markets was a necessary and acceptable component of a national development strategy. There was pragmatic acceptance that institutions and policies that raised national economic output had a valid place in China—summed up in Deng's rehabilitation of an early Maoist exhortation to 'seek truth from facts'. These strands were drawn together in the 1987 Party Congress' acceptance of General Secretary Zhao Ziyang's definition of China as a backward country in the 'primary stage of socialism', in which the first national objective had to be the strengthening of the national economy.

The new political environment after 1978 saw foreign trade, direct foreign investment, and the utilisation of external technological cooperation and capital in all forms become acceptable components of national policy. Local experiments with new forms of organisation of agricultural production were legitimised, leading within a few years to the virtually complete replacement of the people's communes with the immensely more productive household responsibility system. Markets became important for exchange for the rapidly expanding agricultural output.

The absence of a comprehensive reform strategy, the eclecticism of economic policy and the gradualism of change have been criticised by foreign observers from time to time over the past two decades. But the absence of a blueprint was an inevitability of China's circumstances, and in practice a virtue.

It was an inevitability because there was no conceptual basis for a market-oriented economy. A few leaders, and a few intellectuals around the edges of policy, had absorbed some of the elements of internationally-oriented growth in Japan, Korea, Taiwan and Hong Kong. But the main understanding grew out of the new patterns of economic development themselves, through observations of the operation of markets within China, and increasing contact with foreign experience and ideas.

Nor was there an ideological basis in the early years for articulation of a model of development based on the operation of markets, deeply integrated into an international economy. Deng Xiaoping's political control of the Chinese Communist Party and the People's Liberation

Army was strong but not unconditional. It was built partly on others' confidence that he stood firmly for continued Communist Party political dominance, and commitment to some undefined minimum core of socialist principles and objectives.

The absence of a blueprint was a virtue because any theoretical model of reform of the centrally planned economy in China would have been deeply flawed. The rapid unwinding of a centrally planned economy, dominated by state enterprises in the cities and communes in the countryside, is fraught with risk of massive dislocation—a reality which was imperfectly understood before the unhappy later experience of Eastern Europe and the former Soviet Union. Some of the great strengths of the Chinese economy in the era of reform came as surprises to Chinese and foreign observers alike and would have been given an inadequate place in a program of reform built upon the received theory and experience of others. First amongst the surprises was the extraordinary dynamism of industrial production in the township and village enterprises that grew from the remnants of the disintegrating people's communes.

Deng Xiaoping used to describe economic reform in China as crossing the river by feeling for stones at each step. Hu Yaobang described reform to Australian Prime Minister Bob Hawke as an experiment without precedent. In the uncertain months following the dismissal of Hu Yaobang from his office of General Secretary of the Chinese Communist Party, Deng alluded uncharacteristically to the Chinese classics in a conversation with the Secretary General of Japan's Liberal Democratic party, Noboru Takeshita, and compared the path of reform to the mission of Guan Yu, who had had to cross five passes and cut down six generals to achieve his noble objective.[1]

These metaphors contain important insights. Chinese reform required transformations in ideology, in ideas about economic development and policy, in law and regulatory systems and in economic institutions. Above all, it required the accumulation of new knowledge and wisdom in a billion Chinese minds, as the Chinese people learned to do new things in an economic and social world that was fundamentally changed.

These transformations in ideology, ideas, policy, law, institutions, knowledge and experience occurred alongside each other, reinforcing each other. Each created problems for others when it ran into trouble itself.

It took great courage, and faith in some abstract and thinly formed ideas, for the Chinese collective leadership to wade into the river of reform. Courage and faith, and a clear view of the reality—that the maintenance of the *status quo* in centrally planned China in the aftermath of the Cultural Revolution meant continued backwardness, vulnerability and eventually instability in a rapidly developing East Asia and changing world.

Upon establishing his pre-eminence in the exercise of political power, Deng Xiaoping identified as his agents in the reform of the Party, and of the State and economy, Hu Yaobang and Zhao Ziyang. As General Secretary of the Communist Party, Hu led the task of replacing the huge cadre of beneficiaries of the Cultural Revolution with others able to lead and support reform. Zhao was the leader of the practical business of policy reform. Each made extraordinary contributions of leadership and intellect, managing change on a scale and at a pace that was rare in human experience. Each was informed by experience to the view that successful economic reform and development would require a widening of the scope for open discussion of policy, for dissent within the limits set by the imperatives of continued Communist Party rule, and for reform of the political system to make policy somewhat more open to pressures from the rapidly changing society beyond the central leadership. Deng eventually came to doubt the will or the capacity of each to secure and enforce the authority of the Chinese Communist Party, causing the dismissal of Hu in early 1987 after the Shanghai student demonstrations, and of Zhao, then Party General

Secretary, in the Party crisis over the management of the Beijing student demonstrations in May 1989.

The succession after the reform leadership crisis of 1987–89, selected by Deng Xiaoping and until his last years sustained by him, placed a higher premium on stability, and on defining and narrowing the boundaries of discussion of political system change. As it turned out, economic reform and change had its own momentum, that carried along continued social and political change in the local sphere. Li Peng's decade-long Premiership, and the Jiang Zemin leadership of the Party, now approaching the completion of its tenth year, are remarkable for the stability and continuity that they reflect. This stability, in turn, reflected the wider leadership's consciousness of the risk of instability, especially in the period bridging the death of Deng Xiaoping. The emergence of a more activist, reformist Premier in 1998, Zhu Rongji, indicates a return to a sense of urgency in reform and structural change.

In the early years of reform, courage and faith, and a clear view of the futility of standing still, were required in leadership of all state institutions. In the great universities, ageing professors, often with pre-revolutionary experience of academic institutions in the West, were called from the disgrace of the Cultural Revolution to the massive and depressing replacement of half a generation lost to disciplined education. Some leaders of pre-revolutionary business who had opted to make their lives in the mainland, and who had mostly been rewarded by humiliation in the years before reform, accepted invitations to lead market-oriented new state businesses, as examples for the huge and cumbersome enterprises that had grown within the framework of central planning. Loyal servants of the state were called to new tasks for which their education and experience had provided no preparation at all.

In one of the boldest of early reform decisions, many tens of thousands of young people were sent or allowed abroad as students—to America, Australia, Japan, Europe and Hong Kong. They became windows of information and of change when they returned to live and work, or more commonly when they returned to visit or simply kept in touch with home.

The conceptual gap that had to be bridged in the course of reform was immense, extending into every corner of economic policy.

To take one corner, the idea that a country can maximise the value of its production and incomes through open trade, relying on imports for goods and services in which the economy has comparative disadvantage, is not intuitively obvious to Chinese any more than to other components of the human species. Even where the logic of comparative advantage is accepted by policymakers, its full reflection in policy is resisted by vested interests that expect to be damaged by it. In China, the usual resistances to specialisation according to comparative advantage were reinforced by the heavy emphasis on autarchy in Communist central planning, by the special Maoist exhortation to 'self reliance', and by the overlay of security concerns about dependence on foreign trade. Inside and outside China there were doubts about the capacity and willingness of the rest of the world to adjust to much higher levels of Chinese exports.

The acceptance of the idea that there are gains in specialisation according to comparative advantage came slowly. Each major sector of the economy became a battleground over acceptance of the concept. The idea gained enough ground for policy change to allow the beginnings of rapid expansion of labour-intensive manufactures balanced by rapid growth in imports of a range of capital-intensive and technologically sophisticated manufactured goods, and of industrial raw materials. The gains from trade then made their own eloquent case for going further. An important milestone was General Secretary Zhao Ziyang's articulation of a coastal economic strategy in early 1988, under which coastal China would expand its export-oriented manufactured export base, building on its relative abundance of labour, and drawing raw materials from international markets.

Resistance to liberalisation remains strong in some sectors, nowhere more so than in grain. But even in grain, the objective has recently been stated by the Ministry of Agriculture as 95 per cent, rather than complete, self-sufficiency. The difference would represent about 10 per cent of world trade in grain.

Reform was constrained by the legacy of Chinese Communist Party ideology—specifically, the elements of ideology associated variously with Marx, Lenin, Stalin, and Mao. The ideological legacy of Mao turned out to be the least constraining for economic reform, once the Party had delivered its verdict that Mao was 70 per cent right and 30 per cent wrong. The 70 per cent was the contribution of the early Mao to building the supremacy of the Communist Party, a strong Chinese state, and the early policy which had been developed with the cooperation of Deng Xiaoping and the other, older leaders of the reform period. The excesses of the Great Leap Forward and the Cultural Revolution comprised much of the 30 per cent, including the elevation of ideological purity above the requirements of economic development. On the legacy of Marx, the theoretical distance of classical Marxism from the practical decisions of state, and its denial of the possibility of socialism in a backward country, weakened the constraint that it placed on reform. Some intellectual gymnastics were required in the mid 1980s to render the operation of a labour market consistent with the labour theory of value. What then remained was a commitment to avoid the extremes of income inequality that the Chinese leadership associated with capitalist developing countries, and a view that the state should continue to own the largest enterprises in key economic sectors. The Leninist legacy of firm Communist Party control through 'democratic centralism' remained a cardinal principle of Deng Xiaoping, has not been successfully challenged and remains a premise of the current leadership. The Stalinist legacy of central planning has had little continuing ideological resonance, at least in the 1990s.

Beyond ideology and policy, there have been immense problems of a highly practical kind, especially in reforming the system of central planning. The practical challenge was how to build the regulatory system, the institutions and the human knowledge and skills to implement reform policy and to make the partially reformed system work. Amongst the most difficult has been the building of an institutional framework to implement monetary and therefore macro-economic stabilisation indirectly, as is necessary in a market economy. Through the first one and half decades of reform, weaknesses in this area had generated a cycle in growth, inflationary and balance of payments pressure that seemed to be widening over time (Garnaut and Ma 1993a). The apparent 'soft landing' after the inflationary boom of 1993–95 is suggestive of progress, although the role that continued to be played by costly direct controls on investment during this episode qualifies the success. By the mid 1990s it was clear to the government that sustained stable growth required the completion of the reform of state-owned enterprises, allowing, finally, enforcement of hard budget constraints. The 1997 Party Congress and 1998 National People's Congress laid a base for rapid progress, which has as yet been only partially utilised.

At the end of the 1990s, the practical problems centred on the threat of contagion from the East Asian crisis. This was—and indeed still is—a massive challenge, threatening stability and growth.

The larger perspective is that the reform and internationalisation of the Chinese economy is an undertaking of such immense dimensions, and unusual character, that it is inevitably challenged in ways that are potentially dangerous to its successful conclusion. The contemporary challenge is dangerous, but not especially large compared with the passes that have already been crossed, and in particular the barriers of ideology, ideas, policy, institutions and practical difficulties that faced the reformers at the beginning.

Economic change

China's real economy expanded strongly with reform. Over these two decades, China has emerged as the most dynamic large player in the world economy. Growth in output and in external economic relations has been as rapid in China as in any of the East Asian economies in their own periods of strongest growth, although China happens to have been excluded from the World Bank's ill-fated *East Asian Miracle* (World Bank 1993).

Figures 1 to 7 summarise the story of growth and structural change in output and foreign economic relations in a series of charts, taken from the standard data accepted and published by the international agencies.

Can we believe the statistics? This question was asked with more urgency as China claimed success in maintaining growth near 8 per cent through the East Asian crisis in 1998.

The external trade and investment data are broadly confirmed from other countries' records of the same transactions. The main questions focus on the domestic output data.

There are some conceptual problems with the conventions of the standard national accounts. They measure increases in stocks as valuable production, even when the discounted present value of future sales is low. This is not only a problem in China—it arises in advanced market economies in recession. But it is a larger problem when stocks held by government-supported state enterprises are rising rapidly. There are problems of valuing non-marketed services in all economies, and a larger problem in economies like China where this sector is large, leading to underestimation of the level, although not necessarily the growth, in output. In all economies there are problems in bringing natural resource depletion and environmental degradation or enhancement to account in assessment of the growth of valuable economic output, and this is especially important in low income developing economies experiencing rapid industrialisation.

The professional quality of China's statistical collections has improved greatly since the early years of reform. Nevertheless, there are continuing problems in China beyond those that are present in all national accounts. One is a difficulty in valuing output, especially in the township and village enterprises. The weight of informed professional opinion suggests that this may lead to over-estimation of real growth on average by up to 2.5 per cent per annum over the reform period. For example, Maddison (1998) measures the over-estimation at 2.4 per cent or 0.1 per cent, depending on the sectoral weights that are applied. The Maddison logic suggests that the over-estimation would be less important at times of low-inflation, such as the present.

There is a difficulty in reconciling reported data on levels of output over time with reported growth rates, and observed levels of consumption, use and trade in a wide variety of commodities in China and in other developing economies. Garnaut and Ma (1993b) examined this issue and concluded that the standard national accounts, converted into foreign currencies at official exchange rates, undervalued Chinese output relative to other developing economies with low and middle incomes by a factor of three. The large real appreciation of the renminbi since early 1994 and especially through the East Asian crisis would have reduced the relative overvaluation substantially.

The overall story is that, leaving aside the general conceptual problems of the national accounts in all countries, the Chinese data substantially understate the size and average incomes of the Chinese economy, moderately overstate output growth rates, and give a reasonable picture of the scale and growth of China's interaction with the international economy.

There is a separate issue concerning the relationship between GDP as measured in the national accounts, and the purchasing power of GDP. The standard national accounts data

Figure 1   **Proportionate increase in real output, 1978–98** (per cent)

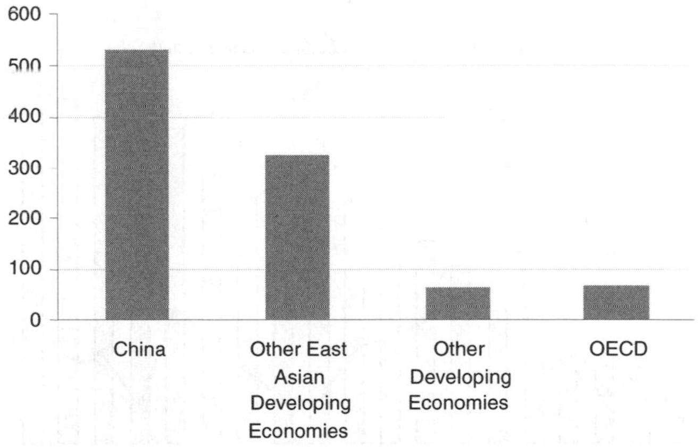

Sources: Author's calculations based on data compiled from World Bank, 1997. *World Development Indicators*, World Bank Publications, Philadelphia [CD-ROM]; International Monetary Fund, (various years). *World Economic Outlook* (various issues), International Monetary Fund, Washington, DC; International Economic Databank, The Australian National University, Canberra.

Figure 2   **Structural changes in China, 1978–97** (industrial output by ownership, per cent of total, total = 100)

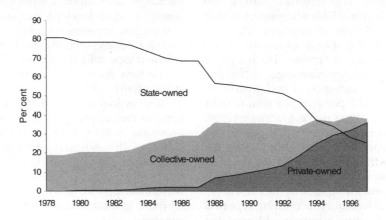

Source: State Statistical Bureau, (various years). *Statistical Yearbook of China*, China Statistical Publishing House, Beijing.

Figure 3   **Employment in township and village enterprises, 1978–97**

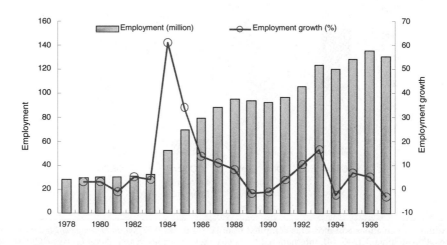

Source: State Statistical Bureau, (various years). *Statistical Yearbook of China*, China Statistical Publishing House, Beijing.

underestimate the purchasing power of lower relative to higher income countries. This simply reflects the lower valuation in the national accounts of labour and non-tradable goods and services in a low-income economy.

This is the reason why China looms much larger in the 'purchasing power parity' estimates of economic size, than it does in the national accounts data. The difference in relative incomes and size resulting from this influence alone is typically a factor of two or three in low income countries. This relative undervaluation of the volume of goods and services produced in low income countries disappears as labour becomes more valuable in the course of economic development. The phasing out of the relative undervaluation explains a general tendency for rapidly growing developing economies to catch up with the world economic frontiers more rapidly than the initial income differences and the growth rate differentials would suggest.

II. China and the East Asian Crisis

China's growth and structural change in the reform era has had much in common with other East Asian economies at corresponding periods of their own development. This was once a comfort, when there was none amongst the East Asian economies that had grown fast enough to double output in a single decade, that had failed to sustain strong growth until they had been lifted to the frontiers of world productivity and average incomes. Growth slowed in Japan from the mid 1970s, and in Hong Kong and Taiwan in the 1990s, but only after these economies' average incomes had entered the range of advanced industrial economies.

Now the question is being asked, whether the crisis in the economies of many of China's neighbours suggests that China can be expected to enter a period of economic instability and slower growth.

Figure 4   Exports of large developing countries and Australia, 1978–98 (US$billion)

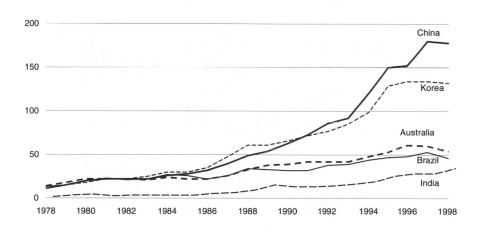

Source: Author's calculations based on data compiled from United Nations COMTRADE database, International Economic Databank, The Australian National University, Canberra.

Figure 5   **Proportionate growth of exports (constant prices), 1978–98** (per cent)

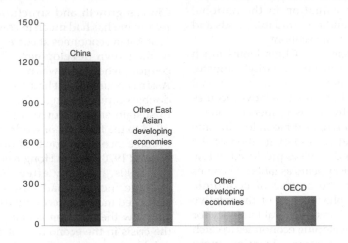

Source: Author's calculations based on data compiled from United Nations COMTRADE database, International Economic Databank, The Australian National University, Canberra.

Figure 6   **China: changes in composition of exports, 1978–96** (per cent)

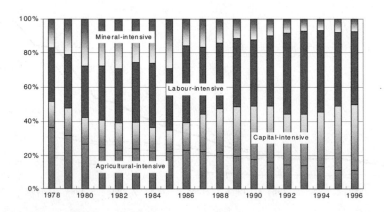

Source: Author's calculations based on data compiled from United Nations COMTRADE database, International Economic Databank, The Australian National University, Canberra.

Figure 7   **Developing economy shares of world trade in labour-intensive manufactures, 1978–96** (per cent)

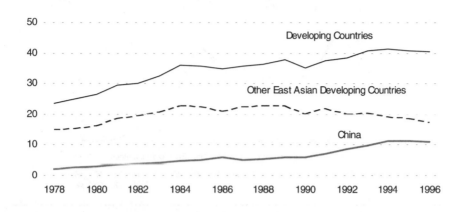

Source: Author's calculations based on data compiled from United Nations COMTRADE database, International Economic Databank, The Australian National University, Canberra.

Certainly the East Asian crisis is the greatest external challenge of the past twenty years to stability and growth in China. So far China has had a relatively good crisis, sustaining growth at high levels (although down on the twenty-year average) in the second half of 1998 through massive fiscal expansion, and winning much international kudos for this and for holding the pre-crisis US dollar value of the renminbi.

At the time of the twentieth anniversary of reform, and still in early 1999, a view was emanating from the foreign community in Beijing and the business community in Hong Kong that China had not really done so well through the crisis, or that it would run into deep trouble in the near future. This view had its origin in incredulity that China, with structural flaws in its financial system as large as any in the region, could avoid the problems that had defeated apparently stronger economies.

The East Asian crisis has certainly been a large blow for mainland China. The East Asian economies that are currently in recession, including China's Northeast Asian neighbours,

Korea, Hong Kong and Japan, account for half China's exports and three-quarters of its direct foreign investment. The East Asian orientation of China's trade and investment was an advantage when the rest of the region was growing strongly. In 1998 it was a large drag on performance, with East Asian imports from the world as a whole declining by 17.3 per cent in 1998 (Figure 8).

In these circumstances, even if China held its share in total imports of other East Asian economies—not an easy task given the heightened competitiveness of others—it would have to expand exports beyond East Asia well above 30 per cent per annum if total exports were to continue to grow at a rate near the average of the reform period. This is simply impractical, if only because of the protectionist response it would generate. In fact, China's export growth slumped through 1998, going strongly and at first sight dangerously into negative territory from October (Figure 9). At the same time, the weak real exchange rates of other East Asian economies through the crisis reduced pressure and capacity for direct foreign investment, including to China.

11

Figure 8   **Growth in East Asian imports, 1985–98** (per cent per annum)

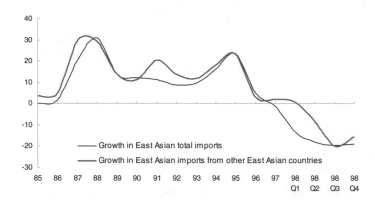

Note: Quarterly data represent change on corresponding period of previous year.
Source: Author's calculations based on data collected from International Monetary Fund, (various years). *Direction of Trade*, International Monetary Fund and International Bank for Reconstruction and Development, Washington; China, (various years). *China Monthly Statistics*, China Statistical Information and Consultancy Service Centre, Peiching; various country sources.

China stood up well to the East Asian crisis, at least through its first year and a half, because its macroeconomic fundamentals were strong at the onset of crisis. Inflation was low in response to the corrective policies applied mid-decade. The current account of the balance of payments, and export momentum were strong. A recent history of high levels of direct foreign investment and reform was generating considerable productivity growth in the export industries. High levels of capital inflow were mainly in the form of direct foreign investment, with controls on capital movement inhibiting inflows of speculative portfolio capital. Foreign exchange reserves were high—second only to Japan in global terms—and rising.

These strengths at the onset of the crisis allowed China to implement a massive fiscal expansion to offset the recessionary impulses from the external sector. This was cutting in powerfully from the third quarter of 1998.

China chose early in the crisis to maintain the US dollar value of the renminbi, at least

through 1998, and perhaps indefinitely. In late 1999, leaders of the government and of the People's Bank of China stated firmly that China intends to maintain the rate at least through 1999.

The motive of the exchange rate policy was primarily domestic: to avoid the inflation and pressure on financial and other businesses that had accompanied massive depreciation elsewhere in East Asia. The maintenance of growth and the old exchange rate parity reduced the pressure on the weak financial system. China's policy of maintaining the exchange rate and supporting growth with fiscal expansion was favourable to eventual stabilisation and recovery elsewhere in the region. China's imports from other East Asian economies held up reasonably well through 1998 (Figure 10). Favourable international feedback encouraged China to persist with the policy.

Can this approach be maintained? Or does the sharp downturn in exports from October 1998 portend an eventual depreciation, abandonment of fiscal expansion, and recession, with the contraction of the economy being intensified greatly by these factors' interactions with a chronically weak financial system?

China could not sustain for many years fiscal deficits on the scale of 1998 and that proposed for 1999. Nor could it sustain indefinitely an appreciation of its real effective exchange rate on the scale of early 1998, against its East Asian trading partners and competitors. This was the reason for its pressure on Japan when the yen was at its weakest point in mid 1998. Eventually the unmanageably large decline in competitiveness can be corrected by declining costs and prices in China, inflation in other countries, faster productivity growth in China than in trading partners and competitors, and by recovery in the economies and re-appreciation in the exchange rates of other East Asian countries.

There are recent signs of favourable movement in several of these parameters. Figure 11 sets out the data for China's average real exchange rate.

Financial markets in the East Asian economies in recession have been stronger since late September 1998. This in itself takes pressure from the Chinese exchange rate and economy, and indicates expectations of recovery in at least some economies. So long as these expectations come to be realised in 1999, China will be able to hold on to its late 1998 strategy.

That is not to say that the weakness of China's financial institutions can be seen as anything other than major potential threats to growth, requiring firm correction. This problem is less urgent in China because the state stands unequivocally behind the banks that it owns, turning a potential financial crisis into a potential budget problem. The Chinese fiscal system currently seems able to handle the load in the immediate future, but not indefinitely.

The Chinese authorities have learned the main lesson of the East Asian crisis—that the strengthening of the regulatory and institutional framework of the banking system is of high national importance and that in China this requires early completion of the reform of state-owned enterprises. They have learned another

lesson as well—that free capital flows carry risks, and that capital convertibility should be placed on hold. This in itself may not impose large costs, but it will do so if capital controls reduce the urgency that is applied to financial sector reforms.

While the exchange rate and fiscal policy responses to the crisis have so far been well judged, the exchange rate may not and the fiscal expansion will not be sustainable much beyond 1999. So 1999 is a window, through which there is a chance to undertake much of the analytic work and some of the policy action in the financial sector that is necessary to support growth into the long-term future.

Already some of the policy actions taken in support of the fixed exchange rate are damaging to growth, including the restoration of much of the earlier large role of state enterprises in grain marketing and price management, and the tolerance of price-fixing cartels to resist falls in prices in a number of sectors in which state-owned enterprises play important producer roles.

One of the objectives of contemporary work on financial reform would be to build the institutions that are necessary smoothly to replace the pegged exchange rate with a floating rate regime. In the first six months of the East Asian crisis there was upward pressure on the foreign exchange value of the renminbi, with foreign exchange reserves rising. The pressure is now strongly downward, with large speculative outflows of capital despite the capital controls. The current downward pressure may intensify, becoming a large problem for domestic economic performance. To move the peg downwards by a discrete amount in response to any such development would risk misjudgment and the intensification of uncertainty.

The best course now would be to let it be known that the authorities were working on the institutional reform that was necessary for a floating exchange rate to be successful. The authorities could then credibly state that the next move in the exchange rate against the US dollar would be a float, and not a discrete devaluation. The authorities could provide assurances that the

Figure 9   **Growth in China's exports, 1985–98** (per cent)

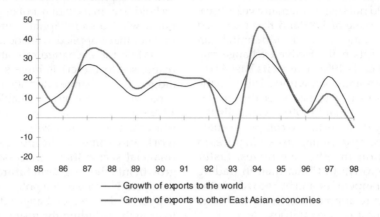

———— Growth of exports to the world
———— Growth of exports to other East Asian economies

Source: Author's calculations based on data collected from State Statistical Bureau, (various years). *Statistical Yearbook of China*, China Statistical Publishing House, Beijing; China, (various years). *China Monthly Statistics*, China Statistical Information and Consultancy Service Centre, Peiching; International Monetary Fund, (various years). *International Financial Statistics*, International Monetary Fund, Washington; various country sources.

Figure 10 **Growth in China's imports, 1985–98** (per cent per annum)

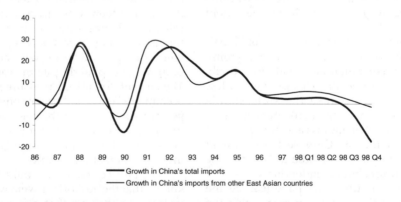

———— Growth in China's total imports
———— Growth in China's imports from other East Asian countries

Note: Quarterly data represent change on corresponding period of previous year.
Source: Author's calculations based on data collected from International Monetary Fund, (various years). *Direction of Trade*, International Monetary Fund and International Bank for Reconstruction and Development, Washington; China, (various years). *China Monthly Statistics*, China Statistical Information and Consultancy Service Centre, Peiching.

Figure 11 **China in the East Asian crisis, competitiveness index, 1990=100**

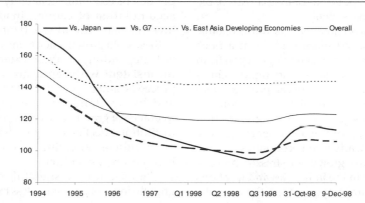

Note: The competitiveness index is a trade share weighted average real exchange rate. It is calculated based on the following formula

$$RER_t^i = \sum_j^n \alpha_{ijt} \left(\frac{e_t^i}{e_t^j}\right)_{index} \bullet \left(\frac{P_t^j}{P_t^i}\right)$$

where RER_t^i denotes country i's real exchange rate at time t, superscripts j denotes trade partner country, α_{ijt} stands for the share of country i's exports to country j in country i's total exports at time t. e_t is country i or j's nominal exchange rate against US$ at time t. P_t is country i or j's consumer price index at time t. The ratio of nominal exchange rate between country i and j is indexed (1990=100) in order to remove the effects of difference in currency units.
Source: Data for trade shares are collected from *Direction of Trade*, International Monetary Fund (IMF). Data for nominal exchange rate and consumer price index are collected from *International Financial Statistics* (IMF) and various country sources; Asia Pacific Economics Group, 1998. *Asia Pacific Profiles 1998*, FT (Asia Pacific), Singapore.

next move would not take place in 1999, and may not take place soon after. The market would be asked to judge upon both the direction and the extent of any change in parity. A mechanism would be on hand to allow flexibility without loss of policy credibility should circumstances over the next few years require it.

III. Where Is Growth Going and When Will It End?

The experience of East Asia in the past half century, and of China in the two decades of reform, tells us that sustained, rapid economic growth is no 'miracle'. Rather, it is a normal part of the human condition in a poor country, which

meets a number of conditions for growth.

Rapid economic growth in the postwar East Asian style is a process of catching up with the world's advanced economies, from a low base. It involves catching up technologically, by drawing on the knowledge and techniques of advanced economies through a range of mechanisms. It involves catching up in the amount of capital available for each worker to use, through high savings and investment and through the use of foreign capital. Accumulation of human capital through education and experience is important to the process. Economic growth involves the allocation of capital and labour to more and more productive uses, through the use of markets at home and open trade that allows international specialisation in line with comparative advantage as it changes over time. All of these conditions require economic policy to deliver a reasonable degree of economic stability.

When the policy conditions allow it, economic growth can proceed more rapidly in a poor country, because a wider technological gap from the world's frontiers allows more rapid technological improvement. Growth can proceed more rapidly in a densely populated poor country because the gains from trade are greater in a country whose resource endowments are very different from the advanced economies.

Rapid economic growth is a stressful process. It forces changes in the industries and locations in which people are employed and the way jobs are done. It churns and re-orders economic and political élites. It can destabilise the political order that is responsible for the policies that sustain it unless the political order itself evolves with the economic structure. At the same time, the capacity to support rising living standards that are generated by economic growth is a salve to the stress of structural change if its benefits are distributed widely. The dispersion of the distribution itself is affected by some factors that are beyond the control of governments. Importantly, a wide distribution of the benefits of internationally-oriented economic growth is facilitated in a densely populated country in which employment and labour incomes grow exceptionally as it opens to foreign trade. This helps China, as it helped other East Asian economies before it. But China's size, poor internal transport and communications, and wide variation in the natural and human resource base for development increase the challenge of maintaining an acceptably broad distribution of the benefits of growth. Acceptable dispersion of the gains from growth in China, more so than in other East Asian economies, is therefore significantly reliant on sound policy choice.

Perfect policy is not a necessary condition for rapid economic growth to proceed. Protectionist policies that reduce the gains from trade, market imperfections that keep some resources in relatively unproductive uses, periods of economic instability that inhibit the accumulation of capital, inadequate public investment in education and infrastructure—all of these hold growth back from attainable levels, but, depending on their extent, may not be inconsistent with rapid growth. As growth proceeds, and the frontiers of world technology and living standards are approached, the tolerance of growth to weaknesses in policy and institutions declines. In particular, the costs of poor policies affecting income distribution become larger over time.

Because it is so stressful, rapid economic growth does not proceed unless the view is widely held in society that it is a prime objective. Growth attained this status in 1978 in China, and has retained it since.

Rapid growth is easier to sustain than to initiate. Rising incomes are more effective in allaying doubts and allaying resistance to change when they are a current reality rather than a hope and a promise. Savings rates rise with rapid growth, supporting the growth process.

Nevertheless, the old as well as the new experience of East Asia, and the older experience of industrialisation in the West, tell us that growth and modernisation do not proceed in logarithmic straight lines. There is a strong tendency for them to proceed until the world's economic frontiers are reached, but they can be broken temporarily or permanently by adverse developments of several kinds. Booms and manias, followed by economic collapse, are ever-present risks of market economies and sometimes result in major lurches in policy that block a return to growth. Poor policy—resulting from professional weakness or political manifestations of resistance to change—can block the continual re-allocation of resources to more productive uses. A failure of the political institutions to adjust to the changing structure and aspirations of the community can undermine social and political cohesion around the objective of growth.

Any one of these risks could emerge to block China's modernisation and continued growth.

It is not likely that these risks will crystallise in China into a collapse of growth as in the East Asian crisis, for reasons that I have already set out. But there will be plenty of other risks and challenges, some arising when China is less well placed to handle them than in 1997.

There is another possibility, that is more closely consistent with the experience of the past twenty years. Within this prospect, ideas about policy, policy itself, institutions, and the knowledge of Chinese people, evolve with the experience of rapid growth, in ways which sustain it. The rapid growth which has been concentrated amongst a few hundred million people in the coastal provinces, spreads inland, as regulatory and infrastuctural barriers to internal trade are removed. It is unlikely, and at odds with the experience of others, that there would be no setback to rapid growth—no recessionary end to a market mania, no large misjudgment of macroeconomic policy, no failure of leadership nerve or judgment on continued market reform. But is it possible that for a long period ahead, as in these past twenty years, the realisation of the national and personal benefits of growth, and awareness of the conditions that sustain it, will be sufficiently widespread and strong to return China to a growth path whenever it is temporarily knocked from it?

Within this prospect, which the experience of the reform period suggests is more likely than not, the average growth of the last two decades will be sustained for several decades more. Output will double each decade. In another two decades, China will be the world's second largest economy by conventional national accounts measures in output and foreign trade, or third if the European Union by then is seen as a single entity. By the end of these two decades, the dynamic coastal provinces—several hundred million people—will enjoy living standards broadly at the level of Taiwan today.

Economic growth can always end with political convulsion that removes the primacy of the growth objective. This would become a greater risk in China if policy were ineffective in allowing the spread of economic growth into the vast inland. This is an avoidable outcome, with awareness of the issue and good policy.

Economic growth in China will not end in global famine, as has been contended famously. Global markets can handle the growing demand for food that rising incomes in China would generate.

It will not end in national environmental catastrophe. Rising incomes are bringing both the will and the capacity to do something about the environmental degeneration that has been associated with urbanisation and industrialisation in China. China's sustained, rapid growth raises larger, global environmental issues, but not just for China.

In two decades, China will face a huge challenge of demographic transition, when the one child family is entering middle age and the number of young workers is shrinking sharply. This will be much on the minds of leaders if there is a 19th Party Congress in 2018, as a threat to the longer term dynamism of Chinese society and economy.

But two decades hence would be an unlikely place for the growth process that began with reform to end. The modernisation of the vast inland of China will be in its early years. It is more likely that Chinese society, aware as never before of the pain and costs of growth, will choose to push ahead. It will be a natural and in no way a miraculous outcome if the growth of China's past two decades continues until most of China's people enjoy living standards and productivity levels close to those in the world's most advanced economies.

Acknowledgements

I am grateful to Xu Xinpeng for assisting me in putting together the statistical material for this chapter, and to Song Ligang for helpful comments on an earlier draft. This paper was delivered to the Australian China Business Council, Melbourne, 25 November 1998.

Note

1. When Takeshita visited the Australian National University in November 1998, I reminded him of the 1987 conversation, reported at the time in the Chinese press. He remembered it more for Deng Xiaoping's imprecision in the numbers and details of economic policy than for his classical allusion!

References

Asia Pacific Economics Group, 1998. *Asia Pacific Profiles 1998*, FT (Asia Pacific), Singapore.

China, (various years). *China Monthly Statistics*, China Statistical Information and Consultancy Service Centre, Peiching.

Garnaut, R. and Ma, G., 1993a. 'Economic growth and stability in China', *Journal of Asian Economics*, 4(1):5–24.

——, 1993b. 'How rich is China: evidence from the food economy', *Australian Journal of Chinese Affairs*, 30:121–48.

International Monetary Fund, (various years). *World Economic Outlook*, International Monetary Fund, Washington, DC.

——, (various years). *Balance of Payments Statistics*, International Monetary Fund, Washington, DC.

——, (various years). *Direction of Trade*, International Monetary Fund and International Bank for Reconstruction and Development, Washington, DC.

Maddison, A., 1998. *Chinese Economic Performance in the Long Run*, OECD Development Centre, Paris.

State Statistical Bureau, (various years). *Statistical Yearbook of China*, China Statistical Publishing House, Beijing.

World Bank, 1993. *The East Asian miracle: economic growth and public policy*, World Bank Policy Research Report series, Oxford University Press, New York.

——, 1997. *World Development Indicators*, World Bank Publications, Philadelphia [CD-ROM].

2 The 'Neither This Nor That' Economy

Geoff Raby[1]

The mixture of half-plan, half-market; neither-plan, nor market; pretend-socialism, pretend-capitalism, with ill-defined borders between legality and illegality; socialist moral codes and principles of market efficiency; neither this nor that; half this, half that; in short a condition of 'market socialism', the NEM [New Economic Mechanism], or 'socialism with Chinese characteristics', is an unstable condition—economically and ethically. Sooner or later (probably sooner) either plan and centralised social property, or market and private property must prevail and dominate the system (Prybyla 1986:43–4).

It is now well over decade since Prybyla argued so forcefully that China's 'neither this nor that' economic system was inherently unstable, and two decades since the process of economic reform was set in train, yet China's system of confusion persists. The economy has continued to go from strength to strength; throughout much of the 1990s it was the fastest growing economy in the world. Foreign trade flourished and the external payments position is strong for a poor country. Foreign investment flooded back after a hiatus following June 1989, reaching levels never approached before for a developing economy. Per capita incomes grew apace and the range and quality of goods in the shops increased at an explosive rate.

More intriguingly, the system has become even weirder in Prybyla's terms, more unlike any other system—whether contemporary or historical. On an international comparison, the non-state industrial sector is big and important in its own right. Moreover, it is the fastest growing industrial sector in the world. When the share of output outside the industrial sector is included, the market accounts for over 50 per cent of China's total output. In the littoral provinces, the expansion of a market economy has gone much further than national indicators reveal. Within China today, by world standards a very large economy operates in response to market signals. This economy did not exist when reform began in the late 1970s.

The creation of a market economy the size of China's non-state sector must rate as a major event in recent world economic history. While the contribution to world resource allocation and efficiency of the return of one prodigal son compared with another cannot readily be established, the creation of the non-plan sector in China is probably worth at least as much as those of East Germany, Poland, and probably Hungary and Romania combined. Yet, at the end of communism, the 'this' or 'that' of the Chinese system, as Prybyla suggests, should not exist. By now, one or the other should have been pushed out.

The conventional wisdom as represented by Prybyla is based on the rather narrow view that markets can only operate within the specific institutional setting of private property. At a time when systems based on collectivist institutions have collapsed around the world, and when fellow travellers have disavowed their past companions on ideological journeys, it is distinctly uncomfortable and out of step to be raising questions about the universal applicability of institutions such as private property rights. Nevertheless, there is in China a big and rapidly growing market economy with private ownership consigned to the margins.

I. Process of Reform

The 'neither this nor that' economy has been the result of the unique process of economic reform in China. The process has had two distinct features which mark out the Chinese reform experience from that of any other Stalinist economy.

First has been the incremental approach adopted by the political leadership. There may be several reasons for this

- a fine balance at the political centre between those seeking rapid tranformation and those wishing to restrain the process
- a generally cautious approach to policymaking etched into the collective consciousness of the leadership by the catastrophes of the Great Leap Forward and the Cultural Revolution
- the fact that rapid and sustained big gains in output and productivity have been achieved despite having followed a risk-averse strategy.

Importantly, public policy has incrementally accommodated pressures on the frontiers of reform. The process looks more like one of reform from below, rather than reform from above as in Russia and some other parts of Eastern Europe.

Second has been the extension of markets while placing narrow limits on private property rights. Markets have been permitted to expand to create a second economy alongside, but increasingly integrated with, the state-owned planned sector of the economy (Garnaut and Liu 1991:20). In the early years of reform, the process seemed more like the extension of the market by stealth. The dynamism of production outside the plan, especially in the dynamic rural and township enterprise sector, led to the continual growth in the share of output produced in the market economy. Integration into the international economy added further pressure for expansion of the market both by the influence of international prices on the traded goods sector and exposure to the methods of markets and market systems. The interests of provincial governments, especially those in coastal areas, have also come to be increasingly identified with the expansion of markets.

China has sustained forward momentum in economic reform since 1978. The aggregate effect of these incremental economic reforms has been the systemic transformation of the Chinese economy. More than any other system since the inception of modern central planning by Stalin in the late 1920s, the Chinese economy has, relatively peacefully, changed systemically (Raby 1989). It has not, however, become a near-market economy but some sort of hybrid.

China's incrementalist approach now stands as an alternative model of reform. The 'shock therapy' of Eastern Europe or Russia would probably have caused massive disruption and, in doing so, would have been extremely wasteful of resources. In view of the political, institutional, infrastructural and other constraints on adjustment, the transition period even under 'cold turkey' could be long and painful.

But, gradualism has its risks and weaknesses as well. A major risk is that regulations associated with an intermediate position may lead to the emergence of interest groups, which derive substantial rents from the transitionary arrangements. Consequently, the process is in constant danger of becoming stuck, as individuals and some provincial and local governments who are able to capture rents invest part of these in attempting to protect their rents by resisting other reform measures (Watson, Liu and Findlay 1992). While reform has created a constituency for further reform, gradual reform is always in danger of creating a constituency for partial reform.

Disjunction between the many steps in reform is endemic to a gradualist process. If all the necessary reforms could be done at once, presumably they would be, and the process would no longer be a gradual one. The main issues then are whether policymakers can minimise tensions created in the reform process and manage the problems these create so that reform does not collapse. In China's case, strong economic growth, willingness of policymakers to accommodate the extension of the market, and internationalisation of the economy have been critical in ensuring that reform has continued.

II. The Path of Economic Reform

It has become accepted to describe the path of economic reform as following a wave-like motion (Harding 1987; Hamrin 1990; Sung 1991). The judgment that economic reform has gone through a constant process of ups and downs, or advances and retreats, rests on a conceptual confusion between systemic economic reform and macroeconomic management (Harding 1987:71). Economic reform has two key features involving institutional change. One expands the scope of markets in allocating resources: the other exposes an economy to international markets and influences. These need to be clearly distinguished from short-term macroeconomic stabilisation measures involving the instruments of monetary and fiscal policy. There are several possible reasons why this confusion has crept into studies.

First has been an assumption that decentralisation of decision-making authority always represents an advance in reform, while centralisation is a retreat. This is not necessarily so. In the mid 1980s, much of the decision-making authority that was devolved did not reach the enterprise level but rather strengthened control by lower levels of government over economic activity in their jurisdictions. Conversely, recentralisation of fiscal responsibility could, for example, support the extension of markets if it removed incentives for maintaining barriers to inter-regional trade flows by provincial governments.

Second have been the instruments of macroeconomic management at the disposal of the central government. Until recently, the only effective stabilisation instruments were quantitative restrictions on credit and administrative interventions. Whenever monetary policy was tightened to correct domestic or external imbalances, the government was forced to rely on these command measures. Their use has created the impression of retreat from reform during periods when the government was seeking to damp demand. The system has not been sufficiently reformed for this to be described as a retreat from systemic reform. Direct, administrative intervention was, and remains, an integral part of macroeconomic management. Such measures are necessary to manage the command part of the economy. Their use involves a choice of whether to control growth in demand or not, rather than whether to advance or retard reform. Over the course of reform, supplementary instruments have been introduced for macroeconomic management, including some limited open market operations and flexible rates on savings and deposit. These have been used in concert with direct interventions, as occurred during the growth recession of 1989.

Third is the overlay of cycles of political reaction on the reform process. These have tended to change the presentation and articulation of policy, sometimes markedly as in the six months following the Beijing tragedy. During such periods, alternative reform policies may gain currency and be adopted but few have been implemented. In the second half of 1989, policies were announced to bias supplies of key inputs and credit towards state-owned enterprises with the scarcely veiled intention being to harm village and township enterprises. Interestingly, the policies were either not implemented or failed. In any event, they were abandoned early in 1990 because of the potential employment consequences.

Another difficulty in describing the path of reform lies in accounting for the myriad of changes that are occurring. How is one to come to a judgment as to the net effect of these on the overall reform process? The example of the 'retrenchment' period at the beginning of the 1980s well illustrates the problem. The government pulled back from reform, yet at the height of retrenchment the open door policies were given a big fillip with the creation of Shenzhen and other special economic zones. At the same time, the share of households under the contract responsibility system rose from 14 per cent in 1980 to 80 per cent in 1982 (Lin 1991). Similarly, during the dark days following June 1989 the market economy expanded its share of output relative to the command economy, the Securities Exchange was launched, and the activities of currency swap centres expanded, to list just three important aspects of reform.

In surveying the course of reform in China, what is most striking is its forward movement. The process seems to have been one of continuous diffusion across an ever widening frontier, albeit with discrete areas undergoing reform at different speeds. The continual unfolding of reform despite the political swings and big macroeconomic fluctuations of the past decade, suggests both significant momentum behind reform and an important degree of inherent stability in the process.

Economic reform began from a narrow base. Through a series of major policy pronouncements the scope of reform was progressively extended until it touched all areas of the economy. No blueprint for reform seems to have been followed, or it may be that numerous blueprints were devised only to be scrapped as conditions changed. Often the major policy pronouncements were providing *ex post* political legitimisation to what had in fact been happening in many parts of the country. The

leadership, wittingly or unwittingly, has accommodated the logic of reform, giving official policy sanction to new streams of reform when necessary, to nurture or sustain previous reforms.

III. Policy Milestones of Reform

Formal presentation and articulation of reform policy has evolved and changed since 1978. The earliest policy statements did not venture beyond providing *ex post* legitimisation for changes made or in progress. Attempting to bring policy up to date with the reality of the economy has remained an important aspect of formal policy. As reform became more firmly entrenched and as it came to be viewed increasingly as the key to China's economic growth, a policy agenda began to emerge in formal statements.

It is, however, necessary to look at much else besides the major policy statements made at times of key plenums or congresses. Throughout the reform period the major political documents have tended to consist mainly of broad generalisations and vague statements of policy. Documents and statements with a lower political profile, often contained specific policies and details for their implementation. On occasions, such documents also moved policy forward, beyond what was set down in the major statements. Accordingly, a review of the milestone statements on reform should include some of these as well.

First stage: policy catching up

The first stage covers the Third Plenary Session of the Eleventh Party Congress in December 1978 to the October 1984 Decision on Urban Reform. The importance of the Third Plenum in 1978 was that it brought to an end the serious policy drift of the Hua Guofeng period. Policy development was confined to the agricultural sector and China's engagement with the international economy, areas of the economy where change was already well underway in advance of policy. Ideological legitimisation was sought by stressing the continuity of the 'new' policies with those of the 1950s.

The document's starting point was Mao's April 1956 speech 'On the ten major relationships' stating that this '…is an objective reflection of economic law and also an important guarantee for the political stability of society. This report still is significant for guidance today' (Liu and Wu 1986:568).

Was this reference to the reform policies of 1956 intended to specify the extent of the 1978 reforms, to circumscribe them by stating how big the bird cage should be, or was it intended to legitimise the reforms which some in the Party hoped to introduce?

It is worth recording that at the Third Plenum a number of the old team, such as Chen Yun, who with Xue Muqiao had been closely associated with the 1956 reform policy, rejoined the Politburo.[2] As things went so badly wrong after 1956, with Mao's swing to what was then known as the 'left', it is likely that those responsible for the Third Plenum intended the document to get things back on track after the unfortunate detour and meandering in policy over the previous 22 years.

The centralisation versus decentralisation debates of 1956–57 saw the first attempt at reforming the centralised command economy. Mao's speech called for more economic authority for lower levels of government, greater scope for markets to allocate resources and provide incentives, a balanced growth strategy with agriculture and light industry keeping pace with heavy industry, and increased decision-making authority for enterprise managers. Another aspect of the policies of this time was profit sharing, or a form of what is now known as the contract responsibility system. This involved a change from all above-quota profits going to the government to a contractual sharing arrangement, which permitted enterprises to retain an agreed flat rate of the profits (Schurmann 1964:79).[3]

The Third Plenum's publicly stated objectives were vague: change management systems, expand economic relations with other countries, adopt new technology from overseas and strengthen education and training in the sciences. Although the touchstone of the post-Mao era is usually the document adopted at the Third Plenary Session of the Eleventh Party Congress on 22 December 1978, the document itself was as remarkable for what it did not say as for what it did (Liu and Wu 1986:564–77). As the document which is often hailed for launching economic reform, it offered little guidance as to what areas would undergo reform.

Agricultural reform. While the Third Plenum emphasised the need to adopt policies conducive to promote agricultural growth, no mention was made of institutional reforms in the agricultural sector. Indeed, the Plenum actually reaffirmed the role of rural communes. It went further, not only was the production team reaffirmed as the basic accounting unit but that '…this should remain unchanged'.

The emphasis of policy was on measures to raise incentives directly. These included admonishments against arbitrary confiscation, guidelines that payment must follow 'the socialist principle' of each according to his work to overcome 'equalitarianism', and that grain quotas must 'never be excessive'. Significantly, official sanction was given for commune members to use for themselves small plots of land and to pursue sideline activities (at the time, non-plan production), and for village fairs to operate.

The biggest boost to incentives, and the most detailed section of the document, dealt with administrative increases in the grain quota and above-quota prices. State purchase prices were also raised for cotton, oil-bearing and sugar crops, animal by-products, aquatic and forestry products and other farm and sideline products. In the case of grain, the quota price was raised by 20 per cent and the above-quota price by 50 per cent. Meanwhile, the prices of manufactured inputs for the agricultural sector were to be cut by between 10 to 15 per cent. Subsidies were to be increased to protect urban consumers from higher grain prices.

Further details of the policies for agriculture were contained in two draft documents circulated at the time of the Plenum and referred to in the Plenum's report.[4] The documents were published widely in 1979 and approved at the Fourth Plenum held in September 1979 (*Beijing Review* 16 March 1979:8–15). They merely provided more specifics on measures to speed up agricultural growth and details on the role and operations of communes within the policy framework presented at the Plenum.

Although the formal documents were silent on systemic reforms, such as changing the basic unit of production in the countryside, deep changes were underway. Some 18 months after the Fourth Plenum it was apparent that the communes were starting to break up, even though official policy as laid down at the Third Plenum had reaffirmed that the production team was the basic unit in agriculture (Ash 1988:537).

More significant extensions of agricultural reform were contained in the first of the annual agricultural policy documents prepared for the Central Committee by the Research Centre for Rural Development. *Document No.1* of 1983 was the first to sanction the household responsibility system officially as a legitimate rural production arrangement, giving it equal status with the work team as one of the basic units of production in agriculture. Of the rural household, the document said

> ...the family operation of a contracted household is only one management level in the collective economy, a new type of family economy. It is essentially different from those small private individual economy in the past about which we must not be confused [*sic*—referring to the individual private plots, as distinct from collective land turned over to the household under contractual arrangements]. Therefore, in localities where the masses have a demand of adopting this form of management, support must be granted in a positive attitude...Various forms of responsibility systems must be allowed to exist side by side... (Central Committee of the Communist Party 1983).

This document also sought to legitimise extension of rural markets by supporting diversification in the composition of agricultural output, thereby encouraging further development of cash crops and sideline production and hence markets. Of past policies and their interpretation at the farm and village level, the document said that these had lost '...contact with reality, [and] are being broken now by the practices carried out by the masses'.

Experimentation with contracts and household responsibility systems had been first acknowledged in September 1980 in the Central Committee's *Document 75*. This recognised that in some poor areas of the country the commune system had broken down. It therefore sanctioned experiments in different organisational forms in poor areas (Riskin 1987:286–7; Ash 1988:534–5). The official numbers on the spread of the household responsibility system show by the end of 1982 that some 80 per cent of production teams had adopted it.

Explicit Party endorsement of the household responsibility system was reinforced with *Document No. 1* of 1984. Its main contribution to reform was to extend minimum leases from three to fifteen years. This was intended to '...encourage the peasants to increase their investment to foster the fertility of soil and practice intensive operation' (Central Committee, *Document No.1* 1984a:2).

The leadership had become worried about farmers mining the soil and investing in more permanent assets off the land (Kueh 1985:128).

Document No.1 of 1984 also gave official endorsement to some activities which had broken with past practices and regulations. Of particular interest, in view of subsequent developments, was the support given to township and village enterprises concerning employment of labour. From the way the policy is expressed, it seems employment of wage labour by rural enterprises was fairly widespread by 1984, but the enterprises lacked legal or regulatory definition and uncertainty prevailed over the 'correctness' of hiring wage labour. This document established broad guidelines for employment and for the legitimate operation of these enterprises.

Foreign trade and investment reforms. From the late 1970s foreign trade reform was carried out under a catch-all label of 'open door policies'. Most of the major policy developments affecting foreign trade and investment were not dealt with in the milestone policy documents. Instead, they seem to have followed something of an independent but parallel evolutionary path to reform in other parts of the economic system.

The Third Plenum of the Eleventh Party Congress in 1978 gave little guidance on foreign trade reform and the development of external economic relations. It merely called for 'expanding economic cooperation on terms of equality and mutual benefit with other countries on the basis of self-reliance, striving to adopt the world's advanced technologies and equipment.' This was followed in July 1979 with the adoption of the foreign joint-venture law and in 1980 the decision to establish four special economic zones. Between then and 1984 many adjustments and refinements to the foreign trade and exchange systems occurred and also to regulations and conditions affecting joint ventures. Early in 1984, an arrangement for sharing foreign exchange between the centre and provinces was formalised. This provided provinces with the right to retain some 25 per cent of foreign exchange earnings. In May 1984, import-licensing regulations were introduced by the Ministry of Foreign Economic Relations and Trade marking a major step forward in decentralising foreign trade to the provincial level (World Bank 1987:8).

Accommodating the market. In September 1982, the Twelfth National Party Congress and the First Plenum of the Twelfth Central Committee held immediately after the Party Congress provided ideological support for limited markets. While the Twelfth Congress was fairly unremarkable except for a subsequently famous statement by Deng on growth targets for the year 2000, it did indicate the direction the leadership wanted the economy to go, at least in general terms. The Congress endorsed the concept that markets, while remaining supplementary to the planned

sector, were an essential part of the economy. The appropriate scope of mandatory and guidance planning was also explained: mandatory planning should be retained for capital goods, essential industries and household necessities; guidance planning could be extended more or less to what was left.[5]

At the First Plenum of September 1982, Hu Yaobang outlined execution patterns which have since become familiar. In what has become a recurring theme, Hu announced that when macroeconomic stability was restored and growth resumed, central and municipal authorities would begin to undertake reform of labour, wages and prices. These reforms were to start early in 1984. Although Hu did not set out in any detail what was intended, both the statements legitimising the role of markets and the broadening of the reform agenda would have sent out powerful messages of support for those wishing to try new, market-oriented ways of doing things.

Although the presentation of economic reform policies at the 1982 Congress was more qualified and less ambitious than what occurred at the October Plenum of 1984, it would have been important in sanctioning the busy and innovative period of experimentation in economic reform which preceded and upon which the 1984 Decision was based.

Second stage: tentatively setting an agenda

The second stage occurred between October 1984 and the Thirteenth Party Congress held in October 1987. During this period, the government attempted to provide more guidance for reform than before. The 1984 Decision on Urban Reform however, did not amount to a major discontinuity in either practice or policy. For example, various forms of contract responsibility systems for enterprises had started before then. Moreover, its main objectives had been anticipated in the documents of the Twelfth National Party Congress and in the First Plenum of the Twelfth Central Committee held immediately after the Party Congress in September 1982.

Urban reform. The Decision on Reform of the Economic Structure, from the Third Plenum of the Twelfth Central Committee, of October 1984, was as important as the 1978 Plenum. It is widely regarded within and outside China as having launched what have become known as 'urban reforms', indicating the formal extension of reform from rural to non-rural areas of the economy.

The Plenum on economic reform had been preceded in May 1984 by the National People's Congress which approved some important new reform policies. Zhao Ziyang's Work Report at the Congress called for a new relationship between the state and enterprises, involving progress on the process begun in 1983 of substituting profit remittances for taxation and introducing a range of new taxes which would be consistent with enterprise managers exercising greater decision-making power (Wong 1985:261–2). Zhao also announced at the Congress that all small-scale enterprises would be contracted out to individuals or collectives to manage. As a further step in enterprise reform, the Congress adopted a policy to commence the gradual introduction of an investment responsibility system by replacing state capital allocation with bank loans in the construction sector.

The significance of the 1984 Decision lay less in terms of actual policy development and more in its attempt to give some strategic guidance to reform outside the agricultural sector. It attempted for the first time to spell out something of a program of economic reform to be applied more broadly than previously. The 1984 Decision identified the problem it sought to address as being a 'rigid economic structure' which stifled economic performance. This was attributed to the five following aspects of the economic system in need of change

- absence of a clear distinction between the functions of government and those of enterprises
- barriers between different industries and sectors

- excessively rigid control by the state over enterprises
- insufficient attention given to the role of markets
- absolute 'equalitarianism in distribution' (*Xinhua* 21 October 1984:5).

As in 1978, the 1984 Decision made an early reference to the correctness of the 1956 economic policies which had attempted to deal with over-centralisation of economic management. As in 1956, and again in 1978, the 1984 Decision also reaffirmed that the central 'task' of socialism was to achieve economic growth. The most important criterion when judging the 'correctness' of economic reform policy was, therefore, whether it promoted economic growth. Importantly, it sought to anticipate arguments over the socialist integrity of specific reform policies, creating a framework for subsequent policy development.

The first major area of reform dealt with in the document was the relationship between state-owned enterprises and government ministries and departments. The document argued that separation of ownership and management was consistent with Marxist theory and the practice of socialism. It then gave official endorsement to the principle of devolution of a wide range of decision-making powers to enterprises. As was typical of this type of document, few details were provided as to what this meant in practice and examples of how the Government intended this to operate were either vague, or qualified, or both.[6]

The document also acknowledged explicitly for the first time that reform of the entire economic system was on the policy agenda. In view of the complexity of the task and the need to phase carefully the introduction of specific reform measures, the reform process was expected to take about five years to complete (*Xinhua* 21 October 1984:11).

As for reform of the planning system, the 1984 Decision argued the case at greater length than did the 1982 Plenum document for the combination of planning and market regulation. It broke with the Chen Yun formula (present in all such statements since 1978) that the market must be subservient to the plan and only play a supplementary role. Instead, it argued that the plan and the market formed a 'unity'. Mandatory planning was to be confined to key sectors and industries; for the rest where products were too numerous to control by planning, either guidance planning or markets were to regulate economic activity.

The document also sought to address an important doctrinal issue. It asserted that the difference between a socialist and a capitalist economy lay not in the extent to which markets or planning operate but in property rights. Capitalism was based on the institutional arrangement of private ownership. China as a socialist economy would stick with public ownership but could extend markets within limits. On this point the Decision was precise and firm '...neither labour power nor land, mines, banks, railways and all other state-owned enterprises and resources are commodities' (*Xinhua* 21 October 1984:13).

The Decision was also unequivocal on the absolute necessity of price reform. This was explained in terms both of allocative efficiency and as a necessary condition for enterprise reform to be undertaken. While it asserted, however, that price reform was the '...key to reform of the entire economic structure', it would only be done gradually.

The principles guiding price reform were vague. Essentially they amounted to a gradual change in price relativities, with enterprises absorbing higher input prices by increasing efficiency and ensuring that if prices of daily necessities for urban dwellers rose so would subsidies to protect real urban living standards (*Xinhua* 21 October 1984:16). The weakest link of this program was the expectation that enterprises would raise productivity and absorb higher input costs, especially while the government did nothing to harden their budget constraints.

Other aspects of reform touched on by the Decision but not developed in an operational or prescriptive way included reform of the wage system with increased reward for 'mental' work, the need to develop various forms of responsibility systems for enterprises, and further reform of the taxation system to reflect the changed, at least, formal relationship between the state and enterprises. The contribution made by collective and individual enterprises was applauded and their further development was encouraged. They were to continue however, to be only an 'adjunct' to the socialist economy (*Xinhua* 21 October 1984:27).

While it did not provide a comprehensive program for implementing reform, importantly it contained a reasonably consistent vision of the Chinese economy (and implicitly administration and government) different from those which had previously prevailed. The vision was incomplete, but it did identify all the major areas of the economy which needed attention, even if it did not give much guidance, as to how to effect change.

Although it did not constitute an abrupt break in either direction or scope of reform, the Decision certainly encouraged further extension of the process. Importantly, it gave official recognition to the inter-relatedness of reform and accepted that reform in one area would require reform in others. Its doctrinal interpretations and ideological legitimisation of reform stretched the political boundaries of what economic activity was acceptable. These contributions would have enhanced the authority of those who were inclined to argue for more market-oriented solutions to economic problems.

Foreign trade reform. Foreign trade reform had been dealt with prior to the Third Plenum. In September 1984, the State Council approved a set of policies that sought to strengthen both existing practice and previous policies. These did, however, constitute a comprehensive set of guidelines for decentralising the administration of foreign trade. Five areas were the main focus of change

• establishing foreign trade corporations as independent accounting units

27

- breaking the monopoly powers of most national foreign trade corporations by establishing local-level competitors
- establishing an agency system for conducting foreign trade in some commodities
- reducing the scope of mandatory planning in foreign trade
- requiring foreign trade corporations to operate financially in the same way as other enterprises.

The intention of these measures taken together was to decentralise the management of foreign trade and expand the number of organisations engaged in trade. The October Plenum endorsed these new policies.

IV. Reform and Reaction

By late 1984, strong growth in agricultural output, the spread of the household responsibility system and the emergence of economically important new organisational forms and activities had created tremendous pressures on the old purchasing, marketing and supply systems in the rural sector. By 1985, these pressures led to 'Stage Two' of agricultural reform which sought to unwind the state's monopsony over rural distribution systems. Effectively, this meant that price reform principles contained in the October 1984 Decision on Urban Reform would also apply in the rural sector.

The official statement of Stage Two of Rural Reform was contained in *Document No.1* of 1985 that introduced the contract responsibility system in the rural sector. On this occasion, government policy seems to have been innovative, rather than merely giving *de jure* recognition to existing practices. In terms of decisions over the composition of output, the policy set out in this document made a major shift towards expanding the scope of markets in the countryside. This was achieved by reversing the long-standing 70:30 ratio, under which 70 per cent of grain, cotton and edible oil production was purchased under

fixed quota prices.[7] Under the new marketing system, only 30 per cent of contract production was to be purchased at fixed prices and 70 per cent was purchased at negotiable prices. At the same time, other quotas, such as those for pigs, vegetables and fruit, and aquatic products would be abolished completely and replaced by market exchange (Ash 1988:546).

Although the year began with some bold strokes on the agricultural reform front, the process became more complicated towards the end of 1985. A fall in grain production led to the now famous speech by Chen Yun at the special Party conference held in September 1985. In this speech he reminded the Party and government that in reforming the agricultural sector and permitting changes in the product mix, it was important not to forget grain.[8] Grain was to remain the 'key link'.

From this time agricultural reform policies became constrained by the requirement that grain self-sufficiency be pursued. Rural reform could only proceed so long as it did not undermine the other policy objective of maintaining grain self-sufficiency.

Accordingly, *Document No.1* of 1986 had as its stated objective the consolidation of policies in the rural sector. In effect, it began to explore ways to raise grain production in the context of the, by then, substantially reformed agricultural sector. Between 1979 and 1984, the problem of agriculture shifted progressively from one of production to consumption; how to match the composition of output more closely with the rising and changing demands of urban consumers and industry as incomes grew. With the sharp fall in grain output in 1985 and the return to being a net importer, policy once again became focused on the production side. Significantly, the response adopted in *Document No.1* of 1986 was not to seek to undo previous reforms but to increase government budgetary allocations to grain production.

The articulation of rural reform policies did not move far beyond the stage reached in 1985, but the policies introduced to that date remained in place. Meanwhile, they were extended throughout the country, modified and refined. Significantly, the influence of a freer system of prices, together with the expansion of voluntary contractual exchanges, contributed to a dramatic increase in the share of agricultural output coming from sideline activities and especially township and village industries.

Meanwhile in 1985, a program for the phased reform of industrial prices was announced. In January, Vice Premier Tian Jiyun, made a major statement on price reform. Unlike other public documents that have been described as blueprints for reform, Tian's document did set out a detailed course of action (Tian 1985). After establishing the case for price reform, the document went on to specify a series of steps to be taken and the conditions conducive to them. This policy for price reform also gave official recognition to the three-tiered pricing system which had been developing with the growth of the non-state owned sector and above-quota production in the state sector. The system consisted of

- state fixed prices for quota production
- negotiated prices for above-quota production
- free-market prices for above-quota production where markets were in equilibrium for products from industries not covered by the plan, and for non-staple food and sideline products produced by peasant households.

The release of Tian's policy was followed by a number of adjustments to the pricing system. These included rapid deregulation of non-staple foodstuff prices during 1985, deregulation of the prices of certain consumer goods, an administrative increase in short-haul transport charges, introduction of a two-tiered price system for raw materials with fixed prices for quota production and market prices for above-quota production, and widespread adoption of flexible or negotiated prices for non-essential industrial products to better reflect differences in quality.

Other areas of domestic reform activity during the period between the Third Plenum and the Thirteenth Party Congress included the spread of incentive-based wages, including piece-work rates, labour assignment and the introduction of contract labour, a wide range of reforms in the financial and banking sectors, and widespread introduction of the contract responsibility system in enterprises.

Concern for the prospects for economic reform were raised with the ousting of then General Secretary Hu Yaobang in January 1987. Despite his dramatic departure, the launching of a campaign against bourgeois liberalisation, and the adoption of macro-stabilisation policies to damp inflation, reform continued. In fact, despite worries in the leadership over the rate of inflation, further measures for advancing price reform were being urged on the government from early in 1987.[9]

During these years, the pressure on the frontiers of reform had become very strong. Growth of the non-planned sectors of the economy and greater exposure to foreign trade and investment kept up momentum behind policy developments. By the end of the period and despite increased political instability the reforms had become extensive.

V. Stage Three: Taking the Lead

Stage three covered the period from the Thirteenth Party Congress held in October 1987 to the Beijing tragedy in June 1989. By 1987 the market sectors of the economy had become important. In particular, rural enterprises and the internationalised sectors had become significant sources of growth in incomes and employment. Addressing ideologically hard areas of reform could no longer be avoided without harming the economy. Greater flexibility was required in the labour and financial systems and in the transfer of use-rights to agricultural land. Importantly, the time had come to give official sanction to income derived from profits and rents in order to provide security and reduce risks from arbitrary action for those operating in the non-state sector.

Zhao Ziyang's Work Report to the Thirteenth Party Congress in October 1987 had as its theme 'acceleration and deepening' economic reform to promote long-term growth (Zhao 1987).[10] It was the most far-reaching statement on reform to that time. It set out an extensive agenda for reform and extended a number of localised reform experiments to the entire economy. In part this was to accommodate pressures for further extension of the market. In part it may also have been a reflection of the leadership's growing confidence in markets and open door policies to drive economic growth.

Doctrinal breakthrough

The main novelty of Zhao's Work Report was its contribution to Party and communist doctrine with its articulation of the theory of the 'primary stages of socialism'. As with all previous keynote statements on economic reform, the historical starting point was the mid 1950s efforts at reform before the deviation from this path because of 'leftist mistakes' (Zhao 1987:9).

The theory of the primary stages of socialism held that socialism in China had been established in an economically underdeveloped country. Socialism, however, could only mature fully by developing the economy. Thus, the document argued a major extension of reform was necessary because China's economy was still too backward for the further development of socialism. For an indefinite period China would need a decentralised system with multiple forms of economic organisation to modernise the economy.

The document concluded that to build socialism in China it was permissible to do whatever was necessary to promote growth. Some of the implications of this were set out in the document, including greater income inequality and the operation of markets in such taboo areas as capital, labour and use-rights to land. The change in policy to accept markets for factors of production marked a major advance in reform thinking and policy over the 1984 Decision that had explicitly ruled them out. The

theory of the primary stages however, provided a more elaborate philosophical cloak for the guiding reform principle that economic performance should be the sole criterion upon which to judge the correctness of policy.

In its discussion of the relationship between planning and markets the Work Report was only a small advance on the 1984 Decision. On the economic mechanism, it repeated the 1984 formula that mandatory planning and markets should coexist, but with the scope of mandatory planning being reduced gradually over time. To the extent that nuances matter in such a document, however, the emphasis is much more on guidance planning in 1987 than in 1984. This was summed up by the slogan, 'the state regulates the market, and the market guides enterprises' (Zhao 1987:15).

Enterprise reform was also stressed, involving the contract responsibility system for enterprise managers and proposing to increase the powers of managers of enterprises. Again, as in 1984, party officials in enterprises were reminded their role was to ensure policies were implemented and to support managers.

Although the primacy of public ownership of property was reaffirmed, collective and private forms were to be expanded. This was an important change in emphasis from previous policy. Prior to October 1987, non-state forms of ownership were to be tolerated as an inevitable aspect of the country's historical conditions, but should not be regarded as permanent features of the economy. Moreover, their expansion was not encouraged. The Work Report also endorsed experiments in shareholding arrangements for state-owned enterprises and contracting and leasing of state-owned property. Procedures for the sale of peasant's leases and methods for compensating peasants for capital improvements were explained in some detail in concurrent public presentations.

Recognition of different forms of distribution was an other major doctrinal advance to legitimise existing practices. While income was mainly to be derived from wages, it was acknowledged for the first time that income could also come from interest on bonds and savings, dividends from shares, and profits from employing labour in the private sector (Zhao 1987). The report also said managers were entitled to receive additional income for taking risks, while piece-rates should be introduced more widely (Zhao 1987).

The limits to reform were also stressed. China was socialist and would remain so: state ownership dominant, wages the main source of income, and continuation of mandatory planning and administered prices in key industries. These strictures were consistent with the guiding principles of reform in both the 1982 Congress and 1984 Plenum documents. In reaffirming the correctness of past reform policies and approaches, the Work Report also reaffirmed ongoing commitment to gradualism and progression through trial and error (Zhao 1987).

Zhao Ziyang's coastal development strategy and foreign trade reform

Foreign trade reform was given less prominence in the Work Report despite the big developments that had taken place (Zhao 1987). The Work Report offered nothing that was new and did not go beyond the policy settings of 1984. It merely confirmed that these had been correct and urged that they be implemented more fully. As on previous occasions foreign trade reforms were dealt with separately. They included accelerated development of coastal provinces, decentralisation of authority to conduct foreign trade and investment, expansion of export-oriented, labour-intensive industries and the opening of foreign-trade corporations to competition. To break out of the 'airlock' separating enterprises that make things for export and the international market, the 1988 reforms set down regulations to permit certain manufacturing firms to export in their own right. A limited role for foreign currency swap centres was also authorised (Zhao 1987).

In January 1988, in somewhat unusual circumstances in Shanghai, Zhao Ziyang announced the coastal development strategy.[11]

The announcement coincided with the promulgation of a major set of measures for reforming the foreign trade system. While the specific reform policies considered adjustments to the existing system, Zhao's coastal development strategy, which was not at the time endorsed formally as policy, represented a significant advance in thinking.

It was a big break with long-standing, mercantilist assumptions about trade. Until then, external economic relations were to effect net transfers to China of resources, especially capital and technology. Zhao's contribution was to suggest China should join the world division of labour according to its comparative advantage in labour-intensive manufactures, permitting international markets to determine the pattern of production and exports.

The coastal development strategy supported more advanced provinces, such as Guangdong and Jiangsu, which were being held back in their development by central government policies requiring provinces to seek self-sufficiency in grain and other key commodities. Provinces which had long been exposed to international markets and prices were increasingly unable to resist pressures for a more rational allocation of resources and were thus beginning to drift towards increasingly specialised patterns of production. This extension of the open door policy tested the limits of political tolerance. After several months of much discussion, public reference to it abated temporarily. The discussion however, had widened policy choices for some coastal provincial governments.

Tiananmen Square and reform

In the year following the Thirteenth Party Congress, leadership struggles and loss of control over the macroeconomy overwhelmed everything else. In May of 1988 a bid by Deng Xiao Pang and Zhao Ziyang to accelerate price reform simply led to an explosion in inflationary expectations, banks and shops were rushed as waves of panic buying swept across the major cities. In September, stringent macroeconomic stabilisation policies were adopted at the Third Plenum.

Although macroeconomic management issues came to be the main focus of economic policy, public discussion of economic reform continued. If anything, concern over inflation intensified public analysis of economic reform policy. Debate focused on whether gradualism had been the correct strategy or whether it had in fact accentuated macroeconomic fluctuations. Prior to the protests of April and May 1989, however, these discussions began to take on a much sharper political edge with increasing questioning of public ownership and gathering calls for privatisation. For the first time, the issue of private ownership was being discussed openly. Public discussion of reform was brought to an abrupt halt on 4 June 1989.

The events of June, ensuing political changes and a return to a trenchant, conservative stance in political and cultural spheres in the six months after June put economic reform to its most severe test. Sabres were rattled over recently acquired decision making and fiscal autonomy in coastal provinces, village and township enterprises and even the rural household responsibility system. The primacy of central planning and concomitantly state-owned enterprises was stressed and their financial difficulties attributed to the non-state sector which had bid up the price of raw materials and energy.

Economic reform stood up well to its most severe political test, indicating the extent to which reform had become firmly bedded down (Raby 1991). Significantly, throughout the period after June 1989, the non-state sector—led by village and township enterprises—was permitted to grow many times faster than the state-owned sector. In an important and real way this extended the market. Each day, more and more economic activity occurred outside the planning system.

Early in 1990, the conservative threat to the reform process was explicitly rejected. Li Peng's Work Report to the National People's Congress in March 1990 (Li Peng 1991) reaffirmed key elements of reform despite the depressing rhetoric of the document. In fact, 1990 saw the continuation of many other important reforms, such as in the financial sector, where secondary bond markets opened. Late in 1990, further foreign trade reforms were introduced and a decision was announced to phase out export subsidies. From December 1989, China has operated its most flexible foreign exchange policy, undertaking two large devaluations and then adopting a floating rate. Meanwhile, the extent of quasi convertibility was extended as conditions for access to the country's many foreign exchange swap centres were relaxed.

After 13 years of economic reform the economy had changed systemically and putting the clock back was no longer an option. In particular, rural industries and the foreign trade sector had over the years of reform become important sources of growth in employment and incomes. These dynamic market-oriented sectors sustained pressure for forward movement of reform.

VI. The 'Neither This nor That' Economy

China's incrementalist approach has worked in terms of delivering sustained growth in real incomes per capita and providing the policy framework for rapid structural change and internationalisation of the economy. It has achieved more than any other centrally planned economy that had attempted economic reform before the collapse of communism in Eastern and Central Europe, Russia and the Newly Independent States. China has maintained forward momentum in economic reform to the middle of the 1990s—even through major political crises. The sum of incremental change has been the systemic transformation of the entire economy. It has not become a near-capitalist economy as many presumed it would in the 1980s, but it is slowly becoming something of a near-market, collectivist system which is capable of sustaining historically and internationally very high rates of growth.

It is likely, therefore, that China will continue with its gradual approach to economic reform. The process has already shown that it has an evolutionary logic, which seems to be shaped and driven by economic necessity and is responsive to reform-induced changes in different parts of the system. More often than not, decision makers have been followers. Frequently, the key documents of reform have supplied the ideological cover for what has gone before. As the confidence and commitment to reform by leaders and the bureaucracy strengthened, documents have become more policy oriented and more prescriptive. Pressure for continual expansion of reform has been sustained by the dynamic sectors which are outside the formal planning system and by the increasing internationalisation of the economy throughout the period of reform.

In view of China's size, low income, infrastructure constraints, and the communist legacy of inefficiency, it is probably in everyone's interest that China reforms gradually, despite the risks and costs which gradualism entails. A 'shock therapy' approach may work for small economies. It is altogether a different matter for big economies, as the recent experience of Russia suggests.

Notes

1. The views expressed in this chapter are solely those of the author and should not be attributed to his employer. The chapter has benefited from comments by Ross Garnaut.
2. Chen was appointed to the Standing Committee of the Politburo, as a Party Vice Chairman and founding Head of the Discipline Inspection Commission. At this Plenum he effectively regained positions he lost in 1969. In 1956, Chen Yun was Minister for Commerce and Xue Muqiao was chief of the State Statistical Bureau (Riskin 1987:103).
3. Franz Schurmann in a remarkable piece of analysis, especially given the paucity of information at the time, and which could easily

be a description of current problems and policy debates, wrote that 'contracts' had played an important role in the workings of the economy ever since the days of the liberation in Manchuria. Contracts had also been important in the Soviet Union to overcome gaps in planned allocations. Commenting on the extent of 'contractual' activity in China in the early 60s, Schurmann wrote that '...it is hard to say what the state of planning is, how much in the way of real production, materials, and commodities the plan actually covers. And...given the continuing discussion of price policy, the least one can say is that there is considerable fluctuations in the price picture. There are even some indications that factory managers have some initiative in setting prices for products' (Schurmann 1964:78).
4. Some questions concerning the acceleration of agricultural development (draft) and Regulations on the work in the Rural People's Commune (draft).
5. Guidance planning refers to the use by the government of indirect measures, such as taxes and subsidies, to influence the size and composition of output.
6. Some of the examples of how this new enterprise responsibility system was to operate in practice included, '...keep and budget funds [the enterprise] is entitled to retain; appoint, remove, employ, or elect its own personnel according to relevant regulations;...[and] set the prices of its products within the limits prescribed by the state.' The enterprise was to do all these things '...on the premise of following the state plans and subjecting itself to state control...' (*Xinhua* 21 October 1984:10).
7. The changes in the grain quota and procurement systems contained in this document marked a departure from the policy on agriculture contained in Hu Yaobang's report to the Twelfth National Congress on 1 September 1982, in which he said '...mandatory targets should...be assigned...in the purchase of grain and other important agricultural and sideline products by the state on fixed quota.'
8. Curiously, Ash, in an otherwise excellent and comprehensive account of the development of rural policy to 1988 does not mention this (Ash 1988).

9. Even before the political dust over Hu Yaobang had begun to settle, *Guangming Ribao* on 14 February was urging that reform of the price system be extended. Veteran economist Xue Muqiao published an article in *Renmin Ribao* on 20 March arguing that problems encountered in implementing price reform were attributable to the partial state of reform of markets and prices, and thus argued for more reform to deal with inflation. Zhao reinforced this message in a major speech in Shanghai in April which was carried in *Xinhua* on 25 April.

10. Advance along the road of socialism with Chinese Characteristics, a report delivered at the Thirteenth National Congress of the Communist Party of China on October 25, 1987 (hereafter, Work Report 1987).

11. Unusual in the sense that the announcement came during a provincial tour and was not apparently connected with a Party meeting, nor did the strategy seem to have the backing of senior Party colleagues, at least in Beijing. It was as if Zhao was attempting to circumvent normal procedures for developing policy.

References

Ash, R., 1988. 'The Evolution of Agricultural Policy', *China Quarterly*, December.

Central Committee of the CPC, 1979a. 'Communiqué of the Fourth Plenary Session of the 11th Central Committee of the CPC', *Beijing Review*, No. 40, 5 October.

Central Committee of the CPC, 1979b. 'Decisions on Some Questions Concerning the Acceleration of Agricultural Development (Draft)', *Beijing Review*, No. 11, 16 March.

Central Committee of the CPC, 1983. Questions of the Current Policies of Rural Economy', Document No. 1, *Research Centre for Rural Development*, January.

Central Committee of the CPC, 1984a. 'A Circular on the Rural Work in 1984…', Document No. 1, *Research Centre for Rural Development*, January.

Central Committee of the CPC, 1984b. 'Decision on Reform of the Economic Structure', *Xinhua*, 21 October.

Central Committee of the CPC, 1985. 'On Ten Points of Policy Concerning Invigorating the Rural Economy…', Document No. 1, *Research Centre for Rural Development*, January.

Central Committee of the CPC, 1986. 'On the arrangements for rural work in 1986…', Document No. 1, Research Centre for Rural Development, January.

Findlay, C. (ed.), 1992. *Challenges of Economic Reform and Industrial Growth: China's wool war*, Allen and Unwin, Sydney.

Garnaut, R. and Liu Guoguang (eds), 1991. *Economic Reform and Internationalisation: China and the Pacific Region*, Allen and Unwin, Sydney.

Hamrin, C.L., 1990. *China and the Challenge of the Future: changing political patterns*. Westview Press, Boulder, Col.

Harding, H., 1987. *China's Second Revolution: reform after Mao*. Brookings Institute, Washington, DC.

Hu Yaobang, 1982. 'Report to the Twelfth National Congress of the Communist Party of China', 1 September.

Kleinberg, R., 1990. *China's 'Opening' to the Outside World: the experiment with capitalism*, Westview Press, Boulder, Col.

Kueh, Y.Y., 1985. 'The economics of the second land reform in China', *China Quarterly*, March.

Li, P., 1991. 'Report on the Outline of the Ten-year Programme and of the Eighth Five-year Plan for National Economic and Social Development', Fourth Session of the Seventh National People's Congress, 25 March. PRT. *Xinhua*, 11 April.

Lin, J.Y., 1991. 'Rural reform and development', in R. Garnaut and G. Liu (eds), *Economic Reform and Internationalisation: China and the Pacific Region*, Allen and Unwin, Sydney.

Liu, S. and Wu Qungan (eds.), 1986. 'China's Socialist Economy: an outline history (1949–1984)', *Beijing Review*, Beijing.

Prybyla, J.S., 1986. 'Mainland China and Hungary: to market, to market', *The Fifteenth Sino-American Conference on Mainland China*, Institute of International Relations, National Chengchi University, Taipei, 8–14 June 1986.

Raby, G., 1989. *Other Economic Systems*, Heinemann, Port Melbourne.

Raby, G., 1991. 'Economic Reform in China: a lesson from Tian'anmen Square', *Asialink*, Melbourne University, Melbourne.

Riskin, C., 1987. *China's Political Economy: the quest for development since 1949*, Oxford University Press, Oxford.

Schurmann, F., 1964. 'China's "New Economic Policy"—transition or beginning?', *China Quarterly*, No. 17, January–March.

Sung, Yun-Wing, 1991. *The China-Hong Kong Connection: the key to China's Open Door Policy*, Cambridge University Press, Cambridge.

Tian, J., 1985. 'Plan for Reforming Price System', BBC, *Summary of World Broadcasts* (SWB), FE/7847/c/1, 12 January.

Watson, A., Liu Zheng and Findlay, C., 1992. 'Collective Resource Management in China: the raw wool industry', in Christopher Findlay (ed.), *Challenges of Economic Reform and Industrial Growth: China's wool war*, Allen and Unwin, Sydney.

Watson, C., 1985. 'The Second Phase of Economic Reform in China,' *Current History*, September.

Wong, C. 1985. 'The second phase of economic reform in China', *Current History*, September.

World Bank, 1987. *China: external trade and capital reform issues and options*, World Bank, Washington, DC.

World Bank, 1990. *China: between plan and market*, World Bank Country Study, Washington, DC.

Zhao Z., 1986. 'Report on the Seventh Five-year Plan', Fourth Session of the Sixth National People's Congress, 25 March, Rpt. *Xinhua* 14 April 1986.

Zhao, Z., 1987. 'Advance Along the Road of Socialism with Chinese Characteristics', *Thirteenth National Congress of CPC*, 25 October.

3 Completing China's Move to the Market

Dwight Perkins

China's economic reform process officially began with the Communist Party Plenum of December 1978. From the outset, China's reforms differed markedly from those of eastern Europe and the Commonwealth of Independent States. China was exhausted from 20 years of dealing with Mao's messianic visions, but it was in no sense ready for revolution. There was nothing comparable to eastern Europe's desire to be like western Europe, the sooner the better. China faced no economic crisis that required immediate and fundamental change, only dissatisfaction with the pace of existing growth, a dissatisfaction fueled in part by increasing awareness of the far better economic performances of China's immediate neighbours. The Communist Party held all of the important reins of power both in 1978 and 15 years later. Where Deng Xiaoping differed from his predecessors was in the strength of his desire to turn China into a wealthy and powerful state and his lack of interest in Maoist ideas of a new kind of society where such things as material incentives would play little or no role. But Deng and his associates had no economic reform blueprint.

In this context, a gradual approach to economic reform was inevitable. Mao Zedong was the believer in 'big bangs'. Mao's successors were willing to try almost anything if it worked. They also had a sense that some sectors, notably agriculture and foreign trade, were more in need of reform than others, such as industry. Mao's bias against foreign technology and foreign products had severely hurt China's modernisation, and per capita grain output in 1978 was the same as it was in the mid 1950s. These latter views led to a sequencing of the economic reforms, first agriculture and foreign trade and only later industry. At no time during the early years of reform did the senior leadership of China think that they were aiming toward a full market system.

It was as much by luck as by design, therefore, that China stumbled on a strategy that has proved remarkably successful in moving the economy from a Soviet-style command system to what by the early 1990s was an economy governed in large part by market forces, however distorted some of those market forces may have been. That the economic reforms initiated in December 1978 and continuing thereafter have been successful cannot be seriously doubted. The data in Tables 1 and 2 tell the basic story. China's gross domestic product grew by over 8 per cent

Reprinted with permission. Dwight Perkins, 1994, 'Completing China's move to the market', *Journal of Economic Perspectives* 8(2):23–46 (with minor editing).

Table 1   **China's GDP and its components**

	1978	1984	1988	1990	1992
GDP (billion 1990 yuan)	669.4	1097.0	1625.9	1769.5	2162.9
per capita (1990 yuan)	695	1051	1464	1548	1846
per capita (index)	100.0	151.2	210.6	225.3	266.6

Growth rates (per cent per year)	1984/1978	1988/1984	1992/1988	1992/1978
Agriculture	7.3	3.1	4.3	5.2
Industry	8.9	14.2	10.4	10.8
Services	10.1	13.5	5.8	9.8
GDP	8.6	10.3	7.5	8.8

Note: The Chinese GDP figures were calculated by applying the indexes in 'comparable prices' for 1978, 1984, 1988, and 1992 to the current price estimates of the three components of GDP in 1990. This produces rough constant price GDP figures for these years and an index that differs slightly from the official Chinese GDP index for this period.
Sources: State Statistical Bureau, 1992:6: State Statistical Bureau, 1991:33, 79; and 'Statistical Communiqué of the State Statistical Bureau of the PRC on the 1992 National Economic and Social Development Plan' February 18, 1993, *Beijing*.

a year for 14 years, or roughly 7 per cent per capita. The 8.8 per cent GDP growth rate figure may overstate the real rate by a small amount (mainly because small-scale industries sometimes only report output figures in current prices which may not always be deflated by the statistical authorities), but there is no question that the growth has been rapid. This rate is roughly double the GDP growth rate of the previous two decades, 1957–1978.[1] The foreign trade story is even more impressive. In the 1970s, China's exports grew by a modest 3.4 per cent a year if one takes away the impact of OPEC-generated increases in the price of petroleum and related across-the-board inflation. This real growth rate rose to 14.1 per cent a year during the first decade of reform and 70 per cent of these exports were manufactures (petroleum and mining products by 1988 accounted for under 8 per cent of exports, as contrasted to 25 per cent in 1980).

China's impressive export performance was partly due to the reforms, but it also reflects the fact that China began its reform period from a more advantageous position than did the reformers of eastern Europe, the C.I.S., and Vietnam. The breakup of the Council for Mutual Economic Assistance (CMEA) forced these latter countries to abandon many of their markets with each other and reorient their trade to the west. China went through a similar process in the early 1960s and it was very disruptive to the economy, but by 1978 China had long since completed this adjustment. China also had no foreign debt to pay off in 1978, unlike the situation in China in 1960 or eastern Europe after 1989. China's other big advantage in 1978 was that it began the reform period with no overt inflation and not much repressed inflationary pressure. Reform did not have to begin with a stabilisation program.

I. Rural Reform

The two principal components of China's rural reforms were the gradual freeing up of the markets for agricultural commodities and the decollectivisation of Chinese rural society.

Table 2   **Growth rate of China's foreign   trade**
           (per cent per year)

| | Nominal | | Real | |
	Exports	Imports	Exports	Imports
1972/1952	7.4	4.8	–	–
1978/1972	19.0	25.0	3.4	13.0
1988/1978	17.2	17.6	14.1	10.2
1992/1978	16.7	15.4	-	-

Sources: Same as in Table 1 plus, for the real rates, China Foreign Trade Yearbook compiling committee, 1984:IV–5; and China Foreign Trade Yearbook Compiling Committee, 1989:303. Appropriate price deflators were not available for the post-1988 period.

The market for secondary crops and household products was freed up almost immediately after the December 1978 party plenum. Free markets, or rural trade fairs as they were called, had existed before 1978 but were tightly controlled when they were allowed to function at all. However, the state retained a near monopoly of the trade in major crops such as grain, until 1985, and state contracts for the purchase of grain and other key agricultural commodities were made voluntary, although the word 'voluntary' as used in China often retains elements of coercion. By the latter half of the 1980s around 60 per cent of agricultural commodities were bought and sold on competitive markets, as compared to only 8 per cent in 1978 (Lu and Timmer 1992). By 1990 this share had risen to about 80 per cent; markets supplied 89 per cent of all aquatic products, 80 per cent of fruits, 76 per cent of vegetables, 68 per cent of meat and eggs, and about half of all grain (*China Daily* December 17, 1992). By 1993 there was talk of freeing up agricultural prices altogether over the next three years and perhaps 10 per cent of the countries had already freed up all prices including grain. The state, however, was still heavily involved in the grain trade and was having trouble fulfilling its purchase quotas and finding cash to pay for the grain it did purchase. The

inability of the state trading companies to get bank credits led them to issue IOU's to farmers that were often not redeemed for months (*China Daily*, 19 April 1993).

Decollectivisation happened more or less spontaneously. What began as experiments to help the poorest areas in certain provinces spread quickly to other regions. Only when lower-level party officials would try to halt or reverse the process did the center move in with orders to let happen what was happening. By the end of 1983, the system of people's communes and the production teams of 20–30 families that had operated as a collective unit had ceased to exist in most of the country.[2] Household agriculture was the norm and the state soon determined that household contracts for the use of the land would last for 15 years.

The response of agriculture to decollectivisation and the freeing up of rural markets was immediate and dramatic. The basic picture can be seen in the data in Table 3. Production of all crops including grain grew at an unprecedented rate—from 1978 to 1984, the growth rate for agricultural value-added was five times what it had been over the previous two decades. Farm income and consumption grew even more rapidly, although the data are less reliable than those for output. Improving terms of trade for agriculture, plus non-agricultural sources of income, account for most of the difference between output versus consumption or income growth.

The raw data for row (4) are from the same sources. The percentage increases in net income were derived from per capita data in current prices divided by the rural retail price index.

These growth statistics also indicate that the agricultural output spurt was a one-shot affair largely exhausted by the end of 1984, when most crop production returned to its long-term growth rate, in part because farmers preferred to invest their resources in rural industry (Huang 1993). Reforms also could not alter the fact that China is attempting to feed 1.1 billion people on less than a tenth of a hectare per capita, and crop yields in the best-endowed provinces are already

Table 3 **Agricultural growth rate** (per cent per year)

	1978/1957	1984/1978	1988/1984	1992/1988
(1) Agricultural value added	1.4[a]	7.3	3.1	4.3
(2) Gross value of crop output	2.9	6.8	1.0	3.7
(3) Grain output	2.1	5.0	-0.8	2.9
(4) Farm household net income per capita (real)	–	15.0[b]	2.3	7.6

[a] The 1957–1978 figure is the growth rate of agriculture's share of net material product.
[b] The changeover from a production team to a household based accounting system makes it difficult to compare net income figures before and after this changeover. Hence the 1978–1984 figure is particularly unreliable
– Indicates data not available to the author.
Sources: Rows (1)–(3) were derived from data in 'Communiqué of the State Statistical Bureau of the PRC on the 1992 National Social and Economic Development, 31–40; State Statistical Bureau, 1989:742–743; State Statistical Bureau, 1991:243, 294–295.
The raw data for row (4) are from the same sources. The percentage increases in net income were derived from per capita data in current prices divided by the rural retail price index.

comparable to those in such advanced agricultural systems as Japan, South Korea or Taiwan. Politically, however, the 1978–1984 spurt gave enormous credibility to market-oriented reforms and to the individuals who designed those reforms. The political lesson for future reformers from China's experience is obvious but often forgotten—try to begin the reform process with a clear winner.

Why did market-oriented reforms work so well and so quickly in agriculture? Five elements are needed to make a market work well, and these five categories also describe the concrete steps that a Soviet-type command economy must take if it is to evolve into a functioning market economy. The five steps are: 1) achieve macro stability, meaning an acceptable level of inflation and a balance of payments not in serious disequilibrium; 2) make inputs and outputs available for purchase and sale on the market, rather than allocated administratively through a state bureaucracy; 3) free up prices to reflect relative scarcities in the economy; 4) remove barriers to market entry so that competition between firms in different localities becomes possible: 5) change key elements of the institutional framework so that decision-makers

in the production unit (farms and industrial or service enterprises) have an incentive to maximise profits by cutting their costs or raising sales.[3]

For Chinese agriculture, achieving the first four elements of a market economy was not particularly difficult. Macro instability was not a problem and there were no effective barriers to entry in farm production. Making goods available on the market was accomplished gradually over a period of a decade and a half, but many goods became available on the market almost immediately. Because rural markets in some form had existed prior to 1978, few had trouble learning how to take advantage of the opportunities offered by the expanded markets. Prices of secondary products were also quickly freed up. Grain prices proved more difficult to liberalise, partly because of the political dangers inherent in a sharp increase in the cost of food to consumers, partly because of the subsidies required from the government budget if producer prices were raised while consumer prices were kept fixed.[4]

The 'household responsibility system' that resulted from decollectivisation embodied some elements of the property rights required to generate market-oriented incentives for farm households, and went a long way toward meeting the fifth profit maximisation criterion of a functioning market economy. Households are natural profit maximises (subject to the usual caveats about uncertainty and risk aversion) provided that they have the right to keep the income that is earned. This objective was achieved by dividing up the commune land and allocating it to individual households who kept all income from that land after meeting certain tax obligations to the government.

However, property rights in rural China were not complete either immediately after collectivisation in the mid 1980s or in the early 1990s. The property rights were both exclusive and enforceable, in the sense that only one farm household should have the right to use a particular plot of land, and that the government would discipline those who didn't respect that right. But property rights should also be secure and transferable, and here the Chinese reformers had greater problems. They did offer a 15-year guarantee of rights to particular plots, plus vaguer promises concerning an extension beyond those 15 years and the right to inherit. But the many twists and turns in Chinese policy over the three decades of Communist Party rule prior to 1979 meant that such promises were not particularly credible.

The issue of transferring land raised the specter of the old landlord system before 1949, and hence such sales were vigorously opposed by many in the Chinese Communist Party. The distinction was made between the right to use the land for a period of time versus ownership. Not until the early 1990s did the state begin to allow the buying and selling of long-term land leases, but only in the urban areas. Acquiring rural land for factory use, in contrast, typically involved laborious negotiations in which the factory guaranteed jobs and other benefits to displaced farmers in exchange for the use of their land. Land transfer within rural areas typically involved guaranteeing a basic grain ration to those giving up their land use rights.[5]

The incomplete nature of property rights in rural China has had a negative impact on agriculture's performance. Because farmers weren't secure that they would keep their property, even over the 15-year lease, they were reluctant to invest in major capital improvements, particularly land improvements such as irrigation systems. Reservoirs and major feeder canals had been a public good and their maintenance had been the responsibility of the collective teams and brigades that no longer existed. Local governments took over some of the functions of the old commune system but left many to a market that was incapable of generating the necessary effort.[6]

The inability to sell land meant that farmers wishing to migrate to urban areas continued to hold onto their land, farming that land using their spare time or elderly relatives simply to maintain their rights. Below market interest rates made it difficult for farmers and many government departments to compete for rural credit against the preferences of local cadres for investment in township and village enterprises. Because township and village enterprises got most of the available credit, one result (as already mentioned) was the use of IOU's to pay farmers for their grain, in effect further lowering the price paid to farmers for that grain.

By the early 1990s, farmers were emphasising higher-valued cash crops and spending more time on off-farm activities, so farm household incomes continued to rise, although not at the same pace as during the 1979–1984 spurt. The largest beneficiaries were farmers in rural areas near cities that could take full advantage of the opportunities to meet the needs of urban markets.

II. The Service Sector

The Chinese, like others following Soviet economic practices, distinguished between productive and non-productive sectors. Most services were in the latter category. Private restaurants and personal services were simply suppressed. Commerce and finance were under state ownership and control but were considered inferior activities in comparison with sectors producing material goods. Where the service sector in a typical low-income developing country constitutes between 35 and 40 per cent of GDP (Chenery and Syrquin 1975:20), the service sector in China in 1978 constituted only 23 per cent (in 1990 prices). By 1988, however, the share of services had risen to 28 per cent of GDP.

From the perspective of China's leadership, services were considered a partial solution to the problem of a labor force rising by 14 million people per year. In addition, by some crude estimates of the number of work days required by the agricultural sector, there were 100 million in the countryside who were already considered to be underemployed. Hence, many of the rules circumscribing small-scale service activities were abolished or ignored. The response was dramatic. The labor force in the service sector doubled during the first decade of reform from 48.7 million people in 1978 to 99.5 million in 1988 (State Statistical Bureau 1991:99).

Traders and transport workers were the first to take advantage of the new opportunities. Then, collectively and individually-owned restaurants and small shops sprung up everywhere. In many cases, state commercial establishments became hollowed-out shells housing private vendors who rented space from the state. Labor contracting services developed in such interior provinces as Sichuan, which provided the construction workers for the job of building millions of new apartments for urban residents. The term 'floating population' was coined to classify people who had migrated to the cities to work but were not formally classified as urban residents. Before 1978, these people could not get food ration coupons and public security officials would quickly pack them back to the countryside. By the mid 1980s these people could buy the food they needed on the market and public security usually ignored them. The floating population nationwide probably numbered in the tens of millions. Some became permanent urban residents, but others moved back and forth between temporary urban jobs and their rural homes.

Small-scale services responded quickly to market forces for many of the same reasons that farmers did. Once these activities were legalised, millions of people were prepared to supply them. Barriers to entry were absent and prices charged for these services, for the most part, could not be controlled. Property rights were not a major problem, because services were not embodied in the people supplying them. (Restaurants and shops required a physical location and sometimes a roof and walls, but one did not have to own the roof and walls or hold a long-term lease to make effective use of them.) With some exceptions, the capital investments required to establish a service activity were modest, like tractors with carts to haul goods to market. There was nothing comparable to the pervasive Mafia-style organisations found in Russia that restricted entry to service markets and extorted payments from those allowed in, although low-level government officials did extract informal payments of various kinds. This boom in small-scale services was readily observable in other former Soviet-style economies, as well; the streets of Hanoi, Warsaw, and Moscow were also teeming with small traders and new shops.

The large-scale service sector did not respond so quickly. Some large commercial establishments in China, like department stores, did respond because they faced direct competition from the collective enterprises and petty traders. The major financial and transport enterprises, in contrast, were very slow to change. The problems with market-oriented reform for banks, railroads, and airlines have much in common with those faced by large-scale state industrial enterprises and will be discussed below.

III. Foreign Trade and Investment

In China's Soviet-style foreign trade system, all trade was handled by government corporations that had a monopoly over all purchases and sales in particular sectors. All foreign exchange was turned over to the Bank of China, the foreign exchange bank. There was an 'air lock' between all producing enterprises and world markets so that prices on world markets had no influence on the domestic price structure. Foreign firms often did not even know to which industrial enterprise the equipment they were selling was going or from which enterprise the items they were purchasing were coming. In addition to this, throughout the Cultural Revolution period (1966–1976) there was active political hostility toward foreign trade in general and foreign technology in particular. Foreign investment did not exist.

After Mao Zedong's death in 1976, policies began to change. The first move was to encourage domestic enterprises to buy inputs from abroad rather then to discourage such purchases. Enterprises responded with such alacrity that China by 1978 found itself with a growing trade deficit, despite increasing prices for China's petroleum exports. Imports in nominal dollar terms rose 51 per cent in 1978 and by 44 per cent in 1979. Clearly, new and increasing sources of foreign exchange had to be discovered.

In 1979, reforms were introduced to facilitate exports of manufactures and (for the first time) to allow for foreign investment (Lardy 1992). In essence, these efforts involved the breakup of the monopoly on foreign trade held by the state corporations, and transferring this authority to regional corporations (but not to producing enterprises for the most part). Special economic zones (export processing zones) were set up to free foreign investors and other exporters from red tape. Various export subsidies were introduced and China's currency was devalued from 1.7 yuan to the US dollar in 1981 to 2.9 yuan to the dollar in 1985 to 4.8 yuan to the dollar in 1990. This 182 per cent rise was much more than the 87 per cent increase in Chinese retail prices or the 40 per cent rise in the ratio of Chinese to US retail prices.

Foreign trade responded to these incentives in dramatic fashion, as indicated by the data in Table 2. The response of foreign direct investment was equally dramatic, as the data in Table 4 indicate. A Soviet-style economy geared to producing low quality goods for a captive domestic market was suddenly competing head-to-head with its East Asian neighbours, the most dynamic exporters of manufactured goods in the world. What accounts for this extraordinary change?

In the sphere of foreign trade, the challenge for a reforming China was how to plug into the international market system, where goods were freely available at market prices. On the import side, as demonstrated as early as 1977 and 1978, all the government had to do was remove barriers to the purchase of foreign products. Exporting of minerals such as petroleum was also straightforward.

The export of manufactures was another matter. Enterprises in China had to acquire the

---

Table 4   **Foreign direct investment in China** (billions of US dollars per year)

	1979–1982	1983–1985	1986–1988	1989–1990	1991	1992
Contracted direct foreign investment	1.50	3.44	3.95	6.10	11.98	58.12
Direct foreign investment actually used	0.29	1.19	2.46	3.44	4.37	11.01

Sources: 'Official predicts $10 billion more in investment', *China Daily*, April 26, 1993, Business Supplement, 1; ' Foreign funds hit record $25 billion', *China Daily*, June 2. 1993:2; State Statistical Bureau, *Zhonguo tongji nianjian*, 1991:629; State Statistical Bureau. *Zhonguo tongji nianjian*. 1992:641; and State Statistical Bureau, *Zhongguo tongji nianjian*, 1993:647.

ability to produce what international markets required, and to make a connection with foreign markets. Rather than simply having enterprises fend for themselves, China did not allow many domestic industrial enterprises to deal directly with foreign markets until well into the 1990s. Instead, the foreign trade corporations were decentralised to the provinces and regions, and allowed to compete for business. By 1993, there were 4,000 foreign trade companies and manufacturing enterprises allowed to deal directly on foreign markets (*China Daily*, 19 April 1993:2). The 'air lock' between domestic enterprises and foreign markets gradually broke down as the international prices were passed through to a liberalised domestic market, and producing enterprises were allowed to retain larger and larger shares of the foreign exchange they earned.

The market for foreign exchange illustrates how market forces gradually come to dominate. In the early 1980s, foreign exchange was tightly controlled by the Bank of China, although black markets for foreign currency existed. Under pressure from foreign investors, who had trouble obtaining foreign exchange with which to buy imported inputs and repatriate profits, the government created 'foreign exchange adjustment centers,' swap markets on which those with surplus foreign exchange, notably joint venture hotels, could sell that surplus to foreign firms at a market-determined rate. Eligibility for participation on these swap markets, initially very restricted, became wider with time and included large numbers of domestic firms.

By 1992, partly because of a desire to become eligible to join GATT, China began talking about moving to a single market-determined exchange rate, but a large capital outflow in mid 1993, much of it technically illegal, led to a sharp divergence in the official and swap market rate. The gap had been about 10 per cent in 1992; by mid 1993, it was more like 75 per cent. However, in March 1993, China for the first time did legally allow individuals to take *renminbi*, the state currency, out of the country and the goal remained

full convertibility at some future date (*China Daily*, 8 February 1993:3). The desire to join GATT also prompted China to reduce import duties and to eliminate many import quotas in favor of tariffs (Li 1993:13–15).

The primary force leading to the capital outflow and the devaluation of the yuan was probably the desire by individuals and organisations to protect the value of their assets against the rising rate of inflation. Real interest rates on deposits and central government bonds were negative by mid 1993, and moving money to Hong Kong was one way to avoid losses. In July 1993, the Chinese government did intervene heavily in the swap markets by selling off dollars, but controlling inflation and/or raising domestic interest rates was likely to be a more effective solution to maintaining an appropriate exchange rate over the long run.

But the opening of China to trade does not explain its success in foreign markets; after all, other countries more open to international market influences than China have not enjoyed China's surge in the export of manufactures. China's exports of manufactures increased from around $5 billion in 1978 to $68 billion by 1992. One cannot prove the point systematically, but connections with Hong Kong probably account for much of China's success. In 1979, 22.6 per cent of Chinese exports went to Hong Kong and 79 per cent of those exports stayed in Hong Kong. By 1987, despite the increasing knowledge of foreign markets on the Chinese mainland, Hong Kong's share of all exports rose to 31.1 per cent (of a much larger total than in 1979) and 62 per cent of these exports to Hong Kong were re-exported. Among manufactures, Hong Kong's share was much higher, ranging from 46 per cent for textile fabric to 62 per cent for clothing and 87 per cent for machinery (Sung 1991). By 1992 Hong Kong's share in total Chinese exports (including re-exports) had risen further to 44 per cent (General Administration of Customs 1993). In the 1990s, a similar process seems to be happening through Taiwan. In effect, the formidable marketing talents of Hong Kong and

Taiwan are being grafted onto the manufacturing capacity of the mainland.

Part of this export performance came from joint venture firms and other firms with various kinds of foreign investment—$17.4 billion in 1992, which marked a 44 per cent rise over 1991. At first glance, China's success in attracting foreign investment is a puzzle. After all, foreign investors have traditionally had little security in China. China does not have a strong legal tradition; in fact, lawyers and most commercial laws were abolished during the Cultural Revolution. The system after 1976 had to be rebuilt from scratch, and the new laws were not very reliable protection against official assaults on foreign property rights. Whatever one's legal rights of ownership, official support was required to gain access to state controlled inputs such as electricity, foreign exchange, or railroad transport. The expansion of the domestic market for many inputs eased this problem but did not eliminate it. After the political crisis caused by the events on Tiananmen on June 4, 1989, there was even reason for foreign investors to expect a reversion to more bureaucratic controls over the economy, not fewer. And yet foreign investment continued to rise.

Investment designed to supply the Chinese domestic market can perhaps be explained by noting that the lure of a billion customers can offset many worries. The rapid growth of export-oriented foreign investment, in the face of insecure property rights, is also easier to understand if one recognises that most of this foreign investment was coming from Hong Kong, and to a lesser degree other overseas Chinese, and was going into Guangdong Province next door to Hong Kong. In 1990, for example, 55 per cent of all realised foreign investment came from Hong Kong and Macao and 46 per cent of all investment whose regional destination could be identified went to Guangdong Province. Fujian Province, with the closest ties historically and culturally to Taiwan, came next with 9 per cent (State Statistical Bureau 1991:630–1). The direct investment of Japan and the United States in 1990, in contrast, was 14 and 13 per cent of the total respectively and no other country had over 2 per cent.

Why did Chinese in Hong Kong and Taiwan move into an area where other investors feared to tread? The primary answer involves at least two components. First, most Hong Kong investments were small in scale and payback periods were short, often three years or less. Property rights don't have to be all that secure if a high rate of return on investment is possible in a short period. The other advantages possessed by the overseas Chinese were their family and other informal ties to their relatives and friends on the mainland. Connections (*guanxi*) are what makes things work in China and connections are based on personal ties. Japanese and American corporations might have better connections at the top of the Chinese pyramid, but nothing comparable to the Hong Kong-Guangdong connections that really counted in day-to-day operations.

Despite the pervasiveness of personal connections, formal rules did matter. The attempt to create rules with which foreign investors could live also had the important side effect of benefiting Chinese investors, too. The special economic zones set up by China illustrate the point. Originally there were only a handful of such zones, all in Guangdong and Fujian provinces, designed to free foreign investors from the various restrictions and red tape of the domestic economy. Rules that made sense for foreigners were increasingly applied to domestic firms, first within the zones and then outside of them. Soon other provinces and coastal cities wanted similar advantages and so more liberal rules spread up the coast. China's interior lagged behind in creating economic rules to attract foreign investors and other exporters, but by the early 1990s they were trying hard to catch up. Foreign investors still got some advantages not available to domestic firms, and vice versa, but these differences were under pressure from such practices as the ability of Chinese firms to launder their money in Hong Kong and bring it back as 'foreign investment'.

Foreign trade and foreign investment, therefore, has played a central role in moving China toward a market economy. Strong vested interests now know how to take advantage of foreign marketing opportunities and have a stake in removing the barriers to trade that still exist.

IV. Industry and State-owned Enterprises

The task of reforming state-owned and private industrial enterprises is not fully analogous to creating market conditions for farm households and small shops. Not only do industrial enterprises have much larger and more complex internal structures, these enterprises are embedded in external institutions, a banking system, a tax system and much else, that are a product of the old command economy. Reforming all of these institutions together is a complex task, but failure to do so carries with it the danger that partial reforms may not lead to sustained increases in industrial productivity, the central goal of the industrial reform effort.

China began a systematic effort to reform industrial enterprises in 1984. In terms of the five components needed for a functioning markets system, the first, macroeconomic stability, was not a problem in 1984. As for components 2 and 3, China made large quantities of industrial inputs available on the market rather than through the administrative allocation system of the government. Inputs (and outputs) allocated by the state were sold at fixed state-set prices, but inputs distributed through the market were sold at much higher market-determined prices. This dual price system soon provided many with the opportunity to earn easy profits and the resulting corruption contributed to urban discontent in 1989. But the dual price system did mean that market-determined prices governed a large share of enterprise allocation decisions. Component 4, opening up the system to competition, was achieved by abolishing the regional monopolies that until then had determined where almost all industrial enterprises, including small ones, could

sell their products. Competition did not result where demand for a product far exceeded its supply at prices that did not allow excessive profits. But where demand was not so strong, as with many consumer goods such as clocks and watches, the more inefficient producers soon found themselves in vigorous competition with efficient high quality producers such as the clock and watch manufacturers of Shanghai.

As for component 5, the enterprise's objective function was changed to emphasise profits rather than gross value output and a myriad of other plan targets. Selling off large state enterprises to private investors was ruled out in both the 1980s and early 1990s, largely on the ideological and political ground that such a move would not be consistent with socialism. The 1988 constitution did include a formal statement allowing private property, and foreign joint ventures and small-scale firms to be private. There was much discussion and numerous experiments with a responsibility system for enterprises which, among other things, was supposed to increase enterprise autonomy vis-à-vis the government ministries. In November 1993, the Central Committee of the Party issued a directive that spelled out terms for moving state enterprises even further toward complete autonomy from the central government, at least on paper (*China Daily*, 17 November 1993:supplement).

The industrial reforms of the mid 1980s had one major success. They led directly to a sustained boom in small and medium-scale industrial enterprises throughout China, particularly along the coast and nearby cities. Because the subject of these enterprises is taken up at length in the essay by Jefferson and Rawski in this symposium, only its relevance to the overall reform effort will be mentioned here.

Making industrial inputs available on a market at market prices was essential to the dynamic growth of what are called the township and village enterprises. Abolition of local monopolies was also important. In 1980, collective and other non-state-owned industries accounted for only 21 per cent of the gross value of industrial output. By 1991 this figure had risen to 47 per cent. Small and medium-scale industrial gross output in 1980, however, was 75 per cent of total industrial output and by 1991 this share had fallen to 66 per cent. Many small and medium-scale firms were, of course, state-owned (State Statistical Bureau 1981:212; 1992:70). All but a handful of the really large firms were state-owned.

As work by Jefferson, Rawski and economists in the Chinese Academy of Social Sciences has shown, total factor productivity after reform rose faster in the non-state sector than in the state sector, but it rose in both (Jefferson, Rawski and Zheng 1992). There is plausible reason to believe that this rise in productivity occurred because the non-state enterprises have solved the problem of getting enterprises to behave according to the rules of the market. Unlike the large-scale state-owned sector, township and village enterprises were not heavily subsidised by the government budget nor by the banking system. They were promoted because they made profits for their workers and for their local governments and, when they made losses, there was little political pressure to keep them open.

How were the property rights defined for small and medium-scale enterprises, or for township and village enterprises in particular? In some cases these firms were started by individuals, but often county or township governments also played a central start-up role. County state-owned firms were the property of the whole county, but they were not the property of the provincial government nor the central government. Collective and private firms were partly owned by their workers and managers but they too paid portions of their earnings to the county or township governments, whatever the tax laws might say. County and township governments did not behave exactly like mini private conglomerates, but there were many features in common. Part of the reason, in the case of townships at least, is that they had been run as production units for some time. The

township, after all, was basically the old commune which had carried out both production and governmental functions. The county and township governments, unlike the central government, could not print money nor, for the most part, could they readily force the banking system to print money to cover their expenses and the losses of local enterprises. Thus the counties, townships, and their local enterprises faced hard budget constraints. In both a positive and a negative sense, therefore, counties, townships, and their enterprises faced incentives to behave in accordance with the rules of the market. If they made profits, someone or everyone in the county or township could keep them. If they made losses, someone or everyone in the county or township bore the losses.

When one turns to the larger state-owned enterprises and the medium-scale state firms under urban or provincial jurisdiction, however, meaningful autonomy and defined property rights fade away. Ownership by 'all of the people' really means a sense of ownership by none of the people. In eastern Europe and Russia, where central governments are weak, the result is often that workers and managers steal state assets and sell them or use them to set up their own firms. Privatisation in that situation becomes necessary simply to preserve the assets of the enterprise. China's state apparatus, although much weaker than in the late 1970s, was still strong enough in the early 1990s to limit this kind of predatory behaviour. But China's large state enterprises in the early 1990s still found themselves halfway between a bureaucratic command system and a market system. Central planning was gone but government intervention in enterprise operations was common. Managers were loaded down with objectives only partially related to the market's requirement to make profits by cutting costs and raising sales. If managers did what government officials wanted them to do, their losses would be made up with bank loans that didn't have to be repaid. Their budget constraint remained soft.

That large state enterprise budget constraints were soft in 1992 and 1993 was no secret, but changing large enterprise behaviour involved many separate but related reforms involving more than just the industrial enterprises themselves. Autonomy and hard budgets could be achieved by simply removing government from the scene and letting enterprises sort the process out on their own at the micro level. But the impact of this approach in eastern Europe, Russia and the Ukraine suggested that the price in human welfare terms could be high. Which institutions must be reformed if large scale industrial enterprises are to be brought in line with what the market requires? A partial list would include some of the following factors.

Financial markets. The formal banking system in China dominated the financial markets. Formally, commercial banks were separated from the central bank early in the reform period, but in reality, the commercial banks continued to follow the direction of the central bank, and of government policymakers in general. These banks took for granted that the central bank would bail them out if they got into trouble, which in turn means that the industrial customers of these banks faced soft budgets.

The fiscal system. Before reform, all but a tiny percentage of profits had simply been turned over to the state and the state then reallocated those funds to investment projects determined by the central plan. After reform, in theory, once fixed rate taxes were paid, enterprises retained the remaining profits and did their own investment. In reality, the fixed tax rates were negotiable and a firm with losses or low profits could usually negotiate a lower rate. This flexibility in the tax system also contributed to the soft budget constraint facing state enterprises.

The legal and regulatory framework. The lack of an established legal tradition in China has already been mentioned. Issues such as how to calculate profits lacked clearcut rules making it easier for managers to divert funds toward their own goals and away from the goals of the nominal owners, public or private. Chinese enterprises used several different accounting systems, none of them really designed for a modern market system, and these somehow had to be changed into one appropriate and enforceable set of rules. China also had a bankruptcy law put in place in the latter half of the 1980s, but there were almost no bankruptcies of large firms until the early 1990s and not many then. Politically, it was difficult to bankrupt companies—particularly given the absence of a safety net for those losing their jobs. Practically, it wasn't easy to decide which enterprises really should be closed down, given price distortions and inadequate accounting rules.

The worker welfare system. In China, both before reform and into the early 1990s, the state-owned enterprises were responsible for the housing, health services, day care, and much else for their workers. Getting rid of the many surplus workers in state enterprises, however desirable from an efficiency point of view, meant depriving people laid off of their homes and health care (Ahmad and Hussein 1989) By the early 1990s, the privatisation and marketisation of housing (making rents reflect market demand and supply) was underway, but the political/equity constraints on doing this quickly were enormous. The Central Committee directive of November 1993 also called for further steps to separate the dependence of the unemployment insurance and the pension system on individual enterprises. How quickly these measures will actually be implemented remains to be seen.

Factor markets. After reform, informal capital markets grew rapidly, ranging from inter-enterprise loans (not always voluntary) to the pooling of the funds of friends and relatives. The market for unskilled labor was also freed up when workers were allowed to move freely from one place to another or, at least, were not effectively prevented from doing so. Only in the 1990s, however, did China begin to loosen the tight controls over the allocation of skilled labor such as university graduates. In 1993, for example, China began to offer college graduates some choice of job, whereas before they had virtually none (*China Daily*, 5 April 1993:3). Enterprises working to gain access to land had a particularly difficult time. The rapid development of the township and village enterprises was partly the result of the fact that they had much easier access to land than did the large urban enterprises. By the early 1990s, however, the need to find more and more land for the rapidly growing industrial sector was leading China to swallow ideology and set up markets for land. As in the case of markets for foreign exchange, it was the need of foreign investors for long-term leases on land at commercial rates that led the way for domestic firms to have the same possibilities.

Ownership and management. China in the early 1990s in general, and in the Central Committee Directive of November 1993 in particular, still rejected across-the-board privatisation. The question then becomes one of whether there is a way of simulating the effect of privatisation while retaining public ownership. In that context, China's experiments with share ownership and the stockmarket take on significance. If managers are picked by shareholders, and the shareholders are concerned mainly with the return on their investment, then the career path of enterprise managers is no longer directly determined by the state bureaucracy. Even if the shares are held by other state enterprises, and thus 'publicly' owned, if those other state enterprises face hard budget constraints and hence are mainly pursuing profits, they will use their membership on the board of directors of the share-owned enterprise to insist on similar profit-oriented behavior by that enterprise's management. Share ownership is spreading in China and is more widespread than the small number of firms registered on the Shanghai and Shenzhen stock markets. But China's large state enterprises are a long way from a system where most shares are held by other enterprises and private individuals and where management is selected by a board of directors independent of the state bureaucracy.

Other analysts might offer a somewhat different list of factors for making large state-owned enterprises responsive to market conditions, but the basic point remains. Getting state enterprise management to behave according to the rules of the market is not just a question of outright privatisation or simulated private behaviour within a system of some kind of public ownership. The whole economic system must be redesigned to be compatible with a market economy. In mixed economies with a high degree of state intervention, such as Indonesia or South Korea, the move toward a more complete market system has taken a decade or longer—and these economies began the reform process with many elements of a market system in place. A nation does not have to complete all of the changes before it has a functioning market system. It must get far enough down the road from a command to a market system so that managers are governed more by market forces than by the wishes of government officials. There is no really reliable measure, however, for telling whether a system is governed more by bureaucratic command than market forces. Determining when market forces are sufficiently dominant for the market to function well is even more difficult, at least in practice if not in theory.

V. Macroeconomic Stability

Enterprise reform is closely related to the problem of controlling inflation without generating a recession or alternative periods of stop and go growth. Enterprise reform is not really feasible until inflation is brought under control by measures other than direct government allocation of credit quotas. Inflation controlled by state-set quotas on bank loans leads quickly back to state intervention in enterprise behaviour in other areas as well. On the other side, without market-oriented enterprise reform, including reform of the institutions such as financial markets, rapid sustained growth tends to lead to bouts of accelerating inflation.

In a market system, inflation is controlled by government actions that determine the amount of high powered money. In turn, the amount of high-powered money determines the supply of money, including deposits of the banking system, that are the main source of supply of loans to business. Business demand for credit determines how many loans are actually made.

In a Soviet-style system, this process actually works in reverse. The central plan determines enterprise credit requirements or demand. The banking system then supplies those credits as spelled out in the plan. Because the central bank and the commercial banks were one and the same—both were components of the People's Bank of China—there is not a question of the banking system being unable to supply the necessary credit, usually at zero or way below market rates of interest. The central bank can print whatever money is required.

In the partially reformed Chinese banking system of the late 1980s and early 1990s, the form of a market system existed, but not the reality. In form, China broke the connection between the central bank and the commercial banks by setting up separate commercial banks and confining the role of the People's Bank of China to central banking. The central planning of credit was abolished and interest rates were raised, although not to market-determined levels. But the process that determined the money supply still worked in reverse from what would be the case in a market system. Enterprises first determined their credit needs. The commercial banks were then expected to supply those needs at below-market interest rates and, in some cases, without much expectation of repayment. The People's Bank of China then created as much high-powered money as was needed to provide commercial banks with the necessary funds.

In such a partially reformed system, controlling inflation by controlling high powered money is possible but inefficient. If the People's Bank tightens up the supply of money, enterprises fight to get as large a share as possible, particularly when interest rates, administratively determined, are kept low. Who actually ends up with credit depends as much on political power as profitability of the proposed investment. Raising interest rates in this context will lead to a reduction in the demand for credit for some enterprises, but the queue for loans is likely to remain long. Too many firms know they won't have to repay the loans if the enterprise makes losses.

Inflation in the context of this kind of system is even more difficult to control when price reform is being carried out simultaneously with partial financial reform. Freeing up prices for previously underpriced inputs such as energy leads to higher costs for enterprises. The enterprises, in the usual cost-push way, pass these costs along in the form of higher prices for their products, and the banking system, where necessary, accommodates increased demand for credit.

The impact of an anti-inflation program with only partially reformed state enterprises was apparent in 1989–1990. With the freeing up of many prices together with a rapid increase in the supply of money, inflation began to accelerate to politically unacceptable levels at the end of 1988, reaching an annual rate by the end of the year of around 30 per cent. In 1989 and 1990, the government instituted a tight money policy by directly setting quotas on credit given by the commercial banks. Inflation fell quickly and in 1990 the retail price index rose by only 2.1 per cent. But output growth in the economy in late 1989 and early 1990 also ground to a halt and unemployment in the cities rose. To avoid the political consequences of rising unemployment, credit was loosened in the latter part of 1990 and the economy resumed growth. In 1991 real GNP rose by 7.3 per cent and then skyrocketed to 12.8 per cent in 1992 and continued at that pace in 1993. But by mid 1993, prices were again increasing at a high and rising pace and another credit crunch was anticipated. No country has shown that it can eliminate cycles in economic activity, but the current wide fluctuations in China's performance could be damped by reform.

In July 1993, the head of the central bank was fired and replaced by Deputy Prime Minister Zhu Rongji. Immediately following the firing, China announced a whole new set of anti-inflation measures. Some of these, such as the raising of bank deposit interest rates, used market methods to dampen down demand. Others involved more administrative interventions to rein in bank lending. But slowing the investment boom in 1993 was more difficult than in 1988–89. The banks were no longer the main source of enterprise capital. Foreign funds, domestic privately held funds, and bonds issued by provincial governments were alternative sources of investment finance by 1993. Simply ordering the banks to lend less and monitoring their performance would not have had the same impact on investment as it did earlier. As in the case of the foreign exchange market, China was being forced to move away from administrative means of controlling prices toward market instruments because the administrative measures no longer worked well in an increasingly liberalised financial setting. In addition, fear of the political consequences of a major slowdown in economic activity made Chinese leaders reluctant to make full use of the anti-inflationary measures that did work. Until the financial system is fully reformed, however, even real GNP growth of 9 or 10 per cent is likely to trigger accelerating inflation followed by retrenchment. Stop and go growth in output and prices appears to be a characteristics of an economy in the twilight zone between command and the market.

VI. Conclusion

China has gone a long way toward a market system, especially in agriculture, foreign trade, and small-scale firms. Most of the problems that stand between the partially reformed Chinese economy of the early 1990s and a full market system reside in the large-scale state enterprise sector, and in the partial nature of the reform of the banking system. Together, these account for the inflation and the stop-go nature of Chinese growth in the 1988–93 period. There are those who believe that the state sector will eventually wither away under competition from the nimble township and village enterprises and locally owned state firms, but this doesn't seem likely. Economies of scale in steel, automobiles, petrochemicals, railroad transport, and electric power grids will ensure the continuance of large firms.

In eastern Europe, the path to reforming large industrial enterprises includes political revolution and across-the-board privatisation. But China is not eastern Europe. The decollectivisation of agriculture substantially reduced the power of local cadres, but it had the full support of the central authorities. The township and village enterprises reduced the power of the central government, but enhanced the resources available to local governments. The centre, after a feeble attempt to rein in the township and village enterprises in 1989–90, gave up. China's State Planning Commission, never as powerful as its counterpart in the Soviet Union, is a shadow of its former self and is increasingly turning to indirect levers of control. Real political power in China, in any case, rests not so much in the economic bureaucracy as in the army, the public security forces, and a party that still has many elements from its revolutionary and rural beginnings.

China has now had 15 years of experience that demonstrates that those who move most quickly toward a market economy will reap the most benefits. Guangdong province has done better than the others and the coastal provinces have done better than those in the interior. The laggards are now scrambling to catch up. Government no longer controls much of the process even where it might like to do so. The dual price system for industrial inputs will disappear because firms don't want to sell their products at below market prices and the state's ability to force them to is dwindling. Foreign exchange will become convertible because the firms earning foreign currency can easily find ways to hold on to it, whatever the wishes of the Bank of China.

What will be left, once the reform of large state enterprises is well along, is a market economy with all kinds of governmental interventions at both the local and central level, perhaps on the pattern of South Korea or Taiwan in the 1970s. The question is whether these continuing state interventions in an essentially market-oriented economy will slow growth markedly, or whether growth will continue at the torrid pace of the first 15 years of reform.

Notes

1. The Chinese net material product indexes for the pre 1978 years are based mainly on 1950s price calculation that give too heavy a weight to the fast-growing industrial sector and hence exaggerate real NMP growth. Following methods similar to those used in Table 1, I recalculated Chinese NMP for the 1952–1978 period using 1978 prices as the base. This recalculation produced NMP growth rates of 4.8 per cent for 1952–1978 or 4.2 per cent per year for 1957–1978 (Perkins 1981).
2. Discussion of this process from a village viewpoint is in the essays by a variety of people who spent time in Chinese villages in the early 1980s (Parish 1985; Zweig 1989).
3. Categories 2–5 are discussed at greater length in Perkins (1988:602–21).
4. Subsidies required for grain alone rose from 3.9 billion yuan in 1978 to 8.4 billion yuan when grain purchase prices were raised for the 1979 harvest and peaked at 23.4 billion yuan in 1984 (Qiao 1990:28). See also the discussion in Lardy (1983). In the early 1980s, one US dollar exchanged for 1.7–1.9 Chinese yuan.
5. I am indebted to Mr Mai Lu for this information.
6. Public health and education were two other public goods that may have suffered because of the abolition of the collective system, although the evidence is far from clear. Barefoot doctors or rural paramedics, the backbone of the rural public health system, for example, declined in number and many became pharmacists selling herbs and other medicines for profit. Whether morbidity or mortality actually increased as a result, however, is unknown.

References

Ahmad, Ehtisham, and Hussein, Athar, 1989. 'Social Security in China: A historical perspective', The Development Economics Research Program, London School of Economics, China Program, No. 4, September.

Byrd, William, A. (ed.), 1992. *Chinese Industrial Firms Under Reform*, Oxford University Press, Oxford.

—— and Qingsong, Lin, (eds), 1990. *China's Rural Industry: structure, development and reform*, Oxford University Press, Oxford.

Chenery, Hollis and Syrquin, Moshe, 1975. *Patterns of Development, 1950–1970*, Oxford University Press, Oxford.

China Foreign Trade Yearbook compiling committee, 1984. *Zhongguo duiwai jingji maoi nianjian 1984*, China Foreign and Economic Trade Publishers, Beijing.

——, 1990. *Zhongguo duiwai jingji maoi nianjian 1989–90*, China Foreign and Economic Trade Publishers, Beijing.

General Administration of Customs, 1993. *China's Customs Statistics*, Series No. 40(1).

Granick, David, 1990. *Chinese State Enterprises: A regional property rights analysis*, University of Chicago Press, Chicago.

Groves, Theodore, Yongmiao, Hong, McMillan, John and Naughton, Barry, 1994. 'Autonomy and incentives in Chinese state enterprises', *Quarterly Journal of Economics*, 109(1):183–209.

He, Jun, 1993. 'Graduates given more freedom to choose jobs', *China Daily*, April 5:3.

Hsu, Robert C., 1991. *Economic Theories in China, 1979–1988*, Cambridge University Press, Cambridge.

Huang, Yiping, 1993. 'Government Intervention and Agricultural Performance in China', unpublished doctoral dissertation, The Australian National University, Canberra.

Hussein, Athar, and Stern, Nicholas, 1991. 'Effective Demand, Enterprise Reforms and Public Finance', The Development Economics Research Programme, London School of Economics, CP:10, March.

Jefferson, Gary H., Rawski, Thomas G. and Yuxin, Zheng, 1992. 'Growth, Efficiency and Convergence in China's State and Collective Industry', *Economic Development and Cultural Change*, 40(2):239–66.

Lardy, Nicholas, 1983. *Agriculture in China's Modern Economic Development*, Cambridge University Press, Cambridge.

——, 1992. *Foreign Trade and Economic Reform in China*, 1978–1990, Cambridge University Press, Cambridge.

Li, Jingwen, 1993. 'Several viewpoints on the present economic situation and the 1993 development trend', in Liu, Guoguang (ed.), *1993 nian zhonguo jingji xingshi fenxi yu yuce*, Chinese Academy of Social Sciences Press, Beijing: 40–50.

Li, Ning, 1993. 'China Moves Closer to GATT', *Beijing Review*, February 8–14, (36)6:13–15.

Lin, Yifu, and Shen, Minggao, 1992. 'A discussion of the shareholding system and the reform of large and medium scale state enterprises', *Jingji yanjiu*, September 20, 9:48–55.

Liu, Chao-nan, 1992. 'The Incentive Structures of China's Enterprises under the Contract Responsibility System, *The Journal of Contemporary China*, Winter–Spring, 2(1):69–81.

Lu, Mai and Timmer, Peter C., 1992. 'Developing the Chinese Rural Economy: experience of the 1980s and prospects of the future', HIID Development Discussion Paper No. 428, AFP, September.

Naughton, Barry, 1992. 'Implications of the State Monopoly over Industry and its Relaxation', *Modern China*, January 18(1):14–41.

Parish, William, L. (ed.), 1985. *Chinese Rural Development: The Great Transformation*, M.E. Sharpe, Armonk.

Perkins, Dwight H., 1981. 'An American View of the Chinese Economy', in Jingji yanjiu compilation group, *Guowai jingji zuezhe lun zhongguo ji fazhanzhong guojia jingji*, China Finance and Economic Publishers, Beijing:4–5.

——, 1988. 'Reforming China's economic system', *Journal of Economic Literature*, 26(2):601-45.

—— and Roemer, Michael (eds), 1991. *Reforming Economic Systems in Developing Countries*, Harvard Institute for International Development, Cambridge:13–33.

Qiao, Rongzhang, 1990. *Jiage butie?*, China Price Publishers.

Rham, Rahman Azizur, Griffin, Keith, Riskin, Carl and Zhao, Renwei, Sources of Income Inequality in Post-Reform China, unpublished manuscript.

Sicular, Terry, 1992. 'Public finance and China's economic reforms', Harvard Institute of Economic Research Discussion Paper No. 1618, November.

State Planning Commission Investment Research Institute, 1992. 'Analysis and forecast of the 1992–1993 investment situation', in Liu, Guoguang, (ed.), *1993 nian zhongguo: jingji xingshe fenxi yu yuce*, Chinese Academy of Social Sciences Press, Beijing: 161–72.

State Statistical Bureau, 1981. *Statistical Yearbook of China*.

——, 1989. *Zhongguo tongji nianjian*.

——, 1991. *Zhongguo tongji nianjian*.

——, 1992. *Zhongguo tongji nianjian*.

——, 1992. *Zhongguo tongji zhaiyao*.

——, 1993. *Zhongguo tongji nianjian*.

——,1993. 'Communiqué of the State Statistical Bureau of the PRC on the 1992 National Social and Economic Development Plan', *Beijing Review*, March 8–14, 36(10):31–40.

Sung, Yun-Wing, 1991. *The China–Hong Kong Connection: The Key to China's Open Door*

Policy, Cambridge University Press, Cambridge.

Tidrick, Gene, and Chen, Jiyuan, 1987. *China's Industrial Reform*, Oxford University Press, Oxford.

Wang, Liansheng, 1993. 'China's Inflation in the 1980s', Centre for Research in Economics and Business Administration, University of Oslo, unpublished manuscript.

Wang, Yijiang, 1991. 'Economic reform, fixed control investment expansion, and inflation: A behavioural model based on the Chinese experience', *China Economic Review*, 2(1):3–27.

Wang, Dayong, and Wang, Zhihong, 1992. 'Improve macro controls, guarantee a successful reform', in Liu, Guoguang, (ed.), *1993 nian zhongguo: jingji zingshi fenzi yu yuce*, Chinese Academy of Social Sciences Press, Beijing:143–45.

Zweig, David, 1989. *Agrarian Radicalism in China, 1968–1981*, Harvard University Press, Cambridge.

4 Foundations for the Future: the building of modern machinery in Shanghai after the Pacific War

Mark Elvin

The transfer of what was, by contemporary standards, high-level foreign engineering technology to Chinese firms in Shanghai was successfully accomplished in the two generations before the Pacific War in 1937. To the extent that mastering modern machine-building technology is the first phase of Kuznetsian modern economic growth, it may be concluded that in a restricted, though important, locality and in a qualitative though not quantitative sense, Chinese society had already created such a core in the pre-Communist period.

The theoretical implications of this fact are of major importance. The structures and values of late-imperial Chinese society were on the whole already well suited to modern economic growth, at least at the entrepreneurial and operational level. Access to the examples, ideas, techniques, personnel, finance, demand and supply of the world market, made possible by the openness of Shanghai, was of crucial importance to the effective transfer of this machine-building technology. Hence any viable theory of late-imperial China's earlier economic retardation relative to the west has to focus primarily on internal inhibiting economic effects (such as those specified by the so-called 'high-level equilibrium trap') or on the economic effects of political

measures (such as the isolation of China from the world outside). Similarly, in the early modern period, economic imperialism may have helped Chinese economic modernisation rather than hindered it.

The real problems facing the communist regime in the 1950s and following decades were those of maintaining the qualitative level of the existing core and of diffusing and generalising what had already been accomplished locally. It is immediately apparent that the relatively greater success of the 1980s was achieved by returning to a less regimented and more internationally open pattern of growth nearer to the late-imperial and early Republican pattern than to the highly controlled and cellularised system of the Maoist period.

I. Shanghai

Shanghai had a number of advantages over other cities and regions in the middle of the nineteenth century in the transfer of technology. These included a sophisticated artisan industry especially in metalworking, major foreign shipyards, and the government's Jiangnan Arsenal. Shanghai was opened as Treaty Port by the Treaty of Nanjing in 1842, and two autonomous foreign settlements—the French and International—were created adjacent to the areas which remained under Chinese rule.

The artisan industry

The traditional artisans of Shanghai and surrounding regions specialised in pre-modern textile machinery, including gins, spindles and spinning-wheels, and in knives for various uses. Between 1850 and 1880, there was a major move of skilled metalworkers into the city, partly in flight from the Taiping Rebellion and partly in response to the growing economic attractions of the city after it had been forced open. These artisans created import substitutes (for example, for foreign tools) and supplied factories with implements. Around the middle of the century, a few large-scale artisan factories appeared, one, for example, producing about 40 thousand sets of iron pots a year, using over a million pounds of metal. There was thus an unusually abundant skilled labour force available to entrepreneurs in the engineering sector.

Foreign shipyards

Foreign shipyards in Shanghai were schools for the first generation of Chinese engineers, especially Boyd's and Farnham's, with workforces in excess of one thousand. They also stimulated metalworking shops with spin off contracts for parts. The expansion of steamshipping created a market for marine repair work that supported many early Chinese engineering firms in Shanghai.

The Arsenal

The Jiangnan Arsenal was founded in 1864–5 by the Manchu-Qing government to produce modern weapons for use against the Taiping rebels. After their defeat, the Arsenal diversified into steam engines, modern lathes and steamships. It was run by a key cadre of foreign engineers and mechanics and trained Chinese workers—a good number of whom later became

engineering entrepreneurs in Shanghai. The China Merchants Steam Navigation Company, founded by the government in 1873, played a comparable role, with its most remarkable member Zhu Kaijia, founding the Qiuxin Company, the most technologically advanced Chinese engineering entrerprise in the city.

II. The Mechanism of Technological Transfer

The foreign presence in Shanghai facilitated the transfer of modern western machine technology. This depended on a number of special factors in addition to the positive feedbacks usually found in any urban concentration. The first was the exceptional depth of the pool of late-traditional technical skills. The second was the direct demonstration of modern techniques in foreign-owned shipyards, factories and workshops as well as the government's Jiangnan Arsenal, and the opportunity to learn new skills through apprenticeships and employment. The third was the chance to learn from running a business that repaired and maintained machinery in foreign firms, executed ancillary tasks and contracts for them, and undertook the assembly of parts. The fourth was the opportunity to copy and adapt foreign machinery imported into Shanghai by foreign firms, often prefaced by part-manufacture combined with the import of key components.

The key factors in the transfer of skills were personal contacts in a working environment and the gamut of opportunities locally available. The latter enabled Chinese entrepreneurs to move towards technological self-sufficiency so as to lessen the risks and difficulties of adopting new processes. The socioeconomic engine for the transfer of technology was damaged by the Japanese wartime occupation. Its post-war reconstruction was made impossible by the communists.

Specific patterns

A few Chinese entrepreneurs served their apprenticeships with a foreign firm. It was more common, however, for them to move to foreign firms later, to gain experience at an intermediate and master level.

Sometimes foreign businesspeople arranged for Chinese workers to be taught industrial skills. After World War I, Chinese entrepreneurs on occasion hired foreign technicians to train the workforce, and attracted Chinese technical personnel working in major foreign companies overseas. At the firm level, a foreign firm could set up a symbiotic relationship with a Chinese firm with technical training provided as part of the deal.

The easy availability of foreign machinery in Shanghai led many Chinese firms to buy and use it. Some examples are silk-reeling equipment, brick kilns, machine tools and electric looms. Shanghai was a sort of permanent industrial exhibition where machines from most industrial countries could be seen in operation, compared, evaluated and purchased.

The familiarity acquired through the purchase and repairing of foreign machines and the manufacture of spare parts for them led to local imitation. This happened for small steamships, cotton gins, silk-reelers and printing presses. Sometimes key components had to be imported as was the case for both Italian silk-reelers and Japanese treadle gins.

Technical difficulties were sometimes overcome by using multifirm combinations. For example, the diesel engine required the collaboration of six companies, and therefore it is not easy to define firm size.

The variety of models available sometimes led to technological eclecticism. The Nanyang Brothers Cigarette Company, after losing its Japanese technicians following the May Thirtieth Movement in 1925, built cigarette-rolling equipment combining Japanese and American characteristics. Some Shanghai businesspeople also engaged in what must be bluntly called technological espionage overseas.

Not all Chinese efforts at reproducing foreign machines were entirely successful. At times, foreign firms losing out to their Chinese imitators would hinder their progress by refusing to supply key parts.

Many of these above themes are evident in the history of the Dalong Engineering Works. It was founded in 1902 with British equipment, and specialised in repairing steamships, silk-reeling equipment, cotton gins, and flour-milling machinery. Skilled labour was enticed from the Arsenal and foreign firms. In response to special orders, it produced soap-making equipment, printing presses, railway trolleys, parts for textile machinery, and engines and transmission systems for river steamers. After World War I, it made machine tools, small-scale petrol and diesel engines based on American models and looms copied from Japanese models. In the years after 1927, it bought five cotton mills to demonstrate its machinery in action for potential customers. By 1937, with a workforce of about 1,300, the Dalong was making every item needed for cotton textile manufacture and opened negotiations for an export order with a Dutch businessman, though the deal was never completed.

While there were some weaknesses in chemicals and the non-ferrous metals sector (copper and tin excluded) and gaps in very advanced domains such as aircraft, Chinese machine-building in Shanghai in the mid 1930s provided a close to complete range of skills for a modern economy of that period (Table 1). In the Chinese-owned modern consumer-goods industries, however, business leaders tended not to have a personal understanding of the technology—unlike engineers—and had a much greater reliance on foreign technicians.

III. A Kuznetsian Type of Economic Growth?

It is generally accepted among economic historians that the Chinese modern industrial sector grew rapidly (greater than 7 per cent a year) up to the mid 1930s, and that the Chinese-owned and operated subsector grew more rapidly than its foreign counterparts. It is not, however, agreed among economic historians as to whether or not the Chinese economy was clearly on the road to a Kuznetsian type of modern economic growth. It is premature to attempt to reach firm conclusions on this

question due to the geographical and sectoral patchiness of solid knowledge; the non-homogeneity of the Chinese economy at this time, including labour markets; and the theoretical impropriety of assuming that amelioration necessarily implies transformation, or that slightly rising living standards plus some proto-industrialisation in the countryside and townships makes an adequate case for an established trend towards transformation. A fourth and more speculative point is that various forms of amelioration, such as the quadrupling of the per person output of handloom weavers by the use of intermediate technology, may actually have strengthened the old economic system's ability to resist full transformation.

Handicrafts

The Shanghai machine-building industry provided the handicraft sector with more productive machinery, usually of an intermediate sort, and created new by-employment such as the manually powered stocking frames. In some ways, it therefore may have strengthened the late-traditional economic system. An example of this is the move of sock production away from the factory and towards the leasing of frames to women who worked at home. Thus hand frames in the countryside tended to co-exist with powered frames in the cities, with a technologically differentiated output.

In the processing of agricultural products, the modern machine sector made a clear contribution to productivity. Examples are hulling of rice, stripping and pressing cotton seeds, cleaning and pressing soybeans, sieving sesame and peanuts, and flour-milling. The nearer the process came to primary production, however, the less effective the contribution of the modern machine industry seems to have been. There is no hard evidence, that the various new ploughs, cultivators, broadcast seeders, sickles, reapers, binders, and maize strippers yielded any major improvements in per person output.

Table 1 **Chinese machine-building expertise in Shanghai during the mid 1930s**

Power sources
    Steam (including turbines)
    Kerosene and internal combustion engines
    Diesel engines
    Electric generators and engines
    Gas engines

Machine tools
    Lathes
    Others

Ferrous metalllurgy
    Iron ore smelters
    Steel
    Producer's goods
    Cotton and silk processing
    Rubber
    Cans and tubes
    Paper
    Printing presses and accessories
    Rice-hulling and flour-milling
    Cigarette rolling

Construction machinery
    Brick kilns, cranes, cement-mixers
    Transport
    Steamships
    Railway locomotives and rolling-stock
    Automobiles (assembly, coachwork, and parts only)

Agricultural machinery
    Water pumps
    Other

Note: These examples are illustrative not exhaustive.
Source: Shanghai-shi gong-shang xingzheng guanli-ju and Shanghai-shi di-yi ji-dian gongye-ju, ed., 1979. *Shanghai minzu jiqi gongye* [The Chinese-owned machine-building industry in Shanghai], Volume I, *Zhonghua shuju*, Shanghai.

Farming

Small engines, using kerosene or diesel fuel, should have been capable of transforming agriculture when attached to pumps and other accessories. It was claimed that the 25-horsepower pump made by the Qiuxin Company in Shanghai could irrigate 32 hectares in 24 hours as against 0.13 hectares in the same time for 2 people, or 0.7 hectares for an ox. In Wuxi it was claimed that one 12-horsepower engine and one 8-inch diameter pump could irrigate about 48 hectares a year. The apparent disparity in these two figures is probably to some extent explained by the limited time periods during which rice farming required pumping.

There is no evidence that the cost of engines, pumps and accessories was outside the financial capacity of landlords and rich peasants. (The total cost of the complete basic assemblage required for pumping was upwards of 500 yuan.)

In fact, the transformation did not happen and the potential output of the Shanghai machine-building factories after about 1910 far outstripped the demand from the agricultural market. Between 1910 and 1931 the total horsepower of the internal combustion engines sold was only slightly over 40 thousand, and only about one-fifth of this capacity was employed for irrigation, the rest being used for presses, saws, mills, generators and the like.

A preliminary examination of the local variation in the rural demand for engines in Shanghai shows that in the few areas where the labour power required for irrigation was exceptionally high, or there was an unusually high proportion of hired farm labour as opposed to family labour, or there were agricultural companies in the market, the demand was quite strong. The tentative conclusion must therefore be that the main inhibiting factor was cheap labour, not technological conservatism, nor the price of the machinery, nor the problems of maintenance.

5 Pre-reform Economic Development in China

Justin Yifu Lin, Fang Cai and Zhou Li

With the implementation of the first five-year plan, the traditional economic system started to take shape. This system solved the problem of how to increase the rate of accumulation to 15 per cent or more in a backward economy,[1] and established in a rather short period of time a relatively complete industrial structure in China. However, in terms of economic efficiency, the cost of implementing this strategy was extremely high.

Under the traditional economic system, China's economic development was repressed in two ways. The first was the distortion of the industrial structure. The preferential development of overly capital-intensive industries prevented the economy from fully exploiting its comparative advantage of an abundant labour endowment, and fortified the dual structure of a traditional sector and a modern sector. As a result, an originally attainable level of employment and urbanisation became unsustainable. In order to support economic growth under such a strategy, a high accumulation rate was required. As a result, the living standard improved very slowly. Moreover, a distorted industrial structure also resulted in an inward-looking economy. Hence, the economy could not

use international trade to exploit its comparative advantage or complement its own comparative disadvantage.

China's economic development was also retarded by low micro-economic efficiency. Under the traditional economic system, all required factors of production were allocated to enterprise by the state, all their products were submitted to the state, all their production costs were settled by the state, and all their profits were remitted to the state. There was no link between the expansion of an enterprise and its economic efficiency, or between its workers' income and their contribution. Such a micro-management institution severely suppressed the incentive to work and caused very low economic efficiency at the micro level. Production could only be carried out inside the production possibility frontier.

Through comparative studies, we can see that not only China but all countries adopting the leap forward strategy performed very poorly economically. None was able to achieve its intended goal of accelerating development. Moreover, all encountered a number of common predicaments. The evidence clearly suggests that the fundamental reason for China's high-cost and

Reprinted with permission. Lin, J.Y., Cai, F., and Hong, Z.L., 1996. *The China Miracle : development strategy and economic reform*, Chinese University Press, Hong Kong, Chapter 3:59–90.

low-efficiency pattern of economic growth before the reform was the choice of an inappropriate development strategy.

I. Rate of Economic Growth Before Reform

From the early 1950s to the late 1970s, China's total economic size increased substantially. The rate of growth in the 1952–78 period was rather high. According to statistics, based on comparable prices, the annual growth rates of total social output value, total output value of industry and agriculture, and national income reached, respectively, 7.9 per cent, 8.2 per cent, 6 per cent (see Table 1). These rates were higher than the average economic growth rates of the world. The rates were not much lower even than those of fast-growing economies, such as those of South Korea and Taiwan. With these rates of economic growth, in the 30 years before the implementation of the reform, China establish-ed a rather complete industrial system on the basis of a predominately agricultural economy, and underwent a dramatic change in economic structure. The percentage of industry in national income increased from 12.6 per cent in 1949 to 46.8 per cent in 1978. The share of agriculture decreased from 68.4 per cent to 35.4 per cent, and the shares of construction industry and transportation increased from 0.3 per cent and 3.3 per cent, respectively, to 4.1 per cent and 3.95 per cent, respectively, whereas commerce decreased from 15.4 per cent to 9.8 per cent, respectively. Between 1952 and 1980, the capital accumulation in industry totalled RMB359.919 billion. The newly added fixed capital amounted to RMB273.45 billion. Calculated on a comparable price basis, the total industrial output value reached RMB499.2 billion in 1980, 17.9 times that of the 1952 value of RMB34.33 billion in 1952 (Hong 1982:79, 153).

The question, however, is why, with such a high rate of economic growth, China did not achieve economic modernisation, and remained a low income developing country. To compare China with nearby countries and regions, in the early 1950s, China's conditions for economic development were roughly similar to those of Korea and Taiwan. From the 1950s to the 1970s, their rates of economic growth were also very similar.[2] However, China's GNP per capita was still very low. According to the official exchange rate, the per capital GNP was US$52 in 1952 and US$210 in 1975.[3] Throughout the period, China was positioned in the bracket of low income developing countries, whose GNP per capita was lower than US$265.[4] In the next two sections we will provide a more detailed analysis of the fundamental reasons for the slow growth of China's real GNP per capita and for its failure to actually leap forward. Here, we simply offer a brief explanation for the existence of an apparently high rate of growth but an actual low level of development.

Without sufficient evidence, it would be unwise to deny the reliability of China's statistics on the economic growth rate in the period 1952–78. However, there are reasons to believe that the growth rate figures for this period do not realistically reflect the development of the Chinese economy. In other words, these figures may help us understand that an apparently high rate of growth in an economy in fact may not represent its actual achievement.

China's economic growth started at a very low level. Based on 1952 prices, the absolute total output value of industry and agriculture in China was only RMB46.6 billion in 1949, and only 82.7 billion in 1952. The per capita total output value of industry and agriculture were RMB86.03 and RMB143.87 yuan, respectively. From the total figures and the per capita figures of the national income, the total social output value, and gross domestic product, we can see that the economy was very weak at that time. By comparing China with many developing economies which became independent after World War II, it can be seen that a relatively low starting level became an important feature of China's economic development. Obviously, the lower the level initially, the easier it is to achieve a higher growth rate (Youjing and Hanzhong 1992). Economies

Table 1 **Basic indicators of economic growth, 1952–78: total social output value***

	Total social output value (%)	Total output value of industry & agriculture (%)	Total output value of industry (%)	Gross domestic product (%)	National income (%)	Rate of accumulation (%)
First five-year period	11.3	10.9	18.0	9.1	8.9	24.2
Second five-year period	-0.4	0.6	3.8	-2.2	-3.1	30.8
1963–1965	15.5	15.7	17.9	14.9	14.7	22.7
Third five-year period	9.3	9.6	12.0	6.9	8.3	26.3
Fourth-five-year period	7.3	7.8	9.3	5.5	5.5	33.0
1976–1978	8.1	8.0	10.1	5.8	5.6	33.5
1953–1978	7.9	8.2	11.4	6.0	6.0	29.5

* The growth rate is calculated on a comparable-price basis. The accumulation rate is calculated on a nominal-prices basis.
Source: State Statistical Bureau, Division of National Economic Balance Statistics, 1987. *Collection of Statistical Data on National Income (1949–1985)*, China Statistical Press, Beijing: 2, 45–46.

with the same economic growth rate but which began at a lower level enjoyed less impressive economic consequences as a result of the same rates of growth. Table 1 shows the changes in the growth rate in different development periods in China. We can see from the table that, as the base of China's economy enlarged, the growth rate tended to slow down. This feature is best illustrated by the changes in the rate of industrial growth. During the recovery period of 1949–52 the average annual growth rate was 34.8 per cent. The rate in the first five-year plan period was 18 per cent. After the huge drop in the 1960s, the growth rate reached 17.8 per cent in 1963–65. Afterwards, it slowed down to 10 per cent in 1965–80.

In addition, economic growth rates were distributed unevenly among different industries in China. Owing to the implementation of the heavy industry-oriented development strategy, the state adopted a biased policy of investment and protection. Industry, particularly heavy industry, grew significantly faster than did agriculture and tertiary industry, and became the driving force behind economic growth. For

example, during the 1951–80 period, the annual growth rate was 11 per cent for industry, 3.2 per cent for agriculture, and 4.2 per cent for commerce.[5] In the industrial section, heavy industry grew especially fast. Between 1949 and 1981, its annual growth rate was 15.3 per cent. Because of its more rapid growth rate, during this period heavy industry led the economy's growth, and its share in the national economy increased. Since the growth rate depended lopsidedly on the growth of heavy industry, it could not produce the effect that could have been obtained had there been more coordinated growth of each industry in the economy. Therefore, a high growth rate of this type does not necessarily mean that the economy's development was substantive.

China also had a very high rate of accumulation. Because the government used the planning method to allocate resources, it could increase the proportion of savings in the national income and decrease that of consumption beyond a level that would have been possible at its stage of development in a market economy. Table 1 shows that China had a very high rate of accumulation in each historical period. The rate was not only higher than the average level in the world but also higher than that of most developing economies which achieved rapid economic growth. The high rate of accumulation, achieved through the government's planning control, undoubtedly contributed to the observed rapid growth. However, because of the bias in the distribution of national income and the investment/consumption structure, personal income and the living standard were persistently suppressed. Moreover, because the industrial structure was biased toward the capital-good industries, the supply of consumer goods was short and the living standard improved slowly. One important aspect of economic development was neglected under the superficially high rate of economic growth.

Lastly, the high growth rate was achieved in a very inefficient manner. We return to this issue later.

II. Distorted Industrial Structure

The intended goal of giving priority to the development of heavy industries was to circumvent the constraints of capital shortage so that the economy could quickly overcome the adverse effect of a weak heavy industry base on the nation's growth and development. It was hoped that in this way the national economy could grow quickly, and could achieve the goal of surpassing advanced economies in the shortest possible amount of time. Through the distortion of product and factor prices to lower the costs of developing heavy industries, and the establishment of a corresponding planned resource allocation mechanism to ensure the supply of resources to the heavy industrial sectors, China was indeed able to make heavy industry grow faster than other sectors. Heavy industry's leading coefficient of growth, which is defined as the ratio of the average annual growth rate of

Table 2   **Changes in investment structure, 1952–78** (in nominal price)

Year	Total fixed asset investment (in hundred thousand)	Total infrastructure investment (in hundred thousand)					Structure of infrastructure investment (%)			
		Total agri-culture	Light indus-tries	Heavy indus-tries	Other sectors	Total	Total agri-culture	Light indus-tries	Heavy indus-tries	Other sectors
First five-year period	611.58	41.83	37.47	212.79	296.38	588.47	7.1	6.4	36.2	50.3
Second five-year period	1,307.00	135.71	76.59	651.71	342.08	1,206.09	11.3	6.4	54.0	28.3
1963–1965	499.45	74.46	16.47	193.71	137.25	421.89	17.6	3.9	45.9	32.6
Third five-year period	1,209.09	104.27	42.62	498.89	330.25	976.03	10.7	4.4	51.1	33.8
Fourth five-year period	2,276.37	173.08	103.03	874.94	612.86	1,763.91	9.8	5.8	49.6	34.8
1967–1978	1,704.96	136.13	74.76	624.49	424.42	1,259.80	10.8	5.9	49.6	33.7

Source: State Statistical Bureau, *China Statistical Yearbook, 1992,* China Statistical Press, Beijing: 149, 158; State Statistical Bureau, Fixed Assets Investment Division, 1987. *The Statistical Data of the Fixed Assets Investment in China, 1950–1985,* China Statistical Press, Beijing: 97.

heavy industry over the average annual growth rate of light industry, was 1.47 for the period between 1953 and 1979. In the sub-periods, the coefficient was 1.68 for the recovery period, 1.97 for the first five-year plan period, as high as 6.0 for the second five-year plan period, 0.7 for 1963–65 due to a structural adjustment prompted by the disaster of the Great Leap Forward Movement, and 1.75 and 1.32, respectively, for the third and fourth five-year plan periods.

The implementation of the heavy industry-oriented strategy led to huge distortion in China's industrial structure. Table 2 shows that during the first five-year plan period the investment ratio of heavy to light industries was 5.7. The ratio rose to 9.1 in 1976–78. The results of under-utilising the advantage of an abundant labour force and of the failure to avoid the disadvantage of capital shortage are as follows

(1) In the industrial structure, the percentage of manufacturing sectors was extra-ordinarily high, whereas that of service sectors was exceptionally small. Tables 3 and 4 show that in the 27 years before the onset of reform, the weight of agriculture in the GNP declined steadily and that of industries increased constantly, whereas the weight of other sectors (construction, transportation, and commerce) increased from 22.75 per cent in 1952 to 24.9 per cent in 1957, and then either declined or stagnated. In 1978 their weight was 7 percentage points lower than it was in 1957. Obviously, such changes were not consistent with the general pattern of an

industrial structural change in economic development.

(2) In the manufacturing industries, the percentage of coarse processing was exceptionally high, whereas that of refined processing was extremely low. Owing to the lopsided pursuit of in-kind indicators and their growth rates, the growth in the capacity of coarse processing far exceeded that in refined processing. Taking the steel industry as an example, the production capacity of steel smelting, which belonged to the category of coarse processing, was growing at a very fast pace. On the other hand, the production capacity of steel rolling—an example of refined processing —was growing rather slowly. Therefore a large quantity of steel ingots piled up, while a large amount of refined steel materials had to be imported.

To illustrate the severity of distortion in the industrial structure, we use the Large-Country Model *á la* Chenery, which was based on the historical changes in the industrial structure of various countries, to compare the deviation of China's economic structure in 1981 to the historical pattern (Huijong and Guanghui 1984:67–8). The Large-Country Model provides the typical economic structures for a large country at a low annual income level (US$300 per capita), lower-middle income level (US$600 per capita), and middle income level (US$1,200), measured in 1981 US dollars (see Figure 1). The per capita GNP in China was estimated to be US$300 or US$350 in 1981.[6] China belonged to the low

Table 3   **Sectoral composition of national income, 1952–1978** (in nominal price)

	1952	1957	1962	1965	1970	1975	1978
Agriculture	57.72	46.80	48.05	46.21	40.39	37.79	32.76
Industry	19.52	28.30	32.79	36.41	40.97	46.02	49.40
Other sectors	22.75	24.90	19.15	17.37	18.64	16.18	17.84

Source: State Statistical Bureau, *China Statistical Yearbook*, 1992, China Statistical Press, Beijing:35.

Table 4   Changes in the employment structure, 1952–1978

Year	Total labour force (in ten thousand)	Agricultural labour force (in ten thousand)	Industrial labour force (in ten thousand)			Labour force in other sectors (in ten thousand)	Percentage of agri-cultural labour force	Percentage of industrial labour force			Labour force in other sectors (in ten thousand)
			Light	Heavy	Total			Light	Heavy	Total	
1952	20,729	17,317	874	372	1,246	2,166	83.5	4.2	1.8	6.0	10.5
1957	23,771	19,310	844	557	1,401	3,060	81.2	3.6	2.3	5.9	12.9
1965	28,670	23,398	866	962	1,828	3,444	81.6	3.0	3.4	6.4	12.0
1978	40,152	29,429	1,825	3,183	5,008	5,715	73.3	4.6	7.9	12.5	14.2

Source: Ma Hong and Sun Shangqing (eds.), 1981. *Research on the Issues of China's Economic Structure*, Beijing: People's Press:104; State Statistical Bureau, 1992. *China Statistical Yearbook*, China Statistical Press, Beijing: 27.

income group, but the manufacturing sector was very highly weighted in the economy. Correspondingly, the tertiary industry was grossly under-developed, accounting for only a very small percentage of the economy.

Such a heavy structure was inconsistent with the comparative advantages of China's endowments,[7] and became an obstacle standing in the way of the development of the Chinese economy and of the improvement in Chinese people's living standard. This was a major drawback of pursuing the traditional economic strategy. In order to analyse the problem in a clearer and more direct manner, we will not consider for the time being the efficiency loss in the traditional economic system (this will be the main theme in the next section), and will assume that through its planning, the government could effectively achieve the goal of developing its priority sectors. We will briefly summarise the economic consequences of the distortion in industrial structure.

(1) The deviation of the industrial structure from the pattern of comparative advantages in resources endowment constrained the speed of economic growth.

If the industrial structure had been built on the market basis, labour-intensive products

would have been relatively inexpensive due to the low wage rate, and they would have been more competitive than capital-intensive products on the domestic as well as the international markets. Induced by profit motives, entrepreneurs would have allocated more resources to labour-intensive industries and would have been more enthusiastic about adopting capital-saving and labour-using technology. Figure 2 illustrates the industrial structure of a two-sector economy. The optimal production mix is at point E, where the distortion-free relative-price line touches the production possibility frontier. The economy will produce OY_0 units of labour-intensive (light industry) products and OX_1 units of capital-intensive (heavy industry) products. Due to the pursuit of a heavy industry-oriented development strategy and to the artificial distortion of factor prices, capital rather than labour became a relatively cheap factor. The government employed the planning mechanism to ensure the allocation of the 'cheap' capital to the heavy industry sector. Despite the fact that it was more consistent with the comparative advantage of the economy, development of light industry was suppressed (this suppression is shown by the Y_1A line in Figure 2). Consequently, the actual production possibility frontier shrunk from

Figure 1   **China's and typical large countries' sectoral structure of GDP**

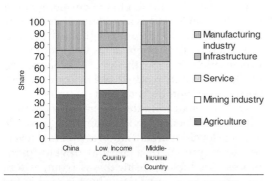

Source: Wang Huijiong and Yang Guanghui (eds), 1984. *Possibility and Alternatives of the Changes and Growth of China's Economic Structure*, Meteorological Press, Beijing:67–68.

CEAD to Y_1AD. The resultant production mix is point A on the production possibility frontier. The corresponding output of the labour-intensive product is OY_1 whereas that of the capital-intensive product is OX_1.

From Figure 2, we can see that the static result of suppressing the comparative advantage sector is a loss of an absolute amount ea or a relative amount ea/eo of GNP, calculated on the basis of constant distortion-free or international prices. A reduction in the GNP implies a fall in the amount that could be used for investment. Assuming that a certain percentage of GNP is used for investment, on the one hand, a reduction in investment will lead to a fall in the total investment by a multiplier effect. This multiplier is the reciprocal of the social marginal propensity to save. On the other hand, assuming that the government's goal of giving priority to the development of heavy industry is achieved through a constant investment ratio between the labour-intensive and the capital-intensive sectors, the production in every new period will also produce a loss of a relative amount ea/eo and an absolute amount of loss which becomes

increasingly larger than ea. The total social investment will decrease by the multiplier effect. This factor greatly suppresses the rate of growth of the economy as a whole. In other words, the faster growth of heavy industries is achieved at the expense of the entire economy's potential for growth. We can conclude that, given a saving rate, the strategy of giving priority to the development of heavy industry causes the rate of economic growth to be lower than it potentially could be. Instead of stimulating economic growth, emphasising heavy industry stunts it.

(2) Distortion in the industrial sector lowers the possibility of reducing the labour force in agriculture and, consequently, reduces the level of urbanisation.

Heavy industry is a capital intensive sector. In other words, for a given amount of capital, the amount of employment heavy industry can absorb is lower than that of other sectors. According to some statistics in China, every RMB1 billion yuan investment in the heavy industry sector provides only 50,000 employment

Figure 2   **Static result of suppressing the economy's comparative advantages**

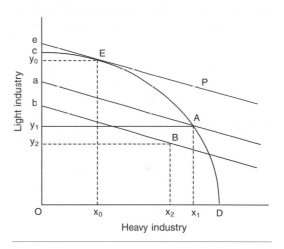

opportunities, which is only one-third of the number provided by the light industry sector. For a one billion yuan investment, state-owned enterprises only create 100,000 employment opportunities, which is only one-fifth the number created by non-state-owned enterprises (Lanrui and Lukuan 1982:10). However, in this period, the increase in the number of people working in heavy industry was 4.1 times that of those working in light industry, and the increase in state-owned enterprises' employment was 3.1 times that of non-state-owned enterprises. From this analysis, we can see that the implementation of the heavy industry-oriented development strategy weakened the economy's ability to provide employment in the non-agricultural sector, and retarded the shift of the employment structure away from the primary industry which would normally have accompanied economic development. The above explanation is the main reason that in the 27 years before reform was instituted, the percentage of agriculture in the GNP decreased from 57.72 per cent to 32.76 per cent, a drop of about 25 percentage points, but the percentage of the labour force in agriculture decreased from 83.5 per cent to 73.3 per cent, a drop of only 10.2 percentage points (see Tables 3 and 4).

Because state policy did not give consideration to the development of rural areas, priority industries were located predominately in large and middle-sized cities. These industries did not require the support of the industries that already existed in the surrounding areas, nor could they accelerate the development of related industries in nearby areas. This led to the development of so-called 'small and self-contained' and 'large and self-contained' pocket-like cities, and obstructed the normal development of urbanisation. In 1980, the level of urbanisation in China had only reached 19.4 per cent, just 6.9 percentage points higher than it was in 1952. This is very different from the general development experience. Chenery and Syrquin (1988) provide average levels of urbanisation at different levels of development in a normal development process (see Table 5). Using this as a comparison, we can see how far behind China lagged in the area of urbanisation. Calculated at 1964 constant prices, China's GNP per capita was about US$154 in 1980 (Fang 1990), which can be compared with the level of urbanisation at a GNP per capita of US$100 or US$200 in the table. In that year, the level of urbanisation was lower than the normal level of urbanisation at US$200. Worse still, it was also lower than the normal level of urbanisation at US$100. The low level of urbanisation led to the severe underdevelopment of the tertiary industry, which made up a far smaller than normal proportion of China's economic structure.

(3) The distortion in the industrial structure resulted in little improvement in the standard of living over more than 20 years.

In this type of economic structure, resources were allocated, to the maximum possible extent, to capital goods sectors, and production of consumption goods was severely restricted. This pattern of resource allocation seriously affected the growth of consumer goods industries. Moreover, for the purpose of accelerating the growth of heavy industries, the limited available foreign exchange was generally not used for importing consumption goods. Therefore, the economy did not have the required material basis for improving people's standard of living. Employees in urban areas faced the policy of low wages and wage freezing. Their income and

Table 5   **Predicted level of urbanisation at different income (GNP) level**

GNP per capita ($US)	100	200	300	400	500	800	1,000
% urban population	22.0	36.2	43.9	49.0	52.7	60.1	63.4

Source: Hollis B. Chenery and M. Syrquin, 1988. *Patterns of Development, 1950–1970*, Economic Science Press, Beijing: 62, 63, 69.

Table 6   **Changes in the level of consumption for urban and rural residents***

Year	The National Income index	The Consumption Index of all citizens	The Consumption Index of farmers	The Consumption Index of urban residents
1952	100.0	100.0	100.0	100.0
1957	153.0	122.9	117.0	126.3
1978	453.4	177.0	157.6	212.6

*The National Income Index and the Consumption Index are calculated on a comparable price basis.
Source: State Statistical Bureau, *China Statistical Yearbook, 1993*, China Statistical Press, Beijing: 34, 281.

consumption level were in a state of slow growth or even stagnation (see Figure 1 and Table 6). And, forced by the government's policy to remain in agricultural activities, farmers faced the problems of under-employment and low incentives in agricultural production. Their per capita production hardly increased. As a result, farmers lacked the necessary material conditions for improving their income and living standard. The underdevelopment of consumer goods industries and the undersupply of agricultural products resulted in a perpetual shortage in the supply of daily consumable goods and foodstuffs. Most basic living necessities had to be rationed. Under such an industrial structure, even if the government wanted to increase the production of consumer goods, it lacked the required resources. People would not work hard because harder work would not bring them a higher income. Therefore, one of the reasons that

people could not improve their living standard was the distortion in the industrial structure.

(4) The inward-looking nature of the economy was reinforced by the deviation of economic structure from the pattern based on the economy's comparative advantage.

Resources were directed towards the production of capital-intensive goods, which was contrary to China's comparative advantage. Therefore, the proportion of capital goods that China had to acquire from the international market decreased. But labour-intensive industries, which were consistent with China's comparative advantage, lacked the necessary conditions for development because of the shortage of inputs allocated to them. The amount of labour-intensive products that China could export to the international market thus also had to decrease. The decline in imports and exports indicated that the economy became increasingly

Table 7   **Changes in international trade, 1952–78**

Year	Total output value of agriculture and industry	Value of import and export	% share of value of import and export in the total value of agriculture and industry
1952–54	2,820	230.2	8.16
1976–78	15,148	891.6	5.89

Source: State Statistical Bureau, *China Statistical Yearbook, 1993*: 57–58 and 633.

inward-looking. Table 7 shows that the share of import and export value in the total industrial and agricultural output value declined from 8.16 per cent in 1952–54 to 5.89 per cent in 1976–78, a drop of 2.27 percentage points.

III. Lack of Incentive and Inefficiency

Apart from the distortion in the industrial structure discussed above, the low efficiency of the traditional economic system was also a result of the low efficiency in resource allocation, lack of competition, and poor incentives.

To begin with, planned allocation caused low resource allocation efficiency. In order to allocate scarce resources according to plans and supervise the implementation of plans, the government established a vertical management system and a horizontal local administration system. The functions of these two systems overlapped. As a result, an orderly linkage based on an input-output relationship between the various sectors and regions was replaced by competition for investments and resources. In fact, the planners were unable to obtain all the information required for forming a plan. Planning often became an ex-post adjustment. Meanwhile, when gaps between the economic structure and the policy goal arose, the planners did not use the price mechanism to adjust it.[8] Instead, planners used distorted prices, various direct and indirect subsidies (soft budget constraints) and quantity-adjustment methods to arrange and adjust the national economy. Therefore, all sectors carried out their production under one of the following two scenarios. As shown in Figure 3a, one type of sector carried out its production with its calculating price (or accounting price) above the equilibrium level.[9] The other type carried out its production with its calculating price below the equilibrium price (shown in Figure 3b). In the former case, because the sector produced at a higher than equilibrium price, a surplus of Q_0Q_1 was the result.[10] The sector's supply curve SS was in fact the sector's marginal cost curve. Therefore, a higher price

actually caused that sector to produce a surplus at a higher marginal cost. In the latter case, the price was lower than the equilibrium level, and a shortage of Q_0Q_1 was the result.

Which sectors were given favourable prices and which were given unfavourable ones? The answer to this question was determined in two ways. In one case, the prices given to a sector depended on its bargaining power, that is, its relative importance in the plans. The more important sectors received favourable prices more frequently. The outputs or services of the agriculture, energy, and transportation sectors were treated as inputs of the heavy industries, and their prices had a strong spillover effect on the prices of other goods. They were frequently given unfavourable prices. This explains why they were bottlenecks for the national economy for a long time. In the other case, sectors which had similar production characteristics were usually equally likely to be assigned favourable or unfavourable prices. Their actual prices, however, depended on the planners' judgment of the economic conditions in the previous period. When the calculating price of a sector was unfavourable, they would under-utilise their capacity. Both caused an efficiency loss.

Lack of competition also contributed to low production efficiency. The policy of giving priority to the development of heavy industry implied the simultaneous implementation of primary import substitution (daily necessities) and secondary import substitution (machinery, equipment, etc.). At that time, China's technological level was very low. Moreover, the strategy did not allow the economy to utilise its own comparative advantage. Therefore, the cost of domestic products had to be very high and was not competitive on the international market. For the purpose of independently developing its own industrial system, China had to protect domestic industries at the expense of efficiency. On the one hand, the resource cost for domestically produced products was much higher than the foreign exchange that could be saved or earned. On the other hand, persistent protection reduced the industrial sectors' opportunity and incentives to improve productivity, and increased the national economy's dynamic loss. The limited size of the domestic market made it impossible for certain industries to exploit their economies of scale. The protected sectors and enterprises were not motivated to innovate either, due to the lack of external competition and the elimination

Figure 3 **Surplus or deficit caused by price distortion**

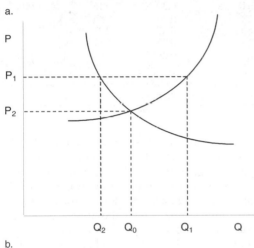

a.

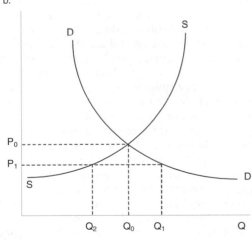

b.

of domestic competition as a result of entry barriers. In particular, when all resources were allocated by plans, all products were sold to and marketed by the state, and all production was carried out according to compulsory plans, enterprises had no incentive to improve their efficiency and upgrade the quality of their products.

In addition, labourer's incentive was low. The incentive to work is positively correlated with reward. To motivate workers, it is necessary to pay those who work hard more. But under the traditional economic system, enterprises could not choose who to hire or fire. Worse still, the wages of urban workers were fixed, and had nothing to do with an individual's effort or an enterprise's performance.

The reason for low incentives in agriculture was different. The production team had the right to control part of its surplus. However, close monitoring of labour was too costly because agricultural production was carried out over a large area and required a long production cycle. These features forced the managers in the people's communes to adopt a low level of supervision. However, it was impossible to accurately measure each worker's contribution without close monitoring. Therefore, workers could not receive rewards that truly reflected their efforts. In fact, the production team set an identical work-point standard (wage rate) for workers of identical ages and genders. A farm worker's reward was independent of his contribution.

Therefore, the incentive to work in the collective production was inadequate and the free rider problem was prevalent (Lin 1988: s199–244).

When we discussed the distortion in the industrial structure created by the traditional economic system, we assumed that there existed no efficiency loss. The economy's production was at a point on the production possibility frontier, such as point A in Figure 2. But, in fact, the efficiency loss created by the poor incentive mechanism was particularly serious. We will use

Table 8   Material consumption rate for per unit of gross domestic product: an international comparison (in 1980 US dollars)

Country	Consumption of per unit gross domestic product			Consumption of per unit output of major industries		
	Energy kg Standard (coal/US$)	Steel (ton/million US$)	Quantity transported (ton km/ US$)	Energy kg standard (coal/US$)	Steel (ton/million US$)	Quantity transported (ton km/ US$)
China	2.90	127.3	3.10	1.06	353	6.74
India	1.77	98.4	1.67	0.99	379	6.43
Korea	1.12	113.8	0.47	0.48	291	1.22
Brazil	0.88	57.1	1.40	0.32	103	4.12
Japan	0.51	63.0	0.41	0.30	146	1.00
France	0.45	30.9	-	0.30	88	-
The United States	1.05	44.8	1.80	0.47	132	5.32
The United Kingdom	0.57	30.0	-	0.23	91	-
Germany	0.49	43.7	-	0.26	95	-

Source: The World Bank, 1984 Economic Study Tour, 1987. 'China: Economic Structure in International Perspective', in China: Long-Term Issues and Options, China Finance and Economics Press, Beijing, Annex 5:23.

an international comparison of efficiency in the use of resources to illustrate this.

The statistics in Tables 8, 9 and 10 show that China's economic growth was grossly inefficient. For the production of per unit gross domestic product, the consumption of energy, steel, and

Table 9   Share of working capital in total capital: an international comparison (%)

	Year	Share of working capital in total capital
China	1981	32.7
India	1979	27.9
Korea	1963	7.0
Japan	1953	19.9
The United Kingdom	1970	12.6
The Soviet Union	1972	29.5

Source: The World Bank, 1984 Economic Study Tour, 1987. 'China: Economic Structure in International Perspective', in China: Long-Term Issues and Options, China Finance and Economics Press, Beijing, Annex 5:23.

transportation in China were, respectively, 63.8–229.5 per cent, 11.9–122.9 per cent, and 85.6–559.6 per cent greater than that of other developing countries. For the production of per unit value of its main industrial products, China's situation was quite similar to the above case, except that India's steel consumption was slightly higher than China's. The differences between China and developed countries were even larger. In the structure of total capital, working capital accounted for the largest share in China and was 4.8 to 25.7 percentage points higher than that of other countries. This implied that inventories of inputs and outputs were larger and inventory was kept longer in China than in other countries. The most important indicator reflecting the high price China paid for economic growth was the extremely low rate of its total factor productivity growth. Between 1952 and 1981, even using the most favourable assumption, the annual growth rate of total factor productivity in China was merely 0.5 per cent. China's rate of growth was the lowest among all countries listed in Table 10. According to the estimation of the World

Bank, between 1957 and 1982, China's total factor productivity was in a state of stagnation or even negative growth (World Bank 1984:145).

From the preceding discussion of the efficiency loss caused by the traditional economic system, we can see that the economy's production was, in fact, located inside the production possibility frontier, such as at point B in Figure 2. This implies that some social resources were wasted. If we take this into consideration, the suppression of economic growth under the traditional economic system must have been much more severe.

IV. Leaping Forward: an international perspective

China's economic growth in the 1950s to the late 1970s suggests that low economic efficiency was caused by two major problems that were endogenous to the adoption of the heavy industry-oriented development strategy and its resultant macro-policy environment, resource allocation mechanism and micro-management institution. The first problem was the distortion in the industrial structure, and the second was the inadequate incentive mechanism. In this

Table 10 Growth rate of total factor productivity: an international comparison (per cent)

Country	Period	Annual growth rate of factor productivity*	Share of total factor productivity growth rate in GNP growth rate*	Country	Period	Annual growth rate of total factor productivity	Share of total factor productivity growth rate in GNP growth rate
China	1952–81	0.53 (–1.0)	8 (–17)	Japan	1952–71	3.8	38
	1952–75	0.3 (–1.1)	5 (–18)		1952–64	5.1	53
	1975–81	1.0 (–0.3)	17 (–5)		1953–71	5.9	58
					1955–71	2.9	25
Brazil	1950–60	3.7	54		1955–70	5.6	55
	1955–70	2.1	34		1966–73	4.5	41
	1966–74	1.6	22				
				United States	1947–60	1.4	38
South Korea	1955–60	2.0	47		1960–73	1.3	30
	1955–70	5.0	57				
	1960–73	4.1	42	USSR	1950–60	1.9	32
					1960–70	1.5	29
					1970–75	0.1	3
				Spain	1959–65	5.0	44
Average of 19 developing countries		2.0	31				
Average of 12 market-economy countries		2.7	49				

* The figure outside the brackets was calculated according to the assumption 0.6 for capital and 0.4 for labour, and the figure within the brackets was calculated according to the assumption 0.4 for capital and 0.6 for labour.
Source: The World Bank, 1984 Economic Study Tour, 1987. 'China: Economic Structure in International Perspective', in *China: Long-Term Issues and Options*, China Finance and Economics Press, Beijing:Annex 5:23.

section, we will examine the economic performance in other developing countries which adopted a similar strategy.

Based on the success of the four Little Dragons which adopted a capitalist system, and of the socialist countries which have one after another changed their economic system, it is easy for people to reach the conclusion that the socialist system is an obstacle to economic growth and development. However, this is an over-simplification. If the success of the four Little Dragons can be attributed to their adoption of a capitalist system, why is it that many other developing countries which also have capitalist systems have not succeeded in becoming newly industrialised economies? If socialism is definitely an obstacle to growth how could China have undergone such a dramatic change in the past 16 years?

And if the sociopolitical system was the cause of slow growth in socialist countries, why are the former Soviet Union and Eastern European countries still undergoing major difficulties after changing their sociopolitical systems?

After examining the experience of economic development in various countries, we find that both capitalist and socialist countries which pursued the leap forward strategy achieved little success in the areas of economic growth and development. As mentioned above, in addition to China, the former Soviet Union and some Eastern European countries, a number of developing capitalist countries also adopted the leap forward strategy. They too implemented the corresponding price-distortion macro-policy environment and the government-intervention resource-management system. Countries adopting the leap forward type of heavy industry-oriented development strategy or import substitution strategy, neither succeeded in achieving economic growth and development nor realised their goal of leaping forward. Latin America's capitalist countries—such as Argentina, Uruguay, Chile, and Bolivia, which were the typical example of import substituting

countries—encountered a whole series of economic difficulties. The polarisation of wealth distribution in their economies increased, and the living standard of their people improved very little after the adoption of the import substitution strategy. The Philippines, which was regarded in the 1960s as the rising star in Asia and second only to Japan, is now in a state of chaos and stagnation. The Philippines' economic troubles are also attributable to the adoption of an import substitution strategy (Ranis and Mahmood 1992).

In a nutshell, the development strategy chosen by the above countries resulted in the following consequences. First, the growth rate was far from satisfactory and the rise in income level was relatively slow. From the annual growth rate of the GDP in 1960–81, we see that the growth rate was 3.5 per cent for India, 5–6 per cent for the Philippines, and 5.4 per cent for Brazil in the first 10 years, and 8.4 per cent in the next 11 years. Uruguay's figures were 1.2 per cent and 3.1 per cent, respectively, in these two periods (World Bank 1983:150–1). These levels of economic growth were not high enough to enable these countries to catch up with, let alone forge ahead of, developed ones. In particular, if we compare these growth rates with those of several other economies that adopted an alternative development strategy, we can see that the former countries' rates were very low.

By looking at the average annual growth rate of per capita GNP in 1960–81, we can see that the growth rate was 1.4 per cent for India, 2.8 per cent for the Philippines, 1.9 per cent for Argentina, and 1.6 per cent for Uruguay. Each country's growth rate was lower than the average growth rate in its respective income group. It is clear that the increase in these countries' levels of development was very slow. Their leap forward attempt was a failure.

In the developing countries alluded to above, the economic and social structures were distorted and, as a result, income distribution deteriorated. Because the growth of heavy industries was given priority, the industrial structure was too heavy and labour absorption was limited. For example, in 1963–69, the average annual growth rate of manufacturing industries was 5.9 per cent for India and 6.1 per cent for the Philippines. For the same period, the average annual growth rate of employment in manufacturing industries in these two countries was 5.3 per cent and 1.1 per cent, respectively (Todaro 1988:317). The slow growth in industrial employment reduced the economy's ability to absorb the seemingly unlimited supply of labour in rural areas. Therefore, the urban wage rate stagnated and most of the labour force remained in poor agrarian jobs. A large low-income population made it impossible to improve the unequal distribution of income with the development of the economy.

Another consequence of adopting the leap forward strategy was low efficiency and loss of welfare. To implement the strategy, the government awarded some industrial sectors a high degree of protection and subsidy. These industries and enterprises became monopolies and were shielded from competition. This caused them to lose the motivation for technological innovation and the incentive for improving management. The result was inefficiency. For example, from 1955–75, the total factor productivity growth rate in India's manufacturing industries was negative (Griffin 1992:157). Furthermore, there was pervasive rent seeking behaviour in these economies. Because the government introduced various kinds of discriminating treatment, such as permits, quotas, low interest loans, price intervention, and so on, once enterprises became the recipients of such preferential treatment or subsidies, they could make an easy profit. Therefore, private entrepreneurs invested a large amount of time, material and money in seeking such institutional rent. Rent seeking not only corrupted government officials, but it discredited the government's reputation, wasted a large quantity of resources, and resulted in a net welfare loss. According to a study, if the loss in GNP due to resource misallocation brought about by protection was 1 per cent in Brazil in 1967, the

loss caused by rent seeking was estimated to be 7 to 9 per cent (Griffin 1992:153). Unfortunately, the leap forward strategy implied giving manufacturing industries long-term, intensive protection.

Yet another consequence of the strategy was the deterioration of the fiscal condition and increased inflation. Countries adopting the strategy attempted to bypass a necessary stage of their development, and relied on government subsidy or direct public investment to develop capital-intensive industries. As a result, the fiscal burden became very heavy and the fiscal deficit grew huge. In order to fill this capital gap, the government had to rely heavily on foreign funds. For example, after the 1970s and particularly at the beginning of the 1980s, for the purpose of achieving a high rate of growth, both Brazil and Mexico unhesitantly borrowed a large amount of foreign funds. As a consequence, they both encountered debt crises, their rates of growth dropped abruptly and their economies suffered a period of negative growth. Moreover, the living standards of their people fell back to the level of over a decade earlier. Inflation was another common disease of many countries that adopted the leap forward strategy. In order to artificially support a high economic growth rate, the government adopted a series of macroeconomic

---

Table 11 Structure of output value in China and India (per cent)

	China (1952)*	India (1950–51)
Total	100	100
Primary sector	58	60
Secondary sector	23	14
Tertiary sector	19	26

* China's output values were calculated from the national income.
Source: State Statistical Bureau, *China Statistical Yearbook*, 1993:33; Peijun, S., (ed.), 1991. *A Comparative Study of Economic Development in China and India*, Peking University Press, Beijing:57.

Table 12   Index of gross agricultural output
value in China and India

Year	China	India
1965–66	172.9	138.1
1980–81	326.7	231.1
1985–6	569.5	270.1

Source: Peijun, S., (ed.), 1991. *A Comparative Study of
Economic Development in China and India*, Peking University
Press, Beijing: 131.

policies to encourage investments and expand
the scale of infrastructure construction. Because
the economic structure was unbalanced, the
consequence of economic overheating was the
appearance of one bottleneck after another. The
shortage of products and factors of production
led to increases in prices and, furthermore,
caused serious inflation. For example, the
average annual inflation rate in Brazil was 46.1
per cent in the 1960s and 42.1 per cent in the
1970s, whereas that of Argentina rose from 21.4
per cent in the 1960s to 134.2 per cent in the 1970s
(World Bank 1983:148–9).

From the above discussion, we can see that
the fundamental reason for the failure of the
developing countries to catch up with and forge
ahead of developed nations was their adoption
of the leap forward strategy, the corresponding
macro-policy environment that distorted product
and factor prices, and the government-
intervention type of management system.

A detailed comparison of the economic
growth and development of China and India
should also prove illuminating. The reasons we
chose India for a comparison are as follows. (1)
China and India are Asia's two neighbouring
large countries. Their populations are ranked as
the first and second largest in the world. (2) Both
China and India are developing countries. They
obtained political power and achieved political
independence at around the same time.
Moreover, the economic development strategies

they chose are quite similar.[11] (3) China and India
have similar resource endowments. They both
have the comparative advantage of a relatively
abundant labour force, and their conditions for
agricultural production both include unequal
seasonal and regional distribution of precip-
itation, and so forth. (4) The bases for economic
development in China and India are roughly the
same. In the 1950s, the economic structures of
China and India were very similar. In 1952,
China's agriculture contributed 57.7 per cent to
the GNP, and the agricultural population made
up 87.5 per cent of the total population. In 1950–
51, these two indicators in India were 59 and 82.7
per cent, respectively. Generally speaking, the
share of secondary industry in China was
somewhat larger than in India but India's share
of tertiary industry was relatively larger than
China's. However, the differences were not very
significant (see Table 11).

One significant area of difference between
the two countries, however, was their micro-
institution for agricultural development from the
1950s to the 1970s. China adopted the highly
centralised people's commune system, but until
the early 1980s, India had only 9,000 agricultural
cooperatives with 250,000 members, 375,000
hectares, and 0.34 per cent of the country's
cultivated land. However, because both countries
adopted the heavy industry-oriented development strategy, in both cases, agriculture faced a
distorted macro-policy environment, and the

Table 13   Employment structure in China and
India in 1980

	China	India
Total	100	100
Primary sector	74	70
Secondary sector	14	13
Tertiary sector	12	17

Source: The World Bank, 1988. *World Development Report,
1988*, China Finance and Economics Press, Beijing: 282.

results of agricultural growth were very similar. In 1950–1980, the average annual growth rate of grain production in China was 3.0 per cent, whereas that of India was 3.08 per cent. Table 12 shows that, if we ignore the rapid output growth in China after the onset of reform, the growth of agricultural output value in both countries was roughly the same. Moreover, from Table 13, we can see that the employment structures in both countries were very close even after 30 years had passed. Perhaps this was one of the reasons why the per capita GNP in China and India both stayed at a level of US$100–$300.

The leap forward strategy failed not only in China and other socialist countries, but also in India and other developing capitalist countries. This suggests that the fundamental reason for the failure in China's economic development before the reform was the adoption of the leap forward strategy.

Notes

1. W.A. Lewis points out that 'the core of economic development is to understand the economic process of how a society in which saving and investment constitute less than 4 or 5 per cent of national income becomes one whose voluntary savings increases to 12 to 15 per cent of GNP' (1989:15; see also Lewis 1954).
2. The per capita GNP in the early 1950s was below US$100 for each of these countries and regions. From 1958–79, the output growth rate in China was 9.3 per cent (World Bank 1984). The annual growth rates of GDP in Korea and Taiwan were 8.9 per cent and 9.3 per cent in 1961–70, and 8.7 per cent and 9.7 per cent in 1971–80 (Asian Development Bank 1990).
3. The World Bank's estimate is US$220 (World Bank 1992:184).
4. In 1980 the Industrial Development Organisation of the United Nations defined developing countries as those whose per capita GNP were lower than US$265 (at the 1975 price level) (United Nations 1980:49).
5. That of commerce was the average annual growth rate from 1952–80.

6. This is calculated and adjusted through a comparison with other developing countries at the level of US$300.
7. Compared to capital-intensive heavy industries, light industries are labour intensive. China's comparative advantage is an abundant labour force. The percentage of light industries in the national economy would have been much higher than that of heavy industries if the macro-policy environment had not been distorted.
8. For the time being, we assume that the structure complies with the policy goals in an equilibrium condition.
9. The calculating price is defined as an accounting indicator which a sector or enterprise uses to calculate its actual profit loss in production. Under the traditional system, owing to the soft budget constraint, the indicator included not only the planned price, but also the planned supply of funds, raw materials, and a series of promoting or suppressing policies which affected the profit or loss of its production.
10. Since the consumer price (P_0) and producer price (P_1) are different here, the surplus is only Q_0Q_1 but not larger. In the following section, when we discuss the shortage of products, this also applies.
11. Nehru, the advocator of the heavy industry-oriented development strategy in India, stressed repeatedly that 'the development of heavy industry is the synonym for industrialisation', and 'the most important thing for industrialisation is to have the machine-building heavy industry.' The actual drafter of this strategy, Mahalanobis, once elaborated in India's second five-year plan that 'the rate of industrialisation and the growth of national economy depend on the overall growth of coal, electricity, iron and steel, heavy machine-building, and heavy chemical industry...Therefore, we have to try all means to develop heavy industries' (Peijun 1991:51–5).

References

Asian Development Bank, 1990. *The Prospect of Development in Asia*, Asian Development Bank, Manila.

Chenery, Hollis B., and Syrquin, M., 1988. *Patterns of Development, 1950–1970*, Economic Science Press, Beijing.

Fang, C., 1990. 'The new phase of urbanisation in China', *Future and Development*, 5.

Griffin, K., 1992. *The Alternative Strategies for Economic Development*, Economic Science Press, Beijing.

Lanrui, Feng, and Lukuan, Zheng, 1982. *The Employment and Wages in China's Cities and Towns*, People's Press, Beijing.

Lewis, W.A., 1954. Economic development with unlimited supplies of labour', *Manchester School of Economics and Social Studies*, 22.

——, 1989. *The Theory of Dual Economy*, Beijing Economics Academy Press, Beijing.

Lin, J.Y., 1988. 'The household responsibility system in China's agricultural reform: a theoretical and empirical study', Economic Development and Cultural Change, 36.3:s199–224.

Ma Hong (ed.), 1982. *Dictionary of Economic Affairs in Contemporary China*, China Social Sciences Press, Beijing.

Ma Hong and Sun Shangqing (eds.), 1981. *Research on Issues of China's Economic Structure*, Peoples Press, Beijing.

Peijun S. (ed.), 1991. *A Comparative Study of Economic Development in China and India*, Peking University Press, Beijing.

Ranis, G. and Mahmood, S., 1992. *The Political Economy of Development Policy Change*, Blackwell, Cambridge, Massachusetts.

State Statistical Bureau, Division of National Economic Balance Statistics, 1987. *Collection of Statistical Data on National Income (1949–1985)*, China Statistical Press, Beijing.

——, Fixed Assets Investment Division, 1987. *The Statistical Data of the Fixed Assets Investment in China, 1950–1985*, China Statistical Press, Beijing.

——, 1992. *China Statistical Yearbook*, 1992. China Statistical Press, Beijing.

——, 1993. *China Statistical Yearbook*, 1993. China Statistical Press, Beijing.

Todaro, M.P., 1988. *The Economic Development in the Third World*, China People's University Press, Beijing.

United Nations, Industrial Development Organization, 1980. *The Condition and Trend of Industrialization in Each Country in the World*, China External Translation Publication Company, Beijing.

Wang Huijong and Yang Guanghui, (eds), 1984. *Possibility and Alternatives of the Changes and Growth of China's Economic Structure*, Meteorological Press, Beijing.

World Bank, 1983. *World Development Report, 1983*, China Finance and Economics Press, Beijing.

——, 1984. *China: Long-term issues and options*, China Finance and Economics Press, Beijing.

——, 1984 Economic Study Tour, 1985. *China: Long-term issues and options*, China Finance and Economics Press, Beijing.

——, 1987. *China: Long-term issues and options*, China Finance and Economics Press, Beijing.

——, 1988. *World Development Report, 1988*, China Finance and Economics Press, Beijing.

——, 1992. *World Table, 1992*, Johns Hopkins University Press, Baltimore.

Youjing, Zheng, and Hanzhong, Fang, 1992. 'A Study on the Trend of Economic Growth', *Economic Research*, 2.

6 A Long-term Appraisal of Country Risk

E.L. Jones

Whether Hungarian politburo members or Chinese students, they have seen the capitalist-imperialist past and it works (Timothy Garton-Ash, *The Spectator*, 27 May 1989).

This paper deals with two sets of issues. The first alludes to the recurrent tendency towards growth within the Chinese economy over the last thousand years. My principal aims are to indicate that southern, or coastal, China's current achievement has not sprung up in the world's least propitious seed-bed, as well as to relate recent changes to preceding episodes. The second set of issues touches on what I have called the 'extricability problem'—whether or not economic growth can proceed successfully in the absence of the political and creative freedoms western history has accustomed us to associate with it.

Modern Chinese experience suggests that this can happen, but that growth will be fragile in the hands of totalitarian political authorities, as well as derivative (meaning somewhat lagging) in technological inventiveness. A lack of political and creative freedoms may not bring development to a halt, but what type of lopsided society will result?

Economic development may, however, contain within itself the antidote through which a 'cultural cycle'—the changing occupational mix required by growth—creates or expands social strata whose demand for freedoms induces some political individuals or factions to supply them. The actual pattern of events deriving from the inherent tension between economics and politics cannot be foreseen. Nevertheless, the forecaster may be able to gauge the probabilities of various outcomes, update the forecasts and refine the understanding of the processes at work.

I. China's Experience

The Needham problem

Under the Song Dynasty (10th–13th centuries AD) China achieved economic growth (Jones 1988). No aggregate statistics exist and this inference is based on a conjunction of developmental indicators lasting as long as a couple of centuries. It is not necessary to know the magnitude of the change as long as we can infer the sign. Any purported macro-statistics are likely to be based on contentious sampling or indirect proxy. Even modern aggregate data—

This paper was presented at the conference 'China's Reforms and Economic Growth', The Australian National University, Canberra, 11–14 November, 1991.

for example, rates of growth in southern China in the 1980s—are insecure and subject to doubt.

The Song growth was caused partly by the state, possibly an emergency marketisation with greater emphasis on money taxes and privatisation. The state fostered market activity, or at any rate removed impediments to it, and provided some overheads. The extent to which this was actually intended remains to be determined.

After the Mongol invasion which overthrew the Song Dynasty there was some degree of recovery. The late Yuan, Ming and Qing Empires were all large, functioning agrarian-commercial empires, though there may not necessarily have been a rise in average incomes. This gives rise to the so-called 'Needham problem' —why did China, rather than Europe, fail to produce the scientific, technological and commercial changes seen in the West, that culminated in the Industrial Revolution? This is not the most pertinent issue (Jones 1990). Not enough distinctions are drawn between the scientific, technological, industrial, and capitalist growth experiences. It is more revealing to consider why China did not re-enact its own Song 'economic revolution'.

What many of the numerous solutions to the Needham problem have in common is a negative appraisal of the role of the Chinese state, although this has recently been challenged by Rowe (1984). Rowe argues that China was a complex society with such varied economic activity that the direction of the whole remains hard to judge. It is worth considering the picture he draws which, although based on nineteenth century Hankow, is far broader in its implications and claims.

Rowe takes a favourable view of the Ming-Qing period, for instance interpreting phases of reduced central government involvement in the economy as deliberate attempts to stimulate the economy by relaxing controls. Privatisation had begun by the seventeenth century and accelerated after the mid-nineteenth century, with self-regulation by merchants superseding direct state control of business. Informal political structures emerged alongside official ones and grew in importance in nineteenth-century Hankow. They were growing before the European arrival at mid-century, which encouraged opportunist Chinese merchants and further stimulated trade.

According to Rowe, China possessed an integrated national market by the mid-eighteenth century. Although this contracted from the latter part of the century, it reappeared after the Taiping Rebellion. Merchants colonised distant regions. In Hankow, some of the native place associations whereby trade usually took place were merging. There were institutional changes to match trade expansion, such as new business institutions and new forms of contract. As Feuerwerker correctly concluded in his study of nineteenth century Chinese industrialisation '...one institutional breakthrough is worth a dozen textile mills or shipping companies established within the framework of traditional society and its system of values' (1970:242). Rowe would claim that society was already mutating. Clearly it was flexible enough to accommodate recurrent economic expansions.

The mere fact of economic expansion in a country whose population had reached 450 million by 1900 would be noteworthy, whether or not any measurable rise in per capita GDP was achieved. Rowe concludes that had the West not intervened so forcefully in the 1890s, China might have developed towards industrial capitalism under its own impetus.

This is a strongly revisionist hypothesis, which solves the Needham problem by saying, in essence, that history ought to have given the process a bit longer. This may be so. Rowe's thesis sits well with the partly Smithian view that I have expressed myself—premodern economies developed on their own, following the dissolving of political rigidities and oppressions (Jones 1988). Early stages of growth could, however, have been encouraged by carefully calculated help from the state, such as more investment in the infrastructure and attention to less tangible conditions for change. This was evident in K'ang

Yu-wei's memorial to the Emperor in 1898, 'I beg your Majesty to adopt the purpose of Peter the Great of Russia as our purpose, and to take the Meiji Reform of Japan as the model for our reform' (Rodzinski 1984:237).

There were precedents for growth in China: the Song economic revolution and the prosperity of the mid-eighteenth century (Jones 1988; Rowe 1984). Too much of the older, more negative, western historiography may reflect the turmoil of the nineteenth and twentieth centuries. This gave rise to interpretations of an unyielding Orient, whereas, Wilhelm sensibly concluded, 'Chinese conservatism is not a symptom of rigidity but rather the result of adaptation to conditions which remained unchanged for thousands of years' (1982:45), which he saw as capable of dissolving rapidly when those conditions changed.

The legal apparatus, or at any rate the condition to which it had reverted during the nineteenth century, may have restricted the achievement of prosperity. A lack of secure commercial law would go some way to explaining the lag in China's development—the heart of the Needham problem—so that its latest growth experiment was truncated and replaced by western quasi-colonialism before it ran its full course. While the central government in the nineteenth century was abandoning regulation, it was not providing supplementary institutions, notably an impersonal law of contract. Something more than an institutional vacuum was desirable if high growth rates were to continue. A distinction should be drawn between the relaxation of regulation to allow growth and the institutional changes needed to establish and hasten the process.

Late Qing China lacked any formal legal code with which to regulate, say, the banking sector. In any case, law in China was not justice. It was likely to involve bribery, extortion and cruelty. Rowe cites examples of individuals beaten to death for business failure. There were no juries, evidence was not weighed and witnesses were never sworn since it was assumed they would lie. If the outcome was in doubt, the litigant or defendant might be beaten or tortured in court. In these circumstances, it is astonishing that magistrates were petitioned as much as they were (Rowe 1984; Bird 1983; Krausse 1900; Coates 1955; Morrison 1985).

This system was compatible with high commercial morality. It demanded great trust and elicited this with its own stern, informal sanctions. Around 1900, banks were lending at 7–12 per cent on personal security, almost never on goods. Krausse (1900) reported that if an employee defrauded a Shansi bank he would be sent home to be tried by his family elders and as punishment might be buried alive.

China has an older, though more interrupted, history of economic growth than Europe. Its failure, however, to create universal institutions slowed and sometimes even stifled, the tendency to return to growth.

The Rawski problem

In the late 1890s, western investment and technology began to instigate a degree of change, including industrialisation. The standard view is that these efforts were heavily concentrated in the Treaty Ports and failed to raise per capita GDP, so that the first half of the twentieth century saw little more than exploitation, foreign intervention and political turmoil. Socialist historians undoubtedly have an interest in portraying China as unable to achieve growth. It is this bleak view that Rawski (1989) seeks to revise.

If Rawski is correct, China has now had almost eight decades of continuous growth, starting long before 1949. Instead of taking over a crumbling, war-torn mess from the Nationalists, the new regime acquired an economy that had already been making a profit since the 1920s and 1930s. Relative evaluations of the communist, or the Maoist, achievement would be correspondingly depressed.

Rawski claims that the communists failed to raise the rate of gross domestic capital formation above the 1930s trend line and conveys the impression that economic growth after 1949 was just a stage in an existing process. In fairness, an allowance should be added by factoring in an income equivalent of the gain in life expectancy since 1949 (Usher 1973). It seems unlikely that this would fail to elevate the post 1949 period to a higher place in the growth stakes than any other time.

The Rawski thesis is that pre-war growth was Smithian, affecting mutually reinforcing sectors, rather than a Schumpeterian gale of 'creative destruction'. Such gradual change would be easily overlooked amidst the political confusion of the times. The economy was civilian, domestic, private and competitive. Foreign and government influences were surprisingly small. Rawski thinks the country performed as well as Japan, give or take differences in timing and the lack of any central government push.

Once Rawski has sharpened our perceptions, observations by other scholars take on greater meaning. Bianco (1971) notes that contrary to the opinion of writers as luminous as Tawney, Chinese peasants may not have been increasingly exploited between the wars. After all, while consumers gained from a 30–80 per cent fall in grain prices between 1929 and 1933, land prices also fell, presumably taking farm rents down with them, while confusing the issue by opening the way for considerable landlord–peasant conflict. Recent work by other writers, such as Brandt and Sands (1990), also portrays a more vigorous republican economy than has been depicted hitherto. Hanson (1988), in expressing scepticism about the desperate poverty of China before World War I, implies that the pre-Republican baseline for growth was higher than had been assumed. The revisionist tendency now stretches back into Qing economic history.

With respect to statistics and method, Rawski has to admit that for lack of sufficient aggregate series, he had to construct amalgams of data. The results, he claims, are no worse than the figures used in debates about a variety of other periods, including the controversy surrounding the Industrial Revolution in eighteenth-century Britain. It is, however, his logic rather than numbers which will succeed or fail to persuade.

An ironic fact which does seem to display Rawski's evidence in a relatively favourable light is that even data for the post-1949 period are not very satisfactory. In the years before the country fell into the hands of a single command system, the standards of record keeping were higher. Malenbaum refers to 'the Confucian quality of the official PRC growth record' (1990: 405). Many of the figures serve to make economic aggregates seem respectable when they are not; have to be supplemented by traditional sources, producing chains of argument with notably weak links; and represent little more than another kind of rhetoric (McCloskey 1983). The conclusion is that although the evident foundations of work on the Chinese economy appear far more satisfactory after 1949, this is to a degree illusory. We are still dealing with economic history and need historical sensitivity.

The most obvious objection to Rawski's favourable conclusion about Republican China is that the period saw undeniable poverty, turbulence and warlordism, not to mention invasion by a foreign power. The revisionist counter is that much of the turmoil was a result of the stresses of the world depression of the 1930s. Growth and depression are always irregular in their impact on classes, occupations and regions and in a country the size of China one need not be surprised at many contradictory tendencies.

The extent of militarism was certainly considerable. Rawski insists, however, that the warlords were not as damaging to the economy as has been reported. The wars cost only a few per cent of output and led to casualties which were tiny in comparison with China's millions. The warlords literally did not have enough guns or ammunition to sustain prolonged fighting and understood that they would not gain by expropriating the merchants. Some warlords actually drew up development plans, and at least one sent students overseas. Indeed, it could be predicted that virtual bandit chiefs would quickly decide to tax rather than expropriate (Olson 1990). But this is a minimalist position, it scarcely assures us that there was real growth.

The population data for the interwar period are not comforting for Rawski's case. The growth rate of population was low (Borrie 1970), and marital fertility was low, possibly because of poor lactation by under-nourished peasant women (Barclay et al. 1976). At the 1953 census, the age composition of the population was heavily weighted towards the younger age cohorts and life expectancy cannot have been high (Borrie 1970). Despite everything that has happened since 1949, including the deaths of 30 million people in the forced collectivisation of 1958–61, life expectancy has risen substantially (Lin 1990). It has reached 70 years at birth, averaged for both sexes. The pre-war period seems to have offered no comparable gain.

There is some reason to hesitate about Rawski's argument that traditional sectors of the economy were genuinely able to compete with the techniques of the modern sector up to, and after, 1949. He claims that the market was already extremely integrated, as a legacy from the past.

There are three possible kinds of integration, physical (in terms of communications), governmental (the legal context) and commercial (private sector substitutes for public infrastructure). By pre-modern standards, large parts of China were bound together by water routes, but this did not embrace the whole economy. There were not enough railways—by 1992 only three tracks linked the 107 million people in Sichuan to the outside world. In 1931, when Fitzgerald was travelling through China, motor roads had not yet connected the whole country. Explaining why he had to take to a cart to travel 80 miles, he pointed out that 'warlord rulers were never very keen to build direct communications with their neighbours and rivals, lest these be used to facilitate invasions' (Fitzgerald 1985:158).

Even granting Rawski's assumption about an integrated market—and in terms of the legal context alone that seems improbable—his conclusion that market access enabled traditional

methods to go on competing, so that new methods and products penetrated slowly, is surprising. This is the opposite of what happened in mainland Europe, where the separation of certain markets protected traditional producers. Otherwise, older methods would have been out-competed much sooner by the British machines of the nineteenth century (Schon 1980).

As Brandt and Sands (1990) conclude in a sympathetic review, the case for economic growth in Republican times is suggested, not proven. The maximum rate claimed, though by historical standards high, would be unimpressive compared with post-war standards especially if an income equivalent of life expectancy gains were incorporated. This is not an endorsement of later communist policies, however, since the scope for further increases in life expectancy is limited. In any case, there are reasons for doubting the ability of communist states to sustain high rates of growth in the long term.

II. China's Political Economy

Market responsiveness

Despite his quantitative methodology, Rawski (1989) finally speculates that Chinese cultural tradition is behind East Asian success. Culture is surprisingly common as the final resting place for economists who seldom refer to it or analyse its implications—they are inclined to accept it as a given. Appeals to fundamental cultural values by themselves cannot explain the timing of events. The transmitted specifics of Imperial China, Rawski says, are the prevalence of the market and related institutions, widespread participation in complex organisations, and harsh social competition in which the strategies of businesses reflect those of families. Thus China may have had an advantage over most developing economies and may still have one today, at least insofar as one believes that present behaviour has been handed down from the past.

Rawski argues that commercially useful institutions and values have been inherited from the pre-communist period, noting the continuity of household-farm enterprises with pre-socialist economic patterns. There is something in this but how much does it really explain? Cultural patterns will surely persist, after all they provide ready, even comforting, algorithms. Continuity in this sense, however, says little more than that the communists were not very effective in eradicating the micro-foundations of China's market system. In any case there is an identification problem. It is not clear how much of the market response was historically conditioned as opposed to being the release of a human impulse (Jones 1988). How specifically Chinese was China's response?

There is a historiographic bias against noticing the minutely contingent aspects of culture, yet value systems do vary in their effects according to political circumstances. Different elements from any complex system can be emphasised, or different meanings may be attached to them. As Wilhelm (1982) pointed out with respect to China, old values are capable of being modified in response to material and political changes much more quickly than is commonly thought.

The upshot is that we do not have to worry about the issue of cultural continuity. Cultural peculiarities may dull or sharpen appetites but *ceteris paribus* they will not be what enables China to enter a capitalist future. That will be the expression of market signals. What may conceivably be explained by 'culture' is the magnitude of the economic response, represented in China by the great upwelling of output in the coastal provinces after 1979. The fundamental and encouraging feature of this change is the underlying human response to incentives.

East Asian regions may be considered, at various stages of a cultural cycle, adjusting modal values and behaviour to needs (Jones 1991). This is an interpretation quite alien to the usual treatment of culture as the independent variable and economic action as the dependent one. Instead, I propose that it is the economy which substantially modifies or even manu-factures culture, the mechanism being the engendering of values, attitudes and behaviour characteristic of the mix of occupations required by a given stage of the product cycle. Just as the product cycle is partly the result of political will, these values in turn have political implications. Already, young urban Chinese and the unemployed are unwilling to enter labour-intensive occupations in textiles, coal mining, building and the metal trades (Liu 1991). In the long run, a new form of economic life may create its own new stage of political life.

Needless to say, even an active market economy will not by itself guarantee sustained high rates of growth. Dynamic technical efficiency requires something more of political society, which the product cycle may eventually provide but totalitarianism must attempt to restrain.

Attitudes engendered by risk

The relationship of economics and politics is a tight spiral. As Ch'i pointed out with respect to warlordism, '...political disintegration had caused economic disintegration in the first place. As time went by, however, economic disintegration in turn retarded political reintegration'.

China's history has been dominated by a high level of risk. It has not been productive in per capita terms, and late Imperial China supported only about two per cent of the population as non-food producers—a smaller proportion than medieval Europe (Jones 1987).

Bland (1912) observed that '...it is not the political agitator who has created unrest, but rather the unrest (chiefly economic in its origin) that has produced the agitator'. Bland's remark reminds us of Rawski's claim that aggression by the warlords was curbed by the limited capacity of the economy to support it. Similarly, the persistence of the guilds during Imperial times was less a tribute to their strength than a sign that the economy was slow to generate enough activity to bypass them (Jones 1988). Despite these economic limitations on politics and institutions, governments have the power to bring about economic growth by removing disincentives for market activity. Usually, though, Chinese governments have been reluctant in this matter.

Ordered disorder—the spontaneous, un-planned order—of an open society is necessary for rapid invention. For innovation, what is needed are property rights, legal frameworks and incentives for investment also characteristic of such societies but less dependent on full openness. In the early stages of growth, these things may be extricable, in other words, some of them may be able to occur without the others. Economic growth does not depend on a full range of freedoms; autocratic, authoritarian and totalitarian regimes have all shown they can manage it. But for growth to be sustained at high levels over many decades, openness is needed.

The Chinese attitude towards openness transcends cynicism, it concerns survival (Bloodworth 1969; Coates 1955). Everything is taken as if meant in a political way: concerning the West, this entails believing that democracy and altruism are either cloaks for interest or evidence of frailty. It is easy to forget that evidence of western corruption is often part of our society's process of self-correction.

Economically, the modal Chinese attitude seems to resemble 'amoral familialism' (Banfield 1958). The response to problems is exit rather than voice. The students rose above this in 1989 but the peasant mass, which did not, was their undoing. The vital question is will growth manage to modify immediate self-interest—that is, stretch out time-preferences—and strengthen demands for the freedoms required for growth to become permanent?

The modal Chinese attitude is the less Chinese the more one accepts the universality of basic motives. Certainly the distortions of the human spirit produced by oppression are not exclusively Chinese. What will change them?

The price of fast, uneven growth

China's economic record of the past twenty years has surpassed expectations. Rapid growth is concentrated in southern coastal provinces and on part of the northeast coast. The government has been unable to tax away the bulk of the resources created in these areas. Some of its anti-reform stance may even be a centralising manoeuvre rather than genuine ideology. It has not succeeded. The fact that growth remains regionally staggered carries the danger of reaction but also has interesting long-term implications (Tsui 1991; Tzeng 1991; Delfs 1991).

If growth in the richer provinces leads to the emergence of a wide stratum demanding further deregulation of the market, the rule of law and representative government, some members of the ruling élite may decide to advance their own careers by supplying them. This process would probably involve greater independence from Beijing.

There are always those who will bend ideology if it seems expedient. Some may use their privileged connections to become private capitalists—the 'nomenklatura buy-out theory' (Garton-Ash 1989). In any event, whole ideologies can shift, probably via cognitive dissonance, to promote behaviour diametrically opposite to that originally propounded. As Collins (1986) concludes on the basis of the comparative history of religion, political considerations eventually come to dominate ideological ones.

The cat and mouse barriers to a single Chinese market act as a centrifugal pressure. Although citizens cannot legally relocate, they may travel and find out what is going on in different provinces. Workers from the country-side do move but more skilled labour, prevented from using exit, will increasingly use voice—making their provincial leaders aware of the requirements of business and the constant need to fend off the tax claims of the central government.

Intra-Chinese trade is not particularly large. Provincial governments would rather have the foreign exchange from export earnings. This links manufacturers in the coastal provinces with overseas markets and exposes them to foreign sources of information. Interior regions are much less involved. This is another centrifugal force.

It must be remembered that independent states, state systems or federations are not sufficient conditions for economic growth. In the very long term, however, they may be necessary conditions, since centralised command economies lack the checks and balances needed to offset the effects of bad decisions at the top.

III. The Eventual Price of Totalitarianism

Worldwide, the association of very low average incomes and a lack of basic freedoms is high. The rule of law, private property rights (including intellectual property), and renewed marketisation will be required for the massive and sustained program of innovation appropriate to China's developmental needs. These conditions will have to be met if there is to be effective trickle down from the coastal provinces to the interior and if an economy trading on full comparative advantage is to replace an administratively decided economic geography.

Meanwhile there are many hazards. Although a *nomenklatura* has more than ideological reasons for not providing legal freedoms, the dangers of semi-marketised economies within corrupt, regulatory states are great. China will forego the full benefits of innovation and entrepreneurship unless it is prepared to trust an impartial legal system for curbing excesses, controlling corruption and enforcing equality before the tax laws.

Corruption is an invitation to political disillusion and hence to the softening of the ideology which the government must value, if only for motivational reasons. Both corruption and ideological blurring are likely to reduce creative energy, especially concerning projects with long gestation periods where the individual would expect to capture a share of the gains. Corruption can also inspire overt political disturbance, but if a counter-revolution ever succeeds there is always the danger that it may take the form of another cleansing regime opposed to the market.

To some extent, governments can find substitutes for private investment. Command economies can continue successfully with major projects on which they are willing to concentrate resources. The preferred activities typically put armaments at the top. Even for a limited number of projects, sustaining the rate of innovation indefinitely is likely to present difficulties but a greater long-run problem for the command economy is sustaining the rate of invention.

The art is not so much to secure some invention to couple with purchased foreign patents and blueprints obtained by industrial espionage. The deeper problem is the likelihood of eventual miscalculation of the direction of research and development. Members of a monopolistic ruling party are trapped in a network where only a dictatorial leader would wish to be first to move (Basu et al. 1987). As a result, real opportunities may be neglected or rejected.

Among the standard ways of evaluating economic performance, consider static technical efficiency, defined as the full use of best-practice techniques with the economy operating on the production frontier. This is a matter of the rate of innovation. Routine scientific work (Kuhn's 'normal' science) does seem possible in relatively organised, factory-like laboratories. Technology can be imported, but at a price, with the likelihood of bias against information technologies. This would eventually result in failing to familiarise enough young people with new methods and types of equipment. Related factors curbing the rate of innovation are income compression, few and insecure property rights, and the curbing of intellectual freedom.

But the ultimate problem lies with dynamic technical efficiency, with pushing out the frontier. Sustaining a high rate of invention over the long run and across the full range of scientific or technological fields, not to mention the social sciences or arts, requires freedom. Such activity is fundamentally heuristic rather than algorithmic. Political considerations and resource scarcities evident in China compound the damage caused by administrative decisions about research, especially in an economy which, if not closed, courts semiclosure by its behaviour towards other people's patents and copyrights. If such a system is rigidly maintained, it will surely lag behind and drift off the course taken by more open societies. Fortunately, there are reasons to think that a growing economy will eventually modify the form of its own governance.

IV. China's Prospects

By definition, growth brings greater personal resources, and changes the institutional set. Given modern technologies of production, the occupational structure must change in favour of skilled workers. Moreover, an unintended concomitant of the restructuring of society is that it reacts back on cultural values. If one chooses, one can look on this as a reassertion of old Chinese commercial virtues. It is neater to see the development as a response to altered structural forces, though the particular menu from which current values are selected may be proffered by China's past. Although we must allow for the theoretical possibility of retreating down the occupational ladder—deindustrialisation—and thus an eventual return to lower expectations, I would expect to see from occupational change a pressure for political liberalisation, or for the type of open society which is the key to sustaining high rates of growth via persistent inventiveness.

The product cycle is enjoined on any economy that opens itself to world trade. Equally, so are its effects. Peasant migrants may sometimes have been returned to the 'cage'—the countryside—in China but '...these "birds" were not the same as before; they had flown and they liked the experience' (Liu 1991:408). Thus, even a limited modernisation such as China's must contain, to a degree, its own corrective to the autocracy which, for instrumental reasons, began it. Moving round the product cycle must create new, more demanding interest groups.

The Chinese have little by way of a tradition of taking individual initiatives in the public sphere. Moreover the process of change is susceptible to all sorts of shocks, the build-up of countervailing resentments, and reversals of the Tiananmen kind. In general, though, I am a long-run optimist and while the changes may take a generation, they could happen more quickly— what Tiananmen showed besides savagery was the build-up of demands. One merit of a long-term study is that the ultimate signal may be heard behind the noise of current events. Another is that relationships may become apparent simply through their repetition.

In the future, China may grow fast by exploiting a backlog of (derivative) technologies, as other economies in East Asia have done. It may improve on some of them by reverse engineering. As currently constituted, however, it is unlikely to contribute its equilibrium share to the world pool of invention. There is a risk of China tripping over its own feet and eventually falling behind. Yet the tendency will be counteracted if the demands for political freedoms, arising from new occupational mixes, are met by opportunistic politicians.

Economically, China has a 'good life' given mildly rosy assumptions about soil fertility, potential arable area, controllable populations, and bolder hopes about the market economy, an opening to trade in food, domestic innovation, and above all the conditions for creativity. The technical difficulties of maintaining momentum from year to year in such a vast and poor economy are not underrated just because we are concerned here with more distant prospects.

Note

The author acknowledges the comments of John Anderson, Tom Fisher, Geoff Raby and Arthur Waldron.

References

Banfield, E.C., 1958. *The Moral Basis of a Backward Society*, Free Press, Glencoe.

Barclay, G. et al., 1976. 'A reassessment of the demography of traditional rural China', *Population Index*, 42:624–5.

Basu, K. et al., 1987. 'The growth and decay of custom: the role of the new institutional economics in economic history', *Explorations in Economic History*, 24:1–21.

Bianco, L., 1971. *Origins of the Chinese Revolution, 1915–1949*, Stanford University Press, Stanford, California.

Bird, I.L., 1983. *The Golden Bird*, Century Books, London.

Bland, J.O.P., 1912. *Recent Events and Present Policies in China*, J.B. Lippincott Co., Philadelphia.

Bloodworth, D., 1969. *Chinese Looking Glass*, Penguin, Middlesex.

Borrie, W.D., 1970. *The Growth and Control of World Population*, Weidenfeld and Nicolson, London.

Brandt, L. and Sands, B., 1990. 'Beyond Malthus and Ricardo: economic growth, land concentration, and income distribution in early twentieth-century rural China', *Journal of Economic History*, 50(4):807–27.

Ch'i, H.S., 1976. *Warlord Politics in China*, Stanford University Press, Stanford, California.

Coates, A., 1955. *Invitation to an Eastern Feast*, Harper and Brothers, New York.

Cohen, B., 1991. 'Freedom and the chain reaction', *The Weekend Australian*, 6 April.

Collins, R., 1986. *Weberian Sociological Theory*, Cambridge University Press, Cambridge.

Delfs, R., 1991. 'Saying no to Peking', *Far Eastern Economic Review*, 4 April.

Feuerwerker, A., 1970. *China's Early Industrialization: Sheng Hsuan-Huai (1844–1916) and Mandarin Enterprise*, Atheneum, New York.

Fitzgerald, C.P., 1985. *Why China? Recollections of China, 1923–1950*, Melbourne University Press, Melbourne.

Garton-Ash, T., 1989. *The Uses of Adversity*, Granta Books, Cambridge.

Hanson, J.R., 1988. 'Third World incomes before World War 1: some comparisons', *Explorations in Economic History*, 25:323–6.

Jones, E.L., 1987. *The European Miracle: environments, economies and geopolitics in the history of Europe and Asia*, Cambridge University Press, Cambridge.

——, 1988. *Growth Recurring: economic change in world history*, Clarendon Press, Oxford.

——, 1990. 'The real question about China: why was the Song economic achievement not repeated?' *Australian Economic History Review*, 30:5–22.

——, 1991. *The Ultimate Significance of East Asian Development*, School of Economics and Commerce Discussion Paper 3/91, La Trobe University, Melbourne.

Krausse, A., 1900. *China in Decay*, George Bell and Sons, London.

Lin, J.Y., 1990. 'Collectivization and China's agricultural crisis in 1958–1961', *Journal of Political Economy*, 98:1228–52.

Liu, A., 1991. 'Economic reform, mobility strategies and national integration in China', *Asian Survey*, 31:396.

Malenbaum, W., 1990. 'A gloomy portrayal of development achievements and prospects: China and India', *Economic Development and Cultural Change*, 38:405.

McCloskey, D.H., 1983. 'The rhetoric of economics', *Journal of Economic Literature*, 21:481–517.

Morrison, G.E., 1985. *An Australian in China*, Oxford University Press, Hong Kong.

Olson, M., 1990. *Autocracy, democracy and prosperity*, University of Maryland, Maryland.

Rawski, T.G., 1989. *Economic Growth in Prewar China*, University of California Press, Berkeley.

Rodzinski, W., 1984. *The Walled Kingdom: a history of China from 2000 BC to the present*, Fontana, London.

Rowe, W.T., 1984. *Hankow: commerce and society in a Chinese city, 1796–1889*, Stanford University Press, Stanford, California.

Schon, L., 1980. 'British competition and domestic change in textiles in Sweden, 1820–1870', *Economy and History*, 23:61–76.

Tsui, K.Y., 1991. 'China's regional inequality, 1952–1985', *Journal of Comparative Economics*, 15:1–15.

Tzeng, Fuh-Wen, 1991. 'The political economy of China's coastal development strategy: a preliminary analysis', *Asian Survey*, 31:270–84.

Usher, D., 1973. 'An imputation to the measure of economic growth for changes in life expectancy', in M. Moss (ed.), *The Measurement of Economic and Social Performance, Conference Proceedings of Income and Wealth*, National Bureau of Economic Research, New York:193–232.

Wilhelm, R., 1982. *Chinese Economic Psychology*, Garland, New York.

7 Economic Growth and Stability in China

Ross Garnaut and Guonan Ma

High inflation and external deficits in the late 1980s in China raised questions about the viability of Chinese official ambitions to sustain strong growth. Inflation helped to set the scene for the political unrest in 1989, which itself raised doubts about the political feasibility of sustained gradual reform. Some commentators drew attention to an apparently deteriorating trade-off between growth and stability through the 1980s, with given rates of growth being associated with higher inflation and external payments deficits later in the decade (Garnaut 1990, 1992).

After a quarter of a century of intermittent high growth with little open inflation and more or less balanced external current payments, the relationship between growth and stability in China changed fundamentally in the reform period. Growth has been consistently, but unevenly, high, and fluctuations in output growth have generated periods of high inflation and substantial deficits in current payments.

In this paper, we address two sets of questions. First, has there been a 'trade-off' between growth and stability in China's economy during the 1980s? If so, did the terms of this trade-off deteriorate through the decade and what are its key features?[1] Second, what are the primary causes of fluctuations in the main macroeconomic variables, and how have they been affected by policy?

I. Growth and Instability

Output, inflation and the current account

High annual growth rates of real GNP have been accompanied by sharp oscillations. Both the peak (13.6 per cent in 1984) and trough (3.6 per cent in 1989) growth rates occurred during the period from 1984, following the accumulation of reform steps that were brought together in the 1984 plenum decisions on urban reform (Raby 1991). There was acceleration of inflation from 1984.[2] Strong growth has tended to be accompanied by high inflation, most emphatically the latter part of the 1980s. When growth has been sluggish, inflation has subsided quickly.

The trade balance has tended to vary inversely with cyclical fluctuations in GNP growth, with some lags. Net exports, expressed as a percentage of GNP, decline when the economy expands rapidly, but increase quickly when growth slows

Reprinted with permission. Extracted from Ross Garnaut and Guonan Ma, 1993. 'Economic growth and stability in China', *Journal of Asian Economics*, 4(1):5–24 (with minor editing).

down. The ratio of net exports to total output has fluctuated a great deal, with the largest trough-to-peak variation being equal to eight percentage points of GNP. These movements are large enough to make the open policy a major element in the overall stability of China's economy.

To explore the possible changing relationship between growth and price stability in the 1980s, Figure 1 plots the annual data for macroeconomic variables. Figure 1 suggests that the data from 1979 to 1990 fall into three sets. The first set, covering the years 1979 to 1984 suggests only a weak tendency for inflation to be higher in years of strong growth. The year 1980 is unusual in this period for its high inflation. Inflation was low in 1982 and 1983 despite relatively strong growth partly because of strong non-inflationary agricultural expansion. These early years preceded urban price reform, and reflected the continued efficacy of the old controls on prices.

The second set of data covers the years 1985–1987 when major urban state enterprise and price reforms unfolded. There appears to have been an increase in the rate of inflation associated with any given rate of growth—a worsening trade-off between growth and price stability. This period may have been influenced by the release, through the price reforms, of previously accumulated and suppressed inflationary pressures. New factors emerging in the reform process started to play an important role.

Then, 1988 and 1989 reveal a sharp deterioration in the relationship between growth and price increases: growth that was high, but within the range of the decade, generated exceptionally high inflation. For any given growth rate, inflation was considerably higher than the earlier period. This is a clear indication that as the economy became more responsive to market pressures, the current economic policy had not yet succeeded in establishing an effective new framework of macroeconomic management to replace the weakened old command controls.

In 1990 and 1991, the relationship between growth and inflation fell back to the range of the early 1980s, with moderate growth being associated with relatively low inflation.

Sources of output fluctuations

What was the source of the output variations of the 1980s? We examine this question by identifying the sectors which contributed most to output changes on the supply side, and the categories which contributed most to changes in aggregate demand.

Agriculture played a major role in production fluctuations during the early 1980s, while changes in industrial output dominated fluctuations for most of the decade. The large, early contribution by the farm sector resulted from a series of supply shocks induced by institutional and pricing policy changes (Lin 1992). The relative role of industrial growth was greater later in the decade, during the period when the trade-off with inflation was less favourable (Khor 1991).

Figure 1   **Relationship between growth and inflation** (per cent)

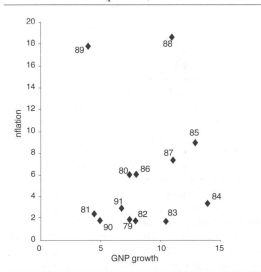

Source: SSB 1991.

On the demand side, the percentage contributions to the overall change in domestic absorption of private consumption expenditure, gross investment and general government spending are compared in Table 1. This table demonstrates that changes in gross investment and private consumption dominated fluctuations in domestic aggregate demand through the 1980s. Variations in general government spending most often had a minor role.

The macroeconomic cycles and monetary fluctuations

Three major cycles are identified by the behaviour of the key macroeconomic variables of output, inflation, trade balance and monetary changes. The three cycles are 1978–1981, 1982–1986 and 1986–1989.

Figure 2 clearly shows the relationship between supply of broad money on the one hand,

Table 1	Sources of domestic absorption fluctuations			
Year	Domestic absorption	Private consumption	Government consumption	Gross investment
1979	100	63.70	-11.05	47.35
1980	100	78.78	11.43	9.76
1981	100	104.03	12.82	-16.81
1982	100	70.84	-12.56	41.76
1983	100	45.33	20.11	34.55
1984	100	42.69	16.33	40.98
1985	100	47.60	-0.76	53.16
1986	100	58.09	-3.73	45.65
1987	100	58.18	-5.09	46.91
1988	100	61.12	2.96	35.92

Source: World Bank 1990a.

Table 1 reveals surprisingly large fluctuations in the contribution of private consumption expenditure to changes in domestic absorption. During the high growth years of 1987 and 1988, the increase in consumption spending was much more important than the increase in investment. This contrasts with 1984 and 1985, when investment was the leading source of increased aggregate demand. An exclusive focus on 'investment hunger', which is common in recent analysis having been influenced by the Eastern Europe experience, misses the role of consumption as a source of excess aggregate demand.

and other major macroeconomic variables on the other (see also Khor 1991).

The first cycle, 1978–1981, ran its course between the late pre-reform era and 1981. Rural reform commenced, if only tentatively in 1978. During 1978 to 1980, state farm procurement prices were raised considerably. Bank loans were used in place of budgetary appropriations for investment financing. Wages rates were raised. There were spurts of high investment associated with ambitious modernisation plans.[3] The old command controls, together with the subordinate financial policy, played an accommodating role, with fiscal deficits surging to 5 per cent of GNP in 1979 and broad money increasing 24 per cent in 1980. This resulted in 8 per cent GNP growth in 1979–1980, and a 6–7 per cent inflation rate.

The first austerity policy of the reform period came in 1981, reducing money growth below 20 per cent. The traditional administrative measures were used to slash state investment and to depress consumer demand by forced sales of treasury bonds. Real GNP growth fell below 5 per cent in 1981, and inflation fell to 2–3 per cent in 1981–1983. The trade balance improved in 1981 and 1982 as growth was dampened and stringent import restrictions were imposed.

The second major cycle occurred between 1981 and 1986. This is the first full cycle in the reform era. The tight policy stance adopted in 1981 continued into early 1983. However, strong performance in the farm sector maintained GNP growth at the considerable pace of 9 per cent per annum during 1982 and 1983, alongside low inflation and a sound external position. In terms of macroeconomic outcomes, these were 'golden years' when high growth was not associated with inflation. The outcome was influenced, however, by the continuation of rigid price (and foreign trade) system controls, which converted current pressures for price increases into fiscal deficits and high forced savings, and hence potential future inflation.[4]

During 1982–1984, enterprises gained much greater autonomy in wage setting and production. The bonus system was widely introduced. Profit taxation and foreign exchange systems were implemented. A central bank was established. A relaxation of financial policy, under the pressures of enterprise investment demand and the ambitious goals set by the party leadership, led to an explosive monetary expansion. Broad money growth jumped from around 20 per cent to well above 40 per cent in late 1984 and early 1985, fueling a huge growth of state investment in 1984 and 1985 (more than 49 per cent). Wage rate growth surged to 18 per cent in 1984–1985. Industrial output increased at an annual rate of

25 per cent in the first half of 1985. GNP expanded more than 12 per cent annually in 1984 and 1985. Inflation was measured in double digits in 1985. The trade balance deteriorated markedly, as the authorities allowed increased imports to dampen excess demand.

In reaction, a slowdown of monetary growth was imposed from mid 1985 to early 1986. Broad money growth slipped to about 30 per cent. Industrial growth soon dropped to a low of five per cent in early 1986. The expansion of state investment remained high for a while, but then fell to 10 per cent. Inflation subsided in 1986, in part through tightening price controls. The trade balance started to improve in 1987. GNP growth dropped from 14 per cent in 1984 to the second 'trough' of 8 per cent in 1986. However, the budget deficit soared again in 1986, and wages continued to increase at a 16 per cent per annum pace. Despite some experimental uses of new macro-management tools, the policy response relied largely on command controls.

Slower growth, the abatement of price increases and mounting fiscal pressure sparked another round of expansionary policy in mid 1986 and set the stage for the third cycle. Monetary growth rose to well above 40 per cent. Growth of industrial production and state investment bounced back quickly, from 5 and 10 per cent respectively to 15 per cent and 20 per cent in late 1986 and early 1987. Inflation accelerated again. A deep short-lived credit squeeze was pursued in late 1986 and early 1987,[5] followed by a burst of monetary growth in early 1988 to 50 per cent. State total investment, industrial output and wage rates rose at an annual rate of 20 per cent. Amidst the overheating of the economy, major price reforms were announced, invoking waves of panic purchases. Inflation remained in double digits throughout this boom, and peaked near 20 per cent in late 1988 and early 1989. Trade deficits doubled in 1988–1989.

Money growth was tightened heavily from mid 1988 to the third quarter of 1989. Interest rates were raised decisively. State total investment

Figure 2 **Quarterly movements in major macroeconomic variables** (quarterly percentage change over four quarters, unless specified otherwise)

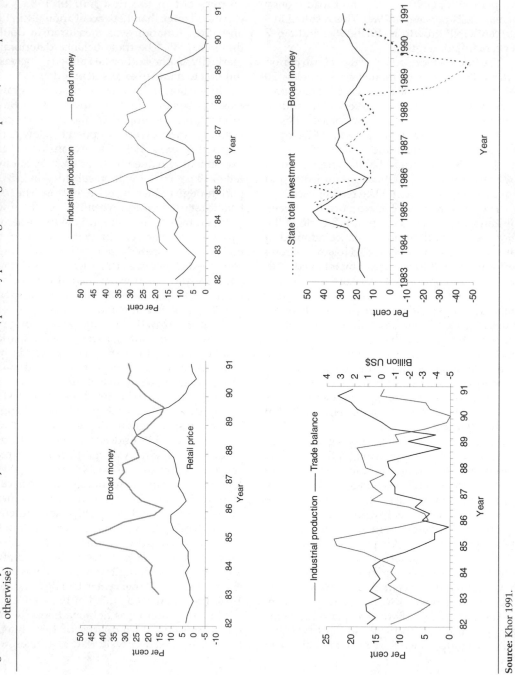

Source: Khor 1991.

92

Table 2   **Budget deficit and its financing**

Year	(1) Deficit (billion yuan)	(2) As a percentage of GNP (%)	(3) Central bank financing (billion yuan)	(4) As a percentage of GNP (%)
1979	20.6	5.2	17.1	4.3
1980	14.8	3.1	12.8	2.9
1981	4.4	0.9	-2.3	-0.5
1982	6.8	1.3	2.9	0.6
1983	9.1	1.6	4.4	0.8
1984	10.4	1.5	4.5	0.6
1985	4.1	0.5	-2.2	-0.3
1986	17.3	1.8	7.1	0.7
1987	23.7	2.1	8.0	0.7
1988	29.1	2.1	7.9	0.6
1989	32.9	2.1	9.2	0.6
1990	35.8	2.1	13.9	0.8

Note: Fiscal expenditure includes interest payments but excludes repayment of principal of government debt outstanding. Fiscal revenue excludes proceeds from debt issuance. Still, some bank financing has not been accounted for due to lack of data.
Source: MOF 1989; SSB 1991.

fell quickly by more than 40 per cent, in part because of forceful bureaucratic actions. Industrial production growth plummeted to zero in early 1990. Inflation abated in late 1989 and through 1990. The trade balance swung into surplus in 1990. The cost of restoring macroeconomic balance was high, with real GNP growth falling to below 4 per cent in 1989, the lowest 'trough' in the 1980s.

From the last quarter of 1989, there was an easing of the monetary stance, leading to a gradual recovery of both industrial output and state investment. Moderately high output growth accompanied by low inflation and trade surplus in 1990 and 1991 seemed at first sight to take the economy back into the more favourable relationship of the early years of reform.[6] Macro-economic outcomes in these years reflected interaction among strong farm output growth, changes in interest rate policy, and for some commodities a return to more restrictive price controls. However, the worsening budget position

in the early 1990s raised the possibility that another inflationary episode was on the horizon.

II. Public Deficits and Monetary Growth

Excess demand can emerge only if pressures to increase expenditures are validated by monetary policy. But simply blaming bad monetary policy for inflation does not advance our understanding of the problems. We need to ask why monetary growth had been high and unstable.

The role of the budget

In many developing economies, excessive public deficits are a principal cause of high money growth (Johnson 1985). The conservative fiscal policies of the Maoist period, having their origins in reaction to the hyperinflation of the late 1940s, cast a shadow into the reform period in China. The authorities have never let official budget outcomes get out of control along the pattern of reforming governments in the former Soviet Union and Eastern Europe.

The state budget has been in deficit since the commencement of reform in 1979 (Table 2 and Figure 3). As a proportion of GNP, the budget deficit has remained below 3 per cent except in 1979–1980. Compared to other economies, this is not an alarming ratio.[7] This proportion fell from 5.2 per cent in 1979 to a low of less than one per cent in 1985. However, since then there has been a noticeable upward trend, reaching more than 2 per cent between 1987 and 1990.

The official data indicate that deficit financing by the central bank (People's Bank of China), expressed as a ratio of GNP, has remained below one per cent since the early 1980s and generally has not been a major source of monetary expansion. The relative importance of central bank credit in budget deficit financing fell considerably during the 1980s.

Some commentators have emphasised a mismatch between price and tax reforms as the price cause of fiscal imbalance and inflation (Naughton 1991); others have emphasised the inelasticity of fiscal revenues between state enterprises to price and income increases under the rules of the enterprise contract system (Blejer and Szapary 1990); and still others have focused on the decentralisation of financial decisions to localities and enterprises, and the banking reform which increased local pressures on allocations through the banking system (Blejer and Szapary 1990; Kojima 1991).

After much peering into the kaleidoscope of structural change and fiscal outcomes through the 1980s, we can find no single dominant cause of fiscal difficulties in the reform period. The factors mentioned by Naughton, Blejer and Szapary and Kojima have all had their hour upon the stage, and have all continued in supporting roles. The general pattern has been for new fiscal holes to emerge as others are filled.

Each source of rising budget deficits as a proportion of total output through the 1980s was constrained by controls or reform within a few

Figure 3   **Budget deficit and broad money growth** (per cent)

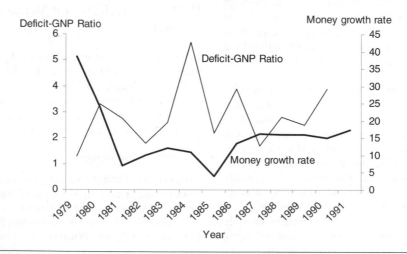

Sources: Khor 1991; Ma 1992.

years, so that it did not become a source of runaway excess demand and inflation. The 'investment hunger' of decentralised enterprises in the early years of reform was limited by considerable hardening of conventional budgets. (As we will see, this shifted rather than solved the problem, as enterprises looked more to state banks to finance investments).

The tax rigidity embodied in the tax/profit contractual agreements between the state and various enterprises had a negative impact on government revenue for a number of years after the start of the urban price reforms in 1984. However, the large increase in the role of sales tax (indirect tax) through the 1980s made the erosion of revenues derived from enterprise profits less crucial to budget outcomes.[8] Revenue from sales tax, like enterprise profit shares and tax, were concentrated disproportionately in the manufacturing sector. Sales tax revenues thus increased with the disproportionate expansion of industrial production as the profit-based tax revenues from the manufacturing sector were eroded by squeezes on profits associated with price adjustments, competition and lax financial discipline.

Decentralisation of fiscal authority to local governments did not in itself contribute to larger budget deficits. It might have weakened the central government's use of the budget as an effective macroeconomic management tool (Blejer and Szapary 1990). And it did create greater incentives for local governments to exert pressure on a more decentralised banking system.

Thus processes of fiscal control and reform have been awkward and arbitrary, contributing to instability in the macro-economy. In the end, however, they have been effective in blocking inexorable fiscal expansion. The direct monetary financing of the official fiscal deficits was not significant for most of the years prior to 1986, but became more important to reserve money growth afterwards (Blejer and Szapary 1990). However, Figure 3 suggests that monetising the formal budget deficit was not the decisive factor

in the expansion of broad money even in the later years. What then has been driving the observed unstable and high monetary growth?

'The smoking gun'

The answer lies in the substantial underestimation of the core public sector financial deficits and the blurred distinction between monetary and fiscal spheres, which gives rise to disguised monetisation of public sector deficits not captured by the formal budgetary process (Ma 1993).

There are four sets of evidence supporting this hypothesis: mounting government arrears, disguised financial losses of state enterprises, pressures on state banks to finance parafiscal operations and a huge overhand of non-performing loans of the state banks.

Government arrears have been rising rapidly since the late 1980s. These involved pre-committed fiscal obligations, mostly in the trade, farm procurement, coal and petroleum sectors. In 1989, government arrears related to the farm procurement and trade sectors were 20 billion yuan. Total government arrears reached 50 billion yuan at the end of 1990, and exceeded 70 billion yuan in 1991 (Ma 1992). In most cases, these government arrears were covered by additional credits by state banks to state enterprises. They were not listed as bank lending to the fiscal authorities. These arrears are one disguised form of budgetary shortfalls financed by bank credits.

Second, there is convincing evidence that the financing of the state enterprise sector has been substantially larger than the official fiscal subventions for this purpose. In 1986 and 1987, the total reported financial loss of state enterprises was 4.17 and 48.1 billion yuan respectively, but the fiscal subsidy for enterprise loss was only 32.4 and 37.6 billion yuan (MOF 1989:19, 146).

The third factor contributing to the under-estimation of budget deficits relates to traditional fiscal obligations being dumped onto the state banking sector. The weak independence of the state banks makes this possible. The share of budget grants in the financing of gross fixed investment declined from 28 per cent in 1981 to less than 10 per cent from mid 1980s. The fixed investment financed by bank credit rose from 14 per cent in the early 1980s to 20 per cent in the late 1980s. Not surprisingly, of the total loan financing of fixed investments, the state sector accounted for almost 80 per cent during the 1980s (SSB 1991).

By 1983, all the working capital of established state enterprises was managed and provided by the state banking sector. Even the liquidity of newly established state enterprises funded by the budget had to be financed by the banks due to fiscal difficulties. As a result, the annual budget provision of working capital fell from five billion yuan in 1979 to around one billion yuan from 1986. By contrast, bank loan financing of enterprise liquidity soared. The annual change in the working capital loan balances increased from 17 billion yuan in 1979 to 78 billion yuan in 1985, and reached 217 billion in 1990.

The problems of requiring the state banks to conduct informal fiscal operations were most pronounced during the anti-inflation episode of 1988 and 1989. When industrial production and capacity utilisation slid, unit costs of output in the state enterprises rose sharply. When falling profits threatened to increase fiscal deficits by denying state enterprises the means of meeting tax commitments to the state in 1989 and 1990, loans were made available for the purpose of paying tax (Editing Committee 1989:206). Beyond business functions, state enterprises in China have welfare (social security) functions, which in an advanced industrial society are the responsibility of the state budget. In 1989 and 1990 banks were ordered to extend loans to these enterprises so that wages could be paid.[9] Using bank loans to pay tax and wages were only two of the many examples of a budget problem being translated into a monetary problem.

'Triangle debts', or inter-enterprise arrears, presented another form of disguised monetisation of the public debt, the untangling of which required a massive injection of bank credit. In 1990, for example, outstanding inter-enterprise debt rose from 150 billion to 200 billion yuan. Since inter-enterprise debts ultimately become losses for China's state-owned banks, the central bank ends up financing these debts through increased lending to the banks. To the extent that the state enterprises are the main source of fiscal revenues, they effectively become the principal intermediary between the state budget and the banking sector (Lardy 1992).

Finally, officially classified and other disguised bad debts of the state banks were estimated to account for about 9 per cent of the total bank loan balances (about 110 billion yuan) by the end of 1991 (Ma 1993). The writing off of these non-performing loans would wipe out the entire equity capital of all the state banks in China. To say the least, a massive recapitalisation of the state banks would be required. These bad loans have been accumulating as normal bank assets since 1981 without being written off. At the same time, the interest accrued on these bad loans continues to be taken as profit in the state bank books.

If we assume that most of the government arrears and bad debts occurred in the late 1980s and early 1990s, then combining government arrears and bad debts of the state banks gives a figure large enough to rival the accumulated adjusted formal budget deficits between 1985 and 1991. This would put China's budget deficit in the range of 4–5 per cent of GNP in recent years. When the bank-financing of enterprise arrears and other undisclosed financial shortfalls of the state enterprises are taken into account, the public sector deficits would reach 5–6 per cent of GNP in the early 1990s (Ma 1992).

Thus, the formal budget deficit is defined too narrowly to reflect the fiscal stress in China. Translating budgetary deficits into monetary expansion without going through the formal budgetary process distorts the relationship between public deficits and monetary growth. A considerable proportion of public debts has been monetised before it shows up in the state official budget. Nevertheless, the budget constraint for the public sector remains important. The links from money, to output, to fiscal revenue, explain the strong pro-cyclical pattern of the high and unstable monetary growth during the 1980s. Public sector deficits, broadly defined, have been the major cause of monetary instability.

Stabilisation policy

The partially reformed economic system of the 1980s generates two types of special problems for macroeconomic management. The first relates to the interactions between fiscal and monetary policies partially through the linkages of credit expansion, industrial growth and fiscal revenues. The second arises because the economy under the plan requires one set of instruments, mainly administrative controls, and the part outside the plan requires another set. There are potential conflicts over short and long term objectives of stabilisation that will have important implications for coordination of monetary and fiscal policies.

Quantitative targets on credit set under the national credit plan still operate, but have at times been little more than indicative guidelines to local bank branches. When the Government has made a determined effort to reduce the temperature of the economy, credit ceilings have been strictly enforced. But when credit ceilings were enforced between late 1988 and early 1989, a huge volume of credit was made available to state-owned enterprises which failed to pay their debts to other enterprises or to meet their debt-servicing obligations with the banking system. An immediate abatement of monetary growth was thus achieved at the cost of greater potential inflationary pressures in the future. Moreover, quantitative restrictions often bias the allocation of resources in favour of the less efficient state enterprises and against the non-state sector.[10]

Market instruments have become much more sophisticated and have been used more effectively with progress in the reforms. The greater willingness to use a range of market instruments attests to the growing confidence of the authorities that indirect measures work in the increasingly important market-regulated parts of the Chinese economy.[11] The Chinese authorities have been learning rapidly the modalities of macroeconomic management in a partially reformed economy. The experience of the late 1980s inflation is likely to lead to earlier corrective action in future inflationary episodes. And market-based instruments of monetary policy will play a greater role as the market share in the economy becomes bigger. The recent greater emphasis on market-oriented financial reforms seems to reflect such a trend.

However, there is uncertainty as to the precise effects of applying market-based instruments to the plan/state sector (Gordon and Li 1991; Naughton 1990; Bowles and White 1989). Greater sophistication of monetary policy, although very useful in managing the emerging inflation, is not a solution for the underlying problem of monetary instability—the public sector imbalance.[12] In fact, the accommodating stance towards state enterprises has been a major obstacle to steady macroeconomic management, whether by market-based or direct instruments. For as long as the government remains strongly committed to sustaining state enterprises, there is an inevitable overflow from fiscal restriction into monetary expansion through one mechanism or another.

The partial economic reform of the 1980s generated great growth momentum, but failed to address the fundamental problem of broad public sector deficits.

The greatest need is to bring state-operated enterprises within the purview of effective, indirect monetary policy. The issue of enforcing market discipline on the public enterprises cannot be avoided. The recent moves to 'push the enterprises into market', bankrupt a few state enterprises in each province, and expand the equity stock system testify to the realisation by the Government of the core problems.

We should note that it is possible for China to experience some non-inflationary monetary expansion, because of the monetisation of the overall economy as a result of the expanding role of market forces and rapid growth. These considerations allow some exploitation of seignorage without risking inflation. There seems to have been significant monetisation in the 1980s. But tapping this source of financing excessively is part of the explanation of the worsening inflation from 1984 to 1989 (Ma 1992, 1993). It is possible that rising inflation itself discouraged monetisation, and that a return to low inflationary expectations would expand the scope for non-inflationary money growth. Higher real interest rates, deriving from increased nominal rates or lower inflationary expectations, would reinforce these effects.

III. Instability and the Open Policy

As the share of exports and imports in GNP and the share of foreign borrowing in the financing of public debt and fixed investment have increased, there has been more potential for interaction between the external sector and domestic macroeconomic performance (Table 3).

A number of arguments have been advanced to the effect that greater openness of China's economy has contributed to greater instability and inflationary pressures in the 1980s. One argument is that as the importance of trade in China's economy increased, international price fluctuations and inappropriate policy responses induced domestic price instability. Export of primary commodities is considered to have worsened the domestic shortage of raw materials and dampened manufacturing profits. Several major yuan devaluations in the 1980s are thought by some observers to have pushed up the overall domestic price level through higher prices for imported merchandise. Finally, the decentralised trading system and the export-oriented development strategy are said to have caused 'excess export' of Chinese goods and services.

None of these arguments stands up to close scrutiny. The declining relative importance of primary goods in both China's exports and imports (Table 4) indicates that any impact of trade on domestic material shortages diminished

during the reform process. Net imports of commodities rose in the inflationary episode of the late 1980s.[13] Even the direct price effects were not all in one direction: unfavourable price movements for some traded goods were balanced by favourable changes in others (for instance, wool prices, and wheat prices reduced by subsidised sales from the United States). However, the terms of trade worsened in the 1980s due to a decline in the international oil price which might have presented difficulties for macroeconomic management.

'Excessive export' could not have generated inflation, because for most of the 1980s China experienced a trade deficit, especially in expansionary episodes from 1984. Although export subsidies could add to fiscal difficulties, they are related to the over-valued exchange rate and their recent abolition means that they will not present major problems in the future. The wide variations in the trade balance moving against changes in total output, must have helped to reduce overall output fluctuations.[14]

The finding by Khor (1991) that broad money leads imports is additional evidence that trade plays a stabilising role in relation to excess aggregate demand.

It is not certain even that the direct price effect of yuan devaluation is inflationary, in the presence of black and swap markets for foreign exchange (Martin 1991).

There is no conclusive evidence that greater openness of China's economy had a net adverse effect on China's domestic stability in the 1980s. Indeed, the variations in net exports have been significantly stabilising over the past decade. Liberalisation of the trade regime could increase this effect in the future, contributing to the loosening of supply bottlenecks and to the improvement of productive efficiency.

IV. Implications and Conclusions

Our examination of the data has confirmed that there was no stable trade-off between growth and instability, and that there was a less favourable

Table 3   **Importance of external factors** (per cent)

Year	Ratio of imports plus exports to GNP	Share of external borrowing in budget deficit financing	Net exports as a percentage of GNP
1980	12.8	14.2	-0.6
1981	15.4	42.1	0.0
1982	14.9	-7.5	1.1
1983	14.8	6.0	0.3
1984	17.3	16.0	-0.6
1985	24.2	5.2	-5.2
1986	26.6	27.3	-4.3
1987	27.3	26.6	-1.3
1988	27.3	37.3	-2.1
1989	26.1	35.6	-1.6
1990	32.0	37.8	2.4

Note: External borrowing refers to borrowing net of retiring debt outstanding.
Sources: SSB 1990 and 1991; SSB 1990b.

trade-off between growth and price stability between 1984 and 1989 than in earlier years. This tendency towards deterioration in the relationship between growth and inflation was broken at the end of the decade by a series of measures that included financial reforms as well as retreat into heavier command controls.

The three major macroeconomic cycles identified in the reform period were closely related to instability of broad money growth.

Progress in reform has made the economy more vulnerable to inflationary pressure from excessive growth in money and domestic demand. Over time, more prices are determined

Table 4   **Changing structure of trade** (per cent)

Year	Exchange rate (US$=100)	Share of primary goods in imports	Share of primary goods in exports	Oil revenue in exports
1980	149.84	34.8	50.2	22.0
1981	170.50	36.5	46.6	22.1
1982	189.25	39.6	45.0	22.0
1983	197.57	27.2	43.3	19.5
1984	232.70	19.0	45.7	21.8
1985	293.67	12.5	50.6	24.8
1986	345.28	13.2	36.4	10.4
1987	372.21	16.0	33.5	10.2
1988	372.21	18.2	30.3	7.1
1989	376.59	19.9	28.7	6.7
1990	478.37	18.5	25.6	6.9

Sources: SSB 1991, 1990b.

in markets. The community is now much more sensitive to decline in the value of money as a store of value.

The experience of the reform period, however, is not of inexorable movement into greater instability. The decline in the relative contributions of state enterprises in national output has constrained these enterprises' claims on monetary expansion. The dynamism of the non-state sector, with its harder budget constraints and therefore greater amenability to monetary policy, has offset to some extent the inflationary contributions of state enterprises. The tendency for real revenues from the profits of state enterprises to fall with inflation has been offset by the increasing relative importance of the indirect tax on industrial enterprises. Fiscal decentralisation has led to more effective collection of revenue from various sources, and has not been a general source of exacerbation of national budgetary problems. And the price adjustments for major foodstuffs and raw materials through 1991 and 1992 have alleviated the pressure of price subsidies on fiscal expenditures.

The increasing integration into the international economy, and the associated, large fluctuations in net exports through the macroeconomic cycle, have been an important stabilizing influence against short-term fluctuations in aggregate demand. Large current account deficits must eventually be corrected, but access to the international economy reduces the danger that excessive demand expansion will explode into high inflation before corrective action has been taken by the monetary authorities.

A variety of reform measures introduced during and after the late 1980s inflationary crises will assist stabilisation in the future. More importantly, the authorities were shocked in 1988 and 1989 by the political reaction to high inflation, and this will encourage timely use of anti-inflationary policies. Overall, the economy is increasingly vulnerable to inflationary responses to excess demand, but the authorities have at hand a wider range of instruments to manage them.

Our analysis highlights the contribution that the monetising of the public sector deficits through formal and informal channels makes to monetary growth. State enterprise deficits persisted and remained large relative to the economic size of state enterprises through the 1980s. Tighter control over budgetary subventions was followed by greater use of bank credit, and when that was regulated more effectively, by inter-firm lending. A large underlying public debt has mean that deficits, however financed, are eventually monetised. The seemingly weak relationship between the state budget deficit and monetary expansion is attributed to the blurred distinction between monetary and fiscal policies. Informal or disguised monetisation may in fact have financed a significant portion of the public debt.

Thus, the greatest risk is still that public deficits, out of control and widening, will be monetised, in the absence of effective financial discipline. While state enterprises' share of total economic activity continues to decline, their effective claim on national financial resources has not declined commensurately. The financing requirements of state enterprises is a continuing threat to economic stability. The maintenance of macroeconomic stability in the process of reform and rapid economic growth through the 1990s, requires strong and effective action by the Government, to reduce decisively broad public sector deficits, extending beyond the formal state budget.

Acknowledgements

We have gained much from discussions with and suggestions by Geoff Raby and from George Fane and Gavin Peebles.

Notes

1. By 'instability' we mean substantial fluctuations in the rate of growth of output and in the imbalance of payments on current accounts, and marked changes in the price level.
2. Inflation will be measured as the rate of change in the general retail price index in this paper unless stated otherwise. See Ma (1992) for a detailed discussion of various measurements of inflation in China.
3. In 1979, state farm prices were raised by 22 per cent. Nominal wage rates were increased by nine per cent in 1979 and 14 per cent in 1980. State fixed investment jumped 22 per cent in 1978 (SSB 1991).
4. Household savings deposits increased at an average rate of 31 per cent between 1981 and 1983 (SSB 1991). The important role of the agricultural sector is consistent with the earlier comments, on its contribution to growth during 1982–83 (See Lin 1992).
5. Monetary growth fell to 15 per cent in early 1987. This time, however, both industrial growth and state investment resisted the monetary acceleration.
6. By the third quarter of 1990 broad money growth reached 30 per cent over the same quarter of the previous year (Khor 1991). GNP grew at five per cent in 1990 and seven per cent in 1991. Inflation was two per cent and three per cent (SSB 1992).
7. For 1984–1987 average, budget deficit as a ratio to GNP was 4.6 per cent for the USA and 8.8 per cent for India (*International Finance Statistic Yearbook 1991*). In the former Soviet Union, it was 12 per cent during 1988–1991 (Ma 1992).
8. The share of profit tax and remittance from state enterprise fell from 60 per cent of budget revenues in 1978 to 45.5 per cent in 1983 and 33.2 per cent in 1988. The share of sales tax rose from 32 per cent in 1978 to 45 per cent in 1988 (World Bank 1990b).
9. Editing Committee 1990:206. These loans are labeled 'Stability and Solidarity Loan'. Still nominal wage rates in the state sector rose at an annual rate of 11 per cent in 1989 and 1990 (SSB 1991:130).
10. The Central Bank injected a massive 24.4 billion yuan credit specifically to the large state enterprises in March, August, September and November of 1989 when the overall financial stance was still contractionary. By the end of the year, bank credit to the urban private sector was cut by more than 20 per cent. Forty thousand key state enterprises alone received 60 per cent of the increase in lending extended by the Bank of Industry and Commerce in 1989 (Editing Committee 1990:53, 204 and 211).
11. Examples include greater flexibility of interest rates and the rediscounting of statutory reserve deposits with the central bank in braking the inflation in 1988 and 1989. To stimulate activity, the Government cut the interest rate in 1990 and again in 1991.
12. At a time of more skillful use of market-based policy tools, the financial loss of the state independent accounting industrial enterprises soared from 8 billion yuan in 1988 to 18 billion in 1989 and to 35 billion in 1990, when credit rationing was favouring these enterprises (SSB 1991:410). Enterprise financial losses appear to have worsened in 1991.
13. Khor (1991) finds that imports are contemporaneously correlated with industrial activities, and that money leads imports.
14. The deep integration of parts of the coastal economy into the international economy may have caused output variations in some regions to correlate with movements in the international economy.

References

Bowles, P. and White, G., 1989. 'Contributions in China's Financial Reforms: The Relationship between Banks and Enterprises', *Cambridge Journal of Economics*, 13:481–495.

Blejer, M. and Szapary, G., 1990. 'The Evolving Role of Tax Policy in China', *Journal of Comparative Economics*, 14:452–472.

Editing Committee, 1986–1990. *Almanac of China's Finance and Banking*, China Finance Press, Beijing.

Feng, J., and Huo, X., 1991. *System, Money and Inflation (Tizhi Huobi vu Tonghuopengzhang)*, China Price Press, Beijing.

Gao, S. (ed.), 1990. *Almanac of China's Economic System Reform–1989 (Zhongguo Jinji Gaige Nianjian)*, The Reform Process, Beijing.

Garnaut, Ross, 1990. 'Recent Developments in the Chinese Economy', *The Australian National University Trade and Development Seminar*, Canberra, August.

——, 1992. 'China's Reform and Internationalisation' in Ross Garnaut and Liu Guoguang (eds), *Economic Reform and Internationalisation: China in the Pacific Region*, Allen and Unwin, Sydney.

Gordon, R. and Li, W., 1991. 'Chinese Economic Reforms, 1979–89: Lessons for the Future', *American Economic Review*, 81(2):202–206.

Hsiao, K.H., 1971. *Money and Monetary Policy in Communist China*, Columbia University Press, New York.

Johnson, O., 1985. 'Growth and Inflation in Developing Countries', *IMF Staff Paper*, December.

Khor, 1991. 'China: Macroeconomic Cycles in the 1980s', *IMF Working Paper*, WP/91/85.

Kojima, R., 1991. 'Achievements and Contradictions in China's Economic Reform: 1979–1988', *Developing Economies*, 28(4):365–389.

Lardy, N., 1992. *Foreign Trade and Economic Reform in China, 1978–1990*, Cambridge University Press, Cambridge.

Lin, Justin Yifu, 1992. 'Rural Reform and Agricultural Growth in China', *American Economic Review*, 82(1):34–51.

Ma, Guonan, 1992. 'Budget Deficits and Fiscal Policy Targets in China', Working Paper, Center for Chinese Political Economy, Macquarie University, Sydney.

——, 1993. 'Macroeconomic Disequilibrium, Structural Changes, and the Household

Savings and Money Demand in China', *Journal of Development Economics*, 41(1), June:115–36.

Martin, W., 1991. 'Reform of the Exchange Rate System', Paper presented at conference on China's Reform and Economic Growth, The Australian National University, Canberra, November.

MOF (Ministry of Finance), 1989. *China Finance Statistics: 1950–1988 (Zhongguo Caizheng Tongji)*, China Financial and Economic Publishing House, Beijing.

Naughton, B., 1990. 'Macroeconomic Adjustment and System Reforms', Mimeo.

——, 1991. 'Why has Economic Reform Led to Inflation?', *American Economic Review*, 81(2):207–211.

Ofer, G., 1990. 'Macroeconomic Issues of Soviet Reforms' in Blanchard and Fisher, eds, *NBER Macroeconomic Annual—1990*, MIT Press, Cambridge, Massachusetts.

Raby, G., 1991. 'The Neither This nor That Economy', paper presented at the conference on China's Reform and Economic Growth, The Australian National University Canberra, November.

SSB (State Statistical Bureau), 1987a. *Statistics of Fixed Investment in China 1950–1985 (Zhongguo Gudingzican Touzi Tongjiziliao)*, China Statistical Publishing House, Beijing.

——, 1981–1992. *China Statistical Yearbook (Zhongguo Tongji Nianjian)*, China Statistical Publishing House, Beijing.

——, 1990b, *Statistics of Domestic and External Commerce in China: 1952–1988 (Zhongguo Shangye Waijing Tongjiziliao)*, China Statistical Publishing House, Beijing.

World Bank, 1990a. *Macroeconomic Stability and Industrial Growth under Decentralised Socialism*, The World Bank, Washington, DC.

——, 1990b. *Revenue Mobilisation and Tax Policy*, The World Bank, Washington, DC.

8 China's Macroeconomic Performance and Management during Transition

Shahid Yusuf

Alone among the former socialist economies, China has led a charmed life. It was not by any means the first to experiment seriously with market institutions—that distinction belongs to Hungary. Nor did it attempt to 'cross the chasm in a single leap'. Nor has China's assimilation of market forms been buffered by a major infusion of resources, as in East Germany. Starting with the agriculture sector (Ash 1993), the country has transformed itself, a step at a time, always ensuring that each economic initiative passed the test of sociopolitical acceptability before it was widely implemented. Instead of a risky Big Bang, China's reform can be most aptly described as a series of small controlled explosions, which maintained the momentum of change while minimising the risk of instability.

On balance, the strategy has paid handsomely. Since 1978, China's macroeconomic performance has rivalled that of Japan, Korea, and Taiwan. When economies are compared using purchasing power parity exchange rates, China is already the third largest economy after the US and Japan (IMF 1993), and if it remains on the current trajectory, there is every likelihood of it moving into first place within the next three decades.

I. Macroeconomic Performance, 1978–93

The process of reforms, first in agriculture and then extending to industry, has been mainly responsible for 9 per cent per annum growth in China's GDP since 1979, as shown in Figure 1. Agriculture boomed first, increasing at an annual average rate of 8 per cent from 1979 to 1984. However, agricultural expansion was slackening by 1984, and as reform efforts widened to embrace manufacturing, the industrial sector moved decisively into the forefront. It has remained the leading sector since then. During this period industry has grown by 12.4 per cent per annum and accounted for 66 per cent of the increase in national product.

Three aspects of China's performance are especially noteworthy. First, although the pace of expansion was unusually rapid, inflationary pressure was largely absent in the earlier years, only becoming noticeable in the second half of the 1980s. But even making allowance for pervasive price controls, which can lead to underestimation of inflation, all indicators— retail, cost of living, and 'market'[1]—show that inflation was in the low single-digit range prior

Reprinted with permission. Extracted (with minor editing) from Shahid Yusuf, 1994. 'China's macroeconomic performance and management during transition', *Journal of Economic Perspectives*, 8(2), Spring:71–92.

Figure 1   GDP, industry, and agriculture growth, 1979–92

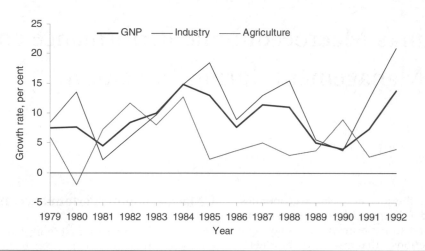

Source: *China Statistical Yearbook*, 1992.

to 1985. Since then, it has approached double-digit levels on the average, though the amplitude of fluctuations have been extremely large, as shown in Figure 2.[2]

Second, China's strong export performance and comfortable exchange reserves have smoothed the road to modernisation. China's success at exporting, combined with the extensive regulation of imports, has led to current account surpluses in all but four years between 1978–92. Except during 1989–91, when access to the foreign capital market was curtailed by the post-Tiananmen political fallout, it is difficult to make the case that development has been hampered by shortages of foreign exchange. In fact, current account surpluses averaging 2.9 per cent of GNP in 1990–92 meant that China's debt/GDP ratio at the end of 1992 was a modest 16 per cent. It had accumulated close to $52 billion in reserves—equivalent to 8 months imports—out of a desire to limit vulnerability to external shocks.

Third, a cycle of economic and political reform has become apparent. The scenario, which has been repeated four times since 1978, commences with a series of reform experiments. As their scope is slowly broadened, investment and growth accelerate and are accommodated by credit policy. Soon the economy is expanding at double-digit rates. Once the fear of overheating is widely acknowledged, the government is empowered to contain reform initiatives and to curb growth by deflating demand. After a year's cooling off, the call for a resumption of reforms and faster growth becomes irresistible, as its benefits have been recognised by a wide constituency. Thus, early successes of reforms have generated a self-perpetuating dynamic.[3]

The first round of liberalisation in 1978–80 led to a tightening of policy and reduced growth in 1981. When the tempo of reform resumed in 1982, it took only a couple of years before the economy was once again showing signs of strain, with a large current account deficit in 1985 compounding the government's concerns. A dose of deflation in 1986 moderated some of the pressures. However, as enterprise and later price reforms gathered momentum in 1987–88, macro stability was once again at stake in 1988 with sharply rising rates of inflation during mid-year. The subsequent deflation, prolonged by the political aftermath of the events at Tiananmen, extended into the second half of 1991. The fourth and most recent cycle of enterprise, price, financial, and trade reforms began in 1991. Together with a relatively permissive monetary environment, they led to a near doubling of GNP growth from 7.2 per cent in 1991 to 12.8 per cent in 1992 and 13.5 per cent in the first three quarters of 1993. Inflation has also rebounded, the urban cost of living index rising from 11 per cent in the second half of 1992 to 20 per cent during 1993 and China may have entered the high growth phase of a new cycle.

The term 'stop-go' has frequently been used to describe China's reform-driven cycles, but downturns have been both short and mild (Hussain and Stern 1991). In no case has deflation pushed growth much below 4 per cent, and when released, the economy has rebounded vigorously, with growth rising by a factor of two or three from trough to peak. This draws attention to the power of growth-inducing forces and to the tremendous elasticity of supply response in this manufacturing-oriented and exceedingly investment-intensive economy.

In sum, the macro scorecard for China is remarkably strong on an absolute as well as on a relative scale. Its growth rate over 15 years is among the highest on record. Growth has been fairly stable, it has been achieved without sacrificing external equilibrium, and inflation has been held in check. No more than a tiny handful of economies can claim as much. Interestingly,

Figure 2   Growth rates of retail prices, cost of living, and market prices[a]

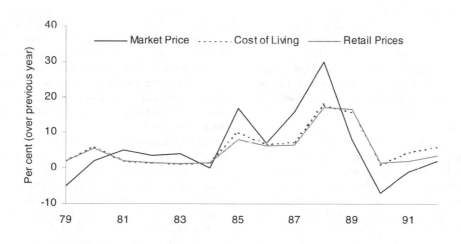

[a] 'market prices' are free-market prices of consumer goods
Source: *China Statistical Yearbook*, 1992.

this pattern of growth and inflation is broadly comparable to Japanese experience during the 1960–74 period and somewhat superior to that of South Korea from 1965 to 1978 (Ito 1992). The comparison is particularly striking when account is taken of the relatively benign policy environment confronting Japan and Korea, neither of which had to juggle simultaneously with systemic reform and macromanagement of a complex, weakly integrated, multiprovincial economy.

II. Growth Stimuli and Sources

Economists are still some years from a sophisticated understanding of the factors responsible for China's recent growth, not the least because the economic data base uses a hybrid combination of accounting conventions.[4] However, pieces of the puzzle are beginning to fall into place.

Decentralisation

The key factor to understanding the process of economic reform, although it may at first sound like an unlikely candidate, is a far-reaching philosophy of decentralisation. Decentralisation has a long history in China; traditionally, the nation was governed by an exceedingly small central bureaucracy which depended on gentry managed, local administrative networks to exercise control.[5] In the mid 1960s, the common rationale for decentralisation was regional self-sufficiency in the event of war and, more prosaically, because centrally administering such a sprawling country posed insurmountable difficulties. This transfer of power from the centre to provincial, municipal, and county governments became more marked after the late 1970s. Once reform had been formally initiated by the Third Plenum of the 11th Party Congress in late 1978, the capabilities of lower level governments were critical for success, chief among them being their close and intimate knowledge of the local economy, their command over the machinery of

political mobilisation, and the organisational resources to implement policies. In general, reform was to be based on local experimentation, and orchestrated by local political machines, which minimised political risks for the central government and the danger of poorly conceived actions being widely applied.[6]

Decentralisation has occurred at three levels. Administrative decentralisation has allowed provincial and local authorities substantial latitude in routine decision-making and the conduct of day-to-day government business. These powers have been progressively enhanced. Local governments have taken on the burden of translating broad reform proposals into a workable reality by modifying existing rules or defining new, market conforming institutions.

Second, fiscal decentralisation, introduced by degrees after 1981 partly in response to demands from lower levels of government, enables provinces to retain and allocate more of the tax revenues collected instead of passing them on to the centre.[7] Local governments can levy surcharges, fees and various duties as well. In addition, they control the budgets of provincially-owned state enterprises and can call upon collective as well as private enterprises for off-budgetary funds. By giving lower level governments a bigger stake in the prosperity of the local economy, fiscal decentralisation has been crucial in cementing their support for increasingly more difficult reforms and for promoting development employing heterodox measures that are expanding the ambit of market forces (Shirk 1993).

Third, industrial policy and supporting investment in infrastructure has been decentralised. In the early 1980s, rural industrialisation (a locally managed affair) entered high gear and enterprise reform began significantly dispersing central control over industrial decision-making to provincial bureaux. This reform did not immediately create a multitude of autonomous firms operating in a price-guided milieu; instead, it allowed power to percolate down to thousands of industrial bureaux, who then joined forces with entrepreneurially minded enterprise managers. Local investment in transport and urban infrastructure financed through augmented revenues has buttressed industrial activity, along with generating demand which attracts additional investment (Yusuf 1993a). For instance, nine-tenths of the intra-provincial road network has been financed locally.

Local entrepreneurship is closely associated with the shift in attitudes towards property rights. Private ownership was formally recognised in 1978, though the so-called 'individually-owned' sector only began achieving some significance in the second half of the 1980s.[8] Of much greater significance has been the informal acknowledgement by local governments of individual ownership of collectives, which constitute the majority of rural enterprises. On paper these have remained the property of the community. But in an increasing number of instances, 'collectives' have either been established by individuals with their own capital or leased to local entrepreneurs. Their ownership claims are tacitly recognised, although in the formal sense rights are fuzzy (Yusuf 1993b; Freeman 1993; Pomfret 1992). In a period of transition, such implicit and uncodified property rights have several advantages: communities can continue to observe ideological norms while implicitly accepting institutions critical for market functioning and resource accumulation; by holding aloft the collective banner, enterprises have gained readier access to credit and other official favours (Young 1991); and fuzzy rights allow a sharing of risks between individual and community in a time of considerable uncertainty. Should market circumstances or political signals change abruptly, the community shoulders some of the responsibility of seeing the enterprise through difficult times. However, when the enterprise earns profits, community officials can claim some of these. Although fuzzy property rights expose enterprises to 'fiscal predation' and might lead to short-sightedness in investment decisions, these have, so far, been outweighed by ownership incentives and risk-sharing.

Decentralisation accelerated the demise of central planning and thus indirectly pushed the economy toward the market. Under some circumstances, giving local officials this power to interfere could easily have resulted in a disastrous upsurge of rent-seeking activity. But in China's case, although anecdotes of bureaucratic corruption and high-handedness abound, the overall results have been positive. Entrepreneurially minded local officials have been most active in soliciting ideas, conducting experiments, disseminating those that succeed, and balancing economic possibilities against political sensitivities—ensuring all the while that the pace of change remained broadly acceptable.

Explaining the success of this decentralised but firm management of transition is far beyond the scope of this paper. Suffice it to say that at least three factors might have contributed: local government accountability, enforced by the comprehensive framework of political monitoring and the demands of social responsibility within communities that until recently have been stable and tightly knit; the emergence of competition between provinces (and within these counties) which possess broadly similar industrial structures; and the disciplining effects on Chinese provinces of participating in export markets and seeking to become a focus of foreign direct investment.[9]

Investment and factor productivity

Although decentralisation has clearly created a climate for vigorous and effective economic reforms, more conventional economic ingredients like factor supply and total factor productivity have also played their part. Among such factors, capital investment is in the forefront. In common with other socialist economies, China maintained levels of gross investment approaching 30 per cent of GNP through the late 1970s. As reforms progressed, the multiplication of profitable opportunities and the difficulty of checking 'investment hunger'[10] in a milieu where budget constraints remain fairly soft[11] pushed gross investment to 35–37 per cent and fixed investment to over 30 per cent. While no precise estimate is available, it seems clear that China's growth from 1978 onwards has been investment-led, and that increased capital investment has probably been responsible for about 40 per cent of growth. This is higher than in Japan during 1960–70 (32 per cent), but it is in about the same range as South Korea and less than in Singapore.

By improving allocative efficiency, agricultural reforms helped raise efficiency and total factor productivity has accounted for the bulk of the sector's growth. With the spread of reforms, productivity has quickened in industry as well, more so in collective than in state enterprises. In collective enterprises, total factor productivity was rising at an annual rate of 5.3 per cent by the second half of the 1980s, contributing a significant share of industrial growth. Table 1 offers some data on growth rates in agriculture, state-owned industry, and collectively-owned industry.

New technology has been brought to China in a variety of ways. Investment in equipment has helped speed up embodied technical progress and introduced more efficient work practices, as suggested by deLong and Summers (1992). Foreign direct investment, especially in manufacturing, has also served as a transmission belt for technology. China has been able to assimilate new practices faster than many other developing countries because of accumulated industrial learning, from the prolonged and single-minded effort at developing heavy manufacturing, starting in the early 1950s.

While the share of total factor productivity in China's industrial growth is on the increase, it does not yet compare with Japan in the 1960s, for a variety of reasons: a sizable share of new fixed investment is in domestically produced equipment of outdated design; managerial techniques are backward; motivation is poor among workers in state enterprises, because of overstaffing and weak incentive mechanisms; market competition is insufficiently strong in many sectors; infrastructure is often weak and the service activities that support manufacturing are sometimes primitive; vertical integration remains very high in medium and large-scale enterprises and is a source of inefficiency; the industrial workforce, though large and experienced, is short of the skills essential to cope with modern technology; and China's large research establishment still lacks a commercial orientation. These factors slow the pace of technical adaptation and innovation. Production functions estimates for selected industries for iron and steel, coal, textiles and clothing suggest that they are operating well within their production sets, achieving no more than 60 per cent of potential output (Wu 1993b).

Table 1   Sources of growth in China

| | Agriculture | Industry | |
		State	Collective
1978–84			
Sector growth	8.0	8.49	14.03
TFP	5.9	3.45	5.2
1984–88			
Sector growth	4.0	10.22	19.86
TFP	3.0	3.01	5.86

Source: Jefferson, Rawski and Zheng 1992.

The labour market contribution to growth

By a rough accounting, capital and total factor productivity may have contributed close to two-thirds of growth during the 1980s, with the share of total factor productivity beginning to climb significantly since the middle of the decade. The remaining one-third of growth is linked largely to an expansion of labour usage. Increased labour force participation and absorption of the unemployed comes first. In China's case, the natural increase of the labour force averaging 2.8 per cent and the vast army of un- or under-employed workers, whose numbers are believed to exceed 100 million, have strongly supported the rapid expansion of manufacturing and service activities.[12] This can be seen most vividly in the spectacular growth of rural industry where employment rose from 70 million in 1985 to 96 million in 1991 (China Statistical Yearbook 1992; Ody 1992). Abundant reserves of labour and the growing integration of the national labour market has also had a dampening effect on wage demands, which has sustained competitiveness while enabling firms to generate large investable surpluses.

The quality of the Chinese workforce has had an important bearing on productivity. Three-quarters of all Chinese are literate and close to 90 per cent of all new entrants into the labour force have primary education. An increasing proportion now also have secondary schooling together with some vocational skills, although the insufficiency of skilled labour does hamper particular industries. The influence of this human capital on work efficiency is considerable and it is convincingly supported by evidence from cross-country studies that have underscored the role of education in growth.

Along with education, discipline, motivation and 'manageability' of the workforce also matter. These traits have been widely observed to matter in East Asia's development success, and are shared by the Chinese workforce, at least in the rapidly expanding non-state sector. In part this is the consequence of a hierarchical culture, which places great stress on obedience. The absence of strikes or other disruption is also a result of the state's policy toward labour institutions. China's constitution specifically permits unionisation, union membership is widespread, and work actions are legal, but pressure from both the government and the Party strongly discourages strikes. Workers' dependence on their unit (*danwei*) for housing and other benefits, the many intersecting bureaucratic controls over an employee's life, and low mobility of urban, state enterprise employees have kept resistance down to very low levels. Overt labour unrest or violence has been minimal and when it has erupted, the authorities have dealt firmly with it. Instead, employee discontent is communicated to managers and bureau supervisors, through both formal and informal channels, in ways which have provided an effective safety valve.

The state has sought to enhance labour discipline and motivation in other ways as well. The urban workforce enjoys many privileges—job security, housing, medical and other benefits generally provided by the enterprise—which serve to accommodate the principal demands of workers. These benefits and the widely-held belief that the Chinese enterprise is there to maximise the utility of its stakeholders, with employees as the dominant group, increase the identification of workers with enterprise. Thus, the institutional elaboration of the internal labour market in a Chinese enterprise has created an environment in many ways similar to Japan or a few of the other east Asian economies, all of which are known for their disciplined workers and the minimum degree of labour unrest. The way in which China differs from these is with respect to the direct involvement of the state in managing labour.

Domestic savings as a source of capital

It was noted above that investment was the principal determinant of growth, and domestic savings have been the main source of finance for this capital accumulation. Gross national savings rose from an already high average of about 33 per cent of GDP during 1978–84 to 38 per cent in the 1985–92 period, thus matching the level and rise of investment discussed already. In the process, its composition also changed significantly. In 1978, government and enterprise savings dominated the picture, at 15.1 per cent and 17 per cent of GDP, respectively, while household savings were only 1.1 per cent of GDP. Since then, government and household savings have swapped places as fiscal reforms which, among other things, allow enterprises to retain a larger share of their earnings, have steeply reduced government revenues. In 1991, government savings were just 1.8 per cent of GDP, while household savings had climbed to 18.7 per cent. (Meanwhile, enterprise savings were 19.9 per cent in 1991.) With this shift, the pattern of savings in China is coming to resemble other east Asian market economies. The rise in the level of savings, and the shift in its composition, raise critical issues for the future (Ito 1992).

One factor altering savings behaviour has been how long-held patterns interact with the new economic reality. For historical reasons, China's culture is oriented toward production rather than consumption. Because of risk perception or low time preference or dislike of conspicuous consumption, household spending adjusts slowly to changes in income. Likewise, under the influence of decades-old austerity policies, Chinese enterprises are prone to accumulate and acquire assets in preference to current outlay. Hence, the rapid increase of incomes has inevitably led to a piling up of savings.

A second factor at work is the changed perception of ownership. Now that households and enterprises perceive themselves as possessing property rights, the incentive to accumulate has been greatly strengthened. Households feel that they have few wealth assets, in relation to their perceived needs. Many existing enterprises recognise that their plant and equipment is outmoded and in need of replacement. And both household and enterprises have

noticed the profitable opportunities created by reforms, especially for small investors.

Demographic trends are also influencing savings behavior and will continue to do so for some time. Average life expectancy in China has risen some 10 years since 1970. It is currently 70 and the trend is upwards. With retirement age still at 55, the middle-aged in particular have every incentive to increase their saving rates to provide for their later years, in the event that pension benefits are either unavailable or prove insufficient. Moreover, fertility has declined sharply since the early 1970s, and with fewer children, households see the need for larger precautionary savings to finance future contingencies.[13]

The emergence of a market economy in China has altered expectations and the structure of wants. Many households are now aspiring to own property, a range of consumer durables and eventually an automobile. Some of the better off expect to send children overseas for education. With financial markets underdeveloped and likely to remain so for the foreseeable future, the vast majority of households expect to have to save in advance of purchase, as was or is the case in Japan, South Korea, and Taiwan. Because the cohorts now entering the labour force and setting up households are so large, the effect on aggregate saving is pronounced.

These are the main reasons behind China's high (but in east Asian terms by no means unprecedented) level of savings. On the east Asian pattern, China's household savings are in a highly liquid form—mostly bank deposits—because of a paucity of financial instruments and the limited sophistication of individual savers. This liquidity and the growing desire of wealthholders for portfolio diversification affects macroeconomic management, a point discussed in the following section.

The role of foreign capital

Although domestic sources of capital have been the dominant source of finance, some mention must be made of foreign direct investment and the resources supplied by multilateral institutions. Until recently, the two combined were a modest addition to China's annual investment during 1985–90—approximately $6.4 billion per year. However, the contribution of foreign investment has been substantial in other ways.

First, these foreign savings have come jointly with a range of expertise. Multilateral institutions have transferred skills on project evaluation, financial analysis, macromanagement and a wide range of technical issues. Industrialists from Hong Kong, Macau, and Taiwan have infused production skills, knowledge of quality control, and background on the logistics of exporting (Sung 1992). Those from Japan and the United States have introduced China to advanced transport and electronics technology and helped it upgrade key service subsectors such as the hotel industry. These skills, plus China's readiness to assimilate them, have helped push the economy into a higher orbit.

Second, foreign capital has had more concentrated impact on the provinces along the southeastern coast, an area which has been primarily responsible for the surge in China's industrial growth. In particular, Guangdong and Fujian have absorbed the lion's share of foreign direct investment, and derived maximum gains from service industries in Hong Kong as well as 'intangible' technology transfers from Southeast Asian economies (Kueh 1992). These eastern provinces have had annual average growth rates in the 1980s in the 15–20 per cent range. Moreover, foreign direct investment along China's southeast rim has stimulated the development of market institutions, and nudged these provincial economies onto the path of export-led growth.

Starting in 1992, foreign direct investment in China moved on to a higher plane. Commitments rose from $7 billion in 1991 to over $100 billion in 1993 and actual disbursements soared from about $3.5 billion in 1991 to nearly $25.76 billion in 1993. This trend appears likely to persist for several years. The main reasons seem to include currency realignments in east Asia, rising labour costs in Japan, Korea and Taiwan, and environ-mental constraints on industrial expansion. Austerity measures, so long as they are moderate, are unlikely to depress the flow of external capital. Of all the developing southeast Asian countries, China has the largest resource base, technological capability and domestic market.

III. Macroeconomic Management

Despite a record of rapid growth, external balance, and relatively low rates of inflation, China's macroeconomic management has aroused continuing concern. Actual outcomes seem to matter less than the perception, which surfaces with some frequency, that macro trends and institutional changes are pushing the country into economic chaos. The fears voiced both inside China and by the community of China-watchers since the early 1980s focus on four possible problems: soft budget constraints and 'investment hunger'; a shrinking tax base; poor monetary management; and a lack of centralised economic power to conduct routine macroeconomic policy. Each of these fears deserves some examination.

Soft budgets and investment hunger

State-owned and collective enterprises in China have long taken 'soft budget constraints' for granted. Furthermore, since capital is very cheap to enterprises with soft budget constraints, they have a strong proclivity to investment. The economic reforms, which gave enterprises more autonomy and discretionary control over their earnings, strengthened their desire to expand capacity, start new projects, and add to the factory's social infrastructure.[14] The upward shift in investment after 1984, when enterprise reforms were introduced, indicates how quickly the 'produce and build' culture responds to a change in signals. After remaining close to 39 per cent of GNP through 1989, investment rates were reduced in 1990–91, but only when the central government used direct administrative controls to regulate the capital spending of state-owned enterprises and limits on credit availability to restrain rural enterprises. Expenditures rose again once checks were eased in 1992 and remained at record levels through 1993.

Soft budget constraints and the associated investment hunger pose risks for macroeconomic stability, but the scale of the problem is diminishing. Provincial action to promote non-state enterprises has been quite successful. In 1980, state-owned firms produced 75 per cent of industrial output, collectively-owned firms another 24 per cent, and other individual and private firms the rest. By 1992, however, the state sector produced only 48 per cent of industrial output, while the collective sector had risen to 38 per cent, and the individual and other to 13 per cent. Hence a smaller part of China's economy is now governed by soft budget constraints. In addition, with the progressive unfolding of enterprise reform, the softness of the budget constraint itself has lessened. An increasing number of state enterprises, particularly the provincially-owned medium- and small-sized ones, have had their budget constraints tightened. Since 1992, governments have shown a willingness to use the bankruptcy law that was passed in 1986, and, what is more common, to merge or restructure loss-making enterprises. The blank check is becoming a thing of the past. Perhaps the most important development in this regard is that state enterprises are being forced to compete against one another and against rural industry. The effects of altered market circumstances are evident in the decline and convergence of state enterprise profits (Naughton 1992; Rawski 1993b). China's state sector is still a distance from operating according to strictly market rules, but the danger of macro-instability from this quarter is less than it used to be, and declining.

Fiscal trends and policy

China's fiscal situation has been criticised in three areas: the steep fall of the revenue/GNP ratio since 1980 (World Bank 1990; Chen et al. 1992); inability to narrow or erase budgetary deficits; and the partial nature of tax reforms.

China's revenue/GNP ratio fell from 32 per cent in 1980 to 17 per cent in 1991. Prior to the reforms, the bulk of government revenues were derived from taxation of enterprise revenues. The latter were deliberately inflated by structuring relative prices so that those of industrial products were biased upwards, allowing enterprises to earn high profits which the government could harvest for the budget. Since the early 1980s, this revenue base has narrowed. Price reforms have diminished the relative price advantages of industrial products. Rising competition has had a further depressing effect on industrial profits. Enterprise reform has given firms latitude to increase compensation for workers and to retain more of their profits (World Bank 1990). These deliberate reform actions account for virtually all the cut in revenues from profit remittances and enterprise taxes.

Furthermore, since provincial governments know that they must share any tax revenues they collect with the central government, they have instead moved to seeking revenue from extra-budgetary sources,[15] which has further reduced the revenue of the central government. When this effect of fiscal decentralisation is factored in, the downward trend in government revenues appears in a very different light. First, the decline inclusive of fiscal extra-budgetary revenues has been moderate—from 32 per cent of GNP in 1981 to 24 per cent in 1990. Second, the redistribution of revenues from budgetary to extrabudgetary classification reflects a political reality; because of the dynamic generated by reforms, more power resides at lower levels of government and the approach to fiscal policy must be rethought to accommodate this. Third, even for the central government the budget may no longer be the primary tool of macroeconomic management— because of its inflexibility (a common character-istic), and because the central authorities control so many more resources through the financial network. China's use of monetary policy as a primary policy tool will be discussed in a later subsection.

Since 1979, China's budget has continuously shown a deficit; the deficit has averaged about

2.3 per cent of GDP between 1987 and 1992, but the size of national debt with respect to GDP is a fairly modest 5 per cent. This is largely because of an inability to contain expenditures on subsidies and administrative expenditures, as well as the imbalances caused by unplanned outlays for flood relief and on reflationary capital spending (in 1991). About a quarter of the deficit financing has come from the central bank, and the remainder either from external sources or the bond market.

While budgetary deficits are frequently associated with inflationary pressure and external imbalance, this does not appear to have happened in China, for three main reasons. First, the deficit is relatively small, its level has been stable, and it has been financed in largely non-inflationary ways. Second, close to one-fourth of budgetary expenditure (4 per cent of GDP) has been on capital construction, which has either built up productive capacity or eased infrastructure constraints. One can argue that an allowance should be made for such outlay in computing the deficit. Third, as in Japan during the latter part of the 1970s, budget deficits helped mop up a very high level of domestic savings, thus helping the economy to realise its growth potential (Lincoln 1988).

Undoubtedly, the tax system is seriously distorted and coverage of non-state enterprises is insufficient. The current system of tax contracting does not clearly separate tax payments from profit remittances. It needs to be replaced by uniform tax rates on enterprise income, with dividend payments to the government on the basis of the contract. Further, the tax base is fairly narrow and needs to be gradually expanded through extension of the value-added tax and the phasing in of income taxes. These deficiencies make adjusting the level or type of tax very difficult; thus, when the threat of instability becomes serious, the government's only policy tool is to apply administrative controls over expenditures. Administrative restrictions forcefully applied on capital spending were critical to stabilising the economy in 1988–89, and the application of administrative brakes will be one of the major stabilising forces in 1994.

The picture with respect to fiscal policy is decidedly mixed. Through its process of fiscal decentralisation, China's budgetary policy has been tremendously effective at stimulating growth, as revenue retention by enterprises and tax-contracting arrangements favouring provincial governments greatly sharpened incentives to develop. As a tool for short-term macroeconomic management, the significance of budgetary policy has been declining for reasons which are by no means peculiar to China. Command over resources exercised through national budgetary policy has declined, although overall control by different levels of the government through various non-budgetary channels has fallen little; tax reforms aimed at raising revenues are proving hard to negotiate. Budget deficits have turned out to be stubborn. On the more positive side, the ongoing attempts at eliminating subsidies promises to reduce claims on the budget over the medium term. These price adjustments will substantially diminish the number of deficit-ridden state enterprises. The most significant loss-making industries are currently coal mining and petroleum extraction, where low administered prices currently lead to some 40 per cent of the total state enterprise losses for the nation (Rawski 1993b).

China's system of planning continues to provide the government with an array of administrative and political levers to regulate spending. When there is a policy consensus, these levers can yield quick results as revealed by the rapidity of adjustment in 1988–90. In 1988, real GDP was growing at 11 per cent, the cost of living was rising at 20 per cent, investment had reached nearly 40 per cent of GDP and the external current account showed a deficit of $3.8 billion. By the second half of 1989, roughly three quarters after deflationary action using predominantly administrative directives was introduced, the situation was reversed. By 1990, growth was down to 3.8 per cent, cost of living increased just 1.3 per cent, gross domestic investment had fallen by 2.5 per cent of GDP, and the current account showed a $12 billion surplus.

Although various steps can be taken to rationalise tax collection, reduce budget deficits, and so on, China is not particularly hamstrung with fiscal disabilities. The main problem lies in the sheer dispersion of fiscal authority, which is making policy coordination exceedingly difficult to achieve, whether for macroeconomic management, infrastructure development or other reform. This issue of coordinating policy between the centre and the provinces will be examined in a later subsection.

Monetary management

China's approach to monetary management resembles its mode of fiscal operation in its appearance of centralisation, and its reality of substantial de facto decentralisation. The People's Bank of China was formally entrusted with central banking functions in 1984 and it has conducted its monetary and regulatory activities through some 2,400 branches located in provinces, counties and major municipalities. Inevitably, in the face of intense demand for financing and the rising power of provincial governments, the expansion of credit has been

rapid (an annual average of 23.6 per cent in 1987–92) and the control exerted by the central bank has been weak. Figure 3 indicates how monetary series have fluctuated relative to price movements and GDP.

A common characterisation of monetary policy during the past eight years is that each level of government, together with state enterprises, has aggressively pursued their development objectives and directed banks to supply the needed financing. By and large, the People's Bank of China is viewed as putting up minimal resistance even when annual credit targets have been breached. Money supply was tightened sharply in 1985 and in 1988–89, but these were years of policy consensus when administrative action was also being used to contain spending, especially on investment. It is highly unlikely that monetary action alone could have achieved such dramatic results without the political agreement between central and provincial governments and the many-layered application of administrative pressure. (For instance, banks and workers in state enterprises were required to buy government bonds.)

Figure 3   **GDP and money growth rates, inflation rate, 1979–92**

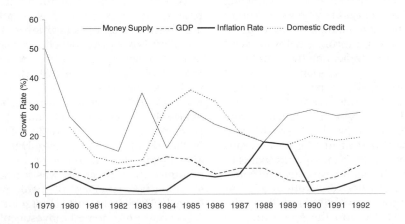

Source: *China Statistical Yearbook*, 1992.

114

Four key factors seem likely to influence the current and future role of monetary policy.

First, as direct subsidies decline, enterprises have become more dependent on financing from banks and financial markets. For instance, state-owned enterprises derive close to half of their funds for fixed capital from banks and an even larger percentage of their working capital. The other side of the coin is that credit allocation is now the major instrument of industrial policy, with approximately two-thirds of all bank loans subject to direction. Thus the role of finance is pivotal.

Second, the very power of credit flows means that their control has become intensely political. As decentralisation has proceeded, the management of credit is determined by political bargaining. All players prefer rapid growth of money, and as yet, the central bank has not been given the political mandate to serve as the autonomous and responsible arbitrator. Only a fear of the political damage which rampant inflation might cause has enabled the central government to impose some restraint on monetary increase.

Third, China is becoming a more monetised economy. In the absence of other financial assets, people have had to hold cash or bank deposits. As a result velocity has drifted downwards, from about 2.5 in 1980 to less than 1 in 1992 (Lau 1992). This downward trend in velocity, which resembles that of Japan in the 1970s and 1980s, implies that if China had heeded the advice to follow a more austere monetary policy, it would have significantly constrained growth and the spread of market activity. The inflationary spikes in 1985 and 1988–89 had little to do with monetary growth; instead, they were tied to sharp changes in expectations following the announcement of reforms. In 1988, for example, anticipations of price adjustment triggered panic buying, which drove up prices. Once the government had retracted earlier statements and expressed a firm commitment to price stability, consumer spending returned to normal.

Fourth, China has promoted a willingness to hold assets in monetary form by adopting a relatively unrepressive interest rate policy (McKinnon 1993). Except for four years when inflation rose rapidly, those holding half- or one-year deposits have earned positive real interest since the start of the economic reforms.[16] This encouraged saving, along with financial deepening. Interest rates were indexed against inflation in 1988.

Looking back over the decade of the 1980s, China's monetary management seems to have been surprisingly effective. Chinese policy-makers responded to a steady decline in velocity by permitting higher rates of credit expansion. They perceived correctly that in an economy in which many prices were set by the state or subject to government guidance, the relationship between money and prices could be manipulated (Peebles 1992). Through much of the period, deposit rates yielded positive returns. And, when a crisis loomed, the People's Bank of China was able to contract credit (using mainly credit ceilings and forced placement of bonds) as a part of a concerted deflationary strategy.

However, in those aspects which are of special relevance for the future, monetary management needs to be reappraised and strengthened. The conduct of a decentralised monetary policy is likely to be particularly problematic in the 1990s for several reasons: (i) continuing rapid growth and the prevalence of strong demand pressure; (ii) a further dismantling of administrative instruments and increased market orientation; (iii) the liquidity of asset holdings and the quick response of asset holders to changes in real return (Hussain and Stern 1991); and (iv) the appearance of new financial instruments which will permit wealthholders to diversify portfolios, but which in conjunction with another round of monetisation (connected with a reform of real estate) will make it difficult to project movements in velocity and calibrate this with the growth of monetary aggregates. These issues will require both institutional reform and the creation of indirect monetary instruments tailored to a market environment. But first, the issues of decentralisation will need to be tackled.

Central-local relations

When igniting reform and achieving an irreversible momentum was a matter of urgency, measures which diluted central control over economic life in China were visibly advantageous. These loosened the bonds of orthodoxy and encouraged experimentation which nudged China marketwards. Now that reform is very much in train, and the economy straining against capacity, the ability to exercise macroeconomic control is taking on a renewed importance. As matters stand, the central government has to build consensus among provincial authorities before deflationary actions can be implemented— fiscal, monetary or administrative.

Persuading the coastal provinces is both crucial and difficult, because they are the ones that must bear the brunt of contractionary policy. Where once the attitude among provincial authorities was unswervingly against inflation, the experience of 1992–93 suggests a certain ambivalence. Faced with the choice of reducing growth by, say, 5 percentage points so as to bring inflation to under 10 per cent, provincial leaders from the coastal provinces are finding the trade-off less attractive. The centre's attempts at forging a consensus have also been undermined by a difference of opinion among senior leaders. This division has encouraged provincial leaders to drag their feet and deflect the government's call to administer deflationary medicine.

With urban cost of living increasing by 20 per cent on an annualised basis, the process of consensus building seemed to reach agreement (with some backtracking) on a deflationary package in late 1993. But the tortuous course of this package has highlighted some operational implications of the decade-long decentralising tendencies and the apparent indispensability of administrative controls on credit and spending.[17]

The administrative leverage exercised by the centre has only limited effect at the provincial level. However, the centre retains considerable power to mobilise support for its views using the Party apparatus, although divisions among the senior leaders can encourage deviance. As a new generation of leaders takes charge, their ability to use the apparatus will depend on their skill at building client networks encompassing the People's Liberation Army and the provincial political machines. If they are unsuccessful in this regard, the centre's authority will be further impaired. Differences in provincial performance are widening economic cleavages between the coastal areas and the interior provinces.[18] If this continues, it will become harder for the various parts of the country to agree on a common set of macro policies and the central government's political mediation will become even more important.

In short, as China has decentralised and assimilated market institutions, the approach to policy formulation has come to resemble that in other large market economies—that is, major macroeconomic policy action must be preceded by consensus building. This may become harder to achieve in the future, but at least over the past seven years China has done better than many countries in this regard. Through intense negotiations, together with a tradition of consensual decision-making, officials have been able to agree on an agenda and then to implement it. Equally important is the absence of powerful interest groups—like labour unions and professional bodies—whose demands interfere with attempts at consensus formation in western countries.

IV. Concluding Remarks

Whether economic achievement is measured by growth rates or stability or macroeconomic management broadly viewed, China's performance appears comparable to that of acknowledged successes like Japan and Korea, if not superior. However, with the demand pressures rising in 1993 and provincial authorities resisting the central government's fiscal and monetary discipline, there is little room for equanimity. If China's high rate of saving is sustained, it can both underwrite growth and, within limits, serve as a cushion against demand shocks. Thus, safeguarding household and public sector savings performance through interest rate, financial and fiscal policies must remain at the heart of the government's strategy.

Decentralisation has reached a point where its advantages with respect to reform are close to being outweighed by the hurdles it puts in the way of policy-making and consensus building. The political rules and their constitutional underpinnings need to be reappraised in the light of changed economic circumstances. Without a new political contract that brings clarity to the rules of centre and provinces, no amount of tinkering with monetary and fiscal instruments will enhance their effectiveness.

Assuming that the central government wins a reaffirmation of its mandate to conduct macroeconomic policy, two kinds of action might yield the greatest long-term results. First, the central bank needs a decent measure of autonomy, which would give it the power to control its branches and the specialised banks. China seems to be edging towards the political agreement which might eventually lead to such autonomy, but these are early days. Second, some rationality needs to be imposed on the budget. In particular, the relevant extra- and off-budgetary items should be brought into the budget, and fiscal responsibilities must be assigned across levels of government in accordance with broadly acceptable rules. Although much work will be required to iron out the details in a way which takes account of international experience and Chinese conditions, such steps are crucial to increasing the centre's managerial capacity. But before that stage is reached, the various parties must settle their political differences. Budgetary policy is an exercise in political economy. Without progress in the political sphere, technical solutions will not work.

China's economic strengths are visible to foreign companies who are rushing to invest in the country, to the international banks who are eager to lend, to China's own citizens who express their confidence in the country's future through their high savings propensities, and to all those who seek to draw lessons from China's experience for other countries. However, it is no easy matter to encapsulate China's many-faceted and highly idiosyncratic experience into neat policy formulae (Chen et al. 1992). For example, it is not useful to tell most of the world's countries to make sure that their geographic neighbours should be as economically dynamic as Hong Kong and Taiwan.

Of the lessons which may have general relevance, five would seem to be most pertinent. First, a widely shared political consensus is critical to success. As Fischer (1993) observed in the Russian context, reform cannot get too far ahead of its political base. Second, the entrepreneurial zeal of local officials, the effectiveness of the local administrative apparatus, and the strength of community cohesiveness have provided a disciplined dynamism.[19] Third, China's high rate of saving has not only helped sustain extraordinary rates of investment, but it has also been the key to stability as well as the ability to absorb shocks. Fourth, a socialist economy in transition must assure the power of administrative tools for macroeconomic management until such time that alternative instruments of sufficient potency are in place. A fifth and related point admits that while the development of market institutions is tremendously important, it takes years to actually happen. And even when such institutions are fully in place, there is no guarantee that an economy such as China's can afford to rely wholly on the market.

Acknowledgements

My thanks to Javed Burki, Peter Murrell, Tom Rawski, and the editors of the JEP for their suggestions. They helped me to strengthen and sharpen the arguments made and improve presentation. Yang Li and Xiaofeng Hua assisted me with the research for this paper and Jean Gray Ponchamni was responsible for seamless production. I am indebted to all three. Shortcomings that remain are, of course, my responsibility.

Notes

1. Initially 'market prices' referred to a small subset of agricultural products and items of daily use sold on 'periodic markets'. The coverage has widened since the mid 1980s to include a wider range of consumer products, but it is still fairly restricted.

2. After peaking at 22 per cent in 1994, the rate of increase of the retail price index fell to 0.8 per cent in 1997. Thereafter, deflationary pressures led to negative rates of price change of close to 2 per cent in 1998 and 2.5 per cent in 1999. By the end of the decade, the inflationary fears of the early 1990s had receded, instead the economy was having to cope with problems associated with falling prices (SY, 8/3/00).

3. This cycle is similar to the demand in several East Asian countries for an outward-oriented development strategy (Krueger 1993).

4. There are several problems with China's national account: (i) conceptual ones related to the partial shift from the Material Product System (MPS) to the System of National Accounts (SNA), (ii) those associated with price deflators; (iii) problems of coverage of services and the real estate sector; and (iv) the accuracy of reporting, especially of rural industry output valued at constant prices. For these and other reasons, the data series, many of which are short and not entirely comparable across periods, must be used with considerable caution (see, for instance, Rawski 1993a; Wu 1993a).

5. Decentralising tendencies occurred towards the latter part of each dynastic period in China. For instance, in the twilight years of the Ching dynasty in the mid- and late-nineteenth century, decentralisation was on the rise and was particularly notable in the first three decades of the twentieth century (Kuhn 1970; Pomeranz 1993).

6. Rural reform in 1978–82 was much more a response to grassroots demand and proposals and not a top-down affair. Later industrial and fiscal and price reforms have been instigated more from the centre, though Beijing is continuously absorbing and responding to initiatives proposed by the provinces. China's success with the bottom-up approach has been linked in an interesting way to the M-form organisation by Qian and Xu (1993).

7. Tax contracts between the centre and provinces are differentiated according to the following characteristics: (i) whether or not the sharing between province and centre is fixed, e.g., Tianjin's share is 46.5 per cent; (ii) whether sharing is combined with an annual per cent increase in the contribution to the centre, as with Beijing; (iii) whether the province pays a fixed tax quota; and (iv) whether the fixed quotas are specially favourable. Guangdong has enjoyed (iv) status.

8. In 1985, the share of individually owned enterprises (mostly rural) in total industrial output was 1.8 per cent. It rose to 5.7 per cent in 1991.

9. These three forms of decentralisation did not affect provinces uniformly. Those along the eastern seaboard, and in particular, the provinces along the south-eastern coast were especially favoured because of their proximity to dynamic East Asian economies, the supply of human capital and because this region was the heir to a strong industrial tradition. The effect on both overall growth and what is perhaps a more sensitive indicator of provincial initiative—growth of non-state industry—was very marked.

10. Because production capacity was critical to meeting and possibly overshooting planned targets (which influences bonuses), socialist enterprises have had a tendency to add plant and equipment wherever possible. The size of production facilities also had a bearing on the allocation of raw material inputs and on the influence of the enterprise managers. Hence, the insatiable demand for investment funding labelled as 'investment hunger.'

11. State enterprises in China, as in other former socialist economies, are insulated from operational losses because the state is prepared to step in and cover them by way of the budget or directed lending through the state-owned banking system. Janos Kornai coined the term 'soft budget constraint' to describe this state of affairs. The hard budget constraint is what one encounters in a market environment, where a firm is responsible for losses incurred and can be driven out of business.

12. The unemployment rate for the formal, urban

work force, whose numbers had reached 152 million in 1991, has ranged from 1.8 per cent in 1985 to 2.3 per cent in 1991. The total workforce, including rural labourers, was 583.6 million in 1991 (China Statistical Yearbook 1992).

13. Savings might also be influenced by the strong sense of intergenerational connectedness in Chinese society, which increases the bequest motive. In China as in Japan, households are motivated to save so as to transfer resources which will benefit their progeny (Hayashi 1986). This desire only reinforces the cautious anti-consumption bent of the average household.

14. Where they can, enterprises have invested heavily in housing for employees and recreational facilities.

15. Local governments derive revenue from surcharges on various taxes and from fees levied on enterprises and particular activities. These revenues are not incorporated in the unified budget but is a side income of the locality.

16. As indicated earlier, the retail price index is a not-entirely-reliable gauge of inflation, especially in the earlier half of the 1980s. However, if that index is applied to the interest rate on one-year deposits, the latter is negative in 1980, 1985, 1988, and 1989. It is zero in 1987.

17. The government's 16-point plan introduced in late July 1993 is aimed at controlling credit by means of ceilings on bank lending and continued placement of bonds. Savings propensities are to be strengthened by raising deposit rates. It seeks to cut public spending by 20 per cent through administrative economies and a reduction of capital spending in the state sector. Further price liberalisation is suspended and some price controls reintroduced. In addition, curbs were revived on the trading of foreign exchange through the swap market. This program resembles earlier deflationary policy actions in its emphasis on administrative means. Whether it is as effective will depend on the willingness of provincial authorities to implement policies and the degree to which administrative intervention remains effective in China's increasingly complex economy.

18. Widening income differentials have also led to increased interprovincial migration. While much of this is of a temporary nature, the restraints on changing residence have weakened and short-term movements could well become permanent. Migration flows are likely to encourage the richer provinces to agree to more fiscal sharing with interior provinces.

19. The experience of Italy, described by Putnam (1993), nicely buttresses this point.

References

Ash, R.F., 1993. 'Agricultural Policy Under the Impact of Reform,' in Kueh, Y. Y., and R. F. Ash (eds), *Economic Trend in Chinese Agriculture*, Clarendon Press, Oxford.

Chen, K., G.H. Jefferson, and I. Singh, 1992. 'Lessons from China's Economic Reform', *Journal of Comparative Economics*, 12:570–91.

China Statistical Yearbook, 1992. State Statistical Bureau, Beijing.

deLong, J.B., and L.H. Summers, 1992. 'Equipment Investment and Economic Growth: How Strong is the Nexus,' *Brookings Papers on Economic Activity*, 2:157–211.

Fischer, S., 1993. 'Socialist Economy Reform: Lessons of the First Three Years,' *American Economic Review*, May, 83(2):390–95.

Freeman, R.B., 1993. 'Labour markets and Institutions in Economic Development,' *American Economic Review*, May, 83(2):405.

Hayashi, Fumio, 1986. 'Why is Japan's Saving Rate so Apparently High?', in Fischer, Stanley, ed., *NBER Macroeconomic Annual*. Cambridge: MIT Press:147–234.

Hussain, A., and N. Stern, 1991. 'Effective Demand, Enterprise Reforms and Public Finance in China,' *Economic Policy*, April, 6(1):142–86.

IMF (International Monetary Fund), 1993. *World Economic Outlook*, Washington, DC.

Ito, T., 1992. *The Japanese Economy*, MIT Press, Cambridge, Massachusetts.

Jefferson, G.H., T.G. Rawski, and Yuxin X. Zheng, 1992. 'Growth, Efficiency and Convergence in China's State and

Collective Industry,' *Economic Development and Cultural Change*, January, 40(2):239–66.

Krueger, Anne O., 1993. *Political Economy of Policy Reform*, MIT Press, Cambridge, Massachusetts.

Kueh, Y. Y., 1992. 'Foreign Investment and Economic Change in China,' *China Quarterly*, September, 131:637–90.

Kuhn, Philip A., 1970. *Rebellion and its Enemies in Late Imperial China*, Harvard University Press, Cambridge.

Lau, Lawrence J., 1992. 'Macroeconomic Policies for Short-term Stabilization and Long-term Growth of the Chinese Economy,' *Asia Pacific Research Center Working Paper Series No. 101*, Stanford University Press, Stanford.

Lincoln, Edward J., 1988. *Japan: Facing Economic Maturity*, Brookings Institution, Washington, DC.

McKinnon, Ronald I., 1993. 'Gradual versus Rapid Liberalization in Socialist Economies: Financial Policies and Macroeconomic Stability in China and Russia Compared,' World Bank Annual Conference on Development Economics, Washington, DC.

Naughton, Barry, 1992. 'Implications of the State Monopoly over Industry and its Relaxation,' *Modern China*, January *18*(1):14–41.

Ody, Anthony, 1992. 'Rural Enterprise Development in China, 1986–90.' World Bank Discussion Paper No. 162, Washington, DC.

Peebles, Gavin, 1992. *Money in the People's Republic of China: A Comparative Study*, Pauland Company Publishers, Concord.

Pomeranz, Kenneth, 1993. *The Making of a Hinterland*, University of California Press, Berkeley.

Pomfret, Richard, 1992. 'The Sequencing of Economic Reform,' Working Paper No. 93/4,

Chinese Economic Research Unit, University of Adelaide, Adelaide.

Putnam, Robert D., 1993. *Making Democracy Work*, Princeton University Press, Princeton.

Qian, Yingyi, and Chenggong Xu, 1993. 'Why China's Economic Reforms Differ,' CP. No. 25, STICERD, London School of Economics, London.

Rawski, Tom, 1993a. 'How Fast Has Chinese Industry Grown?', World Bank PRE Working Paper Series, No. 1194, World Bank, Washington, DC.

——, 1993b. 'Progress Without Privatization,' World Bank, Washington, DC, mimeo.

Shirk, Susan L., 1993. *The Political Logic of Economic Reform in China*, University of California Press, Berkeley.

Sung, Yun-Wing, 1992. *The China-Hong Kong Connection*, Cambridge University Press, Australia, New York.

World Bank, 1990 *Between Plan and Market*, World Bank, Washington, DC.

Wu, Harry X., 1993a. 'The 'Real' Chinese Gross Domestic Product for the Pre-Reform period 1952–77,' *Review of Income and Wealth*, 39(1):63–86.

Wu, Yonrui, 1993b. 'The Measurement of Efficiency: A Review of the Theory and Empirical Applications to China,' Working Paper No. 93/1, Chinese Economy Research Unit, University of Adelaide.

Young, Susan, 1991. 'Wealth but not Security: Attitudes towards Private Business in China in the 1980s,' *Australian Journal of Chinese Affairs*, 25:115–37.

Yusuf, Shahid, 1993a. 'The Rise of China's Non-state Sector,' World Bank, Washington, DC.

——, 1993b. 'Property Rights and Non-state Sector Development in China,' World Bank, Washington, DC, mimeo.

9 Plan and Market in China's Agricultural Commerce

Terry Sicular

The change in leadership following the death of Mao Zedong brought with it a shift in accepted views about the role of markets in a socialist system. For much of the previous three decades, Chinese leaders believed that markets should play a minimal role. Instead, output should revert to the state, which would then arrange for its distribution. Domestic commercial policies reflected this view. A large proportion of trade was carried out through state channels in accordance with economic plans. Quotas governed the procurement of agricultural and industrial goods, and rationing or direct allocation governed their distribution. Procurement and distribution prices were set by the state.

Since 1978 Chinese leaders have acknowledged that the government cannot effectively plan for all allocation. Although planning is still considered essential, they believe that markets can allocate numerous commodities among numerous economic agents more efficiently than state plans. Commercial policies have shifted accordingly, encouraging markets to develop alongside state-planned commerce. For example, after 1978 the government gradually loosened restrictions on private trade for agricultural products, permitting producers to engage in private trade provided they fulfilled their delivery quotas. In response to these policy initiatives, market trade has expanded rapidly, and China has evolved into a 'mixed' economic system, that is, a system in which planned and market exchange coexist. Chinese economists believe that the mixture of market and planning is appropriate to China's present stage of development, and they take pride in what they consider a uniquely Chinese approach to socialist economic development.[1]

Despite certain successes, China's shift toward a mixed system has not been smooth. Market prices have been unstable, state price subsidies have ballooned, and plan fulfillment for some commodities has become difficult to enforce, while for others government stockpiles have grown too large. Certain distributional inequities have also emerged. These problems have arisen in part because the Chinese did not fully foresee the consequences of introducing market allocation alongside the existing planning apparatus and in part because they are not sure exactly how the two should be best combined.

Such problems have led some observers to believe that a mixed system is inherently unstable and that sustaining state planning in the presence

Reprinted with permission. Terry Sicular, 1988. 'Plan and market in China's agricultural commerce', *Journal of Political Economy*, 96:283–307 (with minor editing).

of markets is difficult, if not impossible. The object of this paper is to show that plan and market are not inherently at odds. Under certain conditions a mixed system of the sort observed in China's agricultural commerce is sustainable, and, furthermore, good reasons can exist for maintaining such a mixed system.

In order to implement a sustainable and desirable mixture, however, the government must take into account interactions between the state plan and markets. Recent trends have demonstrated that the emergence of markets can affect the way in which state planning functions. Markets place pressures on plans, and they influence the economic effects of planning. Similarly, state planning can influence price and quantity trends in markets. In designing a plan or in analysing the economic effects of a plan, such interactions should be considered.

Past work on China's economy has not, in general, examined interactions between planning and markets. Most of the literature on China's economy concentrates on state planning and either ignores private markets or treats them only superficially. The reasons for this are fairly obvious: until recently little information about private trade was available, and for many years the level of private trade was very low. Thus the lopsided emphasis on planning was, for the most part, unavoidable.

Exceptions include Perkin's classic work *Market Control and Planning in Communist China* (1966), which examines developments in the 1950s and early 1960s as China moved away from a market system. This paper is concerned with issues similar to those he discussed but focuses on the recent reemergence of markets. A second notable exception is the recent research of Byrd (1987), who examines the mixed allocation system in Chinese industry.

This paper examines the sorts of interactions that occur in a mixed system such as that observed in Chinese agriculture. The first section discusses recent reforms in commercial policies and points out some of the problems that have emerged in the mixed commercial environment.

The second section presents a simple, stylised, analytical model of the sort of mixed system that existed in Chinese agriculture between 1979 and 1985. This model clarifies key ways in which plan and market interact in such economies. A concluding section discusses implications of the analysis for plan design.

The central conclusions of this analysis are as follows:

1. Markets place pressure on the state to choose planned prices so that they do not deviate too far from market prices. If the state tries to set a planned price that exceeds the market prices, then the state will incur budgetary losses. If state prices are considerably lower than market prices, plan evasion can become a problem. In either case, plan sustainability may be sacrificed.

2. In the presence of markets and if quotas are enforceable, state-planned prices and quotas cause lump-sum transfers among producers and consumers and among sectors. They also cause lump-sum transfers between the government and non-government sectors of the economy. Commercial planning can thus serve as an efficient redistributive and tax mechanism.

3. In the presence of markets, state-planned prices and quotas will not, except in certain cases, directly affect levels of production and consumption. Except in cases in which the state price or quota is 'too high' (to be defined below), producers and consumers will look at market prices, not state prices and quotas, in allocating their resources.

4. Although state prices and quotas do not affect production and consumption directly, they nevertheless influence them indirectly through their effects on the distribution of income and equilibrium market prices.

These conclusions point out some of the ways in which markets affect planning and planning affects markets. When choosing levels of planned prices and quotas, the government will want to take such interactions into account.

I. Recent Reforms in Commercial Policies

Reform of policies governing trade in agricultural products began in 1977 and has passed through two stages. First, between 1977 and 1982, the state maintained the existing design of state commercial planning for major agricultural products but adjusted state-planned quotas and prices, permitted markets to revive, and introduced state trade at negotiated prices. In the second stage the design of commercial planning was modified. The story of these commercial reforms illustrates how the original planning structure became increasingly problematic as markets emerged, prompting a second round of reforms.

Prior to and during the first stage of commercial reforms, the state set mandatory minimum delivery quotas. For grain and oilseeds, these quotas specified minimum absolute quantities to be delivered to the state at planned prices. Quota levels were reduced between 1978 and 1982. Over these 4 years the national grain quota and tax were reduced 20 per cent (Ministry of Commerce 1984:386–87), with reductions to some extent targeted regionally to benefit low-income and disadvantaged areas.

As before, no maximum limit was set on deliveries to the state: the state promised to buy as much as producers wished to sell at state prices. The state also continued to distribute these products in a planned way, primarily to urban consumers and industrial users. Rural areas for the most part did not receive allocations of agricultural products, and those allocations that did occur went primarily to areas well suited for production of commercial crops.

The state paid a fixed price for quota deliveries and a higher bonus price for deliveries beyond the quota. In 1979, state-planned prices for quota farm deliveries were raised by more than 20 per cent, and the percentage price bonus for above-quota deliveries enlarged from 30 per cent to 50 per cent for grain and oil-bearing crops. A new 30 per cent above-quota price bonus was instituted for cotton. State retail prices for grain and edible vegetable oils remained at their original levels, while retail prices of meat, vegetables, and several other non-staple foodstuffs were increased.

Policies on free markets were revised in two respects. Local and long-distance market exchanges were allowed and even encouraged to develop. In addition, the number of products that could be exchanged in free markets was enlarged. By the early 1980s the state permitted market trade in all agricultural products but cotton, and this last restriction was later removed. Producers were, however, allowed to sell their products on the market only after they had met their delivery quotas. In response to these policies, market trade developed rapidly. Between 1977 and 1985, the number of markets more than doubled, rising from 30,000 to 61,000, and the volume of trade more than quadrupled.[2] By 1984 more than 18 per cent of all purchases of agricultural products took place at market prices (Table 1).

Concurrently, the government took steps to make state commerce somewhat more responsive to market forces. The first step in this direction was to expand the role of 'negotiated' state trade. The state began to offer negotiated purchase prices agreed on jointly by the producer and local state commercial agents for voluntary above-quota deliveries to the state. Negotiated purchase prices were to be decided on the basis of regional, yearly, seasonal, varietal, and quality consider-ations and to basically follow supply and demand trends; however, they were in general not to exceed local market prices (Wang 1985:53). The state commercial organs could then sell goods purchased at negotiated prices at negotiated retail prices, which were to be set equal to the negotiated purchase price plus reasonable transport and handling fees.

The revival of negotiated price procurement gave the state commercial system more flexibility in responding to market conditions and, together with negotiated price sales, was to provide a lever for influencing prices in the free market. Moreover, in areas where earnings from new sideline and non-agricultural work opportunities

Table 1   **National market statistics**

	1977	1978	1979	1980	1981	1982	1983	1984	1985
Number of markets (total)	29,882	33,302	38,993	40,809	43,013	44,775	48,003	56,500	61,337
Urban	0	0	2,226	2,919	3,298	3,591	4,488	6,144	8,013
Rural	29,882	33,302	36,767	37,890	39,715	41,184	43,515	50,356	53,324
Volume of trade* (billion yuan)	10.5	12.5	18.3	23.5	28.7	33.3	38.6	47.1	70.5
Percentage of total purchases of agricultural products carried out at market prices	n.a.	5.6	n.a.	n.a.	9.4	10.2	10.5	18.1±	n.a.

* At current prices
± Includes purchases by commercial, industrial, and other sectors at market prices.
Sources: Ministry of Commerce (1984:558); State Statistical Bureau (1985:86–7; 1986:93).

threatened to divert labour from agriculture, local officials could use the higher negotiated purchase prices to make agriculture competitive and maintain government procurement.[3] The importance of negotiated price procurement grew quite rapidly. For grain, negotiated price procurement rose from less than 3 per cent of net state purchases in 1978 to roughly 17 per cent in 1983 (State Statistical Bureau, Department of Commercial and Price Statistics, 1984:156, 329).

These policies contributed to rapid growth in levels of agricultural production and incomes, but by 1982 certain problems with the design of commercial planning began to emerge. The higher prices and wider scope of bonuses and negotiated prices for above-quota deliveries encouraged evasion of quotas. Producers preferred to sell at the above-quota, negotiated, and market prices, and they found ways to do so. One was to switch from planting crops with relatively high quotas to those with low or no quotas. Fields subject to grain quotas were converted to cotton or other economic crops, and vice versa. Another evasion tactic was to save output for 1 or 2 years and then deliver it all at once, or for several families to transfer their output

to one family for delivery to the state. Finally, local officials, under pressure from their neighbours, occasionally succumbed to the temptation of carrying out unauthorised reductions in quota levels. Such sorts of behavior resulted in underfulfillment of quotas at the same time that deliveries at above-quota and negotiated prices increased (Table 2) (Xu, Chen, and Liang 1982:121–4, 216–7; Guo and Gu 1983:34; Xue 1985:42). Although total deliveries of grain to the state grew at more than 10 per cent a year,[4] quota fulfillment declined from 94.6 per cent in 1979 to 82.4 per cent in 1980 to 80 per cent in 1981.[5] Farmers obviously benefited from these trends, but the state paid higher prices for farm products than it had anticipated.

A second problem was that the procurement system was designed to operate in a shortage economy and was ill suited to handle emerging agricultural surpluses. Under the existing quota system, the government was obliged to buy as much output as farmers wished to sell. As surpluses grew, the government found itself committed to buying ever-increasing quantities of products at high, above-quota prices. This problem became especially severe in the early

1980s when free-market prices for grain began to fall. The design of the procurement system thus contributed to growing state inventories of grain and further exacerbated state losses on the trade of agricultural products.[6]

An additional related problem arose in the new surplus environment. In the shortage economy that had existed for most of the previous two decades, matching supply to demand had never been a major concern because people would buy whatever was offered for sale. In the early 1980s, with growth in incomes leading to increasing selectivity of demand and with the improved availability of foodstuffs, this was no longer true. The state began to find itself holding surplus stocks of undesirable commodities and was unable to meet consumer demand for a variety of higher-quality, non-staple items. The procurement system's inability to pass on demand signals to producers became increasingly evident with time.

Finally, the procurement system created inequities. Quota levels varied among regions, and so the accrual of above-quota price awards was unequal. Regions with low quotas were able to sell more at above-quota and market prices and so received higher average prices, while those with higher quotas received lower average prices. For example, cotton farmers in the North, especially the Yellow River Basin, faced low cotton quotas and were receiving average prices of 200 yuan per ton or more from the state. In the southern provinces, such as Hubei, quotas were higher, and average state prices were less

Table 2   Various components of state grain procurement

| Year | Quota and tax* | Degree of quota fulfilment (%) | Shares (%) of total deliveries procured at | |
			Quota price (including tax grain)	Above-quota or negotiated prices
1955	40.00			
1965	36.25			
1966	36.25			
1967	36.25			
1968	36.25			
1969	36.25			
1970	36.25			
1971	38.25			
1972	37.75			
1973	37.75			
1974	37.75			
1975	37.75			
1976	37.75			
1977	37.75			
1978	37.75		68.5	31.5
1979	35.00	94.6	49.5	50.5
1980	34.33	82.4	46.5	53.5
1981	30.38	80.0	40.0	60.0
1982	30.32		30.0	70.0
1983	...		27.6	72.4

Note: * Quota and tax grain are in trade (husked) grain equivalent, measured in millions of metric tons.
Sources: Wu (1982:5); Xu et al. (1982:217); Ministry of Commerce (1984:386–7); Walker (1984:62); Wang and Wang (1984:30); Lardy (1985:31); Wang (1985:52).

than 140 yuan (Guo and Gu 1983:34). Planned commerce similarly contributed to inequality between urban and rural sectors since the urban population was the primary beneficiary of low-priced state sales of agricultural products.

These various problems prompted Chinese planners to carry out further commercial reforms. The second-stage reforms were distinct from those that had occurred earlier in that their aim was to modify the design of procurement planning and greatly reduce the scope of planned commerce for agricultural products. Redesign of the state procurement system began in 1983 when the government eliminated the price distinction between quota and above-quota deliveries for oilseeds and began to pay a single price for both quota and above-quota deliveries. Although the new price for oilseed varied somewhat by region and variety, in general it was a weighted average of 40 per cent of the old quota price plus 60 per cent of the old above-quota price (Wang 1985:52). Similar reforms occurred for cotton in 1984 (Almanac of China's Economy 1984:IV–50, IX–132; Wang 1985) and then for grain in 1985. For grain, the new price was set equal to 30 per cent of the quota price plus 70 per cent of the above-quota price.[7]

In conjunction with these pricing modifications, in early 1985 the government announced that, except for a few products, it would no longer send down procurement quotas to farmers. For grain and cotton, quotas were to be replaced by a program of contract and market purchases. State commercial departments were to negotiate purchase contracts with farmers before the sowing season and, when necessary, carry out supplemental procurement on the free market. The prices of these contracts were fixed at the new, weighted prices mentioned above. In theory, farmers could choose freely whether or not they wished to enter into contracts. Products not under contract could be sold on the market or to the state at a low, guaranteed price (equal to the old quota price) at harvest time. The state no longer promised to buy as much as farmers wished to sell at the higher above-quota or contract prices.

Planned procurement of agricultural products other than grain and cotton was to be gradually eliminated and replaced by free-market allocation. In general, state commercial departments would increasingly buy and sell on the market. Through market participation, state commercial departments could not only make supplementary purchases to meet the need for exports and continued planned supply to urban areas but also exert influence on free-market trends (*Jiage lilun yu shijian*, no. 4, 1985:51.

The full effects of the second-stage commercial reforms are still unclear. Recent reports suggest that, in practice, the grain contracts are not always voluntary and often closely resemble the old procurement quotas except that state procurements are limited to the contract amount (Oi 1986:284–90; also author interviews). The program has probably been successful in reducing state procurements and easing state storage and budgetary problems.[8] Lower grain production in 1985 and 1986, however, has raised questions about the new procurement and price system.

II. An Analytical Framework

The sorts of commercial problems that emerged after 1978 can be understood using standard economic tools. For this purpose, a general equilibrium-type approach is useful because it permits market prices to be determined endogenously given the presence of state commercial planning. The model presented below follows in the spirit of standard general equilibrium theory. It contains numerous producers and consumers who choose levels of production and consumption in response to price levels; markets exist for all goods, and market price levels are determined by demand and supply.

This model differs from the standard general equilibrium approach in two important ways. First, it includes not only market exchange but also state commerce. Producers and consumers can trade on markets at market prices or with the state at state-planned prices. Second, the model is not, in some sense, completely closed. For any set of state prices and quotas, the model will yield market prices that set all excess demands in private markets equal to zero. Supply need not equal demand, however, in state commercial activities. In equilibrium the state can hold unsold inventories and need not have a balanced budget. Therefore, in equilibrium overall supply and demand need not balance. Whether or not overall supply and demand balance will, as shown below, depend on the levels of state-planned prices and quotas.

The plan is specified exogenously to the model. For any set of planned prices and quotas, the model yields equilibrium market-clearing prices, levels of production, income, and consumption, and levels of state stockpiles and net budgetary revenues. This approach permits direct analysis of the effects of planning on markets but only indirect analysis of the effect of markets on planning. One could alternatively make the plan endogenous by specifying the government as an optimising agent that chooses optimal prices and quotas in accordance with some objective function. Whether or not the Chinese government is, in fact, an optimising agent is debatable. Suffice it to say that the reform process described above portrays a government that does not optimise globally but adjusts pre-existing state prices and quotas from time to time to meet specific goals or when visible problems arise. Under this sort of adaptive or partial optimisation, imbalances emerge. The theoretical approach taken here allows for such imbalances.

The model does not incorporate uncertainty or information problems, although such problems are undoubtedly relevant. Nor is plan evasion explicitly included, although the model provides insights as to when and where plan evasion is likely to occur. Further research to analyse the effects of uncertainty, information asymmetries, and evasion would probably yield fruitful results, but in-depth analysis of these issues is not within the scope of this paper.

Related work within the general equilibrium literature includes articles that examine equilibrium in the presence of price or quantity rigidities, such as Drèze 1975), and general equilibrium in the presence of Soviet-style planning, such as Feltenstein (1979). For the most part, however, the related general equilibrium literature does not treat the case in which planned and market allocation exist for the same good or goods. Exceptions include Sah and Srinivasan's (1988) examination of the rural food levy in India and Byrd's (1987) analysis of plan and market in China's industrial sector.

The basic model

The model contains two sectors, urban and rural, and three goods. The urban sector consists of industrial producers and urban consumers, and the rural sector consists of farm households that both produce and consume. For simplicity, agents of each type are assumed to be identical. This permits the individual agents to be aggregated into an aggregate industrial producer ($j = 0$), aggregate urban consumer ($j = 1$), and aggregate farm household ($j = 2$). Hereafter agents will be referred to as aggregate agents.

The model contains three goods, a manufactured good ($k = 1$) produced by the industrial producer, an agricultural good ($k = 2$) produced by the aggregate farm household, and a third good ($k = 3$) that is not produced but of which both the urban consumer and the farm household hold initial endowments $\overline{w}_{j3}$. This third good can be thought of as human time, land, or some aggregation of various endowed assets. For convenience, it will be referred to here as human time or labour/leisure. All three goods can be traded on markets.

Consumer preferences in both sectors are defined over consumption of the three goods. The utility functions $u_j = u_j(x_{j1}, x_{j2}, x_{j3}), j = 1,2$ are assumed to have the usual properties, that is, to be continuous, convex, and monotonic. Preferences of the urban consumer and rural household can differ. The urban consumer maximises his or her utility subject to income derived from his or her endowment. The rural household maximises its utility subject to its endowment income plus net income or profits from agricultural production. The industrial producer is assumed to maximise profits.[9]

Industrial profits are not distributed to consumers but go directly into the state budget. This is in accordance with actual practice in China, where, until recently, all industrial profits reverted to the state. In fact, industrial and commercial profits have in the past constituted the major single source of government revenues.[10] Although reforms since 1978 have permitted industrial enterprises to retain a portion of their profits, a majority of their earnings still revert to the state.

Production is given by

industrial: $q_{01} = f^1(q_{02}, q_{03})$,
agricultural: $q_{22} = f^2(q_{21}, q_{23})$.

The manufactured good is produced using inputs of the agricultural good and human time; the agricultural good is produced using inputs of the manufactured good and human time. These production functions are assumed to be regular and quasi-concave.

In the absence of commercial planning, maximisation of profits by the industrial producer and of utility by the urban consumer and rural household would yield the usual supply, input demand, and consumer demand functions:

Supply/input demand functions: $q_{jk} = y_{jk}(p)$,
Urban consumer demand: $x_{1k} = d_{1k}(p, p_3 \overline{w}_{13})$,
Rural consumer demand:
$x_{2k} = d_{2k}(p, p_3 \overline{w}_{23} + R_2(p))$

where $j = 0, 2, k = 1, 2, 3$, and R_2 is maximum profits from farming:

$$R_2(p) = p_2 y_{22}(p) - p_1 y_{21}(p) - p_3 y_{23}(p).$$

Market equilibrium would occur at prices $p^* = (p_1^*, p_2^*, p_3^*)$ that sets excess demands equal to zero for all goods.

State planning

State commercial planning is designed to reflect the structure of agricultural planning used in China to the most recent (1985) stage of reforms. The government set prices $\overline{p} = (\overline{p}_1, \overline{p}_2, \overline{p}_3)$ and fixes quotas $\overline{r}_{jk}$ and procurement quotas $\overline{s}_{jk}$. Ration quotas specify maximum state sales of the manufactured good to the urban consumer ($\overline{r}_{11}$) and rural household ($\overline{r}_{21}$), of the agricultural good to the urban consumer ($\overline{r}_{12}$) and urban producer ($\overline{r}_{02}$), and of labour time to the urban producer ($\overline{r}_{03}$). Ration quotas constitute a maximum constraint on purchases from the state: agents can purchase less than their ration but not more. If r_{jk} represents purchases of good k by agent j from the state, the ration quota constraint can be written as $r_{jk} \leq \overline{r}_{jk}$. The state does not sell manufactured goods to the urban producer, agricultural goods to the rural household, or human time to either the urban consumer or rural household.

Similarly, procurement quotas constitute minimum constraints on deliveries of goods to the state. Each agent is required to deliver at least its quota amount to the state. The state guarantees to purchase as much of the goods as agents wish to sell beyond their quotas. Thus if s_{jk} represents the actual amount of good k delivered to the state by agent j, a procurement quota constraint can be written as $s_{jk} \geq \overline{s}_{jk}$. Procurement quotas are set for sales to the state of the manufactured good by the urban producer, of the agricultural good by the rural household, and of labour time by the urban household. The state does not buy a good from an agent unless that agent has a procurement quota for that good. In other words, the state buys good 1 only from the urban producer, good 2 only from the rural household, and good 3 only from the urban household.

Deliveries to and purchases from the state take place at state-planned prices. For simplicity, I assume that there are no transfer costs and that for each good the state sales price is set equal to the state purchase price. In addition, I assume that for each particular good the sum of procurement quotas is equal to the sum of ration quotas:

$$\overline{s}_{01} = \overline{r}_{11} + \overline{r}_{21}, \overline{s}_{22} = \overline{r}_{02} + \overline{r}_{12}, \overline{s}_{13} = \overline{r}_{03}$$

In other words, the state plans for its purchases to exactly equal its sales when all quotas are binding.[11]

As long as they do not violate their quotas, agents are permitted to buy and sell freely on the market. Goods purchased on the market can be sold to the state, and goods bought from the state can be sold on the market. In this model, then both state and market trade exist for all goods. All three agents can trade all three goods on the market, and each agent can trade some, but not all, goods with the state.

Agent maximisation and market equilibrium for a subset of plan levels

For the purpose of exposition, it is useful to first consider a subset of all possible state-planned price and quota combinations. Let us define the subset U^1 of planned price and quota combinations as that in which, in equilibrium, all state prices are strictly less than market prices p':

$$U^1 = \left\{ (\bar{p}, \bar{r}, \bar{s}) \mid \bar{p}_k < p'_k \quad \text{for all } k \right\}$$

In the presence of such a plan, market prices will guide marginal decisions. State prices and quotas will not directly affect levels of production and consumption. The plan will, however, affect levels of trade on the market and with the state, income distribution, and equilibrium market prices.

Consider first the behaviour of the aggregate rural household in the presence of such a plan. Its utility maximisation problem is as follows:

$$\max_{x,r,s,q} \quad I_2 = u_2(x_2) - \theta_2 \begin{bmatrix} p_3 \bar{w}_{23} + (p_1 - \bar{p}_1) r_{21} - \\ (p_2 - \bar{p}_2) s_{22} - p_1 x_{21} - \\ p_2 x_{22} - p_3 x_{23} + \\ p_2 f^2(q_2) - p_1 q_{21} - p_3 q_{23} \end{bmatrix}$$

$$- \alpha_2(\bar{r}_{21} - r_{21}) - \beta_2(s_{22} - \bar{s}_{22}).$$

First-order conditions of this problem yield

$$\frac{\delta u_2 / \delta x_{2h}}{\delta u_2 / \delta x_{2k}} = \frac{\delta f^2 / \delta q_{2h}}{\delta f^2 / \delta q_{2k}} = \frac{p_h}{p_k} \quad \text{for all } h, k.$$

Thus marginal decisions are guided only by market prices. State prices and quotas do not directly influence the production and consumption choice.

The rural household's supply and demand functions are identical to those that would exist in the absence of planning, except that rural

income now includes an extra component:

$$q_{2k} = y_{2k}(p),$$
$$x_{2k} = d_{2k}(p; p_3 \bar{w}_{23} + R_2(p) + T_2).$$

Commercial planning changes rural income by a transfer T_2 equal to the sum of trade levels with the state times the differences between state and market prices:

$$T_2 = (p_1 - \bar{p}_1) r_{21} - (p_2 - \bar{p}_2) s_{22}.$$

In fact, in equilibrium T_2 will be a lump-sum transfer equal to the sum of the quota levels times the differences between market and state prices:

$$T_2 = (p'_1 - \bar{p}_1) \bar{r}_{21} - (p'_2 - \bar{p}_2) \bar{s}_{22}.$$

This holds because when all state prices are strictly less than equilibrium market prices, then all quotas are strictly binding. For goods purchased from the state, if the state price is lower than the market price, the consumer will buy as much as he or she can, the full amount of the ration quota, from the state and then sell whatever he or she does not consume at the higher market price. For goods sold to the state, if the state price is lower than the market price, the consumer will sell as little as possible, the quota amount, to the state.

The microeconomic behaviour of the urban producer and consumer is similar to that of the rural household. For the urban producer we have

$$\max_{r,s,q} \quad R_0 = p_1 f^1(q_0) - p_2 q_{02} - p_3 q_{03} - (p_1 - \bar{p}_1) s_{01}$$
$$+ (p_2 - \bar{p}_2) r_{02} + (p_3 - \bar{p}_3) r_{03} - \alpha_0(s_{01} - \bar{s}_{01})$$
$$- \beta_0(\bar{r}_{02} - r_{02}) - \sigma_0(\bar{r}_{03} - r_{03}).$$

The urban producer's supply and input demand functions are the same as those that would exist in the absence of state planning, $q_{0k} = y_{0k}(p)$. In equilibrium, the producer's maximum net income will equal maximum profits plus the lump-sum transfer T_0:

$$T_0 = -(p'_1 - \bar{p}_1) \bar{s}_{01} + (p'_2 - \bar{p}_2) \bar{r}_{02} + (p'_3 - \bar{p}_3) \bar{r}_{03}.$$

The urban consumer's maximisation problem is

$$\max_{x,r,s} \quad L_1 = u_1(x_1) - \theta_1 [p_3 \bar{w}_{13} + (p_1 - \bar{p}_1) r_{11} + (p_2 - \bar{p}_2) r_{12}$$
$$- (p_3 - \bar{p}_3) s_{13} - p_1 x_{11} - p_2 x_{12} - p_3 x_{13}] - \alpha_1(\bar{r}_{11} - r_{11})$$
$$- \beta_1(\bar{r}_{12} - r_{12}) - \sigma_1(s_{13} - \bar{s}_{13}).$$

Like the rural household, it sets the ratios of marginal utilities equal to the ratios of market prices. Urban consumer demands are

$$x_{1k} = d_{1k}(p; p_3\overline{w}_{13} + T_1),$$

where urban income includes a transfer that in equilibrium equals

$$T_1 = (p_1' - \overline{p}_1)\overline{r}_{11} + (p_2' - \overline{p}_2)\overline{r}_{12} - (p_3' - \overline{p}_3)\overline{s}_{13}.$$

Equilibrium in this mixed plan and market environment occurs when excess demands on the market equal zero. Each agent's excess demand on the market will be a function of market prices and will equal total excess demand plus (or minus) the relevant quota. Equilibrium market prices are therefore those that solve the following set of market-clearing equations:

$$0 = -y_{01}(p) + d_{11}(p; p_3\overline{w}_{13} + T_1) + y_{21}(p)$$

$$+ d_{21}(p; p_3\overline{w}_{23} + T_2 + R_2) + \overline{s}_{01} - \overline{r}_{11} - \overline{r}_{21},$$

$$0 = y_{02}(p) + d_{12}(p; p_3\overline{w}_{13} + T_1) - y_{22}(p)$$

$$+ d_{22}(p; p_3\overline{w}_{23} + T_2 + R_2) + \overline{s}_{22} - \overline{r}_{02} - \overline{r}_{12},$$

$$0 = y_{03}(p) + d_{13}(p; p_3\overline{w}_{13} + T_1) - \overline{w}_{13} + y_{23}(p)$$

$$+ d_{23}(p; p_3\overline{w}_{23} + T_2 + R_2) - \overline{w}_{23} + \overline{s}_{13} - \overline{r}_{03}.$$

Under the assumption that the state chooses quota levels so that for each good the sum of procurement and delivery quotas equals zero, the last terms in these equations drop out. Markets clear, therefore, at prices $p' = (p_1', p_2', p_3')$ identical to the equilibrium prices that would occur if the state did not engage in commercial planning but implemented lump-sum transfers T_j.[12] In other words, when the state plan belongs to U^1, the mixed plan and market equilibrium is equivalent to that in a pure market economy with lump-sum transfers T_j.

In summary, if a plan belongs to U^1, then state-planned prices and quotas will not directly affect levels of production and consumption. They can have an indirect effect on these variables, however, because they change incomes by lump-sum transfers T_j and so can alter equilibrium market prices. Furthermore, quotas will directly affect each agent's levels of trade with the state

and on the market. Levels of trade with the state will exactly equal quota levels, and market trade for each agent will equal its excess demand minus the ration quota, or plus the procurement quota.

These conclusions will hold no matter how high the state sets quotas. State quotas can, in fact, exceed production levels without directly influencing production. This is possible because producers can meet their quotas by either producing or buying on the market. If the producer buys on the market, which it will if the quota level is so high that the marginal cost of production exceeds the market price, then it will buy from consumers. The consumers in turn will have obtained their goods from the state, which originally purchased them from the producers. Thus a high quota can be met simply by the circulation of goods between the producer, state, and consumer and then back to the producer, which once again delivers them to the state.

Maximisation and market equilibrium when state prices are too high

Now let us consider another possible subset of planned price and quota combinations, specifically, that set for which one or more state-planned prices are greater than or equal to the market price. The set U^2 of state plans in which one or more state prices are 'too high' is defined as

$$U^2 = \left\{ (\overline{p}, \overline{r}, \overline{s}) \middle| \overline{p}_k \geq p_k' \quad for \quad one \quad or \quad more \quad k \right\}$$

On closer inspection, it becomes apparent that a state price can equal, but not exceed, the equilibrium market price. This can be shown using a *reduction* argument. Suppose the state sets $\overline{p}_1 > p_1'$. Then industrial producers could increase their income by buying good 1 for a low price on the market and selling it to the state for a higher price. They would, in fact, continue to buy low and sell high as long as the market price was less than the state price. Such activity would drive up the market price until it exactly equaled the state price. The same argument holds for 2 and 3. Consequently, in equilibrium, state prices can be less than or equal to, but not greater than, market prices.

The argument above reveals that if a state price is 'too high', the quotas associated with that good may no longer be binding. For such a good, agents with procurement quotas are likely to sell more than their quotas to the state, and agents with ration quotas are likely to buy less than their quota amounts from the state. In either event, the state will buy more than it sells and so end up holding unsold inventories.

State planning when a price is too high will, as for state planning when all prices are strictly less than market prices, continue to cause lump-sum transfers among agents. For any good whose market price exceeds its state price, the quotas will be binding, and so the income transfer term is as above. For any good whose state price is too high, the state price must equal the market price, and so the income transfers associated with such goods will be zero. Regardless, then, the income transfer will equal the sum of quota levels multiplied by the differences between state and market prices.

When one or more state prices are too high, therefore, in equilibrium all state prices must be less than or equal to their corresponding equilibrium market prices. For goods whose state prices are strictly less than their market prices, all quotas are binding and state procurement will exactly equal state sales. For any good whose state price is too high, the market price will be driven up to equal the state price. Markets clear at this high market price because the excess of market supply over demand is absorbed by state procurement.

Income transfers in the mixed system

The extent to which the distribution of income in the mixed plan and market environment differs from that in the pure market environment depends both on equilibrium levels of the transfers T_j and on the difference between equilibrium prices without planning p^* and with planning p'. The total changes in income between the pure market and the mixed plan and market situations equal the sum of these transfers plus the changes in income attributable to differences

between equilibrium market prices with and without planning:

$$Y_0' - Y_0^* = T_0,$$

$$Y_1' - Y_1^* = T_1 + (p_3' - p_3^*)\overline{w}_{13},$$

$$Y_2' - Y_2^* = T_2 + (p_3' - p_3^*)\overline{w}_{23}.$$

Profit terms do not enter these equations because competition drives profits from production to zero in both the pure market and the mixed plan and market environment.

These expressions indicate that state commercial planning can change incomes by more or less than the lump-sum transfer. For example, even if the state sets prices and quotas so as to effect a negative lump-sum transfer from the rural sector, that is, so that $T_2 < 0$, rural income need not be reduced from its pure market level. Such a planning strategy will not reduce rural income if the imposition of planning raises the price of good 3 by enough to offset the negative lump-sum transfer.

The conclusion that mandatory agricultural procurement at low prices can raise rather than lower rural income has been discussed elsewhere. Millar's (1974) and Ellman's (1975) empirical studies of the introduction of mandatory procurement in the USSR during the First Five-Year Plan (late 1920s and early 1930s), for example, conclude that reductions in rural income due to low state prices were offset by higher farm profits following a rise in the free-market prices for agricultural goods. The tax burden was as a result shifted to the urban residents who purchased farm products in free markets. Hayami, Subbarao, and Otsuka (1982) reach a similar conclusion with respect to state mandatory procurement of cereals in India. The conclusion here differs somewhat from those of these other studies in that the increased market prices enhance rural incomes by raising the value of the rural endowment, and not by raising farm profits. Farm profits will not increase even if the market prices of agricultural goods rise because in equilibrium competition drives profits to zero.

Equilibrium and plan sustainability

The question of plan sustainability in a mixed plan and market economy would be addressed more fully by a dynamic model; still, the static framework employed here sheds light on the issue. Plan sustainability in this framework depends on two factors: the extent of state budgetary losses due to commercial planning and the extent of plan evasion. In practice, state budgetary losses from commercial planning can be sustained if the government has sources of revenue other than those discussed here. Such losses could be financed, for example, by income or excise taxes borne by urban consumers and rural households, by sales of surplus state stockpiles in international markets, by foreign aid, or by the issuing of money. International demand and the availability of foreign aid, however, are not particularly reliable sources of revenues, while other taxes and the issuing of money can have negative distributive, inflationary, and efficiency consequences. Large budget losses due to commercial planning, then, are likely to be difficult to sustain and so ultimately will induce plan revisions or reform. Such, in fact, has been the case in China during the recent reform period.

In the model presented here, total state net budgetary earnings due to commercial planning have two components. The first is the income transfer to industry T_0, which goes into the state budget. The second is net earnings C in state commercial activities:

$$C = \bar{p}_1(r_{11} + r_{21} - s_{01}) + \bar{p}_2(r_{12} + r_{02} - s_{22}) + \bar{p}_3(r_{03} - s_{13}),$$

where C equals revenues on state sales minus expenditures on procurements. Total net state budgetary earnings due to commercial planning B are thus given by $B = T_0 + C$.

Since state purchase and sales prices are equal and the government cannot sell more of a good than it has purchased, net commercial revenues C must be less than or equal to zero. Net commercial revenues, in other words, cannot show a strict surplus. They will be negative if the state sells less of any good than it has

purchased, that is, if it holds unsold inventories. Such is likely to be the case if one or more state prices are too high.

The size of the transfer to industry T_0 will depend on quota levels and the differences between state and market prices. The transfer will be larger when the state prices of the agricultural good and human time are low, and of the industrial good high, relative to market prices. Thus the state can earn revenues by undervaluing agricultural output and maintaining low state wages. Such, in fact, has been government policy since the 1950s.[13] Similarly, the transfer will be larger if industry's delivery quota is low and its ration allocations are high.

The state will suffer a deficit from its commercial planning if the transfer to industry is negative or if it is positive but insufficiently large to offset losses in commercial activities. Such a deficit is probable when state and market prices are close together, and especially when state prices for the agricultural good or human time are too high. In this situation not only will the state lose money in its trade of these items, but also the non-negative terms of industrial transfer associated with its ration quotas will be equal to zero.

The marginal income gain from quota evasion equals the difference between the market and state prices. The utility gains to consumers from evasion depend further on the marginal utilities of their income. Consider, for example, the rural household's marginal gain from evading its procurement quota. First-order conditions tell us that the marginally utility from an incremental change in the quota equals

$$\beta_2 = \theta_2(p_2' - \bar{p}_2).$$

Thus the incentive for the rural sector to evade is greater when the difference between the state and market prices is large and when rural income is low (assuming that the marginal utility of income is inversely related to the level of income).

In the urban sector, similar temptations exist to evade the ration quota, that is, to try to buy more that the rationed amount of good 2. If urban income is higher than rural income, however, the marginal utility of evasion will be lower than that in the rural sector. Furthermore, evasion of a ration quota requires that a state official in charge of planned distribution be willing to sell under the counter. In general, then, problems of evasion are more likely to emerge for quota constraints applying to the rural (lower-income) sector and for procurement rather than ration quotas.

Problems of plan sustainability can arise, then, when state prices are set either too low or too high. If the former, agents will be tempted to evade plans. If the latter, the state might hold unsold inventories and incur losses on its commercial activities. The standard by which prices are judged to be low or high is the market equilibrium prices p'.

The effects of changes in state prices and quotas

The effects of a change in the state plan on market prices and income distribution are ambiguous.[14] Equilibrium market prices can increase or decrease when the government alters a planned price; similarly, market prices can increase or decrease when the state alters a quota level. Whether equilibrium market prices increase or decrease depends on the signs of fairly complicated expressions containing the derivatives of sectoral demands and supplies with respect to incomes and prices.

The lack of straightforward comparative results means that the effects of changes in planned prices and quotas are difficult to predict and could contradict the planners' intentions. For example, if planners wished to raise rural incomes, they might consider increasing the state price of the agricultural good. However, since market prices can either increase or decrease with $\bar{p}_2$, an increase in $\bar{p}_2$ could conceivably reduce rural income. This can be seen mathematically from the expression for a change in rural income given a change in the planned price:

$$\frac{\delta Y_2}{\delta \bar{p}_2} = \frac{dp_1'}{d\bar{p}_2}\bar{r}_{21} + \left(1 - \frac{dp_2'}{d\bar{p}_2}\right)\bar{s}_{22} + \frac{dp_3'}{d\bar{p}_2}\bar{w}_{23}.$$

If $dp_k'/d\bar{p}_2 = 0$ for all k, then an increase in $\bar{p}_2$ would have an unambiguously positive effect on rural income. A rise in the state price, however, could cause the market price for good 1 or 3 to fall or the market price for good 2 to rise. If these changes in market prices were sufficiently large, rural income would decline. Whether rural income ultimately increases or decreases will depend on how market prices change with the state price and on the levels of the rural household's quotas and endowments.

Similarly, rural income can rise or fall with a change in the procurement quota level:

$$\frac{\delta Y_2}{\delta \bar{s}_{22}} = (\bar{p}_2 - p_2') + \frac{dp_1'}{d\bar{s}_{22}}\bar{r}_{21} - \frac{dp_2'}{d\bar{s}_{22}}\bar{s}_{22} + \frac{dp_3'}{d\bar{s}_{22}}\bar{w}_{23}.$$

If market equilibrium prices do not change with $\bar{s}_{22}$ and if the market price exceeds the state price, then a reduction in the quota will unambiguously raise rural income. However, if the adjustment in the quota causes sufficiently large offsetting changes in p_1', p_2', or p_3', rural income would fall.

III. Conclusions

Recent developments in China's agricultural commerce can be understood in terms of the theoretical analysis above. The oversupply of grain to the state and the rapid accumulation of unsold state grain stockpiles in the early 1980s occurred because the state above-quota price for grain became too high. State prices may not have been too high initially, but they became so as decollectivisation and increased scope for regional specialisation shifted the grain supply curve outward, thus depressing market prices. Price seasonality, in particular, low market prices at harvest time, the most active season for state procurement, reinforced these problems.

The theoretical analysis also sheds light on other aspects of China's recent commercial experience. With the convergence of market to state above-quota prices, losses on state trade grew. Government revenues from industry were also shrinking because of concurrent reforms permitting enterprises to retain some of their profits and because changes in state and market prices had reduced the lump-sum transfer going to industry. These factors contributed to increasing budgetary deficits.

In the new environment income transfers associated with procurement and ration quotas became more noticeable, and the resulting inequities began to cause concern. In addition, quota evasion grew to unprecedented levels. Such were the consequences of the widened differential between quota prices and the prices received on the market or for above-quota deliveries. It is not surprising that in the wake of these developments the government chose to eliminate the two-tier price structure and set a cap on procurement of farm products.

The theoretical analysis above yields several general conclusions about the nature of a mixed plan and market system of the sort observed in China. The first is that commercial planning need not cause inefficiency or a Pareto-inferior allocation of resources. A plan in which all state prices are lower than equilibrium market prices and in which the transfer to industry T0 is zero (or is used in an optimal way) can achieve a Pareto-optimal equilibrium allocation of resources.[15] Furthermore, since planning causes lump-sum transfers among agents and between agents and the state, the government can use planning as an efficient means to pursue distributional or tax objectives. Adjustments in state prices and quotas affect not only the size of transfers but also equilibrium market prices; therefore, planners should understand that resulting income changes in the values of endowments caused by shifts in equilibrium market prices.

In a mixed system, plan and market interact in several ways. State prices and quotas affect equilibrium market prices and quantities traded privately. Similarly, markets influence the operation of planning. If state-planned prices are too low or too high relative to equilibrium market prices, evasion or budgetary deficits may erode plan sustainability. Furthermore, whenever market prices exceed state prices, state prices and quotas will no longer directly influence production and consumption.

Allowing markets to emerge alongside state planning, then, both enhances and limits the power of planning. Markets enhance planning's distributional function and improve allocational efficiency in the mixed economy. Yet markets also limit the state's ability to direct production and consumption by means of planned quotas and prices.

Acknowledgements

I wish to thank participants in the ACLS–SSRC-sponsored conference on Price and Wage Reform in the People's Republic of China, June 1986, Washington, DC, for comments on an earlier version, and also John Geanakoplos, Herbert Scarf, Robin Cowan, and an anonymous referee for their helpful suggestions. This research was supported in part by the Food Research Institute, Stanford University, and also by grants from the Rockefeller Brothers Fund and the Joint Committee on Chinese Studies of the ACLS–SSRC with funds provided by the Andrew W. Mellon Foundation.

Notes

1. Such opinions have been expressed in articles by Chinese economists and policy-makers (Liu 1986; Dai 1986; Xue et al. 1986).
2. Real growth in the volume of market trade over this period was slightly less than what is indicated by these nominal figures since the level of market prices rose during this period. Available evidence on market price levels indicates that prices rose by a total of 3–4 per cent between 1977 and 1984 (State Statistical Bureau, Department of Commercial and Price Statistics, 1984:395–97; State Statistical Bureau, 1985:95). The increases in the market price were relatively modest because under the restricted market situation prevalent in 1977, free-market prices were already quite high.
3. Huang (1983:36–7) discusses use of negotiated pricing for this purpose in Guangdong province.

4. With the exception of 1980, when grain output fell 3 per cent and deliveries to the state declined by less than 1 per cent.
5. Note that the degree of underfulfillment increased despite the fact that quota levels were being reduced.
6. A second important factor contributing to losses in state agricultural trade was the inversion of state procurement and retail prices.
7. *Jiage lilun yu shijian*, 1985, no 4:51. This change to a single-price system not only eliminated some of the structural problems with the above-quota bonus method but also effectively lowered the marginal prices the state paid for above-quota deliveries.
8. In 1985 state grain procurement declined by 16 per cent, and the government budgetary deficit was reduced (Sicular 1986:38a; State Statistical Bureau 1986:545, 595).
9. Research by Granick (1986) and Wong (1986) suggests that industrial producers in China have to some extent been guided by profits, especially in the reform period, but still are not simple profit-maximising agents. For the purposes of this paper, however, profit maximisation is a useful assumption.
10. The close link between industrial profits and government revenues also applies in certain other socialist economies.
11. I make these assumptions for notational simplicity. In China the prevalent policy has been to set the purchase price higher than the sales price for agricultural products and the sales price higher than the purchase price for industrial products. Furthermore, the sums of purchase and sales quotas probably do not all equal zero. Differences between state purchase and sales prices and non-zero sums of quotas can be incorporated into the model quite easily. They will change the equilibrium solution but will not qualitatively alter the conclusions.
12. If state procurement and ration quotas did not sum to zero, then market-clearing prices would equal those that would occur if the government carried out lump-sum transfers and injected (or subtracted) some fixed quantity of output on to (from) the market.
13. See Sicular (1986:36–41) for a discussion of China's use of prices for implicit taxation.
14. The mathematical derivation of the comparative

statics results discussed here will be provided by the author on request.
15. This result may not hold if the plan design is different from that assumed here or is difficult to enforce, if rent-seeking behaviour of the sort described by Krueger (1974) emerges, or if markets are permitted for some but not all goods.

References

Almanac of China's Economy Editorial Board, 1984. *Zhongguo jingji nianjian*, 1984 (Almanac of China's economy), Jingji Guanli Chuban She, Beijing.

Byrd, William, A., 1987. 'The Market Mechanism and Economic Reforms in Chinese Industry', PhD dissertation, Harvard University.

Dai, Yuanzhen, 1986. 'Jingji tizhi moshi zhuanhuan guocheng zhongde shuangzhong jiage' (Two kinds of pricing in the process of changing our economic structural model), *Jingji yanjiu*, (1):43–8.

Drèze, Jacques, H., 1975. 'Existence of an Exchange Equilibrium under price Rigidities', *Internal Econon. Rev.* June, (16):301–20.

Ellman, Michael, 1975. 'Did the Agricultural Surplus Provide the Resources for the Increase in Investment in the USSR during the First Five Year Plan?' *Econ. J.* December, (85):844–63.

Feltenstein, Andrew, 1979. 'Market Equilibrium in a Model of a Planned Economy of the Soviet Type: A Proof of Existence and Results of Numerical Simulations', *Rev. Econ. Studies*, October, (46):631–52.

Granick, David, 1986. 'Prices and the Behaviour of Chinese State Industrial Enterprises: Focus on the Multi-Price System', June, 17–18, Paper prepared for ACLS–SSRC Workshop on Wage and Price Reform in the People's Republic of China, Washington, DC.

Guo, Zhiqiang, and Gu, Jianshi, 1983. 'Mianhua chaogou jiajia cujinle shengchan, dan yeyou bibing' (Above-quota price bonuses for cotton have promoted production, but also have drawbacks), *Jiage lilun yu shijian*, (5):34–5.

Hayami, Yujiro; Subbarao, K., and Otsuka, Keijiro, 1982. 'Efficiency and Equity in the Producer Levy of India', *American J. Agricultural Econ.* November, (64):655–63.

Huang, Liwu, 1983. 'gongfuye fazhan dui nongchanpin jiagede yinxiang' (Development of industry and sidelines influences agricultural product prices), *Jiage lilun yu shijian*, (6):36–7.

Krueger, Anne O., 1974. 'The Political Economy of the Rent-seeking Society', *AER*, June, (64):291–303.

Lardy, Nicholas, R., 1985. 'Agricultural Reform in China', Manuscript, Seattle University, Washington, DC.

Liu, Guogang, 1986. 'Price Reform Essential to Growth', *Beijing Rev.* August 18, (29):14–18.

Millar, James, R., 1974. 'Mass Collectivisation and the Contribution of Soviet Agriculture to the First Five-Year Plan: A Review Article', *Slavic Rev.* December, (33):750–66.

Ministry of Commerce, Institute of Commercial Economic Research, 1984. *Xin Zhongguo shangye shigao* (A short history of commerce in new China), Zhongguo Caizheng Jingji Chuban She, Beijing.

Oi, Jean, C., 1986. 'Peasant Grain Marketing and State Procurement: China's Grain Contracting System, *China Q.* June, (106):272–90.

Perkins, Dwight, H., 1966. *Market Control and Planning in Communist China*, Harvard University Press, Cambridge, Massachusetts.

Sah, Raaj Sumar, and Srinivasan, T.N., 1988. 'Distributional Consequences of Rural Food Levy and Subsidised Urban Rations', *European Econ. Rev* 32(1):141–59.

Sicular, Terry, 1986. 'Grain Pricing: A Key Link in Chinese Economic Policy', Manuscript. Stanford University, Stanford, California.

State Statistical Bureau, 1985. *Zhongguo tongji zhaiyao* (China statistical abstract), Zhongguo Tongji Chuban She, Beijing.

——, 1986. *Zhongguo tongji nianjian* (China statistical abstract), Zhongguo Tongji Chuban She, Beijing.

——, Department of Commercial and Price Statistics, 1984. *Zhongguo maoyi wujia tongji ziliao, 1952–1983* (China commerce and price statistical data), Zhongguo Tongji Chuban She, Beijing.

Walker, Kenneth R., 1984. *Food Grain Procurement and Consumption in China*, Cambridge University Press, New York.

Wang, Dahuai, 1985. 'Nongchanpin jiage zhishi jiangzuo: Liangshi he youliao jiage (shang); (A course of lectures on agricultural prices: Grain and oilseeds prices [first half]), *Jiage lilun yu shijian*, (2):50–3.

Wang, Zhenzhi, and Wang, Yongzhi, 1984. 'Woguo jinnianlai nongchanpin jiage wenti taolun quinguang pingjie' (A review of the state of discussion on recent agricultural price problems in our country), *Jiage lilun yu shijian*, (2):28–30.

Wong, Christine P.W., 1986. 'The Economics of Shortage and the Problem of Reform in Chinese Industry', *J. Comparative Econ.* 10:363–87.

Wu, Zhenkun, 1982. 'Several Issues in the Continued Reliance of Agriculture on Economic Planning' (in Chinese), *Renmin Ribao*, May 27:5.

Xu, Yi; Chen, Baosen; and Liang, Wuxia, 1982. *Shehui zhuyi jiage wenti* (Price questions under socialism), Zhongguo Caizheng Jingji Chuban She, Beijing.

Xu, Changrong, et al. 1986. 'Woguo jiage guanli moshide jige wenti' (A few questions regarding our country's model of price management), *Jiage lilun yu shijian*, (2)17–20.

Xue, Muqiao, 1985. '1979 Nian yilai wending he tiaozheng wujia wenti' (Problems of stabilising and adjusting prices since 1979), *Jingji yanjiu*, (6):39–53.

10 Rural Reforms and Agricultural Growth in China

Justin Yifu Lin

China's agricultural growth in the socialist period prior to the reforms starting in the late 1970s was sluggish. Despite stress on self-sufficiency, grain production and agricultural output barely kept pace with population growth. This picture changed in 1978, when China began a series of fundamental reforms in the rural sector. Growth rates in all major sectors of agriculture were accelerated to levels several times higher than the long-term averages over the preceding period (see Table 1).

The dramatic growth during 1978–1984 was a result of a package of market-oriented reforms. As the rural reforms were so successful, the government was encouraged to take a bolder approach to reforms in both rural and urban sectors in 1985. Although agriculture as a whole still grew at a respectable rate of 4.1 per cent per year thereafter, rapid growth in the subsector of crops, especially grain and cotton, came to a sudden halt (see Table 1). Since most prominent leaders in China have an obsession with the idea of grain self-sufficiency, the disappointing performance of grain production has endangered the future of the market-oriented reforms.

Much has been written about China's economic reform.[1] There are disagreements among students of the Chinese economy about the main reasons behind the remarkable agricultural growth since 1979. The major changes are as follows. The state procurement prices for major crops, on the average, were raised 22.1 per cent in 1979. The change from the collective system to the individual household-based farming system, now called the household-responsibility system (hereafter HRS), began in 1979 and was essentially completed by the end of 1983. The government has also introduced several other changes in its policies of grain procurement and marketing since 1979. Moreover, in addition to the aforementioned reforms, the availability of purchased inputs, particularly chemical fertilisers, increased substantially during this period.

Identifying the sources of the rapid agricultural growth during 1978–1984 is important for the future course of rural reforms in China. If the change from the collective system to HRS was the major factor underlying the sudden output growth, then future reforms should be oriented toward strengthening the position of household farms. On the other hand, recollectivisation would be the logical course if the shift to HRS was detrimental to production,

Reprinted with permission. Justin Yifu Lin, 1992. 'Rural reforms and agricultural growth in China', *American Economic Review*, 82(1), March:34–51 (with minor editing).

Table 1   Average annual growth rates of agriculture, 1952–1987

	Annual growth rate (percentage)		
Subsector	1952–1978	1978–1984	1984–1987
Crops	2.5	5.9	1.4
Grain	2.4	4.8	-0.2
Cotton	2.0	17.7	-12.9
Animal husbandry	4.0	10.0	8.5
Fishery	19.9[a]	12.7	18.6
Forestry	9.4	14.9	0
Sidelines	11.2	19.4	18.5
Agriculture (overall)	2.9	7.7	4.1

Notes: In 1952, the weights of the five agriculture subsectors were: crops, 83.1 per cent; animal husbandry, 11.5 per cent; fishery, 0.3 per cent; forestry, 0.7 per cent; sidelines, 4.4 per cent. In 1987, the weights were: crops, 60.7 per cent; animal husbandry, 22.8 per cent; fishery, 4.7 per cent; forestry, 4.8 per cent; sidelines, 7.0 per cent. For sidelines, outputs from village-run enterprises were excluded.
[a] The low base level in 1952 is the main reason for fishery's high average annual growth during 1952–1978.
Source: Ministry of Agriculture Planning Bureau (1989:112–5, 146–9, 189–92) and Ministry of Agriculture (1989:28, 34).

its harmful impact simply being compensated by rapid output growth arising from rises in price, increases in inputs, and other reforms. The main purpose of this paper is to disentangle the contribution to output growth of the HRS reform from those of other reforms, as well as from that of increased input availability.

Few attempts have been undertaken to assess the effects of particular components of the reforms. Exceptions include Lin (1989), Wen (1989), and McMillan et al. (1989). All three studies identify HRS as the main source of the dramatic output growth. However, there are serious drawbacks with each of these three studies.[2]

This paper applies the production-function approach proposed by Griliches (1963) to evaluate the effects of the various components of reforms on agricultural growth. The data used in this study are the province-level panel data from 1970 to 1987 for 28 of the 29 provinces in mainland China. The novelty of the present study, however, is the inclusion of separate proxies for changes in institution, prices, crop patterns, cropping intensity, and technology in the production function to assess the impacts of these changes.

I. Rural Reforms in China

Broad changes in rural policy began at the end of 1978. The government's original intention was to improve agricultural production through raising the long-depressed state procurement prices for major crops, modifying management methods within the collective system, and increasing budgetary expenditure on agricultural investments. The change from the collective system to the household-based farming system— the most far-reaching change to date in China's economic reforms—was explicitly prohibited in 1978.

Price reform

Before the reforms, two distinct prices existed in the state commercial system: quota prices and above-quota prices. Quota prices applied to crops sold in fulfillment of procurement obligations; above-quota prices applied to crops sold in excess of the obligation. Effective in 1979, quota prices for grain, oil crops, cotton, sugar crops, and pork were raised an average of 17.1 per cent. In addition, the premium paid for above-quota delivery of grain and oil crops was increased from 30 per cent to 50 per cent of the quota prices, and a 30 per cent bonus was instituted for above-quota delivery of cotton.[3] The weighted average increase was 22.1 per cent. If only the marginal prices, that is, the above-quota prices, are considered, the increase was 40.7 per cent (see column 1, Table 2).

Corresponding to the increase in procurement prices, retail prices for pork, fish and eggs were raised one-third, but no changes were made in grain and edible-oil prices. To compensate for this, each urban resident received a 5–8 yuan subsidy per month (State Statistical Bureau. 1988a:12). As a result, the government's price subsidies increased substantially. The financial burden became especially unbearable when an unexpected growth in output began to emerge in 1982. The price subsidies increased from 8.4

per cent of the state budget to 24.6 per cent of the state budget in 1984 (*China Statistical Yearbook* 1988:747, 763). As a way to reduce the state's burden and to increase the role of markets, the mandatory quotas were abolished (for cotton in 1984 and for grain in 1985) and replaced by procurement contracts which were supposed to be negotiated between the government and the farmers. The contract price was a weighted average of the basic quota price and the above-quota price. This change resulted in a 9.2 per cent drop in the price margin paid to farmers (see Table 2). Following the decline of grain and cotton production in 1985 and stagnation thereafter, however, the contracts were made mandatory again in 1986.

Alongside state commercial channels, market fairs have always existed and played an

Table 2 **Price index** (1978 = 100)

Year	State above-quota price index (1)	Rural-market consumer price index (2)	Rural industrial-product price index (3)	Ratio of state above-quota price to industrial-product price index (4)	Ratio of market price to industrial-product price index (5)
1970	97.2	80.4	101.9	95.4	78.9
1971	98.4	87.4	100.4	98.0	87.1
1972	98.4	94.6	99.8	98.6	94.8
1973	98.1	99.6	99.8	98.3	99.8
1974	98.4	101.4	99.8	98.6	101.6
1975	98.7	105.5	99.8	98.9	105.7
1976	99.4	109.7	99.9	98.5	109.8
1977	100.0	107.0	100.0	100.0	107.0
1978	100.0	100.0	100.0	100.0	100.0
1979	140.7	95.5	100.1	140.4	95.4
1980	140.4	97.4	100.9	139.2	96.5
1981	145.1	103.0	101.9	142.3	101.1
1982	144.3	106.5	103.6	139.3	102.8
1983	144.9	110.9	104.6	138.6	106.1
1984	142.5	110.5	107.8	132.1	102.5
1985	129.4	129.5	111.3	116.2	116.3
1986	130.1	140.0	114.9	113.3	121.9
1987	130.2	162.8	120.4	108.1	135.2

Sources: Lin, Justin Yifu, 1992. 'Rural reforms and agricultural growth in China', *American Economic Review*, 82(1), March:34–51.

important role in rural China. Farmers, after fulfilling their quota obligations, could sell their produce in market fairs. With rare exceptions, the market prices are higher than the state procurement prices, even measured with the above-quota premiums. Moreover, as Table 2 shows, market prices and state procurement prices do not always move in the same direction. Table 2 also reports the time-series of state procurement prices and market prices relative to the prices of manufactured inputs in rural markets, which will be used in Section III to estimate the impact of price changes on agricultural growth.

Institutional reform

The change in farming institution from the collective system to HRS was not originally intended by the government. Before the reform, agricultural operations were organised in the production-team system. Each team consisted of about 20–30 neighbouring households. Because of difficulties in monitoring agricultural work in a team, rewards to individual farmers were not tied directly to their efforts, and incentives to work were thus very low (Lin 1988).

It was acknowledged in 1978 that the key to improving the farmer's incentives was to solve the managerial problems in the team system. However, the government at that time considered subdivision of collectively owned land into individual household tracts to be opposed to socialist principles, and thus it explicitly prohibited this practice. Nevertheless, toward the end of 1978, a small number of production teams, first secretly and later with the blessing of local authorities, began to try out the system of contracting land, other resources, and output quotas to individual households. A year later, these teams brought in yields far larger than those of other teams. The central authorities later conceded the existence of this new form of farming but required that it be restricted to poor regions. However, most teams ignored this restriction. Full official acceptance of HRS was eventually given in late 1981, when 45 per cent

of the production teams in China had already been dismantled. By the end of 1983, 98 per cent of production teams had adopted HRS (see column 1 in Table 3). Thus, the shift in the institutional structure of Chinese agriculture by and large evolved spontaneously in response to underlying economic forces (Lin 1987). Under HRS, collectively owned land was assigned to individual households with contracts of up to 15 years.[4]

The government so far still stresses its intention of maintaining the stability of the newly instituted HRS. However, the doctrine of equating advanced technology with big tractors and efficiency with large farm size is still deeply rooted in the minds of many scholars and prominent leaders in China (Ash 1988). Due to increasing discontent with the stagnation of grain production after 1984, the call for recollectivisation has emerged, under the guise of enlarging operational size to exploit returns to scale. In some localities, this call has resulted in disruption of contracts before expiration without the consent of farmers (Yaping Jiang 1988). It is thus possible that farmers may be deprived of the economic independence and greater freedom they have been given in the past 10 years (Johnson 1990:Ch. 8).

Market and planning reform

The third most important element of the reforms is the greater role given to markets in guiding agricultural production. The prevalence of planning in agriculture before the reforms was a result of self-sufficiency in grain. Because grain procurement prices were depressed to levels lower than prevailing market prices, the more grain an area sold to the state, in effect, the more tax it paid. Areas with a comparative advantage in grain production were thus reluctant to raise their grain output levels. Consequently, grain-deficient areas had to increase grain production themselves if local grain demand increased due to growth in population or income. The national self-sufficiency policy thus degenerated into a policy of local self-sufficiency. To guarantee that

Table 3   **HRS, crop pattern, and cropping intensity**

| Year | Household responsibility system (1) | Sown area (percentage) | | | Multiple cropping index (percentage) (5) |
		Grain crops (2)	Cash crops (3)	Other (4)	
1970	0	83.1	8.2	8.7	141.9
1971	0	83.1	8.2	8.7	144.7
1972	0	81.9	8.5	9.6	147.0
1973	0	81.6	8.6	9.8	148.2
1974	0	81.4	8.7	9.9	148.7
1975	0	81.0	9.0	10.0	150.0
1976	0	80.6	9.2	10.2	150.6
1977	0	80.6	9.1	10.3	150.5
1978	0	80.4	9.6	10.0	151.0
1979	0.01	80.3	10.0	9.7	149.2
1980	0.14	80.1	10.9	9.0	147.4
1981	0.45	79.2	12.1	8.7	146.6
1982	0.80	78.4	13.0	8.6	146.7
1983	0.98	79.2	12.3	8.5	146.4
1984	0.99	78.3	13.4	8.3	146.9
1985	0.99	75.8	15.6	8.6	148.4
1986	0.99	76.9	14.1	9.0	150.0
1987	0.99	76.8	14.3	8.9	151.3

Note: Column 1 indicates the proportion of production teams in China that had adopted the household-responsibility system.
Sources: The data for column 1, 1979–1981, are from *Economic Weekly News* [Jingjixue Zhoubao] (11 January 1982). Figures for 1982–1984 are taken from *China Agricultural Yearbook* (1984:69; 1985:120). Figures for 1985–1987 are inferred from the fact that no major change has occurred in the farming institution since 1984. Columns 2–5 are taken from Ministry of Agriculture Planning Bureau (1984:132; 1989:130–1, 335–7) and *China Statistical Yearbook* (1988:224, 243, 276).

each region would produce enough grain for its needs, planning in agricultural production was extensive. Mandatory targets often specified not only acreage for each crop, but also yields, levels of inputs, and so on. As planners gave priority to grain, insufficient consideration was given to profitability and regional comparative advantage. To increase grain output to meet state procurement quotas or local demand, local governments often expanded grain acreage at the expense of cash crops or raised cropping intensity to a level that brought net losses to farmers.

At the beginning of the reforms, the government recognised the losses in allocation efficiency caused by the self-sufficiency policy.

The decision to increase grain imports, cut down grain procurement quotas, and reduce the number of products included in agricultural planning reflected an intention to increase the role of markets.[5] Moreover, the government loosened restrictions on private interregional trade in agricultural products. Special measures were also taken to encourage areas with traditional comparative advantage in cotton production to expand cotton acreage.[6]

All the aforementioned reforms reduced the role of state intervention and increased the function of markets in guiding agricultural production. As a result, cropping patterns and cropping intensity changed substantially between 1978 and 1984. The area devoted to cash crops increased from 9.6 per cent of total sown acreage in 1978 to 13.4 per cent in 1984, a 41.6-per cent increase; meanwhile, the multiple cropping index declined from 151 to 146.9 (see Table 3).

The climax of the market and planning reform was the declaration at the beginning of 1985 that the state would no longer set any mandatory production plans in agriculture and that obligatory procurement quotas were to be replaced by purchasing contracts between the state and farmers. The restoration of household farming and the increase in market freedom prompted farmers to adjust their production activities in accordance with profit margins. The acreage devoted to cash crops further expanded, while grain acreage declined (see Table 3). The expansions in animal husbandry, fishery, and subsidiary production were even faster. As a result of these adjustments, agriculture still grew at a respectable rate of 4.1 per cent annually during 1984–1987, although, the crop sector stagnated (see Table 1).

The market-oriented reforms had aroused anxiety in some sectors of the government from their very beginning. Concerns over 'loss of control' were widely reported in the early 1980s (Sicular 1988). In the wake of unprecedented success between 1978 and 1984, the pro-market group was able to push the reforms further in the market direction. However, when growth rates slowed down and grain output declined in 1985 and thereafter, the government retreated from its position. The voluntary procurement contract was made mandatory again. Throughout the period 1985–1991, administrative intervention in market and production has been increasing.

The above events are the major components of the rural reforms since 1978. As described, the

Table 4   **Index of crop output and inputs** (1978 = 100)

Year	Crop output	Farm labour	Labour in cropping sector	Land	Capital	Chemical fertilisers
	(1)	(2)	(3)	(4)	(5)	(6)
1970	77.10	99.09	103.04	101.76	51.73	36.30
1971	82.82	101.16	104.00	101.29	58.60	41.55
1972	80.48	100.78	102.04	101.20	64.04	47.94
1973	88.25	102.91	103.76	100.80	69.02	58.52
1974	91.50	102.93	104.21	100.50	75.05	55.08
1975	94.22	100.81	103.35	100.11	79.97	60.87
1976	92.43	100.65	102.46	99.98	85.55	66.06
1977	91.47	100.05	100.41	99.82	93.09	73.09
1978	100.00	100.00	100.00	100.00	100.00	100.00
1979	107.10	102.17	103.66	100.10	104.22	120.15
1980	102.36	104.75	107.63	99.91	122.12	134.29
1981	108.52	107.81	111.58	99.44	131.74	141.44
1982	119.60	109.48	112.82	99.21	141.16	156.00
1983	129.42	111.22	115.34	98.89	153.40	169.06
1984	142.23	111.35	114.69	98.89	165.29	171.62
1985	139.52	106.65	104.56	97.46	176.65	167.38
1986	140.76	107.06	95.79	96.81	191.09	183.10
1987	148.21	108.48	88.70	96.47	209.71	192.10

Sources: Lin, Justin Yifu, 1992. 'Rural Reforms and Agricultural Growth in China', *American Economic Review*, 82(1), March:34–51.

reforms were highly successful up to 1984 but have encountered some problems since then. How much of the output growth during 1978–1984 can be attributed to various components of the reforms and what factors have been responsible for the slowdown since 1984 are the focuses of the following sections.

II. Data

The data used in this study include observations for 28 of the 29 provinces in mainland China for 1970–1987.[7] A number of adjustments were required in order to make the data suitable for this study. Detailed information on sources and adjustments is given in the Appendix. Here, I only report a summary description of the data set.

In this study, agricultural output refers to crop outputs.[8] Values of crop output for each province are calculated from the physical outputs of seven grain crops and 12 cash crops, using official prices of 1980 as weights for aggregation. Nationally, these 19 crops accounted for 92 per cent of total acreage and 72.5 per cent of the cropping sector's output value in 1980.[9]

Inputs in the data set include four categories: land, labour, capital, and chemical fertiliser. Land refers to cultivated land; cultivated land is used rather than sown acreage because I also want to see how changes in cropping intensity affected outputs. Labour refers to the number of workers in the cropping sector. Capital includes tractors and draft animals, measured in horsepower. Chemical fertilisers refers to the gross weight of nitrogenous, phosphate and potash fertilisers that each province consumed in each year. The output and input series are summarised in Table 4.

In addition to the four conventional inputs, five other factors are included to reflect various components of the reforms. These measures are the ratio of production teams converted to HRS, the index of above-quota prices and market prices relative to manufactures input prices, the percentage of sown acreage for non-grain crops, and the multiple cropping index (the ratio of sown acreage to cultivated acreage). These measures are used to capture, respectively, the impacts of farming institutional change, state procurement price adjustments, and market reforms. The price indexes are the national indexes, and the other three measures are provincial-level observations.[10]

The total number of observations for each variable is 504. However, since information on the number of production teams converted to HRS in each province in 1980 is not available, that year's observations are deleted, and the actual number of observations that will be used in the analysis is 476. This data set presents an unusual opportunity for undertaking a careful analysis of the impacts of reforms on agricultural growth, as well as an opportunity for estimating the Chinese agricultural production function econometrically.[11]

III. Functional Form Specification and Results

If production were purely an engineering relationship between inputs and outputs, any variation in inputs, except for those due to random shocks, would be a result of changes in inputs. However, the observed production function in general is an economic relationship, as the intensity with which observed resources are utilised depends on economic decisions made by workers as well as managers in response to institutional arrangements, profitable opportunities, and so on (Leibenstein 1966; Carter 1984; McMillan et al. 1989). Therefore, the technical efficiency of production can be altered by economic reforms.

Changes in relative prices are expected to affect not only the level of input use, but also the choice between work and leisure as in standard microeconomic analysis. Adjustments in crop patterns in response to soil, temperature, rainfall, and other region-specific characteristics are a major source of productivity growth in agriculture.[12] Changes in the multiple cropping index reflect, in a way, how intensively land and labour inputs are utilised. Finally, any change in

143

farming institution alters the compensation scheme and is expected to affect the level of effort supplied by each farmer.

The agricultural-production function estimated is a Cobb-Douglas function with four conventional inputs: land, labour, capital, and chemical fertiliser (Fert). In addition, six other variables are included in the function: the proportion of teams that have changed to the household responsibility system (HRS), the index of market prices relative to manufactured input prices (MP), the index of above-quota prices relative to manufactured input prices (GP), the percentage of total sown area in non-grain crops (NGCA), the multiple cropping index (MCI), and a time trend (T) (see the Appendix for variable definitions). The non-conventional variables are incorporated to assess the impacts of farming institutional change, price adjustments, market reforms, and technological changes. Because the productivity of conventional inputs also depends on some omitted time-persistent region-specific variables (e.g. soil quality, rainfall, irrigation, temperature, average education level, etc.), 27 provincial dummies are included in the production function in order to obtain consistent estimates. This specification gives rise to the estimation equation:

$$\ln(Y_{it}) = \alpha_1 + \alpha_2 \ln(\text{Land}_{it})$$
$$+ \alpha_3 \ln(\text{Labour}_{it})$$
$$+ \alpha_4 \ln(\text{Capital}_{it}) + \alpha_5 \ln(\text{Fert}_{it})$$
$$+ \alpha_6 \text{HRS}_{it} + \alpha_7 \text{MP}_{t-1} + \alpha_8 \text{GP}_t$$
$$+ \alpha_9 \text{NGCA}_{it} + \alpha_{10} \text{MCI}_{it} + \alpha_{11} T_t$$
$$+ \sum_{j=12}^{39} a_j D_j + \varepsilon_{it}$$

(1)

where the α's are the parameters to be estimated, and ε is the error term. The output and the four conventional inputs are in natural-logarithm form. Because size of province varies greatly, to prevent the heteroscedastic problem, the output as well as the conventional input variables are normalised by the number of teams in each province in 1980. Theoretically, the relevant price

variables should be the expected prices. For the government procurement price, the current prices at each year are the expected prices at that year, because changes in the state procurement prices are announced prior to the beginning of the production season. However, for the market prices, price expectation is a complicated function of past experience and other information on the economy (Muth 1961). Since no information about the structure of market-price expectation in China is available, the market prices are taken simply as the prices in the previous year.

The above specification is in the form of a one-way fixed-effects model. For comparative purposes, a two-way fixed-effects model, which includes both regional dummies and year dummies in the specification, will also be estimated. In the two-way fixed effects model, the price variables have to be deleted because they are region-invariant national indexes. The coefficients of time dummies capture partly the impacts of year-to-year price changes on productivity. The resulting specification is as follows:

$$\ln(Y_{it}) = \alpha_1' + \alpha_2' \ln(\text{Land}_{it})$$
$$+ \alpha_3' \ln(\text{Labour}_{it})$$
$$+ \alpha_4' \ln(\text{Capital}_{it})$$
$$\alpha_5' \ln(\text{Fert}_{it}) + \alpha_6' \text{HRS}_{it}$$
$$\alpha_7' \text{NGCA}_{it} + \alpha_8' \text{MCI}_{it}$$
$$+ \sum_{j=9}^{36} \alpha_j' D_j + \sum_{k=37}^{52} \alpha_k' T_k + \varepsilon_{it}'.$$

(1')

Expression (1) is designed with the intention of estimating the impacts of reforms in institution, price, and the role of markets on *productivity*. However, application levels of conventional inputs, the crop pattern (NGCA), and cropping intensity (MCI) may be endogenous to the shift to HRS and to price changes. If this is so, the impacts of HRS and price changes on *production* may be over- or underestimated in the specification of expression (1). Therefore, to assess their total impacts on agricultural production, I will also estimate a supply-response function in the form:

144

(2)

$$\ln(Y_{it}) = \beta_1 + \beta_2 \mathrm{HRS}_{it} + b_3 \mathrm{MP}_{t-1}$$
$$+ b_4 \mathrm{GP}_t + \beta_5 T_t$$
$$+ \sum_{i=6}^{33} \beta_i D_i + \mu_{it}.$$

T in this specification will capture not only the trend in technological change, but also the trend in the availability of inputs.

The appropriate method for obtaining consistent estimates of expressions (1) and (2) depends on the structure of disturbances ε_{it} and μ_{it}. If ε_{it} and μ_{it} are spherical disturbances, the covariance estimator of ordinary least squares (OLS) is the best linear unbiased estimator. If production is inside the efficiency frontier and the disturbance can be specified as the difference of two independent terms, one with a normal distribution and the other one with a positive-half normal distribution, the stochastic-frontier regression developed by Aigner et al. (1977) will produce consistent estimates of parameters. If there exist intertemporal correlations and the covariance matrix is unknown, then the appropriate method for fitting expressions (1) and (2) is estimated generalised least squares (EGLS).

As a first step, I apply both OLS and the stochastic-production-frontier model to estimate expression (1). The results are reported in columns 1 and 2 of Table 5. For the sake of simplicity, the estimates for regional dummies are not presented. Except for the index of above-quota prices (GP), all other estimates have the expected positive sign in both models, and except for capital, the index of market prices (MP), the index of above-quota prices (GP), and the time trend (T), all other estimates are highly statistically significant. Moreover, the estimates resulting from the stochastic-production-frontier model differ little from the least-squares estimates.

The last row of column (1) reports the estimated intertemporal correlation of the disturbance:

$$r_{it,it-1} = \left(\sum_{i=1}^{28} \sum_{t=1}^{17} e_{it} , e_{it-1} \right) \left(\sum_{i=1}^{28} \sum_{t=1}^{17} e_{it} \right)$$

where e_{it} represents the estimates for ε_{it}. The resulting $r_{it,it-1}$ is −0.15. Under the null hypothesis of no intertemporal or spatial correlation, $r_{it,it-1}$ has a standard error $N^{-1/2}$, where N is the number of observations (Judge et al. 1985:319). There are 476 observations in the sample, and the standard error under the null hypothesis is 0.046. Hence, the evidence suggests that intertemporal correlations exist in the disturbances. Although OLS still produces unbiased estimates for regression coefficients, the significance tests for the estimated coefficients are invalid.

In a one-way fixed-effects model with unknown intertemporal covariance, the individual effects cannot be consistently estimated when the time period is fixed. Kiefer (1980) suggested that one could first eliminate individual effects by subtracting group means from both regressand and regressor and then estimate regression coefficients and the asymptotic variance-covariance matrix by EGLS. The estimates resulting from applying Kiefer's estimator to expression (1) are reported in column 3 of Table 5. As expected, the estimated coefficients differ little from those estimated using OLS, and their associated standard errors are uniformly smaller than those of OLS. While the estimates for market prices (MP), above-quota procurement prices (GP), and time record (T) are still not significantly different from zero, the estimate for capital is statistically significant at the 0.05 level (asymptotic $t = 1.85$). Column 4 reports the estimates when the insignificant variables MP, GP, and T are dropped. The resulted estimates are basically the same as those in column 3. I shall adopt the estimates in column 4 for growth accounting in the next section.[13]

Column 5 of Table 5 reports the results of applying Kiefer's estimator to expression (2). The estimates for HRS are almost identical to those in columns 3 and 4. However, the estimated coefficients for the index of market prices (MP), the index of above quota prices (GP), and time trend (T) are larger than those in column 3 and, in fact, are highly statistically significant.

145

Table 5   **Estimates of production and supply response function** (dependent variable = LN (value of crop output in constant prices))

Explanatory variable	One-way fixed-effects					Two-way fixed-effects
	OLS	Stochastic frontier	EGLS			
	(1)	(2)	(3)	(4)	(5)	(6)
ln(Land)	0.65	0.59	0.67	0.67		0.58
	(0.07)	(0.05)	(0.04)	(0.04)		(0.09)
ln(Labour)	0.14	0.11	0.14	0.13		0.15
	(0.03)	(0.03)	(0.02)	(0.01)		(0.03)
ln(Capital)	0.037	0.057	0.050	0.070		0.10
	(0.040)	(0.034)	(0.027)	(0.015)		(0.04)
ln(Fert)	0.18	0.18	0.20	0.19		0.17
	(0.02)	(0.02)	(0.01)	(0.01)		(0.02)
Proportion in household farming (HRS)	0.19	0.22	0.19	0.20	0.18	0.15
	(0.03)	(0.03)	(0.01)	(0.01)	(0.01)	(0.05)
(Market price)/ (input price) at time $t-1(MP_{t-1})$	0.00038	0.0010	0.00051		0.0034	
	(0.00123)	(0.0013)	(0.00061)		(0.0007)	
(Government price)/ (input price) at time t (GP_t)	-0.00067	-0.00054	-0.00058		0.0021	
	(0.00055)	(0.00059)	(0.00035)		(0.0004)	
Multiple cropping index (MCI)	0.0020	0.0018	0.0015	0.0020		0.0020
	(0.0009)	(0.0011)	(0.0006)	(0.0006)		(0.0008)
Percentage of non-grain crops (NGCA)	0.0067	0.0093	0.0068	0.0078		0.0078
	(0.0023)	(0.0023)	(0.0015)	(0.0013)		(0.0022)
Time trend (T)	0.0065	0.0005	0.0028		0.021	
	(0.0065)	(0.0068)	(0.0042)		(0.003)	
Regional dummies	yes	yes				yes
Time dummies						yes
Adjusted R^2;	0.961					0.966
Log likelihood:		430.35				
$R_{it,it-1}$:	-0.15					

Notes: Numbers in parentheses are standard errors or estimated asymptotic standard errors. The estimated coefficients of 27 provincial dummies in columns 1, 2 and 6, and of 16 year dummies in column 6 are not reported.

The results of fitting the two-way fixed-effects model of expression (1′) are presented in column 6. All the estimated coefficients are in the same range as the estimates in column 4. These results support the use of the estimates in column 4 for growth accounting in the next section.

From the evidence presented in columns 3, 4, 5, and 6 of Table 5, one can conclude that the shift from the production-team system to HRS had a positive and significant effect on agricultural growth, which came primarily from the change in total factor productivity. The changes in both state procurement prices and market prices also had significant effects on agricultural growth. However, in contrast to the case of institutional reform, these effects derived from impacts on levels of input usage, cropping intensity (MCI), and crop composition (NGCA). The estimated coefficient of the time trend (T) is not statistically significant in column 3, but it is positive and highly significant in column 5. This implies that there was no increasing trend in technological change but that there was a positive trend in agricultural output growth during 1970–1987. The latter trend might stem from the increasing availability of inputs such as chemical fertilisers. The positive and significant estimates of cropping intensity (MCI) and crop composition (NGCA) in columns 3, 4, and 6 suggest that, given the inputs and other variables, an increase in the cropping intensity or in the proportion of non-grain crops will also result in an increase in output.

IV. Sources of Agricultural Growth During 1978–1984 and 1984–1987

This section attempts to assess the relative contributions of the various components of reforms and changes in inputs to agricultural growth in 1978–1984 and 1984–1987. Table 6 reports the growth accounting based on the estimate of the agricultural production function in column 4 of Table 5, and Table 7 reports that based on the supply-response function estimated

in column 5. In Table 6, the sources of output growth are divided into three categories: change in conventional inputs, productivity change due to reforms, and unexplained residual. The first two categories are in turn subdivided into several items. In Table 7, the sources of output growth are divided into the shift to HRS, the changes in market prices and state procurement prices, the time trend, and the residual.

The total output growth during 1978–1984 was 42.23 per cent. From the accounting in Table 6, it appears that 45.79 per cent of this output growth came from increases in inputs. The most important source of growth from inputs was the increase in the application of fertiliser, which alone contributed to about one-third (32.2 per cent) of the output growth during 1978–1984. The growth derived from increases in labour and capital and the adverse impact on growth resulting from reduction in cultivated land were minor. Rural reforms also contributed significantly to output growth during 1978–84. The productivity change resulting from various reforms made up 48.64 per cent of the output growth. Among the various components of reform, the shift from the production-team system to HRS is clearly the most important one. This institutional reform alone produced 48.69 per cent of the output growth, as much as the combined effects of input increases. The changes in cropping intensity (MCI) and crop pattern (NGCA), which might partially reflect the effect of reforms in the role of planning and markets, had small impacts on growth (one negative and one positive). In this growth accounting, 5.57 per cent of the output growth was unexplained residual.

Although the changes in market prices and state procurement prices during 1978–1984 did not affect the total factor productivity, the growth accounting in Table 7 indicates that the substantial increase in the state procurement price had a significant impact (probably through input use, cropping intensity, and/or crop mix) on output growth, contributing 15.98 per cent of the growth. However, compared to the estimated

42.20 per cent that could be attributed to HRS in the supply-response function, the impact of price changes on output growth was not spectacular.[14]

Tables 6 and 7 also attempt to account for the slowdown in output growth after 1984. Several causes might be responsible for such a change.

As Table 6 shows, the dominant reasons for the spectacular growth during 1978–1984 were HRS reform and the sharp increase in the use of chemical fertilisers. The HRS reform was completed in 1983–1984. Therefore, even without any other cause, the rate of output growth would

Table 6   **Accounting for crop output growth: production function**

Explanatory variable	Estimated coefficient (1)	1978–1984		1984–1987	
		Change in explanatory variable (2)	Contribution to growth (percentage) (3) = (1) x (2)	Change in explanatory variable (4)	Contribution to growth (percentage) (5) = (1) x (4)
Inputs			19.34 (45.79)		-0.42 (-9.97)
Land	0.67	- 1.1	-0.74 (-1.75)	-2.4	-1.61 (-38.24)
Labour	0.13	14.7	1.91 (4.52)	-22.7	-2.95 (-70.07)
Capital	0.07	65.3	4.57 (10.82)	26.9	1.88 (44.73)
Fertiliser	0.19	71.6	13.60 (32.20)	11.9	2.26 (53.71)
Productivity			20.54 (48.64)		2.05 (48.69)
Household-farming reform (HRS)	20.00	0.99	19.80 (46.89)	0	0
Multiple cropping (MCI)	0.20	-4.1	-0.82 (1.94)	4.4	0.88 (20.90)
Ratio of non-grain crops (NGCA)	0.78	2.0	1.56 (3.69)	1.5	1.17 (27.79)
Residual			2.35 (5.57)		2.58 (61.28)
Total growth:			42.23 (100.00)		4.21 (100.00)

Notes: The estimated coefficients are taken from column 4 of Table 5. HRS, multiple cropping index (MCI), and percentage of non-grain crop area (NGCA) are in a semilog form in expression (1). To calculate the contributions of these variables to output growth in terms of percentage, the estimated coefficients of these variables are multiplied by 100. For land, labour, capital, and fertiliser, 'change in explanatory variable' refers to the percentage growth of that variable. For HRS, multiple cropping index (MCI), and percentage of non-grain crop area (NGCA), the change refers to the difference in magnitude of that variable between t_1 and t_2. Changes in output and input are calculated from Table 4; changes in HRS, MCI, and NGCA are from Table 3. The numbers in parentheses are the percentage shares of contribution to total output growth, with total output growth set at 100.

have fallen to about half of the previous level. The growth rate of chemical-fertiliser input dropped from 8.9 per cent per year during 1978–1984 to 3.7 per cent during 1984–1987. If fertiliser use had continued to increase at the previous rate, its contribution to output growth would have been 5.54 per cent of the 1984 level, instead of the 2.26 per cent that actually occurred. Moreover, there was a swift outflow of the labour force from the cropping sector to other sectors. The growth rate of the labour force dropped from 2.3 per cent per year during 1978–1984 to –8.6 per cent per year during 1984–1987. This outflow of labour force alone caused output to fall 2.95 per cent compared to the 1984 level. Table 7 shows that the sharp drop in the state procurement prices relative to input prices was probably the determining factor behind

the decrease in the growth rate of chemical-fertiliser usage and the exodus of labour. The change in state procurement prices resulted in a 5.04 per cent drop in output in 1987 compared to the 1984 level. The adverse effect of the drop in state procurement prices on output growth, however, was compensated for by the rise in market prices, which lifted the 1987 output level 5.36 per cent over that of 1984.

V. Concluding Remarks

This paper attempts to evaluate the impacts of various components of reform on agricultural growth in China. The findings indicate that the dominant source of output growth during 1978–1984 was the change from the production-team

Table 7   Accounting for crop output growth: supply-response function

		1978-1984		1984-1987	
Explanatory variable	Estimated coefficient (1)	Change in explanatory variable (2)	Contribution to growth (percentage) (3) = (1) x (2)	Change in explanatory variable (4)	Contribution to growth (percentage) (5) − (1) x (4)
Household-farming reform (HRS)	18.00	0.99	17.82 (42.20)	0.00	0.00
[Market price]/ [input price] (MP)	0.34	-0.93	-0.32 (-0.76)	15.71	5.36 (127.32)
[State procurement price]/ [input price] (GP)	0.21 (15.98)	32.14	6.75 (-119.72)	-24.03	-5.04
Trend (T)	2.10	6.00	12.60 (29.74)	3.00	6.30 (149.64)
Residual			5.38 (12.74)		-2.41 (57.24)
Total growth:			42.23 (100.00)		4.21 (100.00)

Notes: The estimated coefficients are taken from column 5 of Table 5. HRS, index of market price (MP), index of state procurement price (GP), and time trend (T) are in a semilog form in expression (2). To calculate the contributions of these variables to output growth in terms of percentage, the estimated coefficients of these variables are multiplied by 100. The change in explanatory variable refers to the difference in magnitude of that variable between t_1 and t_2. Changes in output and input are calculated from Table 4; change in HRS is from Table 3; and changes in MP and GP are from Table 2. The numbers in parentheses are the percentage shares of contribution to total output growth, with total output growth set at 100.

system to HRS. It is also found that the change in crop pattern away from grain to non-grain crops had a positive impact and that the decline in cropping intensity had a negative impact on growth during 1978–1984. However, both effects were very small in magnitude. The results also suggest that the changes in state procurement prices and market prices had a significant impact on output growth, probably through their influences on application levels of inputs, cropping intensity, and/or crop pattern. However, not all the increases in input use during 1978–1984 could be attributed to the rise in state procurement prices; part of them come from improvements in availability, as revealed by the positive time trend in the supply-response function.

It is worth noting that this paper measures only the one-time discrete impact of the HRS reform on productivity and output growth. The shift from the production-team system to HRS, however, also improves farmers' incentives to adopt new technology and may thus be expected to speed the diffusion of new technology (Lin 1991). Therefore, HRS would also have a long-term, dynamic impact on the growth of agricultural productivity, which is not measured in this paper.

This study also attempts to account for the slowdown in output growth after 1984. In addition to the fact that the one-time discrete effect of the HRS reform had ended in 1984, the evidence suggests that the rapid exodus of the labour force from the cropping sector and the sharp decline in the growth rate of fertiliser usage were responsible for the stagnation. The sharp reduction in state procurement prices is probably the reason for both trends.

The above findings have wider implications than simply improving the understanding of rural reforms in China. An important issue that confronts most developing countries is how to develop agriculture rapidly in order to support industrialisation and to meet the ever-increasing food demand brought on by explosive population growth. Small and fragmented holdings, which

characterise the landscapes in most densely populated developing countries, are often regarded as a great obstacle for mechanisation, irrigation, plant protection, efficient allocation of inputs, and so forth. Consequently, many policy-makers and scholars, not only in China but also in many other developing countries, consider collective farming an attractive method for land consolidation and productivity improvement. However, my findings suggest that the household farm has advantages of its own. Since the household farm leads to a more productive use of inputs, it may be a more appropriate institution for the growth of agriculture in developing countries, including China.

Appendix

For Appendix data sources and adjustment see original source.

Acknowledgements

Justin Yifu Lin is a Senior Fellow, Department of Rural Economy, Development Research Center, 9 Xihuangchenggen Nanjie, Beijing 100032, China, and Associate Professor, Economics Department, Peking University. He thanks two anonymous referees for very helpful comments and suggestions on earlier drafts and Robert Ashmore for exposition improvement.

Notes

1. For a survey of papers by western economists, see Perkins (1988). In addition, there are several books and conference proceedings devoted exclusively to the economic reforms: see for example, Perry and Wong (1985), *Journal of Comparative Economics* (1987), and *China Quarterly* (1988).

2. Lin (1989) employs a production-function approach. The results are suspect due to strong multicollinearity in the estimated production function. The multicollinearity problem arises from the fact that the panel data employed only

cover the period from 1980 to 1983. Wen (1989) estimates a supply-response function. His estimate, based on only 35 observations, is not very credible. McMillan et al. (1989) use a Dennison-Solow-type growth-accounting technique to analyze the national aggregated time-series from 1978 to 1984. The customary criticisms against the Dennison-type growth accounting are applicable to their studies (see Griliches 1963). In addition, their decomposition of the growth in total factor productivity into a price component and an incentive component requires strong assumptions about the form and parameters of the utility function, and their results are sensitive to these assumptions. Furthermore, the price used in their analysis should, theoretically, be marginal price, but they use instead the state above-quota procurement prices, which in general are lower than the prices prevailing in rural markets. Moreover, these two prices often move in opposite directions.

3. For a detailed chronology of the price changes in 1979 and thereafter, see Sicular (1988).

4. For a chronology of the policy evolution, see Ash (1988). For a summary of the development from various types of responsibility systems to HRS, see Yak Yeow Kueh (1984). For a discussion of some new issues related to HRS, see Kojima (1988).

5. For example, net grain imports increased from 6.9 million tons in 1978 to 14.9 million tons in 1982 (Ministry of Agriculture Planning Bureau 1989:522, 535), grain purchase quotas were reduced 2.5 million tons in 1979 (Ash 1988), and the categories of planned products were reduced from 21 in 1978 to 16 in 1981 and were reduced further to only 13 categories in 1982 (Kueh 1984).

6. In 1979, the government instituted a policy that awarded above-quota delivery of cotton with low-priced grain sale. This policy made a substantial expansion of cotton acreage possible in the traditional cotton-producing regions.

7. Tibet is excluded because of the lack of output data.

8. In Chinese statistics, agriculture includes cropping, animal husbandry, forestry, fishery, and sideline production. Forestry, fishery, and sideline production are in general not included in agricultural productivity studies. Animal husbandry is not included, mainly for two

reasons. First, data for the relevant output and input series of animal husbandry previous to 1979 are not available. Secondly, most activities of animal husbandry were carried out by individual households even before the HRS reform; therefore, the institutional reform should not have a direct impact, even though there might have been indirect effects.

9. Those crops excluded from the data set are mainly vegetables and fruits, which command higher value than grain and cash crops.

10. Using the national index as a proxy for state procurement prices will not cause any trouble in the estimation, because the prices are set by the state and implemented uniformly in each province. However, market prices vary across provinces, although the general trends are the same. Using the national market-price index thus may reduce the sharpness with which the influence of market prices on output can be estimated.

11. As pointed out by Perkins and Yusuf (1984:46), attempts by other scholars to estimate the Chinese agricultural production function empirically have not yielded plausible estimates due to the lack of cross-sectional data. A floppy disk containing my data will be provided to researchers upon request.

12. This factor is especially emphasised by Lardy (1983). He attributes much of the stagnation in Chinese agriculture before the recent reform as well as the rapid growth after the reforms to the loss and gain of regional comparative advantages.

13. It would have been preferable to perform a test for the joint insignificance of MP, GP, and T before dropping them from the regression. However, this was not possible because the test statistic for Kiefer's EGLS estimator has not been developed.

14. If one follows the convention of growth accounting and treats residuals as productivity change, then, based on Table 6, the increase in total factor productivity during 1978–1984 was 22.89 per cent, and 89.73 per cent of this increase was attributable to HRS. McMillan et al. (1989) estimated the increase in total factor productivity as 41 per cent and attributed 78 per cent of the increase to HRS. McMillan et al.'s larger estimate for improvement in total factor

productivity is mainly due to the fact that output in their study includes not only crops, but also animal husbandry, fishery, and forestry. According to their definition, the output growth during 1978–1984 was 61.76 per cent. However, with the exception of livestock feed, they employed only those inputs used for crops to construct the index of current inputs and capital. Animal husbandry, fishery, and forestry all had higher rates of growth than crops. Moreover, animal husbandry and fishery are in general more intensive in current inputs and capital than crops. Therefore, McMillan et al.'s estimate of growth in total factor productivity had an upward bias.

References

Aigner, Dennis J., Lovell, C. A. Knox and Schmidt, Peter, 'Formulation and Estimation of Stochastic Frontier Production Function Models', *Journal of Econometrics*, July 1977, *6*, 21–38.

Ash, Robert F., 'The Evolution of Agricultural Policy', *China Quarterly*, December 1988, (116), 529–55.

Carter, Michael R., 'Resource Allocation and Use Under Collective Rights and Labour Management in Peruvian Coastal Agriculture', *Economic Journal*, December 1984, *94*, 826–46.

China Agriculture Yearbook [*Zhongguo Nongye Nianjian*], Beijing: Agriculture Press, 1981–1988 (annual).

China Quarterly, December 1988, (116).

China Statistical Yearbook [*Zhongguo Tongji Nianjian*], Beijing: China Statistical Press, 1981–1989 (annual).

Economic Weekly News [*Jingjixue Zhoubao*], 11 January 1982.

Griliches, Zvi, 'The Source of Measured Productivity Growth: United States Agriculture, 1940–60', *Journal of Political Economy*, July 1963, *71*, 331–46.

Jiang, Yaping, 'All We Want Is To Cultivate Land: An On-The-Spot Report of a Dispute of Land Contract in Shunyi County, Beijing' [in Chinese: 'Wo men bu gou yao zhong di: beijing shunyixian yiqi chengbao tudi hetong jiufeng jishi'], *People's Daily* [*Renmin Ribao*], 26 October 1988.

Johnson, D. Gale, *The People's Republic of China: 1978–1990*, San Francisco: ICS Press, 1990.

Journal of Comparative Economics, September 1987, *11* (3).

Judge, George G., et al., *The Theory and Practice of Econometrics*, 2nd Ed., New York: Wiley, 1985.

Kiefer, Nicholas M., 'Estimation of Fixed Effect Models for Time Series of Cross-Sections with Arbitrary Intertemporal Covariance', *Journal of Econometrics*, October 1980, *14*, 195–202.

Kojima, Reeitsu, 'Agricultural Organization: New Forms, New Contradictions', *China Quarterly*, December 1988, 116, 706–35.

Kueh, Yak-Yeow, 'China's New Agricultural-Policy Program: Major Economic Consequences, 1979–1983', *Journal of Comparative Economics*, December 1984, *8*, 353–75.

Lardy, Nicholas R., *Agriculture in China's Modern Economic Development*, Cambridge: Cambridge University Press, 1983.

Leibenstein, Harvey, 'Allocative Efficiency vs. 'X-Efficiency',' *American Economic Review*, June 1966, *56*, 392–415.

Lin, Justin Yifu, 'The Household Responsibility System Reform in China: A Peasant's Institutional Choice', *American Journal of Agricultural Economics*, May 1987, *69*, 410–5.

——, 'The Household Responsibility System in China's Agricultural Reform: A Theoretical and Empirical Study', *Economic Development and Cultural Change*, April 1988, *36* (supplement), S199–S224.

——, 'The Household Responsibility System in China's Rural Reform', in Allen Mauder and Alberto Valdes, eds., *Agriculture and Governments in an Interdependent World: Proceedings of the XX International Conference of Agricultural Economists*, Aldershot, UK: Dartmout, 1989, pp. 453–62.

——, 'The Household Responsibility System Reform and the Adoption of Hybrid Rice in China', *Journal of Development Economics*, October 1991, *36*, 353–72.

McMillan, John, Whalley, John and Zhu, Lijing, 'The Impact of China's Economic Reforms on Agricultural Productivity Growth', *Journal of Political Economy*, August 1989, *97*, 781–807.

Ministry of Agriculture, *China Agriculture Statistical Material, 1987* [in Chinese: *Zhongguo Nongye Tongji Ziliao, 1987*], Beijing: Agriculture Press, 1989.

Ministry of Agriculture Planning Bureau, *A Comprehensive Book of China Rural Economic Statistics, 1949–1986* [in Chinese: *Zhongguo Nongcun Jingji Tongji Ziliao Daquan, 1949–1986*], Beijing: Agriculture Press, 1989.

——, *Agricultural Economic Data, 1949–1983* [in Chinese: *Nongye Jingji Ziliao, 1949–1983*], Beijing: Ministry of Agriculture, 1984.

Muth, John, 'Rational Expectations and the Theory of Price Movement', *Econometrica*, July 1961, *29*, 315–35.

Perkins, Dwight H., 'Reforming China's Economic System', *Journal of Economic Literature*, June 1988, *26*, 601–45.

—— and Yusuf, Shahid, *Rural Development in China*, Baltimore: Johns Hopkins University Press, 1984.

Perry, Elizabeth J. and Wong, Christine, eds., *The Political Economy of Reform in Post-Mao China*, Cambridge, Massachusetts: Harvard University Press, 1985.

Sicular, Terry, 'Agricultural Planning and Pricing in the Post-Mao Period', *China Quarterly*, December 1988, 116, 671–705.

State Statistical Bureau, 1980a. *National Agricultural Statistics for the 30 Years Since the Founding of the People's Republic of China, 1949–1979* [in Chinese: *Jianguo 30 Nian Quanguo Nongye Tongji Ziliao, 1949–1979*], Beijing: State Statistical Bureau.

——, 1980b. *Scheme for Computing Gross Agricultural Value* [in Chinese: *Nongye Zongchanzhi Jisuan Fangan*], Beijing: State Statistical Bureau.

——, 1984a. *National Agricultural Statistics (Continuation), 1978–1983* [in Chinese: *Quanguo Nongye Tongji Ziliao (Xubain), 1978–1983*], Beijing: State Statistical Bureau.

——, 1984b. *China Trade and Price Statistics, 1952–1983* [in Chinese: *Zhongguo Maoyi Wujia Tongji Ziliao, 1952–1983*], Beijing: China Statistical Press.

——, 1987. *A Compilation of National Income Statistics, 1949–1985* [in Chinese: *Guominshouru Tongji Ziliao Huibain, 1949–1985*], Beijing: China Statistical Press.

——, 1988a. *A Compilation of Price Statistics Documents* [in Chinese: *Wujia Tongji Wenjian Huibian*], Beijing: China Statistical Press.

——, 1988b. *China Price Statistical Yearbook, 1988* [in Chinese: *Zhongguo Wujia Tongji Nianjian, 1988*], Beijing: China Statistical Press.

Wen, Guanzhong James, 1989. 'The Current Land Tenure and Its Impact on Long Term Performance of the Farming Sector: The Case of Modern China,' PhD dissertation, University of Chicago.

11 How Should China Feed Itself?

Yongzheng Yang and Yiping Huang

I. Introduction

When China embarked on economic reform in 1978, its agricultural sector began a transition from a central planning regime to a market-oriented household farming system. With the dismantling of the communes and the release of market forces, agricultural output increased dramatically in the first six years of reform. Food shortages disappeared rapidly. With the deepening of industrial reform since the mid 1980s, strong growth in food demand has continued. Alongside official price liberalisation, food prices, especially grain prices, have increased rapidly and are now approaching world levels. Until this occurred, the choice of direction for China's agricultural policy was simple. Increases in farm prices boosted farm output and improved national economic welfare as agricultural production was discriminated against.

The choice that China now faces is a much more complicated one. Any further significant increases in domestic prices will require higher border barriers to prevent such increases being nullified by rising imports. In addition, price increases no longer improve China's national economic welfare, as they did in the past. Without increased border protection, however, China will face a further decline in food self-sufficiency—a long-held national objective and a political imperative. Should China decide to protect its agriculture, there will be less incentive for farmers to move out of the agricultural sector—a natural, yet necessary, economic process for continued industrialisation. Without out-migration of farm population or government intervention, farm income is doomed to grow more slowly than non-farm income, a result of both relatively inelastic demand for farm products and of domestic structural change (Martin and Warr 1993).

As China continues to pursue outward-oriented growth and moves to join the World Trade Organisation (WTO), it is constrained in the policies that it can adopt. With the conclusion of the Uruguay Round multilateral trade negotiations, countries which now have agricultural protection will gradually have to liberalise and those which do not protect their agriculture will find it difficult to introduce protection. If world trade liberalisation continues in the future, China has to choose either comprehensive engagement with the world

Reprinted with permission. Extracted from Yongzheng Yang and Yiping Huang, 1996. 'How should China feed itself?', *The World Economy*, 20(7), November:913–34 (with minor editing).

Figure 1   **International and Chinese market prices: wheat, rice and maize January 1993-August 1996** (US$/tonne)

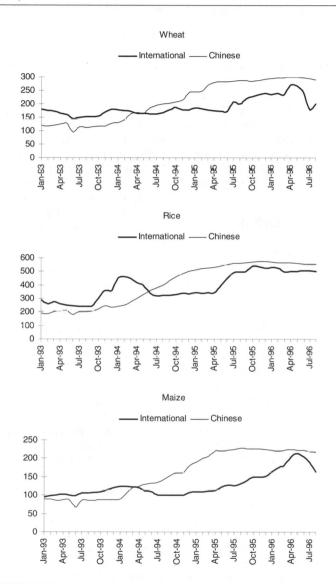

Note: China domestic prices are market prices in rural and urban fairs converted using the swap exchange rate and international prices are f.o.b. Gulf No. 1 hard red winter (ordinary protein) for wheat, f.o.b. Bangkok, white milled 5 per cent broken for rice and f.o.b. Gulf No. 2 yellow for maize.
Sources: Garnaut, Cai and Huang (1996); personal communications with the State Planning Commission, China; IMF (various issues).

economy, or reverse to the inward-looking development of the past.

This paper examines the implications of China's agricultural policy in a changing domestic and world economy. Using the global general equilibrium model GTAP, we find that with reasonable assumptions about productivity growth, China's agricultural self-sufficiency is likely to decline in the next decade if its rapid economic growth continues. To retain agricultural self-sufficiency at the present level by the year 2005 would entail considerable economic costs. In addition, agricultural self-sufficiency through border protection cannot be used to halt the growing gap between rural and urban incomes.

II. The Domestic Policy Debate

China's agricultural reforms in the early years resulted in a nation-wide grain surplus in 1983 and 1984. The grain market, however, saw a dramatic turnaround after 1985 when reforms were gradually extended to the rest of the economy. While supply growth slowed because of increasing competition for resources by other booming sectors such as cash crops and rural industries, demand rose rapidly as income growth started to accelerate. In the following ten years, both grain prices and imports increased considerably. In 1992, in an attempt to liberalise the grain market, the government abolished administrative restrictions on grain production and consumption and brought consumer prices in line with producer prices. From the end of 1993, however, market prices for grain rose dramatically. Price inflation for grain reached an all-time high of about 50 per cent in 1994. This led to a historical change in China's agricultural development (Garnaut et al. 1996). The domestic market prices were pushed from below international prices to levels similar to those on world markets (Figure 1).

Several studies suggested that future increases in the imports of grain were inevitable if China's rapid economic growth continued and trade barriers were not raised (Yang and Tyers 1989; Anderson 1990; and Garnaut and Ma 1992). China has about 7 per cent of the world's arable land[1] but 22 per cent of the world population, and it therefore does not have a comparative advantage in land-intensive products. China's experience in the past decade has shown that rapid industrialisation has not only accelerated grain demand but has also shifted resources away from grain production. This position on China's grain economy is, in general, shared by a number of studies, including the International Food Policy Research Institute (Rosegrant et al. 1995; and Huang et al. 1996), the Organisation for Economic Cooperation and Development (Huang 1995), the Overseas Economic Cooperation Fund of Japan (OECF 1995) and the Worldwatch Institute (Brown 1995).

These studies, especially that by Lester Brown (1995), caused anxiety among Chinese policymakers and economists. Brown forecasts that China's total grain deficit will rise to 370 million tonnes in 2030, nearly double current world total exports, if it does not stick to its self-sufficiency strategy. It follows that unprohibited imports by China would send international grain prices sky-rocketing and starve the rest of the world, especially poor countries, many of which have to rely on the world market for their food grain.[2]

The Chinese government welcomes the warning by Brown and others about the importance of the grain issue but reiterates that China will be able to feed its population through increases in domestic production. Wan Baorui (1996), Vice Minister of Agriculture, has recently announced that the food self-sufficiency rate is to be maintained at above 95 per cent.[3] Most Chinese economists are indeed more optimistic than their international counterparts about the potential of China's grain production and its ability to realise it. Hu Angang, for example, points to the dramatic gains made in grain production since 1949 and argues that China had an enormous potential for expanding its grain production (Hu 1996). A major study of China's agricultural scientific research priority and grain yield potential led by Justin Lin claimed that the grain yield potential is in general two to three times the current yield levels (Lin 1995). It is suggested that if the areas sown to grain remain constant, total grain output grows faster than the population by one percentage point and grain supply can meet demand for the next 50 years. Mei Fangquan contends that China will be able to maintain grain self-sufficiency for another decade or two (Mei 1996).

Chinese economists have proposed a number of strategies by which China could balance its grain demand and supply. Some Chinese economists advocate participation in international grain markets. While China is losing its comparative advantage in grain production, it is gaining comparative advantages in labour-intensive and some capital-intensive manufactured goods. It is therefore in China's best interests to exchange manufactured exports for grain in the world market. Many others, however, stress the importance of producing the bulk of grain products at home. The measures recommended to increase domestic production include: improvement in agricultural infrastructure, increases in investment, more inputs into agricultural research, land consolidation, establishment of a unified domestic grain market, increase in input (fertiliser) use, and introducing price protection for grain production (Guo 1995).

There are two major objectives of these recommendations for increased production: food security and improved farm income (Ministry of Agriculture 1996). Food security is largely a political consideration. Chinese policymakers are concerned about the consequences of reliance on world grain markets. They fear that fluctuations in the world market might be transmitted to the domestic market. If grain prices rise on the world market, China may not have sufficient foreign exchange to buy grain, and even if it could afford it, major agricultural exporting countries might impose export embargoes if they themselves experienced domestic shortages or were in conflict with China.

The second objective is an equity consideration. Fear of social unrest resulting from rising income inequality is a prime motivation behind this policy objective. Like their counterparts in many industrialising economies, Chinese farmers have been heavily taxed to finance the country's industrialisation. There is strong sentiment among agricultural policymakers and economists that farmers should now be protected to compensate for their sacrifice in the past. They argue that without such protection, farmers increasingly become disadvantaged in the Chinese society.

These discussions pose three important questions for economic analysis. First, to what extent will China's grain self-sufficiency decline if it does not intervene in the domestic market? It must be noted that if China's grain demand outpaces its supply, domestic prices will increase, which will reduce demand as well as stimulate supply. The world grain market has a similar mechanism for balancing demand and supply (Mitchell et al. 1997). If China's demand for grain imports rises, it will push up world prices. Price increases will suppress world demand, but at the same time boost supply. Thus, any projections that ignore the equilibrating effect of price changes are biased. The extent to which China's grain self-sufficiency will decline is an empirical question, and can only be estimated with careful analysis.[4]

Second, what costs will China have to pay if it is to maintain a high level of grain self-sufficiency? If China's grain imports are to increase, as predicted by many observers, self-sufficiency means that increased government interventions in the grain economy will become necessary. To produce more grain than economic efficiency dictates, more resources such as land, labour and capital will have to be diverted to agricultural production from other economic activities.

Finally, is protection or any other form of price intervention in agriculture an effective and efficient policy instrument to support farm incomes? Similar to the grain self-sufficiency policy, price intervention in agriculture for income distribution purposes will reduce China's economic welfare and may not be in the interest of farmers in the long run.

III. Projections of Self-sufficiency

China currently has an overall self-sufficiency in food. Given China's land endowments, most forecasts suggest that China's grain self-sufficiency rate will decline in the future as its economy grows. In this section, we use a 10x17 version[5] of the GTAP model[6] to further examine these forecasts by projecting the world economy from the model base year (1992) to the year 2005. The projections here will also provide a baseline for subsequent simulations of China's food trade policies. In the projections, primary factor accumulation and GDP growth are exogenously determined. Also exogenously estimated in the projections are sector-specific productivity changes, but economy-wide productivity changes are endogenous to take up any slacks in the GDP forecasts.

A set of estimates of factor accumulation and a set of GDP growth rates are compiled for the projections (Table 1). These estimates are broadly in line with those assumed by other studies.[7] We have also assembled a set of sector-specific productivity forecasts which represent the likely pattern of productivity change over the period of our forecast (1992–2005). These estimates are based on past productivity performance estimated by a number of studies, particularly

those surveyed by Tyers and Yang (1997) and McKibbin and Huang (1996). In the case of China, most estimates based on the post-reform period would probably overstate future productivity performance. Much lower productivity progress is therefore assumed for the forecasts. However, these forecasts are comparable with most other studies (see Fan and Agcaoili-Sombilla 1997, for a review of various forecasts). These revised estimates are judgmental, as are estimates for all other regions. In addition, in light of historical evidence (Hayami and Ruttan 1985; Fecher and Perelman 1992; Martin and Mitra 1993), we have assumed that in developing countries land productivity improves faster (by 0.3 per cent per annum) than that of capital and labour. For industrial countries, we assume that labour productivity grows 0.3 per cent per annum faster than that of land and capital.

The standard GTAP closure is used in the projections and all subsequent comparative static simulations. In particular, all prices and quantities are endogenously determined except for the price of savings—the numeraire. Thus, any price changes in the simulations are relative to the price of savings. Land, labour and capital are all exogenous. Labour and capital are perfectly mobile across sectors while land is only partially mobile. This means that expanding sectors can

Table 1   **Projected annual average growth of macroeconomic variables, 1992–2005 (per cent)[a]**

	Population	Land	Labour	Capital	Real GDP
Australasia	0.7	-0.1	0.6	2.1	2.5
North America	0.7	-0.6	0.9	2.8	2.7
EU-12	0.2	-0.4	0.2	1.3	2.2
High income Asia	0.5	-2.1	0.4	3.6	3.0
ASEAN	1.6	-0.4	2.2	6.8	6.8
China	1.1	-3.8	2.4	9.3	8.9
South Asia	1.8	-0.2	2.4	5.5	5.2
Latin America	1.7	-0.3	2.2	1.2	3.6
Africa and Middle East	3.0	-0.3	3.1	2.6	3.0
Rest of the world	1.3	-0.3	2.4	2.5	3.0

Note: [a] Numbers for land are total change over the period.
Sources: Hertel et al. (1996), Yang (1998) and Anderson et al. (1996).

Table 2   **Self-sufficiency ratios and their changes over the period 1992–2005** (per cent)[a]

| | High Growth with Uruguay Round Reform | | | Low Growth with Uruguay Round Reform | |
	1992	2005		2005	
Paddy rice	100	100	(0)	100	(0)
Wheat	88	66	(-25)	75	(-15)
Other grains	104	99	(-6)	100	(-4)
Non-grain crops	104	86	(-170)	92	(-11)
Wool	5	2	(-66)	2	(-49)
Other livestock products	103	95	(-8)	98	(-5)
Forestry	95	71	(-25)	82	(-13)
Fishery	112	67	(-40)	82	(-26)
Processed rice	102	102	(1)	103	(1)
Meat	107	99	(-7)	100	(-6)
Milk products	82	74	(-10)	76	(-7)
Other food products	105	87	(-16)	89	(-15)
Grains	100	93	(-6)	96	(-4)
Agriculture	102	89	(-12)	94	(-8)

Note: [a] Numbers in parentheses are percentage changes in self-sufficiency rates.
Source: Simulations of the GTAP model.

easily draw labour and capital away from contracting sectors. The elasticity of transformation between sectoral land uses is unity. Because GTAP is a one-period model, investment does not augment productive capital stock in the current period, although it affects final demand. For this reason, capital stock is exogenously augmented in the projections. The balance of trade is endogenously determined.

Two scenarios for projections are tested. In the first scenario, exogenous macroeconomic forecasts used in the simulation are shown in Table 1. In particular, China's GDP growth is forecast to grow at 8.9 per cent per annum from 1992 to 2005. The second scenario assumes a one-third lower economic growth (6.0 per cent per annum) for China. The growth of capital accumulation is also lowered by one-third. In both scenarios, the Uruguay Round reforms are incorporated.

China's agricultural self-sufficiency ratios are projected to decline over the next decade (Table 2). If our projections under the high-growth scenario eventuate, by 2005 one-third of China's

wheat consumption would have to come from imports, down from a self-sufficiency rate of 88 per cent in 1992. China is projected to maintain its current self-sufficiency in rice, but it may turn from a significant net exporter to a small net importer for other grains. Despite an above average increase in the output of non-grain crops, the average self-sufficiency rate for these crops is projected to fall considerably because of the rapid increase in demand. However, it must be noted that this commodity category is highly aggregated.[8] It is possible that some products in this category have great potential for export and their self-sufficiency may not decline, or can even increase in the future, if projected separately. This is equally true for 'other food products', which also comprise diverse products. Some argue that China may well have a comparative advantage in these products as they tend to be labour-intensive rather than land-intensive (Lu 1996).

The largest falls in the rates of self-sufficiency are seen in wool, fish and forestry products, the three relatively income-elastic commodities. The similarly high income elasticities also drive down the self-sufficiency rate for livestock food products. The meat industry is projected to turn from a significant net exporter to a marginal net importer. China is currently a large net importer of milk products, partly as a result of United Nations food aid whose supply has been largely sourced in industrial economies. High income growth will further increase China's reliance on the imports of milk products.

China's self-sufficiency rate for grain as a whole falls to 93 per cent if high income growth is maintained. This translates into 56 million tonnes of grain imports in 2005. Although this does not represent alarming reliance on grain imports, it is a decisive departure from an overall grain self-sufficiency of the past. The overall agricultural self-sufficiency rate drops to 89 per cent, reflecting greater excess demand for more income-elastic livestock and other agricultural commodities.

Slower economic growth in China will reduce the declines in grain and agricultural self-sufficiency, but it does not reverse the trend towards greater reliance on international markets. Even with slow growth, a quarter of China's wheat consumption may have to be imported from overseas by 2005. Overall grain self-sufficiency falls to 96 per cent in the low growth scenario, instead of 93 per cent in the high growth scenario. Grain imports increase to 31 million tonnes. Again, overall self-sufficiency for agriculture falls more than grain, to 94 per cent.

Our forecasts are similar to the forecasts of Garnaut and Ma (1992), Huang et al. (1996), Tuan (1994) and OECF (1995), and higher than those by Rosegrant et al. (1995) and Mitchell, Ingco and Duncan (1997), but much smaller than Brown's (1995) forecast of 108 million tonnes (extrapolated from his 2030 forecast).

IV. Implications of the Agricultural Self-sufficiency Policy

Chinese policymakers regard reliance on food imports as a security and hence, political problem. Current thinking among policymakers is overwhelmingly in favour of food self-sufficiency.[9] It is not clear, however, how this will be achieved. There are several options available to the government. One would be to increase government spending on agricultural investment and research. The recently revealed overstatement of grain yield as a result of the under-reporting of arable land suggests that China has greater potential to increase its land productivity than the previously over-reported yield levels suggest. Other options include further development of factor markets in rural China. At present, there are considerable distortions in credit, land and labour markets. These and other options have been comprehensively summarised by Wan (1996). However, these supply side policies are unlikely to halt China's declining comparative advantage in grain production, especially if rapid economic growth continues.

There are also price-based policy options. One would be to increase farm subsidies (including output and/or input subsidies). This policy may face opposition from the non-agricultural sectors. However, price controls on output and inputs as practised in the past make the implicit subsidies less visible to the non-agricultural sectors and consumers and may prove politically more popular than increases in farm investment. Another price-based policy option to boost food self-sufficiency is to introduce and/or increase import barriers. The costs of this option are less obvious than increased agricultural investment and farm subsidies, especially if tariffs and/or quotas are used. Increases in tariffs or tightening of quotas (assuming auctioned), are likely to increase government revenues, instead of competing for revenues with other industries.

These various policy options have very different implications for China's external economic relations. Should China continue to pursue WTO membership, there are limits on what China can do in relation to its farm policy. If China is admitted as a developing economy, certain subsidies to agricultural inputs and investment are permitted under the Uruguay Round Agreement on Agriculture, but direct output subsidies are not. There are, of course, considerable 'green box' exemptions that China can explore.

Price interventions will not only increase China's political costs for international engagement, but also the economic costs for its own economy. Whether the government is able or willing to afford such costs is an important factor in the process of political decision-making. In this section, we examine the economic costs of maintaining grain and agricultural self-sufficiency. Two sets of experiments are carried out. In the first set, we explore the implications of food grain self-sufficiency. China is assumed to follow other East Asian industrialised economies (Japan, Republic of Korea and Taiwan) in its pattern of agricultural protection. Starting from the two projected 2005 equilibria, we ask the question: what would the Chinese economy look like if it was to maintain the self-sufficiency rates for rice and wheat (the so-called staple food) at their 1992 levels? Note that in this case, self-sufficiency is not required for other agricultural commodities. We explore this policy setting again under two growth scenarios for China: high (8.9 per cent) and low (6 per cent) GDP growth. In both scenarios, commodity-

specific import tariffs are used as the policy instrument to achieve self-sufficiency. The welfare implications of these two scenarios are reported in the first two columns of Table 3.

High growth in the economy will lead to lower self-sufficiency in staple food in 2005 than low growth. To maintain the 1992 levels of self-sufficiency in the year 2005 will therefore entail greater losses of economic efficiency in the high growth scenario. The cost of this policy is in the order of half a billion dollars per year by 2005. Assuming a population of 1.3 billion in 2005, this amounts to 3 yuan per person at the current exchange rate (8.3 yuan per US dollar).

Interestingly, the world as a whole benefits from China's self-sufficiency in staple food. But this seemingly paradoxical outcome is a second best result for the world economy. First, China presently maintains net subsidies on agricultural imports, especially on rice and wheat. Any tariff increases which offset these subsidies will improve China's economic welfare. Once import subsidisation turns into taxation, however, economic welfare begins to decline. Beyond a certain point of import protection, the level of economic welfare becomes lower than in the

---

Table 3   **Welfare impact of China's food self-sufficiency, 2005** (equivalent variation in millions of US$)

	Food grain self-sufficiency				Agricultural self-sufficiency			
	High growth		Low growth		High growth		Low growth	
Australasia	-62	(-0.01)	-33	(-0.01)	-631	(-0.14)	-248	(-0.06)
North America	170	(0.00)	90	(0.00)	-3325	(-0.04)	-1269	(-0.01)
EU-12	554	(0.01)	265	(0.00)	2016	(0.02)	667	(0.01)
High income Asia	372	(0.01)	178	(0.00)	1845	(0.03)	466	(0.01)
ASEAN	64	(0.01)	27	(0.00)	-192	(-0.02)	-218	(-0.03)
China	-465	(-0.04)	41	(0.01)	-8188	(-0.76)	-2464	(-0.32)
South Asia	26	(0.00)	13	(0.00)	115	(0.02)	39	(0.01)
Latin America	11	(0.00)	5	(0.00)	-568	(-0.03)	-270	(-0.01)
Africa and Middle East	76	(0.01)	39	(0.00)	-382	(-0.03)	-143	(-0.01)
Rest of the world	48	(0.00)	22	(0.00)	-884	(-0.05)	-356	(-0.01)
World	793	(0.00)	648	(0.00)	-10194	(-0.03)	-3796	(-0.01)

Note: Numbers in parentheses are equivalent variation as percentages of GDP.
Source: Simulations of the GTAP model.

initial situation with import subsidies. This is what has occurred in this experiment. In the low growth scenario, however, moderate protection required to maintain staple food self-sufficiency improves China's welfare compared with initial subsidy distortions.

While self-sufficiency in staple food will increase perceived food security, the Government will have to extend this policy to other food products if the continuous decline in overall agricultural self-sufficiency is politically unacceptable. In the second set of experiments, we restore the 2005 self-sufficiency ratios for all agricultural commodities to their 1992 levels. Again, commodity-specific tariffs are used as the policy instrument to achieve this outcome. The resulting economic costs of such a policy will be much larger than those resulting from self-sufficiency in staple food only. The last two columns in Table 3 show that the annual cost of agricultural self-sufficiency in the year 2005 ranges from US$2.5 billion to US$8.2 billion, depending on the rate of economic growth over the period 1992–2005. Complete agricultural self-sufficiency will no longer lead to a second best welfare improvement for the global economy. Instead, the world as whole suffers a loss between US$4 and US$10 billion. All other economies except for net food-importing South Asia and the highly-protected economies of high income Asia and the EU are worse off. It should be noted that while grain-importing developing countries do benefit from China's self-sufficiency, their producers suffer from it as world prices are depressed. China's agricultural self-sufficiency will not benefit food-importing developing countries if these countries have the potential to become net food exporters once their domestic policies discriminating against agriculture are removed and agricultural protection in many industrial countries is reduced.

Agricultural self-sufficiency will turn China's import subsidisation into import taxation for most commodities (Table 4). This turnaround raises China's agricultural protection levels toward those prevailing in other East Asian industrial economies. It is not known whether these levels of protection will exceed those offered by China during its WTO membership negotiations.

Self-sufficiency inevitably leads to higher domestic prices, especially if economic growth is high. If only staple food self-sufficiency is maintained, the price effects are marginal except for wheat (8 per cent), whose large quantities of imports have a significant impact on domestic prices. In the low-growth scenario, the price increase for wheat is halved. If complete agricultural self-sufficiency is maintained, price increases for all agricultural commodities are higher than under staple food self-sufficiency. The largest price hikes are seen in wheat, non-grain crops, wool, meat, milk products and 'other food products'. Larger price increases under complete self-sufficiency result from greater competition for scarce land resources. This pushes up costs for all crops. In fact, rice may not be able to maintain self-sufficiency if prices for other crops continue to rise, a point also noted in an early study by Yang and Tyers (1989).

In two separate experiments, we also examined costs of agricultural self-sufficiency using output subsidies. Sector-specific subsidies were introduced to maintain the 1992 levels of self-sufficiency in 2005 for all agricultural commodities. As expected, this policy alternative is more costly than border protection as it is a less direct policy instrument for achieving the objective of self-sufficiency. China's economic welfare is US$20 billion worse off in the high-growth scenario, and US$6 billion in the low-growth scenario. In the high growth scenario, a nine per cent tax on all non-agricultural commodities is required to finance subsidies to the farm sector. The resulting rate of output subsidy ranges from one per cent for rice to 58 per cent for wool. For other primary commodities, a subsidy between 15 and 43 per cent is required. As a result of increased subsidies to primary commodities, processed food industries would require lower subsidies or can even achieve self-sufficiency with higher taxes. Under the low-growth scenarios, changes in both subsidies and taxes are considerably smaller.

Table 4   **Nominal tariff rates to achieve food self-sufficiency in 2005** (per cent)

| | 1992 | Food Grain self-sufficiency, 2005 | | Agricultural self-sufficiency, 2005 | |
		High Growth	Low Growth	High Growth	Low Growth
Paddy rice	-35	-86	-34	-85	-11
Wheat	-13	31	13	42	18
Other grains	10	8	8	81	25
Non-grains crops	-9	-9	-9	143	75
Wool	15	11	11	96	62
Other livestock products	-33	-33	-33	49	13
Forestry	8	5	5	59	38
Fishery	28	22	22	154	89
Processed rice	-35	-35	-35	-62	-100
Meat	-33	-33	-33	-5	-22
Milk products	29	22	22	50	40
Other food products	26	20	20	107	80

Source: Simulations of the GTAP model.

V. Maintaining Farm Incomes

While food security remains a paramount concern for Chinese policymakers, rural income has become an increasingly political issue. Since the mid 1980s, farm income growth has decelerated considerably, after a period of rapid growth between 1978 and 1984. At the same time urban income growth has accelerated with deepening urban reforms. In 1995–96, rural income grew slightly more rapidly than urban income. However, it is doubtful that this represents a long-term trend.

Leaving aside the effect of government policy on farm incomes in recent years (such as the declines in agricultural investment) and the booming township enterprises which provide an increasing proportion of rural incomes, increases in the rural–urban income gap should not have come as a surprise. With rapid industrialisation and hence capital accumulation, manufacturing income is expected to grow more rapidly than agricultural income. On the demand side, demand elasticities for crops, especially rice and wheat, are substantially lower than those for

manufactures. Rice consumption per capita has stagnated since the mid 1980s. In this regard, China's consumption pattern resembles that of an economy two-to-three times its per capita income levels. It is this consumption pattern which leads some economists to argue that China's per capita income levels are about three times as high as official statistics suggest (Garnaut and Ma 1992). This conclusion is supported by income comparisons using purchasing power parity methods (Summers and Heston 1991; and Ren and Chen 1995).

Although the growing income disparities between rural and urban populations are fundamentally a result of structural change, there is growing demand for price intervention to boost farm income. One policy that has been advocated is to increase import restrictions. Given that this policy is also consistent with the government's food self-sufficiency policy, it holds great attraction for policymakers. But apart from the constraints that China will face under the WTO Agreement on Agriculture, one has to ask whether border policies will be effective in protecting farm income. The answer is no. Border policy can be implemented only to the extent of achieving autarky in the agricultural sector. If the Chinese economy continues to grow, structural change in favour of the non-agricultural sector will continue, and hence relative farm income growth will continue to lag behind non-farm income growth even without imports.

In one projection experiment, we attempted to maintain the relativity of farm and non-farm income (defined as value added by all primary factors of production in agricultural and non-agricultural sectors, respectively) over the period 1992–2005 through increasing border protection[10] It turned out that this simulation did not have a solution, implying that farm income cannot be made to grow at the same rate as non-farm income if import tariffs are the only policy instrument used. Empirically, it is not difficult to interpret this result. Imports are small relative to output for most commodities. Increases in tariffs can easily wipe out all imports. Furthermore, as imports are prohibited, increases in domestic prices hold back exports, leading to complete autarky in the farm economy. Once tariffs are prohibitive, any further increases in protection will no longer affect domestic market prices; these prices will be entirely determined

by domestic demand and supply conditions. Given the fundamental structural change we described earlier, domestic prices resulting from market clearing cannot sustain income relativity between agricultural and non-agricultural sectors over the period 1992–2005.

If border protection cannot maintain farm and non-farm parity, China has to look to the European model to boost farm income, instead of the East Asian model. China has in the past attempted to use farm support programmes similar to those in Europe and North America. However, with ever-increasing domestic prices, the floor prices have been rarely effective. The government has also been hesitant to increase the floor prices due to cost considerations.

In this section, two experiments are undertaken to evaluate the impact of a farm support policy which will maintain current farm and non-farm income inequality. Only aggregate farm income is required to grow at the same rate as aggregate non-farm income; incomes from individual farm sectors are not required to keep pace with non-farm income. In our previous projection experiments, farm income relative to non-farm income declined by nearly 8 per cent (relative grain sector income declined by 25 per

Table 5   **Welfare impact of maintaining 1992 income inequality between farm and non-farm sectors, 2005** (equivalent variation in millions of US dollars)

	High growth		Low growth	
Australasia	-227	(-0.05)	-93	(-0.02)
North America	-1287	(-0.02)	-466	(-0.01)
EU-12	470	(0.00)	248	(0.00)
High income Asia	518	(0.01)	235	(0.00)
ASEAN	68	(0.01)	79	(0.01)
China	-2671	(-0.25)	-1284	(-0.17)
South Asia	42	(0.01)	20	(0.00)
Latin America	-246	(-0.01)	105	(-0.01)
Africa and Middle East	-107	(-0.01)	-21	(0.00)
Rest of the world	-311	(-0.02)	-82	(0.00)
World	-3751	(-0.01)	-1470	(0.00)

Note: Numbers in parentheses are equivalent variation as percentages of GDP.
Source: Simulations of the GTAP model.

Table 6   Output subsidies to maintain 1992 income inequality between farm and non farm sectors, 2005
(per cent of market price)

	1992	High Growth 2005	Low Growth 2005
Paddy rice	-0.9	6.1	3.2
Wheat	-1.0	5.9	3. 1
Other grains	-2.5	4.3	1.5
Non-grain crops	-4.1	2.6	-0.1
Wool	-0.8	6.2	3.3
Other livestock products	-0.9	6.1	3.2
Forestry	-9.4	-3.0	-5.6
Fishery	-4.5	2.2	-0.6
Processed rice	-4.6	2.1	-0.5
Meat	-2.5	4.4	1.6
Milk products	-7.4	-0.9	-3.5
Other food products	-3.6	3.2	0.4

Source: Simulations of the GTAP model.

cent) in the high growth scenario. The corresponding declines are 6 per cent and 15 per cent in the low growth scenario. In the two comparative static experiments undertaken in this section, we reverse these declines using production subsidies. To finance the subsidies, output taxes on all non-agricultural activities are raised to maintain government revenues at a constant share of national income.

Under the high growth scenario, it costs China US$2.7 billion in 2005 to maintain the 1992 level of farm and non-farm income parity, and under the low growth scenario, the cost is about half the magnitude of the high-growth scenario (Table 5). Most other regions lose from this policy. The EU gains as a result of a second best improvement, while High Income Asia, ASEAN and South Asia gain due to an improvement in their terms of trade, resulting from lower world food prices.

It is interesting to note that the global welfare impact of this farm subsidisation policy is similar to the self-sufficiency policy. Both policies reduce China's agricultural imports, but to a much greater extent in the case of agricultural self-

sufficiency. On the other hand, China's exports of agricultural commodities increase substantially under the subsidisation policy, whereas they decline dramatically under self-sufficiency policy.

To maintain the current farm and non-farm income parity, a seven per cent increase in subsidies on all agricultural commodities is required under the high-growth scenario. For example, the current one per cent production tax on rice will have to turn into a six per cent subsidy in order to maintain self-sufficiency in rice and other agricultural commodities (Table 6). A 2.5 per cent increase in taxes on all other non-agricultural commodities is necessary to finance these subsidies. In the low growth scenario, only 1.5 per cent tax increase will be necessary.

Subsidies on agricultural activities lead to considerable increases in agricultural output (Table 7). There are, however, substantial variations across sectors. Wool has the largest increase, followed by milk and meat products. Wheat also sees a significant rise in output, but rice production expands only marginally. These increases in agricultural output come at the expense of non-agricultural output. Manufactured output declines by as much as five per cent, and minerals by three per cent in the high-growth scenario.

Agricultural subsidies reduce consumer prices across all agricultural commodities, although the extent of price declines in the low-growth scenario is considerably smaller. However, the subsidies fail to increase producer prices significantly. In fact for a number of agricultural commodities, producer prices fall. Nevertheless, farm revenues increase for all agricultural sectors because of output expansion. Farm value added is boosted substantially by increases in land prices. Due to the assumption that labour and capital is perfectly mobile, their prices change to the same extent throughout the economy. At the same time, producer prices for non-agricultural commodities decline. Combined with price falls for these commodities, this leads to significant falls in relative non-agricultural revenues. Since the rural reform in the late 1970s, an increasing

proportion of rural household incomes has come from rural industries. Thus, subsidies on agriculture will adversely affect this part of rural income as more resources are diverted to agriculture.

VI. Policy Implications

The simulation results of this paper are indications of direction of change and should be interpreted with caution because of the large number of assumptions underpinning these results. In particular, the results are conditional on the forecasts of economic growth, factor accumulation, and productivity growth, in addition to the magnitude of elasticities used in the model. These forecasts and assumptions are broadly in line with those used by most other studies. Bearing these caveats in mind, several policy implications can be drawn from the results.

Table 7   **The effects on agricultural prices of maintaining farm income, 2005** (per cent)

	Output		Consumer prices		Producers prices	
	High growth	Low growth	High growth	Low growth	High growth	Low growth
Paddy rice	2.3	1.4	-6.5	-4.2	0.1	-9.2
Wheat	10.6	6.1	-4.8	-3.2	1.9	0.8
Other grains	5.4	3.5	-5.9	-3.8	0.7	0.2
Non-grain crops	4.2	2.4	-5.6	-3.8	1.0	0.2
Wool	29.8	19.0	-5.3	-3.4	1.3	0.6
Other livestock products	3.0	1.8	-7.3	-5.0	-0.8	-1.1
Forestry	11.3	4.5	-9.2	-5.8	-2.8	-2.0
Fishery	18.1	9.7	-9.1	-5.9	-2.8	-2.0
Processed rice	6.3	3.7	-11.9	-7.5	-5.7	-3.7
Meat	5.1	3.9	-12.3	-8.0	-6.1	-4.2
Milk products	18.0	11.3	-12.0	-7.7	-5.8	-3.9
Other food products	16.5	10.6	-11.3	-7.2	-5.1	-3.4
Beverage and tobacco	2.5	1.8	-1.7	-1.2	-4.2	-2.7
Minerals	-2.9	-1.9	-0.3	-0.2	-2.9	-1.7
Textiles and clothing	-2.3	-1.4	0.3	0.2	-2.2	-1.4
Other manufactures	-5.4	-3.6	0.9	0.6	-1.7	-0.9
Services	-1.1	-0.7	0.3	0.2	-2.3	-1.3
Land	0.0	0.0	8.9	5.1	8.9	5.1

Source: Simulations of the GTAP model.

Chinese policymakers are facing a dilemma. On the one hand, China would like to internationalise its economy to sustain its strong growth of manufactured exports. A most effective way to increase market access for its manufactured goods is an early entry into the World Trade Organisation. On the other hand, strong export-led growth in the manufactured sector means declining comparative advantage in agriculture and makes China's food self-sufficiency policy economically unviable. Price interventions seem inevitable if food self-sufficiency is to be maintained. While Chinese policymakers may be prepared to pay the price of self-sufficiency, the newly concluded WTO Agreements make it difficult to introduce or increase agricultural protection once tariffs are bound. Unlike in the previous rounds of GATT negotiations, China cannot choose which WTO agreements it wishes to sign; all WTO agreements, including the one on agriculture, have to be accepted.

Protection is going to be ineffective and expensive for reducing rural–urban income disparities. Farm subsidy is a more effective and efficient instrument than protection, but as with protection policy it is not the fundamental solution, nor is it generally permitted by the WTO should China become a WTO member. The fundamental cause of the growing rural–urban income gap is the relative decline of China's agricultural sector as a result of sustained economic growth. If farm income is of concern for political considerations, income policies should be used, instead of trade or industrial policies.

Acknowledgements

Yongzheng Yang and Yiping Huang are from the National Centre for Development Studies, Australian National University, Canberra. They would like to thank David Vincent, Peter Warr, Ross Garnaut and other participants at the two workshops on China's food policy, held in Beijing on 10-11 October, 1996, and in Canberra on 15-16 April, 1997, for their valuable comments on an early version of this paper. We are also grateful to an anonymous referee for helpful comments. Financial support from the Australian and Asian Institutional Linkages Program of the Australian Department of Foreign Affairs and Trade is gratefully acknowledged. This paper also benefited from Yiping Huang's visiting fellowship at the China Centre for Economic Research, Peking University.

Notes

1. A recent Chinese report puts China's arable land area 40 per cent larger than reported by the State Statistical Bureau (*People's Daily*, 24 June, 1996:2), This, however, does not alter the fact that China is a land-scarce economy.
2. For a critique of Brown's book, see Alexandratos (1996).
3. When asked about how 'food' was defined at a conference in Beijing in October 1996, Wan did not elaborate. Thus, food could mean all food commodities in its broadest definition or food grain only to its narrowest. Chinese officials often talk about agricultural self-sufficiency as well.
4. The impact of China's growth on world food markets are dealt with in another paper (Yang and Huang 1996) because of space constraints.
5. See Table 1 for the region details. Commodities included in the model can be found in Table 8.
6. The GTAP model was developed at the Global Trade Analysis Project led by Thomas Hertel of Purdue University. Interested readers are referred to Hertel (1997) for more details of the model.
7. See Fan and Agcaoili-Sombilla (1997) for a survey of the various assumptions.
8. Further disaggregation of this category is impossible given the current version of the GTAP database.
9. See endnote 3 for the ambiguity of the official definition of food in this context.
10. Since there is only one household in the GTAP model, we cannot define income distribution by income groups. The approach adopted here essentially captures the relative incomes of urban households and the rural households whose income comes predominantly from agriculture.

References

Alexandratos, N., 1996. 'China's Projected Cereals Deficits in a World Context', *Agricultural Economics*, 15, 1–17.

Anderson, K., 1990. 'China's Economic Growth, Changing Comparative Advantages and Agricultural Trade', *Review of Marketing and Agricultural Economics*, 58, 56–75.

——, Dimaranan, B. Hertel, T. and Martin, W., 1996. 'Asia-Pacific Food Markets and Trade in 2005: A Global, Economy-wide Perspective', Seminar Paper 96–05, Centre for International Economic Studies, University of Adelaide, South Australia.

Brown, L., 1995. *Who Will Feed China?* Earthscan Publications, London.

China State Statistical Bureau, 1995. *China Statistical Yearbook*, China Statistics Publishing House, Beijing.

Fan, S.G. and Agcaoili-Sombilla, M., 1997. 'Why Projections on China's Future Food Supply and Demand Differ', *Australian Journal of Agricultural and Resource Economics*, 41(2):169–90.

Fecher, F. and Perelman, S., 1992. 'Productivity Growth and Technical Efficiency in OECD Industrial Activities', in R.E. Caves (ed.) *Industrial Efficiency in Six Nations*, MIT Press, Cambridge.

Garnaut, R. and Ma, G., 1992. *Grain in China*, Australian Government Publishing Services, Canberra.

Garnaut, R., Cai, F. and Huang, Y., 1996. 'A Turning Point in China's Agricultural Development', in R. Garnaut, S. Guo and G. Ma (eds), *The Third Revolution in China's Countryside*, Cambridge University Press, Cambridge.

Garnaut, R., Guo, S. and Ma, G., (eds.) 1996. *The Third Revolution in China's Countryside*, Cambridge University Press, Cambridge.

GATT, 1993. *An Analysis of the Proposed Uruguay Round Agreement, with Particular Emphasis on Aspects of Interest to Developing Economies*, November, Geneva.

——, 1994. *News of the Uruguay Round of Multilateral Trade Negotiations*, April, Geneva.

Gehlhar, M., 1997. 'Historical Analysis of Growth and Trade Patterns in the Pacific Rim: a Validation Exercise', in T. Hertel (ed.), *Global Trade Analysis Using the GTAP Model*, Cambridge University Press, Cambridge.

Guo, S., 1995. 'Grain Policy in China', Paper presented at the International Workshop on Grain in China, September, East-West Center, Hawaii.

Hayami, Y. and Ruttan, V.W., 1985. *Agricultural Development: An International Perspective*, revised and expanded edition, Johns Hopkins University Press, Baltimore.

Hertel, T., (ed.) 1997. *Global Trade Analysis Using the GTAP Model*, Cambridge University Press, Cambridge.

——, Martin, W., Yanagishma, K. and Dimaranan, B., 1996. 'Liberalising Manufactures Trade in a Changing World Economy', in W. Martin, and A. Winters, (eds), *The Uruguay Round and the Developing Economies*, Cambridge University Press, Cambridge.

Hu, A., 1996. 'China Can Realise its Objective of Self-sufficiency in Grain', in L. Ying (ed.), *Can China Feed Itself?*, Economic Science Press, Beijing, 35-8.

Huang, Y., 1995. *China's Grains and Oilseeds Sectors: Major Changes Underway*, Organisation for Economic Cooperation and Development, Paris.

Huang, J., Rozelle, S. and Rosegrant, M.W., 1996. China's Food Economy to the 21st Century: Supply, Demand and Trade, IFPRI Discussion paper, Washington, DC.

International Monetary Fund (various issues), *International Financial Statistics*, IMF, Washington, DC.

Lin, J.Y., 1995. 'Grain Yield Potential and Prospect of Grain Output Increase in China', *People's Daily*, 10 March.

Lu, F., 1996. 'Grain versus Food: A Hidden Issue in China's Food Policy Debate', Economic Division Working Papers, East Asia, 96/2, Australian National University, Canberra.

Martin, W. and Mitra, D., 1993. 'Technical Progress in Agriculture and Manufacturing' October, IECIT World Bank, Washington, DC.

Martin, W. and Warr, P.G., 1993. 'Explaining the Relative Decline of Agriculture: A Supply-side Analysis for Indonesia', *World Bank Economic Review*, 7, 381-401.

McDougall, R.A., 1997. *Global Trade, Assistance, and Protection: The GTAP 3 Data Base*, Center for Global Trade Analysis, Purdue University, West Lafayette.

McKibbin, W. and Huang, Y., 1996. 'Liberalisation and Growth in China: Implications for the World Economy', paper presented at the International Conference *China and WTO: Issues and Impacts on China and the East Asian and Pacific Economies*, 8–9 May, Tokyo.

Ministry of Agriculture, China, 1996. *China Agricultural Development Report '96*, Publishing House of Agriculture, Beijing.

Mitchell, D., Ingco, M. and Duncan, R., 1997. *The World Food Outlook*, Cambridge University Press, New York.

OECF (Overseas Economic Cooperation Fund), 1995. 'Prospects for Grain Supply-demand Balance and Agricultural Development Policy in China', OECF Discussion Paper No. 6, The Overseas Economic Cooperation Fund, Tokyo.

Ren, R. and Chen, K., 1995. 'An Expenditure-based Bilateral Comparison of Gross Domestic Product Between China and the United States', Policy Research Working Paper, World Bank, Washington, DC.

Rosegrant, M.W., Agcaoili-Sombilla, M. and Perez, N.D., 1995. 'Global Food Projections to 2020: Implications for Investment', Food, Agriculture, and the Environment Discussion Paper 5, International Food Policy Research Institute, Washington, DC.

Summers, R. and Heston, A., 1991. 'The Penn World Trade Table (Mark 5): An Expanded Set of International Comparisons, 1950–1988', *The Quarterly Journal of Economics*, 106:327–68.

Tuan, F., 1994. *China: Situation and Outlook, International Agricultural and Trade Reports*, WRS-94-4, Economic Research Service, USDA, Washington, DC.

Tyers, R. and Yang, Y., 1997. 'Trade with Asia and Skill Upgrading: Effects on Factor Markets in the Older Industrial Countries', *Weltwirtschaftliches Archiv*.

UNCTAD, 1995. *An Analysis of Trading Opportunities Resulting from the Uruguay Round in Selected Sectors: Agriculture, Textiles and Clothing, and Other Industrial Products*, UNCTAD, Geneva.

Wan Baorui, 1996. 'Prospect and Policy of China's Agricultural Development'. Keynote speech by Agricultural Vice Minister Wan Baorui on the international symposium, *China's Grain and Agriculture: Prospect and Policy*, 7 October, Beijing.

Yang, Y., 1998, 'China's Textile and Clothing Exports in a Changing World Economy', Economic Division Working Paper, East Asia Series, 96/1, *Developing Economies*, 36(1) March:3–23.

Yang, Y. and Huang, Y., 1996. 'The Dilemma for China's Agricultural Policy', Paper presented at the workshop China's Food Problems in a Changing Economy, 10–11 October, China Agricultural University, Beijing.

Yang, Y. and Tyers, R., 1989. 'The Economic Costs of Food Self-sufficiency in China', *World Development*, 17:237–53.

12 Township, Village and Private Industry in China's Economic Reform

William Byrd and Alan Gelb

For most economists, seventeen articles and a book on comparative economic systems and reform would constitute a sizable volume of output. In the case of Béla Balassa, this work is dwarfed by his prodigious output in other areas. Nevertheless, his deep interest in this topic is only natural. From its early stages, he has analysed the Chinese economic reform process, comparing it with developments in Eastern Europe, especially his native Hungary. A notable characteristic of Balassa's analysis, for example, in 'China's Economic Reforms in a Comparative Perspective' (1987), is a strong focus on the incentive structures linking performance and rewards. This emphasis, natural to one so involved in analysing trade (and other) regulatory regimes, provides a unifying thread for analysis of the spread of 'responsibility systems' in agriculture and industry and of the evolving balance between planning and markets for both products and factors that characterise the reform process.

Next to the decollectivisation of agriculture, the most striking economic transformation in China since 1978 has been the rapid growth of rural non-state industry. Firms in this sector are owned by a hierarchy of local government units below the county level—towns (or townships), villages, and in some areas production teams—and to a lesser extent by private individuals and groups. Reflecting their mix of ownership, these firms are referred to here as TVPs,[1] while that part of the TVP sector that is owned by township and village community governments (that is, not privately owned) will be referred to as township and village community enterprises (TVCEs).

China had attained a certain degree of rural industrialisation by the late 1970s, but this occurred within the confines of an administrative straitjacket. This earlier industrialisation has been dwarfed by the burst of activity that followed the easing of ideological and political prohibitions against rural non-agricultural activities after 1978. Private industrial and other non-agricultural ('sideline') activities came to be permitted, even encouraged. In 1987, limits on the size of private firms, which had been only sporadically enforced, were lifted. Following several years of spectacular growth, by 1987 TVPs accounted for some 23 per cent of total

Reprinted with permission. William Byrd and Alan Gelb, 1991. 'Township, village, and private industry in China's economic reform', in de Melo and Sapir (eds), *Trade Theory and Economic Reform: North, South, and East: Essays in honor of Béla Balassa*, Blackwell, Oxford and Cambridge, Mass.:327–49 (with minor editing).

industrial output value of Chinese industry. Some rural areas that only a few years back had relied almost entirely on agriculture have become overwhelmingly industrial communities, with agriculture continuing as a marginal activity subsidised out of industrial income.

What does the growth of TVP sector mean for China's overall reform? To what extent does it represent a broadening of the market mechanism outside agriculture and a potential source of competition for state industry? How compatible with a market economy are the patterns of incentives for TVP owners, managers, and workers? What are the regional implications of TVP development? We examine these questions here, drawing on the results of a recent collaborative research project between the World Bank and the Institute of Economics of the Chinese Academy of Social Sciences.[2]

The extent and characteristics of rural industrial development differ greatly among China's many counties. The project therefore involved in-depth fieldwork in four counties selected for their diversity in development stages and organisational features.[3]

As suggested by Table 1, two of the counties, Wuxi and Nanhai, are relatively industrialised. Wuxi, in Jiangsu Province near Shanghai, has for a long time been the most industrialised rural county in China and offers a good example of a 'traditional' system of tightly integrated local government-owned firms. Neither labour nor land markets have developed Wuxi, although there are elements of a capital market. Nanhai County, situated in the booming coastal province of Guangdong with its more freewheeling economy, has also industralised rapidly and has benefited from expanding links with foreign business, especially through Hong Kong. Labour markets are relatively open, and a *laissez-faire* attitude prevails concerning private versus local-government ownership of firms. Jieshou County in Anhui Province represents a more-or-less average level of TVP development for China, but its policies toward the sector are unusual in that private enterprises have been encouraged and even sponsored by local governments. An active land market has developed, as have 'specialised villages', a new mode of rural industrial development. Shangrao County in Jiangxi Province represents a level of TVP development below the national average, with 'traditional', and unsuccessful, management of the sector.

This examination of the TVP sector looks briefly at the rise of the sector, its relationship with agricultural reform, and the patterns of labour absorption in the sample counties. Next it considers the market environment for TVPs— the extent to which these firms compete on an equal basis in free product and factor markets— and summarises what is known about the efficiency of different ownership types. A look

Table 1 **TVP ownership structure in four counties of China, 1985** (percentage of total gross industrial output value of TVPs)

Type of TVP	Wuxi	Nanhai[a]	Jieshou	Shangrao	China
Township firms	48	43	36	43	45
Village firms	47	31	13	22	38
Team firms	2	16	-	-	9
Private firms	3	10	51	35	8
Total (millions of yuan)	3,705	1,421	127	31	175,008

Note: TVPs are firms owned by township or village governments or by private individuals or groups.
[a] Shares in gross revenues of industrial TVPs.
Source: Fieldwork of World Bank/Institute of Economics of the Chinese Academy of Social Sciences research project.

at the incentives for owners of TVPs follows this discussion. As the owners are mainly various levels of local governments, an important question in judging the significance of the TVP sector is the extent to which such firms will behave differently from those owned by the state.[4] The research indicates some important differences between state ownership and ownership by 'small' units of government, which suggests that looking at the TVP sector as simply another form of state enterprise is misleading. This examination ends with a consideration of the incentives for labour and patterns of labour payments in the TVP sector.

I. The Rise of the TVP Sector

The development of China's TVP sector during the past thirty years can be divided into several phases. The Great Leap Forward of the late 1950s led local governments to establish numerous rural small-scale industrial firms, but most of them turned out to be unsustainable. As a result, the TVP sector shrank drastically in the early 1960s. A new wave of TVP development began in 1970, based on the government's desire to promote production of key inputs for the mechanisation of agriculture (agricultural tools and implements, tractors, other agricultural machinery, chemical fertiliser, and the like). But this development spread beyond the limits set by government, and a few parts of the country, like southern Jiangsu Province, achieved rural industrialisation on a self-sustaining basis. In its third phase, TVP development has been an integral part of rural and agricultural reforms since 1978.

The production responsibility system

Agricultural reforms have had a major impact on the TVP sector. Prices of farm products were raised substantially, improving agriculture's terms of trade. Mandatory quotas for areas planted, output, and compulsory procurement were eliminated or reduced. Most important, in the early 1980s the commune system gave way to the production responsibility system, under which most communal land was divided equally on per capita or per worker terms.[5] The obligations of the household were limited to tax payments, procurement quotas at set prices, and contributions to social funds. As noted by Balassa (1987), quotas were often set in absolute terms, providing a strong incentive for increasing production.

The response to these reforms is well-documented. Although acreage shifted away from grain production, per capita grain output rose and overall per capita gross agricultural output grew by two-thirds. About half the increased output between 1978 and 1984 could be attributed to increased inputs and half to growth of total factor productivity (Johnson 1986 was presented in Balassa 1987). Lin (1986) found that growth of output was correlated with the extent to which the production responsibility system was introduced.

China's rural communities were profoundly affected by the production responsibility system. A major consequence was to make apparent the extent of surplus rural labour and so to generate pressures to address the employment problem. With continuing controls on mobility (forestalling a major population shift to urban areas), job creation in rural areas was needed not only for social stability but to enable the potential productivity gains of the production responsibility system to be fully realised. At the same time, increased rural incomes boosted the demand for consumer goods and housing, creating markets for products suitable for production by smaller firms, while rural savings, deposited in the local banking system, offered a growing source of capital to finance industrial investment. Demand and supply factors thus combined to impel rural industrialisation.

Incentives for labour and potential owners of industrial firms also changed markedly after 1978. Many TVPs had previously paid wages directly to worker production teams, and the workers had then participated in year-end

172

collective income distributions. This greatly diluted incentives. Even in enterprises that paid workers directly, fixed-time wages were usual. Under the production responsibility system, however, firms could shift to direct, performance-related pay in a variety of forms (although, as described below, the income of a community still has an important influence in setting the terms of these payments). For local governments, the benefits of owning successful industrial firms were boosted by progressive decentralisation of the fiscal system. In areas like Wuxi County, the response to this confluence of forces was to further promote existing local-government-owned industry; other localities like Nanhai sought a mix of government and private initiatives; and still other places turned to primarily private enterprise-based rural industrialisation.

Output growth in the TVP sector

Between 1978 and 1987 the value of rural gross industrial output is estimated to have increased by about 26 per cent annually (Table 2). During this time the price level, as measured by the consumer price index, increased by 5 per cent a year. Gross fixed assets of TVCEs rose at over 20 per cent a year and bank loans to TVCEs at the remarkable rate of 44 per cent. Fieldwork suggests that early profit opportunities, which were clearly very high, were progressively whittled away by increased competition within the TVP sector. This is confirmed by aggregate data, which show profits rising more slowly than output, assets, and wage payments.

Employment in rural non-agricultural activities rose sharply in this period, from 22 million in 1978 to 77 million by 1986 (including seasonal and part-time workers). Much of this increase was due to service activities, however, and the industrial TVP sector posted more modest increases. In the more advanced localities, in particular, rural industrialisation has accompanied declines in the agricultural labour force. For example, in Wuxi County during 1978–85 the industrial labour force grew by 19 per cent a year while the agricultural force declined by 13 per cent a year. Average wages paid by TVPs, which were initially well below state-firm levels, rose rapidly but then moderated to slightly below the rate of increase in the state sector. In 1978–87, the average real TVP wage rose by almost 8 per cent a year.

Table 2 **Selected indicators of growth in the TVP sector in China, 1978–83 and 1983–87** (average annual percentage change)

Indicator	1978–83	1983–87	1978–87
Rural industrial output	19.7	41.5	26.4
Rural industrial labour force	3.1	15.9	7.4
Fixed assets[a]	15.7	26.7	20.5
Bank loans[a]	34.7	55.4	43.8
Profits before tax[a]	7.4	14.1	10.3
Employment	2.7	9.8	5.8
Wage bill	15.2	24.9	19.4
Average wage	12.1	13.7	12.9
Memorandum items			
Average wage, state firms	6.1	15.6	10.2
Inflation (CPI)	3.1	7.6	5.1

Note: TVPs are firms owned by township or village governments or by private individuals or groups.
[a]TVCEs only (TVCEs are town and village-government-owned TVPs).
Source: State Statistical Bureau of China (various years); *China Rural Statistical Yearbook* (various years).

Table 3   **Ownership structure of Chinese industry, selected years** (percentage of total industrial output value)

Category	1971	1978	1983	1987
State	85.9	77.6	72.6	59.7
Urban collective	10.9	13.7	14.4	14.6
Urban individual[a]	-	-	0.1	0.6
Urban other	-	-	0.8	2.0
Rural non-state (TVP)	3.2	8.7	12.1	23.1
Township	1.6	4.8	6.3	9.3
Village				8.4
Below village	{1.6	{3.9	{5.8	5.4
Individual firms				3.3

Note: TVPs are firms owned by township or village governments or by private individuals or groups.
[a] Includes partnerships.
Source: State Statistical Bureau of China (various years). *China Rural Statistical Yearbook, Statistical Materials on China's Industrial Materials*.

As a result of rapid TVP growth, the ownership structure of China's industry as a whole has changed markedly (see Table 3). The share of the TVP sector has increased sharply, from only 3 per cent in 1971 to over 23 per cent by 1987, while the share of state enterprises has declined considerably. All types of TVPs have seen an increase in their share, but growth has been most marked for private firms. There has been a corresponding shift in the composition of rural gross output. Whereas in 1978 crop cultivation represented 53 per cent and industry only 19 per cent of output, by 1987 the share of crop cultivation had fallen to 30 per cent while that of industry had risen to 35 per cent. Smaller gains were posted by other farming activities and by construction, transport, and commerce.

The share of TVPs in the output of specific product groups varied greatly, although they were active in virtually all broad product groups by 1985. Considering only TVCEs shows that in 1985 they accounted for 26 per cent of the gross value of industrial production in machine building, 19 per cent in construction materials, and 13 per cent in textiles. They produced some

80 per cent of all bricks, almost 20 per cent of cement, and nearly 25 per cent of paper and cardboard made in China.

II. Markets and Administrative Structure

Market environment

Does the rise of the TVP sector represent a strengthening of market forces? Or do TVPs, like their state counterparts, operate largely according to mandatory or 'guidance' plans? Insofar as they are market based, are their markets fragmented by 'local protectionism' policies implemented by local governments, or are their markets regional or national?

The answers to these questions differ for product and factor markets. Surveys provide ample evidence that planned output as a share of total output is minimal for most TVPs. Furthermore, they are 'outward oriented' with respect to their home communities, as might be expected given the very small size of their home markets. For example, in Wuxi only 4 per cent of sales of industrial TVCEs occurred within the home township in 1985. Large majorities of sampled firms in all four counties sold at least 40 per cent of their output outside the home province. In any case, communal governments have little scope for protecting their enterprises from outside competition. TVPs also rely heavily on the market mechanism for intermediate inputs, with the partial exception of electric power.

On the factor side, however, the TVP sector is heavily community oriented. All firms (including private enterprises) must obtain land and financial capital (usually in the form of bank loans) through the good offices of their local governments.[6] Although a labour market is emerging in some areas, labour allocation still takes place in many localities. In particular, technically skilled labour tends to be allocated by governments, rather than bid for by potential employers. Except for labour in some areas, TVPs in different localities do not generally compete for factors on the basis of price.

The efficiency of the TVP sector therefore depends both on the efficiency of factor allocation *within* individual localities and on the degree to which locking productive factors into small administrative units induces misallocation of resources *between* localities. The first issue is related to the incentives faced by TVP owners, managers, and employees. Extensive treatment of the second issue is beyond the scope of this brief coverage of TVPs, but it appears that decisions on location and scale of TVPs are seriously, and sometimes adversely, affected by the dispersion of ownership across communities and by the limited scope of joint ventures between communities. Small communities also faced increased risk from concentration of their resources in one or two large firms.

Overall, there is considerable anecdotal and statistical evidence that the TVP sector's market environment and orientation lead to efficient performance by Chinese standards. In many industries, TVPs outcompete state enterprises or at least hold their own. Production function estimates (both Cobb-Douglas and translog) for sample enterprises suggest that TVPs have experienced rapid technical progress (or

improvement in X-efficiency) over time and that they operate under increasing returns to scale. Interestingly, productive efficiency does not seem to vary systematically with type of ownership (Svejnar 1990), which suggests that the general market orientation and the community ties common to nearly all TVPs dominate any impact of different forms of ownership.

Local government and enterprise hierarchies

With property rights still undeveloped in China, some degree of association between the bureaucratic status of the owners of an enterprise and the status of the firm is not surprising. By and large, there is little discrimination against local TVCEs by county governments, as they have a strong interest in promoting local industrialisation. At higher levels of government, however, unfavourable policies such as abrupt curtailment of credit have sometimes been imposed.[7] Within the hierarchy of local governments, there is often some degree of favouritism for enterprises owned by the corresponding government unit, because of the strength of fiscal and other ties. Considerable rivalry may exist between local governments at similar levels.

Lowest on the bureaucratic totem pole are, of course, the private enterprises. Competition for technically and administratively skilled personnel is normally the most severe source of conflict between private firms and local TVCEs, especially where, as in Wuxi, local governments seek to closely regulate firms and their pay scales. The formation of private firms and their entry into specified lines of activity can be restricted in many ways, such as through regulations on energy use and zoning or sanctions on skilled workers wanting to leave TVCEs for private firms. The extent to which private firms are encouraged or discouraged varies widely among localities, reflecting differences in the extent to which traditional community-owned firms are protected from private sector competition. But even in areas supportive of private enterprise, such as Jieshou, the weakness of property rights can lead to numerous problems. These may include 'collectivisation' of private firms under pressure from workers and local authorities and more voluntary changes of ownership based on improved administrative status and security for the original proprietors.

III. Incentives for TVP Owners

Spatial inequality

Most of China's rural population is rooted in small communities with little prospect for permanent migration, although seasonal or temporary labour flows are somewhat more common. Financial resources raised from within a community are seen as a local resource, and intercommunity flows are limited by a 'gap' system of credit allocation and the determination of leaders to use local funds for local investments. Under these conditions, substantial inequalities in factor rewards, especially personal incomes, might be expected between communities.

Evidence on the dispersion of personal incomes in China and the United States is presented in Table 4. While urban incomes in China are distributed relatively evenly, the dispersion of rural incomes among provinces is markedly larger than the dispersion of average

Table 4   Dispersion of personal income: spatial income inequality in China and the United States, selected years

Area	Year	Percentage of mean		Coefficient of variation (%)[a]
		Highest	Lowest	
Provinces and states				
China urban[b]	1983	137	75	13
China rural[c]	1980	194	70	28
	1985	195	62	31
United States[d]	1981	134	72	14
	1986	140	70	17
Chinese counties				
Anthus urban[e]	1984	128	87	8
Jiangsu urban[e]	1985	127	85	10
Anhui rural[f]	1984	163	49	23
Jiangsu rural[g]	1985	164	62	23
US states				
Michigan	1981	164	60	17
Mississippi	1981	163	65	16
Oregon	1981	137	81	12
South Dakota	1981	183	39	21

Notes:
[a] Standard deviation divided by mean.
[b] Average per capita income of urban residents in the capital cities of each of the twenty-nine provinces, based on household surveys.
[c] Average per capita income of rural residents in each province from household surveys.
[d] Average per capita income by state.
[e] Average wage per member of the urban work force.
[f] Average per capita income for the rural population.
[g] Average gross value of agricultural output (GVAO) per member of the rural population.
Source: State Statistical Bureau of China (1985:62, 1986:202, 1987:204); US Government (1983); *Washington Post* (August 21, 1987:C2); *Anhui Jingji Nianjian* 1985; *Jiangsu Jingji Nianjian* 1986.

incomes across US states. A similar pattern is evident for dispersion of average incomes among counties within individual provinces or among states. The level of TVP development is probably the primary determinant of rural per capita incomes in China; in 1985, the correlation between the value of rural industrial output per head and average income per head across China's provinces was 0.91.

Income inequality within Chinese counties, however, is usually much lower than inequalities between counties. For example, in Nanhai County the coefficient of variation of income per head among districts was only 7 per cent in 1985.[8] And within districts and smaller administrative units, a range of measures, including compensating payments made to agriculture out of industrial profits, keeps income inequality within a fairly narrow range (as is shown also by the wage equations discussed below). China may thus be characterised as a 'locally equal' society.

Among the four sample counties, the degree of spatial inequality is striking (see Table 5). Average per capita income in Nanhai county is 3.6 times that in Jieshou. The per capita wage bill of TVCEs in Wuxi is 28 times that in Jieshou.

TVCE profits are even more unevenly distributed. These patterns point to the uneven pace of rural industrial development across China and the effect of low labour mobility.

An interesting question concerns the extent to which greater capital mobility could compensate for labour immobility. There are some examples of TVP firms relocating to poorer regions in response to lower labour costs, while balance sheet analysis confirms that rents in the TVP sector have indeed fallen with greater competition in product markets. However, such a process is likely to be slow, partly because of the importance of personal connections in establishing and operating businesses. In the meantime, the large rural inequalities, which appear to have widened with industrialisation, are likely to continue. The degree of inequality may seem especially surprising given China's strong ideological commitment to equality and the powerful redistributional instruments available to the state. But whereas government can exert a strong influence over urban wages and incomes, it has no comparable instrument for equalising rural incomes although, as noted below, some redistribution does take place through the fiscal system.

Table 5   **Selected economic indicators in four counties, 1985** (yuan per capita of agricultural population)

Indicator	Wuxi	Nanhai	Jieshou	Shangrao	China
Average per capita income of rural population	754	1,029	285	322	398
Rural gross value of industrial output	4,656	2,313	244	49	207
Gross value of agricultural output	604	610	210	266	429
TVCE gross profits	512	208	9	4	24
TVCE wage bill	364	276	13	23	36

Note: TVCEs are town and village-government-owned enterprises. For China as a whole, the figures are per member of the rural population. The agricultural population is an administratively defined category used at local levels, which includes people engaged in non-agricultural activities but not receiving grain subsidiy rations or other subsidies.
Source: Information from fieldwork of World Bank/Institute of Economics of the Chinese Academy of Social Sciences research project; State Statistical Bureau of China (1986).

Incentives for government leaders

Without the deep involvement of community government leaders, China TVP sector could not have grown nearly as rapidly as it has. The incentives for government leaders to establish and promote local industries are therefore crucial for an understanding of the characteristics of the sector. Following the approach of public choice theory, local governments and individual public decision makers are considered here as self-interested entities whose actions are geared toward maximising their own benefits.[9] This involves analysing the role of TVPs in their communities and the incentives for developing TVPs and using them to support other goals.

Fiscal linkages and discretionary powers. China's highly centralised pre-reform public finance system dated back to 1950. While even under this system certain extrabudgetary funds were mobilised and used by local governments, extrabudgetary funds in China as a whole in 1953 were equivalent to only 4 per cent of the state budget. This proportion rose to over 35 per cent by 1977, but it was not until 1980 that China began to decentralise actively and to offer more financial autonomy to local governments and state enterprises. By 1985 extra-budgetary funds were equivalent to 85 per cent of the state budget.

In many rural communities, especially the more advanced, TVP industry has become the primary source of extrabudgetary funds, in the form of profit remittances and management fees paid by the firms to the local government. In Nanhai and Wuxi counties, industry provided 100 per cent of these resources in the mid 1980s; even in Jieshou it provided 73 per cent and in Shangrao 51 per cent despite their low levels of industrial development.

For local governments, access to extra-budgetary funds is important. These funds represent their only substantial source of fiscal autonomy, since budgetary funds are mostly earmarked for specified expenses, notably salaries and administrative costs. In some respects, local governments in China resemble ministates because of their stable population bases. Yet they face important limitations on their powers. Deficit financing by any level of local government is not permitted, and they do not have the right to establish any new tax instruments or to set tax rates. Community governments therefore face a relatively 'hard' budget constraint.

Typically, township governments now can retain for their own discretionary use a portion of above-quota tax revenues collected in their communities, which allows them to tap into part of the budgetary revenue generated by TVP development. Townships can retain 8–12 per cent of above-quota tax collections in Wuxi, 20 per cent in Nanhai, and 50–100 per cent in Shangrao. The quotas themselves are increasingly being set according to a fixed percentage increase from some baseline level.

Typical financial flows among township firms and township and county institutions are shown in Figure 1. Township firms pay direct and indirect taxes to the township. They pay management fees (actually a tax) to their supervisory agency, the township industrial corporation, which is best thought of as a community holding company under the direction of a township economic commission. Part of their after-tax profits is reinvested and part is turned over to the township industrial corporation. The township industrial corporation constitutes an important source of funding for government salaries and overhead, discretionary spending, and reinvestment in other township firms. It allocates these reinvested funds between firms (in our sample, investment by township governments accounted for more than 30 per cent of start-up funds for township enterprises. The township investment corporation also assumes the debts of failing township firms and reallocates them to healthy firms to ensure their continued service.[10]

A tale of two townships. To illustrate the disparity in the degree of development among China's rural communities, comparative statistics for two townships are presented in

Figure 1   **Township revenue flows and community-owned firms in China**

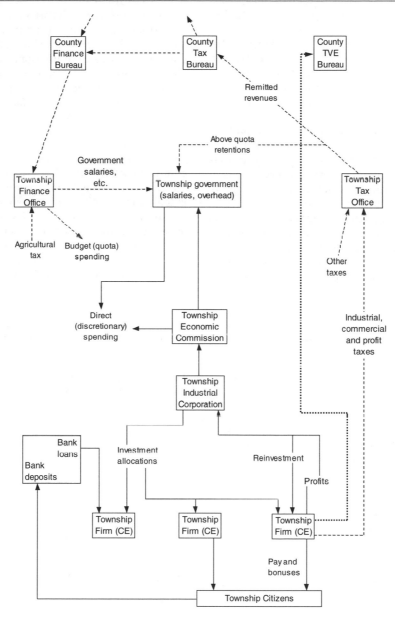

Table 6. Township A is the most industrialised in Wuxi. Township B, in Shangrao Province, is one of the poorest townships visited during fieldwork; it has an average per capita income one-seventh that of Township A. Most of this disparity is due to differences in industrial output per head. The most astonishing differences are in local revenues and expenditures per head, which in Township A exceed those in Township B by a vast margin.

A breakdown of resource generation and use between the two townships is shown in Table 7. In Township A, the vast bulk of tax revenues is remitted to the county, whereas very little is in poorer Township B, which receives a supplemental allocation from the county budget. Nevertheless, remittances from enterprises in Township A dwarf all budgetary allocations.[11] The differences between townships in government spending are also substantial (Table 7). In Township A, almost 70 per cent of expenditures

are plowed back into industrial investment, whereas in Township B, 86 per cent are used for services and administrative expenditures. Nevertheless, the amount spent on services and administration is greater in Township A, and its government is far more autonomous since almost all its resources are extrabudgetary. This ability to increase the autonomy of local government appears to be an important factor motivating them to promote TVPs.

Rewards to community government officials. The personal rewards and career prospects of community officials also depend greatly on income, employment, and revenue mobilisation in their communities. These personal benefits can be divided into two types: pay, bonuses, and informal earnings, and prospects for promotion. *Pay, bonuses, and earnings* of community leaders and factory directors in TVCEs vary significantly across communities with the average level of

---

Table 6   **Selected economic indicators for two townships in Wuxi and Shangrao Provinces, China** (in yuan)

Indicator	Township A (Wuxi, 1985)	Township B (Shangrao, 1986)	Ratio A/B
Population (number)	18,779	23,396	0.8
Average per capita income of rural population	907	131	6.9
Gross value of agricultural output per capita	399	197	2.0
Gross value of industrial output per capita	11,268	17	662.8
Sales income of township enterprises per capita	5,846[a]	14	418.0
Local revenue per capita[b]	1,268	9	417.6
Expenditure per capita	522	18	29.0

Notes: [a] Industrial enterprises only.
[b] Includes both budgetary and nonbudgetary revenues but not additional budgetary funds provided by the county for quota budget expenditures.
Source: Fieldwork of World Bank/Institute of Economics of the Chinese Academy of Social Sciences research project.

incomes and TVP development in their communities. This variation tends to be greater for villages and production teams than for townships. In contrast, socially acceptable limits to pay differentials appear to exist within communities, although these may be vague and change over time.

In Wuxi, the pay of a factory director is generally limited to twice the average pay of factory employees. Pay and supplements for village leaders are also about twice average pay levels in village factories. Workers' wages are linked to enterprise profits (as described below), so there is a relationship between enterprise

profitability and the income of community leaders.

In Nanhai, leaders' pay is typically two to three times average income per worker at the town and village levels in their community. In one township, government leaders earned about 2,500 yuan a year, whereas incomes for village leaders ranged from 2,000 yuan to 6,000 yuan a year and appear to be linked directly to the profits of 'their' enterprises. In some cases, such as in Xiqiao town, detailed incentive pay schemes have been promulgated for leaders of subordinate villages. With an annual base pay for a village leader of 660 yuan,[12] the possibility

---

Table 7   Government income and expenditure in two townships in Wuxi and Shangrao Provinces, China

Income/expeditures	Township A (Wuxi, 1985)		Township B (Shangrao, 1986)	
	Yuan (thousands)	Per cent of total	Yuan (thousands)	Per cent of total
Income				
Tax revenues	13,428	56.1	193.5	46.4
Less remitted to county	12,978	54.5	1.7	0.4
Retained	450	1.9	191.8	46.1
Refund from county	–	–	209.8	50.4
Remittances by township enterprises	10,390	43.6	13.2[a]	3.2
Less remitted to county	1,035	4.4	–	–
Total resources	9,805	100.0	414.8	100.0
Expenditures				
Investment in township enterprises	6,720	68.5	19.3[b]	4.6
Support to agriculture	900	9.2	26.0	6.3
Public and social services	1,050	10.7	285.7	68.9
Administrative expenditures	138	1.4	70.8	17.1
Unidentified (residual)[c]	1,097	11.2	13.0	3.1
Total expenditures	9,805	100.0	414.8	100.0

Notes:
– not available
[a] Township B's enterprise had net losses totalling 13,759 yuan in 1986. These remittances were financed by additional bank borrowing and by drawing from depreciation allowances.
[b] It is assumed that all budgetary expenditure 'in support of production' other than items clearly specified as agricultural was for investment in township enterprises.
[c] Total expenditures are assumed to be exactly equal to total township revenue resources, with the unidentified portion of expenditures derived as residual.
Source: Fieldwork of World Bank/Institute of Economics of the Chinese Academy of Social Sciences research project.

of earning up to 1,100 yuan for meeting various economic targets and 10,000 yuan or even more on the basis of enterprise profits created strong incentives for village leaders to Xiqiao to develop community enterprises and operate them profitably. The top pay of village leaders in Nanhai appeared to be about 15,000 yuan (some thirty times the typical wage in Shangrao), in a village where workers received about 5,000 yuan per year.

In Jieshou, owners of private firms (who are also managers) appear to be able to earn high salaries only by paying their workers much higher wages than warranted by local labour market conditions. In Shangrao there is also some linkage between local income levels and leaders' pay, but the incentive effects seem to be weaker because of the low general level of incomes and the consequently greater influence of state wage scales for officials down to the township level. Given the poor record of profitability of TVPs in Shangrao, there appears to be very little relationship between the performance of firms and rewards to their directors.

It is impossible to gauge the magnitude of informal incomes with any precision, but rewards of this type are typically an important part of total compensation. More common than outright bribery is consumption of community government or enterprise resources, from cigarettes to banquets to housing construction. Since more funds, especially more discretionary funds, are available in richer areas, leaders undoubtedly have an additional incentive for stimulating TVP development.

The interaction of national pay scales with sharp differences in local income levels causes *promotion and career incentives* to operate quite differently in different parts of China. In rich areas such as Wuxi and Nanhai, successful community leaders are generally unwilling to be promoted to higher levels because of the greater influence of the national wage scale at those levels and prohibitions against business involvement by township-level officials on their own account. In poor, backward areas, promotion

incentives are far more potent. Not only is there little loss of income for promoted leaders, but the change in household residency status for those promoted to township or county level is of inestimable value.[13] In Jieshou and Shangrao, lower-level leaders actively strive for promotion. The criteria for promotion are undoubtedly subjective, but it is clear that at least since 1980 the economic performance of the community for which the leader is responsible has carried great weight.

Immediate financial incentives and career incentives therefore appear to complement each other, with financial incentives being more powerful in rich areas and career incentives more powerful in poor areas. Fieldwork indicates that, despite these differences in the mix of incentives, under almost any circumstances local leaders have had strong personal as well as bureaucratic incentives to develop a successful TVP sector of some kind. This is broadly true, even where TVP development has lagged or failed. Thus the main factors that determine the success of development must be sought in the patterns of constraints facing local leaders and the interaction of these constraints with the incentive structure.

The dual roles of community governments

Local governments play a dual role in industrial development, being both owners of firms and administrators of the local community. This can lead to tensions and inefficiencies in the operation of the TVCE sector, as well as bias against private enterprises. In certain cases, it can cause the linkages between enterprises and governments, described above as having favourable incentive effects, to operate perversely. In this situation, which is more likely in poorer areas, local governments can become an impediment to successful industrialisation rather than a powerful force in its favour. This practice of excessive government exploitation of local firms can be termed 'fiscal predation'.

The household responsibility system radically altered the composition of property under the control of local governments.

Agriculture, and the community population as a whole, became much less exposed to fiscal predation, leaving industry as the only major source of financing for extrabudgetary spending. Especially in the more advanced areas, government underwent a successful transition from landlords to industrialists. But where enterprise development has not reached a self-sustaining stage, community governments have been tempted—in some cases even impelled by the inelasticity of basic services expected from local government—to extract funds from and through their enterprises to support their own consumption expenditures. Funds are levied from TVCEs regardless of their financial performance. Loss-making firms meet these requirements by transferring their depreciation funds (in effect 'eating' their capital stock) or by additional borrowing, which means that local governments are indirectly using the banking system to finance their deficits. Such was the case in Shangrao, where enterprises made payments to local government (see Table 7) despite very poor financial performance by firms.

Instances of 'political' interference in the operation of community enterprises seem to be fairly widespread in rich areas. In Wuxi, for example, many enterprise directors admitted that their enterprises were overstaffed, occasionally by margins as high as 50 per cent, and firms are often required to pay various expenses, including entertainment of guests, on behalf of the local government.[14] Nevertheless, the conflict between the two roles of community government is far more severe in poor areas, and this raises the issue of how rapidly the benefits of rural industrial development can be expected to diffuse under a policy of local self-reliance.

The independence of the banking system from local pressures in China and clear commitment to property rights (including accountability for losses) will be important in maintaining a tight budget constraint for local communities and holding the TVP sector to market-based behavior.[15] Although the problem of predation is most severe for poor areas that seek to use their enterprises

to borrow from the banking system to fund current expenses, it could spread to more prosperous areas should China experience a major economic downturn.

IV. Labour Markets and Incentives

Labour markets for rural industry

Labour markets are still fragmented in China, with significant obstacles to both rural–urban and rural–rural migration. The extent to which the TVP sector is contributing to a loosening of the labour market and the extent to which rural firms face a reasonably competitive labour market are important issues in assessing the incentives for participation in the sector and the sector's place in economic reform.

Some indication of the mobility of labour in the four sample counties is provided by data on the original area of residence of employees in sampled enterprises (Table 8). The most striking contrast is between the two advanced areas, Wuxi and Nanhai. In Wuxi, very few employees come from outside the towns or villages of their current employment; in Nanhai, almost half came from outside the community and 15 per cent from other counties or provinces. This finding is especially striking since Wuxi County is considered to have a scarcity of labour, which is being reflected in an increasing capital intensity of production. The situation in the two less developed counties, Jieshou and Shangrao, lies somewhere between these two extremes.

This indication that Wuxi and Nanhai represent opposite points in the spectrum of rural labour markets is reinforced by other survey information. TVP industry in Wuxi relies almost entirely on workers who describe themselves as 'permanent' whereas this category represents only 40 per cent of employees in Nanhai, 76 per cent in Jeishou, and 79 per cent in Shangrao. Further, great shifts have taken place in the relative shares of permanent and casual workers in Nanhai, indicating major changes in the operation of the labour market. Permanent workers represented 92 per cent of the total in 1980, 76 per cent in 1983, and only 40 per cent in 1985. Nanhai workers are more mobile than workers in Wuxi: 27 per cent plant to leave their firm within three years and, probably because of this, there is far stronger pressure to distribute profits to the workforce as opposed to reinvesting them. Indeed, as noted below, pay is higher in Nanhai TVP industry relative to Wuxi, essentially because the presence of a substantial private sector forces government industries to compete for labour.

Are workers allocated to their firms, or are they hired in a voluntary manner? Given the limits on choice because of population immobility, this distinction can be difficult to make very rigorously. A breakdown of recruitment according to various modes that correspond reasonably well to these concepts shows that voluntary hiring is most prevalent in Nanhai and Jieshou and lowest in Wuxi (Table 9). Older employees are more likely to have been allocated to their firms, and so, interestingly, are the higher-paid workers.

Labour mobility and earnings distribution within local industry both appear to be heavily influenced by the presence of private enterprises. Few workers are allocated to private firms, and in booming, labour-short areas such as Nanhai, private enterprises provide a source of competition for government-owned TVCEs that is absent in the more tightly regulated Wuxi model. Thus, in 1985 average income in sample firms was higher in Nanhai than in Wuxi, and the dispersion of income was significantly greater. In a poor, labour-surplus county like Jieshou, however, the existence of an active labour market has much less effect in boosting workers' incomes.

With respect to labour dismissals, the survey found that most TVP employees have a fairly long time-horizon for employment with their firms: 75 per cent plan to stay with their firms for at least five years and, possibly because the bulk of them are first-generation industrial workers, most appear to be basically content in their firms. As described below, TVP firms, whether public or private, appear to have some 'communal' characteristics that distinguish them from most firms in advanced market economies. Nevertheless, enterprises whose directors claimed to have the power to dismiss employees accounted for 97 per cent of all directors surveyed in Jieshou, 82 per cent in Wuxi, 73 per cent in Nanhai, and 68 per cent in Shangrao. The actual number of employees dismissed for any reason was extremely small in all four counties, however, and it was clear, especially in Wuxi and Shangrao, that the power to dismiss employees was severely curtailed by local community governments. In labour-surplus Shangrao, such intervention in labour markets is more understandable than in labour-scarce Wuxi.

Table 8   **Original residence of employees in sample TVP enterprises in China, by county** (percentage of total)

County	Same township/ village	Other township/ village in county	Other county	Other
Wuxi	94.0	3.0	1.6	1.4
Jieshou	79.7	12.7	4.8	2.8
Nanhai	50.9	33.8	14.2	1.1
Shangrao	80.9	14.8	2.1	2.2

Note: TVPs are firms owned by township or village governments or by private individuals or groups.
Source: Meng Xin (1990).

Incentives and pay structures in TVPs

Pay systems differ considerably among TVPs, with those in the more advanced counties tending to be more complex. Surveys show that time rates are not the main method of payment for most workers. Piece rates are common, and bonuses are important for all but 19 per cent of the sample. Whatever the specific form of payment, however, employees across all counties and types of firm perceive a clear relationship between their incomes and the profitability of their firms; only 10 per cent see no such relationship while 71 per cent consider it to be a strong one. There was also evidence of consider-

able willingness of employees to buy stock in their firms, should this become possible.

Despite the wide distribution of income levels reported by the sample, only 2 per cent of respondents described their incomes as high relative to levels in their community and only 9 per cent saw them as low. Furthermore, there was no systematic relationship between incomes and perceptions of relative level. This suggests that pay in TVPs tends to be set largely with reference to the general income levels in the community. TVPs thus have some of the characteristics of cooperative firms, although survey results indicate clearly that they are far from worker-managed.[16] There is surprisingly little difference

Table 9   **Recruitment of workers in sample TVP enterprises in China by selected categories**

Category	Allocation	Voluntary	Total
By county			
Wuxi	270	191	461
Jieshou	84	209	293
Nanhai	99	154	253
Shangrao	78	66	144
Total	531	620	1,151
By age			
Under 20	40	114	153
20–29	233	320	554
30–39	168	117	258
40–49	71	57	128
50+	19	12	31
Total	531	620	1,151
By ownership			
Public	398	380	778
Private	33	111	144
Total	431	491	922
By pay (yuan per year)			
Less than 625	82	180	262
625–1,249	180	263	475
1,250–2,499	173	142	315
2,500–4,999	44	31	75
Total	531	620	1,151

Note: TVPs are firms owned by township or village enterprises or by private individuals or groups. Chi square = 73.4 for counties, 54.9 for age, 38.9 for ownership, and 51.5 for pay. All are significant at 0.1 per cent.
Source: Fieldwork of World Bank/Institute of Economics of the Chinese Academy of Social Sciences research project.

between public and private firms in terms of reported pay, pay differentials, labour relations, and similar variables, except that private firms tend to be smaller and to have fewer technical or highly skilled workers.

The variables that determine pay may be considered in several classes. *County dummy* variables can be used to represent the stage of development of the area, and *ownership dummy* variables can represent ownership of the firm. If the firm is closely identified with a community, *firm dummy* variables can be used instead. Other firm characteristics are size (number of employees) and profitability (ratio of profits to sales). *Individual variables* include age (or experience), gender, number of workdays, occupation, and education.

A variety of statistical models was fitted to the data to explain log (pay) using the sample of 1,172 workers. County dummy variables alone account for 30 per cent of pay variance, and introduction of a simply public-private ownership dummy adds little to this. Profitability of the firm enters significantly, and with the expected positive sign. Using firm dummy variables alone results in an R^2 adjusted for degrees of freedom of 0.57. Much of the observed dispersion of pay can therefore be accounted for by differences between firms. Moreover, non-parametric statistical tests suggest that average pay levels in firms rank positively with growth of the labour force, of output, and of output value per worker. They thus arise from the 'pull' effect of labour productivity gains in the more dynamic firms in the presence of slowly responding labour markets.

Adding firm size, profitability, and individual variables to the model with firm dummy variables boosts the adjusted R^2 to 0.70. Women receive 14 per cent lower pay than men, and apprentices receive 26 per cent less than regular workers; group leaders and technical staff receive between 10 and 40 per cent more. The effect of adding in an education variable is surprising, in that it indicates that employees with some college education receive *lower* pay than would be expected on the basis of other variables. In this connection, it is interesting to note that highly skilled employees are more likely to have been allocated to their firms and that the few college graduates in the sample are by far the most likely to want to leave their firms. This suggests that the market for human skills has not yet opened up for TVPs. Indeed, this is true of China as a whole, and examples encountered during fieldwork showed many ingenious ways in which firms sought to get around the problem of the missing markets for technological, management, and marketing knowhow.

V. Conclusions

Combining elements of public and private enterprises, China's dynamic TVP sector has become an important part of the country's rural economy as well as a major actor in industry. TVPs have been at the forefront of economic reforms. They are essentially market oriented on the output and material input sides, and they are outward oriented because of the tiny size of their home markets. TVPs represent an increasingly important source of competition for the state sector, while the potential for economically beneficial interactions between the two (for example subcontracting) is also great.

This review has highlighted some of the distinctive characteristics of TVPs, which are related primarily to their close ties to China's largely fixed-membership rural communities and to the local governments' relatively hard budget constraints. Almost irrespective of form of ownership, there is a close relationship between individual incomes and firm and community economic performance, and most individuals expect to stay in their firms for relatively long periods of time. In some ways, TVPs are akin to the so-called Z-firms, which follow Japanese models of labour relations and operate successfully in other market economies.[17]

The incentives for community governments to promote TVP development are extremely strong. Where the opportunities and resources have been present, the result has been an extraordinary burst of rural industrialisation. In the more backward areas local government may have been an obstacle to rural development. Since the legitimisation of private enterprise in the mid 1980s, some of the poorer areas have resorted to this option and achieved much more dynamic TVP growth than earlier.

The community orientation of TVPs also leads to certain problems, resulting from the fragmentation of markets for capital and labour and the multiple, sometimes conflicting roles of community governments. Even if resources are used relatively efficiently *within* rural communities, immobility of factors of production can lead to increasingly serious misallocations and inequalities *between* communities. A gradual opening up of capital and labour markets will be a priority task in the next stage of reform. A weakening of the involvement of community governments in managing rural industrialisation is likely to be a gradual, long-term process. A strengthened legal framework within which TVCEs and private firms can securely operate will be needed.

National government policy toward the TVP sector has played an important, but essentially passive, role in stimulating TVP development. In the future, an important need will be to avoid government policies and practices that do major harm to TVPs; this is even more important than any positive measures (including allocation of public resources) to support the TVP sector. Discrimination against TVPs and, within the TVP sector, against private enterprise by government legal and regulatory apparatus should be minimised, with the elimination of differential treatment as a long-term goal.

Notes

1. Rural communities in China exist at three levels: the *township* (formerly the commune), which typically has 15,000–30,000 people; the *village* (formally the brigade), which typically has 1,000–2,000 people; and the *production team*, which has about 100–200. There are substantial variations in

size and economic power among communities in different parts of the country.

2. The results of the project are detailed in Byrd and Lin (1990).

3. In the course of the project, five qualitative and quantitative surveys and numerous interviews were carried out. Data were collected and analysed on a sample of 122 rural industrial firms, 1,174 employees, and 67 rural townships to complement aggregate statistics at county, provincial, and national levels.

4. Despite rapid growth of private firms, by 1987 they still reproduced only one-seventh of the total industrial output of the TVP sector. Moreover, in most cases, the extent to which private firms could be established and could grow was still very much determined by the attitude of local government and its willingness to permit their use of land and other factors and to guarantee bank loans.

5. Strictly speaking, the right to use land rather than its ownership was assigned on an individual or household basis.

6. With interest rates held below market-clearing levels, China tends to experience excess demand for funds. Rural bank deposits are considered local resources, and communal governments exert a large influence on their use. Nevertheless, the more industrialised areas such as Wuxi have, for some years, been net borrowers from other areas.

7. TVPs have also benefited, relative to state enterprises, from more favourable tax treatment, although this advantage is being eliminated. The effect of mid 1989 policy changes, which apparently discriminate against TVPs in favour of state firms, remains to be seen.

8. Regional income inequality in the United States has fallen greatly over the past 50 years as result of increased interregional mobility. For discussion of this topic, see Barro and Sala i Martin (1989). In rural China, by contrast, it has remained high because of limited mobility.

9. For reviews of public choice theory see Buchanan (1975) and Mueller (1976). This approach diverges from the more traditional view that government benevolently designs policies for society.

10. Local governments are slow to close loss-making firms partly because the debts of these firms represent a fixed cost.

11. Remittances in Township A are mostly out of enterprise profits. In Township B, enterprises

actually made a loss but were still compelled to remit funds to the township government. This is characteristic of the 'fiscal predation' practised in some poor areas.

12. Village leadership positions are considered to be part-time jobs, which explains this low base pay.

13. Urban registration opens up access to cities for the official and his family and descendants and also carries with it a package of benefits.

14. A peculiar practice contributing to overstaffing is the compensation of farmers whose land is lost because of industrial development and those who have worked on construction without pay with lifetime jobs in the new firms. This was a particular problem in the hydro plants of Shangrao, where employees exceeded those necessary to operate the installations by large margins.

15. This is a sharp contrast, for example, to the self-managed enterprises in Yugoslavia, which have some similarities with the TVPs (especially TVCEs). The most important difference is in the nature of the local budget constraint. The self-managed enterprises are larger and tend to control banks; social ownership of capital further weakens local accountability in Yugoslavia relative to China and contributes to the softening of local budget constraints. This has resulted in poor enterprise performance, deteriorated portfolios and a large deficit in the captive banking system.

16. Workers do elect their directors in some Shangrao firms; this innovation was introduced in an attempt to lessen the degree of political interference in management.

17. The term 'Z-firm' was introduced by Ouchi (1982) to describe firms following Japanese patterns of labour relations sometimes referred to as 'lifetime employment'. In contrast, 'Taylorist' firms follow a 'hire-and fire' labour policy.

References

Balassa, B., 1987. 'China's Economic Reforms in a Comparative Perspective', *Journal of Comparative Economics*, 11:410–26.

Barro, R., and Sala i Martin, X., 1989. 'Economic Growth and Convergence Across the United States', Paper presented at the National Bureau of Economic Research Conference on Economic Growth, October 6–7, Cambridge, Massachusetts.

Buchanan, J.M., 1975. 'Public Finance and Public Choice', *National Tax Journal*, 28 (December):383–94.

Byrd, W., and Qingsong, Lin (eds), 1990. *China's Rural Industry*, Oxford University Press for the World Bank, New York.

Johnson, D.G., 1986. 'Economic Reforms in the Peoples Republic of China', paper prepared for the Anniversary Conference of the Graduate Program in Economic Development, October, Vanderbilt University, Nashville, Tennessee.

Lin, J.Y., 1986. 'The Household Responsibility System in China's Agricultural Reform: A Theoretical and Empirical Study', paper prepared for the Anniversary Conference of the Graduate Program in Economic Development, October, Vanderbilt University, Nashville, Tennessee.

Meng, Xin, 1990. 'The Rural Labour Market', in W. Byrd and Lin Qingsong (eds), *China's Rural Industry: Structure, development, and reform*. Oxford University Press for the World Bank, New York:299–322.

Mueller, D.C., 1976. 'Public Choice: A Survey', *Journal of Economic Literature*, 14 (June):395–433.

Ouchi, W., 1982. *Theory Z: How American Business Can Meet the Japanese Challenge*, Avon, New York.

State Statistical Bureau of China, various years. *Statistical Yearbooks of China*.

Svejnar, J., 1990. 'Productive Efficiency and Employment', in W. Byrd and Ling Qingsong (eds), *China's Rural Industry: Structure, development, and reform*, Oxford University Press for the World Bank, New York:243–54.

US Government, 1983. *US County and City Data Book*, US Government Printing Office, Washington, DC.

13 Surrounding the Cities from the Countryside

Christopher Findlay and Andrew Watson

In the late 1920s and early 1930s Mao Zedong developed a revolutionary strategy of 'surrounding the cities from the countryside'. The strategy, forged in the midst of intense debate within the Chinese Communist Party, was based on an evaluation of the relative political strengths of city and country in achieving the aims of the revolution.[1] A key issue in the reforms since 1978 has also been the relationship between city and countryside, though the strategic goal this time has been to accelerate economic growth through economic reform. The rural reforms have provided the stimulus for a phase of rapid growth and, simultaneously, presented new challenges for the urban economy. One of the most significant aspects of this process has been the impact of the growth of non-agricultural rural enterprises on state-run urban industry. These enterprises, which have profoundly influenced the economic relationship between China's cities and countryside, are leading to structural changes in the economy and generating new types of conflict between urban and rural industrial systems. In terms of the strategic aims of the reforms, they offer again, in some ways, a chance to surround the cities from the countryside and help solve some of the difficult problems of urban enterprise reform.

I. The Development of Township Enterprises

Definition

China's rural enterprises, commonly known as township enterprises, are economic entities established by various levels of local government in the countryside or by the peasants themselves. They may be run by towns (*zhen*), townships (*xiang*), districts (*qu*) or villages (*cun*), or by peasants, acting either as individuals, in partnerships, or in cooperation with their villages. Their undertakings encompass all types of economic activity, including agriculture, industry, construction, transport, commerce and services.[2] Since Chinese statistics provide a breakdown based on ownership of, or responsibility for, the assets, it is possible for us to distinguish between rural and urban enterprises, since rural enterprises are owned by the successors to the commune system and the peasants while urban enterprises are owned by the various levels of state government and urban residents.[3]

Rural enterprises operate outside the state plan. Unlike urban state enterprises, they are subject to 'hard budget constraints' in that their owners (the peasants or the townships) do not

Reprinted with permission. Extracted from Christopher Findlay and Andrew Watson, 1992. 'Surrounding the cities from the countryside', in R. Garnaut and G. Liu (eds), *Economic Reform and Internationalisation: China and the Pacific Region*, Allen & Unwin, Sydney:49–78 (with minor editing).

Table 1   **Rural enterprises: numbers, workers and real output value, 1978–89**

	Number of rural enterprises (million)	Number of workers in rural enterprises (million)	Total real output value of rural enterprises (billion yuan)
1978[a,b]	1.5242	28.2656	49.3070
1979[b]	1.4804	29.0934	54.8410
1980	1.4246	29.9967	56.6900
1981	1.3375	29.6956	74.5300
1982	1.3617	31.1291	85.3080
1983	1.3464	32.2464	101.6830
1984	6.0652	52.0811	170.9890
1985	12.2245	69.7903	272.8390
1986	15.1513	79.3714	354.0870
1987	17.4464	87.7640	474.3100
1988	18.8816	95.4546	649.5660
1989	18.6863	93.6678	742.8380

Notes: [a] 1978–83 covers township and village levels only; 1984–89 covers all rural enterprises.
[b] 1978 and 1979 data are in terms of 1970 prices. Data from 1980 onwards are in terms of 1980 prices.
Source: State Statistical Bureau, *Chinese Statistical Yearbook* 1988:292; 1990:250, 390–401.

have any guaranteed income from the budgets of higher levels of government. They buy inputs and sell outputs in free markets, without having to fulfil plan obligations to the state. Despite this market orientation, however, their origins in the collective system mean that they commonly have a strong linkage with governments at *zhen* level and below.[4] Governments at county and higher levels also have strong interests in the performance of rural enterprises within their region. Rural enterprises can form an important source of revenue. They can also develop close relationships with other local and regional government-owned industries, acting as processors and subcontractors and enabling the regional economy to take advantage of the labour and other resources within its administrative area. This connection has significant implications for patterns of trade within China and therefore between China and the rest of the world.

Rural enterprise growth

As a result of rural reforms of 1978 township enterprises experienced unprecedented rapid development.[5] As shown in Table 1, the total number of enterprises increased more than tenfold, from 1.5 million in 1978 to 18.7 million in 1989 (Figure 1). The total labour force of the enterprises rose from 28.3 million to 93.7 million (Figure 2), while from 1980 to 1989 their total output value grew from 56.7 billion yuan to 743 billion yuan in constant prices.[6]

By 1987 the total output value of these enterprises accounted for over 50 per cent of rural social output value, exceeding the total output value of agriculture for the first time, and accounting for 21 per cent of national social output value.[7] These shares were stable for the period 1987 to 1989 (Chen, Watson and Findlay 1991, Table 4). As noted above, preliminary figures for 1990 claimed that the output value of rural enterprises was 950 billion yuan, though it is not clear which statistical series was used (Summary of World Broadcasts (SWB), FE/WO159/A/1, 19 December 1990). If reliable, this represented a much higher 26 per cent of national output value, suggesting that the economic problems of 1989–90 had not undermined the momentum of rural enterprise development. Furthermore, the statistical communique on the 1990 performance also claimed that non-agricultural activities accounted for 54.6 per cent of gross rural social output (SWB, FE1005/C1/2, 25 February 1991). The national figures, however, disguise significant regional variations.[8] This trend in the share of rural industries in output is expected to be particularly marked in the coastal provinces with low per capita land ratios, dense populations, better infrastructure and the potential for rural enterprises to build profitable links with existing industries. As discussed below, coastal provinces also offer greater stimulus to township and village enterprises through international trade.

The data in Table 1 refer to output value. In the Chinese statistical system, output value includes the value of intermediate products and therefore possibly presents a distorted picture of the growth of manufacturing activity. A more accurate set of indicators is therefore the volume of other inputs into rural industry. These indicators are shown in Table 2.[9] However, they show that between 1980 and 1989 there was nearly a sixfold increase in the value of assets in

these enterprises, nearly a fivefold increase in the wage bill, and a fourfold increase in value added (defined as payments to capital, labour, plus taxes). The final statistic implies that value added was increasing by about 17 per cent a year— 9 per cent a year in real terms (see Figure 3)[10]— over that period. By contrast, Chen, Watson and Findlay (1991) report that for state-run enterprises profits and taxes nearly doubled between 1980 and 1989, at an average growth rate of about 8 per cent, while the wage bill grew at 13 per cent a year (to 1987) and value added grew at 9 per cent a year (about 5 per cent in real terms). Thus value added in township and village enterprises was growing over the 1980s about twice as fast as that in state enterprises. It accounted for 29 per cent of that in state enterprises in 1984 but rose to 36 per cent in 1987. In other words, by 1987 rural enterprises contributed about a quarter of national value added.

Origins of rural industry growth

Chen, Watson and Findlay (1991) map out the shifts in policy towards rural enterprises through three stages in their development. In the first

---

Figure 1   **Number of rural enterprises, 1984–89**

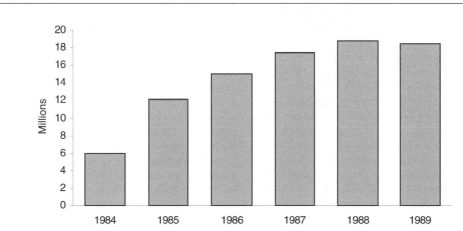

Source: Table 1.

Figure 2   **Number of workers in rural enterprises, 1984–89**

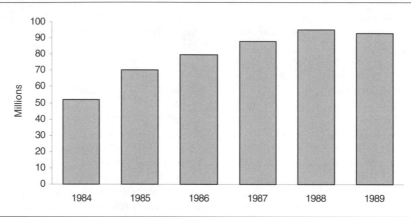

Source: Table 1.

stage after 1949 rural enterprises were engaged mainly in handicraft production and the processing of primary products. The establishment of the communes in 1958 marked the start of the second phase when the government called for large-scale development of rural industries. From this time until the late 1970s these industries emphasised support of agricultural production, either providing mechanical inputs or processing outputs. The third stage dates from when the rural reforms began.

In late 1978 the Central Committee's 'Decision on Some Problems in Accelerating the Development of Agriculture' stressed that the new rural development strategy relied on the comprehensive development of agriculture, industry and commerce. It also pointed out that commune and brigade-run enterprises needed to expand in order to promote the growth of small towns in rural areas (China Agricultural Yearbook Editorial Group 1981:57–63). This decision recognised that rural policy should have a wider perspective than its previous concentration on crop farming. Subsequently, in March 1984 the Central Committee and the State Council approved the 'Report on Creating a New Situation in Commune and Brigade-run Enterprises', which signalled a new phase of development for township enterprises (Zhongguo Nongye Nianjian Editorial Department 1986:343–56). The report envisaged that the former collective enterprises, now run by townships and villages, together with the cooperative and private undertakings that had grown up since 1978, would become the focus of a new phase of integrated rural development, providing inputs for agriculture, absorbing rural labour, helping to raise rural incomes and producing for the market. It stressed that the enterprises were responsible for their own profits and losses but that their development should be supported and encouraged by government at all levels. As shown in Tables 1 and 2, rural enterprise then entered a phase of unprecedented development.

The shifts in policy sanctioned investment in rural enterprises. Wu (1990) identifies a number of factors which made a rapid increase in the accumulation of assets in rural industry possible. One, noted above, was the rapid increase in rural incomes, following the reforms in the agricultural sector and the growth in savings.

Table 2   **Main financial indicators of enterprises run by townships and villages** (billion yuan)

	Original value of fixed assets	Net value of fixed assets	Circulating funds	State taxes (A)	Net profits (B)	Total wages (C)	Value added (A+B+C) (D)	Total wages value added (CD)x 100
1977	22.960			2.200	8.810	8.660	19.670	32.87
1978	28.920			2.260	10.450	10.380	23.090	37.38
1980	32.630		17.720	2.570	11.840	11.940	26.350	45.31
1981	37.540		20.100	3.430	11.280	13.060	27.770	47.03
1982	42.930		23.050	4.470	11.550	15.330	31.350	48.90
1983	47.570	37.982	26.250	5.890	11.780	17.580	35.250	49.87
1984	57.500	44.567	39.870	7.910	12.870	23.930	44.710	53.52
1985	75.040	58.975	59.010	10.360	17.130	30.140	58.130	51.85
1986	94.675	74.316	76.981	13.774	16.103	35.551	64.428	54.34
1987	122.665	95.977	113.464	16.808	18.775	42.768	78.351	54.59
1988	158.430	123.450	154.060	23.650	25.920	54.120	103.690	52.19
1989	192.070	148.620	189.010	27.250	24.010	58.070	109.330	53.11

Sources: Ministry of Agriculture, *Yearbook of Rural, Social and Economic Statistics of China*, 1986:228; Ministry of Agriculture, *Chinese Encyclopedia of Township Enterprises*:656; Ministry of Agriculture, *Chinese Encyclopedia of Rural Economy (1949–86)*, 1989:286–9; State Statistical Bureau, *Chinese Statistical Yearbook*, 1988:287; 1990:355.

The question arises why those funds were not invested in either agriculture or enterprises located in urban areas, closer to the traditional industrial bases of China. The bias against agricultural investment was due in part to the forces leading to diminishing returns to investment in agriculture. This long-run development process was further exaggerated in China by a combination of price distortions which worked against agriculture, and the deceleration in institutional reforms in agriculture, especially concerns about the lack of tenure over land. Similar price distortions led to biases against investment in raw material production, as noted above in our discussion of the effects of the escalating pricing structure for processed products as compared to raw materials. There was also a rapid decline in investment in rural infrastructure, reflecting the distorted prices for agricultural products and the incentives facing local governments, which, by this time, were faced with a greater responsibility for raising finance.[11]

In principle, the funds accumulated in rural China could have been reinvested in urban industry, either in the state or the private sector. Peasants could have accumulated savings in the formal financial system, which would have recirculated those funds. However, high yielding investments were available in the rural economy following the policy changes outlined above. Increasingly, wealthy peasants could have also contributed funds to the setting up of private businesses in urban areas above the township level. However, the attitudes of policymakers as well as investors towards private business have waxed and waned in China since 1986 in ways that are unlikely to make the rural population want to invest in distant cities with the constant threat of policy change (Young 1991). Without the appropriate contacts, access to cheap labour, buildings and land and so forth, the prospect of making a profit through urban investment must also seem much more remote to rural entre-preneurs. For these reasons, funds accumulated in the rural areas tended to be used in the rural sector.

The sources of funds for rural industry are considered in detail by Chen, Findlay and Watson (1991). Investment is typically funded about 60:40 from debt and equity, where the debt is raised from the banking system and the equity funds are provided mainly by township and village government. Tam (1991) shows the importance of the growth of the informal capital market in China for raising these funds.

The financing structure has left rural industry especially sensitive to credit squeezes. Until the reforms, state-run industry was funded directly by central budget allocations and was not influenced by credit policy. Now, however, the shift to interest-bearing loans for state industry and the decentralisation of budget authority to local government has changed this situation. State enterprises at all levels have become much more sensitive to the costs of capital and to credit availability, and this has happened at a time when the overall demand for capital is high. Nevertheless, planned allocation still applies to many of the inputs for state industry, and the fact that it is operated by governments at county level and above means that state industry's sources of capital are much less unstable.

The effect of the credit squeeze from late 1998 onwards is evident in Table 1, as well as in Figures 1, 2 and 3, which show the fall in real output value of rural enterprises, as well as the drop in employment and the number of enterprises. Real value added in rural enterprises also fell by about 11 per cent in 1989. This fall in output value, and the evidence of a drop in retail sales by all (not just rural) collectively-owned enterprises (SWB, FE/1005 C1/4, 25 February 1991), at the same time as an apparent export boom, indicates that rural enterprises were able to continue to develop their links with the world market during the 1989–1990 slump, as discussed below.

II. Rural and Urban Economies

The rationale for a two-way division

Barriers to the movement of labour in China created by the household registration and grain rationing systems suggest that the Chinese economy can be analysed as if split into two sub-economies, one rural and the other urban. There has been a relatively small permanent shift of

Figure 3   **Real value added in township and village enterprises, 1984–90** (1984 = 100)

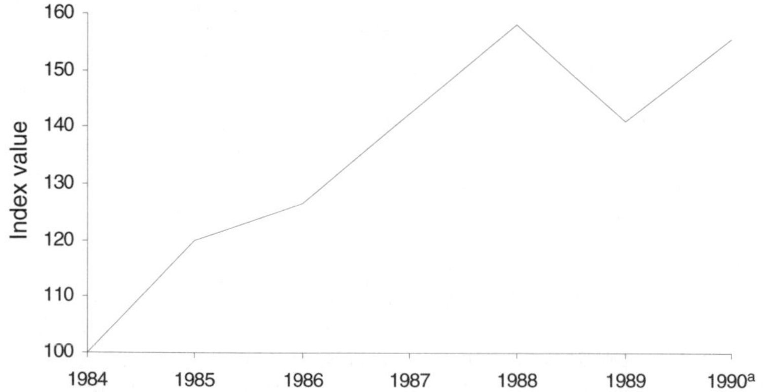

Note: [a] Estimate
Source: Tables 1 and 2

194

rural labour to urban areas in China in the years since 1949. Rural workers faced much higher costs of living in urban areas because of their lack of access to subsidies for, or to rationed supplies of, either food or housing. These higher costs lowered real wages and created incentives to cut long-term migration to urban areas, despite a desire by many peasants to move. The origins of this situation and its implications have been discussed by Anderson (1990) and Wu (1990). At the same time, the government used strong administrative measures (household registration and travel controls) to reinforce these economic pressures. Population movement, such as during the Great Leap Forward and afterwards, has mainly taken place as a result of policy decisions and has been strictly regulated. Although movement is now much freer, especially between the countryside and the smaller towns, the economic factors discussed above continue to apply.

This geographic division of the China economy tends to correspond to the concentration of firms of different types of ownership. The rural economy is primarily collective or private, and the urban economy is primarily state run. As we pointed out above, this transformation of firms classified by ownership is not perfect but it is close enough to facilitate the analysis.

The basic features of goods and factor flows between the rural and urban economies are, in some ways, typical of relations between nation states which are also members of a customs union. The conditions in China can be character-ised as follows:

1. goods and raw materials can flow between the rural and urban economies, with a consequent tendency to similar relative prices;

2. each is open to trade with the rest of the world as well as with each other, and the same policies for the management of trade with the rest of the world apply to both sub-economies;

3. the main sectors in the rural economy are agriculture (including raw material production) and a variety of

manufacturing activities, while manufacturing activities dominate the urban sector (the service sector is ignored for simplicity);

4. labour mobility between the different ownership sectors is tightly controlled and, at times, impossible; and

5. capital can move between the two sub-economies, albeit imperfectly, but capital is highly mobile between sectors within each economy.

Differences in factor intensity

Before examining various aspects of the economic relationships between these two sub-economies and their implications for China's trade with the rest of the world, a prior step is to compare the factor intensities of enterprises in the two economies. Technologies employed in the urban economy are much more capital-intensive than in the rural economy for two reasons. One is the hangover from the pre 1978 investment strategies, involving a focus on heavy industry in urban areas. The second is the current relative endowments of labour and capital in rural and urban areas. As indicated by the gap between incomes per head, rural areas are better endowed with labour than capital. In 1990 average income per head in rural China, even allowing for own consumption (SWB, FE/1005 C1/4, 25 February 1991) was about half that in urban areas. Therefore, new projects in rural areas will tend to be more labour-intensive.

The factor intensities of rural enterprises on average compared to urban enterprises have been examined by Chen, Watson and Findlay (1991) and by Zhang (1991b). One measure of labour intensity is the share of wages paid in value added, the balance being profits and taxes. More labour-intensive activities tend to have larger wage bills compared to value added. Data on this ratio for rural enterprises are reported in Table 2 and illustrated in Figure 4. Two points are evident from these data. First, the ratio of wages to value added is about 50 per cent, which is about 20 percentage points higher than in

Figure 4   **Labour and capital shares of value added in township and village enterprises, 1978–89** (per cent)

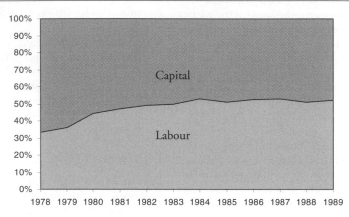

Source: Table 2.

urban industry. Second, the share of wages in value added is rising. This is the result of the higher productivity of labour and hence the rising real wages in the process of industrialisation which so far has not been offset by a shift to more capital-intensive methods of production.

Another indicator of factor intensity is the availability of capital per worker. The ratio of assets to workers is 9 times higher in state industry than in rural enterprise (although this gap is diminishing over time) and the average size of a state-run enterprise in terms of its asset value is hundreds of times larger than an average rural enterprise (Chen, Watson and Findlay 1991).

One qualification to bear in mind when considering the national average data on the labour intensity of rural industry is that there is considerable variation between regions of China.

In summary, the technologies employed in the rural economy appear to be much more labour-intensive than those employed in the urban economy. In the light of the characteristics of goods, labour and capital flows between the two sub-economies, what are the implications for their patterns of specialisation and the changes in the relationships between them as the Chinese

economy grows? The outcome will depend on the degree of integration between the rural economy and the rest of the world. The first step is therefore to evaluate the degree of international orientation of the rural economy.

International orientation

In 1989 exports by rural enterprises accounted for 20 per cent of export earnings (*Renmin Ribao* [overseas edition], 8 June 1990:3). Total rural enterprise export earnings of US$10.5 billion in 1989 represented an increase of 30.1 per cent over 1988 and a rise of 17 per cent to 20 per cent of total national export earnings (*Jingji Xiaoxi Bao*, 1 September 1990:3). By 1990 the share of rural enterprises in national exports had risen to 25 per cent (SWB, FE/WO159/A/1, 19 December 1990; *Zhongguo Xiangzhen Qiye Bao*, 12 December 1990:3). Given the 18 per cent growth in national exports over this period, these reported changes in shares imply that rural enterprise exports grew by 48 per cent in 1990 over 1989. The growth in rural enterprises exports therefore accounted for about a third of China's total export growth in 1990. It is not surprising to find that as a result of this potential, from 1988 onwards China's leaders and economists began to pay increasing attention to the role of export-oriented rural enterprises in the growth of the Chinese economy (see, for example, He 1988, Tao and Zhao 1988, Zhong 1988, Hu 1988, and Chen 1988). By the time of the second national conference on rural enterprise exports in 1991, State Councillor Chen Junsheng was stressing the need to improve the channels for rural enterprises to link with the foreign trade structure and to form joint ventures with foreigners (SWB,FE/1085, B2/2–3, 30 May 1991).

As in the case of total output value noted above, however, this national figure again disguised significant regional variations. The proportion of rural enterprise exports in coastal provinces more closely involved in international trade was much higher.[12] According to one report, in 1988 some 84 per cent of rural enterprises exports came from the nine coastal provinces (State Council Research Unit Rural Economy Group and the Rural Development Research Institute of the Chinese Academy of Social Sciences 1990:175).

Composition of rural industrial output and trade

The discussion so far of conditions in labour and capital markets suggests that rural enterprise would have incentives not only to use labour-intensive methods of production but also to specialise in industries where production is more suited to labour-intensive methods. A corollary is that the industry mix in the countryside would be very different from that in urban industry.

Zhang (1991b) estimates that in 1985, 59 per cent of the net output value of township enterprises was produced in industries which he classifies as labour-intensive. In comparison, those industries accounted for only about 34 per cent of national net output value in that year. Thus the mix of output in rural industry is relatively labour-intensive.[13]

Given this situation, we would expect the exports of rural industry to be concentrated in labour-intensive products. Data on trade of rural enterprises classified by factor intensities is scarce. The limited evidence available to us, however, indicates that the situation is as expected. Table 3 shows some data on the composition of merchandise exports for 1989, where activities have been classified into factor intensity groups, based on Zhang's (1991a) scheme for Chinese industry. These data are illustrated in Figure 5. The labour-intensive group accounts for nearly 75 per cent of total exports, compared to about 62 per cent in national manufactures exports, so the rural economy reveals a comparative advantage in labour-intensive production.

In summary, rural enterprises are growing rapidly. Their output and exports are concentrated in labour-intensive product groups. The reforms to the foreign trading system have removed some of the 'airlocks' between world markets and domestic producers in China. At the same time, the Chinese administrative system is encouraging ways of increasing rural enterprise participation in trade. These developments also provide stronger incentives for these enterprises to pursue their comparative advantage. Warr and Zhang (1990) identified a closer orientation between China's comparative advantage and its trade pattern in the latter half of the 1980s. The growth of rural enterprises will have contributed to that shift. Rural enterprise will also continue to make a major contribution to the growth of China's exports of labour-intensive products. At the same time, the Chinese authorities are moving to encourage attention to quality of products in order to ensure greater competitiveness for rural enterprise exports. In May 1991, for example, a national survey of rural enterprise product quality was launched.[14]

Rural–urban specialisation and trade

Chen, Watson and Findlay (1991) also examine the production structure of rural industry compared to urban industry. One unexpected aspect is that rural industries appear to have a surprisingly similar industrial structure to that of urban industries. The indicators of industrial structure which they report are based on

Table 3   Composition of industrial exports of rural enterprises

Type	Value (billion yuan)	Share (%)	Increase over 1988 (%)
Labour-intensive			
Textiles	6.114	16.5	42.6
Clothing	4.894	13.2	62.2
Handicrafts	4.824	13.0	27.2
Other light industrial	3.848	10.4	33.9
Foods	3.492	9.4	28.7
Silk products	1.955	5.3	49.9
Animal products	1.472	4.0	27.9
Native products	0.685	1.8	41.8
Capital-intensive			
Chemicals	2.076	5.6	37.9
Machinery	1.782	4.8	58.7
Minerals	1.915	5.2	41.0
Others	4.087	11.0	25.1
Total	37.144	100.0	39.3

Source: *Jingji Xiaoxi Bao*, 1 September 1990:3.

comparisons of the rankings of importance of various industries. They show that the rankings are similar in both rural and urban China. For example, the top three activities in both sub-economies are food processing, construction materials and machinery production. These results are not necessarily inconsistent, however, with those of Zhang (1991b). It is possible that industries included in the rural and urban economies are similar and that their rankings by size are also similar but that the rural economy output contains a larger share of output among labour-intensive products. The rural chemical industry, for example, is likely to be rather different from major state enterprises producing chemical inputs for other state enterprises. The results do imply, however, that so far there has been a smaller degree of specialisation in production in the rural and urban economies than might have been expected according to our outline of the factor endowments and the scope for trade between them.

A number of factors have led to this lack of specialisation in the structure of production.

These include: the major development of the construction materials industry in both sectors; the distorted pricing structure for processed products compared to raw materials, which encourages local processing in order to extract the profits available; barriers to internal trade, such as transport congestion; and the incentive for local administrations to develop their own comprehensive industrial network.

The lack of reliability of planning mechanisms to deliver various intermediate products encourages local governments to diversify their industrial structure and develop comprehensive local systems. The growth of rural industry thereby threatens the stability and guarantees of the urban sector. Indeed, the competition offered can been seen as a means of forcing greater efficiency on urban industry (Zhang et al. 1988:5–6). These economic factors also bear on social and political issues since they ultimately imply an undermining of the preferential treatment given to the urban population. In this situation, many major social and political issues require careful consideration.

Figure 5   **Composition of rural enterprise merchandise exports, 1989**

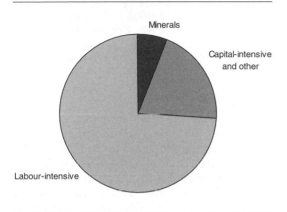

Source: Table 3.

To some extent, this competition may be overstated. It is often alleged, for example, that the rural enterprises compete with urban enterprises for energy. One study, however, reports that the energy produced by rural enterprises far exceeds the amount they use (State Council Research Unit Rural Economy Group and the Rural Development Research Institute of the Chinese Academy of Social Sciences 1990:54). Nevertheless, the lower degree of specialisation between rural and urban economies than might have been expected has two important implications, one for raw materials trade and the other for trade in intermediate, or semi-processed, products.

Raw materials trade

In the distribution of industrial intermediate products, efforts are made to ensure that the needs of urban industry are guaranteed first. Urban and rural industries can then compete in the market for the remainder (Zhang et al. 1988:6). The quantity of the surplus is thus influenced by the speed of urban development. When it is slow, the volumes available for market distribution are relatively greater, and rural industries have greater opportunities. When urban development is rapid, however, supplies are scarce. The quantity distributed through administrative allocation tends to grow and rural industries face higher prices, while urban industries obtain more guaranteed supplies at lower plan prices.

In terms of our analogy of trade between two sub-economies within China, this situation is similar to that which arises when one economy, in this case the urban economy, tries to exploit its bargaining power to alter its terms of trade with its trading partner, in this case the rural economy. It does this by employing a discriminatory purchasing policy typical of a monopsonist, or a discriminatory selling policy typical of a monopolist. The end result has been a structure of relative prices within China which are biased against raw materials.

This situation provoked a couple of reactions, once the rural enterprise sector was released from its previous policy shackles. First, goods 'leaked' from the planned sector for sale at higher market prices, a process which involves the corruption of those with power over distribution. In other words, goods are 'smuggled across the borders' between the two economies.

Second, and more importantly, policy-makers in the rural economy retaliated. Local authorities tried to restrict the flow of industrial raw materials out of their area in order to ensure supplies go first to their own rural industries on which they depend for income. The profits which can be earned from local processing are much higher than those available from the sale of raw materials, because of the distortions in the price structure. So, in retaliation, the rural economy put embargoes on its 'exports', especially its exports of raw materials.

The implications for the trade in raw materials within China have been chaotic. The situation is described by a commentator as one in which 'feudal lords contend, regions set up blockades, trades practise monopolies and wars are continuous'. There are numerous examples

199

of these wars in the raw materials trades, such as the 'wool war', discussed by Watson, Findlay and Du (1989), the cotton, silk, hemp and tobacco 'wars' and the 'cashmere chaos'. In other words, the issues arose mainly in relation to raw materials consumed by labour-intensive processing industries.

These issues were also important in the events of 1989. As part of the subsequent policy of economic adjustment, efforts were made to restrict the growth of rural enterprises (*Dongfang Ribao* [Hong Kong], 15 July 1989:6), especially those believed to be wasteful and polluting, and to protect supplies of raw materials, transport and energy to urban industries. Given the credit restrictions already in place, this was a strong attack on the growth of rural enterprises. Such policies therefore represented an attempt to protect urban industries. The fact that urban industries have found it difficult to improve productivity and that the rural and regional economies were weakened by this policy eventually forced a relaxation of such an approach during 1990 and a reassertion of the significance of the rural enterprise and private sectors. These policy debates reflect the way the structural economic changes in the countryside have affected the urban–rural economic balance and entail significant policy issues, thus recalling Mao Zedong's dictum on 'surrounding the cities from the countryside'.

In summary, the distorted pricing structure and the rents it created led to significant shifts in the patterns of trade in raw materials in China. These shifts were magnified by the policy shifts which relaxed constraints on the growth of rural industry. The ensuing struggles over raw materials supplies were resolved by a greater reliance on the world market, especially in the coastal areas; a process which was facilitated by a series of foreign trade reforms. Therefore, the initial policy initiative of promoting rural industrial growth had the important side-effect of contributing to the reinforcement of the reforms in China's international trading system.

These events may not have resulted in much difference in the national processing capacity in China or the net trades in raw materials. Without them, however, there may have been a greater concentration of processing capacity in coastal urban areas than occurred. This raises some issues about the efficiency of the development pattern of rural enterprises, as noted below.

The conflict of interests between the rural and urban economies in the trade in raw materials might also be resolved by a greater degree of specialisation between them.

Urban enterprises will have the incentive to subcontract the production of some stages of their production process to rural enterprise. By doing so they will attain access to cheaper labour, and they may be able to circumvent constraints on supplies of some critical inputs, even electricity, which are binding in their urban locations. The reason is that local governments may have more power to relax those constraints in rural jurisdictions. Furthermore, subcontracting the production of components, for example, promotes the development of relationships which enhance efficiency and spread risks involved in the production process. The development of these links will be accompanied by flows of capital back from the urban economy to the rural economy.

In sum, the nature of the goods, raw materials and capital flows, even in the absence of labour mobility, is not consistent in the longer run with the apparently low degree of specialisation between the rural and urban economies. The opening up of market transactions and greater use of subcontracting will facilitate specialisation and trade. As that occurs, the pressure for further market-oriented reforms will increase.

Location and efficiency

The previous discussion has focused on some aspects of the process of development, structural changes at an aggregate level and the role of enterprises in the rural economy. It should be borne in mind, however, that there are still many problems associated with the rapid growth of rural enterprises. We briefly review some of them here.

Wu (1991) argues that the management structure of rural enterprise and their market orientation are forces for greater levels of efficiency (in terms of ratios of outputs to inputs) compared to state enterprise. We made a similar point in relation to the responsiveness of rural enterprise to shifts in relative prices. However, as Wu also notes, there are some offsetting sources of inefficiency.

The geographical distribution of rural industries not only affects their capital costs and market linkages but also relates to their potential to develop economic cooperation with urban industries. The great majority of rural industries are located across the countryside in the townships and villages which own them. This strong community identity is a major factor influencing their distribution and freedom to merge or link with enterprise from different areas. In other words, trade within the rural economy is also restricted, since the local government intervenes to maintain its local enterprises. Within the same prefecture, and even within the same county, there may be duplication of investment in enterprises, further stretching the demand for resources in short supply. At the same time, resources needed elsewhere may be kept idle to protect local interests (Zhang et al. 1988:7).

Duplication of effort has been a common characteristic of rural industries in every region (Zhang et al. 1988:7). The result distorts markets and investment, and the problem extends from local communities up to provincial level.[15] At the same time, this pattern of development increases the overall costs by requiring infrastructure investment in all areas. Local industries in each village or township require their own roads, electricity supply, transport and communications links and other services. Economies of scale or agglomeration could be lost, and pollution and marketing costs are increased. However, these are empirical issues, since the alternatives involve a greater concentration of the population in some urban areas. It is not clear that those areas, if expanded, would continue to show declining unit costs for the provision of all the necessary infrastructure.

One of the policy responses to this situation is to propose that the development of rural industries should be concentrated in small towns and that clusters should grow up around cores made up of urban industry (Zhang et al. 1988:7). The issue then arises of whether enterprises that have grown up in rural settings using highly labour-intensive technologies will be able to become good partners in the process of cooperation, subcontracting and technology transfer. There is some evidence that they can. In the Yangzi and Zhujiang Deltas, particularly, rural industries have evolved as small clusters, cooperating with urban industry in various ways. Although these two areas have a developed infrastructure and strong links with foreign trade and are not typical of the country as a whole, the results have formed the most dynamic urban–rural industrial networks in China, with sustained rates of growth.

III. Conclusions

The growth of rural enterprises is significant for a number of reasons. First, it is a part of the overall process of industrialisation in China. The out-of-plan character of rural enterprises means that the patterns of investment and trade of this sector are much more likely to match China's comparative advantage. The rapidly growing importance of these firms in the economy means that in the last few years they have started to have a large impact on the growth and composition of China's trade. Their emergence has been an important institutional development which has shifted the pattern of development in China to one much closer to that observed in the rest of East Asia.

There has been both conflict and cooperation in the relationship between the rural and urban economies. The tensions have emerged more strongly in the trade in raw materials. These tensions have led to a greater degree of local protectionism and thus to barriers to trade between urban and rural economies. In some cases, the promotion of the construction of processing capacity in the rural economy also raises serious issues about efficiency of the operation of plants and their location.

Cooperation has been a feature of the trade in intermediate products between the rural and urban economies. This trade is likely to develop and lead to a greater degree of specialisation between the two economies than has been observed so far. As a whole, therefore, the growth of rural enterprises offers the opportunity to exploit an alternative pattern of economic development, leading to a reshaping of both the urban and the rural economies.

Finally, the emergence of rural enterprise has important political implications. A vast new constituency, building on the support for the reform process generated by the rise in agricultural incomes, has been created by the promotion of rural enterprise. A strong coalition of support among local officials and enterprise management and staff is in favour of further enterprise and pricing reform. Indeed, the release of rural industry from its shackles has turned out to be a major force for further economic change and for 'surrounding the cities from the countryside'.

Notes

1. Mao stated that this was his strategy from 1927 to 1949 in a speech to the second session of the Seventh Plenum on 5 May 1949. See *Renmin Chubanshe* (1968: 1316–17).
2. In the following sections, we sometimes distinguish between rural enterprises in total and those run by townships and villages. The latter are a subset of the former, the other subset being those enterprises which are run by individuals or cooperatively. In 1988 township and village-run enterprises accounted for about 64 per cent of total income in rural enterprises, but only 9 per cent of employment (Chen, Watson and Findlay 1991). Another issue is that the term 'rural enterprises' refers to all types of activity, regardless of the sector of the economy in which the enterprise operates. In 1989 less than 2 per cent of rural enterprise output value

came from sectors classified as agricultural (Chen, Watson and Findlay 1991).
3. It should be noted that this classification of enterprises by type of ownership and control does not always correspond precisely to a classification by location. For example, not all urban enterprises will be within the state plan. In the urban economy, there are some collectively or privately-owned enterprises that are outside the plan, but their significance is small in urban economies relative to state enterprises. Furthermore, some rural enterprises may operate in or close to urban areas.
4. There are major issues involved in the ownership and control of these enterprises. Rural enterprises have become very important sources of revenue for basic levels of rural government. These topics are explored in detail in Chen, Watson and Findlay (1991). Aspects of the organisation of the enterprise and their links with local government also affect their behaviour, such as their scale and efficiency. However, these effects lie beyond the scope of our discussion. What is of interest is the use of policy instruments by local governments to promote the interests of enterprises within their region. Some examples are provided in what follows.
5. For a useful discussion of all aspects of rural enterprise development during the 1980s, see the State Council Research Unit Rural Economy Group and the Rural Development Research Institute of the Chinese Academy of Social Sciences (1990). The growth of rural industry in the first half of the 1980s was reported in pioneering work edited by Byrd and Lin (1990).
6. There is some uncertainty over the actual content of the output value series and whether they are in current or constant prices. The figures cited are from the State Statistical Bureau statistical system and, according to Li (1991), the data since 1980 are in terms of 1980 prices. A comparison with the current year prices in the Statistical Bureau's 1991 statistical survey tends to confirm this point. Other sources give different figures. The Ministry of Agriculture gave 840 billion yuan for 1989 (see *Jingji Ribao*, 10 May 1990:3). A recent report gave 950 billion yuan for 1990 (SWB, FE/W0159/A/1, 19 December 1990). These data may be in current

prices. Some economists also argue that the Ministry of Agriculture series may be more reliable since the Ministry statistical system reaches more deeply into the countryside. As we discuss below, a better evaluation of performance is value added.

7. Chen, Watson and Findlay (1991) caution that the data in Table 1 are distorted by changes in the industrial classification system. But they note that the continual adjustment of categories reflects both the changes in ownership and management taking place as the reforms evolved, and the rapid growth which was occurring outside the existing categories, thereby forcing the continual changes in statistical methods. They conclude it is reasonable to assume that the overall rise in numbers from 1978 to 1989 shown in Table 1 closely represents the long-term growth taking place, even though the jumps from 1.35 million in 1983 to 6.06 million in 1984 and again to 12.22 million in 1985 reflect changes in statistical procedures rather than the actual growth for the years concerned.

8. In Shandong, for example, the output value of rural industries in the first five months of 1990 accounted for 50 per cent of all industrial output value, up 6 per cent over the same period of the previous year (*Zhongguo Xiangzhen Qiye Bao*, 25 June 1990:1). In Guangdong it was anticipated that the output value would account for 30 per cent of provincial industrial output value in 1990 (*Ao-gang Xinxi Bao*, 9 October 1990). In Zhejiang the proportion was nearly 51 per cent in 1987 (*Zhongguo Xiangzhen Qiye*, No. 9, 1988:21–6).

9. These data refer only to enterprises run by townships and villages, not to all rural enterprises.

10. Figure 3 includes a data point for 1990. We estimated the real 1990 output growth over 1989 as 10 per cent, based on recent press reports of gross value of output (see note 7), after an allowance for inflation of about 3 per cent in 1990.

11. The process of revenue contracting and its implications are discussed in more detail in Chen, Watson and Findlay (1991).

12. Aggregate data on this issue are not easily available but there are many local reports. *Ao-gang Xinxi Bao* (9 October 1990:1) claims that Guangdong rural enterprise exports account for one-fifth of the national total for all such

exports; *Zhongguo Xiangzhen Qiye Bao* (11 April 1990: 1) reports that rural enterprise exports accounted for one-third of Tianjin's export value in 1989; *Zhongguo Xiangzhen Qiye* (1988:21–6, No. 9) reports that in Zhejiang the proportion was 16 per cent in 1987, with a target of 30 per cent for 1990.

13. These data refer to only township enterprises. The aggregate of all rural enterprises, including private would be even more labour-intensive. See note 2.

14. See the speech by Chen Junsheng, SWB, FE/1085, B2/2–3. The adoption of a new law on product quality attestation is also aimed at improving product reputation and quality generally (SWB, FE/1094, C1/1–3). The survey was reported in *Zhongguo Xiangzhen Qiye Bao*, 27 May 1991:1.

15. See Watson, Findlay and Du (1989) for examples in the textile industry.

References

Anderson, K. (1990) 'Urban household subsidies and rural out-migration: the case of China' *Communist Economies* Vol.2, No.4

Byrd, W.A. and Qingsong Lin (eds) (1990) *China's Rural Industry: Structure, Development and Reform* Oxford: Oxford University Press, for the World Bank

Chen, Chunlai, A. Watson and C. Findlay (1991) 'One state—two economies: current issues in China's rural industrialisation' *Chinese Economy Research Unit Working Paper* No.91/15, University of Adelaide, Adelaide

Chen, Guohua (1988) 'Shi lun neidi xiang-zhen waixiang qiye de fazhan zhanlue' [A tentative discussion of the development strategy for export-oriented township enterprises in the interior] *Zhongguo Xiangzhen Qiye* No.7, pp.8–11

China Agricultural Yearbook Editorial Group (1981) *Zhongguo Nongye Nianjian 1980* [China Agricultural Yearbook 1980] Beijing: Nongye Chubanshe

He, Kang (1988) 'Kaichuang xiang-zhen qiye chukou chuanghui gongzu de xin jumian'

[Create a new situation in the work on township enterprise exports and foreign currency earnings] *Jingji Gongzuo Tongxun* No.2, pp.9–11

Hu, Ping (1988) 'Ba xiang-zhen qiye tuixiang waimao chukou shengchan de zhu zhanchang' [The main battle in pushing township enterprises towards foreign trade and exports production] *Jingji Gongzuo Tongxun* No.2, p.12

Li, Bingkun (1991) 'Jiushi niandai xiangzhen qiye de jiankang fazhan yu hongguan tiaokong' [The healthy development and macro-control of township enterprises in the nineties] *Zhongguo Gongye Jingji Yanjiu* No.7, pp.43–9

Ministry of Agriculture, Planning Bureau (1989) *Zhongguo Nongcun Jingji Tongji Ziliao Daquan, 1949–1986* [A Comprehensive Book of China's Rural Economic Statistics, 1949–1986] Beijing: Agriculture Press

Renmin Chubanshe (1968) *Mao Zedong Xuanji* [Selected Works of Mao Zedong] Beijing: Renmin Chubanshe

State Council Research Unit Rural Economy Group and the Rural Development Research Institute of the Chinese Academy of Social Sciences (eds) (1990) *Bie Wu Xuanze— Xiangzhen Qiye yu Guomin Jingji de Xietiao Fazhan* [There is a Choice—The Co-ordinated Development of Rural Enterprises and the National Economy] Beijing: Gaige Chubanshe

State Statistical Bureau (1988) *Zhongguo Tongji Nianjian 1988* [China Statistical Yearbook 1988] Beijing: China Statistical Press

—— (1990) *Statistical Yearbook of China* Beijing: Zhongguo Tongji Chubanshe

Summary of World Broadcasts (SWB), Far East (various issues), British Broadcasting Corporation Monitoring Service, Reading

Tam, On Kit (1991) 'Capital market development in China' *World Development* Vol.19, No.5, pp.511–32

Tao, Junchang and Jie Zhao (1988) 'Xian-zhen qiye zouxiang shijie de jinqi zhanlue' [The short-term strategy for linking township enterprises with the world] *Caijing Wenti Yanjiu* No.2, pp.50–5

Warr, P. and Xiaoguang Zhang (1990) 'Chinese trade pattern and comparative advantage' Paper presented to the Chinese Students Society for Economic Studies, Macquarie University, November

Watson, A., C. Findlay, and Yintang Du (1989) 'Who won the "wool war"? A case study of rural product marketing in China' *China Quarterly* No.118 (June), pp.213–41

Wu, Yanrui (1990) 'Rural industrialisation in China: a general equilibrium analysis' *Chinese Economy Research Unit Working Paper* No.90/2, Univeristy of Adelaide, Adelaide

—— (1991) 'Efficiency analysis of Chinese enterprises: a case study of the steel industry' *Chinese Economy Research Unit Working Paper* No.91/xx, University of Adelaide, Adelaide

Young, S. (1991) 'Wealth but not security: attitudes towards private business in China in the 1980s' *The Australian Journal of Chinese Affairs* 25 (January), pp.115–38

Zhang, Gensheng et al. (1988) 'Wo guo xiangzhen qiye zhongchangqi fazhan guoxiang' [Thoughts on the medium and long-term development of China's township enterprises] *Zhongguo Nongcun Jingji* No.1

Zhang, Xiaohe (1991a) 'The classification of China's industries by factor intensity and the corresponding trade pattern of China' *Chinese Economy Research Unit Working paper* No.91, University of Adelaide, Adelaide

—— (1991b) 'The urban-rural isolation policy and its impact on China's production and trade pattern' *Chinese Economy Research Unit Working Paper* No.91/xx, University of Adelaide, Adelaide

Zhong, Borong (1988) 'Xiang-zhen qiye yao jinru guoji da xunhuan' [Township enterprises must enter international circulation] *Xuexi Yu Sikao* No.1, pp.3, 14

Zhongguo Nongye Nianjian Editorial Department (1986) *Zhongguo Nongcun Fagui 1984* [China Rural Laws 1984] Beijing: Nongye Chubanshe

14 The Nature of the Township–Village Enterprise

Chun Chang and Yijiang Wang

I. Introduction

In the past 15 years, the total output of the township–village enterprises (TVEs) in China has grown at an average rate of 30 per cent per annum. In 1993 TVEs produced about 40 per cent of the nation's total industrial product and provided employment to 112 million people.[1] Questions have been raised regarding the nature of township–village enterprises: Are they private firms or state-owned enterprises disguised under nominal collective ownership? How do they differ from producer cooperatives? What explains their ownership structure?[2]

In this paper we follow Grossman and Hart (1986) and study the ownership structure of the TVE along two dimensions: the residual control right and the residual benefit right. We conclude that the TVE is controlled by the township–village government (TVG), not by its nominal owners, the local citizens. Moreover, with explicit rules specified by the centre regarding profit distribution, residual benefits of the TVE are shared between the local citizens and the TVG. This ownership structure of the TVE is compared to

that of four other more familiar types of enterprises, producer cooperatives (PCs), state-owned enterprises (SOEs), Japanese firms (J-firms), and large American corporations (A-firms), to demonstrate the uniqueness of the ownership structure in the TVE.

We argue that the rationale for assigning the control right to the TVG reflects the costs and benefits of giving control to various parties. For example, under the existing Chinese system of highly concentrated political powers, private citizens may find it difficult to obtain key resources that are critical for the success of the TVE.[3] Giving control to the citizens thus leads to a less promising future for the TVE. The more difficult question is why local citizens, rather than the state or the TVG, should be the nominal owners of the TVE. We view the citizen's nominal ownership as a means by which the centre makes a commitment to policies and rules that guarantee to local agents, the TVG and local citizens, the main benefits from the operation of the TVE. This commitment provides local agents with strong incentives to make sure that the TVE succeeds. Finally, to prevent the TVG from appropriating

Reprinted with permission. Chun Chang and Yijiang Wang, 1994. 'The nature of the township–village enterprise', *Journal of Comparative Economics*, 19(3):434–52 (with minor editing).

excessive benefits, the centre makes some explicit rules as to how the profit of the TVE should be distributed.

The TVG's control distinguishes the TVE from genuine private enterprises and workers' co-operatives. Local ownership and its distributional effect distinguish the TVE from SOEs and explain differences in their performance.[4] Consequently, it seems natural and useful to view the ownership structure of the TVE as the centre's solution to a design problem in which the objective is to improve the welfare of local citizens subject to two constraints. One is that the present political system in China must be preserved.[5] The other is that local agents must be provided with economic incentives. The first constraint explains why the government prefers the TVE to a genuine private sector. The second constraint explains why the TVE is locally, not nationally, owned, as are the SOEs.

Two points should be clarified immediately. First, to say that the centre wants to improve the citizens' welfare does not have to mean that the centre is caring and benevolent. It is perfectly logical to think of a self-interested centre caring about the citizens' welfare because the centre views improving citizens' welfare as part of its effort to sustain and strengthen its political power.[6] Second, to say that the TVE is the centre's solution to a design problem does not mean that the centre had a well-calculated plan before it developed TVEs. In fact, for a long time the centre focused largely on improving the SOEs' efficiency, but this task proved very difficult, to say the least. Meanwhile, genuine private enterprises and foreign-owned firms have played relatively unimportant roles in Chinese economic growth until recently. In contrast, the TVEs, growing at an average annual rate of about 30 per cent since 1978, demonstrated powerful dynamics from the very beginning. There is little doubt that the enthusiasm and initiatives of the TVGs and local citizens were among the major reasons for the impressive performances of the TVEs. The success of the TVEs forced the centre to pay more attention to them, to rely upon them

for development, and also to formulate systematic policies regarding them. In spite of this rather passive role of the centre, it is important to keep in mind that the centre has the ultimate power to veto initiatives from below and to force TVEs in directions of its choice. It follows that the policies regarding the TVEs must have reflected the centre's preferences. It is in this passive sense that we say the centre designed the TVE.

It is also worth pointing out that the TVEs are a complex phenomenon, and the study of them is still in an early stage. Our analysis is a simplified treatment of the TVEs with many rich elements left out. Our purpose is to emphasise the most important factors such as communist monopoly over political power and government control over key economic resources in order to see how they affect the design of the TVEs.

II. The Ownership Structure of the TVE

The TVE is nominally owned by the local citizens. To understand the meaning of ownership it is important to know who has the residual right of the control and who enjoys the residual benefit of the TVE (see Grossman and Hart 1986).

The right of control

Most observers seem to agree that the control right of the TVE is in the hands of the TVG.[7] As noted by Weitzman and Xu (1994:132).

> Many Chinese economists report that TVEs are usually controlled by local governments and typically there is no separation between the communal government and the TVEs. These reports describe a situation where many TVEs do not have genuine autonomy in business transactions; the communal government has major influence in the determination of managerial personnel and employment.[8]

Upon closer examination, there seem to be two ways in which the TVG can exercise control, one direct and the other indirect. In the early stages of the TVE's life, the TVG is more likely to play a direct managerial role in the TVE. It will choose or approve projects, raise or help raise funds, mobilise manpower and other resources within its jurisdiction to support the project, and supervise the construction process. This is what Song (1990:396) calls a father–son relationship between the TVG and the TVE.

After the initial stages of the life of a TVE, the TVG may decide to delegate some authority to professional managers and not remain in direct control of the daily operations of the TVE. Even if a TVG delegates full operational responsibilities to management, this does not mean that the management has the control right in the TVE, independent of the control of the TVG. This is so because the TVG keeps the power to appoint managers. The managers of the TVE thus often find it in their own best interest to make major decisions in close consultation with the TVG and not to resist decisions made by the TVG.

Workers in the TVE sometimes do have the nominal right of voting to approve or disapprove the TVG's choice of a manager. For at least two obvious reasons, hwever, this right semes to be largely cosmetic. First, usually the TVG has to initiate a vote. If it is satisfied with a manager, the TVG is not required to initiate a vote. The manager can thus remain in office indefinitely. Second, the TVG controls many other aspects of a local citizen's life—which are discussed below—including who can work in the TVE. Workers of the TVE, therefore, would rarely want a confrontational relationship with the TVG. Hence managerial nominees of the TVG are rarely, if ever, disapproved by the workers. It is not surprising that, in a survey, Song (1990:399) found that 83.3 per cent of township–village enterprise managers believe that they were appointed by the TVG.[9]

Since the TVE is officially owned collectively by the local citizens, control by the TVG means that there is a separation of ownership and control in the TVE. This, however, is not unusual in modern business enterprises because the separation of ownership and control is common in both capitalist firms, for example, A-and J-firms, and SOEs. What differentiates the TVE from these other firms are the source and the completeness of the control right of a non-owner.[10] In capitalist firms, managerial control is derived from the voluntary delegation of the right by the owners through private contracting in a mutually beneficial manner. Usually when the control right is delegated, mechanisms are also designed to force the manager to give up the right should the firm consistently perform below an expected level. Managerial control in capitalist firms, therefore, may be said to be conditional or incomplete. In contrast, the control right of the centre over SOEs is derived from state power. Unless the centre chooses to give it up, there is almost no means by which citizens can take the right back from the centre. Thus the control of SOEs by the centre is almost unconditional and most complete. The TVG's officials are appointed by higher government authorities. Their control over the TVE is also derived from state power. This is similar to the case of SOEs but different from those of capitalist firms. Since there is no mechanism for the local citizens as the nominal owners to take control back from the TVG, the TVG's control over the TVG is more complete than managerial control of capitalist firms.

Benefit distribution

The right to derive benefits from propertry is considered to be another essential dimension of ownership. The question of who are the residual benefit claimants in the TVE can be difficult to answer, especially when it is addressed from a static point of view.[11] From a dynamic point of view, however, it seems fairly clear that the residual benefits produced by the TVE are shared between the TVG and the citizens.

Post-tax profits of the TVE are divided into three parts. The centre requires that the largest share, about 60 per cent of the profit, be retained by the firm for production expansion (see Ministry of Agriculture 1990).[12] The distribution of the remaining 40 per cent is not explicitly regulated by the centre, nor can its division be found in available statistics. In many cases, however, a relatively small portion is used as bonuses for workers, while a large portion is paid as fees to the TVG.[13]

The fees paid to the TVG are used for two purposes. One is for the support of communal social programs and infrastructure projects, such as education and construction of roads and irrigation systems.[14] The other supports the operation of the TVG. This often covers many benefits enjoyed by TVG officials, such as nice offices, generous travel expenses, banquets, and government vehicles for private use.[15] It thus seems fair to view the fees paid to the TVG as a benefit shared between the TVG and the citizens, with a significant amount going to each party.

It is important to know who benefits from the retained profit used for further development of the TVE, which accounts for 60 per cent of the total net profit. The local citizens seem to benefit most from these retained profits through three channels. First, development of TVEs means improved job security for TVE workers. Second, it provides new job opportunities for other citizens in the township–village. Given the substantial wage differentials between agricultural and industrial labour in China, finding employment in the industrial sector for more family members is a way by which rural households can increase their incomes rapidly. For many of them, the TVE offers the most accessible and desirable industrial job opportunities.[16] Finally, if the share of the TVG's expenditure for communal welfare programs remains stable, increased profit also means expanded social programs.[17]

Of course, the budget that the TVG officials can use for their own perk consumption will also increase because the retained profits contribute to the growth of TVEs and to greater profits in the future. TVG officials, therefore, also benefit from the retained profits of the TVEs.

Two additional factors should be considered when we think about how the TVG and the citizens share the benefits of the TVE. One is that the TVG officials have shorter time horizons than

the citizens. As government officials, they may work in a particular township or village for a limited term, say 5 or 10 years, and then be moved to another government position. This means that they cannot enjoy the benefits that the retained profits will produce after they leave. In contrast, most local citizens and their families will live in the same township or village for their lifetimes.[18] They can thus benefit for their entire lives from social projects such as a better-educated population, better roads, irrigation, and other infrastructures. The jobs they obtained at the TVE are also likely to be theirs for as long as the TVE remains healthy.

The other factor has to do with the effort of TVG officials. As indicated earlier, the TVG is responsible for many social programs. To finance these programs, a typical practice is for the TVG to charge the citizens fees. The citizens, however, often find these to be excessive. Their resistance can be so severe that it sometimes becomes a major source of social unrest.[19] Increased profits from the TVE can make this difficult part of a TVG's job much easier. As profits are paid to the TVG, the fees that need to be collected from the citizens to finance these programs are reduced accordingly. At the same time, as their incomes increase with growing employment in the TVE, citizens' resistance to these fees becomes weaker. An increase of total resources within the township–village, therefore, whether as fees to the TVG or as citizens' private incomes, can be said to improve the TVG's utility in a broader sense.

Ownership structure: a summary

Most people seem to agree that the TVE is controlled by the TVG, not its nominal owners, the local citizens. It follows that, as in modern capitalist firms and SOEs, ownership and control are separated in the TVE. It seems fair to say that the residual benefits of the TVE are shared between the TVG and the citizens, with the citizens the main beneficiaries. An important factor that guarantees this division of benefits is the centre's policy that 60 per cent of the TVE's profit must be retained within the TVE for development. Another important policy is that the TVG should spend sizeable amounts of fees from the TVE's profits for rural social programs and infrastructure. Such rules are imposed by an authority that has the power to enforce them. They are also relatively simple rules to enforce.

Table 1 summarises the above discussion on the nominal ownership, control right, and distribution of benefits in the TVE. The features of four other types of firms along the same dimensions are also provided for comparison. Many writers have likened the TVE to the PCs. The table, however, seems to suggest that the ownership structure of the TVE bears a greater resemblance to that of the A-firms in many aspects. First, in both the TVE and the A-firms there is a separation of ownership and control, as seen in the fact that Row 1 and Row 2 in the table are occupied by different parties. Such a separation is not as obvious in PCs. Second, in both the TVE and A-firms, nominal owners are the main beneficiaries from improved performance of the firm. This is not true in SOEs and J-firms. The main difference between the TVE and A-firms is that, instead of professional management appointed by owners, the TVG as a government institution is in control of the TVE. Separation of ownership and control also exists in J-firms and SOEs. Workers in J-firms, however, have more control of the firm than their counterparts in the TVE or a A-firms. Their compensation is also more directly related to the

performance of the firm.[20] We thus see more consistency between Line 2 and Line 3 for J-firms, but not between Row 1 and Row 3, as in the cases of the TVE and A-firms. A situation similar to that in J-firms is found in SOEs, where the government has the control rights and also benefits the most from improved performance of SOEs. The comparison between the TVE and SOEs suggests that nominal ownership has more distributional significance in the TVE than in SOEs, as shown by the consistency between Rows 1 and 3 for the TVE but not for the SOEs.

III. Rationale for the Ownership Structure in the TVE

Benefits and costs of the TVG's control

The gist of Grossman and Hart (1986) is that the allocation of the residual control right has incentive effects, and every ownership structure has both costs and benefits due to these effects.[21] Their theory can be used to explain why in the TVE the control right is vested in the TVG, because under the current political and economic system in China the inputs of the TVG are far more important than those of the citizens for the success of the TVE. It is, therefore, more beneficial for the TVG to control the TVE.

The TVG makes at least three critical contributions to the TVE. The first is safety. China is a country with a long tradition of authoritarian government. This tradition has been developed

Table 1 Ownership structure in different types of firms

	TVE	PC	SOE	J-firm	A-firm
1. Nominal owner	Local citizens	Workers	People of nation	Shareholders	Shareholders
2. Control right	TVG	Workers and managers	Centre	Workers and managers	Managers
3. Main beneficiaries	Citizens and TVG	Workers	Centre and citizens	Workers and shareholders	Shareholders

to an unprecedented extreme under the rule of the Communist Party. To ensure so-called comprehensive proletarian dictatorship, Mao devised a political system that gives the Communist Party the right to intervene in every aspect of a citizen's life. The TVGs in the Chinese countryside are parts of a large government institution with broad power given by the fundamentals of the political system. They can, and often do, use this power to enforce their policies.[22] For this reason, the full support of the TVG can provide the citizens and other stakeholders in the TVE a sense of security needed for long-term development.

The second contribution of the TVG is managerial inputs. In a society where the market has been systematically suppressed, ordinary citizens with immediately identifiable managerial talents are a scarce resource. In contrast, the TVG is the figure that is in charge, organising major activities in its jurisdiction. Many TVG officials are well-educated and informed. Giving control to the TVG, therefore, seems very natural to most citizens. The TVG's authority, based on the broad sociopolitical power it enjoys, also gives it great managerial advantages that are not available to an ordinary citizen with managerial talents (see Murrell and Wang (1993) for a detailed discussion). For example, choosing the location of a TVE often involves conflicting interests. The noise, water, or air pollution is likely to be more severe for the nearby villages than for more distant parts of the town. Without a market or other social mechanism to compensate those who bear most of these adverse consequences, the TVG is often the only available local institution that has the authority to mediate negotiations to settle these controversies. Otherwise the land, water, or other resources needed by a TVE may not be as readily available.[23]

The third contribution of the TVG is access to outside resources such as bank loans that are critical for the development of the TVE. In an authoritarian communist system, resources are highly concentrated and tightly controlled by the government. This means that, without the

approval of the government, citizens are often denied access to resources required to accomplish any major project. Establishing and operating a TVE is no exception.[24] For example, because private banking in China is undeveloped, the TVEs rely primarily on the state banking system for loans.[25] Since private citizens have almost no access to the state banking system, the role of the TVG is critical for gaining access to credit.[26]

Compared with those of the TVG, the inputs of citizens are less critical and more easily replaceable. An important resource that citizens contribute to the TVE is their labour. Since labour is an abundant resource in China, any individual withdrawing his labour would have a very limited effect on the development of the TVE. With the low skill requirement for the kinds of products that most TVEs produce, the skills that citizens possess are unlikely to be in serious shortage. In many cases, citizens also contribute their financial resources to TVEs through *jizhi*, that is, pooling financial resources, especially at the initial stages of some TVEs. However, without the power and reputation of the TVG, *jizhi* may be difficult to organise.[27] Also, for sustained development of TVEs on a scale that can benefit a large portion of the local citizens in significant ways, bank loans are clearly more critical. Because citizens' resources are relatively unimportant for the development of the TVE and more easily replaceable, granting them the control right does not seem to have many significant benefits. The costs associated with the citizens' control right, however, may be large and numerous. All the benefits associated with the control by the TVG would be lost. A field study by Zhou and Fang (1989) describes the difficulties that private enterprises in Wenzhou faced. They found that after decades of government anticapitalism propaganda and efforts to eliminate the private sector altogether, the owners of private enterprises faced enormous social pressure and distrust. They bore considerable social stigma and were afraid of being labelled as selfish or exploiters. They worried about a possible reversal of the government policy that allowed them to exist. They paid taxes at a rate 250 per cent higher than did the TVEs. They had to obtain bank loans from the government bureau in charge of the TVEs, not directly from the banks. They paid the market rate for electricity when it was available to them, while the TVEs paid the low government-regulated price. Otherwise they had to generate their own electricity at a cost twice as high as the market rate. Few rights were guaranteed to them, and their operation was hampered by all kinds of government institutions. In addition, the owner-managers of these private enterprises were not very well educated. In a sample of 50 such private enterprises, Zhou and Fang found that 42 per cent of the owner-managers had less than six and 90 per cent had less than nine years of education. It can be noted that although the actual discriminatory practices against private businesses vary from place to place in China, the overall situation is that they all have to overcome many great difficulties in order to survive and grow.

A third candidate who may have the control right over the TVE is a government authority higher than the TVG, for example, the centre itself. If the centre has the control of the TVE, as it does in many SOEs, it will certainly be able to enjoy all the benefits that the TVG enjoys, but the costs will also be higher. One cost results from the agency problem. The centre, without giving the control right to the TVG, cannot ensure the support and cooperation of a TVG so that a TVE located within its jurisdiction can perform well.[28] Another likely problem associated with direct control by the centre is the soft-budget constraint. As the party who controls the TVE, the centre will also bear the consequences of its decisions. If the TVE is not performing well financially because of a decision by the centre, the centre will be obliged to bail it out through additional loans or reduced taxes. Because the bank is also controlled by the centre, it would be difficult for the bank to resist the centre's order to extend a loan.[29] The same is true with the tax system. As the experiences of SOEs suggest, the TVE is likely

to become very inefficient once it develops an expectation of a soft-budget constraint.

The above analyses suggest that giving the TVG the control of the TVE is an arrangement that generates more benefits at a smaller cost than does giving control to either the citizens or the centre.

Citizens as nominal owners

We now explain why the local citizens should be made the nominal owners of the TVE instead of, for example, making the TVE into a local SOE controlled by the TVG but owned by the people of the whole nation.

The answer to this question would be straightforward and somewhat trivial if a change in nominal ownership would also alter the current pattern of distribution. For example, if the distribution of benefits from the TVE becomes very egalitarian among a much larger population after the TVE is changed into an SOE, it is natural to expect the kind of incentive problems typical in a partnership to emerge. A more interesting and also more challenging question is whether the TVE would perform worse if the centre were to take ownership away from the local citizens but keep the distribution system exactly the same. The issue involved here is the credibility of the centre's promise that the sharing rule will not be changed. The question thus becomes whether making the local citizens the owners leads to a better commitment to the distributional rule that guarantees that the local agents are the main beneficiaries of the TVE. While an entirely satisfactory answer to this question is probably still beyond the reach of economics, the prevailing social psychology and moral standard of our time are that property rights should be respected. If the centre takes from the owner too much of the return to a property, or forcefully changes ownership in order to gain a better share in distribution, it is likely to lead to strong resistance from the citizens. The centre could also suffer a great loss of reputation. Changing a promised distributional rule for benefits produced by a government property will also lead to a loss of reputation, but probably to a lesser extent. In the history of Communist China, the centre has used both methods for redistribution purposes. In 1949 and the following years, it first confiscated land from the landlords and gave it to poor peasants, and then collectivised farming. In 1956, it coerced most capitalist enterprises into joint ownership with the state and then forced the capitalist owners to accept a fixed interest payment for their share. In all these events, the social and economic shocks were enormous and their consequences were disastrous. The tax policy of the centre regarding the SOEs has also changed from time to time. These changes have impacts but not nearly as great as those on occasions when property rights were directly violated.[30]

A good reputation is important even for an authoritarian government because many of its policies cannot be implemented without voluntary cooperation from various other parties. At present, the Chinese government is campaigning for modernisation. To achieve this goal, it wants to encourage private business and foreign investment. The incentives of domestic and foreign private investors to respond positively to this policy depend on the reputation of the Chinese government as a protector of property rights. With so many other things at stake, whatever the centre may gain by violating the property rights of the TVE, it would probably lose more by scaring away many potential investors. For this reason, the centre's commitment to a distributional rule based on ownership seems to be a commitment with a higher stake, and thus it is also a commitment with better credibility.

Ownership in the TVE as a design problem for the centre

We have argued that the rationale of the ownership structure in the TVE can be understood by looking at the costs and benefits of alternative arrangements. For such an analysis to be valid, the premise that the centre, which has the ultimate power to determine the ownership structure in the TVE, cares about production efficiency in the TVE must be true.

Yet, if using whatever given amount of resource to produce the largest possible output is the centre's objective in the design of the TVE, then it can probably better achieve it by giving most benefits to the TVG instead of the citizens. The centre can achieve such a goal by making the TVG the nominal owner or by not regulating the distribution of the TVE so that the TVG with control right will automatically give itself the largest share of the benefit. However, the centre did set explicit rules to guarantee that most benefits accrue to the citizens even though this may mean some loss of incentives on the part of the TVG. This seems to suggest that the centre must have the citizens' welfare in mind.

Control is given to the TVG for the benefits associated with it. These benefits exist, however, largely because, in China, the government has control rights over too many other things. At a local level, the TVG is given a very broad power over citizens' private, social, political, and economic lives as a means to preserve the authoritarian political system. The continued existence of various benefits that the TVE can derive from the TVG's control, therefore, depends negatively on the extent to which the centre is willing to relax its control over other aspects of citizens' lives. We can think of a complete relaxation of these controls as being equivalent to a fundamental change of the Chinese political system. Since, at the present, this seems to be something that the centre is reluctant to do, the broad and general control rights of the TVG within its jurisdiction can be viewed as a constraint on the centre's problem of achieving efficiency in the TVE.

The above discussion has touched several issues related to the ownership structure in the TVE. The following model seems to most coherently summarise all these aspects. In this model, the centre faces the problem of designing an ownership structure in the TVE. Its objective is to maximise local citizens' welfare. It gives the control right to the party whose inputs are the most critical for the success of the TVE, that is, the TVG. The centre also takes two measures to provide incentives for the local agents. First, it assigns nominal ownership to the township–village citizens as a commitment that most benefits produced by the TVE will be retained locally. Second, it specifies explicit sharing rules that at the same time provide the TVG officials with incentives to improve the performance of the TVE and prevent these officials from abusing their power and giving excessive benefits to themselves.

Some empirical implications

The rationale of the ownership structure in the TVE generates some empirical implications for variations and the dynamics in Chinese rural enterprises' ownership structures. It suggests that enterprises with a low capital requirement are more likely to be privately owned than those with a higher capital requirement. This is so because access to the state banking system, and hence also the role of the TVG, is not as critical in enterprises with lower capital requirement. Also, smaller enterprises are more likely to be privately owned, while collective ownership and TVGs' control are more likely in larger enterprises. This is so because smaller enterprises need less capital, less managerial talent, and can more easily satisfy their input needs from family members, relatives, and friends. All these reduce the benefits that once can expect from giving the TVG the control right.

Many casual observations support the above predictions. Due to limited space, we cite the result of only one study here. Hu (1989:303) compared the patterns of rural enterprises in southern Jiangsu province ('Sunan model', or S-model) and the Gengche area in northern Jiangsu province ('Gengche model', or G-Model). He made the following observation.

S-model is based on productive power needed for producing modern machinery and electronic products. Technologies in these industries are capital intensive (in Kunshan county where the development

of TVEs is at an average level, capital requirement for starting a new TVE exceeds one to two million yuan, or even tens of million yuan for larger projects) …Firms in G-model are mostly based on handicraft skills. They have low capital needs, are simple to manage, and do not consume too much energy. It is therefore appropriate for them to develop family-based small scale enterprises. We thus see a boom of private economy [in the Gengche area]. On the other hand, in the S-model…the absolute dominance of collectively-owned enterprises at the township and village levels developed naturally.

Dynamically, our theory suggests that the historical and present government policies and the extent of reforms also matter. Private ownership is more likely in places where the centre and its local representatives have a more hands-off policy or where the political system has deteriorated more quickly, because in these places citizens are likely to feel safer about their properties, face less social pressure, and find resources more readily available. The reverse is more likely to be true where government control remains strong. For the same reason, as economic reforms continue, resources become more easily available through the market instead of through bureaucratic mechanisms. Citizens are also likely to gain more confidence in the safety of their property. Therefore, more private ownership can be expected as a result of continued reforms in China. Byrd (1990:195), for example, reports that, in 1985, the share of industrial output produced by private firms was 10 per cent in Nanhai County, whereas it was only 3 per cent in Wuxi. Both Wuxi and Nanhai belong to those areas in China where TVEs have been most successful. Nanhai, however, is in Guangdong province where reforms started the earliest and have been the most profound in China, whereas Wuxi is in southern Jiangsu province where government control has remained very tight. Byrd (1990:211) also reports that, starting from zero, the share of total gross income generated by rural private enterprises increased steadily in both a sample of four counties and in China as a whole from 1978 through 1986. The trend of increasing importance of private ownership in Chinese rural enterprises since the inception of the reforms seems clear.

IV. Concluding Remarks

The ownership structure of TVEs is not the result of free contracting among private agents as in a market economy. It is, instead, a product of an environment in which an authoritarian government with monopolistic political power plays a dominant role in economic life. In such an environment, a cost-benefit analysis explains why the right of control is given to the TVG. In this sense, the ownership structure in the TVE is chosen in the same manner as it is in a private firm. The underlying factors that affect benefits and costs, however, are fundamentally different. In the case of private firms, a cost-benefit analysis of control is closely associated with such concepts as unverifiable information, uncontractible contingencies, moral hazard problems, and hold-up threats. In the case of the TVE, concentrated economic and political power under the communist system largely explains the most important costs and benefits under alternative control arrangements.

The future of the TVE is ambiguous. On the one hand, since a fundamental change in the Chinese political system is unlikely in the near future, the TVE will likely continue to play an important role in the Chinese economy. On the other hand, as economic reforms continue to undermine the traditional political system in China and move the economy toward a more market-oriented system, the TVE will probably become a less desirable form of organisation in the future. This raises the possibility of a need for privatising at least some of the existing TVEs in the future. How such a privatisation scheme should proceed is an issue of great policy concern.

Another question of interest and importance regarding the future of the TVE is how successful it can continue to be within the confines of its current ownership structure. Observers have noticed that the growth rates of employment at TVEs have declined dramatically in the past few years while their output growth rates continued to be high.[31] Many observers believe that TVEs have been prematurely substituting capital for labour. It is easy to infer from our discussion above a strong local bias in the TVE's behavior. Due to such a bias, wages paid to a worker who is a local citizen will have a higher value than the wages paid to a worker who is an outsider. It is thus reasonable to think that the TVE will demonstrate one pattern of labour employment before full local employment is reached but another after it is. This leads us to speculate that the low growth rates of labour employment in the past few years have something to do with full local employment in places where TVEs have been the most successful and with a lack of adequate growth of TVEs in places where TVEs have been less successful. Our intention here is not to fully address the issue; issues like this can be better addressed by theoretical modelling of the TVE's behavior and systematic empirical work. We hope that the discussion in this paper on the nature of the TVE will contribute to a more solid theoretical foundation on which future modelling of the TVE's behavior and empirical works on the TVE can be conducted.

Acknowledgements

We thank Changzhen Gong, Shuhe Li, Dwight Perkins, Louis Putterman, Christine Wong, two anonymous referees, Josef Brada, and the participants of the 1993 Meeting of the Chinese Economist Society, the Center of Entrepreneurial Studies, and the Freeman International Forum at the University of Minnesota for helpful comments. We also thank Gary Jefferson, Yingyi Qian, Martin Weitzman, and Chenggang Xu for useful discussions about township–village enterprises. We are deeply indebted to numerous local government, bank, and township–village enterprise officials in Changsha for their warm hospitality that made a field study conducted there in June 1993 most fruitful and enjoyable. Wang also gratefully acknowledges partial financial support provided by the IPD, Carlson School of Management, and the China Center at the University of Minnesota.

Notes

1. See *People's Daily* (Overseas Edition, January 8, 1994:1).
2. The main results of some earlier efforts to address these questions are included in Byrd and Lin (1990). Recently, Weitzman and Xu (1994) examined why township–village enterprises can be so successful without clearly defined property rights.
3. Ruttan (1991) emphasises the need to consider the interactions between political and economic developments.
4. Besides its distributional effect, local ownership also makes the state less obligated to bail a TVE out when it is losing money.
5. Note that the centre's objective and the first constraint agree well with the pronounced goal of Deng Xiaoping's reforms, economic prosperity under the political control of the Communist Party.
6. Technically speaking, maximising the citizens' welfare subject to the political constraint may be considered the dual problem of maximising the centre's benefit associated with preserving the current political system subject to the constraint that citizens' welfare is not too low.
7. In some coastal areas, for example, Wenzhou and Guangdong, private control of rural firms is relatively strong, and local government authorities do not interfere in enterprises' affairs as much as they do in the rest of China. See Section III for the factors that cause variations in ownership structures in Chinese rural enterprises.
8. A referee, however, has pointed out that managers and skilled workers now have much of the control right in many TVEs. Shifting control from the TVGs to the managers and skilled workers is part of the dynamic process of change in the TVEs. Our theory makes some predictions about the dynamic process but does not fully address it.

9. In an interview we had in June 1993. Mr M.J. Lai, the director of the Loan Department, Changsha Municipal Branch of the Agriculture Bank, gave us some information regarding management change in his jurisdiction. According to Lai, 30 per cent of the TVE managers in the Changsha municipal area have been changed in the past three years because of poor performance or for various other reasons, for example, 'a corruptive life' lived by a manager. In each case, the change was proposed and supervised by the TVG. At the same time, many managers have stayed in their positions since the start of the firm 10 or 15 years ago. These are cases in which the TVG has so far not proposed a change or another election. Changsha municipality consists of the city of Changsha, four rural counties, and a surburban district. In 1992 about one-third of the municipal's industrial output was produced by the TVEs, which was about the national average.
10. The term completeness of control is used here to describe how difficult it is for the owners to take back the right after delegating control to a non-owner.
11. Weitzman and Xu (1994:133) note that '[t]here is no residual claimant in the traditional sense. The typical resident waits passively to receive or to enjoy the benefits…Even for the income distributed to the residents, which accounts for less than forty per cent of the after-tax profits, the residents still do not have the full rights of disposing with it as they please, since it is intended for social purposes'.
12. This policy seems to have been follwed well in general. In 1990, for example, the TVEs' post-tax profit was 23 billion yuan, of which 12.8 billion yuan, or more than 55 per cent, was used for 'production expansion'. See *A Statistical Survey of China* (Bureau of Statistics 1991:65).
13. This observation is based on personal interviews with TVE and local government officials in the Changsha municipal area. The magnitudes and forms of fee payments vary from town to town. For example, a fixed amount, instead of a fixed rate, may be paid to the TVG. An accurate breakdown of this part of TVE's profit, however, is not crucial for the analyses that follow.

14. In fact, the centre requires the TVG to undertake many of these social and agricultural projects. It also requires the TVG to use income from the TVE's profit to partially finance these projects. In 1990, nearly 2.4 billion yuan of the TVEs' total post-tax profit was spent for rural welfare programs, while another slightly less than 1.5 billion yuan was spent for rural education. These two items counted for more than 16 per cent of the TVEs' total post-tax profits in that year. (See *A Statistical Survey of China*, Bureau of Statistics 1991:65).

15. Statistics of TVG officals' benefits are not available, but anyone who observes the extravagant lives of TVG officials in places where TVEs have been very successful cannot doubt the sizeable benefits these officials receive.

16. According to a *People's Daily* report (Overseas Edition, December 15, 1993:1), of the Chinese rural population's income increase in 1993, 60 per cent was due to the growth of the TVEs. The other 40 per cent was attributable to factors such as improved agricultural productivity and incomes from employment in cities. In the past few years more and more rural people have started to seek employment in the citites. The TVEs, however, still absorb many more workers. In 1993, 70 million rural people worked in the cities, while employment at the TVEs was 112 million workers. China is estimated to still have 150 million surplus rural workers (*People's Daily*, Oveseas Edition, December 16, 1993:8; January 8, 1994:1). Besides limited opportunities, most rural people have to work and live under harsh conditions in the cities. Their jobs in the cities are also mostly temporary and unstable.

17. Indeed the shares of the TVEs' post-tax profits spent for welfare programs, rural education and infrastructures was fairly stable over time. According to a *People's Daily* report (Overseas Edition, December 15, 1993:1), in the first 11 months of 1993, total revenue of the TVEs increased 55 per cent over that from the same period of 1992. The TVEs' profit used for construction of agricultural projects in this period increased 50 per cent. From 1985 to 1990, the total post-tax profit of the TVEs increased 35.8 per cent. During the same period TVEs' income spent for rural welfare programs increased 21.3 per cent, that for rural education

145 per cent, and that for township infrastructure 108 per cent (See *A Statistical Survey of China* (Bureau of Statistics 1991:65).

18. Only a small portion of the rural population works in the cities. Furthermore, the majority of them are only temporary workers in cities. They leave their wives, elderly parents, and children behind in their rural homes. Many of these workers also return to their rural homes for traditional holidays such as the Spring Festival and during the planting and harvest seasons to meet the peak demands for agricultural labour.

19. On June 5, 1993, peasants' complaints of fee burdens led to a riot in a county in China's most populous Sichuan province.

20. According to Freeman and Weitzman (1987), bonuses based on the firm's profit account for one-quarter of Japanese workers' total incomes. Our casual observation suggests this figure is much lower in the TVEs.

21. See Ben-Ner and Jones (1992) and Putterman (1993) for discussion of this idea in different types of firms.

22. A *People's Daily* article (Overseas Edition, August 28, 1993) illustrates what broad power the party head in a model village in northern Chinese Tianjin enjoyed. He could hire or fire people from jobs in the village as he liked and could arrest and physically punish people even for personal reasons. He went so far as to order the beating of two people to death at different times. After the second person was beaten to death, the municipal government felt it necessary to intervene. The party head was arrested and sentenced to 20 years in jail. Of course this is an extreme case, but it does illustrate how far a local government official can abuse power before it becomes a problem.

23. When the construction of a cement plant was being planned in Changsha, villagers living around the chosen site expressed strong objection because of the water and air pollution such a plant would cause. The TVG called the leaders of all villages together to discuss the problem. They agreed that, as a form of compensation, young people in the nearby villages be given priority to work in the plant.

24. We are describing here a picture that better corresponds to the situation in China before the mid 1980s. Economic reforms have significantly

changed the situation but not yet fundamentally. We will discuss what reforms mean to ownership structure in Chinese rural enterprises later in this section.

25. In 1978 and 1979, bank loans counted for 23 and 27 per cent, or about one-quarter, of the TVEs' total circulating capital at the respective year ends. The corresponding figure was 37 per cent for 1983 and has fluctuated around 50 per cent since. Besides bank loans, retained profits are the most important sources for the TVEs' working capital. See Byrd (1990).

26. Loans from the state banking system to the private sector have been negligible. See the case given by Zhou and Fang (1989) below.

27. More often than not *jizhi* is not voluntary. Instead, it is conducted in a manner similar to the one used by the TVG to collect fees for social programs. The TVG orders how much each houschold must contribute.

28. A local government authority is capable of affecting the performance of any firm within its jurisdiction because of the sweeping power it has over people's lives. For example, a TVG may ask an SOE within its jurisdiction to use its resources, money, skills, or equipment to help a local project. If the executives of the SOE do not accommodate this request at least to some extent, they may find their families living in a very hostile environment.

29. We suggest thinking of a discontinuity between the influence of a TVG on a state bank's lending decisions and that of the county government immediately above it, with the influence of the TVG being much weaker. This is so because the state banks have no branches below the county level; they have only office outlets to serve private individuals. Since major lending decisions have to be made at a county or higher bank branch, it is harder for a TVG to assert its influence on banks' lending decisions than for a county or higher government authority. The concept of a soft-budget constraint was first used by Kornai (1992) to describe socialist SOEs' lack of financial responsibilities. Dewatripont and Maskin (1990) explain the phenomenon of informational asymmetry between the centre and the managers.

30. As a recent example, the contracting and responsibility system [*chengbao zheren zhi*] that

implements tax–profit sharing between the government and SOEs was introduced in the mid 1980s to replace the old hand-in-everything system. There has been discussion of whether the new system has led to improved performance of the SOEs. For example, the results of Xiao (1991) and Woo et al. (1994) tend to suggest that reforms led to very limited productivity improvement in SOEs. The work of Chen et al. (1988) shows the opposite. In contrast, when there is a widespread change in ownership, its effect on productivity is often obvious from simple statistics and hardly disputable.

31. See Pitt and Putterman (1992) for a study of employment and wages in TVEs.

References

Ben-Ner, Avner, and Jones, Derek, C., 1992. 'A New Conceptual Framework for the Analysis of the Impact of Employee Participation, Profit Sharing and Owner-ship on Firm Performance', IRC Working Paper 92–10, University of Minnesota.

Bureau of Statistics, 1991. China, *A Statistical Survey of China*, China Statistics Publishing House, Beijing.

Byrd, William, 1990. 'Entrepreneurship, Capital, and Ownership', in W. Byrd and Q. Lin (eds), *China's Rural Industry: Structure, Development and Reform*, Oxford University Press, New York.

—— and Lin, Qingshong (eds), 1990. *China's Rural Industry: Structure, Development and Reform*, Oxford University Press, London/New York.

Chen, Kang, Jefferson, Gary, Rawski, Thomas, Wang, Hongchang, and Zheng, Yuxin, 1988. 'Productivity Change in Chinese Industry: 1953–85', *J. Comp. Econom.* 12(4):570–591, December 1988.

Dewatripont, Mathias, and Maskin, Eric, 1990. 'Credit and Efficiency in Centralised and Decentralised Economies', Discussion Paper 1512, Harvard University, August.

Freeman, Richard, and Weitzman, Martin, 1987. 'Bonuses and Employment in Japan', *J. Japan. Internat. Economies* 1:168–194.

Gelb, Alan, and Svejnar, Jan, 1990. Chinese TVEs in an International Perspective', in W. Byrd and Q. Lin, Eds, *China's Rural Industry: Structure, Development and Reform*, Oxford University Press, London/New York.

Grossman, Sanford, and Hart, Oliver, 1986. 'The Costs and Benefits of Ownership: A Theory of Vertical and Lateral Integration', *J. Polit. Economy* 94(4):691–719, August.

Hu, Tonggeng, 1989. 'Factors Determining the Ownership Structure of Township and Village Enterprises and Its Tendency, in J. Cheng and D. Xia, Eds, *Studying Models of Township and Village Enterprises [Xiangxhen Qiyie Moshi Yianjiu]*, Chinese Social Science, Beijing.

Kornai, Janos, 1992. *The Socialist System*, Princeton University Press and Oxford University Press, Princeton, NJ, and London/New York.

Ministry of Agriculture, China, 1990. *The PRC (People's Republic of China) Regulations of Rural Collectively-Owned Enterprises (RRCOE) [zhonghua renmin gongheguo xiangcun jiti suoyou zhi qiye tiaoli]*, People's Press, Beijing.

Murrell, Peter, and Wang, Yijiang, 1993. 'When Privatization Should be Delayed: The Effect of Communist Legacies on Organizational and Institutional Reforms, *J. Comp. Econom.* 17(2):385–406, June.

Pitt, Mark, M. and Putterman, Louis, 1992. 'Employment and Wages in Township, Village, and Other Rural Enterprises', Mimeo, Brown University.

Putterman, Louis, 1993. 'Ownership and the Nature of the Firm', *J. Comp. Econom.* 17(2)243–263, June.

Ruttan, Vernon W., 1991. 'What Happened to Political Development', *Econom. Develop Cultural Change*, 39(2)265–292, January.

Song, Lina, 1990. 'Convergence: A Comparison of Township-Run Firms and Local State Enterprises', in W. Byrd and Q. Lin (eds), *China's Rural Industry: Structure, Development and Reform*, Oxford University Press, London/New York.

Weitzman, Martin, and Xu, Chenggang, 1994. 'Chinese Township Village Enterprises as Vaguely Defined Cooperatives', *J. Comp. Econom*, 18(2):121–145, April.

Woo, Wing Thye, Hai, Wen, Jin, Yibiao, and Fan, Gang, 1994. 'How Successful has Chinese Enterprise Reform Been?', *J. Comp. Econom.* 18(3):410–437, June.

Xiao, Geng, 1991. 'Managerial Autonomy, Fringe Benefits, and Ownership Structure— A Comparative Study of Chinese State and Collective Enterprises', World Bank Research Paper Series 20.

Zhou, Qunfeng, and Fang, Haiyue, 1989. 'Problems in and Thoughts about Economic Development in Wenzhou, in *Zhongguo Jingji Wenti [China Economic Issues]*, 3:45–49.

15 Public versus Private Ownership of Firms: evidence from rural China

Hehui Jin and Yingyi Qian

I. Introduction

In studying economies in transition from planned to market, no single issue has received more attention from economists and policymakers than the one of property rights and ownership of firms. In Eastern Europe and the former Soviet Union, one observes mass privatisation of old state-owned enterprises (SOEs) and the emergence of new private (including newly privatised) enterprises. In China, old SOEs also declined even without privatisation, and new private enterprises flourish. However, there is a puzzle concerning China's successful Township–Village Enterprises (TVEs).

TVEs are not private enterprises, nor SOEs. While SOEs are (central government-owned) national public firms, TVEs are rural (community government-owned) local public firms controlled by community (township or village) governments. Between 1979 and 1993, the TVE share of the national industrial output expanded from 9 per cent to 27 per cent, while the share of rural private enterprises increased from 0 to 9 per cent (*China Statistical Yearbook* 1994). Combining TVEs with private enterprises in

1993, rural industries as a whole produced 36 per cent of the national industrial output, and rural industries and services employed 123 million people, accounting for about one-half of the national non-farm employment. Rural industries, and in particular TVEs, have made major contributions toward sustaining China's 10 per cent annual growth during its transition to markets.

Why are there many community publically owned TVEs? The conventional theory on the ownership of firms has largely focused on private and national public enterprises. Recently, several new theories have been proposed to explain TVEs. A large body of this literature has viewed TVEs as local (that is, community) government ownership taking advantage of the existing institutional environment to achieve certain government goals.

Several possible objectives of community government are studied. In the context of rural China, the three most relevant goals of a community government are considered to be the community government's revenue (for example, Byrd and Gelb 1990; Oi 1992 and 1994 and Che and Qian 1998b), non-farm employment (for example, Rozelle and Boisvert 1994), and per

Reprinted with permission. Hehui Jin and Yingyi Qian, 1998. 'Public versus private ownership of firms: evidence from rural China, *Quarterly Journal of Economics*, 113(3), August:773–808.

capita income, which provide its financial and political support. Theories suggest that community government ownership of TVEs can be a more effective instrument than private ownership in achieving the government's objectives when contracts are incomplete (for example, Schleifer and Vishny 1994 and Che and Qian 1998b).

Theories also relate the ownership of firms to the specific institutional environment during the process of transition and development. Three institutional factors are emphasised that might give more political and economic advantages to TVEs rather than to private enterprises, given the goals of the community government: the central government's influence, the community government's power, and underdevelopment of the market. These factors can operate through several channels. Theories suggest that TVEs are favored in credit rationing by the central government or in the imperfect capital market (for example, Wong 1988, 1991; Byrd 1990 and Che and Qian 1998a), and TVEs may use their political connections with the central government-owned SOEs to smooth transactions when the product market is underdeveloped (for example, Nee 1992 and Otsuka 1996). Another possibility is that TVEs are vehicles for the community government to cash in the value of land under its control in the absence of asset markets (Naughton 1994, 1996). Other theories propose that TVEs are better protected politically by the community government's power in the absence of secure property rights under the rule of law (for example, Chang and Wang 1994; Li 1996 and Che and Qian 1998b), and TVEs benefit from the community government which was empowered by the initial collective assets and experiences before the reform (for example, Chang and Wang 1994; Putterman 1994 and Luo 1990).

All of these theories seem plausible, but none of them has been investigated empirically.[1] In this paper we use a set of provincial data to carry out an empirical analysis on TVEs versus private ownership of firms. Inspired by the above theories but limited by the data available, we will focus on two empirical issues. First, how do the three factors concerning the institutional environment of firms explain the observed provincial variation of ownership distribution between TVEs and private enterprises? And second, how effectively does community government ownership of TVEs, as opposed to private ownership, help the community government to achieve the three objectives?

We find that TVEs, relative to private enterprises, are favored in a province where the central government's influence is greater through a larger state supply of credit and more state industrial enterprises. TVEs are also favored where the community government's power is stronger through having more collective assets under its control at the beginning of the reform and stronger local political strength. On the other hand, private enterprises, relative to TVEs, are more likely to develop in the environment of less antimarket ideology and better market development through more product market expansion and urbanisation. We also find some evidence on the effectiveness of TVE ownership in pursuing the community government's goals: the TVE share in the rural non-farm sector increases the community government's share of revenue, and somewhat surprisingly, the state's (all governments above the township level) share of revenue as well, but more so for the former. The TVE share also raises rural non-farm employment and rural real per capita income, but it does not increase income for the given levels of non-farm employment and local public goods provision.

These results help in understanding the nature of TVEs and private enterprises and provide several insights that may have implications beyond China. First, the distribution of firms between local public and private ownership reflects the institutional features in the process of transition from plan to markets and economic development, which can be summarised by three factors: the central government's influence, the local community government's power, and market development.

Second, ownership of TVEs may serve as an effective instrument for both the community and central governments to raise more revenue and for the community government to retain a larger share. This provides some evidence on the incentives of all levels of government, especially the community government, to develop TVEs. Indeed, development of TVEs helps the government avoid revenue crises that are often observed in other transition and developing economies. Third, although TVEs generate a higher level of rural non-farm employment and a higher revenue share for the community government than private enterprises, they do not increase per capita income for the given levels of non-farm employment and local public goods provision. Because of the relatively high capital-labour ratio in TVEs, this finding may indicate that TVEs are not so efficient as private enterprises.

The rest of the paper is organised as follows. Section II provides a brief description of TVEs and their roles in China's economic reform. Section III summarises theories on ownership of TVEs and their major testable implications. Section IV discusses estimation methods. Section V describes the construction of regression variables. Section VI presents results on the provincial variation of the relative share of TVEs versus private enterprises in rural industry. Section VII reports results of the effect of TVE ownership on the community government's objectives. Section VIII concludes.

II. TVEs and China's Economic Reforms

The Chinese economy is divided into 'urban' and 'rural' areas, which is an administrative rather than economic concept inherited from the planning era. Firms in the urban area consist of state-owned, collectively owned, privately owned, and 'other' (including foreign) firms. State-owned enterprises are national public firms owned by the central government and supervised by the four upper levels of government: central, provincial, prefecture, and county (a municipality can have a rank of the latter three). Firms in the rural area are called rural enterprises, which consist of two ownership types: community public firms (TVEs) and private firms. In China, the state sector refers to SOEs in urban areas, and the non-state sector refers to the rest.

Between 1978 and 1993 the share of the state sector in the national industrial output declined from 78 per cent to 43 per cent, while the share of rural enterprises increased from 9 per cent to 36 per cent (the rest came from other urban enterprises such as collectives, private, and foreign firms) (China Statistical Yearbook 1994). These relative share changes have occurred without any privatisation of old SOEs. In 1993 total rural enterprise employment reached 123 million, accounting for about one-half of the national non-farm employment. Clearly, rural enterprises have played an essential role in China's economic reform.[2]

Within the rural enterprise sector, both TVEs and private enterprises flourish, but until recently, TVEs have played more important roles in rural industrialisation than private enterprises. At the end of 1992, China had about 50,000 townships and 800,000 villages. On average, each township (with a population of about 18,000) had 8.2 township-run enterprises, and each village (with a population of about 1,000) had 1.4 village-run enterprises (China Statistical Yearbook 1993). In 1993 there were about 1.5 million TVEs with 52 million employees, and the shares of TVE output and employment in rural industry were 72 per cent and 58 per cent, respectively, with the remaining shares coming from private enterprises (China Township Enterprises Statistical Yearbook 1994). The TVE subsector is indeed significant by both absolute and relative measures.[3]

TVEs are local community public firms owned and controlled by the township or village government (Chang and Wang 1994; Che and Qian 1998a). TVEs are not private enterprises. As compared with private enterprises, TVEs receive substantial assistance from the community government (see Section III below) and also suffer from problems typically found in public firms, such as weaker managerial incentives and greater political intervention from the community government (Zhang 1996).

On the other hand, the local community government-owned TVEs differ significantly from the central government-owned SOEs. Although both the theoretical and empirical parts of our paper are about TVEs and private enterprises and are not about the comparison between TVEs and SOEs, it is worthwhile to summarise the important differences between TVEs and SOEs as useful background.

Some works in the empirical literature have found that TVEs are much more efficient than SOEs in terms of productivity growth (for example, Jefferson and Rawski 1994). At the enterprise level, TVEs differ from SOEs in the following three aspects. First, TVEs have not been under state allocation plans for either input or output. In the early periods the central government tolerated TVEs for the purpose of agricultural mechanisation; indeed, many TVEs started as agricultural machine repair shops. Later, TVEs expanded their scope of operation to pursue local industrialisation. Second, TVE workers are not state employees who receive job security and welfare from the state. Unlike SOE employees, TVE workers can be laid off.[4] Third, although TVEs have softer budget constraints than private enterprises, they have much harder budget constraints than SOEs. TVEs have been receiving proportionally many fewer loans than SOEs, and they were badly hurt during the retrenchment period.[5]

A more thorough understanding of the difference between TVEs and SOEs requires a deeper knowledge about township and village governments.[6] Under China's highly decentralised fiscal system, fiscal 'self-sufficiency' has been a basic principle for the rural community governments (Wong 1997). On the one hand, these community governments retain and use a large proportion of the revenues they generate on the other hand, they receive no or very few

fiscal budgetary transfers from higher level governments.[7] At the same time, the authority of township and village governments in some important aspects is more constrained as compared with the central government and even to higher level local governments such as provincial governments. For example, although township and village governments may have connections with SOEs and exert some influence on the state financial institutions, they do not control them. Moreover, township and village governments are unable to erect trade barriers since their jurisdictions are geographically too small. Therefore, as compared with the central and higher level local governments, township and village governments have more constrained authority and have relatively hard budget constraints from the fiscal and financial channels. These are possibly fundamental reasons for TVEs to perform better than SOEs, although both are government-owned (Qian and Weingast 1996; Che and Qian 1998a).

III. Theories of TVEs

Due to their unconventional features and relative success, China's TVEs have recently stimulated quite a lot of research. The traditional theory on public ownership postulates that benevolent governments as owners of firms maximise social welfare to cure market failures in the presence of monopoly power or externalities. In contrast, theories on TVEs are positive in nature. Most theories intend to explain TVEs as local (that is, community) government firms taking advantage of the existing institutional environment to achieve certain government goals.[8]

Because the community government plays a central role in TVEs, theories about them start with the goals of the community government in developing TVEs. In the late 1970s rural China was characterised by a large amount of surplus labour, a low level of income, and a poor local government revenue base. Economic reform has since proceeded in the direction of fiscal decentralisation, under which township and village governments were able to retain a large portion of their revenues while obtaining few revenue transfers from the higher level. Consequently, the most relevant objectives of a community government are considered to be an increase in government revenue, creation of non-farm employment, and an increase in rural income. Conceivably, the first provides financial support, and the latter two provide political support for the community government.[9]

All of the aforementioned objectives of the community government can be achieved by rural industrialisation. However, it is not obvious whether community government-owned firms (TVEs) or private firms are more effective in achieving the government's goals. An important consideration is the incompleteness of contracts, which entails the relevance of allocation of ownership of firms in general and government ownership of firms in particular (Shleifer and Vishny 1994; Hart, Shleifer and Vishny 1997; Che and Qian 1998b). Theories on TVEs relate the ownership of firms to the specific institutional environment in which the firms are operating. During the process of transition and development, both government and market institutions are problematic. Three factors concerning the institutional environment of firms that might give more political and economic advantages to TVEs rather than to private enterprises are the central government's influence, the community government's power, and underdevelopment of the market.

In what follows, we first discuss several channels through which the three institutional factors may play important roles in the development of rural industrial firms. They are financing of investments, transaction costs, urbanisation, security of property rights, and collective heritage. We then discuss the three objectives of the community government for developing TVEs.

Ownership and the institutional environment

The first theory proposes that TVEs have distinct advantages in financing investment compared with private enterprises because of the central government's influence, or underdevelopment of the capital market, or both. The start-up capital for private enterprises comes mainly from owners, with little coming from bank loans. Given the limited amount of personal financial resources, private enterprises have difficulty growing. In contrast, TVEs are able to access a larger pool of capital, in particular, bank loans, with the help of the community government (Wong 1988, 1991).

TVEs may have an advantage over private enterprises in financing investment because the community government can make use of its political connections with the central government-owned state banks to channel loans to TVEs. The state banks are also more willing to lend to TVEs because ideological discrimination against private enterprises makes lending to the latter politically more risky. TVEs may also have possible advantages in financing investment due to the underdevelopment of market financial institutions and the imperfect capital market (Byrd 1990; Che and Qian 1998a). For example, the community government is able to share risks by cross-subsidisation among its many diversified enterprises, thus reducing the default risks borne by banks. The community government can also reduce agency costs in borrowing because of its larger endowment in physical and financial assets. From both perspectives, this theory implies that the relative share of TVEs is positively correlated with the supply of credit from state financial institutions to all rural enterprises, but negatively correlated with the extent of financial market development.

Second, the 'transaction costs' theory similarly relates TVEs to the partial liberalisation of the economy with the coexistence of the central government's influence and underdevelopment of the market. Nee (1992) contends that China's economy is characterised by declining but still functioning central government planning institutions on the one hand, and emerging but weak market institutions with poorly specified and enforced property rights, on the other. TVEs, with help from the community government, have a lower transaction cost in dealing with the existing SOEs, which enables them to access the SOEs' technology and materials. Quite often TVEs and SOEs establish a long-term relationship through subcontracting (Otsuka 1996). On the other hand, private enterprises have lower transaction costs in dealing with other enterprises in competitive markets because, for example, private entrepreneurs have higher marketing ability. This theory suggests a positive relationship between the share of TVEs and the importance of links with the state industrial sector, and a negative relationship between the TVE share and product market development.

Third, Naughton (1994, 1996) views developing TVEs as vehicles for the community government to convert community assets (that is, land) to cash flow under the situation in which the development of asset markets lags behind that of product markets. He implicitly assumes an imperfection of the land rental market so that the only way of transforming land value into income streams is to directly operate businesses on it. He argues that because land close to urban areas is more valuable, communities closer to them have more incentive to transform assets into income streams by developing TVEs. However, one may also argue that a higher degree of urbanisation can be associated with better market development, and thus reduce the disadvantages of small private enterprises in doing business through more accessible outlets for output, increased support for specialised inputs, labour market pooling, and technological spillovers. Naughton's testable hypothesis is the positive correlation between the share of TVEs in a community and its 'urban proximity', which is a measure of the proximity of the community to urban centres weighted by urban population.

The fourth theory concerns the security of property rights of firms and associates the advantages of TVEs over private enterprises with the local community government's power for political protection. China's reform has proceeded in an environment without a rule of law. As part of the political institutions, the community government can provide better political security to their own enterprises (Chang and Wang 1994). The community government's protection of TVEs becomes more effective than that of private enterprises because ownership gives the community government better information about the operation of firms (Li 1996).

Che and Qian (1998b) endogenise the community government's role in securing TVE property rights under a predatory state. Under TVE ownership the community government integrates government activities (that is, community public goods provision) and business activities, and it can better serve the interests of the central government. Consequently, the central government is less predatory toward community government-owned firms (TVEs) than private firms, and property rights under TVEs become more secure. In such a case, both the central government and the community government can benefit from TVE ownership.[10] This theory implies that the share of TVEs versus private enterprises is positively correlated with the local political strength of the community government against pressure from the central government, but negatively correlated with the change of nationwide ideology in favor of the market economy.

The fifth theory relates TVEs to the history of China's economic planning and development. Because twenty years were spent implementing the commune system, the community government in rural China had already accumulated an unusual amount of physical and human capital by the late 1970s. One might argue that this particular historical experience empowered the community government, and thus gave TVEs organisational advantages over private enterprises (Chang and Wang 1994; Putterman 1994). However, one might also argue that this legacy provided more incentives for the community government to suppress private enterprises instead—in order, for example, to reduce competition in the skilled labour market (Luo 1990). In either case, the 'history matters' theory implies that the relative share of TVEs in the late 1980s and early 1990s should positively correlate with the strength of the rural collective sector at the beginning of reform, which is the community government's initial power base.

Ownership and the community government's objectives

First, several studies have emphasised the revenue goals of the community government in developing TVEs. Both Byrd and Gelb (1990) and Oi (1992, 1994) stress the effect of fiscal decentralisation that has made community governments independent fiscal entities. Community governments are able to retain and use a large proportion of the revenues they generate, and they are also subject to hard fiscal budget constraints due to limited fiscal revenue transfers from the higher level government. These authors then argue that, under this circumstance, community governments turn to TVEs for a revenue source.

However, these authors did not explain why the revenue objectives of the community government can be better achieved by developing TVEs. Conceivably, in a developed market economy, government ownership of firms may not help increase government revenue, and even worse, the inefficiency associated with public ownership is likely to decrease both profits and government revenue as compared with private ownership. One plausible explanation for the positive linkage between TVE ownership and community government revenue is based on incomplete contracts (Che and Qian 1998b). Due to inadequate accounting and taxation institutions, the community government finds it hard to tax private firms. However, the community government can better extract revenue from TVEs because ownership gives it control over, and information about, operation of the firms. In the model of Che and Qian (1998b), because the community government also carries out revenue-enhancing local government activities by providing local public goods, both the community government and the central government can benefit from TVEs in terms of their own revenues. This theory implies that we may not only expect a positive correlation between the TVE shares and the revenue share of the community government, but also a positive correlation between the TVE shares and the revenue share of the central government.

Second, creation of non-farm employment in a community ranks very high on the list of community leaders' concerns (Rozelle and Boisvert 1994), and is often a motive claimed by the community government itself for developing TVEs. Reduction of rural underemployment is especially important in China because of some restrictions on costs of labour migration from the rural to urban areas. Although an increase of non-farm employment is generally efficiency-enhancing in rural China, there may also be the possibility of inefficient excess employment. Whether developing TVEs is more effective than developing private enterprises to increase non-farm employment depends on the net effect of several factors. On the one hand, because TVEs are able to mobilise more capital than private enterprises, they may bring in more capital investment which leads to more non-farm employment. In addition, the ownership rights give the community government the power to force TVEs to employ workers at the high level it desires. On the other hand, private enterprises typically have much lower capital-labour ratios (Zhang and Ronnas 1996), and thus they may provide more employment opportunities for a given level of capital investment.

The third often claimed objective of the community government in developing TVEs is raising per capita income within the community. Because of the restrictions on costs of labour migration, one way TVEs could contribute to raising per capita income is through increased local employment opportunities. Another way TVEs could contribute to raising per capita income is through an increased local public goods provision due to the improvement of the community government's revenue, because local public goods are usually undersupplied in the rural areas. On the other hand, inefficiency associated with the community government's political intervention may reduce per capita income. Therefore, developing TVEs could also be less effective than developing private enterprises to increase rural income.

IV. Estimation Method

The above theories inspired us to address the following two empirical questions. First, suppose that the community government's objectives are the same across provinces. Then, how do the three factors concerning the institutional environment of firms explain the observed provincial variation of ownership distribution between TVEs and private enterprises? Second, how effectively do TVEs, as opposed to private enterprises, help the community government achieve the objectives of increasing government revenue, non-farm employment, and per capita income?

We use provincial data from 1986 to 1993.[11] There are 28 provinces, excluding Tibet and Hainan. We incorporate Hainan into Guangdong in our data because Hainan separated from Guangdong and obtained a provincial status only in 1988. An advantage of such comprehensive data, as compared with survey data from a few provinces, is that it covers the entire country which varies greatly across provinces.

We use the following econometric model to examine the provincial variation of ownership distribution. Let p_{it} be the probability of observing a worker (or unit of output) being employed (or produced) by TVEs, rather than private enterprises, in province i in year t, and X_{it} represent various aspects of the factors concerning the institutional environment of firms. We assume that p_{it} is a logit function of X_{it}:

$$p_{it} = \exp(\alpha_i + \gamma_t + X'_{it}\beta + u_{it}) /$$

$$[1 + \exp(\alpha_i + \gamma_t + X'_{it}\beta + u_{it})],$$

where α_i's represent provincial fixed effects, γ_t's yearly fixed effects, and u_{it}'s are error terms. This formulation has the property that the 'odds ratio' has a log-linear functional form

$$\ln[p_{it} / (1 - p_{it})] = \alpha_i + \gamma_t + X'_{it}\beta + u_{it}. \quad (1)$$

Equation (1) is a reduced form, where the endogenous variable p_{it} is regressed on exogenous variables X_{it}. Clearly, u_{it}'s of the same province in different years are highly correlated. Furthermore, there may also be a provincial specific error component and the variances of u_{it}'s may vary across provinces. To address these problems, we compute Huber-White robust standard errors allowing for group errors by provinces using the procedure suggested by Deaton (1995). We report ordinary-least-squares estimation results with t-ratios based on Huber-White robust standard errors.

As described below, several of our variables (for example, initial collective assets) are not time varying, and thus they would be absorbed into provincial fixed effects α_i's in the estimations including all provincial dummies. Therefore, instead of using all provincial dummies, we use six region dummies in our regressions to capture some pre-existing regional differences. We group the 28 provinces into 6 regions according to geographic location: North, South, Southwest, Northwest, Coastal, and huge cities (for details see next section). We also report estimation results from regressions without these region dummies.[12]

To investigate the effectiveness of TVE ownership in achieving the alternative government's objectives, we estimate the structural equations with causality going from the share of TVEs to government revenues, non-farm employment, and per capita income. The general form of the equations we use is given by

$$y_{it} = \alpha_i + \gamma_t + p_{it}\theta + Y'_{it}\delta + Z'_{it}\gamma + v_{it}, \quad (2)$$

where y_{it} represents the dependent variables we are interested in, that is, the community government's and the state's shares of revenue, rural non-farm employment, or per capita income; p_{it} is the share of TVEs relative to private enterprises; Y_{it} is endogenous variables including a subset of y_{it}'s; Z_{it} is exogenous variables, for example, per capita cultivated land and urbanisation; and v_{it} is an error term. We again use six region dummies to capture some pre-existing regional differences.

The error term v_{it} in equation (2) may be correlated not only with Y_{it}, but also with p_{it}, the TVE shares. This arises from the possibility that, while the ownership distribution may indeed have an effect on the government's revenues, employment, and income, there may be another structural equation, say $p_{it} = g(y_{it}, Z_{it})$, where the causality runs from the latter to the TVE shares. For example, community governments with a higher share of revenues may have a larger capability to finance their enterprises, which in turn leads to a higher share of TVE ownership. Thus, both Y_{it} and p_{it} should be treated as endogenous variables in equation (2). To correct for the endogeneity problem, we use an instrumental variable method to estimate equation (2). The set of instrumental variables includes X_{it} from equation (1) and Z_{it} from equation (2), as well as all region and year dummies. In addition, we also report the results from the ordinary-least-squared estimations. For both ordinary-least-squared and instrumental variable estimations, we report t-ratios based on Huber-White robust standard errors allowing for provincial group effects.

In our specification, some variables in X_{it} which have direct effects on TVE shares are not present in equation (2). This differentiates them from the equations with reverse causality running from the government revenue to the TVE shares and thus makes them identifiable. In fact, these equations are overidentified. It is arguable that some of the instrumental variables should be included as independent variables. To address this issue, we perform an over-identification test (Newey 1985). An insignificant χ^2 statistic will justify the exclusion of these instruments from the equations, and will also indicate that any proper subset of the instruments should produce the same estimation of coefficients. Because our panel data have grouped errors, we adjust the test statistics as recently suggested by Hoxby and Paserman (1997).

V. Construction of Variables[13]

To examine provincial variation of ownership, we use the relative share of TVEs versus private enterprises in rural industrial employment and output, respectively for p_{it}. We focus on industry (and thus exclude services) to avoid the further problem of heterogeneity of technologies between industry and services. The X_{it} includes the following variables representing various aspects of the three factors concerning the institutional environment of firms.

We have two variables representing the central government's influence. The first is the state supply of credits. The credit here refers to 'rural enterprise loans' from the Agricultural Bank of China (ABC) and Rural Credit Cooperatives (RCCs), which are the two major credit sources for both TVEs and private enterprises. This variable is then normalised to represent the amount of loans per employee in real terms obtained by all rural enterprises from state financial institutions.

The second variable is the size of state industry measured by the per capita state industrial real output in a province. It serves as an index of the potential linkage of a rural enterprise with SOEs in the province. Because TVEs developed much later than SOEs, this variable is exogenous to TVEs.[14]

For the local government's power, we also have two variables. The first is collective heritage which is measured by the per capita collective fixed assets in 1980. It indicates the initial base of the rural collective sector and is a proxy for the accumulated physical and human capital under the control of the community government at the beginning of reform. Because few private assets existed at the time, it was also an approximate value of per capita wealth. However, since this wealth was under direct control of the community governments, it captures elements of collective heritage.

The second variable concerns local (that is, community) political strength. The political strength and organisational capability of local community leaders are hard to measure. We use the following measurement as a proxy for community political strength: the percentage of rural households in a province NOT adopting the *Dabaogan* form of the Household Responsibility System in agriculture at the end of 1983. The *Dabaogan* form is based on fixed renting, and community governments are not involved at all in any production decision-making and revenue-sharing arrangements with households.

The *Dabaogan* form initially started spontaneously in the late 1970s in a few provinces, and it was soon welcomed enthusiastically by households across the country. The central government endorsed the *Dabaogan* form as early as 1980. For three consecutive years starting in 1982, the Party Central Committee issued three No.1 Party Circulars to put pressure on community governments across the country to adopt this form, and by the end of 1984, nearly 100 per cent of households had done so. Communities which had not adopted it by the end of 1983 demonstrated the community governments' political strength to resist pressure from both above and below. We interpret this resistance as coming from community governments rather than higher levels of local governments because adoption of this form was not uniform at the county and provincial levels.

We have three variables to measure market development. The first is private financial assets at the end of the previous year to indicate financial market development.[15] Because the data for total private financial assets are not available, the total rural household savings deposits are used instead,[16] which is a reasonably good proxy if the amount of household savings deposits is roughly proportional to the amount of total household financial assets. We normalise private household savings deposits in a province by its

rural gross output. This measure is parallel to the usual measure for 'financial deepening', which is the ratio of total financial assets in the economy to total GDP. Therefore, our index of private financial assets is not an index of the level of private wealth, but the level of the development of rural financial markets.

The second variable is product market development. We use the total transaction volume in rural free markets in a province divided by its total rural gross output to measure the development of the product market. The transaction volume in the rural free market indicates overall private trading activities in the markets of farm products and consumer goods, as well as producer goods. A higher index means a better opportunity for enterprises to obtain a supply of materials from, and to sell their outputs to, the market. Because the local industrial enterprises only account for a very small proportion of the total transactions in these markets, this index can be thought of as exogenous.

Finally, urbanisation is also potentially associated with the extent of market development. We use the index of urbanisation measured by the share of urban population in the total population. We use the 1990 census data because they are the most appropriate for our purposes.[17] A related, but different, index for urbanisation is the urban proximity index constructed by Naughton (1996), which is a weighted average of the inverse of distance from the centre of a province to selected major cities, using the city population as weight. The two indexes give very similar results so we will only use urban population in our reports.

In addition, we use year dummies for each year between 1987 and 1993 to capture any changes over one particular year as compared with the previous year. Because macroeconomic policy changes over years have been somewhat controlled by the variables such as the state credit supply, we interpret time dummies as representing the nationwide shift of official ideology regarding plans and markets due to changes in the Party line. From 1986 to 1993 the overall trend of the Party line was moving in a more liberal direction with the major exception of 1989 due to the Tiananmen Square incident. The years of 1992 and 1993 were particularly so when Deng Xiaoping made his famous trip to southern China to promote market-oriented reform and the Chinese Community Party subsequently endorsed the 'socialist market economy' as its official Party ideology.

We use 6 region dummies to capture pre-existing regional differences among 28 provinces. We divide China into North and South (according to climate and pattern of agricultural activities) and East and West (the West is mountainous and the East is relatively flat) to obtain four regions: North and South in the East, and Southwest and Northwest in the West. We then separately list six coastal provinces as one region because they were one step ahead in reforms and opening up to foreign trade and investment. Finally, we single out the three huge cities of Beijing, Tianjin, and Shanghai because they are small in geographical size and do not have large rural areas like all the other provinces.

In examining the community government's objectives, consider first the government's revenue. The net income of the rural economy is generated from three sources. The first two sources are the income generated by farm households and private enterprises, respectively. Part of this income is paid to the state (all governments above the township and village level) as taxes, part goes to community governments under the names of 'collective reserves' and 'administrative fees', and the remaining part is retained by households. The third source is the income generated by TVEs. Part of this income is submitted to the state as taxes and fees, but a major part goes to households as wages and bonuses, and the remainder (including retained profits) is controlled by community governments. From the destination perspective, the net income of the rural economy is distributed among three entities: the state (all governments above the township and village level), the community

(township and village) government, and households. The state's revenue includes all state taxes and fees remitted to the government above the township. The community government revenue is the income received by township and village governments, including retained profits from TVEs. The remaining income belongs to households.[18]

In addition to the community government's and the state's shares of revenue, our dependent variables also include rural non-farm employment and the rural income level. We use share of the rural non-agricultural labour force in the total rural labour force to measure the level of rural non-farm employment. We measure the income level by the rural real per capita income at the 1980 price.

We use the share of TVEs in rural enterprise employment in both industry and services as our independent variable to measure the importance of TVE ownership relative to private ownership. This is because our dependent variables concerning income and employment also include the sources from both industry and services.

The summary statistics of the above variables are reported in Table 1. Our data set has a much smaller sample variation over time than across provinces. This is not surprising because most variables are characterisations of the institutional environment that shift slowly over time at the provincial aggregate level and our data covers only eight years. Three variables, local political strength, the share of urban population, and initial collective assets, are not time varying. Among the rest, the variances over time of the share of TVE industrial employment and output account for about 2 per cent and 8 per cent of total variances, respectively, and those of the revenue shares of the community government and the state represent about 8 per cent and 12 per cent of the total variances, respectively. Only the variances over time of the state supply of credit and private assets are significant, accounting for about 42 per cent and 34 per cent of the total variances, respectively.

VI. Estimation Results: provincial variation of ownership

Table 2 reports the regression results for the provincial variation of ownership distribution between TVEs and private enterprises. We initially included in our regressions the variables of adult education (measured by the percentage of the rural labour force having at least primary schooling) and the per capita cultivated land. They are not significant, and we later dropped them. Table 2 also reports the regression results by excluding region dummies, which show slight changes only.[19]

First, the coefficients for the supply of credits from state financial institutions are positive and significant, while the coefficients for private financial assets are not significant. This gives some support to the financial theory of TVE ownership. A large supply of state non-agricultural loans can increase the relative share

of TVEs because, with the help of the community government, these loans are more likely to go to TVEs to support their development. However, the more important private financial assets in the rural economy, which indicates more developed informal financial markets, seems to affect both TVEs and private enterprises equally.

Second, the coefficients of product market development are all negative and significant, which suggests that product market development favors private enterprises. On the other hand, the effect of the size of state industry on TVEs is positive and significant. Therefore, a larger state industrial sector seems to favor TVEs, for example, through subcontracting. These results seem to be consistent with the transaction cost theory of TVEs.

Third, we were able to reproduce Naughton's (1996) result of a positive correlation between the share of TVEs in a province and its 'urban proximity' (or our urbanisation index) in

Table 1   **Summary statistics of variables**

	Mean	Minimum	Maximum	Standard deviation
Employment share of TVEs in rural industry	0.585	0.226	0.970	0.169
Output share of TVEs in rural industry	0.681	0.342	0.990	0.140
State supply of credit	1.006	0.243	6.238	0.816
Size of state industry	0.101	0.024	0.584	0.109
Log of initial collective assets	4.926	3.523	6.231	0.547
Local political strength	0.094	0.002	0.606	0.128
Private financial assets	0.139	0.014	0.318	0.055
Product market development	0.084	0.008	0.241	0.044
Share of urban population	0.311	0.147	0.732	0.162
State share in rural net income	0.073	0.025	0.283	0.048
Community government share in rural net income	0.082	0.011	0.255	0.056
Share of non-farm employment in total rural labour force	0.233	0.068	0.771	0.148
Rural per capita real income	0.317	0.167	0.829	0.128
Share of TVEs in rural enterprise employment	0.494	0.198	0.970	0.180
Per capita community government revenue	0.072	0.003	0.885	0.118
Per capita cultivated land	1.441	0.476	4.824	1.074

Note: Precise variable definitions and sources are presented in the Appendix.

univariate regressions for our extended sample period. Casual observation often gives the impression that TVEs are predominant in provinces with a high degree of urbanisation or proximity to major cities, which is indeed captured by the univariate regressions.

However, the positive correlation no longer holds when other variables are controlled for. By adding the size of state industry, the coefficient of urbanisation becomes insignificant in the output equation, suggesting that urbanisation picked up some effects from the size of state industry in univariate regressions. By further adding any one of the four variables—initial collective assets, local political strength, state supply of credit, and product market development—the coefficient of urbanisation becomes negative in the output equation and insignificant in the employment equation. With all explanatory variables included, we find that the coefficient of urbanisation (and that of Naughton's urban proximity index as well, which is not reported here) becomes negative and significant. This provides some evidence showing that urbanisation favors private enterprises through better market development. For example, private enterprises can take advantage of being located near urban areas for a more accessible outlet for output, increases support for specialised inputs, labour market pooling, and technological spillovers.

Fourth, the local political strength seems to play an important role in favoring TVEs, as indicated by its positive and significant coefficients. A greater capability of community leaders to resist pressure from higher levels of government provides more effective political protection for TVEs relative to private enterprises, and therefore favors their development. As will be shown in the next section, a higher share of TVEs gives the community government more revenue; therefore, the community government has incentive to provide more protection to TVEs than to private enterprises. The evidence seems to support the theory of the security of property rights.

Examining the year dummies we find a general trend of decline in TVEs relative to private enterprises in this time period. The evidence also indicates that the political retrenchment in 1989 stopped this decline temporarily, but it did not reverse this trend. On the other hand, there is some evidence of an acceleration of private enterprises relative to TVEs after 1992. It seems that a nationwide ideology shift toward conservatism does not effectively reduce the share of private enterprises in the rural economy immediately, but an ideology shift in a liberal direction leads to significant prosperity for private enterprises. Perhaps the mere removal of existing restrictions on private enterprises induces an instant response, but adding new restrictions has little immediate effect, as it takes time to establish effective enforcement.

Finally, the initial collective assets have a positive and significant effect on the TVE's shares in later years. According to one interpretation, those provinces with a larger base of accumulated physical and human capital controlled by the community government prior to the reform tend to give organisational advantages to TVEs relative to private enterprises. According to the alternative interpretation, a larger collective base provides community governments with higher incentives to suppress private enterprises. Both interpretations are consistent with the view that the community government's initial power base is crucial in the development of TVEs. They seem to accord well with the 'history matters' theory of TVEs and demonstrate the 'path dependent' nature of institutional changes in agreement with North (1991).[20]

In the above regressions there may be a potential endogeneity problem concerning the variables of 'state supply of credit' and 'private financial assets'.[21] The state supply of credit may rise when TVEs demand more credit,[22] and similarly, private assets would be higher with more private firms.[23] We dealt with this problem in two ways. First, we ran regressions by excluding these two variables, and the results are

Table 2 **Ownership and the institutional environment: the logit model**

	Share of TVEs in rural industrial employment			Share of TVEs in rural industrial output		
Intercept	-2.076 [2.547]	-1.596 [2.217]	-2.195 [2.069]	-0.444 [0.455]	0.370 [0.592]	-0.577 [0.476]
State supply of credits	0.274 [5.200]	0.480 [4.687]	0.363 [3.650]	0.538 [4.365]		
Size of state industry	0.746 [1.324]	1.322 [2.170]	1.487 [2.902]	1.866 [2.529]	2.957 [3.972]	2.846 [4.523]
Log of initial collective assets	0.698 [3.838]	0.563 [3.318]	0.690 [2.929]	0.522 [2.444]	0.292 [1.625]	0.506 [1.928]
Local political strength	1.532 [3.739]	2.062 [4.049]	1.356 [3.732]	2.319 [4.679]	2.902 [4.329]	2.079 [4.065]
Private financial assets	-0.009 [0.006]	-2.785 [2.375]	-0.102 [0.057]	-2.506 [1.507]		
Product market development	-7.476 [5.782]	-5.452 [2.998]	-6.586 [4.536]	-7.503 [4.441]	-5.155 [2.439]	-6.375 [3.247]
Share of urban population	-1.977 [2.627]	-1.636 [1.605]	-1.574 [1.938]	-3.440 [2.855]	-3.137 [2.220]	-2.913 [2.285]
Region dummy for huge cities	0.568 [2.057]	0.788 [2.525]	0.509 [1.070]	0.806 [1.483]		
Region dummy for coastal	0.391 [3.177]	0.572 [3.737]	0.283 [1.426]	0.520 [2.259]		
Region dummy for Southwest	0.253 [1.751]	0.251 [1.411]	0.312 [1.457]	0.307 [1.332]		
Region dummy for Northwest	-0.243 [1.730]	-0.208 [2.456]	-0.201 [1.024]	-0.164 [1.049]		
Region dummy for North	-0.349 [2.181]	-0.308 [1.875]	-0.482 [2.530]	-0.433 [2.130]		
Year dummy for 1987	-0.041 [1.221]	-0.015 [0.523]	-0.022 [0.838]	-0.082 [1.735]	-0.062 [1.325]	-0.058 [1.564]
Year dummy for 1988	-0.083 [4.434]	-0.083 [4.635]	-0.077 [4.266]	-0.060 [2.915]	-0.065 [3.258]	-0.052 [2.433]
Year dummy for 1989	-0.006 [0.282]	0.002 [0.104]	0.006 [0.316]	-0.012 [0.390]	-0.006 [0.196]	0.003 [0.113]
Year dummy for 1990	-0.105 [3.282]	-0.102 [2.544]	-0.048 [1.917]	-0.201 [3.748]	-0.193 [3.516]	-0.127 [2.429]
Year dummy for 1991	-0.047 [0.930]	0.009 [0.224]	-0.009 [0.485]	0.021 [0.261]	0.067 [0.923]	0.069 [1.417]
Year dummy for 1992	-0.121 [3.986]	-0.177 [4.898]	-0.050 [2.570]	-0.164 [3.938]	-0.216 [5.063]	-0.071 [2.677]
Year dummy for 1993	-0.123 [2.700]	-0.236 [4.153]	-0.055 [1.600]	-0.125 [1.762]	-0.222 [2.881]	-0.034 [0.682]
R^2	0.929	0.875	0.911	0.847	0.782	0.815

Notes: (a) The functional form of the dependent variable is given by equation (1) in Section IV. (b) Sample size is 224. (c) The *t*-statistics are in parentheses, which are based on Huber-White robust standard errors allowing for group errors by provinces.

reported in Table 2. The results show that our estimations of other coefficients are not sensitive to the inclusion of these two variables. Second, we also looked at the 'average TVE share' over our sample period as a function of 'ex ante' provincial characteristics from the period before our sample. We first used only initial collective assets (1980), local political strength (1983), and the 1982 share of urban population as ex ante characteristics, and later added the 1986 data of state supply of credit, private financial assets, product market development, and the size of state industry as additional ex ante characteristics. We report the results, which are quite similar to our previous findings, in Table 3. This again shows that our results are not driven by the potential endogeneity problem.

In summary, our results seem to suggest that the variation in the share of TVEs versus private enterprises among provinces can be explained by three factors: the central government's influence, the community government's power, and the extent of market development. TVEs, relative to private enterprises, are favored in provinces where the state supply of credit is large and the potential linkages with the state industry are large. TVEs are also favored where the community government's political strength is strong and the initial collective assets under its control are large. On the other hand, private enterprises, relative to TVEs, are more likely to develop if there are more developed product markets, more urbanisation, and a less hostile ideological environment toward markets.

What can be said about the magnitudes of the estimates? By looking at the effect of a 1 per cent increase in the independent variables at the mean on the change of the TVE share, we find that the most significant variables in the employment equation are initial collective assets (0.17 per cent), urbanisation (0.15 per cent), and product market development (0.15 per cent). In the output equation, the most significant variables are urbanisation (0.23 per cent), product market development (0.14 per cent), and initial collective assets (0.11 per cent). In other words, the most

significant variables concern the local government's power and market development.

We also looked at how much actual inter-provincial differences can be explained by the alternative independent variables in order to make some assessment of their economic importance. Take the pair of Shanghai (with the highest share of TVEs) and Guizhou (with the lowest share of TVEs) as an example. All the variables together (excluding region and year dummies) explain about 86 per cent of the difference in the TVE share in employment and 89 per cent in output. The two most important variables are the initial collective assets and product market development for employment (together they explain 69 per cent of the difference), and the initial collective assets and the size of state industry for output (together they explain 65 per cent of the difference). We also take a less extreme pair, Jiangsu (a coastal province) and Sichuan (an inland province), both having state industrial sectors of a moderate size. In this case, all the variables together (excluding region and year dummies) explain 73 per cent of the difference in the TVE share in employment and 58 per cent in output. The two most important variables are the initial collective assets and the product market development for both employment and output; together they explain 62 per cent of the difference for employment and 44 per cent of the difference for output. Again, the local government's power and market development seem to be the most important factors.

VII. Estimation Results: ownership and the community government's objectives

Table 4 reports the results from ordinary-least-squares and instrumental-variable estimations for the effect of TVE ownership on the government's revenue. The table also reports χ^2 statistics for the overidentification test, adjusted for group errors. The null hypothesis that all the instruments are legitimate and can be excluded

Table 3   **Ownership and the institutional environment: the logit model** (average TVE shares and 'ex ante' provincial characteristics)

	Share of TVEs in rural industrial employment		Share of TVEs in rural industrial output	
Intercept	-3.913	-2.498	-2.367	-1.046
	[4.192]	[3.288]	[2.362]	[1.094]
State supply of credits	0.499	0.448		
	[3.457]	[1.744]		
Size of state industry	1.692	0.151	2.787	1.126
	[2.737]	[0.399]	[3.867]	[1.264]
Log of initial collective assets	0.833	0.771	0.663	0.632
	[3.677]	[4.793]	[2.778]	[2.928]
Local political strength	1.324	1.246	1.924	1.957
	[6.653]	[4.073]	[4.492]	[2.816]
Private financial assets	-1.261	-1.594		
	[0.566]	[0.510]		
Product market development	-7.782	-7.696		
	[6.328]	[4.713]		
Share of urban population	-1.590	-2.025	-3.320	-4.158
	[1.815]	[4.928]	[2.576]	[4.263]
Region dummy for huge cities	1.239	1.064	1.486	1.342
	[3.075]	[3.739]	[2.286]	[2.755]
Region dummy for coastal	0.786	0.412	0.723	0.387
	[2.835]	[3.171]	[2.339]	[2.027]
Region dummy for Southwest	0.324	0.034	0.416	0.450
	[1.266]	[1.987]	[1.773]	[1.730]
Region dummy for Northwest	0.123	-0.110	0.185	-0.027
	[0.512]	[0.679]	[0.788]	[0.116]
Region dummy for North	0.022	-0.242	-0.077	-0.326
	[0.078]	[1.555]	[0.275]	[1.791]
R^2	0.892	0.959	0.838	0.907

Notes: (a) The functional form of the dependent variable is given by equation (1) in Section IV. (b) Shares of TVEs are averages over 1986–1993; share of urban population is the 1982 data; state supply of credit, private financial assets, produce market development, and size of state industry are the 1986 data; and local political strength is 1983 data and initial collective assets are 1980 data as in the rest of the paper. (b) Sample size is 28. (d) The t-statistics are in parentheses, which are based on White heteroskedasticity consistent standard errors.

from the revenue share equations cannot be rejected at the 10 per cent level. The following discussions are based on the instrumental variable estimations.

The state's share of revenue is positively related to real per capita income, which seems to be consistent with similar trends in other countries. For a given level of real per capita income, the TVE share in rural enterprise employment has positive effects on both the community government's and the state's shares of revenue, and more so for the community government. This seems to suggest that ownership of TVEs is an effective instrument for both the community government and the state to raise more revenue, and for the community government to obtain a larger share.

These results provide some evidence on the fiscal incentives of the community government in developing TVEs, which tends to confirm numerous previous finding from anecdotal stories and case studies (for example, Byrd and Gelb 1990 and Oi 1992, 1994). However, somewhat surprisingly, our results indicate that the state also benefits from TVEs in terms of its own revenue.[24] This result provides some evidence on the fiscal incentives of the central government for having more TVEs developed. Together, these findings give some support to the theory of the revenue goals of both the community government and the central government in developing TVEs (Che and Qian 1998b).

The revenue effect of TVEs may have some implications for transition and developing economies. All transition economies have been experiencing government revenue shortfalls due to the collapse of the planning-based mechanism of revenue extraction. At the same time, all levels of government often find it difficult to tax new private firms due to the lack of market-based taxation institutions (McKinnon 1991). On the other hand, the governments in developing economies, for political reasons, often bias the revenue allocation toward urban areas which hinders rural development (Bates 1987). The above results provide some empirical evidence

that TVEs helped reduce the severity of these two problems.

Interestingly, local political strength has a negative effect on the state's share of revenue and positive effects on the revenue shares of the community government and households, given the TVEs share in rural enterprise employment.[25] These results may suggest a conflict of interest between the community government and the central government (but not between the community government and households). For the given level of a TVE share, the political strength of community leaders plays an important role in increasing the combined community income at the expense of state taxes. This result shows that our variable of local political strength captures the ability of local resistance to pressure from above rather than below.

But stronger local political power also has an indirect positive effect on the state's revenue through the increased TVEs share, as is shown in Section VI. Therefore the total effect of local political strength on the state's share of revenue is not necessarily negative. We have run alternative regressions in which the state's share and the community government's share of revenue are regressed on all exogenous variables X_{lt} in equation (1), and found that the total effect of local political strength on the state's and community government's shares of revenue is, respectively, positive and significant. This suggests that both the central government and the community government benefit from local political strength. This looks paradoxical, but it is consistent with the predictions of models considering commitment problems (for example, Aghion and Tirole 1997 and Che and Qian 1998b). In such a situation, one party may gain by giving away some information or power to another party. Thus, we can view the local political power of community governments as a device to secure their revenues against the central government's arbitrary extraction and at the same time also make the central government better off through, say, improved incentives of the community government.

Table 5 reports the results of the effect of TVE ownership on rural non-farm employment and per capita income from both ordinary-least-squares and instrumental variable estimations. The table also reports χ^2 statistics for the overidentification test, adjusted for group errors. The null hypothesis that all the instruments are legitimate and can be excluded from the employment and income equations cannot be rejected at the 10 per cent level. The following discussion is based on instrumental-variable estimations.

The TVEs' share in rural enterprise employment has a positive effect on the share of rural non-farm employment in the total rural labour force even with the control of per capita community government revenue (a proxy for local public goods provision). This provides some evidence that TVEs are able to create more non-farm employment opportunities than private

Table 4 Ownership and the community government's objectives: the government's revenue

	OLS		IV	
	State share	Community government share	State share	Community government share
Intercept	-0.066	0.001	-0.098	-0.074
	[3.879]	[0.042]	[7.356]	[3.255]
Share of TVEs in rural	0.108	0.112	0.114	0.242
enterprise employment	[3.690]	[4.292]	[3.896]	[4.316]
Net per capita rural income	0.181	-0.055	0.285	-0.006
	[3.741]	[0.957]	[7.742]	[0.108]
Local political strength	-0.073	0.026	-0.095	0.018
	[2.819]	[0.966]	[5.468]	[0.811]
Region dummy for huge cities	0.048	0.126	0.019	0.056
	[3.197]	[4.426]	[1.679]	[2.549]
Region dummy for Coastal	0.003	0.039	-0.010	0.008
	[0.267]	[2.497]	[1.795]	[0.639]
Region dummy for Southwest	0.008	-0.010	0.013	-0.002
	[1.002]	[1.278]	[1.496]	[0.144]
Region dummy for Northwest	0.003	0.002	0.008	0.004
	[0.458]	[0.212]	[1.193]	[0.423]
Region dummy for North	0.014	0.032	0.015	0.039
	[2.376]	[4.615]	[2.779]	[3.897]
χ^2 [dof]			4.532 [5]	2.354 [5]
Standard errors	0.015	0.021	0.016	0.024

Notes: (a) A full set of year dummies is included in each specification. (b) Endogenous variables are the share of TVEs in rural enterprise employment and net per capita rural income. Instruments are local political strength, region dummies, year dummies, state supply of credit, size of state industry, private financial assets, product market development, share of urban population, log of initial collective assets, and per capita cultivated land. (c) Sample size is 224. (d) The t-statistics are in parentheses, which are based on Huber-White robust standard errors allowing for group errors by provinces. (e) The χ^2 statistics are for the overidentification test for the legitimacy of the instruments, adjusted for provincial group errors.

Table 5 **Ownership and the community government's objectives: non-farm employment and per capita income**

	OLS				IV			
	Share of non-farm employment in rural labour force		Net per capita rural income		Share of non-farm employment in rural labour force		Net per capita rural income	
Intercept	-0.005	-0.034	0.2197	0.156	-0.009	-0.096	0.371	0.131
	[0.148]	[0.856]	[4.508]	[3.465]	[0.188]	[1.946]	[3.773]	[3.646]
Share of TVEs in rural enterprise employment	0.348	0.402	0.047	0.202	0.356	0.532	-0.531	0.255
	[5.003]	[5.286]	[0.517]	[2.448]	[3.444]	[6.685]	[2.311]	[4.265]
Share of non-farm employment in rural labour force			0.507				0.892	
			[2.238]				[1.690]	
Per capita community government revenue	3.182		2.700		3.792		6.697	
	[4.410]		[2.406]		[3.414]		[2.026]	
Per capita cultivated land	-0.036	-0.037	0.015	-0.005	-0.036	-0.037	0.031	-0.005
	[3.331]	[3.282]	[1.029]	[0.360]	[3.418]	[3.578]	[1.149]	[0.415]
Share of urban population	0.081	0.091	0.144	0.198	0.080	0.095	0.088	0.200
	[0.785]	[0.825]	[1.958]	[1.349]	[0.805]	[0.925]	[0.494]	[1.441]
Region dummy for huge cities	0.124	0.203	-0.022	0.148	0.100	0.144	-0.081	0.125
	[2.123]	[2.964]	[0.233]	[1.462]	[1.926]	[2.210]	[0.817]	[1.693]
Region dummy for Coastal	0.055	0.061	0.027	0.063	0.049	0.036	0.015	0.053
	[2.247]	[2.384]	[0.807]	[2.183]	[1.983]	[1.321]	[0.867]	[2.377]
Region dummy for Southwest	-0.031	-0.032	-0.014	-0.031	-0.030	-0.025	-0.143	-0.028
	[1.381]	[1.244]	[0.862]	[2.859]	[1.491]	[0.768]	[0.306]	[2.122]
Region dummy for Northwest	0.035	0.036	-0.055	-0.035	0.035	0.040	-0.078	-0.034
	[1.618]	[1.568]	[2.751]	[1.890]	[1.668]	[1.489]	[1.962]	[1.878]
Region dummy for North	0.081	0.089	-0.054	-0.003	0.080	0.095	-0.112	0.001
	[3.249]	[3.416]	[2.145]	[0.131]	[3.459]	[3.457]	[1.997]	[0.006]
χ^2 [dof]					7.454	5.439	0.363	7.461
					[4]	[5]	[3]	[5]
Standard errors	0.037	0.041	0.043	0.052	0.037	0.042	0.058	0.053

Notes: (a) A full set of year dummies is included in each specification. (b) Endogenous variables are the share of TVEs in rural enterprise employment, share of non-farm employment in rural labour force, net per capita rural income, and per capita community government revenue. Instruments are per capita cultivated land, region dummies, year dummies, local political strength, state supply of credit, size of state industry, private financial assets, product market development, share of urban population, and log of initial collective assets. (c) Sample size is 224. (d) The t-statistics are in parentheses, which are based on Huber-White robust standard errors allowing for provincial group errors. (e) the χ^2 statistics are for the overidentification test for the legitimacy of the instruments, adjusted for provincial group errors.

enterprises. Thus, although private enterprises generally have a lower capital-labour ratio than TVEs, perhaps a lack of access to capital may be sufficiently severe to hinder their ability to increase non-farm employment. Although our result seems to support the theory that TVEs help increase non-farm employment, it does not necessarily mean that TVEs are more efficient in creating non-farm employment than private enterprises, given that capital is scarce and labour abundant in rural China.

We also find that the TVEs' share in rural enterprise employment has a positive and significant effect on per capita income when not conditioned on the non-farm employment of the rural labour force and local public goods provision. But for a given share on non-farm employment in the rural labour force and the level of local public goods provision, that effect becomes negative. These results seem to indicate that the effect of TVEs on increasing per capita income works only through expansions of non-farm employment and local public goods provision. Furthermore, taking into account the fact that TVEs have a higher capital-labour ratio than private enterprises, these results seem to indicate that TVEs are not as efficient as private enterprises.

In summary, we find some evidence on the effectiveness of TVE ownership in pursuing the community government's goals: TVEs seem to increase the revenue shares of the community government and the state, as well as to increase rural non-farm employment and income, but they do not increase income given the levels of non-farm employment and local public goods provision.[26]

VIII. Concluding Remarks

We found evidence that the variation in the share of TVEs among provinces can be explained by the central government's influence, the community government's power, and market development. We also found evidence on the effectiveness of TVE ownership in pursuing the

community government's goals of the government's revenue, non-farm employment, and rural per capita income.

While our focus in the paper is the variation among provinces in China, it is useful to emphasise the common institutional elements throughout China under the reform. As already mentioned in Section II, common to all provinces, township and village governments are all independent fiscal entities under fiscal decentralisation: they are subject to hard fiscal budget constraints, and they are able to retain a large proportion of the revenue they generate. In addition, township and village governments have the authority as well as the responsibility to participate in enterprise development. These considerations help explain why we do not observe many TVE-types of firms in other transition and developing economies. In those economies the fiscal systems are typically very centralised so that local governments are not independent fiscal entities, and relatedly, local governments are often prohibited from becoming directly involved in enterprise development.

Since 1994 TVEs themselves have been evolving, and some of them have been transformed into a new corporate form known as a 'joint-stock cooperative', which is a mix of employee/manager ownership and cooperatives. These changes deserve further research.

Acknowledgements

We are grateful to Takeshi Amemiya, Masahiko Aoki, Avner Greif, D. Gale Johnson, Anjini Kochar, Michael Kremer, Lawrence Lau, David D. Li, Guo Li, John McMillan, Jonathon Morduch, Barry Naughton, Douglass North, Albert Park, Dwight Perkins, Louis Putterman, Jan Svejnar, Frank Wolak, two referees, especially Lawrence Katz and Andrei Shleifer, and seminar participants at University of Southern California, Harvard University, Stanford University, the Universities of California at Berkeley and San Diego, University of Michigan, University of Pittsburgh, and the World Bank for helpful comments and discussions.

Appendix   **Definitions and data sources of variables**

Employment share of TVEs in rural industry: TVE employment divided by total employment in rural enterprises (TVEs plus private enterprises) in industry. 1986 figures are taken from TESM (1986) and others from CTESY (1988–1994).

Output share of TVEs in rural industry: TVE output divided by total output in rural enterprises (TVEs plus private enterprises) in industry. 1986 figures are taken from TESM (1987) and others from CTESY (1988–1994).

State supply of credit: total volume of 'rural enterprise loans' from the ABC and RCCs at the end of the previous year (CRFSY 1989–1993) divided by TVEs output price index, and then normalised by the total rural enterprise (TVE plus private enterprises) employment (1,000 yuan/employee) (CTESY 1988–1994). The TVEs output price index is constructed based on the gross output value of TVEs in current and constant prices (CTESY 1986–1994).

Size of state industry: gross industrial real output of state enterprises (CSY 1987–1994) divided by population (CPY 1991–1994) (10,000 yuan/person).

Initial collective assets: collective fixed assets in 1980 (TESM 1986) divided by rural population (CAY 1981) (yuan/person).

Local political strength: share of rural households NOT adopting the *Dabaogan* form of the Household Responsibility System in agriculture at the end of 1983 (CRSY 1985).

Private financial assets: total rural household savings deposits at the end of the previous year (CRFSY 1989–1993) divided by total rural gross social products (CRSY 1987–1994).

Product market development: total transaction volume in rural free markets (CICAS 1990, CDTSY 1991–1994) divided by total rural gross social products (CRSY 1987–1994).

Share of urban population: urban population in the 1990 census divided by total population (CPY 1991). The 1982 data used in Table 3 are urban population in the 1982 census divided by total population (CPY 1983).

State share in rural net income: state (governments above the township level) taxes and fees collected in rural areas (CAY 1987–1994) divided by rural net income (CAY 1987–1994).

Community government share in rural net income: township and village government revenue from all sources and retained profits in TVEs, divided by rural net income (CAY 1987–1994).

Share of non-farm employment in total rural labour force: total rural labour force minus rural agricultural labour force divided by total rural labour force (CRSY 1987–1994).

Rural per capita real income: rural net per capita income (CAY 1987–1994) deflated by rural consumer price index (1980 = 1, constructed based on annual rural consumer price indexes from CSY 1981–1994) (1,000 yuan/person).

Share of TVEs in rural enterprise employment: TVE employment divided by total rural enterprise (TVE plus private enterprise) employment in industry and services (TESM 1986, CTESY 1987–1994).

Per capita community government revenue: township and village government revenue from all sources and retained profits in TVEs, divided by rural population and deflated by rural overall price index (CAY 1987–1994) (1,000 yuan/person).

Per capita cultivated land: total cultivated land divided by rural population (CRSY 1987–1994) (mu/person).

Region dummies: Huge Cities (Beijing, Tianjin, and Shanghai); Coastal Region (Liaoning, Shandong, Jiangsu, Zhejiang, Fujian, and Guangdong); South Region (Hunan, Hubei, Jiangxi, and Guangxi); Southwest Region (Sichuan, Guizhou, and Yunnan); Northwest Region (Shaaxi, Gansu, Ningxia, Qinghuai, and Xinjiang); and North Region (Heilongjiang, Jilin, Inner Mongolia, Shanxi, Anhui, Hebei, and Henan).

Notes

1. The only empirical work on the issue that we are aware of is that of Naughton (1996), who, in univariate regressions, finds a positive correlation between the share of TVEs in a province and its 'urban proximity'. We show later that his result will not hold in multivariate regressions.

2. This is in accord with the general East Asian model of rural-based development (Hayami 1996).

3. However, TVEs and rural industrialisation in China were not planned and actively supported by the central government at the initial stage. This historical fact is reflected in the following quote from Deng Xiaoping on June 12, 1987: 'The greatest achievement that was totally out of our expectation is that rural enterprises [both TVEs and private enterprises] have developed' (*Economic Daily*, June 13, 1993).

4. In fact, in response to a central government austerity program, total TVE employment fell from 48.9 million in 1988 to 47.2 million in 1989, and further to 45.9 million in 1990. In contrast, employment in the state sector increased during the same period (*China Statistical Yearbook* 1992).

5. During the late 1980s and early 1990s, the total size of SOE industry output was about twice that of TVEs. However, for each year between 1986 and 1992, loans to all rural enterprises accounted for only about 8 per cent of all non-agricultural loans, while loans to SOEs accounted for about 86 per cent. During the retrenchment period in the late 1980s, the share of new loans to rural enterprises in total non-agricultural areas declined from 10.2 per cent in 1988 to 6.8 per cent in 1989, and the share of new loans to SOEs increased from 82.9 per cent in 1988 to 90.5 per cent in 1989 (*Almanac of China's Finance and Banking* 1993).

6. Before 1994, the leaders of village (township) governments were appointed by township (county) governments. Evidence suggests that community economic performance, especially TVE performance, is an important criterion used for appointments (Whiting 1995). After 1994 the leaders of village governments have been directly elected by village residents, but those of township government are still appointed by county governments.

7. Byrd and Gelb (1990) report a high correlation between county (one level above township) revenues and expenditures within a province in the 1980s, which leads to what they called 'ineffective redistribution' across counties and townships in the rural area. Wong (1997) also reports that in the 1990s the rural sector is still very much neglected by the fiscal system. Counties face hard fiscal budget constraints, and, on average, they have inadequate revenues to finance their expenditure responsibilities.

8. In an alternative approach, Weitzman and Xu (1994) point to the Chinese culture for the success of TVEs which they view as vaguely defined cooperatives. We leave this theory out because we are unable to measure variations of the Chinese culture across provinces inside China.

9. Consider other possible objectives of government. Maximisation of the budget is not quite relevant given the fixed and limited fiscal transfers from higher level government; maximisation of votes is irrelevant because the leaders of townships and villages were not elected before 1994; lobbying for central government projects is not very realistic because the central government usually does not have projects located in rural areas; and promotion to counties does not look very attractive compared with running a profitable enterprise, given the low salary for civil servants and limited power of those offices (on the last point, see Byrd and Gelb (1990)).

10. This would imply that it is possible that local political strength can also benefit the central government.

11. Data on many variables before 1986 are not available. Data after 1994 are not available at the time of this writing. Even if data exist, they may present some problems because since 1994 a new category of ownership known as 'joint stock cooperatives', emerged, in addition to TVEs and private enterprises, but no unified national rule has yet been established to distinguish this form from TVEs and private firms.

12. In addition, we have also run all corresponding regressions for single years and for the averages

over 1986–93. The results are similar and are reported in the earlier version of the paper.

13. The Appendix describes the precise construction of regression variables and their sources.

14. An alternative index would be the total transaction volume between SOEs and the rural industry within a province, but no such data are available. Even if such data were available, they might not be able to capture all aspects of the linkages between SOEs and rural enterprises because such linkages have many dimensions through subcontracting, technology transfers, skill training, trade credit, etc.

15. Outside the state financial institutions, the rural financial market has developed rapidly since the mid 1980s. A study estimates that the capital flows through the informal financial markets were larger than those through the formal state financial institutions after 1990 (Liu 1993).

16. Although rural household savings deposits are the main liability components of the ABC and RCCs, loans to rural enterprises constitute only a small part of their assets as agricultural loans are the major part. Hence, the household savings deposits and state credit to rural enterprises are two different variables.

17. Two other more readily available sets of data are from the *China Statistical Yearbook*, one a non-agricultural population and the other a population of designated cities and towns. But neither of them is appropriate: the former is downward biased, and the latter is upward biased.

18. A more refined approach would distinguish further between farm and non-farm incomes accrued to the three entities. Unfortunately, no such data are available.

19. We also estimated the linear probability model, and the results (available upon request) are similar.

20. The 'history matters' theory is supported by additional evidence. Simply examining the data over the eight year period reveals that TVEs grew faster than private enterprises in the provinces where they were initially strong, but more slowly in the provinces where they were initially weak.

21. It is also possible that local political strength is enhanced by TVEs. But our variable of 'local political strength' poses less of a problem because it is from 1983 and the dependent variables are after 1986.

22. This might be the case if the state banks had preferred to lend to TVEs and, if there are few TVEs, diverted the loans for other purposes rather than lending to private enterprises. However, because most other loans in rural areas are agricultural loans, which are known to be less attractive to banks than loans to rural industry (including private enterprises), this consideration is less likely to be important.

23. Private assets would also be lower with more TVEs if TVEs had raised a large part of their capital directly from households because household bank deposits would be correspondingly reduced. In the period we consider here, however, this kind of direct financing is not significant (Zhang and Ronnas 1996).

24. In comparison, Oi (1994) reports from her fieldwork that county government sometimes complained that their revenue was squeezed by TVEs.

25. The results on the household revenue share equation can be derived from the state's and community government's revenue equation because the three revenue shares add up to one.

26. In the estimations including provincial fixed effects, the effect of TVE ownership on the state's share of revenue remains positive and significant while that of the community government's share of revenue becomes insignificant; and the effect of TVE ownership on non-farm employment remains positive and significant while that on income is insignificant. These results (available on request) are consistent with the above findings.

References

Aghion, Philippe, and Jean, Tirole, 'Formal and Real Authority in Organizations', *Journal of Political Economy*, 105(1):1-29, February, 1997.

Almanac of China's Finance and Banking (Zhongguo jin rong nian jian), Beijing, 1993.

Bates, Robert, *Essays on the Political Economy of Rural Africa*, Berkeley: University of California Press, 1987.

Byrd, William, 'Entrepreneurship, Capital and Ownership', in William Byrd and Qingsong Lin (eds.), *China's Rural Industry: Structure, Development, and Reform*, Oxford: Oxford University Press, 1990.

Byrd, William and Allen Gelb, 'Why Industrialize? The Incentives for Rural Community Governments', Chapter 17 in William Byrd and Qingsong Lin, eds, *China's Rural Industry: Structure, Development, and Reform*, Oxford: Oxford University Press, 1990.

CAY, *China Agricultural Yearbook*, 1981–1994, Beijing: China Agricultural Press.

CDTSY, *China Domestic Trade Statistical Yearbook*, 1991–1994, Beijing: China Statistical Press.

Chang, Chun and Yijiang Wang, 'The Nature of the Township Enterprise,' *Journal of Comparative Economics*, 19:434–452, 1994.

Che, Jiahua and Yingyi Qian, 'Institutional Environment, Community Government, and Corporate Governance: Understanding China's Township-Village Enterprises', *Journal of Law, Economics, and Organization*, April 1998a.

Che, Jiahua and Yingyi Qian, 'Insecure Property Rights and Government Ownership of Firms', *Quarterly Journal of Economics*, May, 1998b.

CICAS, *China Industrial and Commerce Administration Statistics 40 Years*, Beijing: China Statistical Press, 1990.

CPY, *China Population Yearbook 1991*, Beijing: China Population Press, 1991.

CRFSY, *China Rural Finance Statistical Yearbook*, 1989–1994, Beijing: China Statistical Press.

CRSY, *China Rural Statistical Yearbook*, 1984–1994, Beijing: China Statistical Press.

CSY, *China Statistical Yearbook*, 1981–1994, Beijing: China Statistical Press.

CTESY, *China Township Enterprises Statistical Yearbook*, 1987–1994, Beijing: China Agricultural Press.

Deaton, Angus, 'Data and Econometric Tools for Development Studies', in J. Behrman and T.N. Srinivasan (eds), *Handbook of Development Economics, Volume III*, Elsevier Science B.V., 1995.

Hart, Olivier, Andrei Shleifer, and Robert W. Vishny, 'The Proper Scope of Government: Theory and an Application to Prisons', *Quarterly Journal of Economics*, CXII(4):1127–62, November, 1997.

Hayami, Yujiro, 'Toward an Alternative Paradigm of Economic Development: An Introduction,' in Y. Hayami (ed.), *Rural-Based Development of Commerce and Industry: Selected Experience from East Asia*, the World Bank, 1996.

Hoxby, Caroline, and Daniele Paserman, 'Overidentification Tests with Grouped Data', mimeo, Harvard University, 1997.

Jefferson, Gary and Thomas Rawski, 'Enterprise Reform in China's Industry', *Journal of Economic Perspectives*, 8(2), 47–70, Spring, 1994.

Li, David D., 'Ambiguous Property Rights in Transition Economies,' *Journal of Comparative Economics*, 23:1–19, 1996.

Liu, Jianjin, 'A Study of Borrowing and Lending Behaviour of Rural Households in China', *China Rural Economy (Zhongguo Nongcun Jingji)*, No.12, 1993.

Luo, Xiaopeng, 'Ownership and Status Stratification', in William Byrd and Qingsong Lin (eds.), *China's Rural Industry: Structure, Development, and Reform*, Oxford: Oxford University Press, 1990.

McKinnon, Ronald, 'Financial Control in the Transition to A Market Economy from Classical Socialism', in C. Clague (ed.) *The Emergence of Market Economies in Eastern Europe*, Oxford: Basil Blackwell, 1991.

Naughton, Barry, 'Chinese Institutional Innovation and Privatization from Below', *American Economic Review*, 84(2):266–270, May, 1994.

Naughton, Barry, 'Why are [some of] China's Rural Industries Publically Owned?', mimeo, University of California at San Diego, 1996.

Nee, Victor, 'Organizational Dynamics of Market Transition: Hybrid Forms, Property Rights and Mixed Economy in China', *Administrative Science Quarterly*, 37:1–27, 1992.

Newey, Whitney, 'Generalized Method of Moments Specification Testing', *Journal of Econometrics*, 29(3):229–256, September, 1985.

North, Douglass, 'Institutions', *Journal of Economic Perspectives*, 5(1):97–112, Winter, 1991.

Oi, Jean, 'Fiscal Reform and the Economic Foundations of Local State Corporatism in China', *World Politics*, 45(1):99–126, October, 1992.

Oi, Jean, *Rural China Take off: Incentives for Reform*, book manuscript, Harvard University, 1994.

Otsuka, Keijiro, 'Rural Industrialization in East Asia', mimeo, Tokyo Metropolitan University, 1996.

Putterman, Louis, 'On the Past and Future of China's Township and Village Owned Enterprises', mimeo, Brown University, 1994.

Qian, Yingyi, and Barry R. Weingast, 'Institutions, State Activism, and Economic Development: A Comparison of State-Owned vs. Township-Village Enterprises in China', in M. Aoki, H. Kim, and M. Okuno-Fujiwara (eds.) *The Role of Government in East Asian Economic Development: Comparative Institutional Analysis*, Oxford University Press, 1996.

Rozelle, Scott and R.N. Boisvert, 'Quantifying Chinese Village Leaders' Multiple Objectives', *Journal of Comparative Economics*, 18:25–45, February, 1994.

Shleifer, Andrei, and Robert W. Vishny, 'Politicians and Firms', *Quarterly Journal of Economics*, CIX:995–1025, November, 1994.

TESM, *Township Enterprises Statistical Material 1978–1985*, Beijing: Ministry of Agriculture, 1986.

TESM, *Township Enterprises Statistical Material 1986*, Beijing: Ministry of Agriculture, 1987.

Weitzman, Martin and Chenggang Xu, 'Chinese Township Village Enterprises as Vaguely Defined Cooperatives', *Journal of Comparative Economics*, 18:121–145, 1994.

Whiting, Susan, *The Micro-Foundations of Institutional Change in Reform China: Property Rights and Revenue Extraction in the Rural Industrial Sector*, PhD dissertation, Department of Political Science, University of Michigan, 1995.

Wong, Christine, 'Interpreting Rural Industrial Growth in the Post-Mao Period', *Modern China*, XIV (1988), 3–30.

Wong, Christine, 'The Maoist 'Model' Reconsidered: Local Self-Reliance and its Financing of Rural Industrialization', in William Joseph, Christine Wong, and David Zweig (eds.), *New Perspectives on the Cultural Revolution*, Cambridge: Harvard University Press, 1991.

Wong, Christine, *Financing Local Governments in the People's Republic of China*, Oxford University Press, 1997.

Zhang, Gang, 'Government Intervention versus Marketization', in Per Ronnas (ed.), *Rural Industries in Post-Reform China: An Inquiry into Their Characteristics*, International Labour Organization and South Asia Multi-Disciplinary Advisory Team, New Delhi, 1996.

Zhang, Gang, and Per Ronnas, 'The Capital Structure of Township Enterprises', in Per Ronnas (ed.), *Rural Industries in Post-Reform China: An Inquiry into Their Characteristics*, International Labour Organization and South Asia Multi-Disciplinary Advisory Team, New Delhi, 1996.

16 Enterprise Reform in Chinese Industry

Gary H. Jefferson and Thomas G. Rawski

The Chinese economy commands attention because of its immense size, and because China's unique combination of dynamic performance and unusual institutional arrangements challenges many popular notions about the reform of socialist systems. Industry, which by Chinese convention includes mining and utilities as well as manufacturing, exemplifies this arresting mix of scale, dynamism, and unexpected structural features. Industry is the largest sector of China's economy, accounting for 50 per cent of total output and 80 per cent of exports, and employing 102 million workers in 1992 (*Zhongguo tongji zhaiyao* 1993). Its robust growth, amounting to well above 10 per cent annually during the 1980s (Table 1), undergirds China's standing as the world's fastest-growing economy.[1]

Since China's initial reform efforts began as experimental changes aimed at improving performance rather than, as in eastern Europe, establishing a Western-style market system, it is not surprising that institutional change has been gradual and uneven, with many features of the pre-reform system surviving even today. Rather than attempting a 'big bang', China's reform path is more akin to 'growing out of the plan' (Naughton 1994).

Industry stands at the core of China's reform problem. Efforts to revitalise and restructure domestic industry are closely linked to the reform of pricing, banking, public finance, ownership, social welfare, and research and development. If China's recent accomplishments carry distinctive implications for policy design, it is industry, where reform has side-stepped privatisation and other standard remedies, that is the most likely source of lessons.

In considering China's experience of enterprise reform, this paper begins by reviewing conditions prior to the reform initiatives of the late 1970s, and then describes the impact of reform policies on structure, conduct, and performance of state-owned industry during the 1980s. Next we examine the growth of industry outside the state sector, and discuss the problems and prospects for industry in the 1990s. Finally, we consider possible implications of China's recent industrial experience for broader issues of reform strategy in transitional economies.[2]

Reprinted with permission. Extracted from Gary H. Jefferson and Thomas G. Rawski, 1994. 'Enterprise reform in Chinese industry', *Journal of Economic Perspectives*, 8(2) Spring:47–70 (with minor editing).

Table 1   Overview of Chinese industrial performance, 1980–1992

A. Real output

| | Index of real output (1980 = 100) | | | | Average annual growth, 1980/92 (per cent) |
	1980	1985	1990	1992	
Ownership type					
State	100	148	210	257	7.8
Collective	100	247	554	914	18.4
Private[a]	100	21,752	126,057	241,455	64.9
Other[b]	100	492	3,530	8,736	37.2
Total	100	176	328	480	13.1

B. Shares of various types of firms in nominal output

| | Share of nominal output (per cent) | | | | Per cent share of incremental output growth, 1980/92 |
	1980	1985	1990	1992	
Ownership type					
State	76.0	64.9	54.6	48.4	43.6
Collective					
Urban	13.7	13.3	10.3	11.8	11.5
Township-village	9.9	18.8	25.3	26.2	28.8
Private[a]	0.0	1.9	5.4	6.8	7.9
Other[b]	0.5	1.2	4.4	7.2	8.3
Total	100.0	100.0	100.0	100.0	100.0
Total output (yuan billion)	515.4	971.6	2392.5	3706.6	

Note: Percentage totals may not check due to rounding error.
[a] Privately-owned firms employing less than 8 workers.
[b] Includes private firms employing 8 or more workers, joint ventures, foreign-owned firms, and other ownership forms.
Source: Yearbook (1993:409, 413); Rawski (1993).

I. Initial Conditions

Studies of Chinese industry during the era of socialist planning reveal many commonalties with the Soviet experience of centrally-directed industrialisation. Managers focused on quantitative targets, especially those concerning physical output volume and total output value, rather than financial objectives. Profitability did not influence the incomes of executives and workers nor the growth prospects of firms.

Chinese socialism also developed its own distinctive features. The national planning apparatus in China was far less comprehensive than in the USSR (Granick 1990). As early as 1979,

for instance, 64 per cent of cement, 41 per cent of coal and 23 per cent of steel were allocated outside the plan system (Fan and Schaffer 1991:9). Although fluctuations in the degree of central control over production and investment decisions date back to the 1950s, broad areas of responsibility were routinely delegated to provinces and localities (Perkins et al. 1977:272–78). Local authorities acquired custodial and usufruct rights over enterprise assets, which were sometimes transferred to enterprise management.[3]

Furthermore, China's mechanism of central planning often failed to determine outcomes within its intended span of control. Naughton (1994) observes that 'the ability of planners to obtain compliance with specific detailed directives had always been limited' by the 'extraordinarily weak planning apparatus'. Hua, Zhang and Luo (1993:71) trace the specific consequences of this fractured structure: '[T]he planning system was so ineffectual that township enterprises…though poorly equipped and funded, developed rapidly from the early 1970s…market transactions[s], or the 'relationship outside the plan' between township enterprises and state-owned enterprises was widespread even under the traditional system'.

Thus, both administrative design and lapses in plan implementation contributed to the pre-reform development of unplanned, semi-market industrial activity under local government auspices. Since the expansion of inherited patterns is easier than the creation of new modes of production and allocation, these atypical features of China's pre-reform industrial system acted to smooth the path of reform.

Beyond these factors, several aspects of China's broader economic environment strongly affected the outcome of partial and gradual industrial reforms. These include the financial, commercial, and technical capabilities of Chinese communities in Hong Kong, Taiwan, and throughout the Asia-Pacific region, which magnified the impact of China's 'open door' policy (Chen, Jefferson and Singh 1992); the broad dispersion of entre-preneurial drive (Cohen 1993), which transformed hesitant reform initiatives into massive change that repeatedly swamped the expectations of China's political leaders as well as foreign onlookers; and the dramatic surge in rural production and incomes following the abandon-ment of collective farming, which relaxed the foreign exchange constraint and gave a huge boost to China's nascent rural industries (Sicular 1991).

II. China's State Industry: system reform in the 1980s

State-owned enterprises are the natural focus of any effort to evaluate the progress of China's industrial reform. The problem is complex: the population of state-owned enterprises is large and diverse; the reforms are partial and uneven; they consist of measures that permit (rather than mandate) new courses of action; and outcomes are ambiguous. A full analysis must penetrate to the enterprise level and transcend the evidence available from anecdotes, small samples, and fragile statistical aggregates.

We adopt the structure-conduct-performance paradigm used in the field of industrial organisation. In applying this framework to the area of socialist reform, we expand the notion of 'structure' to include not just the nature of product and factor markets, but the whole environment surrounding and conditioning enterprise operations (Jefferson and Xu 1991). Since data are inevitably limited and uncertain, we hope that consistent findings across three analytic dimensions can offer more convincing evidence of progress or stagnation than any single perspective. We begin with structure.

Structure

At the outset of reform, China's state-owned enterprises functioned as passive agents of the state economic bureaucracy. Managers had little authority over research and development, product innovation, investment planning, marketing, or even such routine matters as production scheduling, material purchases, wage structures, and employment levels (Komiya 1987). Ten years of reform brought dramatic changes in the allocation of industrial products, the procurement of inputs, the character of incentives, and the degree of competition. By the end of the 1980s, enterprise managers had gained control of most business decisions. Even the largest state-owned enterprises were deeply enmeshed in markets driven by decentralised forces of demand and supply. The new structural environment facing China's state-owned enterprises evolved in response to two distinct policy initiatives.[4]

The first reform effort, implemented around 1980, consisted of tentative steps designed to improve performance within a framework dominated by mandatory output planning and administrative allocation of inputs and products. On the domestic side, state-owned enterprises gained the right to retain a modest share of total profits. They also obtained unprecedented control over any output beyond mandatory plan targets. Decentralised, semi-market transactions, long tolerated as a sort of grey market, were now encouraged as a means of stimulating firms to manage their affairs more actively. On the external side, a new 'open door policy' dismantled long-standing barriers to international trade and investment, with southern provinces enjoying special incentives to expand foreign economic contacts.

The second set of reforms, dating from 1984, centred on two innovations: dual pricing and the enterprise contract responsibility system. Dual pricing partitioned supplies of industrial products into plan and market components. Under the dual pricing regime, most state enterprises transacted marginal sales and purchases on markets where prices responded increasingly to the forces of supply and demand. At the same time, bank loans began to replace budgetary appropriations as the chief source of external funding for industrial enterprises, signalling the emergence of embryonic factor markets.

New forms of contracting gradually supplanted annual plan targets even for the largest firms. Under the contract responsibility system, the enterprise manager, a group of managers, or sometimes the firm's entire workforce agree to fulfill specific obligations, typically involving targets for total profit, delivery of profit to the state, and productivity increases, in return for extensive control over enterprise operations, including full or substantial retention of excess profits.

The most visible consequence of these reforms was a shift from planning toward the market. Surveys of state-owned enterprises show that between 1980 and 1989, the share of material inputs purchased through the market rose from 32 to 59 per cent (Dong 1992), or from 12 to 66

per cent (Zou and Wang 1993). The same surveys show the share of output sold on the market rising from 49 to 60 per cent (Dong 1992), or from 13 to 66 per cent (Zou and Wang 1993). Surveys also show that enterprise funds and bank loans replaced state budgetary grants as the chief sources of investment finance during the 1980s (Dong 1992; Fan and Woo 1992). The overall impact of reform on the structural environment surrounding state-owned enterprise operations emerges from a review of three categories: autonomy, incentives and competition.

Autonomy. As the scope of mandatory planning declined, the managers of state-owned enterprises acquired growing authority over decisions about the quantity and variety of output, production methods, and selling price. A host of market-supporting institutional developments enhanced enterprise autonomy by increasing choice and reducing transaction costs, thereby expanding the capacity of state enterprise managers to restructure business arrangements. These included the creation of markets for industrial materials; the deregulation of trucking and wholesale trade; the erosion of barriers to commercial arrangements involving foreign participants; expanded opportunities to hire consultants and temporary or contract workers; new mechanisms for enforcing contracts and resolving commercial disputes; patent and copyright legislation; the commercialisation of scientific and technical research; the growth of trade and professional associations; and the expansion of advertising, insurance, banking and telecommunications.

Greater enterprise autonomy has not eliminated intrusive regulation. State agencies sometimes refuse to allow enterprises to exercise their new 'rights', especially with respect to foreign trade, employment and financial management. Government officials sometimes manipulate remaining controls in ways that effectively nullify the expansion of enterprise autonomy (Enterprise 1993). There are also complaints that state-owned enterprise managers seek responsibility only for profits and expect the state to cope with financial losses (Liu and Zou 1992). Despite these limitations, autonomy has expanded. Survey data from the late 1980s show that the decision-making authority of state firms, previously subject to tight government controls, is no different from the autonomy reported by managers of urban and suburban collectives (Jefferson, Rawski and Zheng 1992b). Groves et al. (1994) use another set of survey data to demonstrate that the grant of autonomy leads enterprises to hire more contract (non-permanent) labour, increase the share of compensation tied to performance, and raise productivity.

Incentives. New incentive mechanisms have reconfigured the relations between effort, financial outcomes, individual reward, and enterprise control over resources. Beginning around 1980, state-owned enterprises were allowed to retain part of their profits. Unlike Hungary and Poland, where similar reforms failed to alter the leveling tendency of tax and subsidy policy (Kornai and Matits 1984; Farrell 1991), Chinese data reveal a substantial and growing link between profit and retained earnings. Data from a World Bank survey of over 900 state enterprises, summarised in Table 2, show that a 10 per cent rise in gross profit led to increases in retained earnings of 7.6 per cent during 1980–83, 8.7 per cent during 1984–87, and 9.2 per cent during 1988–90. Many enterprises now retain 100 per cent of earnings in excess of fixed quotas for profit remittance.

Table 2   Measures of state enterprise conduct, 1980–1990

Regression results $\ln Y = \alpha + \beta \ln X + \varepsilon$		1980–83	1984–87	1988–90
An increase of 1% in *gross profit*	$\hat{\beta}$	0.76	0.87	0.92
(X) yields a rise in	t	(71.84)	(110.15)	(137.25)
retained profit (Y) of	R^2	0.67	0.79	0.76
An increase of 1% in *labour*	$\hat{\beta}$	0.04	0.13	0.18
productivity (X) yields a rise in	t	(8.76)	(19.11)	(25.69)
the *average wage* (Y) of	R^2	0.03	0.11	0.22
An increase of 1% in *labour*	$\hat{\beta}$	0.22	0.37	0.51
productivity (Y) yields an increase	t	(17.02)	(25.38)	(27.75)
in per capita bonus (X) of	R^2	0.09	0.18	0.26
An increase of 1% in *gross profit*	$\hat{\beta}$	0.97	1.01	0.99
(X) yields an increase in the *per*	t	(58.02)	(68.36)	(43.69)
capita bonus (Y) of	R^2	0.56	0.62	0.50
An increase of 1% in *current* (X_1)	$\hat{\beta}_1$		0.23	
or *lagged value* (X_2) *of retained*	t		(3.72)	
earnings yields an increase in	$\hat{\beta}_2$		0.50	
investment (Y) of	t		(7.62)	
	R^2		0.50	

Note: The final set of estimates covers 1984–90; the estimating equation is $\ln Y = \alpha + \hat{\beta}_1 \ln X_1 + \hat{\beta}_2 \ln X_2 + \varepsilon$
Source: World Bank Survey, covering approximately 900 firms.

Table 3   **Eight-firm concentration ratios for industrial products, 1980–1988**

Product	China 1980	China 1985	China 1988	Japan 1980	United States 1982
Beer	16.2	8.1	10.2	98.9	64.0
Cement	5.7	3.8	2.5	46.0	24.0
Cotton yarn	4.1	3.9	2.8	28.0	44.0
Diesel engines	22.6*	15.6*	16.2*	60.1	n.a.
Machine tools	12.5	10.5	n.a.	n.a.	22.0
Nylon	76.0	62.4	51.2	n.a.	78.0
Refrigerators	42.3	35.7	26.1	73.3	82.0
Steel	37.1	34.7	32.5	65.0	n.a.
Structural glass	40.6	33.6	25.6	100.0	90.0
Televisions	35.8	21.2	19.8	59.2	n.a.

*Three-firm concentration ratios.
Source: Chen et al. 1991:196–97.

Despite continuing support of loss-making enterprises and their employees from direct budgetary subsidies, flexible tax rates, and 'soft' bank lending, new incentive arrangements began to generate penalties as well as rewards. Morris and Liu (1993) find that while subsidies rose in response to deteriorating profit performance during the later 1980s, there was a considerable reduction in the softness of budget constraints for state firms. The recession initiated by the anti-inflation policies of 1988–90 forced many state-owned enterprises to curtail bonuses, furlough some workers at a fraction of their basic wage, and pay others in kind rather than in cash. Even in the boom year of 1988, one study of the coal industry, where price controls ensure widespread losses, noted that if 'enterprises accumulate large losses, this cannot but influence workers' living standards' (*Jiage lilun yu shijian* 1988).

Competition. Reform has meant an expansion not only of markets, but also of competition. Naughton (1992) observes sharp reductions in both the level of state enterprise profits and the dispersion of profitability across branches of Chinese industry. He attributes the decline and convergence of profit rates to the continuing erosion of barriers that formerly protected state enterprises against competition from collective firms, from imported products, and from innovative rivals within the state sector. As a result of past efforts to build 'complete sets' of industries in every province, eight-firm concentration ratios for Chinese industry tend to fall considerably below comparable figures for the United States and Japan; they also show a declining time trend (Table 3). With military industries converting to civilian production, barriers to internal trade in decline, import penetration on the rise, and the prospect of sweeping reductions in import restrictions if China joins the GATT, we see rival markets as a well-entrenched fixture of China's industrial economy.

Conduct

Changes in the structure of Chinese industry have, in turn, induced changes in conduct. There is little room to doubt that profit has become the dominant objective of managers in China's state industries. Dong Furen (1992:4) summarises the outcome of one large survey effort by noting that 'enterprises arrange production plans according to market conditions with the objective of increasing profit'. Many authors echo this view. Some writers accuse state enterprise managers of excessive attention to short-run financial outcomes (Liu and Wang 1993; Gu and Cao 1993); the frequent inclusion of investment and product innovation targets in management contracts indicates that supervisory bodies share this concern. But other observers note a tendency for large firms and enterprise groups to sacrifice current profit for longer-term strategic advantage (Jiang et al. 1993).

Changing attitudes toward the planning system offer another perspective on the objectives of state-owned enterprises. Beginning in the late 1980s, state enterprise leaders sought relief from 'unfair' competition with collective firms owned by local governments (*Touzi yanjiu* 1991). Their complaints had a strange sound, coming from the very firms that had benefited for decades from preferential allocations of funds, equipment, foreign exchange, university graduates, skilled labour, and scarce materials. In our view, these demands reflect the growing conviction among state-owned enterprise managers that the costs of continued participation in the planning system had come to outweigh the benefits.

Some observers, struck by rapid increases in wages and benefits for workers in state enterprises, argue that worker incomes outweigh profits in the minds of state enterprise managers (Woo et al. 1993). Indeed, average monetary compensation of state-owned enterprise industrial workers rose by 252 per cent between 1980 and 1992. But nominal labour productivity rose by 231 per cent over the same period, or nearly as much as wages, so that labour's income share (wages plus bonuses) of gross output rose only slightly, from 7.0 to 7.5 per cent (*Zhongguo tongji nianjian* 1993:107, 130, 412). Even if we assume that a full accounting of labour's share, including housing and other benefits paid in kind, might double the ratio of labour income to total output, labour's effective income share is unlikely to exceed 0.15, the figure around which estimates of labour's (gross) output elasticity appear to cluster.

Hay and Liu (1992) reach a similar conclusion. Working with panel data, they find that standard neoclassical cost functions can successfully model the behavior of state enterprises. Their results indicate that state firms respond to changing factor prices as anticipated by standard theory, that enterprises located near the production frontier conform more closely to cost minimising behaviour than other firms, and that the widely criticised system of bonus payments 'appears to have been highly effective...in improving efficiency and keeping costs down'.

If the profit motive dominates decision-making in state enterprises, how do managers distribute the fruits of higher profits and productivity? Table 2 uses survey data from a World Bank project to illustrate the evolution of several key relationships during the first decade of reform. The first line of the table illustrates the growing link, noted earlier, between gross profits and retained earnings. The next three lines indicate that wage payments (including base wages and bonuses) have become increasingly responsive to changes in profits and productivity.

The last set of results shows that during 1989–90, investment responded significantly to current or lagged profit performance. This critical link between profitability and capacity expansion is a central requirement for long-term economic success. It is precisely this connection that was absent in Kornai and Matits' (1984) investigation of Hungarian firms' investment behaviour between 1975 and 1980. Morris and Liu (1993) confirm the link between profitability and capacity expansion among Chinese state enterprises during the 1980s.

Performance

How have these changes in industrial structure and enterprise conduct affected industrial performance? Rapid growth is the most obvious feature of recent industrial activity. Although the share of the state sector in total industrial output has declined, the real product of state industry more than doubled during the 1980s; expansion continues apace. But rapid, high-cost growth at the extensive margin is the hallmark of socialist systems. So rapid growth of state industry alone cannot demonstrate the efficacy of China's unorthodox reforms.

Expansion of overseas sales offers a more convincing test, especially in view of the recent removal of direct export subsidies.[5] Comprehensive information about the exports of state-owned enterprises is available only for 1985. Available data show, however, that the combined exports of state-owned enterprises and urban collectives grew at an annual rate of about 16 per cent during 1985–90. Since the output of state-owned enterprises was nearly five times that of urban collectives in 1985 and somewhat higher in 1990 (Table 1), it seems evident that the exports of state-owned enterprises grew rapidly during the latter half of the 1980s.

Information about export composition, which shows swift expansion in categories dominated by state-owned firms (power-generating equipment, textile machinery, machine tools), reinforces this impression, as do survey results showing state enterprise exports growing at annual rates of 20 per cent during the later 1980s

(Rawski 1993). Data from a World Bank survey indicate that the ratio of state-owned enterprise exports to value-added rose during the 1980s to levels that match comparable aggregates for US manufacturing. Apparently, many of China's state-owned enterprises are gaining ground in the international marketplace.

Trends in total factor productivity offer another perspective on the performance on state-owned enterprises. Using aggregate data, K. Chen et al. (1988) found that total factor productivity in state industry stagnated from the mid 1950s to the late 1970s, but increased during the reform period. We have identified 13 studies of total factor productivity in China's state industry during the 1980s, most based on sample surveys. Nine studies report annual growth of total factor productivity within the range of 2–4 per cent. Of the remaining four studies, two show higher rates and two obtain lower rates of productivity change. Table 4 summarises the results of our own work, which is based on aggregate rather than sample data.

Can we corroborate indications of rising total factor productivity with micro-level evidence of

Table 4   **Estimated rates of annual productivity growth in Chinese industry (per cent)**

	1980–84	1984–88	1988–92
A. Total factor productivity			
State sector	1.8	3.0	2.5[a]
Collective sector			
Urban and township	3.4	5.9	4.9[a]
Township-village	7.3[a]	6.6[a]	6.9[a]
B. Labour productivity (real terms)			
State sector	3.8	6.2	4.7
Collective sector			
Urban and township	8.6	7.0	13.8
Township-village	5.8	14.4	17.7

[a]Preliminary results.
Source: Jefferson, Rawski and Zheng 1992a; Yearbook, 1993; authors' calculations.

increases in static or dynamic efficiency? We can investigate static efficiency by identifying statistical relationships that should exist in a market system and then testing for their emergence during the reform process.

Market forces create a tendency to equalise financial returns to factors employed in different lines of business. Several studies identify measurable improvements of this sort. China has seen sharp reductions in the dispersion of profitability across branches of industry (Naughton 1992) and across different ownership types (Rawski 1993). There is also evidence of convergence in financial returns to capital, labour and materials across ownership types (Jefferson, Rawski and Zheng 1992a) and among large and medium-size state-owned enterprises (Jefferson and Xu 1991). The dispersion of total factor productivity across enterprises has declined during the reform period, with the greatest convergence evident among enterprises with sales fully disengaged from the plan (Jefferson and Xu 1991). A study of province-level total factor productivity trends for state industry finds 'a pattern of convergence among measures of provincial efficiency levels both nationally and across...the coast, the centre, and the west' (Hsueh, Rawski and Tsui 1992).

Total factor productivity can also grow in response to improved dynamic efficiency, by which we mean accelerated expansion of production frontiers through the adoption of new products, new processes, and new organisational arrangements. Although studies of socialist industrial reform devote little attention to the sources of technological change, a variety of evidence indicates that reform has substantially accelerated innovation in China's state enterprises.

Export growth is perhaps the most visible outcome of successful innovation. During the 1970s, visitors agreed that Chinese manufactures seemed unlikely to penetrate markets in the United States, Japan, or other economies where buyers value style, packaging, finish, service, and prompt delivery as well as low cost and

functionality. The recent surge of exports from China's state industries, noted above, includes large sales to the United States and Japan. In apparel and other fields, Chinese export producers have begun to adopt features of 'just-in-time' production.

Reform has also increased the effectiveness of innovation efforts. China's government has eased the long-standing split between the efforts of state-sponsored research institutes and the commercial needs of industry by the simple expedient of cutting the budgets of research organisations. This has created a powerful stimulus for researchers 'to better serve the economy' (Suttmeier 1992). Enterprise funds have replaced state appropriations as the major source of finance for research and development: the share of state grants in research and development spending by large and medium enterprises dropped to 11 per cent in 1987 and only 7 per cent in 1991 (*Zhongguo xiangzhen qiye nianjian 1978–1987* 1990:251; *Zhongguo tongji nianjian* 1992:749).

Survey research confirms the acceleration of innovative activity within state industry. One study found enterprises focusing on 'the development of new products and the abolition of old products' (Dong 1992); another survey found over 90 per cent of large and medium enterprises engaged in some form of innovative activity, with 81 per cent developing new products (*Zhongguo tongji* 1993); a third showed that the output share of new products rose substantially during the 1980s (Jefferson, Rawski and Zheng 1992b). Over 90 per cent of the state-owned, urban-collective and township-village enterprises in the latter survey cited state-owned enterprises as the principal innovators in their product lines.

This review leads to the conclusion that reform has pushed China's state-owned enterprises in the direction of 'intensive' growth based on higher productivity rather than expanded resource consumption. Although the production of unwanted goods and other characteristic socialist flaws persist (Liu 1993), we observe a consistent picture of improved results—higher output, growing exports, rising total factor productivity, and increased innovative effort—against a background of gains in static and dynamic efficiency that reflect the growing impact of market forces.

Our survey reveals a massive shift from planning toward market coordination, vigorous competition in product markets, substantial gains in performance, and a distinct, albeit gradual and uncoordinated 'corporatisation' of China's state industries. Despite these achievements, certain dysfunctional aspects of the former planning regime remain more or less intact. In particular, weaknesses in the financial system perpetuate costly resource misallocation and threaten macroeconomic stability, while the continued absence of well-defined property arrangements compromises incentives and autonomy. Although these defects have not prevented China's state-owned enterprises from increasing output, exports, productivity, and efficiency; the cost of failing to grapple with these issues appears large. Before considering these matters, we turn to a survey of developments outside the state sector.

Beyond the state sector

No review of China's recent industrial experience can overlook the large and beneficial contribution of enterprises outside the state sector. These enterprises have fortified national economic statistics with substantial increases in output, exports, productivity, and employment. The dynamic performance of enterprises outside the state sector has reduced the share of state-owned firms in total industrial output from more than three-fourths at the beginning of the reform to less than half in the early 1990s (Table 1).

The entrepreneurial firms that have undercut the dominance of state-owned producers are widely described as 'non-state' enterprises. The data in Table 1 make it clear that most of the output in the non-state sector comes from collective firms. These collectives, which are typically controlled by local governments, are part of the public sector. Despite the falling output share of state-owned firms, public enterprise continues to dominate China's industrial scene. The contribution of genuinely private firms, although difficult to measure, is in the vicinity of 10 per cent. We focus our study of non-state industry on collective firms, particularly rural collectives, widely known as 'township and village enterprises'.

Rural collectives expanded during the 1980s on foundations established by the earlier efforts of local governments to promote rural industry (Perkins et al. 1977). Like their predecessors, township or village industrial departments contribute start-up funds, appoint managers, and 'are intimately involved in major strategic decisions' (Wong 1993:9; Ody 1991:iv). The growth of township and village enterprises benefited from the success of China's agricultural reforms, which greatly expanded the supply of rural savings, freed millions of workers to seek non-farm employment, and boosted rural demand for consumer goods.

Table 5 describes the scale, capital intensity, and labour productivity of firms operating under different ownership regimes: state, collective, private and 'other' (a residual category including joint ventures with foreign participation). We focus on data for 1987 because they permit a breakdown of state-owned enterprises based on farm size. The data show a steady downward progression of scale (measured by workers per firm), capital intensity, and labour productivity as we move from large to small state enterprises and then down the administrative ladder to include collectives organised in cities, townships (xiang), and village (cun). A dynamic perspective would show both the collective and private sectors gaining ground on state-owned enterprises, especially the smaller units, in terms of total output, enterprise scale, capital intensity and labour productivity. Nominal labour productivity in the collective sector (excluding village-level units), for example, jumped from 60 to 76 per cent of the average for state enterprises between 1987 and 1992 (Survey 1993:81).

Table 5   Characteristics of state and non-state industrial enterprises, 1987

Category	1987 gross output (billion yuan, current prices)	Workers per firm	Fixed assets (yuan per worker) original cost	net value	Labour productivity (thousand yuan per worker)
I. State-owned enterprises					
All state firms	825	4,110	19,142	13,070	20.6
Firms employing over 5,000	261	9,851	30,080	19,750	21.3
Other large and medium firms	304	1,492	17,620	12,310	24.6
Small state enterprises	263	256	11,760	8,470	16.0
II. Non-state enterprises					
A. Collective ownership					
Urban collectives	167	110	4,670	3,380	11.3
Rural enterprises					
Township	141	61	3,052	2,388	8.9
Village	120	25			6.8
B. Private ownership					
Urban firms[a]	5	2	n.a.	n.a.	5.6
Rural households[a]	80	3	n.a.	n.a.	4.1
C. Other ownership[b]	28	202	n.a.	n.a.	35.3

[a]Privately owned firms employing less than 8 workers.
[b]Includes private firms employing 8 or more workers, joint ventures, foreign-owned firms, and other ownership forms.
Source: Rawski 1993; Yearbook 1989; TVE 1989; Industry 1988.

The achievements of China's non-state enterprises can be summarised briefly. Output has risen explosively, although standard data probably exaggerate real growth (Ody 1991; Rawski 1991). Growing production has absorbed tens of millions of workers. The exports of township and village enterprises (including some non-industrial goods) shot up from US$3.9 to US$12.5 billion between 1985 and 1990, the latter figure amounting to over one-fifth of China's total exports for 1990 (Lardy 1992). Although efforts to measure productivity growth in the collective sector are impeded by inadequate output deflators and inconsistencies between statistical measures of output and employment, it appears that the growth of output per worker, output per unit of capital, and total factor productivity in the collective sector—and especially among township and village enterprises—has outstripped comparable measures for the state sector. Table 4 contains a set of productivity comparisons that includes township-village enterprises.

The expansion of non-state enterprises has served as a lever forcing often reluctant state firms in the direction of market-oriented behaviour. Our own calculations and those of Singh, Ratha and Xiao (1993) show that profitability within the state industry is lowest in provinces where the output of non-state industry has grown most rapidly. Singh, Ratha, and Xiao also find that large provincial shares of non-state industrial output are associated with high levels of total factor productivity in state industry, suggesting that robust growth of the non-state sector both squeezes profits and motivates greater efficiency in the state sector.

The impact of competition extends even to industries like steel and petroleum that face little rivalry from collective enterprises. The continuing fall in profit rates throughout industry, coupled with the expansion of enterprise claims on profit flows, has caused government, the chief holder of industrial capital, to suffer a crushing decline in revenue growth. Fear of inflation has left the state with little choice but to restrict the growth of subsidies and push an ever-growing list of industries into the hurly-burly of the marketplace.

The success of China's collectives has sparked growing interest in measuring and explaining their conduct and performance. Recent studies direct attention to several features that distinguish rural collectives from state enterprises: 1) information channels linking (government) principals with (managerial) agents tend to be shorter and simpler for non-state firms than for state-owned units (Groves et al. forthcoming); 2) local officials and non-state enterprise managers focus sharply on financial objectives (profit plus local tax revenues), while managers of state enterprises, burdened with responsibility for housing and other social services[6] as well as industrial operations, face a more complex set of objectives (Byrd and Gelb 1990:3) Because localities lack the centre's borrowing capacity, enterprises under local jurisdiction face harder budget constraints than state-owned enterprises and often fall into bankruptcy (Qian and Xu 1993).

Several researchers have also suggested that, despite the absence of well-specified private property rights, the demographic stability of China's rural communities promotes the emergence of 'invisible institutions' to provide a 'moral framework for rights' or a 'cooperative culture' that serves to reduce problems of shirking and monitoring found in most public enterprises (Byrd and Lin 1990; Yusuf 1993a; Weitzman and Xu 1993).

It is not clear that these considerations can explain the vibrancy of the township and village enterprise sector. Ties with the state sector represent an important and widely neglected ingredient in the successful development of non-state firms. Collective units rely on the state sector as a source of capital, materials, equipment, specialised personnel, technology, sub-contracting arrangements, and sales revenues. In southern Jiangsu province (near Shanghai), a centre of booming rural enterprise development, 'more than two-thirds of township and village enterprises...have established various forms of economic and technical cooperation arrangements with industrial enterprises, research units, and higher educational institutions in larger cities' (Xu, Mao and Yuan 1993). Officials attempting to develop industry in poor localities are encouraged to pursue 'joint operations with scientific research organisations or large-and medium-scale enterprises' (Du, Huang and Chen 1992). Survey results indicating near-equality of financial returns to the employment of engineers in urban state firms and suburban collectives provide some quantitative measure of the extent to which reform-induced developments have broken long-standing patterns of market segmentation (Jefferson, Rawski and Zheng 1992b).

The erosion of entry barriers associated with China's industrial reform has created a domestic product cycle in which new products, materials, and processes introduced by innovative state firms are adopted by non-state enterprises which use their cost advantages to erode state sector profits and forces state industry toward fresh innovations. Chinese manufacturers are enmeshed in multi-layered innovation ladders that link international firms and their Chinese branches to small and unsophisticated township and village enterprises through the agency of state-managed factories, laboratories, and universities (Jefferson and Rawski 1994).

Despite the important contribution of non-state firms to China's recent industrial achievements, it is too soon to conclude that China's collectives represent an enduring organisational innovation. The dependence of non-state enterprises on resources from the state sector, the tendency for non-state enterprise operations to cluster at the low end of the scale and technology spectrum, and the somewhat artificial nature of the domestic cost advantages enjoyed by non-state firms all suggest that their rapid gains owe much to the specific circumstances of China's economy in the 1980s. Some authors predict that, as underlying economic conditions change, rural industry will also give way to large domestic firms, enterprise groups, and joint venture companies during the course of the 1990s (Jiang et al. 1993; Pan 1993).

Chinese industry in the 1990s

The 1990s have brought an unprecedented and virtually unrestrained push toward the market. This dynamic draws on the extraordinary success of China's southern regions as well as a new vision, shared even by the Communist party, of a market-dominated system in which the state's contribution is limited to indirect macroeconomic controls, microeconomic regulation, passive ownership of assets, and the enunciation of overall economic priorities.

Regulations on 'Transforming the Management Mechanisms of State-Owned Industrial Enterprises' reflect this new attitude, formalising the autonomy of state-owned enterprises and their responsibility for the financial consequences of independent business decisions and of market-driven economic change (US Department of Commerce 1992). The text allows firms to 'reject' or 'refuse' official instructions, including mandatory plan directives, that fall outside narrowly defined boundaries. Overzealous officials who encroach upon enterprise autonomy will 'bear responsibility for a criminal act' (FBIS 1992). Enterprises can dismiss managers and technicians or assign them to blue-collar positions. They can 'select employees according to their merits' and 'dismiss and fire workers and state' (US Department of Commerce 1992).

Official foot-dragging has effectively denied these 'rights' to some units, especially large firms in the state sector. Even so, managers have begun to address the difficult and politically sensitive issue of redundant workers in state industry. In 1992, China's coal industry cut its workforce by 4 per cent, while large and medium enterprises in Liaoning province, the heart of China's industrial 'rust belt', reduced employment by over 6 per cent (*Wall Street Journal*, December 27 1993:8; Liaoning 1993). State industrial enterprises are transferring a growing number of redundant personnel to newly established units, most engaged in service organisations, which will gradually sever their financial ties with the parent units.

The reform of incentives has also expanded the gap between winners and losers. Contrary to the expectations of Chinese managers, who concealed huge profits in advance of negotiations for the renewal of enterprise responsibility contracts in 1990/91 (Wang Haibo 1992), the new contracts appear to have avoided 'ratchet effects' that would have penalised successful firms (Jefferson and Singh 1993). With state subsidies fixed in nominal terms despite substantial inflation and rising enterprise losses, workers and managers attached to unsuccessful firms face growing financial pressure. While some managers may have expected 'virtually unlimited budgetary subsidies' in the past (Ody 1991:30), financially troubled enterprises now face growing uncertainty about their access even to partial compensation for financial losses, price shocks, or falling profits.

In addition, the central government has expanded the role of market transactions in coal, petroleum, steel, and other sectors formerly regarded as bastions of mandatory planning. By 1993, central plans controlled only 7 per cent of industrial output value (Su 1993). Even these mandatory commodity allocations often 'depend on market prices' (Zhang Zhiping 1993:14). These initiatives, along with a continuing inflow of foreign technology and equipment, have contributed to the continued outward shift of industry's efficiency frontier.

While China's industrial economy is rapidly acquiring many characteristics of a market system, important weaknesses remain. We must differentiate between fundamental issues that could potentially block the path of reform and the myriad distortions and bottlenecks that create difficulties without threatening to derail the reform process.

III. Conclusions

The governments of eastern Europe have clear economic objectives: they hope to build Western-style economic systems that will reward their citizens with income levels comparable to those enjoyed in western Europe and qualify their nations for membership in the European Economic Community. China's leaders initiated industrial reform in the hope of eliciting better performance, but with no specific vision of a desirable post-reform industrial system. Not surprisingly, China's reforms have followed an evolutionary path marked by frequent shifts of direction and ad hoc responses to unanticipated outcomes. Bottom-up initiative, experimentation, learning, and adaptation stand at the core of the reform process in Chinese industry.

We view the implementation of substantive economic reform measures from the perspective of the microeconomic theory of investment (Jefferson and Rawski 1993). If investment decisions cannot be costlessly reversed, we expect a firm that faces uncertain demand prospects and uncertain returns to changes in technology, product mix, and capital stock to invest more gradually than an enterprise with a sharply delineated vision of demand conditions and project outcomes (Pindyck 1991). This approach provides a purely economic explanation for China's seeming hesitancy to move decisively toward market-style institutions.

If China's circumstances suggest a theoretical case for a more gradual approach to reform than what we see in nations like Poland or the Czech Republic, China's recent history proves that gradual reform of state industry is a feasible policy alternative that is capable of generating very substantial results. We do not deny that reform is a 'seamless web' in which the rate of progress in one direction affects the consequences of reform efforts in other directions (Dhanji 1991). But this does not imply that every reform component, however desirable in the long run, must be initiated at once. In the reform of socialist economies, as in earlier episodes of industrial-isation (Gerschenkron 1962) and development (Hirschman 1958), a comparative approach demonstrates that there is no unique recipe for successfully managing economic change.

The technique of building a market system is not one of fixed proportions. Temporary recourse to semi-market arrangements like China's systems of dual pricing and management contracts may produce outcomes that dominate the result of immediate efforts to achieve comprehensive price liberalisation or rapid privatisation of state enterprises. China's industrial gains of the past 15 years are partly attributable to favourable initial conditions. But the contrast between China's trend of buoyant increases in industrial output, real wages, employment, and exports and the performance of industry in states that have attempted to accelerate the pace of institutional change is too large to be explained solely by differences in initial conditions. We cannot avoid speculating that China is not the only venue in which the optimal path from plan to market might involve a lengthy interlude of gradual reform and a succession of transitional structures that deviate widely from standard market institutions.

During the past 15 years, China's industrial economy has achieved important progress toward building a market system. The accumulation of market experience and the confidence inspired by large increases in living standards have created a consensus favouring a market-based economy with a limited role for state ownership, government planning, and bureaucratic regulation of economic activity.

This new sense of purpose, which did not exist ten, five, or even three years ago, is itself a consequence of gradual reform. The emergence of a widely shared vision of China's post-reform economy has broadened the scope of feasible policy alternatives. Both the government and the Communist party have approved a new reform agenda that promises to install many elements typical of a full market system. The new reform push has begun with the creation of a unified exchange rate and a sweeping reduction in price controls for industrial goods. China's leaders now seem intent upon pursuing more complex and difficult industrial reform objectives, including the commercialisation of bank lending, the expansion of domestic markets for industrial labour and capital, the creation of genuinely independent business management, and the reduction of government staff in industry-related fields to levels appropriate to the needs of strategic planning rather than micro-management of individual enterprises.

China has deployed an unorthodox strategy of industrial reform to great advantage. An initial round of partial reforms opened the door to growing competition involving old and new forms of public enterprise. During the 1980s, competition emerged as a powerful force for beneficial change in all segments of China's semi-market industrial system. As a result, this episode of partial reform raised the level of industrial output and enhanced the economic welfare of China's factory workforce while creating the foundation for a market system.

Starting from the semi-market economy of the early 1990s, the current acceleration in the tempo of industrial reform, with its new focus on establishing conditions similar to standard market economy arrangements, may open the way to harnessing China's potential for further gains in industrial productivity without creating intolerable political tensions or social costs.

Acknowledgements

We gratefully acknowledge research support from the Woodrow Wilson International Center for Scholars, the John Simon Guggenheim Memorial Foundation, the Henry Luce Foundation, Brandeis University's Mazer Fund, the University of Pittsburgh's University Center for International Studies, and the World Bank. We also thank Joseph Berliner, Alan Gelb, Alan Krueger, Nicholas Lardy, Derek Morris, Peter Murrell, Barry Naughton, Dwight Perkins, Carl Shapiro, Timothy Taylor, Shahid Yusuf and Yuxin Zheng for detailed comments on our initial drafts.

Notes

1. We refrain from detailed comment on the accuracy of Chinese economic statistics, except to note that officially compiled data on industrial inputs and outputs typically convey the order of magnitude of relevant levels and rates of change.
2. Other discussions in this vein include Chen, Jefferson and Singh (1992); Gelb, Jefferson and Singh (1993); and McMillan and Naughton (1993).
3. Yusuf (1993b) decomposes ownership into four basic rights: custody, or deciding how assets are used; usufruct, which entitles the holder to control income streams; alienation, determining the sale or transfer of assets; and destruction, affecting the ultimate disposition of assets.
4. For more detailed accounts, see Hua, Zhang and Luo (1993); Naughton (1994); and *Zhongguo qiye gaige shinian* (1990).
5. Indirect subsidies remain, including low-interest bank loans to favoured exporters (Lardy 1993).
6. Du and Shang (1993) note that state enterprises provide housing for 93 per cent of their employees and 51 per cent of all urban residents.

References

Byrd, William A. and Alan Gelb 1990. 'Why Industrialize? The Incentives for Rural Community Governments'. In *China's Rural Industry: Structure, Development, and Reform*, edited by William A. Byrd and Qingsong Lin. New York: Oxford University Press:338–358.

Byrd, William A. and Qingsong Lin 1990. 'China's Rural Industry: An Introduction.' In *China's Rural Industry: Structure, Development, and Reform*, edited by William

A. Byrd and Qingsong Lin. New York: Oxford University Press:3–18.

Chen, Kang, Gary H. Jefferson and Inderjit Singh 1992. 'Lessons from China's Economic Reform.' *Journal of Comparative Economics*, vol. 16:201–25.

Chen, Kuan et al, 1988. 'Productivity Change in Chinese Industry, 1953–1985,' *Journal of Comparative Economics* 12 (1988): 570–591.

Chen Xiaohong et al 1991. 'Preliminary Overview and Analysis of Concentration in Chinese Industry.' In *Chanye zuzhi ji youxiao jingzheng: Zhongguo chanye zuzhi de chubu yanjiu* (Industrial organization and effective competition: a preliminary study of Chinese industrial organization) edited by Wang Huijiong and Chen Xiaohong. Beijing: Zhongguo jingji chubanshe:191–209

Cohen, Myron L. 1993. 'Cultural and Political Inventions in Modern China: the Case of the Chinese 'Peasant'.' *Daedalus*, Spring issue:151–70.

Dhanji, Farid 1991. 'Transformation Programs: Content and Sequencing,' *American Economic Review*, May:323–28.

Dong Furen, 1992. 'Behavior of China's State-owned Enterprises Under the Dual System.' *Caimao jingji* (Finance and Economics) no. 9:3–15.

Du Haiyan and Shang Lie 1993. 'Distribution of Fringe Benefits for Employees of State-owned Enterprises.' *Zhongguo gongye jingji yanjiu* (Research on Chinese Industrial Economics) no. 2:46–52, 30

Du Miaodeng, Huang Shiqiu and Chen Xuewen 1992. 'On the Management of 'High Starting Point' Enterprises in Poor Townships and Districts.' *Jingji guanli* (Economic Management), no. 12:55–57.

Enterprise 1993. 'How Has the Self Management Right of Enterprises Been Implemented?' *Jingji cankao* (Economic reference news), February 22:1.

Fan, Gang and Wing Thye Woo 1992. 'Decentralized Socialism and Macroeconomic Stability: Lessons from China.' Department of Economics, University of California-Davis. Working Paper Series No. 411.

Fan, Qimiao and Mark E. Schaffer 1991. *Enterprise Reforms in Chinese and Polish State-owned Industries*. London School of Economics Development Economics Research Programme, STICERD, CP No. 13.

Farrell, John P., 1991. 'Monitoring the Great Transition.' *Comparative Economic Studies* 23.2: 9–28.

FBIS 1992. 'More on [Minister] Chen Jinhua Comments on State Firms Law.' US Dept of Commerce. Foreign Broadcast Information Service. *Daily Report: China*, July 28:27.

Gelb, Alan, Gary H. Jefferson and Inderjit Singh, 1993. 'Can Communist Economies Transform Incrementally?', *NBER Macroeconomics Annual 1993*, MIT Press, Cambridge, Massachusetts:87–132.

Gerschenkron, Alexander 1962. *Economic Backwardness in Historical Perspective*. NY: Praeger.

Granick, David 1990. *Chinese State Enterprises: A Regional Property Rights Analysis*. Chicago: University of Chicago Press.

Groves, Theodore, Yongmiao Hong, John McMillan and Barry Naughton, 1994. 'Autonomy and Incentives in Chinese State Enterprises', *Quarterly Journal of Economics*, 109(1):183–209.

Gu Shutang and Cao Xuelin, 1993. 'Create the Conditions for Surmounting Difficulties: On Enlivening State Enterprises to Escape Contradictions.' *Jiage lilun yu shijian* (Price theory and practice), no. 2:12–17.

Hay, Donald A. and Guy S. Liu 1992. 'Cost Behaviour of Chinese State-owned Manufacturing Enterprises During the Reform Period, 1979-1987', Applied Economics Discussion Paper No. 134, Institute of Economics and Statistics, Oxford University.

Hirschman, Albert O. 1958. *The Strategy of Economic Development*. New Haven: Yale University Press.

Hsueh, Tien-tung, Thomas G. Rawski and Kai-yuen Tsui 1992. 'The Impact of Reform on China's State Industry: A Regional Perspective.' Paper presented to a conference on 'Productivity, Efficiency, and Reform in China's Economy,' Chinese University of Hong Kong, August 1992.

Hua, Sheng, Xuejun Zhang and Xiaopeng Luo 1993. *China: From Revolution to Reform.* Houndsmills: Macmillan, 1993.

Jefferson, Gary H. and Thomas G. Rawski, 1993. 'A Theory of Economic Reform,' University of Pittsburgh, Department of Economics, Working Paper No. 273.

——, 1994. 'Institutional Change and Industrial Innovation in Transitional Economies.' Paper presented at the Annual Meeting of the Allied Social Science Associations, Boston, Massachusetts.

Jefferson, Gary H., Thomas G. Rawski and Yuxin Zheng, 1992a. 'Growth, Efficiency, and Convergence in China's State and Collective Industry', *Economic Development and Cultural Change*, 40.2:239–66.

—— 1992b. 'Innovation and Reform in Chinese Industry: A Preliminary Analysis of Survey Data (1)', paper delivered at the annual meeting of the Association for Asian Studies, Washington DC, April 1992.

Jefferson, Gary H. and Inderjit Singh 1993. 'China's State-Owned Industrial Enterprises: How Effective Were the Reforms of the 1980s?', World Bank, Washington, DC.

Jefferson, Gary H. and Wenyi Xu 1991. 'The Impact of Reform on Socialist Enterprises in Transition: Structure, Conduct, and Performance in Chinese Industry,' *Journal of Comparative Economics* 15 (1991):45–64.

Jiage lilun yu shijian (Price Theory and Practice) 1988. 'A Study of China's Policy on Coal Prices, Part 1.' no. 6:40–46.

Jiang Xiaojuan et al 1993. 'New Features of China's Industrial Growth and Structural Change.' *Zhongguo gongye jingji yanjiu* (Research on Chinese Industrial Economics) no. 8:32–40.

Komiya, Ryutaro 1987. 'Japanese Firms, Chinese Firms: Problems of Economic Reform in China, Part 1,' *Journal of the Japanese and International Economies*, 1.1:31–61.

Kornai, Janos and Agnes Matits, 1984. 'Softness of the Budget Constraint—An analysis relying on data of firms.' *Acta Oeconomica* 32 (3–4):223–49.

Lardy, Nicholas R. 1992. 'Chinese Foreign Trade.' *China Quarterly* no. 131:691–720.

Lardy, Nicholas R. 1993. 'China's Foreign Trade Reform in the 1990's.' Paper presented to the Association for Asian Studies, Los Angeles.

Liaoning 1993. 'Increase the Developmental Stamina of Large and Medium State-Owned Enterprises.' *Shengchanli zhisheng* (Voice of Productive Forces), No. 5:6–7, 12.

Liu Li 1993. 'Analysis of Industrial Results for 1992 and Thoughts on the Strategy for Industrial Development.' *Jingji guanli* (Economic Management), no. 2:12–14.

Liu Lili and Wang Shengjiao 1993. 'Strengthen the Management of State-owned Coal Resources, Perfect the Mechanism of Contract Service.' *Zhongguo nengyuan* (China Energy) no. 1:21–23.

Liu Renxiu and Zou Bailin 1992. 'We Must Smash the Problem of Enterprises Taking Responsibility for Profits and not for Losses.' *Jingji yanjiu* (Economic Research), no. 12:22–24.

McMillan, John and Barry Naughton 1993. 'How to Reform a Planned Economy: Lessons from China.' *Oxford Review of Economic Policy* 8.1:130–43.

Morris, Derek and Guy Shaojia Liu 1993. 'The Soft Budget Constraint in Chinese Industrial Enterprises in the 1980s.' Unpublished ms. Oxford University. January 1993.

Naughton, Barry, 1992. 'Implications of the State Monopoly Over Industry and its Relaxation.' *Modern China* 18.1:14–41.

Naughton, Barry, 1994. *Growing Out of the Plan: Chinese Economic Reform, 1978–1993*. NY: Cambridge University Press.

Ody, Anthony J. 1991. 'China: Rural Enterprise, Rural Industry, 1986–1990.' Unpublished paper. Washington DC: World Bank.

Pan Xining 1993. 'Development of Rural Industry Confronts Nine Big Issues.' *Shengchanli zhisheng* (Voice of Productive Forces), No. 7:33–34.

Perkins, Dwight H. et al 1977. *Rural Small-Scale Industry in the People's Republic of China*. Berkeley: University of California Press.

Pindyck, Robert S. 1991. 'Irreversibility, Uncertainty, and Investment.' *Journal of Economic Literature* 29.3, pp. 1110–1148.

Qian, Yingyi and Chenggang Xu, 1993. 'Why China's Economic Reforms Differ: The M-form Hierarchy and Entry/Expansion of the Non-State Sector.' *Economics of Transition*, 1(2):135–70.

Rawski, Thomas G. 1991. 'How Fast Has Chinese Industry Grown?' Research Paper Series, No. 7, Socialist Economies Reform Unit, Country Economics Department, World Bank.

Rawski, Thomas G. 1993. 'An Overview of Chinese Industry in the 1980s.' Unpublished, University of Pittsburgh.

Rawski, Thomas G. 1994. 'Progress Without Privatization: The Reform of China's State Industries.' In *The Political Economy of Privatization and Public Enterprise in Post-Communist and Reforming Communist States*, edited by Vedat Milor. Boulder: Lynne Rienner:27–52.

Sicular, Terry 1991. China's Agricultural Policy During the Reform Period.' In US Congress, Joint Economic Committee. *China: Economic Dilemmas in the 1990s: The Problems of Reforms, Modernization, and Interdependence*. Washington, DC: US Government Printing Office. Vol. 1:340–64.

Singh, Inderjit, Dilip Ratha and Geng Xiao 1993. 'Non-State Enterprises as an Engine of Growth: An Analysis of Provincial Industrial Growth in Post-Reform China.' Working Paper, Transition and Macro Adjustment Division, the World Bank.

Su, Ning 1993. 'China's Industrial Policy During Economic System Transformation.' Paper delivered to an International Conference on Macroeconomic Management,' Dalian China.

Suttmeier, Richard P. 1992. 'High-Technology Development in China: Some Critical Issues.' Unpublished paper. University of Oregon.

Touzi yanjiu (Investment Research) 1991. 'Speed Up the Pace of Technical Reform at Large and Medium State Enterprises: Summary of a Meeting on "Policy Toward Enterprise Technical Reform" Organized by the China Association of Investment Studies.' no. 7:45–48.

US Department of Commerce, 1992. 'Text of Regulations on Transforming State Enterprises, Foreign Broadcast Information Service. *Daily Report: China*. July 28:27–36.

Wang Haibo 1992. 'Now is the Time to Strengthen the Unity Between High Speed Growth and Raising Efficiency.' *Zhongguo gongye jingji yanjiu* (Studies in Chinese Industrial Economics) no. 10:23–28.

Weitzman, Martin and Chenggang Xu 1993. 'Chinese Township and Village Enterprises as Vaguely Defined Cooperatives.' Unpublished ms. Harvard University

Wong, Christine 1993. 'Economic Reform in China.' Unpublished ms. University of California, Santa Cruz.

Woo, Wing Thye et al. 1993. 'The Efficiency and Macroeconomic Consequences of Chinese Enterprise Reform', *China Economic Review*, 4(2):153–68.

Wood, Adrian 1991. *Joint Stock Companies with Rearranged Public Ownership: Invigoration of China's State Enterprises Further Considered.* Programme of Research into the Reform of Pricing and Market Structure in China. London: STICERD.

——, 1993. 'Joint Stock Companies with Rearranged Public Ownership: What Can We Learn from Recent Chinese Experience and East European Experience with State Enterprises?' Paper delivered at the International Symposium on Economic Transition in China, Haikou.

World Bank Survey. Industrial Reform and Productivity in Chinese Enterprises, a research project administered by the Transition and Macro-Adjustment Division, World Bank, Washington, DC.

Xu Fengxian, Mao Zhichong and Yuan Juying 1993. 'New Development a la Sunan.' *Jingji yanjiu* (Economic Research) no. 2:49–55

Xu, Liqing, Robin Sherbourne and Xue Mei 1992. *Industrial Development and Reform in Changzhou City: A Case Study.* London: London School of Economics Development Economics Research Programme, STICERD, CP No. 13.

Yusuf, Shahid 1993a. 'The Rise of China's Nonstate Sector.' Unpublished ms.

Yusuf, Shahid 1993b. 'Property Rights and Non-State Sector Development in China.' Unpublished ms.

Zhang, Zhiping 1993. 'Capital Goods Turn to Free Market.' *Beijing Review* 36.27 (July 5–11):13–16.

Zhongguo kexue jishu sishinian (tongji ziliao) 1949–1989 (Statistics on Science and Technology of China 1949–1989), 1990. Beijing: Zhongguo tongji chubanshe.

Zhongguo tongji (China's Statistics) 1993. 'Technical Development in Large and Medium Industrial Firms—Innovative Activity Develops Universally.' No. 4:10.

Zhongguo tongji nianjian (China Statistical Yearbook),1989, 1992, 1993. Beijing: Zhongguo tongji chubanshe, annual.

Zhongguo qiye gaige shinian [Ten Years of Enterprise Reform in China], 1990. Beijing: Gaige chubanshe.

Zhongguo xiangzhen qiye nianjian 1978–1987 [Yearbook of China's village and township enterprises, 1978–1987], 1989. Beijing: Nongye chubanshe.

Zhongguo tongji zhaiyao 1993 (A Statistical Survey of China 1993). Beijing: Zhongguo tongji chubanshe.

Zhou Shulian 1993. 'Stock-holding is the Way to Transform the Operating Mechanism of State Enterprises.' *Zhongguo gongye jingji yanjiu* (Studies in Chinese Industrial Economics) no. 4:8–13.

Zou, Gang and Zhigang Wang 1993. 'Marketization and Productivity Change.' Unpublished, University of Southern California.

17 Autonomy and Incentives in Chinese State Enterprises

Theodore Groves, Yongmiao Hong, John McMillan, Barry Naughton

I. China's Industrial Reforms

In deciding the best way to reform a planned economy, one of the crucial questions is about the prospects for improvements in state-owned firms' notoriously low productivity. Can changes in policy induce state firms to perform better? We shall offer evidence that in one reforming economy, China, state-owned firms' productivity has been significantly improved by the introduction of some elementary incentives.

Beginning in 1978 and continuing throughout the 1980s, China reformed its industrial sector. Enterprises that had been largely controlled by the state were given some market or market-like incentives (though by the end of the decade, twelve years into the reforms, they were still a long way from looking like capitalist firms). State-owned enterprises were allowed to keep some fraction of their profits, where before all profits had to be remitted to the state. Enterprises began to sell some of their outputs and buy some of their inputs in free markets, rather than selling and procuring everything at state-controlled prices. Managers were given monetary rewards

explicitly based on their firm's performance, and the right to decide what to produce, how much to produce, and how to produce it was shifted from the state to the enterprise (Byrd 1991; Naughton 1995).

Workers' lack of motivation has been a major problem in Chinese enterprises. That productivity could be improved by strengthening the workers' incentives is suggested by anecdotal accounts of inactivity in pre-reform Chinese factories—of workers idling away the day after fulfilling some minimal quota. One of the reforms tried in China was the shifting of responsibility for output decisions from the level of the state to the level of the firm. Another was to increase the fraction of its profits that the firm could retain. The hypothesis to be developed and tested here is that a firm's manager should respond to these increases in autonomy by strengthening the workers' performance incentives, and as a result, the firm should become more productive.

Reforms can be ineffective. Managers may fail to respond to the opportunities created by their expanded autonomy. Partial efforts at reform may be contradictory either with

Reprinted with permission. Theodore Groves, Yongmiao Hong, John McMillan, Barry Naughton, 1994. 'Autonomy and incentives in Chinese state enterprises', *Quarterly Journal of Economics*, 109(1):183–209 (with minor editing).

themselves or with the remnants of the planning system. It is often argued that partial reforms are useless. 'I am relatively pessimistic about the effectiveness of reforms that rely on shifting decision making and financial responsibility to the enterprise level until there is a fundamental reform of the price system', says Johnson (1988:S241–S242), for example: 'Planned control by the centre of inputs and output may well be a superior nth best solution to decentralised decision making with an inappropriate price structure'. We ask whether China's partial reforms—shifting decision responsibilities to managers while leaving the firms state-owned—has resulted in perceptible improvements in enterprise productivity.

Our empirical analysis will ask whether, when the responsibility for deciding output levels was shifted from the state to the firm, and when the firm's marginal profit-retention rate was increased, managers of Chinese state-owned enterprises responded by strengthening the discipline imposed on workers (by increasing the proportion of workers' income paid in the form of bonuses, or by increasing the fraction of workers whom, being on fixed-term contracts, it was in principle possible to fire). We shall then ask whether the new incentives were effective. Did productivity increase significantly with the stronger incentives? The next set of questions will be about who benefited from the reforms. Did the increased autonomy result in higher incomes for workers or managers? Was autonomy followed by more investment by the enterprises? Did autonomy result in smaller subsidies or larger remittances to the state?

Chinese industrial productivity growth accelerated markedly in the reform period of the 1980s. Before the reforms, industrial productivity had been almost stagnant. Total factor productivity grew at an annual rate of only 0.4 per cent between 1957 and 1978 (according to Chen, Hongchang, Wang, Zheng, Yuxin, Jefferson, and Rawski 1988), but this changed after the reforms began. Between 1978 and 1985 industrial productivity grew at an annual rate

of 4.8 per cent (Chen et al.), and it continued to grow strongly after 1985. For the firms in our sample, between 1980 and 1989 total factor productivity rose at an average annual rate of 4.5 per cent.[1]

Not all of this improvement in productivity is attributable to the particular reforms we investigate here. A large number of reforms were introduced in gradual and piecemeal forms. Changes in behaviour were the result of the total impact of these incremental reforms. An important source of gains is the extra discipline resulting from the increased product-market competition that these firms have faced, both from other state firms and from new, non-state firms (McMillan and Naughton 1992). Gains also came from better methods of selecting managers and from linking managers' pay and career prospects to their firms' performance (Groves, Hong, McMillan and Naughton 1995b). The reforms we analyse here are only part, but an important part, of a broad process of change.

II. The Costs of Hierarchy

In order to learn about costs so as to decide on appropriate output quantities, and in order to learn how to organise production so as to minimise costs, the ultimate decision-maker (the central planner in a planned economy, or the firm's manager in a decentralised economy) must rely in part on information that comes from below. Information about how high costs are, whether workers could be reassigned to increase productivity, whether excessive inventories are being held, what improvements in production techniques could feasibly be introduced, how well newly introduced techniques are working, and so on must be gathered from workers and supervisors. Information inevitably becomes distorted as it moves up through the organisation. Bargaining costs are created as people try to use any information they have to influence the decisions that will be based on that information (as Milgrom and Roberts (1988, 1990) noted in their theory of influence costs). Costs of hierarchy arise from the fact that information becomes distorted within the firm as it is transmitted from production to management, and in the case of firms subject to central planning, the information is further distorted in the communications between the firm and state agencies, as has been noted by observers of Chinese enterprises. 'The basic problem is that the narrow channels connecting subordinates to superiors become clogged with pseudo-information, which is often intentionally distorted. While the system continues to report thousands of 'bits' of data, the actual information content is quite limited' (Naughton 1991). 'In their dealings with industrial bureaus and government agencies, managers engage in continual face-to-face bargaining over the setting of mandatory production plans…, and in procuring low priced supplies, subsidised credit and tax breaks. The bargaining, invariably including a measure of deception, and sometimes the cultivation of official favour, has several goals' (Walder 1987:36).

People's proclivity to exploit any information they have affects the incentive system offered within a firm. In the McAfee-McMillan (1995) model of the interaction of hierarchy and incentives, informational asymmetries and the rents they create result in workers being given incomplete performance incentives. The incentives imposed on production workers will be more stringent, according to this analysis, the shorter the hierarchical distance between the production floor and the ultimate decision-maker. The logic of this result is that informational distortions increase cumulatively as information moves up a hierarchy, as each person through whose hands the information passes uses the information to gain some bargaining advantage. The shorter the hierarchy, therefore, the less concerned the top decision-maker need be about giving incentives for information transmission, so the more the decision-maker can focus on providing performance incentives. The mere fact that the right to make output decisions is shifted from the state to the enterprise ought by itself to result in stronger worker incentives and consequently improved productivity. In what follows, we use data on reform-era Chinese state enterprises to test this proposition.

Managerial decision-making autonomy would be meaningless, however, if the enterprise were required to remit all its profits to the centre. Conversely, the larger the fraction of its profits the enterprise is allowed to retain, the stronger the manager's incentives to improve productivity. We shall look at the effects on internal incentives of increases in the enterprise's marginal profit-retention rate.

Differences in managers' and bureaucrats' objectives provide an additional reason why the granting of output autonomy will be followed by a strengthening of workers' incentives. The industrial bureau may want to maintain excessive employment at the expense of productive efficiency (Boycko, Shleifer and Vishny 1996). The shifting of decision-making rights to the manager will result in production being organised more efficiently, provided that the manager is at the same time given a stake in the firm's profits (which increases in the marginal profit-retention rate and other managerial reforms did achieve—see Groves, Hong, McMillan and Naughton (1995b).

Bonuses, having been denounced in China as politically unacceptable in 1966, were revived in 1978 (Walder 1987:23–24). But giving managers the right to offer bonuses to workers did not ensure that they were immediately used: bonus payments did not suddenly increase but rather rose steadily through the 1980s. It is personally costly for a manager to institute an incentive-payment scheme, in that it creates contention between workers and management, as well as among different groups of workers. Rewarding performance usually means increasing disparities among different workers' remuneration. Disputes arise over how to assess performance, how much to reward seniority, whether it is fair to create income inequalities, and so on. In the wage adjustments that occurred in 1977–1978 and 1979–1980, for instance, the 'evaluations often became conflict-ridden, dragging on month after month, affecting morale, and creating dissatisfaction among those not chosen to receive raises' (Walder:27). Thus, managers may be reluctant to introduce incentive schemes, even if they are being encouraged to do so by the state. The managers must be given some positive inducement to bear the costs involved in introducing workers' incentives. In addition, the rules that govern bonuses may affect the ability of managers to institute effective incentive-payment schemes. When bonuses were first revived, the total amount that could be paid in bonuses was fixed at a specified percentage of the wage bill, typically 10 per cent. With total incentive payments limited, and growing only as rapidly as the basic wage, workers correctly treated bonus distribution as a zero-sum game and resisted differentiation. In 1984 the limit on bonuses was replaced by a progressive bonus tax paid by the enterprise. With this change, workers may have begun to perceive bonus distribution as a positive-sum game, reducing the costs incurred by management in instituting effective incentive-payment schemes. During the course of the 1980s, increased authority and autonomy granted to managers may have increased the effectiveness with which bonuses were used to elicit work effort.

Granting the manager autonomy changes the manager's incentives over the design of the workers' incentive system, according to the McAfee-McMillan (1995) model. Making it the manager's role to decide output, rather than merely to pass information up to the centre, changes the manager's personal calculus. When decisions are made at the centre, they are made using information supplied by the manager. It is in the manager's interest to exploit whatever bargaining power is to be obtained from his information. Thus, the information on which the centre bases its decision is distorted. When the buck stops at the manager, more efficient decisions are made because there are now fewer steps in the information-transmission chain. In particular, the manager would be expected to

introduce performance payments to induce more effort from workers.

As well as immediate monetary rewards, workers can be given effort incentives by facing the prospect of losing their job. An additional consequence of output autonomy, therefore, is that managers will expand their ability to fire workers. Most workers in Chinese state enterprises have permanent jobs, but an increasing number have been hired on fixed-term contracts. It is easier for a manager to refuse to renew a worker's contract at the end of his or her term than it is to fire a permanent worker. According to aggregate data, a contract worker in 1989 was six times as likely to have a contract terminated as a permanent worker was to quit or to be fired (State Statistical Bureau 1990a:204, 218).

The introduction of an incentive-payment mechanism does not by itself guarantee that a factory's productivity will rise. It might be that in practice bonuses are paid out equally, regardless of individual productivity, so that they have no incentive effect. Often it is difficult to define adequate output measures, and basing payment on the wrong measures of performance can be counterproductive. Workers might collude against management, subverting attempts to reward good performers by imposing social sanctions on anyone who works too hard. Similarly, although workers on contracts in principle can be laid off at the end of their term so that they have some incentive to exert effort, in practice it may be that their contracts are always renewed, and thus they are effectively the same as permanent workers. Thus, it is necessary to look at the data to see whether the strengthening of worker incentives was real or just apparent and whether the new incentives actually succeeded in improving productivity.

III. Trends in Autonomy, Incentives and Productivity

The data we use come from surveys conducted by the Institute of Economics, Chinese Academy of Social Science (CASS), in consultation with the authors of this paper as well as economists from the University of Michigan and Oxford University. Annual data for 1980–1989 for 769 enterprises in four provinces (Sichuan, Jiangsu, Jilin, and Shanxi) give details of the firms' internal incentives, the firms' cost and revenue accounts, and the nature of the relationship between the firms and the state.

All the firms sampled are state-owned, and large firms are overrepresented in comparison to state-owned firms in general. The sample therefore covers the core of the traditional state-run economy, the set of enterprises for which it is generally held that progress in reforms has been modest, compared with the small-scale, non-state sector. The sample appears reasonably representative of state-run industry as a whole in dimensions other than enterprise size. Output per employee in 1980, the first year of the sample, was 11,329 yuan, 6 per cent below the national average. By 1989 output per employee had increased to 18,891 yuan (in constant 1980 prices) and was now 3 per cent above the national average. Between 1980 and 1989 real output per employee increased 67 per cent in the CASS sample, slightly better than the 52 per cent increase recorded for state-run industry as a whole.

Beginning in 1979, the Chinese government began granting expanded autonomy provisions to selected enterprises nationwide. Initially, enterprises were granted rights to retain a share of profits and to sell some output outside state delivery quotas. Additional autonomy provisions were extended throughout the 1980s. Most state-owned firms in China are controlled by provincial and municipal governments, and expansion of autonomy occurred unsystematically. The factory managers answering the questionnaire were asked when they achieved autonomy to plan activity in six areas: value of output, physical quantity of output, product mix, production technology, production scheduling (quarterly or monthly), and exports. With the exceptions of production scheduling, which came earlier, and exports, which came later, the

answers to the questionnaire show that the other four types of autonomy were tightly clustered, usually being achieved simultaneously. In the regressions reported below, we take as one of our main explanatory variables the date of achieving autonomy to plan output value.

Autonomy is a multidimensional construction, but output autonomy is a crucial element, particularly in the Chinese context. The grant of output autonomy implies that the enterprise's production activity is clearly separated from the obligation to turn over a certain amount of output to state delivery channels. With production autonomy, the state delivery plan is a compulsory contract, rather than the basis for surveillance and control of firm activity by government superiors. In other respects, the firms achieved a measure of 'autonomy' very early in the reform process. By the early 1980s nearly all firms were retaining a share of profits and had the authority to sell some portion of their output outside the plan. We hypothesise that, in such an environment, the grant of output autonomy was a crucial component required for a qualitative increase in overall autonomy, since it allowed firms to integrate incentives, sales, and production. (Conversely, most firms by the end of the 1980s still did not have clear rights to fire permanent workers.)

There is considerable diversity across the firms in the CASS sample as to when they were granted output autonomy. The number of firms in the sample receiving output autonomy in each year is shown in Figure 1. In each year between 1980 and 1989 some firms were granted output autonomy, but it occurred most commonly between 1984 and 1988. While a few of the firms had output autonomy before 1980, some had not received it by the end of 1989.

Firms with output autonomy still operate with a number of obligations to bureaucratic superiors. Firms must deliver output at state set-prices according to contracts signed with their superiors. These contracts are in practice compulsory, and are typically tied to the supply of inputs, also at state-set prices. Such contracts,

Figure 1 **Output autonomy**

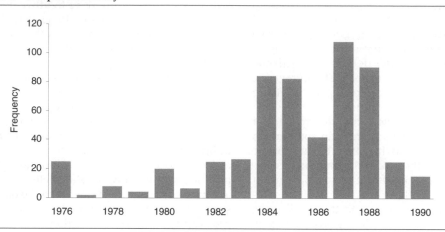

however, are invariably set at below full capacity levels. Firms then establish production schedules for additional output, typically transacted at market or near-market prices, using inputs also purchased from the market. Firms with output autonomy have the authority to establish their own production schedules for all output, subject only to the constraint that they fulfil their contracts. The proportion of enterprise transactions for 1989 carried out at planned prices, which reflects the share of compulsory state contracts, is shown in Table 1. Enterprises in all five industries listed in Table 1 report that state controls affect a larger proportion (in value terms) of their outputs than their inputs, but all

industries report a large volume of transactions outside state contracts and price controls. (For more on the dual-track system, see McMillan and Naughton 1995).

Additional autonomy came through increases in the proportion of profits that the enterprises were allowed to retain. The CASS survey gives data on ex ante marginal profit-retention rates, which is the appropriate measure of profit retention from the point of view of economic incentives. (Marginal profit-retention rates are given directly in the survey: the survey asks the firm's manager for the '*ex ante* rate of profit sharing from profit increase'.) Most enterprises operated under a profit-contract system, in which

Table 1 **Proportion of transactions value at plan price, 1989**

Industry	Inputs (per cent)	Outputs (per cent)
Textiles	53.0	73.0
Chemicals	32.0	62.0
Building materials	19.0	43.0
Machinery	34.0	51.0
Electronics	23.0	58.0

Figure 2   *Ex ante* profit retention, 1980–1989

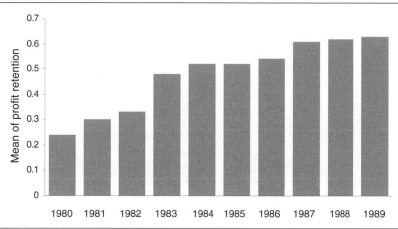

marginal retention rates differed from—and were generally higher than—average retention rates. In the extreme case, some enterprises had a lump-sum profit delivery obligation and 100 per cent retention on the margin. Marginal profit-retention rates steadily increased over the decade, rising from a mean (across firms) of 24 per cent in 1980 to a mean of 63 per cent in 1989 (see Figure 2). In other words, by 1989 the typical firm was remitting 37 per cent of its marginal profits to the state. The average numbers conceal considerable variation across enterprises in marginal profit-retention rates, however. While some enterprises were retaining 100 per cent of their marginal profits by 1989, others were still remitting all their profits to the state.

Worker incentives changed steadily over time. The proportion of worker income received as bonuses, averaged over all the firms in the sample, doubled over the decade, increasing from just over 10 per cent of remuneration in 1980 to over 19 per cent in 1988, and dropping back slightly to just over 18 per cent in 1989 (see Figure 3). (Bonuses are distinguished from base wages, which a worker receives merely for showing up, in that they are, in principle, discretionary from the standpoint of the manager. The worker

receives a bonus only if he or she meets some performance standard. Of course, there is nothing that prevents the manager from setting the performance standard so low that everyone qualifies. But, as a matter of definition, there is a clear distinction between bonuses and base wages: bonuses are contingent on some kind of performance standard; base wage are absolutely not contingent.) The fraction of workers on fixed-term contracts, averaged over all the firms in the sample, increased from 8 per cent of total workers in 1980 to 23 per cent in 1989 (see Figure 4). Evidently, in these two respects the instruments available to managers potentially to provide worker incentives were strengthened over the reform period (though, as noted, they need not necessarily have been used in such a way as to generate effective incentives).

Total factor productivity for the firms in our sample rose at an annual rate of 4.5 per cent between 1980 and 1989, as already noted. Considerable variation across industries underlies this aggregate growth. Total factor productivity (measured as described in the next section) rose between 1980 and 1989 at annual rates of 2.5 per cent in the textile industry, 2.7 per cent in the chemicals industry, 3.4 per cent in the building

Figure 3   **Bonuses as a fraction of pay**

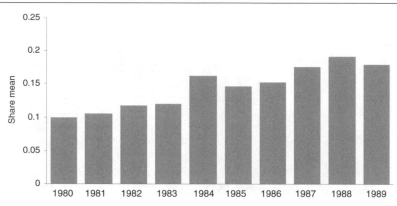

materials industry, 6.1 per cent in the machinery industry, and 7.9 per cent in the electronics industry.

IV. Estimation Method

We look econometrically at three questions. Did managers respond to autonomy by strengthening worker's incentives? Did the stronger workers' incentives translate into higher productivity? Did autonomy result in higher returns to the stakeholders, that is, workers, management, and the state?

We use a subset of the CASS sample: the five industries for which the industry-level sample sizes are reasonably large (textiles, with 103 enterprises; chemicals, with 80 enterprises; building materials, with 52 enterprises; machinery, with 158 enterprises; and electronics, with 44 enterprises; for each of which we have a ten-year time series, 1980–1989).

We use two different econometric models. The regressions not involving productivity estimates are as follows. (Models of this sort underlie Tables 2, 4 and 5.) The reforms are characterised by a set of indices or variables. Let X_{it} be a k-vector representing the reforms affecting firm i at time t, $i = 1, 2, ...N$, and $t = 1, 2,$

..., T; the grant of autonomy, for example. Let Y_{it} represent the results of the actions of firm i at time t, bonus payments, for example. In order to look for the effects of X_{it} on Y_{it}, we use the following program-evaluation model:

$$Y_{it} = \alpha_i + \beta_{tj} + \gamma'_j X_{it} + \zeta_j d_{it} + \varepsilon_{it}; \quad (1)$$
$$i = 1, ..., N; j = 1, ..., 5; t = 1, ..., T_i.$$

The α_i, the individual time-invariant coefficients, are the same for a given firm through time but differ across firms; examples are the technology of firm i and the attributes of firm i's management. The β_{tj}, the industry-specific time dummies, are the same for all firms in a given industry at a given point in time but change through time and across industries; examples are prices and interest rates that are the same for all firms, technological progress, and government policies that are common to all firms. The elements of the p-vector γ_j are assumed to be parameters that are constant over time for all firms within a given industry, the j subscript denoting the industry (the prime denotes a transpose). The ε_{it} represent the effects of the omitted variables that are peculiar to both firms and time periods. We allow for different total time periods T_i for different firms in order to be able to handle possibly missing data.

Figure 4　**Fraction of contract workers**

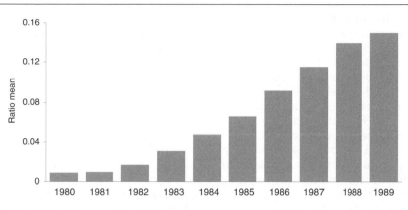

Autonomy may not be randomly assigned by the industrial bureau. Conceivably, firms that are unusually productive might pay out more than other firms in bonuses, and they might be selected by the government for earlier autonomy than other firms. This might produce correlations between bonuses and productivity that seem to support our theoretical model, but such support would be spurious (because good firms might pay more in bonuses, rather than autonomy generating bonuses, as our model predicts). To try to avoid the effects of this possible selection bias on the estimation of γ_j, we include a dummy variable d_{it} representing autonomy occurring two years in the future (with an industry-specific coefficient ζ_j). In other words, d_{it} is equal to one if firm i receives autonomy in year $t + 1$ or $t + 2$. If it is the case that a firm that did well in the previous two years is given autonomy, and that good firms pay more in bonuses, then this dummy will help filter out this source of correlation (compare with Heckman and Hotz 1989).

Some of our regressions (those underlying Table 3 to follow) involve estimates of productivity. We seek a measure of productivity that accounts for the effects of increases in capital stock and material inputs, technical innovation, and reforms other than those investigated here.

We run regressions that simultaneously estimate a production function for each industry and test for any efficiency changes attributable to the reforms. We use the loglinear production function.

$$\ln Y_{it} = \alpha_i + \beta_{tj} + \gamma'_j X_{it} + \delta'_j Z_{it} + \varepsilon_{it}, \quad (2)$$

where $\ln Y_{it}$ is the log of output (in 1980 constant prices); $X_{it} = (L_{it}, K_{it}, M_{it})$, are labour, capital, and material inputs; and Z_{it} represents potential determinants of increased productivity (such as bonus payments and contract workers). The industry-specific time dummy is included to capture the effects of technological change and other, non-modeled, reforms. We estimate a joint production function for all five industries together, with coefficients γ_j and δ_j, corresponding to industry j.

Some manipulation of the data was required before the production function (2) could be estimated. The questionnaire gives gross output data in 1980 constant prices. The enterprise accountant who answered the questionnaire was required to convert output sold at varying current prices into constant prices based on an official list of 1980 prices. Measurement of material inputs and fixed capital required a more elaborate deflation procedure. The questionnaire collected data on prices paid for

271

material inputs and investment goods. Material input deflators were then calculated for each of the five sectors. In calculating the fixed capital stock, the increment to productive fixed capital in each year was deflated by that year's investment-goods deflator and added to the previous year's deflated capital stock. In this way a new series of fixed capital at 1980 prices was created. Labour is measured as the number of workers, averaged over the year. (For more details on the data, see Groves et al. 1995a.)

Equation (2) is a structural equation, with causality going from incentive mechanisms to productivity. If the theory outlined above holds, then the coefficient δ_j should be strictly positive. Thus, we shall test the hypothesis that the vector δ_j is equal to zero.

A difficulty with equation (2) is that the disturbance term ε_{ij} may not be uncorrelated with the independent variables Z_{it}. This arises from the possibility that, while the incentive mechanism such as bonus payments may indeed have effects on productivity as our model predicts, any increases in productivity may in turn increase the bonus payments (simply because more productive firms are able to pay their workers more). If this is the case, the ordinary-least-squares estimator for δ_j will be biased. To correct for this, we use instrumental variables estimators for δ_j. Specifically, we use one-year lagged variables Z_{it-1} as instrumental variables. These work as instruments because the increased productivity in the current period cannot cause increases in the previous year's bonuses and contract workers, so the Z_{it-1} are uncorrelated with ε_{ij}. Also Z_{it-1} is highly correlated with Z_{it}, and so it will give efficient estimates. It is also possible that ε_{ij} is serially correlated. If this is the case, then Z_{it-1} will still be correlated with ε_{ij}, and it would therefore not be a valid instrument variable. For this reason, we also tried using a two-year lag, Z_{it-2}, as the instrumental variable, and found similar results, so that our results seem to be robust to first-order serial correlation.

V. Estimation Results

Table 2 shows the estimation results for the effects of autonomy on the provision by management of worker incentives (Table 2 also shows, for the sake of completeness, the estimated coefficients for the loglinear production functions, that is, the γ_j of equation (2)). The two independent variables, X_1 and X_2, are, respectively, a dummy variable representing the presence or absence of output autonomy, and the enterprise's ex ante marginal profit-retention rate. (Thus, for example, the variable X_i takes on the value zero for the years prior to and including the granting of output autonomy to the firm, and one for all subsequent years.) These are the regressors for, first, real[2] bonuses per worker and, second, the number of contract workers as a fraction of the total number of workers. In the following discussion, we take 10 per cent as the cutoff level for significance tests. Our model suggests that autonomy increases productivity. An alternative possibility is that some firms are inherently better than others, and good firms both pay more in bonuses and are granted autonomy early. Our regressions include firm-specific fixed effects, so that any positive association we find cannot be attributed to inherent firm characteristics. In two of the five industries (machinery and electronics) bonuses as a fraction of total wage bill were significantly positively associated with output autonomy, and in three (chemicals, building materials and machinery) bonuses as a fraction of the total wage bill were significantly positively associated with the profit-retention rate. With a different normalisation, bonuses per worker were positively associated with output autonomy in two industries (again, machinery and electronics), and positively associated with the profit-retention rate in all five industries. In one industry (chemicals) the fraction of contract workers was significantly positively associated with output autonomy; and in another (textiles) it was significantly positively associated with the profit-retention rate. There is some evidence,

Table 2   **Effects of autonomy on incentives**

	Textiles	Chemical	Building materials	Machinery	Electronics	N	R^2
Bonuses/total wage bill						1630	0.62
X_1	-0.008	0.012	-0.006	0.020	0.038		
	[-0.72]	[0.83]	[-0.38]	[2.11]**	[2.36]**		
X_2	0.017	0.045	0.073	0.046	0.036		
	[1.35]	[1.76]*	[1.99]**	[2.83]***	[1.48]		
Real bonuses per employee						1464	0.64
X_1	-18.69	11.82	-15.01	34.66	60.22		
	[-1.26]	[0.63]	[-0.71]	[2.86]***	[2.93]***		
X_2	430.8	659.9	938.8	812.3	857.4		
	[2.61]***	[2.02]***	[2.02]***	[3.88]***	[2.77]***		
Contract workers/permanent workers						1446	0.85
X_1	0.052	0.143	0.031	0.002	0.002		
	[1.46]	[3.17]***	[0.60]	[0.06]	[0.04]		
X_2	0.305	-0.019	-0.001	-0.071	0.043		
	[7.54]***	[-0.24]	[-0.01]	[-1.41]	[0.57]		

Notes: X_1 = output autonomy, X_2 = marginal profit retention, *, **, and *** represent 10 per cent, 5 per cent, and 1 per cent significance levels, respectively. N = the total sample size.

therefore, that managers were induced to strengthen worker discipline by receiving output autonomy and by having their profit-retention rate increased.

What is the effect of worker incentives on total factor productivity? Our two measures of worker incentives are the fraction of employee remuneration paid as bonuses, X_1, and the fraction of contract workers, X_2. A positive correlation between bonuses and productivity is, of course, consistent with both directions of causality. Higher bonuses could generate higher productivity, and an increase in productivity could be paid out to workers as higher bonuses. (For the incentives to work, the causality has to be working in both directions. The promise of bonuses might lead to greater productivity, but if the incentives are genuine, the higher productivity must then result in higher actual

bonus payments.) Conceivably, however, a correlation between bonuses and productivity might merely reflect the fact that the workers get a share of any rents that go to the firm, and the bonuses may not be awarded in such a way as to generate incentives. To check whether the causality goes from bonuses to productivity— that is, whether there is an incentive effect as Section II's model suggests—we use instrumental variables estimation (as described in the previous section) to filter out the opposite causality. The instruments we use are bonuses and contract workers lagged by one year. The regressions include firm-specific fixed effects, so the effects of any variations across firms in inherent productivity are filtered out. Table 3 shows the estimation results based on equation (2). The first three rows of Table 3 show the production-function coefficient estimates for labour, capital, and materials. The last two rows show the effects of the incentives variables. In four of the five industries (all except chemicals), bonuses are significantly positively associated with productivity. In three industries (chemicals, building materials, and electronics) contract workers are significantly positively associated with productivity. To check whether our results seem to be robust to first-order serial correlation, we repeated these regressions using two-year lagged bonuses and contract workers as the instruments: the results (not reported here) were similar. Additionally, we tried omitting the instrumental variables and running an ordinary-least-squares panel regression of productivity on bonuses, together with firm and time dummies, that is, equation (2). In this case, not reported here, all five industries were found to be very strongly positively significant, suggesting, as would be expected, that causality goes both ways—from productivity to bonuses as well as from bonuses to productivity.

The results in Tables 2 and 3, therefore, provide some support for the hypotheses outlined in Section II above. In all five industries there is evidence that firms respond to either the grant of output autonomy or increases in the marginal profit-retention rate (or both) by strengthening worker incentives (either paying more in bonuses, or hiring more contract workers, or both). And in all five industries at least one of these incentive variables generates increased productivity.

We also looked at a reduced-form version of these questions, asking whether autonomy and profit retention affect productivity. The results of this regression, which includes time and firm fixed effects, are given in Table 4. The results are less clear-cut. In two industries (chemicals and building materials) productivity is significantly positively associated with autonomy, but for profit retention there is only one significant interaction, and that is negative (in machinery). Our theory says that autonomy and profit retention do not affect productivity directly, but only indirectly, through their effects on worker incentives, and the results of Table 2 and 3 are consistent with this. Nevertheless, the relationship could be expected to carry over into the reduced form, and it is a puzzle why in most cases shown in Table 4 it does not. Perhaps there is too much unmodeled variation across firms

---

Table 3   **Effects of incentives on productivity**

	Textiles	Chemicals	Building materials	Machinery	Electronics
	IV estimation	$N = 3047$	$R^2 = 0.97$		
L	0.482	0.267	0.306	0.698	0.193
	[4.84]***	[2.54]**	[1.66]*	[2.31]**	[1.45]
K	0.143	0.232	0.214	-0.030	-0.018
	[2.46]**	[4.16]***	[3.27]***	[-0.71]	[-0.24]
M	0.459	0.455	0.256	0.606	0.431
	[10.86]***	[13.80]***	[6.42]***	[22.3]***	[9.69]***
X_1	1.860	0.926	1.358	1.324	1.967
	[1.72]*	[1.53]	[1.68]*	[2.11]**	[2.48]**
X_2	-0.037	0.332	0.343	-0.642	0.591
	[-0.35]	[3.96]**	[1.93]*	[-1.02]	[2.08]**

Notes: L, K, M = log-labour, log-capital, and log-material. X_1 = bonuses/total wages bill; X_2 = contract/total workers. *, **, and *** represent 10 per cent, 5 per cent, and 1 per cent significance levels, respectively. N = the total sample size.

	Textiles	Chemicals	Building materials	Machinery	Electronics
		$N = 1402$	$R^2 = 0.97$		
X_1	0.093	0.125	0.127	0.019	0.001
	[1.02]	[1.69]*	[1.68]*	[0.40]	[0.01]
X_2	-0.0003	-0.0004	0.0007	-0.0011	0.0013
	[-0.34]	[-0.41]	[0.75]	[-1.66]*	[0.90]

Table 4   **Effects of autonomy on productivity**

Notes: X_1 = output autonomy; X_2 = marginal profit retention; *represents the 10 per cent significance level; N = the total sample size.

(picked up in the regressions by the firm and time fixed effects) for the reduced form to show much interaction.

Who benefited from the improvements in productivity that followed autonomy? Tables 5 and 6 show the results of some regressions (based on equation (1)) that ask this question. The independent variables are the two autonomy measures: the output-autonomy dummy X_1 and the profit-retention rate, X_2. Table 5 shows the effects on profits, remittances to the state, and investment from retained earnings. (In the following, the dependent variables are measured in per employee terms to permit comparability across different firms.)

There is some weak evidence that output autonomy has increased enterprise pretax profits, but increasing the marginal profit-retention rate had mixed effects on pretax profits. Real profit per employee is significantly related to output autonomy in one industry (building materials), is significantly positively related to the profit-retention rate in two industries (electronics and textiles), and is significantly negatively related in one industry (building materials). The reforms, therefore, seem to have had a weakly positive effect on profits.

State-run industry has been the main source of the Chinese government's revenue, accounting for over 80 per cent of budgetary revenues in the late 1970s (Naughton 1992). The government's

budget does not seem to have benefited from the reforms. The government-approved subsidy for losses per employee rose in one industry (machinery) and fell with output autonomy in one industry (electronics). Subsidies did not significantly change with increases in marginal profit-retention rates. Thus, there is little evidence that the government was able to reduce its subsidy burden by grants of output autonomy to enterprises. (The government subsidy for losses is simply the payments made by the government to cover losses on non-profitable products. In the still partially planned economy, the government recognises some of the responsibility for losses resulting from its role in setting prices.) Similarly, there is no evidence that the amount of profit remitted to the state increased with reform. Remitted profit per employee was positively associated with output autonomy in one of the industries (building materials), and it was significantly negatively associated with marginal profit-retention rates in two industries (building materials and electronics). No Laffer-curve effect occurred following the reduction in marginal 'corporate tax' rates, therefore, even though the 'tax' rates initially were at or close to 100 per cent.

Increased autonomy did, however, appear to increase the resources available to the enterprise. The production development fund, drawn from enterprise profit, showed no

Table 5   **Effects of autonomy on enterprise finances**

	Textiles	Chemicals	Building materials	Machinery	Electronics	N	R²
Real profit per employee						1464	0.68
X_1	0.0015	0.031	0.063	-0.001	0.025		
	[0.67]	[1.10]	[1.95]*	[-0.04]	[0.83]		
X_2	0.049	0.006	-0.158	-0.027	0.148		
	[1.99]**	[0.13]	[-2.26]**	[-0.85]	[3.16]***		
Real government subsidy per worker						1216	0.51
X_1	-0.000	0.000	-0.001	0.006	-0.011		
	[-0.00]	[0.23]	[-0.25]	[2.26]**	[-2.83]***		
X_2	0.000	-0.007	-0.002	-0.008	0.007		
	[0.00]	[-0.92]	[-0.20]	[-1.55]	[1.23]		
Real profit remitted to state						1374	0.62
X_1	0.003	-0.003	0.060	-0.011	0.015		
	[0.19]	[-0.11]	[2.39]**	[-0.076]	[0.61]		
X_2	0.020	-0.040	-0.179	0.032	-0.072		
	[0.99]	[-0.88]	[-3.30]***	[1.25]	[-2.01]**		
Real product development fund per worker						1415	0.51
X_1	-0.002	0.002	0.001	0.002	-0.002		
	[-0.35]	[0.36]	[0.06]	[0.40]	[-0.24]		
X_2	0.017	0.003	0.003	0.018	0.087		
	[2.97]***	[0.29]	[0.18]	[2.32]**	[8.02]***		

Notes: X_1 = output autonomy; X_2 = marginal profit retention. *, **, and *** represent 10 per cent, 5 per cent, and 1 per cent significance levels, respectively, N = the total sample size.

significant interaction with output autonomy, but it rose significantly with the profit-retention rate in three industries (textiles, machinery, and electronics). (The production development fund is money retained by the enterprise, out of profits, that is used for fixed investment—construction and purchase of machinery—within the enterprise.) This increase in investment suggests that managers viewed the reforms as likely to be permanent rather than temporary.

Much of the benefits of autonomy seem to have gone to the enterprise's workers. Table 6 shows the effects of autonomy on employee's earnings (inclusive of bonuses). The workforce as a whole seems to have benefited from output autonomy and increases in the marginal profit-retention rate. Real average employee wages

(computed by dividing the total wage bill by the total number of employees and deflating with the urban consumer price index) rose significantly in one industry (machinery) with output autonomy and in three (textiles, machinery, and electronics) with the profit-retention rate. In the machinery industry, for example, the simple grant of output autonomy was associated with an increase in the average wage of 90 yuan, 8 per cent of the mean industrial wage in the average year of output autonomy, 1986.

This increase in remuneration seems to have accrued mainly at the level of workers rather than managers. Average production-worker remuneration was not significantly associated with output autonomy, but rose with the profit-retention rate in three industries (textiles, building materials, and electronics). The evidence suggests that managerial personnel did not take advantage of the grant of autonomy to increase their incomes. Average management-personnel wages fell with output autonomy in one industry (textiles) and showed no significant interaction in the others, and there was no significant interaction with the profit-retention rate in any industry. The finding that managerial wages do not rise with autonomy seems surprising. Managerial wages, however, did rise less than production-worker wages between 1980 and 1989. (Production-worker wages rose in real terms at 3.2 per cent annually for the firms in the CASS sample, while managerial wages rose at 1.8 per cent.) The 1980s saw the rise of a managerial labour market in China and considerable turnover in managers (Groves et al. 1995b). Perhaps the slow rate of increase of managers' pay, and its lack of responsiveness to autonomy, reflects the increased competition for managerial jobs. Table 6 leaves unexplained, therefore, what it was that motivated the managers to introduce more efficient methods of production. The answer seems to be that, even

Table 6   **The beneficiaries of autonomy**

	Textiles	Chemicals	Building materials	Machinery	Electronics	N	R^2
Real wage per employee						1471	0.78
X_1	-67.93	45.23	-14.16	90.58	92.94		
	[-1.62]	[0.86]	[-0.24]	[2.64]***	[1.61]		
X_2	172.65	91.07	136.71	219.52	168.16		
	[3.71]***	[0.99]	[1.04]	[3.74]***	[1.92]*		
Real wage per production worker						1110	0.76
X_1	-7.564	10.58	-10.25	21.22	-4.13		
	[0.13]	[0.14]	[-0.14]	[0.32]	[-0.25]		
X_2	346.53	169.00	12.76	137.26	362.80		
	[4.57]***	[1.18]	[0.08]	[1.79]*	[2.89]***		
Real average management wage						1164	0.74
X_1	-407.52	-25.51	-82.18	125.20	136.86		
	[-2.44]**	[-0.12]	[-0.37]	[0.93]	[0.59]		
X_2	-267.78	434.33	2543844	191.48	440.06		
	[-1.21]	[1.07]	[0.52]	[0.91]	[1.22]		
Real welfare fund per worker						1402	0.52
X_1	-0.001	0.002	0.002	0.002	-0.004		
	[-0.68]	[0.97]	[0.78]	[1.13]	[-1.73]*		
X_2	0.001	0.005	0.011	0.005	0.023		
	[0.58]	[1.11]	[2.01]**	[1.71]*	[6.14]***		
Real management expenses per worker						1391	0.51
X_1	-0.041	0.004	-0.016	0.0105	-0.024		
	[-2.13]**	[0.18]	[-0.60]	[0.68]	[-0.93]		
X_2	0.055	-0.021	0.021	0.030	0.092		
	[2.62]***	[-0.46]	[0.34]	[1.17]	[2.39]**		

Note: X_1 = output autonomy; X_2 = marginal retention. *, ** and *** represent 10 per cent, 5 per cent and 1 per cent significance levels, respectively, N = the total sample size.

if the level of manager pay did not rise much, the responsiveness of pay to performance did rise. The manager is an agent of governmental superiors, and his pay is determined by his contract with the industrial bureau. Managers' pay and promotion prospects through the 1980s became increasingly sensitive to the firms' profits and sales (as shown by Groves et al. 1995b).

Table 6 gives some weak evidence that the nonpecuniary rents enjoyed by the enterprises' managers, however, did increase. Enterprise management expenses per employee (which include office expenses, travel, etc.), although showing a significant negative association with output autonomy in one industry (textiles), showed a significant positive association with the profit-retention rate in two industries (textiles and electronics). The welfare fund, drawn out of retained profits and used to supply workers' housing and other benefits, fell with autonomy in one industry (electronics) and rose in per employee terms in three industries (machinery, building materials, and electronics) with the profit-retention rate. Employees' welfare benefits seem therefore to have increased with the reforms.

So far we have been asking how the firms responded to given reforms. Another set of questions is whether there are any systematic patterns in the industrial bureau's decision-making over the imposition of the reforms. (This is a question both about the political economy of reform and about potential selection bias in the econometrics.) According to the model of Laffont and Tirole (1986), if the government wanted to maximise the revenue it earned from firms, but could not distinguish firms with inherently high productivity from those with inherently low productivity, then it should offer a range of different contracts, with firms that claim to have high productivity being given high marginal profit-retention rates (together with high fixed-profit delivery obligations). Similarly, the government might have tried to achieve early reform success by giving autonomy first to the firms that were inherently the most productive. In fact, did good firms get high marginal profit-

retention rates or early autonomy? We performed some simple statistical analysis to look for such selection effects.[3] First, we ran panel-data regressions with, as the dependent variable, the marginal-profit retention rate and, as the independent variable, the production-function residual from the previous year (the residuals coming from panel estimates without firm fixed effects). No significant interaction was found, either for the pooled sample or industry by industry. Second, we computed, for all firms receiving autonomy in a given year, the average production-function residual in the previous year. If more productive firms received autonomy early, this average residual would fall over time. In the case of the machinery industry, but none of the others, there was an apparent tendency for more productive firms to receive autonomy early. With this one exception, output autonomy seems to have been imposed arbitrarily.

VI. Conclusion

Unlike in agriculture, where China's economic reforms have been spectacularly successful (McMillan, Whalley and Zhu 1989), progress in industry has been less clear. Some (Stepanek 1991 for example) go so far as to argue that the industrial reforms have been a failure. Industrial reforms, it is commonly argued, are more difficult than agricultural reforms, because of the greater complexity of the industrial management system and the multiple constraints to which enterprise managers are subject. While there have been large-scale changes in ownership and use rights in agriculture, there has been virtually no change in ownership relations within state-run industry. Reforms in industry have been implemented in a gradual, piecemeal, but sustained, fashion over more than a decade. A continuous series of measures, each slightly enhancing enterprise autonomy, has been enacted, but at different rates in different industries and regions. In many cases implementation was partial or inadequate; in other cases, individual changes seem trivial. It has been hard for outside observers to discern whether the cumulative impact of these changes has been meaningful.

Our analysis leads to the conclusion that the industrial reforms have in fact met with significant success. While enterprises remain subject to many of the problems associated with state ownership in Eastern Europe and elsewhere, increases in enterprise autonomy have induced measurable changes in behaviour at the enterprise level. With autonomy in output decisions and with higher marginal profit-retention rates, enterprises increased their use of bonus payments and hired more fixed-term contract workers. This strengthening of workers' incentives was correlated with higher productivity. The improved productivity raised the workers' incomes (but not the manager's incomes), and resulted in more investment by the enterprises, but did not lower subsidies or increase profits.

Acknowledgements

We thank Julian Betts, Takeo Hoshi, Gary Jefferson, Alex Kane, Wei Li, James Rauch, Glenn Sueyoshi, as well as Lawrence Katz and three referees for comments, and the Ford Foundation for research support.

Notes

1. Production-function estimates from other data sets show similar increases in state firms' productivity. Gordon and Li (1989) estimated, using a sample of 400 state enterprises, that productivity rose by 4.6 per cent annually over 1983–87. Dollar (1990) estimated, using a sample of twenty state enterprises, that productivity rose by 4.7 per cent annually over 1978–82.
2. Nominal values are deflated using the urban consumer price index, from State Statistical Bureau (1990b:250).
3. In the regression reported in Tables 2, 5 and 6, we sought to avoid the potential selection bias that this could have caused by, as discussed in

Section IV, including dummy variables representing autonomy occurring two years in the future.

References

Boycko, Maxim, Shleifer, Andrei, and Vishny, Robert, W., 1996. 'A Theory of Privatisation', *Economic Journal*, 106(435) March:309–19.

Byrd, William, 1991. 'Contractual Responsibility Systems in Chinese State-Owned Industry', in *Advances in Chinese Industrial Studies*, Vol. II, JAI Press, Greenwich, CT.

Chen, Kuan, Hongchang, Wang, Yuxin, Zheng, Jefferson, Gary H., and Rawski, Thomas, G., 1988. 'Productivity Change in Chinese Industry: 1953–1985', *Journal of Comparative Economics*, XII:570–91.

Dollar, David, 1990. 'Economic Reform and Allocative Efficiency in China's State-Owned Industry', *Economic Development and Cultural Change*, XXXIV:89–105.

Gordon, Roger, and Li, Wei, 1995. 'The Change in Productivity of Chinese State Enterprises, 1983–1987', *Journal of Productivity Analysis*, 6(1):5–26.

Groves, Theodore, Hong, Yongmiao, McMillan, John, and Naughton, Barry, 1995a. 'Productivity Growth in Chinese State-Run Industry', in *China's State-Owned Enterprise Reforms*, Dong Fureng, Tang Zhongkuan and Du Haiyan, Beijing: People's Press (in Chinese).

——, 1995b. 'China's Evolving Managerial Labor Market', *Journal of Political Economy*, CIII:873–92.

Heckman, James, J., and Hotz, Joseph, V., 1989. 'Choosing Among Alternative Nonexperimental Methods for Estimating the Impact of Social Programs: The Case of Manpower Training', *Journal of the American Statistical Association*, LXXXIV:862–80.

Jefferson, Gary, and Xu, Wenyi, 1991. 'The Impact of Reform on Socialist Enterprises in

Transition: Structure, Conduct, and Performance in Chinese Industry', *Journal of Comparative Economics*, XV:45–64.

Johnson, Gale, D., 1988. 'Economic Reforms in the People's Republic of China', *Economic Development and Cultural Change*, XXXVI:S225–S246.

Laffont, Jean-Jacques, and Tirole, Jean, 1986. 'Using Cost Observation to Regulate Firms', *Journal of Political Economy*, XCIV:6124–41.

McAfee, Preston, R., and McMillan, John, 1995. 'Organizational Diseconomies of Scale', *Journal of Economics and Management Strategy*, 4, Fall:399–426.

McMillan, John and Naughton, Barry, 1992. 'How to Reform a Planned Economy: Lessons from China', *Oxford Review of Economic Policy*, VIII:130–43.

——, 1995. 'Evaluating the Dual Track System', in *China's State-Owned Enterprise Reforms*, Dong Fureng, Tang Zhongkuan and Du Haiyan, Beijing: People's Press (in Chinese).

——, Whalley, John, and Zhu, Lijing, 1989. 'The Impact of China's Economic Reforms on Agricultural Productivity Growth', *Journal of Political Economy*, XCVII:781–807.

Milgrom, Paul, and Roberts, John, 1988. 'An Economic Approach to Influence Activities in Organisations', *American Journal of Sociology*, XCIV:S154–S79.

——, 1990. 'Bargaining and Influence Costs and the Organisation of Economic Activity', in J. Alt and K. Shepsle, eds., *Rational Perspectives on Political Economy*, Cambridge University Press, Cambridge, UK.

Miljus, Robert C., and Moore, William, M., 1990. 'Economic Reform and Workplace Conflict Resolution in China', *Columbia Journal of World Business*, XXV:49–59.

Myerson, Roger B., 1979. 'Incentive Compatibility and the Bargaining Problem', *Econometrica*, XLVII:61–74.

Naughton, Barry, 1991. 'Hierarchy and the Bargaining Economy: Government and Enterprise in the Reform Process', in M. Lampton and K. Lieberthal, eds., *Bureaucracy, Politics, and Decision-Making in Post-Mao China*, University of California Press, Berkeley.

——, 1992. 'Implications of the State Monopoly over Industry and its Relaxation', *Modern China*, XVIII:14–41.

——, 1995. *Growing out of the Plan: China's Economic Reform 1978–1992*, Cambridge University Press, Cambridge, UK.

State Statistical Bureau, 1990a. *China Labor and Wages Statistical Yearbook 1990*, Zhongguo Tongji, Beijing.

——, 1990b. *Statistical Yearbook 1990*, Zhongguo Tongji, Beijing.

Stepanek, James, B., 1991. 'China's Enduring State Factories: Why Ten Years of Reform Has Left China's Big State Factories Unchanged', in *China's Economic Dilemmas in the 1990s: The Problems of Reforms, Modernisation, and Interdependence*, Study Paper Submitted to the Joint Economics Committee, Congress of the United States, US Government Printing Office, Washington, DC.

Walder, Andrew, G., 1987. 'Wage reform and the Web of Factory Interests', *China Quarterly*, CIX:23–41.

Wong, Thomas, T., 1989. 'The Salary Structure, Allowances and Benefits of a Shanghai Electronics Factory', *China Quarterly*, CXVII:135–44.

18 The SOE Sector Under Reform

Jeffrey Sachs and Wing Thye Woo

China's reform of its state enterprise sector has been undoubtedly incremental and experimental. Reforms have typically taken the form of new practices being allowed for a small number of SOEs, and then being more widely adopted over time. Furthermore, before full coverage was reached, another set of new measures would be implemented on an experimental scale which might then in turn be expanded in scope. So, at most points in time, there may be the preponderance but not exclusive existence of a particular reform configuration.

Market socialism has been the guiding force behind SOE reform, and this explains why the general reform direction has been the steady expansion of the operational autonomy of the SOEs with almost no serious discussions (until very recently) of privatisation as a reform option. From 1979 onward, managers received in piece-meal fashion the rights to make decisions about bonuses, how and what to produce, pricing, marketing, and investment. In parallel with this expansion of managerial autonomy was the steady decontrol of prices; with the prices of final goods being gradually liberalised since 1979, and the prices of inputs liberalised via the dual-track system since February 1985.

The fiscal relationship between the SOE and the state has exhibited bigger twists and turns, however. Before the reform period, Chinese state enterprises operated under the state plan with little autonomy, and the state did little to create a hard-budget constraint[1] because there was no need to do so. By 1983, a de facto contract responsibility system (CRS) had emerged. An SOE would sign an individually-negotiated contract with its supervising agency specifying the annual amount of revenue (tax-cum-profit) to be turned over to the state, thereby supposedly giving the firm the incentive to maximise its financial surplus. However, SOEs remained subject to a soft-budget constraint, being absolved of the responsibility of paying the contracted amount if the financial outcome was poor. As a result, the state found the decline in revenue expressed as a per cent of GDP to be much larger than anticipated.

In 1983, the state began to replace the CRS with an income tax (the *ligaishui* reform). This income tax system was short-lived however because it not only failed to arrest the decline in revenue-GDP ratio, but its positive marginal tax rate was also perceived to be a damper on economic growth. By 1986, SOEs were reverting

Reprinted with permission. Extracted from Jeffrey Sachs and Wing Thye Woo, 1997. 'Understanding China's economic reform', NBER Working Paper 5935, May, Cambridge (with minor editing).

to an expanded CRS. The CRS was again replaced by an income tax in January 1994.

None of the preceding SOE reforms fundamentally altered the ownership structure of the enterprises, through they did significantly affect the control structure. A fundamental change in official philosophy about SOE reform occurred at the end of 1993 when the Central Committee of CPC identified the ambiguity of property rights to be an important cause of the unsatisfactory performance of SOEs, and decided that:

> Large and medium-sized State-owned enterprises are the mainstay of the national economy;...[for them,] it is useful to experiment with the corporate system...As for the small State-owned enterprises, the management of some can be contracted out or leased; others can be shifted to the partnership system in the form of stock sharing, or sold to collectives and individuals.[2]

By the end of 1995, the above decision had been formulated into the slogan of 'holding on to the large SOEs, and freeing the small SOEs (*zhua da, fang xiao*).' The current debate on SOE reform in China is over the definition of 'large', and the optimal form of 'letting go', or privatisation, of the 'small' SOEs.

Assessments of the above decentralising reforms on SOE performance have differed widely. Adherents of the experimentalist school accord great success to the state enterprise reforms in China, while adherents of the convergence school tend to see chronic failures in SOE reforms.[3] On the experimentalist side, Jefferson and Rawski (1994:58) have concluded that:

> ...reform has pushed China's state-owned enterprises in the direction of 'intensive' growth based on higher productivity rather than expanded resource consumption ...we observe a consistent picture of improved results—higher output, growing exports, rising total factor productivity, and increased innovative effort—against a background of gains in static and dynamic efficiency that reflect the growing impact of market forces.

However, China's own leadership has been much more pessimistic. Vice-Premier for the Economy, Zhu Rongji, announced in 1996, that the SOE sector is deeply plagued with problems. According to the Vice Premier:

> The current problems of SOEs are: excessive investments in fixed assets with very low return rates, resulting in the sinking of large amounts of capital; low sales-to-production ratio giving rise to mounting inventories. The end result is that the state has to inject an increasing amount of working capital through the banking sector into the state enterprises.[4]

Vice-Premier Zhu's pessimistic verdict represents the dominant view of Chinese economists and officials throughout the reform period—a view shared by foreign economists of the convergence school. According to Naughton (1995), though, who continues to defend the results of the state enterprise reforms, this negative assessment is the result of ignorance on the part of Chinese observers and of ideological prejudice on the part of some foreign observers:

> Focusing on profitability, [state bureaucrats] see the erosion in state sector profits as a profound crisis of the state sector. Without good measures of total factor productivity, they conclude that state sector performance is deteriorating. Foreign observers, hearing the cries of alarm from the state planners, shake their heads knowingly as they perceive still further evidence that state ownership is intrinsically inefficient. Neither party sees that the difficulties are the result of an ultimately beneficial transition to a different type of economy, and are entirely compatible with gradually improving efficiency.

Opinions about SOE performance are strongly split and the facts are hotly disputed. The main propositions of the experimentalist school *vis-à-vis* SOE performance are that:

(1) China's state enterprise reforms have improved productivity growth (particularly total factor productivity (TFP) growth) in the SOEs;

(2) China's state enterprise reforms have improved the sectoral allocation of production and investment; and

(3) China may be able to avoid privatisation of the SOEs in the future.

The convergence school, on the other hand, holds that:

(1) China's state enterprise reforms have failed to improve productivity performance;

(2) China's state enterprise reforms have failed to improve the financial performance of the SOEs;

(3) China's state enterprise reforms have failed to improve the sectoral allocation of production and investment; and

(4) China will need to pursue a strategy of privatisation in the future, both for purposes of fiscal balance and allocative efficiency.

I. Has TFP Growth Accelerated in the SOEs?

The productivity performance of the SOEs remains a highly contentious issue. Some see improvements, while other researchers do not. Before reviewing the debate, however, it is worthwhile to remember two important points of agreement: (1) SOE productivity growth has been lower than non-state productivity growth; and (2) improvements in the TFP, if any, have been modest in magnitude. Nonetheless, a debate has raged as to whether TFP growth in the SOEs has in fact risen in the course of China's reforms.

The first generation of empirical studies were generally of the opinion that the post 1978 SOE reforms did not raise TFP growth.[5] The picture has become cloudier since then with roughly three sets of results. The first set found 'high' TFP growth rates, for example, Jefferson, Rawski and Zheng, JRZ (1992), and Groves, Hong, McMillan, and Naughton, GHMN (1995a).[6] The second set found little or deteriorating technical changes, for example, Woo, Hai, Jin and Fan, WHJF (1994).[7] The third set found results in between the first

two sets, often with a slowing down of TFP growth after 1985.[8]

The wide range of TFP estimates in the literature could be caused by a wide array of factors which include the choice of data set (for example, geographical and sectoral represent-ation, time period),[9] the specification of the production function (for example Cobb-Douglas, Griliches-type), the assumption of technical change (for example, Hicks-neutral, labour-augmenting), the estimation method (for example, OLS, stochastic frontier), the selection of deflators for output and inputs, and ad hoc exclusion of observations. Another serious problem is that all the studies we know estimate TFP by using the size of the capital stock and the labour force instead of using the actual hours of equipment operation and the actual labour hours spent in production. This mis-measurement is particularly serious because energy shortages have varied according to time period, region and firm ownership. So an increase in the availability of energy could increase TFP estimates that were derived from stock rather than flow data of actual capital and labour usage.

In the debate between WHJF and JRZ on their different results, the main focus has come to rest on two inter-related issues: the validity of the output and input deflators used in the studies, and the degree to which the production structure of China's industrial SOEs differ from those of industrial enterprises in other countries. The attention on these two issues arose when WHJF (1994) found that the implicit value added deflator (VAD) constructed from the nominal value added series and the real value added series in JRZ (1992) declined secularly in the 1980–86 period in contrast to the secularly rising consumer price index (CPI). WHJF considered this opposite trend movement in CPI and JRZ's VAD to be 'anomalous' because it was internationally unprecedented. WHFJ argued that the apparent rise in TFP in the SOEs was due to an overstatement of value added caused by two biases, the overstatement of gross output and the understatement of the intermediate inputs used in production.[10] JRZ (1996) defended their deflators for gross output and intermediate inputs, and attributed the declining VAD to the unusual production structure of China's manufacturing sector. However, JRZ's (1996) claim is no longer true when the industrial census data they used are adjusted to be compatible with economy-wide input-output flows.[11]

Though the debate over TFP performance continues, the broader conclusion that SOE productivity performance lags behind non-state productivity performance continues to win much wider assent. As Andrew Walder (1995) notes of the TFP debate, the 'dispute so far appears inconclusive, *especially given the small productivity increases under dispute*' (emphasis added). While Putterman (1995) is impressed by the 'robustness' of the positive findings of efficiency gains in the state sector, he too emphasises the 'widespread agreement in China at least that...previous reforms in the sector had accomplished far too little'. Similarly, Nee and Matthews (1996) have recently declared 'the need to remain skeptical about overly optimistic assessments [by Jefferson, Rawski and Naughton] of the prospects for successful adaptation to a marketising economy by large state-owned firms. The industrial heartland of Northeastern China dominated by state-owned enterprises, is following the path of the state-owned firms in the former Soviet Union.'

II. The Issues of Allocative Efficiency

Even allowing for some increase in TFP, the SOE sector is widely challenged by the convergence school on two other grounds: allocative efficiency and financial performance (with consequent threats to macroeconomic stability). According to Bai, Li and Wang (BLW 1997), TFP improvements (if any) have not increased economic welfare in China, and this is why the Chinese general public and Chinese leaders have continued to see SOE reform as failure. BLW pointed out that TFP growth is a good index of welfare improvement only:

> in the context of profit-maximising and market-oriented firms. However, for

SOEs under reform, these conditions are not satisfied (in fact, this is the very reason for SOE reform)...One of the important non-profit objectives of the managers is their excessive pursuit of output.

In BLW's judgement, Kornai's (1992) observation that 'SOE managers are embedded in a bureaucratic hierarchy, in which the size of the firm, or output level, is a proxy for status', still applies to China. Furthermore, in China where the soft-budget constraint is real, it is to the managers' advantage to make their SOEs 'too big to be allowed to fail', GHMN's (1995b) finding on SOE managers' compensation that 'sales are significant in explaining wages over full sample period but that profits are just insignificant' reveals the existence of incentives to Chinese managers to attach importance to the output level, as well as to profits.[12]

When both output and profits were included in the objective function of SOE managers, BLW found that 'a higher productivity as measured by the TFP growth may actually lead to lower profitability and therefore, in many cases, lower economic efficiency'. The image of some Chinese SOEs producing undesired goods, but with greater efficiency, finds some support in the aggregate data on inventories. Inventory investment in China averaged 7 per cent of GDP in the 1980–93 period, compared to an average of 2 to 3 per cent for the OECD countries. Only some Eastern European countries prior to 1990 had such high inventory investment rates. These high inventory levels suggest considerable production that is simply not marketable.

Even if one believes that SOE managers in China are mainly maximising profits, technical innovations comprise only one method of maximising an SOE's profits. It may be financially even more rewarding for an SOE manager in China to spend time developing good relations with the state bureaucracy than increasing production efficiency. Until the 1990s, the large and medium-sized SOEs had to fulfill production quota at below-market prices, and they received subsidised inputs in return. If the amount of subsidised inputs was high, the quota system would generate a positive rent to the enterprise. Li (1994) estimated that an SOE which made positive market profits on its above-quota production in the 1986–88 period received a rent that was 2.7 times that of its market profit.[13] Bureaucratic haggling was vastly more profitable than competing in the market! Li's rent estimate may be the lower bound because it did not include the rent that an SOE received from tax bargaining, a practice so pervasive that an SOE paid an effective income tax rate of 33 per cent instead of the legal rate of 55 per cent then in force.

Taken together, these arguments suggest that there are likely to be serious problems of allocative efficiency within China's SOE sector which the TFP index would not measure. These allocative efficiency problems have not been adequately discussed or measured in the literature.

III. Financial Performance of the SOE Sector

There has been a steady increase in SOE losses since additional decision-making power were given to SOE managers in the mid 1980s. The situation stabilised in the 1990–91 period when the state attempted to recover some of the decision-making power devolved to the SOEs. In 1992, decentralising efforts accelerated at the initiative of local leaders after Deng Xiaoping called for faster economic reforms in order to avoid the fate of the Soviet Union. The unexpected event was that the faster economic growth was accompanied by larger SOE losses. About two-thirds of Chinese SOEs ran losses in 1992 when output growth in that year was 13 per cent. These enterprise losses cannot be blamed on price controls because price controls covered only a small proportion of SOEs in 1992. State enterprise losses have continued to accelerate since then. In the first quarter of 1996, the SOE sector slid into the red for the first time since the establishment of the People's Republic of China in 1949, it reported a net deficit of 3.4 billion yuan.[14]

The literature has identified three possible factors as being responsible for the disappearing SOE profits. The first factor is the emergence of competition from the non-state enterprises,[15] the second factor is the failure of the SOEs to improve their efficiency despite the new profit incentives from the decentralising reforms,[16] and the third factor is the over-compensation of SOE personnel.[17] The difference between the experimentalist school's explanation and the convergence school's explanation for the sharp collapse in SOE profit rates lies in the different weights that they put on each of the above three factors. The experimentalist school, as exemplified by Naughton (1995), considered only the first and second factors, and dismissed the empirical importance of the second factor on the basis of the empirical work of GHNM (1994, 1995a and 1995b) and JRZ (1992 and 1996) reviewed earlier. The convergence school, on the other hand, sees similar forces behind the mounting SOE losses during the decentralising reforms of pre 1990 EEFSU and post 1978 China: the increasing ability of SOE insiders to appropriate the income and assets of the SOEs, and the continued inefficiency of the SOEs.

Naughton's (1995) evidence in support of competition being the only factor behind the SOE's losses consisted of showing the sector-wide (average of SOEs and non-SOEs) rates of return to capital in different sectors of industry in 1980 and 1989. In 30 out of 38 cases, the 1989 profit rates were lower than in 1980. The main difficulty with Naughton's explanation that increased competition is driving down the profit rates is that the profit rates of SOEs in sectors of industry that experienced little entry by non-SOEs have shown the same dramatic drop as the profits rates of SOEs in sectors with heavy penetration by non-SOEs. Fan and Woo (1996) compared the SOE profit rate and the proportion of output sold by SOEs in different sectors of industry in 1989 and 1992. In four of the five cases where the degree of SOE domination was unchanged, the profit rates were lower in 1992, for example, the profit rate of the tobacco industry dropped 82 percentage points, and that of petroleum refining dropped 13 percentage points. The 1992 profit rates were lower in six of the seven cases where the degree of SOE domination had declined by less than five percentage points. A regression estimation of the change in SOE profit rate on the change in SOE market share yield an insignificant negative relation between the two variables and an R^2 of 0.3.

The convergence school emphasises the 'spontaneous appropriation' of firm profits by managers and workers as the most important cause for the general decline in SOE profits. With the end of the central plan and the devolution of financial decision-making power to the SOEs, the key source of information to the industrial bureaux regarding the SOEs were reports submitted by the SOEs themselves. This reduction in the monitoring ability of the state in a situation of continued soft-budget constraints meant that there was little incentive for state-enterprise managers to resist wage demands because their future promotion to larger SOEs was determined in part by the increases in workers' welfare during their tenure.[18]

One of the earliest attributions of the erosion of SOE profits to the decentralising reforms was a 1986 report by the China Economic System Reform Research Institute (*Tigaisuo*) which pointed out the emerging tendency of SOEs to over-consume and over-invest through various book-keeping subterfuges.[19] Woo, Hai, Jin and Fan (1994), Woo (1994), Fan and Woo (1996) used various samples and national data to show that the sum of direct income (wages and bonuses) and indirect income (for example, subsidies, and in-kind distribution) increased more than labour productivity growth. Minami and Hondai (1995) found that the labour share of output in the machine industry started rising with the acceleration of decentralised reforms in 1985 and exceeded the estimated output elasticity since 1988. Bouin (1998) calculated that the marginal product of labour of industrial SOEs increased by 5 per cent in 1989–93 while the product wage of industrial SOE workers rose by 7 per cent. Meng and Perkins (1996) studied the determin-

ants of wage and labour demand in 149 industrial SOEs and 139 non-state firms in Guangzhou, Xiamen, Shenzhen and Shanghai (four coastal economies that are marked by more intense market competition) in the 1980–92 period. Meng and Perkins found that the SOEs were maximising income per employee (by dipping into profits) like labour-managed firms, while non-state firms were maximising profits like capitalist firms.

Naughton (1994) was skeptical of the excessive compensation explanation because 'the SOE wage bill, including all monetary subsidies, has remained approximately unchanged at about 5 per cent of GNP since 1978'. There are two difficulties with this point of view. The first is that the correct test for the excessive compensation hypothesis is to normalise the SOE wage bill by value-added in the SOE sector and not by economy-wide GDP. The second difficulty is that direct cash income is only a part of the total package of labour compensation, and that the main categories of direct cash compensation have been under strict state regulation in order to control inflation and embezzlement. The wage and bonus regulations have forced the SOEs to increase workers' income through indirect means like better housing, improved transportation, new recreational facilities, and study tours.[20]

The financial weakness of SOEs has destabilised the macroeconomy by increasing money creation through three channels. The first channel is the monetisation of the growing state budget deficits caused by the declining financial contribution from the SOE sector. SOE paid income taxes that amounted to 19.1 per cent of GDP in 1978, 6.6 per cent in 1985 and 1.7 per cent in 1993; and they remitted gross profits of 19.1 per cent, 0.5 per cent and 0.1 per cent respectively; World Bank (1995, Table 7.3; and 1996, Table 23). The second channel for money creation is the financing of mounting SOE losses by bank loans. The third channel is the disbursement of investment loans to the SOEs to make up for their shortage of internal funds to finance capacity expansion and technical upgrading.

Fan and Woo (1996) have argued that the general reform strategy of decentralisation is intrinsically inflationary. Decentralisation necessarily worsens the principal-agent problem, and given the soft budget constraint the SOEs' appetite for investment soars because they can now, to a much larger extent, privatise the profits and socialise the losses. The local governments, in the interest of local development, inevitably lobby the local branches of the state banks to grant the SOEs' application for investment loans. The evidence overwhelmingly shows that the local bank branches have generally not been able to resist the demand for easy money.[21]

The 'disappearing profits' at the SOEs have also contributed to social instability. In December 1995, the State Administration of State Property reported that asset-stripping in the SOE sector 'has been about 50 billion yuan [annually] since the early 1980s'.[22] This would mean that the cumulative loss of SOE assets in 1983–1992 was equivalent to some 34 per cent of the net value of fixed assets in the SOE sector in 1992. In our opinion, this steady stripping of state assets may subvert political legitimacy much more than a transparent method of privatisation would.

It is notable that the original demands of the 1989 Tiananmen demonstrators were reduction of inflation and corruption. We therefore think that the oft-given justifications for the absence of privatisation in China on the grounds of preserving social stability may be overlooking the social tensions being created by the asset stripping, corruption, and macroeconomic instability caused by the unreformed ownership structure of the SOEs. (Of course, corruptly managed privatisation, as in the case of natural resources in Russia, can also lead to profound inequities and social instability.)

IV. The Emerging Response to the SOE Crisis

There can be little doubt that the Chinese leadership recognises the increasingly serious economic and political problems created by the agency problem innate in the decentralising reforms of market socialism. This is why the debate between the conservative reformers and the liberal reformers has progressed from 'whether privatisation is necessary' to 'what is the optimal amount and optimal form of privatisation'. In late 1995, the most market-oriented of the conservative reformers were in favour of keeping the 4,000 large industrial SOEs and 10,500 medium industrial SOEs under state ownership, and privatising the more than 87,700 small industrial SOEs; while the most radical of the liberal reformers were in favour of the state keeping ownership of only the 1,000 largest industrial SOEs. There are now 25 official property rights exchanges and about 150 unofficial property rights exchanges where state assets are sold to the public, with the latter disappearing temporarily whenever there appears to be a swing back to more orthodox socialism at the centre, Fan (1995).

Recent reports indicate that full-scale sales of small and medium SOEs have occurred in several places. The best known example is Zhucheng city in Shandong province which started privatising SOEs in 1992 when two-thirds of its SOEs were losing money or just breaking even.[23] Almost ninety per cent of county-supervised SOEs in Zhucheng have already been privatised. Sichuan province has been steadily selling off money-losing SOEs, and Guangdong province has been selling profitable SOEs as well in order to finance local infrastructure and clear the debts of unprofitable SOEs to prepare them for sale. Heilongjiang province has just announced plans to privatise 200 SOEs after having sold 160 successfully.[24]

The acceleration in SOEs' conversion to joint-stock companies reflects the leadership's opinion that partial privatisation through public offering in the stock markets and through joint ventures with foreign companies would be an improvement over the contract responsibility system. The important point about partial privatisation is that the movement of the stock price of the firm is a publicly available indicator of the firm's relative performance. The existence of this objective indicator limits the supervising agency's ability to impose non-economic objectives on the firm, and places more pressure on the supervising agency to monitor the returns to state assets.

As is clear from the above, China has not been an exception to absorbing the positive international experience with privatisation of SOEs. However, it is a serious concern of the Chinese Communist Party that more explicit and larger-scale privatisation under its leadership may undermine its political legitimacy. The likely outcome of this political concern is that privatisation would continue under the protection of a terminological haze.

Notes

1. A hard-budget environment is when the firm has autonomous responsibility for its own financial results.
2. 'Decision of the CPC Central Committee on issues concerning the establishment of a socialist market economic structure', *China Daily*, Supplement, November 17, 1993.
3. These two schools represent the two broad competing explanations of China's post-1978 economic performance. The experimentalist school credits China's impressive economic growth to economic experimentation that discovered new, non-capitalist economic institutions that are optimal for China's economic circumstances and may be transferable for use in other transition economies; whereas the convergence school credits the impressive growth to the convergence of China's economic institutions to those of modern capitalist market economies, and to the dominance of peasant agriculture in China's economy in 1978.
4. 'Guo you quye sheng hua gaige ke burong huan', (No time shall be lost in further reforming state owned enterprises), speech at the 4th meeting of the 8th People's Congress, *People's Daily, Overseas Edition*, March 11, 1996.
5. For example, Dernburger (1988), and Rawski (1986).
6. JRZ (1992) found that annual TFP growth

averaged 2.4 per cent in the 1980–88 period; and JRZ (1996) revised it to 2.5 per cent for the 1980–92 period. GHMN (1995a) estimated annual TFP growth in the 1980–89 period to range from 2.3 per cent in the food products sector to 7.9 per cent in the electronic sector.
7. Huang and Meng (1997) found the annual TFP growth rate to be negative 2 per cent in the 1986–290 period, and the number of skilled workers in SOEs to be excessive. WHJF (1994) found TFP growth to be zero in the 1984–88 period; and Bouin (1998) found annual TFP growth to range from -0.7 to 0.2 per cent in the 1989–93 period.
8. Wu and Wu (1994) found TFP to increase in the 1979–84 period but to be stagnant in the 1985–92 period. Perkins, Zheng and Cao (1993) established that there were significant regional variations in TFP growth: for the Special Economic Zone of Xiamen, the TFP index went from 100 in 1980 to 139 in 1985 and then to 131 in 1988; for Shanghai, it went from 100 in 1985 to 99 in 1988; and, for Beijing, it went steadily down from 100 in 1983 to 74 in 1988. The overall national picture was that the TFP index rose from 100 in 1981 to 104 in 1985 and then declined steadily to 81 in 1989. Using samples for medium and large state-owned construction enterprises, Parker (1995, 1997) found annual TFP growth to average 1 per cent in the 1985–91 period but to decline significantly over time.
9. Because most samples are collected through contract with the State Statistical Bureau, the absence of independent monitoring raises the possibility of Potemkin datasets.
10. The phenomenon of declining VAD also applies to the empirical works of GHMN, see Naughton (1994). In fact, Naughton (1994) was sufficiently concerned about GHMN's survey data that he warned readers that: 'Reliance on retrospective reconstruction might bias inflation rates for intermediate inputs upward if managers idealise the pre-inflation period. This would produce a corresponding upward bias in the TFP growth rates…'.
11. Specifically, JRZ (1996) claimed that China's manufacturing sector had an usually low gross value added (GVA) to gross output value (GOV) ratio. They computed the (GVA/GOV) ratio to

be 46 per cent for the United States, 40 per cent for Japan, 45 per cent for West Germany and 44 per cent for the United Kingdom compared to the (GVA/GOV) ratio for China which was 33 per cent in 1980, 31 per cent in 1984, 29 per cent in 1988, and 25 per cent in 1992. However, JRZ's finding of an unusual Chinese industrial structure for China appears to be a fragile one. Specifically, JRZ's proposition which is based on Industrial Yearbook data does not hold when the 1987 Input-Output Table data are used instead. Ren Ruoen (private communication) found that the ratio of gross value added to gross output value for the industrial sector was 44 per cent for the United States, and 42 per cent for China when Input-Output Table data were used. The fact is that the US Census definition of GVA includes the cost of services purchased outside of the manufacturing sector whereas the usual Chinese definition of GVA does not. Ren Rouen's estimates were obtained after adjusting the Chinese Input-Output Table definition of GVA to make it consistent with the US Census definition estimates. JRZ's low ratios for China suggest to us the Chinese measure of GVA is inconsistent with the US measure that they use for comparison. JRZ's declining ratios suggest to us the increasing appropriation of capital income by SOE personnel over time—an issue that we will discuss later.

12. However, GHMN also found indicators that the importance of sales decreased over time while that of profits increased. Parker's (1997) finding of over-usage of capital and labour in Chinese state-owned construction firms confirms that such 'growth for growth sake' type of incentives did have an impact on firms' operations.

13. So total profits equaled the sum of market profits plus rent.

14. 'Record loss suffered by state sector', *South China Morning Post International Weekly*, June 29, 1996.

15. For example, Naughton (1995) and Jefferson and Rawski (1994).

16. An exasperated view commonly found in official Chinese statements, for example, Vice-Premier Wu Bangguo stated that: 'The situation as regards the economic efficiency of [state] enterprises has remained very grim...And the prominent feature is the great increase in the volume and size of losses' (*The Washington Post*,

'Losses of State-Owned Industries Pose Problems for China's Leaders, November 3, 1996).

17. For example, Reynolds (1987) and Fan and Woo (1996).

18. This SOE tendency to over-reward workers received official acknowledgement in 1984 when the government introduced a progressive bonus tax to control the generous dispensation of bonuses that began in 1979. An annual bonus of up to 4 months of basic wages were exempted from the bonus tax; but a fifth month bonus would require the SOE to pay a 100 per cent bonus tax, a sixth month bonus would be subject to a 200 per cent bonus tax, a seven month bonus would be subject to a 300 per cent bonus tax, and so forth.

19. This report has been published in English as Reynolds (1987). *Tigaisuo* was disbanded when Zhao Ziyang was ousted as Party Secretary after the 1989 Tiananmen demonstrations.

20. These indirect transfers are listed under either production costs or investment expenditure financed from depreciation funds. The ingenuity of disguising extra compensation can be quite impressive. Chen (1994) reported that 'in some enterprises, [workers'] shares, with promised interest rate higher than bank deposit rates in addition to fixed dividend payment, are simply a device to raise the level of wages and bonuses which have been regulated by the government to control inflation'.

21. The institutional reforms of the central bank and the state banks implemented in July 1993 as part of an austerity campaign have not been successful in changing things. Chen Yuan (1996), Deputy Governor of the central bank, reported that 'the enthusiasm for economic growth in some localities is so strong that it is very difficult to stop completely excessive investment financed through *forced* bank credit' (emphasis added).

22. 'State asset drain must end', *China Daily*, December 13, 1995. See also 'State toughens stand to protect its possessions', *China Daily*, June 2, 1995; 'Asset checks can stop fiddles', *China Daily*, June 7, 1995; and 'Market investigated for losing State assets', *China Daily*, June 2, 1995.

23. 'China City Turns Into a Prototype for Privatisation', *Wall Street Journal*, June 10, 1995.

24. 'Heilongjiang puts 200 firms on the block', *China Daily*, June 7, 1996.

References

Bai, Chongen, Li, David and Wang, Yijiang, 1997. 'Why Can Productivity Analysis be Misleading for Gauging State Enterprise Performance? *Journal of Comparative Economics*, 2(2) June:269–71.

Bouin, Oliver, 1998. 'Financial Discipline and State Enterprise Reform in China in the 1990s', in Oliver Bouin, Fabrizio Coricelli and Francoise Lemoine (eds*)*, *Different Paths to a Market Economy: China and European Economies in Transition*, OECD, Paris:115–52.

Chen, Aimin, 1994. 'Chinese Industrial Structure in Transition: The Emergence of Stock-offering Firms', *Comparative Economic Studies*, 36(4):1–19.

Chen, Yuan, 1996. 'Opening Remarks', in Manuel Guitian and Robert Mundell (eds), *Inflation and Growth in China*, 23–28, IMF, Washington, DC.

Dernberger, Robert, 1988. 'Financing China's Development: Needs, Sources and Prospects', in Robert Dernberger and Richard Eckaus, *Financing Asian Development 2: China and India*, University Press of America:12–68.

Fan, Gang, 1995. 'China's Incremental Reform: Progress, Problems and Turning Points', paper presented at CEPR/CEIPP/OECD conference on Different Approaches to Market Reforms: A Comparison between China and the CEECS, Budapest.

—— and Woo, Wing Thye, 1996. 'State Enterprise Reform as a Source of Macroeconomic Instability', *Asian Economic Journal*, November.

Groves, Theodore, Hong, Yongmiao, McMillan, John, and Naughton, Barry, 1994. 'Autonomy and Incentives in Chinese State Enterprises', *Quarterly Journal of Economics*, 109(1):185–209, February.

——, 1995a. 'Productivity Growth in Chinese State-Run Industry', in Fureng Dong, Cyril Lin and Barry Naughton (eds), *Reform of China's State-Owned Enterprises*, MacMillan, London.

—— 1995b. 'China's Evolving Managerial Labor Market', *Journal of Political Economy*, 103(4):873–892, August.

Huang, Yiping and Meng, Xin, 1997. 'China's Industrial Growth and Efficiency: A Comparison between the State and the TVE Sectors', *Journal of the Asia Pacific Economy*, 2(1):101–121.

Jefferson, Gary and Rawski, Thomas, 1994. 'Enterprise Reform in Chinese Industry', *Journal of Economic Perspectives*, 8(2):47–70.

——, Zheng, Yuxin, 1992. 'Growth, Efficiency, and Convergence in China's State and Collective Industry', *Economic Development and Cultural Change*, 40(2):239–266.

——, 1996. 'Chinese Industrial Productivity: Trends, Measurement Issues, and Recent Developments', *Journal of Comparative Economics*, 23:146–180.

Kornai, Janos, 1992. *The Socialist System*, Princeton University Press, Princeton, NJ.

Li, David, 1994. 'The Behaviour of Chinese State Enterprises under the Dual Influence of the Government and the Market', University of Michigan, manuscript.

Meng, Xin and Perkins, Frances, 1996. 'The Destination of China's Enterprise Reform: A Case Study from a Labor Market Perspective', Australian National University, August.

Minami, Ryoshin and Susumu Hondai, 1995. 'An Evaluation of the Enterprise Reform in China: Income Share of Labor and Profitability in the Machine Industry', *Hitotsubashi Journal of Economics*, 36(2), December:125–43.

Naughton, Barry, 1994. 'What is Distinctive about China's Economic Transition? State Enterprise Reform and Overall System Transformation', *Journal of Comparative Economics*, 18(3):470–490.

——, 1995. *Growing Out of the Plan: Chinese Economic Reform, 1978–1993*, Cambridge University Press.

Nee, Victor and Matthews, Rebecca, 1996. 'Market Transition and Societal Transformation in Reforming State Socialism', *Annual Review of Sociology*, 22:401–435.

Parker, Elliott, 1995. 'Shadow Factor Price Convergence and the Response of Chinese State-Owned Construction Enterprises to Reform', *Journal of Comparative Economics*, 21(1):54–81.

——, 1997. 'The Effect of Scale on the Response to Reform by Chinese State-Owned Construction Units', *Journal of Development Economics*, 52(2):331–53.

Perkins, Frances, Zheng Yuxing and Cao Yong, 1993. 'The Impact of Economic Reform on Productivity Growth in Chinese Industry: A Case of Xiamen Special Economic Zone', *Asian Economic Journal*, 7(2):107–46.

Putterman, Louis, 1995. 'The Role of Ownership and Property Rights in China's Economic Transition', *The China Quarterly*, 144:1047–1064, December.

Rawski, Thomas, 1986. 'Overview: Industry and Transport', in US Congress, Joint Economic Committee, *China's Economy Looks Toward the Year 2000: Volume 1. The Four Modernizations*, May.

Reynolds, Bruce (ed.) 1987. *Reform in China: Challenges and Choices*, ME Sharpe, New York.

Walder, Andrew, 1995. 'China's Transitional Economy: Interpreting its Significance', '*The China Quarterly*, 144:963–979.

Woo, Wing Thye, 1994. 'The Art of Reforming Centrally-Planned Economies: Comparing China, Poland and Russia', *Journal of Comparative Economics*, 18(3):276–308.

Woo, Wing Thye, Wen Hai, Yibiao Jin, and Gang Fan, 1994. 'How Successful Has Chinese Enterprise Reforms Been? Pitfalls in Opposite Biases and Focus', *Journal of Comparative Economics*, June:410–37.

World Bank, 1995. *China: Macroeconomic Stability in a Decentralised Economy*, Washington, DC.

——, 1996. *The Chinese Economy: Fighting Inflation, Deepening Reforms*, Washington, DC.

Wu, Harry Ziaoying and Wu, Yanrui, 1994. 'Rural Enterprise Growth and Efficiency', in Christopher Findlay, Andrew Watson and Harry Wu (eds), *Rural Enterprises in China*, St. Martin's Press, New York.

19 China's Industrial Growth and Efficiency: a comparison between the state and the TVE sectors

Yiping Huang and Xin Meng

I. Introduction

China has experienced two rounds of industrialisation —a Soviet-style, heavy industry-oriented industrialisation in the pre-reform period and an East Asian-type, labour-intensive manufacturing-oriented industrialisation during the reform period. As a result, two major industrial sectors—the state and the rural township and village enterprises (TVE)—have been successively established over the last four decades.[1]

The share of the state sector in national industry was as high as 80–90 per cent in the twenty years before economic reform, but fell to 65 per cent in 1985 and 48 per cent in 1992 (Table 1). The TVE sector has had extraordinarily rapid growth.[2] In 1992, the state and the TVE sectors together produced 81 per cent of the country's industrial outputs.[3] Employment in the two sectors was already comparable in 1984, with each employing about 40 per cent of total industrial workers (State Statistical Bureau (SSB),

various years). In 1992, the TVE sector employed about 40 per cent more workers than the state sector. The state sector, however, was still dominant in terms of capital stock, although its share declined from 87 per cent in 1985 to 81 per cent in 1992.[4]

These two major groups of industrial enterprises are different in various ways: in the cause of establishment, their institutional settings and their technological development. A set of interesting questions concerning their relative efficiency and growth performance naturally arises. Firstly, are the sources of growth (total factor productivity growth versus factor expansion) the same for the two sectors, and if not, how do they differ? Secondly, which sector is technically more efficient? Thirdly, is factor allocation between the two sectors efficient from an industry-wide perspective? Answers to these questions are important for a clearer understanding of Chinese industrial growth, as well as for policymaking purposes.

Reprinted with permission. Yiping Huang and Xin Meng, 1997. 'China's industrial growth and efficiency: a comparison between the state and the TVE sectors', *Journal of the Asia Pacific Economy*, 2(1):101–21 (with minor editing).

Table 1   **Some development indicators of China's industrial state and TVE sectors**

| | State sector | | TVE sector | |
	Value	Share (%)[b]	Value	Share (%)[b]
Capital stock (billion yuan)[a]				
1985	398	87.1	59	12.9
1992	1,098	80.9	259	19.1
Labour (thousand persons)				
1985	38,150	39.4	41,367	42.7
1992	45,210	34.6	63,364	48.5
Output (billion yuan)				
1978	329	77.6	n.a.	n.a.
1985	630	64.9	183	10.7
1992	1,782	48.1	1,364	32.5
Output growth (% per annum)				
1952–78	14.3	-	n.a.	-
1979–83	6.7	-	13.5	-
1984–92	8.8	-	23.0	-

Notes:
[a] Capital stock is in current prices.
[b] All shares are proportions in total Chinese industry except for the capital stock where the two sectors' shares sum to 100 per cent because capital stock data for other industrial sectors (mainly the urban collectives and joint ventures) are not available.
Sources: State Statistical Bureau.

Substantial studies have been undertaken on the issues of China's economic reform and industrial growth. Comparison of growth performance between the state and non-state industrial sectors has been one of the central interests in the literature. While all the studies conclude significant and positive total factor productivity (TFP) growth in the collective and TVE sector (Jefferson 1989; Svejnar 1990; Jefferson et al. 1992; Xiao Geng 1991; Wu and Wu 1994; Woo et al. 1994),[5] the evidence for the state sector is mixed. Some studies find that economic reform has failed to end the stagnant TFP growth in the Chinese state industry (World Bank 1985; Tidrick 1986; McGuckin et al. 1992; Woo et al. 1994). Other studies discover either a positive rate or an acceleration of TFP growth in the state sector during China's reform period (Chen et al. 1988a; Lau and Brada 1990; Dollar

1990; Jefferson and Xu 1991; Jefferson et al. 1992; Wu and Wu 1994).[6]

The following important points distinguish the current study from the previous ones. Firstly, most previous studies compared the performance of the state sector with that of the collective sector (Jefferson 1989; Jefferson et al. 1992; Xiao Geng 1991),[7] whereas this study focuses on the comparison between the state sector (the one mostly representing the planned economy) and the TVE sector (the most market-oriented sector in China's industry).

Secondly, the only studies comparing directly the state and TVE sector are by Wu and Wu (1994) and Woo et al. (1994). The study by Woo et al. (1994), however, emphasises an estimation of productivity growth in the state sector and not much attention is paid to detailed comparison between the two sectors. The findings by Wu and Wu (1994) are subject to three types of weaknesses of their study.

1. They use national data in analysis and, therefore, miss out useful firm level information through aggregation.

2. Their study employs a simple Cobb-Douglas production function without any validity test.[8]

3. Because of failing to derive a significant coefficient for capital, they used coefficient estimates for the TVE sector to infer the productivity growth in the state sector.

Thirdly, in all the previous studies, labour is treated as an aggregate factor of production. While this treatment is conventional and useful, it fails to tell a differentiated story about skilled and unskilled labour in the whole comparison. Skilled labour and unskilled labour are separated in this study to capture their different contributions to production and their different productivity in the two sectors.

Fourthly, the data set used in this study is more representative compared to those used by the previous study.[9]

Fifthly, this study applies the meta-production function approach introduced by Hayami and Ruttan (1970, 1985) and developed by Lau and Yotopoulos (1989). The strength of the meta-production function approach is its recognition of the same potential production technology available to different industrial sectors. At the same time, it allows for variation in coefficients given the fact that different sectors may produce using different techniques (of the same technology) because of the different economic environment they face.

II. Some Hypotheses

China has experienced two rounds of industrialisation in the past four decades which resulted in the development of its two major industrial sectors—the state and the TVE sectors.

The first round was launched in the early 1950s. Following the former Soviet Union, the Chinese government adopted a heavy-industry-oriented development strategy. Resources were drawn from other sectors to build large-scale, heavy industry factories. Existing enterprises (both industrial and commercial) were taken over by the government through a so-called 'socialist transformation' movement and the newly established firms were exclusively owned and managed by the State (Xue 1981). The quantities and prices of inputs (including capital investment, employment and raw material) and output were determined centrally. This first round of industrialisation seemed very successful in the beginning. The average annual growth rate of the state industry was 36 per cent during 1952–60,[10] but fell significantly to 3.7 per cent during 1960–70 as a consequence of the 'Great Leap Forward' and the Cultural Revolution.[11] The growth rate recovered to 8.1 per cent between 1970 and 1978.

Concentrating resources on heavy industry development was, in fact, not unique among developing countries in the 1950s and 1960s. What was unique was that, while the urban economy was being rapidly industrialised,[12] farmers were restricted from moving out of their villages.[13] The first round of industrialisation, therefore, failed to absorb surplus agricultural labour.

The second round of industrialisation was initiated in the mid 1980s when the government gradually relaxed its restrictions on non-agricultural activities in the rural areas. Because the restrictions on labour movement, especially to urban areas, remained (more or less) in place,[14] farmers started to combine their own surplus labour and capital to build small industrial processing workshops using very simple techniques to produce labour-intensive goods. These TVE firms utilise resources outside the government plan. They are highly market-oriented, less subject to state regulations and enjoy less in the way of preferential government treatment. Their growth momentum is, however, extremely strong, recording an average growth rate of 24 per cent during 1985–94.

Attempts have frequently been made to improve the performance of the state sector during the reform period.[15] Various forms of contract systems and profit-sharing have been introduced. Although those reforms granting greater autonomy to enterprise managers and allowing product market competition achieved some positive results, they have failed to create an effective system of governance. Old problems, such as enterprise losses, have grown and some new problems such as the haemorrhage of state assets, have arisen (Hussain 1994). The high recorded growth rate (8 per cent) in the reform period was partly a consequence of government protection.[16]

Now the state and the TVE sectors leave roughly comparable scales. At the same time, they have important distinctive characteristics. The most significant difference lies in the institutional settings. The development of the state sector was government-driven, while the TVE sector is purely market driven. The two sectors also vary in their ability to adjust levels of input and output. State firms, for instance, often find it difficult to dismiss an employee,[17] while it is relatively easier for the TVE firms to do so. Meanwhile, the state firms are heavily supported by the government while the TVE firms receive little government support.[18] While bankruptcy of TVE firms is common, it is extremely hard to bankrupt a state enterprise.

Secondly, when established, the state enterprises were targeted at advanced technologies, but most TVE firms applied the simplest production techniques. The capital-labour ratio is much higher in the state sector than in the TVE sector. In 1992, the per capita capital stock (at current prices) was 24,300 yuan in the state sector and 4,100 yuan in the TVE sector. The state sector also has a larger proportion of skilled labour in its labour force.

The two sectors are also different in their history of development. With forty years of history the state sector is already an old industry in China, the TVE sector, on the other hand, was newly established in the 1980s.

Based on these key differences and their likely impact on growth performance and productive efficiency, we formulate the following three working hypotheses.

Hypothesis I: Sources of growth

Both the state and TVE sectors experienced positive growth during the reform period. While it is uncontroversial that TFP growth dominated the development of the TVE sector, TFP growth in the state sector is inconclusive. It is interesting to examine productivity growth in the two sectors for the period 1986–90 using our enterprise data. The hypothesis is that TFP growth in the TVE sector is significantly higher than that in the state sector due to its highly market-oriented institutional setting. Furthermore, improvement in productivity was probably the most important factor contributing to growth of the TVE sector. In the state sector, however, TFP growth may be insignificant or even negative given its continuous poor economic performance.

Hypothesis II: Overall technical efficiency

Because the state sector was targeted at more advanced technologies and the TVE sector usually adopted simple production techniques, it is reasonable to hypothesise that the overall technical efficiency was still higher in the state sector than that in the TVE sector, at least in the mid 1980s. If Hypothesis I is confirmed, however, we would be able to observe a convergence of overall technical efficiency between the two sectors.

Hypothesis III: Industry-wide allocative efficiency

Industry-wide allocative efficiency can be examined through a comparison of the marginal productivity of individual factors in the two sectors. Industry-wide allocative efficiency exists when marginal products are the same (or at similar levels) between the two sectors.[19] Allocative inefficiency is present when the marginal products of one factor are significantly different between the two sectors, which implies that reallocation of that factor from one sector to another can immediately improve the overall efficiency and increase total industrial output. Although still highly distorted, the factor markets in China have experienced significant reform. Our hypothesis is that marginal returns to individual factors in the two sectors converged over the period under study and that the Chinese industry as a whole moved towards industry-wide allocative efficiency.

III. The Model, Data and Estimation Results

Model specification

The concept of meta-production function is based on the simple but appealing hypothesis that all producers (sectors) have potential access to the same technology portfolio, but that each may choose to operate with a different part of it depending on specific circumstances such as the qualities and quantities of factor endowments, the relative prices of inputs, and the basic environment (Lau and Yotopoulos 1989).

The meta-production function was first used to examine technological progress in agricultural sectors across countries (Hayami and Ruttan 1970, 1985; Lau and Yotopoulos 1989); it was later applied to analyse sources of economic growth (Boskin and Lau 1990). In this study, it is applied to investigate the efficiency and the sources of growth in the state and the TVE sectors in the Chinese economy.

The meta-production function in this study is defined as the common underlying production function representing the 'efficient-equivalent' input-output relationship of a given firm in China:

$$y_{it}^* = f(x_{i1t}^*, x_{i2t}^*, \ldots, x_{imt}^*) \quad (1)$$

where y_{it}^* and x_{ijt}^* are 'efficient-equivalent' quantities of output and input respectively of the ith firm in the ith period. The 'efficient-equivalent' quantity of output for each firm is not

directly observable and is linked to the measured quantities of outputs, y_{it}, and inputs, x_{ijt}, through firm-specific augmentation factors

$$A_{ij} \quad (i = 1,2,\ldots,n; \, j = 1,2,\ldots,m):$$

$$y_{it}^* = A_{i0} y_{it} \quad (2)$$

$$x_{ijt}^* = A_{ij} x_{ijt} \quad (3)$$

The production function, in terms of the measured quantities of outputs and inputs, can therefore be rewritten as

$$y_{it} = (A_{i0})^{-1} f(A_{i1} x_{i1t}, A_{i2} x_{i2t}, \ldots, A_{im} x_{imt}) \quad (4)$$

Following Boskin and Lau (1990), a flexible functional form—the transcendental logarithmic (translog) functional form—is chosen to accommodate the wide variation in the quantities of inputs in the pooled inter-firm data and to allow the possibility of non-neutral returns to scale and technical progress. The meta-production function with three inputs, capital (k), skilled labour (s) and unskilled labour (u), takes the form:

$$\ln y_{it}^* = \ln y_0 + \alpha_k \ln k_{it}^* + \alpha_s \ln s_{it}^* + \alpha_u \ln u_{it}^*$$

$$+ \beta_{kk} (\ln k_{it}^*)^2 / 2 + \beta_{ss} (\ln s_{it}^*)^2 / 2$$

$$+ \beta_{uu} (\ln u_{it}^*)^2 / 2 + \beta_{ks} \ln k_{it}^* \ln s_{it}^* \quad (5)$$

$$+ \beta_{ku} \ln k_{it}^* \ln u_{it}^* + \beta_{su} \ln s_{it}^* \ln u_{it}^* + \delta_i t$$

Substituting equations (2) and (3) into equation (5) gives the production function in terms of the observable variables

$$\ln y_{it} = \ln y_0 + \ln A_{i0}^* + \alpha_k \ln k_{it} + \alpha_s \ln s_{it} + \alpha_u \ln u_{it}$$

$$+ \beta_{kk} (\ln k_{it})^2 / 2 + \beta_{ss} (\ln s_{it})^2 / 2 + \beta_{uu} (\ln u_{it})^2 / 2$$

$$+ \beta_{ks} \ln k_{it} \ln s_{it} + \beta_{ku} \ln k_{it} \ln u_{it} + \beta_{su} \ln s_{it} \ln u_{it} \quad (6)$$

$$+ \alpha_k^* \ln k_{it} \alpha_s^* \ln s_{it} + \alpha_u^* \ln u_{it} + \delta_i t$$

where $\ln A_{i0}^*$ and α^* for each i are unknown constants that are functions of α, β, A_{i0} and A_{ij}. At least one sector's augmentation factors, A_{i0} and A_{ij}, can be assumed to be identical to unity (or any other constants), which reflects the fact that 'efficient-equivalent' outputs and inputs can be measured only relative to some standard. Without loss of generality the A_{i0} and A_{ij} for the state sector are taken to be identically unity. This assumption implies that

$$\alpha_k^*, \alpha_s^*, \alpha_u^* = \begin{cases} \alpha_k^*, \alpha_s^*, \alpha_u^* & \text{if } i \in tve \\ 0 & \text{if } i \in state \end{cases} \quad (7)$$

$$A_{i0}^* = \begin{cases} A_0^* & \text{if } i \in tve \\ 1 & \text{if } i \in state \end{cases} \quad (8)$$

The final functional form becomes

$$\begin{aligned}
\ln y_{it} = {} & \ln y_0 + \ln A_0 D_{tve} + \alpha_k \ln k_{it} + \alpha_s \ln s_{it} + \alpha_u \ln u_{it} \\
& + \beta_{kk} (\ln k_{it})^2 / 2 + \beta_{ss} (\ln s_{it})^2 / 2 + \beta_{uu} (\ln u_{it})^2 / 2 \\
& + \beta_{ks} \ln k_{it} \ln s_{it} + \beta_{ku} \ln k_{it} \ln u_{it} + \beta_{su} \ln s_{it} \ln u_{it} \qquad (9) \\
& + \alpha_k^* D_{tve} \ln k_{it} + \alpha_s^* D_{tve} \ln s_{it} + \alpha_u^* D_{tve} \ln u_{it} + \delta t + \delta^* D_{tve} t
\end{aligned}$$

Data description

The survey data used in this study were collected originally by the Institute of Economics (IE) of the Chinese Academy of Social Sciences (CASS) and the former Development Institute (DI) of the Research Centre for Rural Development (RCRD) with support from the World Bank. The aim of the survey was to provide a statistical base for investigating the impact of China's economic reforms on the performance and behaviour of Chinese industrial enterprises. The survey covered 967 state firms, 360 urban collective firms and 300 TVE firms among the 30 cities and 39 industries. All the firms in the sample were surveyed each year from 1984 to 1990 for the TVE sector and from 1986 to 1990 for the state and the urban collective sectors.[20] In the empirical work, we use only the data for the state and the TVE enterprises. To retain consistency between the sectors, observations of TVE firms for the years 1984 and 1985 are dropped. After deleting the missing and invalid values, we have 5,393 observations in total.[21]

The variable means of the sample firms are reported in Table 2. Comparing these two groups with the national firm population, we find that both the sample state and TVE firms were larger than the national average in terms of number of employees. In 1990, the national average number of employees for the state and the TVE firms were larger than the national average in terms of number of employees. In 1990, the national average number of employees for the state and the TVE firms were 418 and 319 persons, respectively, which were far less than the sample averages (SSB). The mean value of outputs (at 1980 prices) of the sample state firms was lower than the national average (12,513 yuan) while that of the sample TVE firms was larger than the national average (84,000 yuan) (SSB).

Not only are the state firms much larger, on average, than the TVE firms in terms of the number of employees, the capital stock and the level of output, but they are also much more capital-intensive and skilled-labour-intensive. During 1986–90, the capital/labour ratio increased from 1.1 (1,000 yuan/person) to 1.5 for the TVE firms while it increased from 2.0 to 2.7 for the state firms. Moreover, the proportion of skilled labour in the total labour force was, on average, about 10 per cent for the TVE firms and 15 per cent for the state firms.

Although both the state and TVE sample firms' outputs grew significantly during the survey period (6 and 8 per cent per annum, respectively), the capital-output ratio increased (from 0.9 to 1.1) for the state firms but declined (from 0.9 to 0.8) for the TVE firms. This implies that for the state sector, to produce one unit of output, more capital input is needed comparing 1990 with 1986. For the TVE sector, however, less capital input is needed.

Finally, it is noted that the total labour force in the TVE sector decreased in some years, especially with regard to unskilled labour. This may be consistent with changes at the national level reflecting consequences of the macro-economic adjustment.[22] But the survey covers only a fixed number of firms, and it does not take into account the employment increase due to newly established enterprises.[23] These characteristics

Table 2   Variable means of the sample firms

	Industrial output (1,000 yuan)	Capital stock (1,000 yuan)	Total (persons)	Labour force Skilled (persons)	Unskilled (persons)
TVE sector					
1986	554	507	465	40	425
1987	729	594	484	43	441
1988	696	585	439	42	397
1989	740	655	429	45	384
1990	825	688	455	50	406
State sector					
1986	6,931	6,051	3,075	433	2,642
1987	7,478	6,786	3,110	451	2,659
1988	8,473	7,401	3,443	504	2,938
1989	8,263	7,711	3,357	501	2,855
1990	8,622	9,376	3,483	542	2,940

Source: Survey data set.

and potential differences between the sample firms and the national population must be kept in mind when interpreting the results.

Empirical results

Equation (9) is estimated using the above data set. Both fixed-effects and random-effects models are estimated. The results are reported in Table 3. A Hausman specification test is conducted and the hypothesis of the random effects being uncorrelated with the regressors is rejected. Hence, the estimation results fixed-effects model are preferable and used for the following analysis.[24] Overall, the model fits well, with an R^2 of 0.8. Most of the coefficient estimates are significant at the 0.01 or 0.05 significance levels.

To validate the functional form used and the sector-specific effects, we impose various restrictions on the unrestricted model. F-statistics are used to test the restrictions and the results are summarised in Table 4. The first test relates to the functional form used. To test whether the translog production function is superior to the Cobb-Douglas functional form, the restriction that coefficients for all the cross and squared-

terms are zero is imposed

$(H_0^1 : \beta_{kk} = \beta_{ss} = \beta_{uu} = \beta_{ks} = \beta_{ku} = \beta_{su} = 0)$.

To test whether the production function has the property of additivity, the restriction that co-efficients for all the cross-terms are zero $(H_0^2 : \beta_{ks} = \beta_{ku} = \beta_{su} = 0)$ is imposed. Both null hypotheses are rejected at the 1 per cent significance level. So we confirm that the translog functional form is better than Cobb-Douglas specification.

The second type of tests is associated with the sector-specific augmentation levels.[25] It is tested whether the augmentation levels are identical between the state and the TVE sectors for capital, skilled labour, unskilled labour and commodities. We conduct the tests by imposing restrictions on the coefficients for capital (α_k^*), skilled labour (α_s^*), unskilled labour (α_u^*) and commodities (A_0^*) so that they are all equal to zero (the terms with a TVE dummy variable, D_{tve}). The restrictions are defined as $H_0^3 : \alpha_k^* = 0$, $H_0^5 : \alpha_u^* = 0$, and $H_0^6 : A_0^* = 1$. The hypotheses of identical augmentation levels for capital, skilled labour, unskilled labour and

298

Table 3   Estimation results of the meta-production function

Variable	Parameter	Fixed effects	Random effects
Const.	$\ln y_0$	1.812*** (-4.59)	0.274 (0.90)
D_{tve}const.	$\ln A_0^*$	-1.870*** (-6.89)	-0.803*** (-3.84)
$\ln k$	α_k	0.256*** (2.77)	0.323*** (3.90)
$D_{tve}\ln k$	α_k^*	0.215*** (5.46)	0.071 (1.97)
$\ln s$	α_s	0.117 (1.02)	0.297*** (2.69)
$D_{tve}\ln s$	α_s^*	0.125*** (2.71)	0.076* (1.67)
$\ln u$	α_u	0.386*** (2.88)	0.520*** (4.31)
$D_{tve}\ln u$	α_u^*	-0.098* (-1.81)	-0.051 (-1.03)
$(\ln k)^2/2$	β_{kk}	0.026 (1.55)	0.025 (1.58)
$(\ln s)^2/2$	β_{ss}	-0.0008 (-0.03)	-0.0008 (-0.03)
$(\ln u)^2/2$	β_{uu}	0.090** (2.46)	0.012 (0.35)
$\ln k \ln s$	β_{ks}	0.039** (1.97)	-0.015 (0.79)
$\ln k \ln u$	β_{ku}	-0.039* (-1.87)	-0.001 (-0.07)
$\ln s \ln u$	β_{su}	-0.046* (-1.83)	-0.047* (-1.88)
$time$	δ	-0.0006 (-0.19)	-0.018*** (-5.55)
$D_{tve}\,time$	δ^*	0.010 (1.19)	0.025*** (2.91)
R^2		0.81	0.86
Number of observations		5,393	5,393
Hausman specification test			$\chi^2(15) = 693.40$

Notes: Numbers in parentheses are t-ratios. Coefficient estimates marked with * are significant at 0.1 significance level, with ** at 0.05 significance level and *** at 0.05 and 0.01 significance level.
Source: Authors' estimation results.

Table 4   **Tests of restrictions: meta-production function**

Tested hypothesis	Degree of freedom	Calculated F-statistic	Critical value of F-statistic	Conclusion
Basic functional form				
1. Cobb-Douglas function	6,5,377	4.25	$F_{0.01}(6,\infty) = 2.8$	rejected
2. Additivity	3,5,377	3.79	$F_{0.01}(3,\infty) = 3.78$	rejected
Identical augmentation level				
3. Capital	1,5,377	36.83	$F_{0.01}(1,\infty) = 6.63$	rejected
4. Skilled labour	1,5,377	45.3	$F_{0.01}(1,\infty) = 3.84$	rejected
5. Unskilled labour	1,5,377	11.33	$F_{0.01}(1,\infty) = 6.63$	rejected
6. Commodity	1,5,377	75.49	$F_{0.01}(1,\infty) = 3.84$	rejected
Technical progress				
7. Same time trend	1,5,377	11.33	$F_{0.01}(1,\infty) = 3.84$	rejected

Sources: Authors' estimation results.

commodities are all rejected at 1 per cent significance level.

The last type of test explores whether the two sectors had the same technical progress during the sample period (represented by a time trend) ($H_0^7 : \delta^* = 0$). The null hypothesis is, again, rejected at the 1 per cent significance level.

IV. Efficiency and Growth Performance

The estimation results contain very important information about efficiency and growth in Chinese industry and can be applied to test the three working hypotheses.

To examine the sources of growth in the two sectors, the estimated co-efficients are applied to a growth accounting exercise (Table 5). For the TVE sample firms, the average growth rate of output during 1986–90 was 10.5 per cent. Inputs of capital increased by 8 per cent per annum, skilled labour 6 per cent and unskilled labour—1 per cent. Growth in inputs together contributed 5.3 percentage points to output growth. Growth in total factor productivity (TFP) contributed 5.2 percentage points (or 49.5 per cent) to output growth.

In the state sector, total output increased by 5.6 per cent on average. The annual growth rate was 12 per cent for capital stock, 6 per cent for skilled labour and 3 per cent for unskilled labour. Growth accounting exercise shows that the output increase in the state sector was mainly supported by an accumulation of capital stock which contributed about 79 per cent of the total output growth. TFP contributed a negative 39 per cent of total output growth.

The growth accounting exercise confirms our hypothesis that TFP growth was the dominant factor behind the rapid growth in the TVE sector and that the state sector experienced negative TFP growth during 1986-90.[26]

We also measured the local returns to scale of both sectors using the estimation results (see Table 6, column 4). Production of the state sector during the second half of the 1980s exhibited roughly constant returns to scale. Meanwhile, production in the TVE sector exhibited clear increasing returns to scale (with the degree of returns to scale being 1.2).

To test the second hypothesis about the overall technical efficiency of the two sectors and its dynamics, we simulate the state sector's

Table 5   **Sources of industrial growth in China, 1986–90** (annual average, percentage at sample means)

	TVE sector			State sector		
	Growth rate (%)	Contribution		Growth rate (%)	Contribution	
		absolute (% points)	share (%)		absolute (% points)	share (%)
Output	10.5			5.6		
Capital	8.0	4.1	39.1	11.6	4.4	78.6
Skilled labour	5.8	1.7	16.2	5.8	3.0	53.6
Unskilled labour	-1.2	-0.5	-4.8	2.7	0.4	7.1
TFP		5.2	49.5		2.2	39.3

Sources: Calculated from sample average and coefficient estimates.

output levels using actual input levels for the TVE sector but coefficients for the state sector, following Boskin and Lau (1990) and Kim and Lau (1994). This exercise provides an idea about how much the state sector would have been able to produce if it were given the same quantities of inputs as the TVE sector (the top diagram of Figure 1). The differences between the simulated output levels and the TVE sector's actual output levels represent the overall efficiency gap between the two sectors. The other exercise, which simulates the TVE sector's output levels using the actual input levels

for the state sector but the coefficients for the TVE sector, is also undertaken (the bottom diagram of Figure 1). Both exercises suggest that although the overall technical efficiency was still lower in the TVE sector than in the state sector in the late 1980s. The gap, however, had narrowed significantly since then and the overall technical efficiency levels of the two sectors were already very close to each other in 1990. This implies that during the period the TVE sector had been catching up very quickly with the efficiency level of the state sector.

The reasons for the rapid catching-up or

Figure 1   **Comparison of production efficiency between the state and the TVE sectors** (1,000 yuan at 1980 prices)

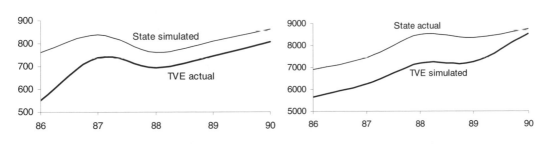

Notes: In the left-hand diagram, the state sector's predicted output is calculated using the TVE sector's mean values of inputs and coefficients for the state sector in the meta-production function. Similarly, in the right-hand diagram, the TVE sector's predicted output is calculated using the state sector's mean values of inputs and coefficients for the TVE sector.

convergence of technical efficiency might be mixed. Because of the relatively backward production techniques applied at the very beginning, the TVE firms probably enjoyed the advantages of 'backwardness' and, therefore, experienced faster improvement in technical efficiency (Dowrick 1992). But most importantly, their institutional advantage probably helped the TVE sector to catch up and gain strong growth momentum. The state firms were much less exposed to market competition. Losses made by a state firm can always be financed by the 'soft' government budget (see Kornai 1980) and, in many cases, the employees and managers cannot fully enjoy the profits they create. The motivation for productivity improvement has been weak and their ability to do so has been limited. On the contrary, in the TVE sector, firms' survival depends solely on their competitiveness. The pressure for efficiency improvement in this sector, therefore, was very high.

The third hypothesis about industry-wide allocative efficiency is tested by comparing the marginal productivities of factors between the two sectors. Marginal products and output elasticities were calculated using the coefficient estimates and variable means (Table 6). It is found that the marginal products of capital are only slightly higher in the TVE sector than in the state. On the other hand, the difference in the marginal product of labour between the two sectors is quite significant: while marginal product of skilled labour is much higher in the TVE sector than in the state sector, the marginal product of unskilled labour is much higher in the state sector than in the TVE sector.[27]

It is clear that industry-wide allocative inefficiency is present in Chinese industry. The substantial gaps in the marginal productivity of skilled and unskilled labour suggest that labour market reforms have not been successful. Relatively speaking, there was a shortage of skilled labour in the TVE sector and a shortage of unskilled labour in the state sector.[28] The restriction on labour mobility has negative impact on the overall allocative efficiency in the industrial sector.[29] Potential gains from policies

Table 6   **Estimated output elasticities and marginal products** (using sample means)

	Shares of returns			Local returns to scale	Marginal products		
	Capital Stock	Skilled labour	Unskilled labour		Capital stock	Skilled labour	Unskilled labour
	(1)	(2)	(3)	(4)	(5)	(6)	(7)
TVE firms							
1986	0.503	0.300	0.444	1.25	0.594	4.757	0.479
1987	0.507	0.296	0.440	1.24	0.627	5.062	0.560
1988	0.514	0.300	0.425	1.29	0.637	5.177	0.624
1989	0.518	0.301	0.418	1.24	0.579	5.614	0.621
1990	0.521	0.300	0.414	1.24	0.615	5.450	0.636
State firms							
1986	0.375	0.162	0.483	1.02	0.510	3.081	1.407
1987	0.378	0.164	0.479	1.02	0.499	3.199	1.492
1988	0.381	0.164	0.477	1.02	0.505	3.296	1.583
1989	0.383	0.165	0.472	1.02	0.473	3.239	1.556
1990	0.389	0.169	0.465	1.02	0.417	3.335	1.576

Sources: Calculated according to the sample averages and coefficient estimates.

facilitating resource mobility between the state and TVE sectors are likely to be large.

V. Concluding remarks

The findings of this study can be summarised as follows:

1. The rapid growth of the TVE sector during 1986-90 was mainly driven by TFP growth (more than 5 per cent per annum) and expansion of capital stock. TFP growth in the state sector was significantly negative (-2 per cent).
2. Although the state sector was technically more efficient in the mid-1980s, the TVE sector had been catching up with, and was about to reach, the level of the technical efficiency of the state sector by 1990.
3. From an industry-wide perspective, allocative inefficiency between the state and the TVE sectors was very significant for both skilled and unskilled labour but less so for capital.

These findings have important implications. Firstly, there was an important policy debate in China, especially around 1988, about the relative efficiency of the state and TVE sectors. It was argued that because of the use of backward techniques the development of the TVE sector reduces overall efficiency of the industry by competing away resources from the 'more efficient' state sector. This argument once dominated the economic and policy-making circles in China and some policy measures were introduced to restrict the development of the TVE sector in 1989, together with an austerity program.[30] This study suggests that the above argument may be right for the early 1980s. The level of technical efficiency of the TVE sector, however, was not significantly different from that of the state sector at the end of the 1980s.[31] Efficiency can no longer be used as an excuse to restrict the development of the TVE sector.

Secondly, the evidence from this study suggests that, at least for the period 1986–90, reform policies for the state sector failed to stimulate productivity growth. TFP was in fact decreasing by 2 per cent per annum. A real growth rate of 5.6 per cent (for the sample) was supported by more rapid expansion of factor inputs and such growth cannot be sustained. More substantial reform measures are required to maintain a positive productivity growth in the state sector.

Thirdly, there is still room for the use of policies to improve the industry-wide allocative efficiency. As the gap of marginal return to skilled and unskilled labour is quite substantial, it would be a Pareto improvement if appropriate policy measures can be designed to facilitate flows of skilled labour from the state to the TVE sector and unskilled labour from the rural to urban sector. The most important strategy for achieving industry or economy-wide allocative efficiency is to establish integrated factor markets for capital, skilled and unskilled labour. Removing restrictions on labour movements between sectors may produce industry-wide benefits.

Acknowledgements

We are grateful to Steve Dowrick, Ron Duncan, Ross Garnaut, Raja Junankar, K. Kalirajan, Paul Miller, George Fane, Warwick McKibbin and seminar participants at the Australian National University for helpful comments.

Appendix

Refer to original source for appendices.

Notes

1. In the literature, TVE is sometimes distinguished from TVP (township, village and private enterprises). In this paper, the TVE sector also includes rural private enterprises. In addition, our discussion here covers only the state and the TVE industrial sectors, while the usual definitions of the two sectors also include other activities apart from the industrial production.
2. It is estimated that the TVE sector accounted for

nearly half of the country's industrial output and exports in 1994 (Wang and Liu 1994).

3. The other major industrial sectors include urban collective enterprises and joint ventures.

4. In Chinese statistics, capital stock is reported only in current prices. If changes in investment prices were the same for the two sectors, we may conclude from Table 1 that the real growth rate of capital stock was higher in the TVE sector than in the state sector.

5. For example, Svejnar (1990) finds that TVEs had an annual TFP growth rate of about 13 per cent in the 1981–86 period. Wu and Wu (1994) conclude that TFP growth of the rural industry averaged 5.5 per cent between 1978 and 1991.

6. By imposing hypothetical factor weights, the World Bank (1985) and Tidrick (1986) report declining total factor productivity (TFP) between 1957 and 1982. Using reconstructed factor input data, Chen et al. (1988a, 1988b) conclude that, after stagnating during 1957–78, TFP (capital and labour) in state industry grew at a rate of 4–5 per cent per annum during 1978–85. Lau and Brada (1990) use these revised data to estimate frontier production functions and conclude a rate of technological progress between 1.8 and 3.6 per cent per year. Dollar (1990) confirmed at the firm level the findings by Chen and others. Jefferson et al. (1992), employing a data set of state industrial sectors at the city/county level, find that annual TFP growth averaged 2.4 per cent in the period 1984–87. In a recent study, Woo et al. (1994) criticise the methods of data construction adopted by Jefferson et al. (1992) and suggest that they might have overstated their case for improved TFP performance. Woo et al. (1994) find that FTP growth in the state industrial sector has been zero at best during 1984–88. Using data from China's 1985 industrial census, McGuckin et al. (1992) conclude that TFP in the state sector declined during 1980–87. The findings by Woo et al. (1994), however, were later questioned by Jefferson et al. (1994), for their choice of deflators.

7. In fact, as pointed out by Wu and Wu (1994), large collective enterprises in the urban areas resemble the behaviour of state enterprises in many respects.

8. The Cobb-Douglas production function is a very restrictive functional form for empirical study because of its unity elasticity of factor substitution and constant factor weights over time.

9. Our data set on the TVE firms is also more representative than that used by Svejnar (1990) which consists of 122 firms from four counties.

10. This extraordinary growth was partly due to the collapse of industry during the civil-war period and partly helped by the taking over of existing firms.

11. During the period of the 'Great Leap Forward', which began around 1958, most able-bodied urban and rural labourers were drawn to backyard, small-scale steel-making plants. This irrational resource reallocation, together with crop failure in the agricultural sector, resulted in an economic collapse in the early 1960s. Industrial production of the state sector fell by 40 and 17 per cent in 1961 and 1962, respectively (Xue 1981; SSB).

12. There were many heavy industrial enterprises which physically located in rural areas. But these firms belonged to the urban system and did not have any economic interaction with the rural agricultural collectives in terms of employment, capital investment or output sale.

13. The restrictions in labour movement partly resulted from the fact that the development of heavy industries did not require many unskilled labourers.

14. Anderson (1990) finds that, apart from the administrative restrictions, subsidies to urban residents were also contributing factors prohibiting labour movement from rural to urban areas.

15. For more detailed discussion about economic reform in China, particularly in its state industrial sector, see Harrod (1992) and Perkins (1992), among others.

16. There have been reports indicating that a large number of state enterprises have kept on producing although they had difficulties in selling their products.

17. Dismissing employees has only been possible in recent years when the workers have violated important rules, disciplines or laws but not

when the firm is overstaffed (Meng 1990).

18. Government support includes financial support as well as more planned (cheaper) inputs, etc.

19. We define industry-wide allocative efficiency here as the equalisation of the marginal productivity of factors between different industrial groups within China's industrial sector.

20. The data set is an extension of two original smaller data sets provided by IE of CASS and DI of RCRD. In order to make the data useful for making comparisons across ownership types and evaluating the impact of specific industrial reforms, the World Bank financed another survey of the original enterprises plus an additional 550 enterprises. A two-stage approach was adopted in a sample selection for the state-owned and collective enterprises. First, for each of the 30 cities participating in the survey, the proportion of enterprises surveyed in the total sample is the same as the city's share in total industrial output of the 30 cities. Second, for each city, this total number of enterprises surveyed was then distributed across 39 industrial branches according to each branch's industrial output share in the city. For the TVW sample, 319 counties were chosen from the 10 provinces. Each county then identified 3–5 TVE enterprises, thus creating a pool of 1,264 enterprises. From this pool, 20 enterprises were randomly drawn from each of the 10 provinces (see China Data Documentation, Transition and Macro-Adjustment Division, World Bank 1993).

21. The data set used for estimation in this study call be supplied in the form of a floppy disk at special request.

22. Total TVE employees decreased from 95.5 million in 1988 to 93.7 million in 1989 and to 92.6 million in 1990.

23. Bankruptcy and establishment of TVE firms are very common. In 1994, for example, there were 0.1 million enterprises bankrupted and 1 million new firms established (Wang and Liu 1994).

24. See Stata *4.0 Reference Manual* (1995) for a detailed explanation of the methods and the Hausman test.

25. Although in A_{i0}^* and α_i^* for each i are functions of α, β, A_{i0} and A_{ij} they are, to a certain extent, influenced by the augmentation levels of $\ln A_{i0}$

and $\ln A_{ij}$. Following Boskin and Lau (1990) we still consider them as mixed augmentation levels. They, in fact, measure the differences in the contributions of each factor between the state and the state sectors.

26. Our results seem to be consistent with the findings by Woo et al. (1994) but differ from findings by Jefferson et al. (1992) and Wu and Wu (1994).

27. There is a puzzling phenomenon which deserves further investigation. While the marginal product of unskilled labour was positive and rising, the TVE sector experienced a negative growth in total numbers of unskilled labour. This happened when there was still a large surplus labour pool in rural areas.

28. If skilled labour were allowed to work for the TVE sector and rural surplus labour were allowed to migrate to the urban area the marginal products of skilled and unskilled labour would have been equalised.

29. It is worth noting though that the skilled labour in the TVE sector may be very different from the skilled labour in the state sector. However, one would presume that the skill level in the state sector is higher than that in the TVE sector. If a skilled labourer in the state sector were to move to the TVE sector he or she would be deemed to be more competent than his or her TVE peers.

30. The austerity program implemented in 1989 aimed at a tight macroeconomic environment to cool down the overheated economy. Restricting bank loans to the TVE sector on the basis of the efficiency argument was at the top of the list of the program.

31. Some participants of our seminars at the Australian National University suggest that capital stocks of the state sector may be down-valued (relative to that of the TVE sector) because of the preferential prices it enjoyed in both the pre- and post-reform period. We are unable to address this issue using our data set. But if this proposition is true, the TFP growth and overall technical efficiency revealed in this study may be overestimated.

References

Anderson, K., 1990. 'Urban household subsidies and rural out-migration: the case of China', *Communist Economics*, 2(4):525–31.

Boskin, M.J. and Lau, L.J., 1990. 'Post-war economic growth of the group-of-five countries: a new analysis', Technical Paper No. 127, Center for Economic Policy Research, Stanford University, Stanford, CA.

Chen, K., Wang, H., Zheng, Y., Jefferson, G. and Rawski, T., 1988a. 'Productivity change in Chinese industry: 1953–1985', *Journal of Comparative Economics*, 12(4):570–91.

——, 1988b. 'New estimates of fixed investment and capital stock for Chinese state industry', *China Quarterly*, 114:24.9–66.

Dollar, D., 1990. 'Economic reform and allocative efficiency in China's state-owned industry', *Economic Development and Cultural Change*, 39(1):89–105.

Dowrick, S., 1992. 'Technological catch up and diverging incomes: patterns of economic growth 1960–88', *Economic Journal*, 102, (May):600–10.

Granick, D., 1990. *Chinese State Enterprises: A Regional Property Rights Analysis*, University of Chicago Press, Chicago.

Harrod, P., 1992. 'China's reform experience to date', World Bank Discussion Paper 180, Washington, DC.

Hayami, Y. and Ruttan, V.W., 1970. 'Agricultural productivity differences among countries', *American Economic Review*, 60:895–911.

——, 1985. *Agricultural Development: An International Perspective*, Johns Hopkins University Press, Baltimore, MD.

Huang, Y and Duncan, R., 1997. 'How successful were China's state enterprises reform?', *Journal of Comparative Economics*, 24(1):65–78.

Hussain, A., 1994. 'China: unfinished agenda of reform', presentation at the Gateway China Forum, Washington Center for China Studies.

Jefferson, G.H., 1989. 'Potential sources of productivity growth within Chinese industry', *World Development*, 17(l):44–57.

—— and Xu, W., 1991. 'The impact of reform on social enterprises in transition: structure, conduct, and performance in Chinese industry', *Journal of Comparative Economics*, 15(1):45–64.

——, Rawski, T., Zheng, Y., 1992. 'Growth, efficiency, and convergence in China's state and collective industry', *Economic Development and Cultural Change*, 40(2):239–66.

——, 1994. 'Productivity change in Chinese industry: a comment', *China Economic Review*, 5(2):235–41.

Kim, J. and Lau, L.J., 1994. 'The sources of growth of the East Asian newly industrialised countries', *Journal of the Japanese and International Economics*, 8(3):235–71.

Kornai, J., 1980. *Economics of Shortage*, North-Holland, Amsterdam.

Lardy, N., 1989. 'Technical changes and economic reform in China: a tale of two sectors', unpublished manuscript.

Lau, Kam-Tim and Brada, J.C., 1990. 'Technological progress and technical efficiency in Chinese industrial growth: a frontier approach', *China Economic Review*, 1(2):113–24.

Lau, L.J. and Yotopoulos, P.A., 1989. 'The meta-production function approach to technical change in world agriculture', *Journal of Development Economics*, 31(2):241–69

McGuckin, R.H., Nguyen, S.V., Taylor, J.R. and Waite, C.A., 1992. 'Post-reform productivity performance and sources of growth in

Chinese industry: 1980–85', *Review of Income and Wealth*, 38(3):249–66.

Meng, X., 1990. 'The rural labour market', in W.A. Byrd and Q. Lin (eds) *China's Rural Industry*, 299–322, Oxford University Press, Oxford.

Perkins, D.H., 1992. 'China's gradual approach to market reforms', paper presented at a conference on Comparative Experiences of Economic Reform and Post-Socialist Transition, 6–8 July 1992, El Escorial, Spain.

SSB (State Statistics Bureau), *China Statistical Yearbook*, 1990–94, China Statistics Press, Beijing.

Stata Press, 1995. *Stata 4.0 Reference Manual*, Stata Press, Texas.

Svejnar, J., 1990. 'Productive efficiency and employment', in William Byrd and Lin Qingsong (eds) *China's Rural Industry: Structure, Development and Reform*, 243–54, Oxford University Press, Oxford.

Tidrick, G., 1986. 'Productivity growth and technological change in Chinese industry', World Bank Working Papers, No. 761, The World Bank, Washington, DC.

Wang, Y and Liu, J., 1994. 'Realise rapid and efficient development', *Economic Daily*, 18 December.

Woo, W.T., Fan, G., Hai, W. and Jin, Y., 1993. 'The efficiency and macro-economic consequences of Chinese enterprise reform', *China Economic Review*, 4(2):153–68.

——, 1994. 'How successful has Chinese enterprise reform been? Pitfalls in opposite biases and focus', *Journal of Comparative Economics*, 18:410–37.

World Bank, 1985. *China: Long-Term Development Issues and Options*, Johns Hopkins University Press, Baltimore.

Wu, X.H. and Wu, Y., 1994. 'Rural enterprise growth and efficiency', in C. Findlay, A.

Watson and H. Wu (eds), *Rural Enterprises in China*, 148–72, Macmillan, London.

Xiao Geng, 1991. 'Managerial autonomy, fringe benefits, and ownership structure: a comparative study of Chinese state and collective enterprises', *China Economic Review*, 2(1):47–73.

Xue, M., 1981. *China's Socialist Economy*, Foreign Languages Press, Beijing.

20 Towards a Labour Market in China

John Knight and Lina Song

I. Introduction

In a sense, China does not yet have a 'labour market'. The Chinese labour system, set up in the 1950s and based on the Soviet model, is characterised by state direction of labour, immobility, lack of incentives, overstaffing, and underemployment. On the other hand, it has avoided open unemployment and serious urbanisation problems, it has provided employees with security, and it has achieved egalitarian objectives. The Chinese government has begun a process of reform designed to improve the mobility, flexibility, incentives, and efficiency of labour. By comparison with other market reforms in China, however, labour market reform is tardy and limited.

The Chinese labour market is characterised by surplus labour in both the rural and the urban sectors (see Box 1). It is a surplus labour economy *par excellence* and the institutions of the labour market have to be viewed in that light. It differs from most developing countries, also, in the invariably disguised nature of unemployment. Open unemployment, normally associated with landlessness, is absent from rural China. The

policy of allocating village land leasehold to all households of the village, usually on a per-capita basis, has eliminated landlessness. In urban China open unemployment is generally avoided in two ways. One is the control of migration from the rural areas and the severe restrictions on urban settlement. The other is through employment policies which result in disguised unemployment and surplus labour in the public sector.

Tables 1 and 2 present a summary view of the Chinese labour force over 40 years. The labour force grew on average by 2.7 per cent per annum: 2.2 per cent in rural areas and 4.7 per cent in urban areas. Urban employees, known as 'staff and workers', increased by 5.7 per cent per annum, from being 8 per cent of the labour force in 1952 to 25 per cent in 1992. Despite the rapid industrialisation and urbanisation, rural labour more than doubled over the 40 years, whereas land was already fully occupied in 1952 and its use could not be expanded significantly. By 1992 there were no fewer than 594 million workers in China, 438 million in the rural and 156 million in the urban areas. Of the 148 million urban staff and workers, 109 million were employed in the state-owned sector and 36 million in urban collective units.

Reprinted with permission. John Knight and Lina Song, 1995. 'Towards a labour market in China', *Oxford Review of Economic Policy*, 11(4):97–117 (with minor editing).

Box 1

A model of the labour market

The labour situation can be depicted very simply, as in Figure 1. The horizontal axis, 00′, shows the amount of labour in the economy, assumed to be fixed. Rural-sector labour is measured rightwards from the origin, 0. The curve MPL_a shows the marginal product of labour in the agricultural (here equated with rural) sector. Industrial (urban) employment is measured leftwards from 0′. In a competitive labour market in which the rural supply curve is given by MPL_a and the urban demand curve by MPL_i, the competitive wage would be w_c and labour allocation OL_2 in the rural and $L_2 0′$ in the urban sector.

Figure 1

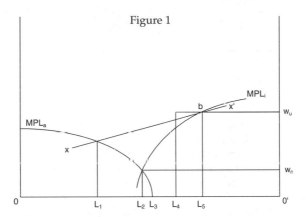

However, the urban wage is set higher than the competitive wage, at w_u. In a market economy this would imply urban employment $L_5 0′$. In a Harris Todaro framework the 'expected wage'—w_u multiplied by the probability of obtaining it—equals the rural supply price. With the probability equal to the ratio of urban employment to urban labour force, rural–urban migration occurs until this condition is satisfied. Given that the curve $xx′$, passing through the point b, is a rectangular hyperbola, urban open unemployment equal to $L_1 L_5$ is created.

This simple story would fit various developing countries with a substantial urban–rural income differential. In China, however, the outcome is different. Government prevents open unemployment by controlling rural–urban migration and by creating surplus jobs, $L_4 L_5$, in the urban state sector. Thus the labour force is divided into OL_4 (rural employment) and $L_4 0′$ (urban employment). The extent of rural disguised unemployment is indicated by the zero marginal product of labour in agriculture at point L_3.

Table 1 **The labour force and its distribution, China, 1952–92** (millions and percentage of total)

	Labour force			Urban employees
	Total	Rural	Urban	
1952 million	207	182	25	16
Percentage of total	100	88	12	8
1962 million	259	214	45	43
Percentage of total	100	83	17	17
1972 million	359	287	72	71
Percentage of total	100	80	20	20
1982 million	453	339	114	113
Percentage of total	100	75	25	25
1992 million	594	438	156	148
Percentage of total	100	74	26	25

Source: State Statistical Bureau (1993):75.

The rest of this paper is organised as follows. Section II is concerned with the urban labour market. It examines the labour system in the pre-reform period and the reforms that have occurred in recent years. It analyses the behaviour of wages during the reform period, and the current structure of wages. Section III analyses the labour situation in rural China. There is a discussion of estimates of the level of and trends in rural surplus labour. We examine the creation of a rural labour market through rural industrialisation, and the structure of wages in that, relatively free, market. There is also an analysis of rising income inequality in rural China and the contribution made by labour immobility. Section IV is concerned with the rural–urban divide in China. We examine the income gap between rural and urban areas—its size, its causes, and its consequences. In particular, an attempt is made to gauge the extent and characteristics of rural–urban migration. Section V considers the obstacles that have to be faced and the problems that have to be solved in the transition to a labour market in China. It ends with an assessment of the prospects for successful labour market reform.

II. The Urban Labour System

The urban labour system was established in the 1950s, influenced by the Soviet model. It replaced the pre-revolution labour market with state direction of labour. In this way the government and the party achieved great economic and social control. Urban labour demand and supply were regulated through the planning system. The labour 'requirements' of each enterprise were based on the plan, which was adjusted to avoid urban unemployment.

The spatial mobility of labour was severely controlled and restricted by means of the residential registration (*hukou*) system.

Mobility of workers among enterprises was also rigidly controlled: the first job was normally the last. Thus a system of lifetime employment within the enterprise was created, giving employees an 'iron rice bowl'. Not only did the enterprise provide secure employment and a wage, but it also provided a 'mini welfare state': housing, medical care, pension, etc. An extremely egalitarian wage structure was laid down for all enterprises, with only slight regional (cost of

Table 2 **The labour force: average growth rates, 1952–92** (per cent per annum)

		Labour force		Urban employees
	Total	Rural	Urban	
1952–62	2.3	1.6	6.1	10.4
1962–72	3.3	3.0	4.8	5.1
1972–82	2.4	1.7	4.7	4.8
1982–92	2.8	2.6	3.2	2.7
1952–92	2.7	2.2	4.7	5.7

Source: State Statistical Bureau (1993):75.

living) and industrial variations. Pay was based mainly on a system of job grades and on employment experience.

We can summarise the urban labour situation during the pre-reform period as follows. The system was heavily directed, providing almost no scope for individual preferences or responses to economic incentives. It was the plan, and not market wages, that governed labour supply and demand. The centralised control of enterprises provided no inducement for the efficient use of labour, and indeed surplus labour was imposed on enterprises. Workers had few incentives to acquire human capital, to work efficiently, or to improve work methods. On the other hand, urban workers occupied a privileged place in Chinese society, enjoying higher incomes, greater security, and better social services than did the rural peasants. Moreover, the system permitted the state to pursue its egalitarian objectives.

Reform of the urban labour system began in 1980, when the state monopoly of labour allocation was replaced by a somewhat more decentralised one. Central and local labour authorities continued to plan the labour requirements of state enterprises and urban collectives, and remained responsible for the placement of college graduates. Under the reform, local authorities and state enterprises established labour service companies. These were made responsible for registration of job vacancies, for

most job placements, and for training. They also established new enterprises to create employment opportunities. The authorities did not place labour in small collectives and private enterprises, a sector which was now permitted to grow. The rigid controls on rural–urban migration were somewhat relaxed after 1980. Migrants from the rural areas were permitted to work temporarily —but not to settle—in the urban areas. College graduates could take jobs in rural industry without losing their urban *hukous*.

In 1983 the 'labour contract system' was gradually introduced to replace lifetime employment in the urban sector. Although it was intended eventually to be generally applicable, it applied largely to newly hired recruits. By the end of 1992 only 17 per cent of the urban labour force was covered. The slow progress reflected accommodating behaviour on the part of the authorities and enterprise managers: managers identified closely with labour, they needed the support of workers, and thus responded to social pressures.

The 'optimal labour reorganisation scheme', designed to reduce surplus labour in state-owned enterprises (SOEs), was extended nation-wide in 1989. The selected enterprises were subjected to reorganisation, redeployment, and retraining of labour. Workers were encouraged to form labour groups to contract for production projects. A combination of training and attrition, that is, no recruitment, were used to avoid open unemployment. By February 1992, 35,000 SOEs, representing 10 per cent of the SOE labour force, were covered.

Wage reform began in 1978, when the bonus system and piece rates were reintroduced. SOEs were given more authority to determine bonuses and thus overall wages. In 1983, as part of the enterprise reforms, SOEs were allowed to redistribute after-tax profits for various purposes, including employee welfare and bonuses, subject to stipulated percentages. The share of the basic wage in total emoluments of SOE employees fell from 85 per cent in 1978 to 45 per cent in 1992. Wage policies became more decentralised, and state controls over wages became less direct. Moreover, the most dynamic sectors of the economy—rural industries and urban private enterprises—were not subject to wage controls.

It is apparent that the urban labour reforms have not proceeded very far. The move has been towards decentralisation of labour management rather than towards a properly functioning labour market. The reforms correspond to a change in the objective function of the Chinese government away from equality towards efficiency objectives. How successful have they been in raising the efficiency of labour?

Consider first whether the reforms have reduced surplus labour in urban enterprises. The best method of answering this question is to measure the extent of surplus labour in a panel survey over time. In the absence of such data, we can examine recent estimates of surplus labour or trends in labour productivity. It is not easy to estimate the extent of surplus labour. The approach of welfare economics is to pose the question: how much labour would be employed by profit-maximising enterprises in competitive markets? Surplus labour is then any employment in excess of the profit maximisation benchmark. If SOEs are asked to measure their surplus labour, they might do so by measuring the excess over the employment required for maximum production or labour productivity, given capacity, rather than for maximum profits. The first criterion is likely to give the smallest estimate and the second the largest.

A recent World Bank report (World Bank 1993:8) cites various estimates of surplus labour from Chinese government sources: one-quarter of SOE employees (by officials in charge of planning and systems reform); 10–12 per cent of urban SOE employees (Ministry of Labour, based on a survey of 15,000 enterprises in 11 provinces); 20–25 per cent of urban SOE employees (estimates of other research institutes); and 20 per cent of employees (in a survey of 45 reforming SOEs in Shanghai). The World Bank mission itself carried out surveys in eight SOEs in Dalian and 11 SOEs in Wuhan. The SOE managers, generally using the concept of maximum production capacity, produced estimates ranging from 3 to 30 per cent but averaging 11 per cent over the 19 enterprises. Jefferson and Xu (1991) conducted a survey of 20 industrial enterprises in Wuhan, of which 13 were SOEs. Factory directors estimated that the number of hours worked each day averaged 5.4, whereas the normal day was 7–8 hours, that is, surplus labour was 23–32 per cent.

Whatever the obstacles to measurement and whatever the sources and methods of estimation, it is difficult not to conclude that there is substantial surplus labour in the public sector in China. Since the same pressures for providing jobs are to be found in the urban collectives, we expect similar problems of urban underemployment to exist in all but the small private wage sector.

Another criterion for judging the effects of the labour reforms is to examine the growth of labour productivity. It is, of course, dangerous to attribute growth of output per unit of labour to improved efficiency of labour—it might instead be due to technical progress, capital accumulation, economies of scale, etc. Nevertheless, labour productivity grew much more rapidly in the period 1978–88 (6.1 per cent per annum) than in the period 1957–78 (2.0 per cent per annum) (Chen et al. 1988). Moreover, Jefferson and Xu (1991) provided evidence that the coefficient of variation of the estimated marginal product of labour fell over the 1980s for various enterprise samples. This they interpreted as the result of increased pressures on and incentives for managers to use labour more efficiently.

A panel study of 359 industrial enterprises shows a statistically significant relationship between the wage per worker and productivity per worker. In 1980 the variance in wages that was explained by labour productivity was only 4 per cent, but in 1987 it had risen to 37 per cent (World Bank 1992a:57). However, this trend does not necessarily represent an efficiency gain as it may have retarded resource transfers towards more efficient enterprises and anyway the criterion for labour efficiency is marginal, not average, product.

A criterion for movement towards a labour market is whether labour mobility has increased. We have data on separations for state and collectively owned enterprises, but only for a recent year, 1989. Excluding death and retirement, total separations were extremely low: 13 and 60 per 1,000 workers, respectively. Those separations

which could be identified as voluntary were lower still: 4 and 25 respectively (People's Republic of China, Ministry of Labour 1990:315–8).

We would not expect real wages to rise significantly in a labour surplus economy. Nor did they in the quarter-century 1952–77: urban real wages grew by less than 0.2 per cent per annum. However, the real wages of staff and workers rose strongly during the period 1977–92 (Table 3). The performance was erratic, with spurts in 1978–80, 1984–86, and 1990–92, and troughs in the intervening periods 1981–83 and 1987–89. The pattern is similar irrespective of ownership form. It is not amenable to statistical analysis, as real wage behaviour was largely a matter of government policy, which was more exogenous than endogenous. The rapid increase between 1977 and 1980 represented a policy change after the long real-wage stagnation during the Cultural Revolution. This was followed by 3 years of consolidation. The most

Table 3   Behaviour of real wages of urban employees, 1977–92

| | Real wage change over previous year | | | | |
	Total	State-owned	Collective	Other	Inflation rate[a] over previous year
1978	6.0	6.2	5.1		0.7
1979	6.6	7.4	5.1		1.9
1980	6.1	6.0	6.9		7.5
1981	-1.2	-1.3	0.5		2.5
1982	1.3	0.9	2.5		2.0
1983	1.5	1.4	2.0		2.0
1984	14.8	16.4	13.1		2.7
1985	5.3	4.8	6.6	22.5	11.9
1986	8.2	8.9	5.5	6.0	7.0
1987	0.9	0.5	1.6	6.0	8.8
1988	-0.8	-0.7	-2.1	5.0	20.7
1989	-4.8	-4.6	-6.1	-2.3	16.3
1990	9.2	9.7	6.6	8.9	1.3
1991	4.0	3.2	5.6	10.5	5.1
1992	6.7	7.0	4.1	5.3	8.6
1977–92	4.1	4.2	3.3	7.8[b]	6.5

Notes: [a]The cost of living index for staff and workers is used to deflate nominal wages. [b]Denotes 1984–92.
Source: State Statistical Bureau (1993):110.

rapid increases in real wages (by 15 per cent) occurred in 1984, as a result of the enterprise reforms which partly decentralised employee compensation decisions. The fall in real wages over the period 1987–89 represented tardy government response to inflation and government concern about the role of wages in increasing costs and demand. Resumed real wage growth since 1989 may reflect a catching up, as inflation decelerated, and a political response to the events in 1989.

We examine the structure of individual urban wages by means of the national household survey conducted by the Chinese Academy of Social Sciences (CASS) in 1988 and reported in Griffin and Zhao (1993). The object is to analyse the operation and efficiency of the labour market as gauged by the outcomes that it generates and the incentives that it provides. The urban sample covered ten provinces and came from a national sampling frame of 90,000 households. It contained 9,000 households and 32,000 individuals, of whom 18,000 were workers receiving income. It is this last group that we analyse here, drawing on the chapter by Knight and Song (1993c). Generally, we use the broadest definition of income (Y_1), which nevertheless excludes certain household benefits in kind not attributable to individual members or not quantifiable. Y_1 averaged 1,754 yuan per annum, of which 982 was regular income (Y_2) and 771 other cash income (Y_3), the most important components of which were bonuses (338 yuan) and subsidies (297 yuan). Table 4 sets out the basic income function of urban workers, with $y_1 (= \ln Y_1)$ as the dependent variable. We examine the more interesting explanatory variables in turn.

The familiar inverted U-shaped age-earnings profile is found in this sample, as in many others. Income rises monotonically to a peak for workers in their fifties (A_8 and A_9), when it is 90 per cent higher than for workers in their teens, and thereafter declines slightly. It is difficult to interpret the Chinese result in the familiar way, that is, human capital acquired through employment experience is rewarded with its marginal product in competitive labour markets. Nor can it be seen as a means of recouping firm-specific training by means of seniority payments: the absence of voluntary mobility in China means that seniority payments are unnecessary for maintaining internal labour markets. The old have power in China—an outcome both of its culture and of its bureaucracy. Great weight has been placed on length of service within the employment unit throughout the period in which the system of wage grades has operated: seniority is a central aspect of the Chinese wage system.

The contrast between regular and other income helps to explain why age is rewarded. Regular income is more responsive to age, whereas other income peaks early (in the age group $A_6 = 41$–5 years) and then declines sharply. The former is likely to be governed by the centrally imposed system of wage grades, whereas the latter depends more on the policy and resources of the employer: concepts of fairness (for example, everyone should receive the same) or productivity (for example, rewards for individual efficiency) are more likely to apply than seniority *per se*. There is some tendency for the returns to age to increase with educational level, and to be greater for non-manual than for manual workers, but these results are open to both human capital and institutional interpretations.

The least ambiguous evidence is to be found by comparing ownership sectors. In the public sector (Ow_1 and Ow_2) wages peak in the age group 66 and over, the highest paid age group earning 117 and 118 per cent more than the lowest paid. In the collective sector (Ow_3) and in the other sectors (Ow_4-Ow_8), the corresponding figures are 69 and 67 per cent and the peak age groups are 56–60 and 41–50 respectively. In the public sectors, wage structures are laid down by the state, whereas in the other sectors employers have more autonomy. This suggests that a major part of the returns to age or employment experience stems from the standardised wage scales imposed from above. However, that only raises the deeper question: why does the system of wage grades reward seniority? It might reflect a culturally based respect for age or it might represent an underlying concern to reward human capital in the absence of a labour market.

Historically, much value was placed on education in China. Entrance to the bureaucracy, offering high status and wealth positions, was by means of competitive examinations. The Confucian stress on education lives on in Chinese culture but the economic motive may dominate: is education rewarded in the labour market? Respondents were classified into eight educational levels, their mean length of education running from one (E_8, the omitted category) to 15 years (E_1). College graduates (E_1) receive 20 per cent more income than the 'uneducated' base group. The premium on education, as measured by the coefficients in Table 4, increases almost monotonically with education. The premium is not consistently higher for regular wages than for other income. More education does mean more income in urban China, but the effect of education on income is remarkably slight by comparison with other countries.

It might be hypothesised that education, if it is productive, will be rewarded more by collective and by private-sector employers than by the state if the latter has weaker profit and efficiency goals and stronger equity goals. The regression results for the different ownership sub-samples are consistent with this hypothesis. Only one education term (E_1) has a significant coefficient in the state-owned sector whereas at least five have significant positive coefficients in the other publicly owned and collective sectors. Moreover, their coefficients are in each case larger than in the state-owned sector, and rise consistently with educational level. The evidence suggests that education is better rewarded where employers have greater autonomy and that the state, where it can, compresses the educational wage structure by comparison with a free-market outcome.

In principle, the occupation-based wage system and lack of occupational mobility should make occupation the most important determinant of wages in China. However, there is a sense in

which wages are attached to individuals rather than jobs. For instance, most manual workers can rise though the manual grades as their years of service increase, irrespective of the precise occupation or its skill level. This suggests that the determinants of initial allocation to the manual, technical, or administrative groups, and their corresponding wage systems, can be important determinants of pay. That is a way in which education can influence pay.

In the absence of a labour market, however, relative pay between the different wage systems is influenced by concepts of fairness, in turn moulded by political and social values and by the employers' practice of creating housing communities for their workers. Occupational wage distinctions are therefore likely to be muted. Seven occupations were distinguished in the survey and are shown in Table 4, manual labourer (Oc_7) being the omitted category. The coefficients on each of the non-manual occupations are positive and significant, although not large. The greatest wage difference, *ceteris paribus*, between a factory director or manager and a labourer, is only 15 per cent. It is probable that technically qualified workers are not paid well enough to provide workers with incentives to acquire qualifications or employers with incentives to economise on the use of qualified labour.

There is a powerful, statistically significant relationship between education and occupation. For instance, the proportion of workers in manual occupations rises monotonically, from 2 per cent in the case of college graduates to 88 per cent in the case of those with less than 3 years of primary education. Education has indeed been an important criterion for allocating workers to occupations, although less so during the Cultural Revolution decade. Education thus raises the income of workers not only directly but also indirectly by improving their chance of allocation to a well-paid occupation. The omission of the occupation terms from the income function therefore shows the combined effect of education on income. The spread of earnings is widened

Table 4   Income function analysis of urban workers, 1988 survey

	Independent variable	Proportion of sample (per cent)	Coefficient
	Constant term	100.00	7.057**
S_2	Female	47.72	-0.081**
E_1	College graduate or above	6.17	0.181**
E_2	Community college graduate	6.24	0.128**
E_3	Professional school graduate	11.07	0.112**
E_4	Upper middle school graduate	24.89	0.098**
E_5	Lower middle school graduate	38.61	0.091**
E_6	Primary school graduate	10.32	0.038
E_7	3 years or more of primary school	1.07	0.006
Ow_2	Other publicly-owned sector	39.05	-0.079**
Ow_3	Collective sector	20.45	-0.175**
Ow_4	Private or individually owned sector	0.23	-0.338**
Ow_5	Sino-foreign joint venture	0.31	0.192**
Ow_6	Foreign-owned sector	0.05	0.022
Ow_7	Other	0.58	-0.124*
Ow_8	Multiple ownership	0.01	-0.392
Oc_1	Owner of private or individual enterprise	0.57	0.029
Oc_2	Owner and manager of private or individual enterprise	0.11	0.080**
Oc_3	Professional or technical worker	16.00	0.073**
Oc_4	Responsible official of government	4.71	0.086**
Oc_5	Factory director or manager	1.79	0.142**
Oc_6	Office worker	23.63	0.037**
A_1	Age below 20	6.29	-0.329
A_2	21–25	10.85	-0.205**
A_4	31–35	17.25	0.151**
A_5	36–40	17.67	0.200**
A_6	41–45	12.62	0.262**
A_7	46–50	12.19	0.290**
A_8	51–55	7.63	0.317
A_9	56–60	3.37	0.317*
A_{10}	61–65	0.49	0.293**
A_{11}	66 and over	0.21	0.275**
F		246.041	
$\bar{R}^2$		0.461	
$\bar{y}_1$		7.390	
N	Number of observations	17,480	

Notes: The dependent variable is the logarithm of total income (y_1). The omitted categories in the dummy variable analysis are male (S_1), less than 3 years of primary school (E_8), not Communist Party member (C_2), Han (M_2), state-owned sector (Ow_1), manual worker (Oc_7), manufacturing (Es_3), management of private or individual enterprise (J_3), age 25-30 (A_3), and Jiangsu (P_{10}). *Denotes statistical significance at the 5 per cent level. **Denotes statistical significance at the 1 per cent level. Explanatory variables included in the equation but not presented in the table are Communist Party membership, ethnic minority, sector, employment status, and province.
Source: Knight and Song (1993c):222–4, drawing on the 1988 CASS national household survey.

from 20 to 34 per cent, but the premium on education remains low in comparison with most developing countries.

It has been government policy in China to remove gender discrimination in both jobs and wages. Labour allocation and administrative wage setting gave government the power to correct the inequalities of the past. There are few 'housewives' in China: in the urban sample women constituted no less than 47 per cent of employees. Female employees are thus not a select group. Nevertheless, women receive on average 16 per cent less income than men, both in their regular wage and in their other income. How is the difference to be explained?

Women tend to be 'crowded' into the lower-paying collective sector, despite pressures from labour bureaux and party branches to overcome managers' prejudices. Since liberation the government has also pursued a policy of providing equality of educational access for boys and girls. Equality has not been achieved, however, except for the youngest age groups in the urban areas. A regression analysis of educational attainment shows that urban women have 1.8 years less of education, *ceteris paribus*, than men (Knight and Li 1993:295). In the urban worker sample, 20 per cent of women had gone beyond upper middle school and 52 per cent had not reached it, the corresponding figures for men being 28 and 47 per cent respectively.

How much of the gender difference in mean wages is due to such differences in characteristics and how much to differences in the income-generating process itself? The coefficient on female sex in the income function (Table 4) implies that women are paid 9 per cent less, *ceteris paribus*. A decomposition analysis shows that differences in characteristics account for some 45 per cent of the wage difference. Men have more favourable education, age, and occupation structures and a higher proportion of them are state employees. Residual differences in coefficients account for some 55 per cent of the wage difference. Do they represent discrimination against women?

We can learn about the nature of the residual component by examining its incidence. The coefficient on female sex is larger for less-educated women. There is very little difference in wage income between men and women with high education at all ages and between young men and women with low education, but the difference emerges and grows consistently from the late twenties onwards for those with low education. It appears that gender is largely irrelevant in the early stages of the working life but becomes important in the later stages. This may be the result of labour-market discrimination against women: for instance, men may receive preference in promotion to better-paid jobs and grades. Similarly, the facts that the sex difference is small in the private and individual ownership sector (much self-employment) and in temporary employment (much piecework) are consistent with the discrimination explanation applying where the sex difference is large, that is, among older, less educated workers. Possession of education protects women against discrimination, apparently because it gives them access to jobs in which there is less discrimination.

Labour-market segmentation among employing enterprises has been growing and is now substantial. No less than 78 per cent of urban workers are employed by publicly owned enterprises, 39 per cent by the national government, and 39 per cent by sub-national governments. The wage difference is minor: the latter are paid 8 per cent less, *ceteris paribus*, than the former. Some state units—the industrial enterprises—earn profits and are therefore in a better position to pay bonuses and other supplements to the basic wage. The collective sector pays 16 per cent less than the state sector, reflecting perhaps their weaker political position and 'hard' budgets. Collective employees tend to be younger, less well-educated, and more frequently female than state employees: collectives are rarely the preferred sector.

The lowest-paying sector is local private or individually owned enterprises, and the highest-paying is Sino-foreign joint ventures. It is the growing number of small private firms that are most likely to pay no more than the supply price of rural labour. Moreover, it is within this group that exploitative relationships are most likely to be found: some employers can take advantage of poorly informed workers coming from a distance on fixed-term contracts. The urban private sector is still small and heterogeneous, having both high- and low-paying segments, one capable of attracting good workers and the other absorbing the disadvantaged. As the size of both segments grows, so their influences are likely to be felt in the labour market.

Being a cross-section data set, the 1988 survey does not permit an analysis of the effects of the enterprise reforms that took place during the 1980s. It is nevertheless possible to examine predictions of the likely effects of the reforms. During the Cultural Revolution there was little relationship between pay and work. Afterwards there was a continuous call to tie pay to individual performance. Enterprise-specific determinants of pay grew in importance during the 1980s as state enterprises were given more autonomy and profit-related bonuses were allowed to grow. As we have seen, real wages increased rapidly if sporadically, and the composition of pay moved away from time-based wages towards perform-ance pay (piece rates, bonuses) and subsidies.

Can we expect individual differences in non-basic pay to represent differences in productivity, that is, to reflect economic rationality? There is little sign that non-basic pay, being less subject to government control and direction, has an economically more rational structure. On the contrary, compared with basic income, Communist Party members are proportionately more and women proportionately less rewarded, and state ownership yields a large premium. The returns to education and the pattern of occupational pay are on a par with those for basic income, yet education and occupation-based skills are surely too little rewarded for economic efficiency. Moreover, Hay et al. (1994) found no tendency for intra-enterprise wage structures to widen in their panel of state enterprises, as enterprises gained more autonomy and were encouraged to reward performance.

These results are consistent with the inter-pretation of Walder (1987), who presented a gloomy assessment of the attempt to introduce performance incentives into the pay structure: a web of factory interests gave rise to a distribution of bonuses unrelated to the productivity of individual workers. Management encouraged worker cooperation by maximising bonuses, and distributed the rewards so as to minimise contention. If bonuses improved incentives, they did so more at the enterprise than at the individual level.

The Gini coefficient of income among workers in urban China is low by international

Table 5	Absorption of the increment to the rural labour force, 1978–88		
		Million	Percentage
Growth in rural labour supply of which:		107.9	100.0
Assigned urban jobs		13.6	12.6
Absorbed in rural areas of which:		94.3	87.4
Employed in rural enterprises		67.2	62.3
Employed elsewhere		27.1	25.1

Note: Rural enterprises are officially defined as rural economic activities having 'stable managerial structure, production or office equipment, and employees' (State Statistical Bureau 1990:251).
Source: Knight and Song (1993b), from official Chinese sources.

standards. It is lower for basic pay (0.20) and higher for other income (0.34) than for total income (0.24). More interesting are the inequality measures for worker incomes 'inside the plan' and 'outside the plan' (Zhao 1993:76–7). The Gini coefficient of the former (state, other public, and collective enterprises) is 0.23; that of the latter (the other ownership forms) is twice as high: 0.49. As this small sector grows in importance, so overall inequality of wage incomes will rise.

III. The Rural Labour Market

China reached the limits of its land availability decades ago. The total land area sown in 1988 was no more than 3 per cent higher than it had been in 1952. Yet population continued to grow. Over the same period the rural labour force increased by 120 per cent: the sown area of land fell from 11.6 to 5.4 mu per rural worker (a mu is a Chinese unit of measurement equalling 0.0667 hectares). Surplus labour existed in the communes but was camouflaged by the work-point system, and became more evident under the 'household responsibility' system. There have been numerous attempts to measure the extent of rural surplus labour in China (surveyed by Taylor 1988). Using various methods, for example taking a base year to indicate efficient labour use or setting norms for labour inputs for each crop, researchers produced a range of estimates of rural surplus labour expressed as a proportion of the rural labour force, but the majority of estimates were of the order of 30 per cent (Taylor 1988:749–53).

The absorption of the fast-growing rural labour force into productive activities is thus a central problem for China. Between 1980 and 1988 it grew by 2.9 per cent per annum, from 318m to 401m. The number of workers in rural non-agricultural enterprises increased by over 15 per cent per annum, from 30 million to 96 million. Table 5 shows how the increment to rural labour supply was absorbed during the decade 1978–88. The remarkable statistic is that more

than 60 per cent entered rural (township, village, and private) enterprises (TVPs) and no more than 25 per cent entered peasant production. By 1988 rural enterprises accounted for 24 per cent of the rural labour force.

The growth rate of the Chinese labour force began to decline in the late 1980s as a result of the prior decline in fertility. Between 1978 and 1985 labour force growth peaked at 3.6 per cent per annum. In the subsequent 5 years (1985–90) it fell to 2.3 per cent, and it was expected to decline further to 1.3 per cent during 1990–5. The projection for 1995–2000 is 1.2 per cent, and further slight falls are expected thereafter (World Bank 1992b:502). The implication is that the labour force, having grown by 176 million over the 1980s, will grow by 93 million over the 1990s. Assuming that the same pattern applies in both rural and urban areas, the projected rate of natural increase of the rural labour force over the period 1988–2000 is shown in Table 6.

The remarkable expansion of rural enterprise employment that had occurred in the previous decade was not repeated over the years 1988–93 (Table 6), in fact, employment stagnated until 1991 and improved only thereafter. The rapid growth of rural industry over the previous decade was basically a response to an acute market disequilibrium, and it could not confidently be expected to continue in the 1990s. Temporary rural–urban migration had become substantial by 1990 (Table 6), and there is much loose evidence that it has continued to grow. Its future will depend on the policies of central government and of local governments, and on the extent of labour retrenchment in the urban sector. It is unclear how the growth of the rural labour force over the 1990s—by 55 million, or 13 per cent—will be allocated among urban employment, rural enterprise employment, and peasant agriculture. Nevertheless, the way in which it is absorbed will be crucial both for the development of labour markets and for rural living standards.

In 1988 employees in rural areas represented 41 per cent of total wage employees. Were these

Table 6   **Projections of the rural labour force, 1988–2000** (millions)

	Rural labour force	Employment in rural enterprises	Rural–urban migrants
1988	401	96	36
1990	420	93	37
1993	437	125	24
1995	448		
2000	475		

Note: Rural–urban migrants are an annualised flow of temporary migrants. The data for 1988 and 1990 were pieced together from various sources and are not comparable with the figure for 1993, which is based on a rural household survey. **Source:** Labour force: official statistics of rural labour force 1988, plus World Bank projections; employment: State Statistical Bureau 1993:360; State Statistical Bureau 1994:85; migrants: World Bank 1992a; Rural Development Institute 1994:110–1.

employees more like their urban counterparts or their rural co-residents in peasant agriculture? For instance, were they effectively part of a rural labour market, with their wages governed by the supply price of workers in household agriculture, or were they an adjunct of the heavily regulated urban wage and employment system, with their wages set by reference to equivalent urban wages?

The data source for our analysis of wages in rural enterprises is the 1988 CASS national household survey. The rural sample contained 10,260 households and 30,810 income recipients of working age, but only 6 per cent of these were employed by enterprises. Table 7 presents an income function analysis, with the logarithm of total cash income (y_1) as the dependent variable. The regression equation is not well fitting, explaining only 19 per cent of the variance in y_1. However, a number of coefficients are statistically significant. Age is rewarded, rising 55 per cent from the youngest age group (A_1) to the age group 56–60 (A_9). Compared with incomplete primary education (E_6 and E_7), the educational groups involving higher education (E_1 and E_2) receive over 20 per cent more income. Higher cadres (Oc_1) receive 26 per cent more pay than manual workers (Oc_7), and ordinary cadres (Oc_6) 12 per cent more. However, the occupation terms are generally small and not significant.

These results suggest that individual characteristics are important in the determination of pay in rural enterprises. The fact that potential human capital variables, such as education and length of employment experience, reward workers is of particular interest, because piece-work payments are common in rural enterprises. For instance, in a 1986 survey of 200 large and medium-sized rural industrial enterprises in ten provinces, the principal form of wage payment was found to be piecework (Li 1986–7:280). The apparent discrimination against women (receiving 14 per cent less, *ceteris paribus*) is more difficult to explain in a piecework system but might take the form of job discrimination. The equation in Table 7 also implies that the enterprise and the economic activity both play a role. The few state-owned enterprises (Ow_1 and Ow_2) in the rural areas pay more than private enterprises (Ow_4) whereas workers in the predominant cooperative sector (Ow_3) are paid on a par with those in the private sector.

Province dummy variables (not shown) representing 28 provinces were also included, and half of them were significantly different from the omitted province, Jiangsu. Searching for a pattern, we regressed p_{it}, the coefficient on the province dummy variable, on y_{it}, the equivalent measure of rural income per capita:

Table 7   Income function analysis of rural enterprise employees, 1988 survey

		Proportion of sample (per cent)	Coefficient
	Intercept	100.00	6.958**
S_2	Female sex	31.87	-0.144**
E_1	College or above	0.79	0.211
E_2	Professional school	3.16	0.231*
E_3	Upper middle school	18.18	0.137
E_4	Lower middle school	44.12	0.112
E_5	Primary school graduate	25.34	0.046
E_7	1–3 years of primary school	4.74	-0.014
E_8	Illiterate	3.51	0.091
A_1	≤20	16.99	-0.251**
A_2	21–25	18.03	-0.065
A_4	31–35	11.46	0.080
A_5	36–40	14.18	0.133*
A_6	41–45	10.42	0.097
A_7	46–50	10.42	0.120*
A_8	51–55	4.74	-0.030
A_9	56–60	2.47	0.189*
A_{10}	61–65	1.04	0.043
A_{11}	≥66	0.54	-0.040
Ow_1	State-owned	2.77	0.228*
Ow_2	Local state-owned	12.99	0.145*
Ow_3	Cooperative	48.67	0.064
Ow_6	Foreign-owned	0.59	0.058**
Ow_7	Household farming	17.24	-0.030
Ow_8	Other	9.29	-0.025
Oc_1	Government or party leader	1.09	0.231
Oc_2	Technical worker	2.52	0.025
Oc_3	Leading official of state or collective enterprise	0.84	-0.152
Oc_4	Ordinary cadre	8.10	0.116
Oc_5	Owner or manager of private enterprise	2.12	-0.052
Oc_6	Township or village cadre	5.93	-0.004
Oc_8	Temporary or contract labourer	14.38	-0.094
Oc_9	Farm worker	17.00	-0.191**
Oc_{10}	Worker in township or village enterprise	34.83	-0.027
Oc_{11}	Manager of local state-owned enterprise	1.00	0.212
F-value			7.0 20
$\overline{R}^2$			0.190
N	Number of observations	2,023	

Notes: The dependent variable is the logarithm of cash income (y_1). The omitted categories are male (S_1), 3 or more years of primary school (E_6), age 26–30 (A_3), private or individually owned enterprise (Ow_4, Ow_5), and ordinary worker (Oc_7). ** denotes that the coefficient is significantly different from zero at the 1 per cent level, and * at the 5 per cent level. Explanatory variables included in the equation but not presented in the table are Communist Party membership, ethnic minority, sector, and province.
Source: Knight and Song (1993b:181–5) drawing on the 1988 CASS survey.

$p_{i'} = 0.174^{**} + 0.413^{**}\, y_i$

($R^2 = 0.246$, F-value = 9.801, SEE 22 per cent, $p_i = 0.032$, N = 28,** denotes statistical significance at the 1 per cent level, and $y_{i'} = \ln Y_i - Y_j$ where i denotes province i and j denotes Jiangsu). The equation implies that a 10 per cent increase in rural income per capita of a province raises the enterprise wage in that province by 4.1 per cent. The positive relationship (albeit less than unity) suggests that labour-market forces are at least part of the story.

There are other reasons to expect that local labour markets are important determinants of pay in rural enterprises. Case-study evidence suggests that in the more developed, labour-scarce (rural) counties, industrial wages and agricultural incomes rose closely together as labour became scarce, and overtook wages in state enterprises, although wages were more directed where community (township and village) government ownership predominated than where private ownership predominated. In less developed, labour-surplus counties, wages were low, and lowest where community government intervention was least (Gelb 1990; Meng 1990). The restricted mobility of labour among rural areas and the operation of labour-market forces in at least some areas creates greater spatial segmentation of wages in the rural enterprise sector than in the urban sector.

It is possible to make a rigorous comparison of employees in rural and urban enterprises using the 1988 household survey. The geometric mean of urban wages is 36 per cent higher than that of rural wages. How much of this is due to rural–urban location? A pooled regression with an urban dummy variable puts urban wages 12 per cent higher, *ceteris paribus*. Comparable earnings functions were estimated using the same set of independent variables (Knight and Song 1993b). A decomposition analysis based on the earnings functions produced different results (7 or 19 per cent higher) according to the decomposition used. Using the urban income function, it is the role of the state as the major employer and a high and age-related payer in

the urban areas, and the tendency for TVPs to employ young people, that explain much of the difference in mean wages. The use of the rural income function, however, leaves a larger residual suggestive of rural disadvantage in wage payments.

The difference in the standardised wages of rural and urban employees is surprisingly small, given their difference in openness to market forces and their likely differences in technology and capital intensity. However, the urban–rural difference in enterprises' labour costs and employees' living standards might well appear greater if we could standardise for hours worked and for payments in kind.

It is not possible to draw a clear distinction between wage earners and others because almost all rural households in receipt of wage income also have non-wage sources of income. The lack of specialisation reflects limited opportunities for wage employment and the policy of allocating some land to each household. According to the 1988 household survey, income per worker in the majority of households without wage income (group two) was only 70 per cent of average income per worker in the minority of households which received wage income (group one).

There are two possible explanations for the apparently limited trade-off between wage income and other income. One is that many Chinese households are characterised by a shortage of land and other resources but a surplus of labour. The other is that wage employees tend to be concentrated in prosperous areas. In favour of the former hypothesis is the fact that group-one households have 30 per cent more cultivated land per non-wage worker, although less land per household. Moreover, an income function for group-one households yielded a coefficient on the number of employees that was five times as great as the coefficient on the number of other workers. Thus wage employment has an opportunity cost in terms of income forgone but its opportunity cost is relatively low. In favour of the latter hypothesis is the evidence that more-prosperous provinces have both higher wage rates and more wage employment (see Box 2).

Wage income from rural enterprises accrues largely to the richer rural households. Thus, the highest income per capita decile of rural households received 62 per cent of wage income in the 1988 rural survey. Many rural workers have an incentive to obtain the scarce wage jobs.

How are these jobs allocated? A logit analysis showed the major determinants of access to be education, male gender, Communist Party membership, and province. For instance, an upper-middle-school graduate had an 81 per cent probability of wage employment, *ceteris*

Box 2

The spatial relationship between wage and other rural income

We examine the spatial relationship between wage and other rural income by means of a province-level analysis using the rural sample of the 1988 CASS survey. The object is to explain various dimensions of the income of households receiving wage income (group one) in terms of the income per worker (Y_2) of households without wage income (group 2). The results are illustrated in Figure 2.

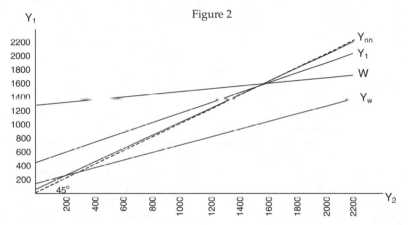

Figure 2

The province mean wage per employee in group one (W) is positively but weakly related to Y_2. Over the relevant range of Y_2 (600–2,170 yuan), W is generally well above Y_2, and is insensitive to Y_2. There appears to be an institutional as well as a market element in the determination of W, which provides a floor to wages where the supply price of wage labour is particularly low. By contrast, the non-wage income per non-wage worker in group one(Y_{nn}) is almost equal to Y_2 throughout the relevant range. This is further evidence that wage employment is no hindrance to the household's other economic activities. Income per worker in group one (Y_1) generally exceeds the corresponding value of Y_2 but the ratio is greatest in the poorest provinces. Wage income per worker in group one (Y_w) is more sensitive to Y_2 than is the wage per employee, indicating that wage employment per worker also rises with Y_2. Thus wage income per worker is high where wage rates and wage employment are high, and these tend to be high in areas of generally high rural income.

paribus, and a primary-school graduate a 9 per cent probability. A similar, household-based, logit analysis showed that access to wage employment increased with the number of household workers, varied inversely with the amount of farming land per worker, and was higher in suburb than in non-suburb rural areas (Knight and Song 1993a:200–11).

There are plausible explanations for these findings. Education is more valuable in TVPs than in other rural activities. Households with many workers or little land may be favoured by local authorities in the allocation of township and village enterprise (TVE) jobs. Insofar as rural industries are concentrated in small towns or suburban areas, such centres are likely to have less surrounding land per worker. The powerful role played by the province variables suggests that the location of rural industry is extremely uneven and, given the restrictions on labour mobility, very important for access to wage employment.

There are at least three reasons why wage employment is concentrated in high-income households. First, the wage rate from employment exceeds income from other rural activities and has a low opportunity cost. Second, rich households are favoured by the common requirement that TVP recruits provide a capital loan or a joining fee to the enterprise. Third, there is a tendency for agriculturally rich areas also to be industrially more developed. An income function analysis of the 2,400 (rural) counties of China showed that non-agricultural product per capita is assisted by agricultural success, standardising for other variables (Knight and Song 1993a). Thus households in prosperous localities have more opportunities for wage employment.

The limitations placed on the mobility of labour even among rural areas contribute to rural differentiation. This is well illustrated at the village level. Village land is normally allocated among village households on an equal per capita basis. Almost all revenue for village investment and village welfare provision must come from the village itself—in the forms of taxes on village people and production, the rent of land or factories, and the profits of village collective enterprises. Particularly where ownership is collective rather than private, village members receive priority in access to industrial employment. Those with a right to live in the village are effectively 'shareholders' in the resources of the village.

Before the rural reforms the main source of income differences among villages was the quantity of agricultural land and other natural resources available to each village. However, the development of rural industry produced a new source of income stratification among villages. Some villages were more successful than others in establishing industry, and some could not industrialise at all. This process of economic differentiation occurred both where rural industrialisation was mainly organised in collectives and where it was mainly left to private initiative. Even within the same county, the varying success of villages in setting up non-agricultural activities depends on the initiative of village leaders in forming collective enterprises, or attracting private investors from outside, or forming links with city enterprises, on the degree of enterprise, skill, and initiative displayed by the villagers themselves, on village location, infrastructure, and transport facilities, and on access to funds.

It seems that a process of cumulative causation is operating, with some villages being launched into virtuous circles of economic growth while others are trapped in vicious circles. For instance, entrepreneurial skills are often acquired through experience, in a process of learning-by-doing, and there are often externalities within a community because the success of one entrepreneur provides an example, information, contacts, and skills for others; training-on-the-job can raise the quality of workers, and village success can improve their attitudes and aspirations; additional village revenues can improve welfare services, such as education and health, with consequent effects on labour quality, and can raise investment in infrastructure such as irrigation, communications, and transport. Profits are available for the expansion of the enterprise or the establishment of new enterprises. If social welfare is not collectively provided in the industrialised villages, village households can afford to buy their own welfare and security, whereas in unindustrialised villages adequate provision cannot be made either collectively or individually.

Industrialisation eventually creates a shortage of labour, and this draws in labour from neighbouring villages or from further afield. The migrants often work for low pay on the farms leased by village industry workers or in the least pleasant, most arduous jobs in village industry, such as brick factories or coal mines. Normally they cannot share, or have to pay fully for, village welfare services. Such in-migration can be only temporary as it is generally impossible for workers and their families to change their place of household registration. Rural labour markets are not competitive but are segmented as between village 'insiders' and 'outsiders'. Thus,

'trickledown' effects do occur among villages but they tend to be diluted by vested interests and restrictions on labour mobility, and consequent lack of open competition.

IV. The Rural–Urban Divide and Migration

There is a very considerable urban–rural divide in China: a great disparity in average living standards as between workers and peasants. This is true not only of measured household income but also of such social provision as education, health, and social security. Rural people, therefore, have a strong incentive to move to the urban areas. In the pre-reform period such movement was very strictly controlled and restricted. One of the consequences of the economic reforms was that the degree of control over the movement of rural labour was weakened. Nevertheless, rural–urban migration remains restricted by comparison with most other developing countries.

Table 8   **Urban and rural net income per capita, and their ratio, 1978–93**

	Urban (yuan per annum)	Rural	Urban (rural = 1.0)
1978	316	134	2.36
1980	439	191	2.30
1981	500	223	2.24
1982	535	270	1.98
1983	573	310	1.85
1984	660	355	1.71
1985	685	398	1.72
1986	828	424	1.95
1987	916	463	1.98
1988	1,119	545	2.05
1989	1,260	602	2.09
1990	1,387	686	2.02
1991	1,544	709	2.18
1992	1,826	784	2.33
1993	2,337	922	2.53

Source: State Statistical Bureau 1991, 1994.

The official household survey yielded a ratio of urban to rural household income per capita in 1993 of 2.53 to 1 (Table 8). The table shows that the ratio narrowed between 1978 and 1984 as the rural reforms bore fruit, but widened again after 1984 as the urban reforms gathered pace. The CASS household income survey, which defined income more broadly, arrived at a ratio for 1988 of 2.42 to 1 (Khan et al. 1993:34), compared with the official ratio in that year of 2.05 to 1. The urban–rural income ratio is greater in poor than in rich provinces as urban wages are standardised across China and not much subject to local market forces.

Education provides another example of the urban–rural divide. The 1988 CASS household survey showed urban adults to average 9.6 years of education and rural adults 5.5 years, a difference of 4.1 years (Knight and Li 1993). The standardised difference was slightly larger, 4.6 years. The explanation is likely to be found in income differences both of governments and of households. In the rural areas considerable emphasis is placed on self-reliance: much revenue-raising is decentralised to local governments, county, and village authorities. Urban areas are more centrally funded.

There are large differences in educational attainment among provinces. An attempt was made to explain the coefficients on the province dummy variables by province mean income per capita (Knight and Li 1993, Table 8.5). No relationship was found for the urban areas, but there was a powerful positive relationship in the rural areas. This reflects the rural dependence on local revenue raising. The quality of rural education also suffers, for the same reason.

These results carry over from educational attainment to educational enrolment. A logit analysis of current educational enrolment in rural China also found that household and provincial income per capita raised enrolment. A rural income function analysis showed the opportunity cost of enrolment (income forgone) to be high for 14–19 year-olds. This helps to explain why only 45 per cent of this age-group in the rural

sample were enrolled in 1986, compared with 75 per cent in urban China.

The disparities between rural and urban China in income, education, and other aspects of the quality of life provide a strong incentive for rural–urban migration. Although the restrictions on migration have been eased since the rigid controls of the commune period, the situation remains one of disequilibrium in the labour market.

The constraints on migration that are specific to China arise from the registration (hukou) system and its implementation. It effectively prevents rural people, other than specially favoured categories, from settling with their families in the cities. Individual migration is possible: there is no effective monitoring system to reject rural–urban migrants, and the abolition of food rationing made it possible to get food in the cities. Nevertheless, temporary migration, mostly without family, is not an attractive life. If rural people wish to settle in the city, they find it very difficult or costly to obtain an urban hukou. Urban residents have first claim on jobs, housing, and social services in the city, and rural–urban migrants are virtually excluded from sharing these rights. Thus the urban labour market in China remains highly segmented and rural–urban migration remains constrained.

The 'floating population' of China are persons who are away from their place of permanent residence, that is, their place of registration. In that sense they are temporary migrants. The floating population is extremely difficult to measure, mainly because of the often transient nature of their jobs and their accommodation. An unpublished World Bank study, based on all the empirical information available in 1991, arrived at estimates of temporary migration of rural people in China. These are not hard estimates but involve numerous assumptions. The numbers rose rapidly over the 1980s—from 35 million in 1980 to 98 million in 1988. Most were away for less than a year. When the flow is converted into an annualised stock, for example, four people migrating for 3 months are converted into one person-year, the stock is seen to have risen from 20 million in 1980 to 58 million in 1988. Not all of the floating population went to the urban areas: the stock in the urban areas rose from 15 million in 1980 to 36 million in 1988.

Perhaps the best estimate of migration from rural China that has so far been made was based on a national household survey conducted in 1994 by the Agricultural Bank of China. 5.84 per cent of rural people went out to work in 1993, their average period of absence being 6.75 months. This implies that there were 49 million migrants, of which 39 million went to urban areas, the annualised flow being 24 million. Remittances from urban areas would have amounted to 10 per cent of rural incomes (Rural Development Institute 1994:110–1).

The growth of rural–urban migrants over the period 1980-86 was no less than 13.5 per cent per annum, and over the period 1986-90 it averaged 4.1 per cent per annum. The fact that the urban/ rural income differential was narrowing in the early 1980s and widening in the late 1980s suggests that the different growth rates were not due to changes in economic incentives. Rather, the economic incentives and disequilibrium existed throughout. The rapid early increase in migration was due to liberalising policy and institutional changes, and the subsequent slow-down may have been due to a combination of diminished disequilibrium, reduced urban construction, the recession of 1989, and a tightening of some controls, especially in the large cities. The signs are that the rate of migration rose again in the 1990s.

The 'urban distribution policy' prescribed strict control of large cities, weaker control of medium cities, and encouragement of the growth of small cities and towns. This policy is reflected—but only weakly—in the rates of growth of migrants in destinations categorised by size. The growth was fastest in rural areas, followed by towns, then small cities, and finally larger cities. However, the variation among these urban categories (ranging from 10.5 to 13.2 per cent per annum over the period 1980–8) was small.

V. Transition and Reform: the prospects

A contrast can be drawn between 'insiders' and 'outsiders', the former being state-employed urban residents and the latter private-sector employees, rural–urban migrants, and rural industry workers. The latter group works in conditions that approximate more closely to a labour market than does the former. The move towards a labour market in China is mainly due to the rapidly increasing importance of the outsiders.

Urban China has not proceeded very far towards a properly functioning labour market. One reason is that the problem is systemic and requires system-wide reform. Labour market reforms inevitably connect with other economic reforms, including fiscal reform, price, enterprise, ownership, bankruptcy, housing, and social security reform. This raises difficult issues of sequencing. A worker who leaves a job has to give up far more than the job. He also loses housing, pension, medical, and other social security benefits. This makes workers reluctant to quit their iron rice bowls, and it also makes employers reluctant to dismiss workers. In the present circumstances attempts to achieve a more flexible labour market and more efficient use of labour could involve severe hardship and accordingly meet resistance from urban workers.

A properly functioning labour market requires that social benefits be separated from the work place. Should the government choose to create such a labour market, it would need not only to decentralise wage and employment decisions but also to centralise the provision of social security and welfare. Consider housing provision. State employees are generally allocated housing at nominal rents. The quality of the housing often depends on the power and profitability of the employing unit, and on the seniority of the employee. The low rents of state employees, the weakness of the housing market, and the high rents and poor housing of the private sector make employees extremely reluctant to leave the state or large cooperative sector. Housing reform, which is only at the early stages, is essential to increase labour mobility even within the state sector, but especially from the state sector.

The current social security arrangements constitute another obstacle to labour mobility. The most important of these are pensions and health insurance. At present, retirement pensions are tied to the employing enterprise. Moreover, retirement benefits are less generous or non-existent outside the state sector. The government is currently encouraging experimentation with retirement pension pools, but until pensions are generally transferable labour mobility will remain restricted. The better access to and subsidies of medical facilities enjoyed by state employees again discourage movement out of state employment.

One of the reasons for underemployment in Chinese enterprises is that the enterprise is responsible for paying unemployment benefit. Tying unemployment insurance to the enterprise makes it more difficult for enterprises to dismiss workers and for government to permit enterprise bankruptcies. The pooling of unemployment insurance has occurred in certain urban areas, which alleviates the direct responsibility of the enterprise for dealing with the hardship of unemployment. Generalised pooling will help to improve the efficiency of labour allocation and use. It is important that adequate social protection be put in place in the early stages of the transition to a labour market.

The economically efficient use of factors of production requires that they be priced at their social marginal products and employed by cost-minimising producers. By this criterion the allocation of resources in China remains deficient in three main respects. First, the incentives for managers to be privately efficient are weak in large segments of the Chinese economy, particularly in the predominant state sector. Persuasive evidence of this is to be found in the extent of underemployment in state enterprises and the extent of loss-making among them.

Second, there remains a great urban–rural income differential, which is to be found—

although muted—also in the wages of urban and rural wage employees. The result is an acute labour market disequilibrium and a potential misallocation of resources between urban and rural areas. The wage gap reflects institutional and political influence on urban incomes which keeps them above the levels at which markets would clear. The institutional and political obstacles to reform are severe.

Third, there is a distortion of relative factor prices within the urban economy. Wages are too high relative to the cost of capital and energy. According to a World Bank report (1992a:70–1), the price of (urban) labour relative to energy in China is three times that in India, and the price of labour relative to capital more than three times. With investment decisions increasingly decentralised and based on profit considerations, inappropriate relative factor prices take on greater importance. The danger is that excessively capital-intensive and energy-intensive technologies will be installed and then operated with excessive labour.

It would be difficult to argue convincingly that China's remarkably high rate of economic growth over the reform period had been held back by tardy labour-market reform. More competitive labour markets are not necessarily more conducive to economic growth. The advantages of dynamic efficiency may dominate the loss from static inefficiency. As has been argued in respect of Japan, internal labour markets and lifetime employment can facilitate skill acquisition, innovation, and cooperative behaviour. Nevertheless, the administered wage system in China does not provide adequate incentives for workers to acquire scarce human capital nor for employers to use it well. Moreover, the various impediments to labour mobility may deter investment wherever labour shortages emerge. Thus the benefits of labour market reform are not merely static efficiency gains.

The reform of the labour system and the creation of an urban labour market in China is likely to be a slow and difficult process. It will require prior or simultaneous reform in other areas, in particular social security reform, housing reform, enterprise reform, and the creation of competitive markets for other inputs. It will require decentralisation in some areas of decision-taking and centralisation in some others. There is likely to be political resistance from urban workers seeking to protect their interests, and government will be fearful of creating political instability, for example, through the growth of unemployment.

It is arguable, therefore, that the reforms may stop well short of creating a competitive labour market in the textbook sense. What may emerge is a dual labour market. In one sector internal labour markets similar to those found in large Japanese companies will be preserved. In the other sector, which is growing and will eventually be predominant, competitive forces— albeit muted by social values and political objectives—will operate more freely.

References

Chen, K., Jefferson, G., Rawski, T., Wang, H.C., and Zheng, Y.X., 1988. 'Productivity Change in Chinese Industry, 1953–85', *Journal of Comparative Economics*, 12, 570–91.

Gelb, A., 1990. 'TVP Workers' Incomes, Incentives and Attitudes', in W. Byrd and Q. Lin (eds), *China's Rural Industry. Structure, Development and Reform*, World Bank/ Oxford University Press, Washington, DC.

Griffin, K., and Zhao, R., 1993. *The Distribution of Income in China*, Macmillan, London.

Hay, D., Liu, G., Morris, D.J., and Yao, S., 1994. *Economic Reform and State-owned Enterprises in China 1979*, 87, Clarendon Press, Oxford.

Jefferson, G.H. and Xu, W., 1991. 'The Impact of Reform on Socialist Enterprises in Transition: Structure, Conduct and Performance in Chinese Industry', *Journal of Comparative Economics*, 15:45–64.

Khan, A.R., Griffin, K., Riskin, C. and Zhao, R., 1993. 'Household Income and its Distribution in China', in K. Griffin and R. Zhao (eds), *The Distribution of Income in China*, Macmillan, London.

Knight, J. and Li, S., 1993. 'The Determinants of Educational Attainment in China', in K. Griffin and R. Zhao (eds), *The Distribution of Income in China*, Macmillan, London.

——, Song, L., 1993a. 'The Spatial Contribution to Income Inequality in Rural China', *Cambridge Journal of Economics*, 17:195–213.

——, 1993b. 'Workers in China's Rural Industries', in K. Griffin and R. Zhao (eds), *The Distribution of Income in China*, Macmillan, London.

——, 1993c. 'Why Urban Wages Differ in China', in K. Griffin and R. Zhao (eds), *The Distribution of Income in China*, Macmillan, London.

Li, G., 1986–7. 'Wage Income and Rural Enterprise Employees', Development Research, Development Research Institute, Beijing (in Chinese).

Meng, X., 1990. 'The Rural Labour Market', in W. Byrd and Q. Lin (eds), *China's Rural Industry. Structure, Development and Reform*, World Bank, Oxford University Press, Washington, DC.

People's Republic of China (Ministry of Labour), 1990. *Statistical Yearbook of Chinese Labour and Wages*, Ministry of Labour, Beijing (in Chinese).

Rural Development Institute and others, 1994. *Green Report. Annual Report on Economic Development of Rural China in 1993 and the Development Trends in 1994*, China Social Sciences Publishing House, Beijing.

State Statistical Bureau, 1990. *Statistical Yearbook of China*, China Statistical Publishing House, Beijing (in Chinese).

——, 1991. *Statistical Yearbook of China*, China Statistical Publishing House, Beijing (in Chinese).

——, 1993. *Statistical Yearbook of China*, China Statistical Publishing House, Beijing (in Chinese).

——, 1994. *Statistical Yearbook of China*, China Statistical Publishing House, Beijing (in Chinese).

Taylor, J.R., 1988.'Rural Employment Trends and the Legacy of Surplus Labour 1928–86', *China Quarterly, 116*, December.

Walder, A. G., 1987. 'Wage Reform and the Web of Factory Interests', *China Quarterly*, 109, March, 22–41.

World Bank, 1992a. *China: Reforming the Urban Employment and Wage System*, Washington, DC (restricted).

——, 1992b. *China Strategies for Reducing Poverty in the 1990s*, Washington, DC.

——, 1993. *China: New Skills for Economic Development. The Employment and Training Implications of Enterprise Reform*, Washington, DC (restricted).

Zhao, R., 1993. 'Three Features of the Distribution of Income During the Transition to Reform', in K. Griffin and R. Zhao (eds), *The Distribution of Income in China*, Macmillan, London.

21 Fiscal Decentralisation and Growing Regional Disparities in Rural China

Loraine A. West and Christine P.W. Wong

I. Introduction

Increasing regional and sectoral inequality and its possible consequences for social and economic instability are of growing concern in China. This is reflected in the ninth Five Year Plan adopted in September 1995, which has included among its key targets the amelioration of regional income disparities during the plan period (1996–2000). A priori, the process of transition to a market economy is expected to produce large income shifts and increase income disparities as the realignment of prices and resource allocation by market forces bring changes to the distribution of income across sectors, regions, and households, and as the mechanisms by which planned economies effect equalisation (such as restrictions on private property rights, wage setting, and trade restriction) are dismantled. In fact, however, one of the pleasant surprises of the Chinese reform experience was the diminution of income differentials during the 1979–84 period (World Bank 1985; Adelman and Sunding 1987; Denny 1991; Sicular 1991; Tsui 1991).

This improvement in income distribution during the early reform period was mainly attributed to ending the bad policies of the plan period and freeing the allocation of resources in the rural sector. Reversal of the extremely costly policy of promoting autarkic development at the national and regional levels enabled rapid economic recovery in some of the poorest provinces, improving income distribution across provinces (Denny 1991).

Raising procurement prices for agricultural products in the late 1970s also improved terms of trade for agriculture and brought a significant decline in urban–rural inequality (Adelman and Sunding 1987; Sicular 1991). Liberalisation of factor allocation and migration policies permitted an exodus of surplus labour from the farm sector, whose earnings from the industrial and service sectors contributed to raising rural household incomes (Wong 1988).

In addition, increased agricultural income and savings supported the rapid growth of township and village enterprises (TVEs), which provided employment and further raised rural incomes in the mid 1980s (Wong 1988; Sicular 1991).

However, since 1984 the terms of trade for agriculture have once again deteriorated and

Reprinted with permission. Loraine A. West and Christine P.W. Wong, 1995. 'Fiscal decentralisation and growing regional disparities in rural China: some evidence in the provision of social services', *Oxford Review of Economic Policy*, 11(4):70–84 (with minor editing).

urban incomes increased rapidly, reversing the earlier beneficent trend and resulting in a widening of the urban–rural income gap (Khan et al. 1992). By the late 1980s, there was also a growing consensus among observers of the rural economy that the benefits of reform were not being equally distributed throughout China (Yang 1990; Khan et al. 1992; Tsui 1993; Rozelle 1994). Growing regional inequality in the rural sector is being driven by non-agricultural activities. In particular, the distribution of TVEs is uneven, with coastal provinces accounting for more than half of all employees and nearly three-quarters of operating revenue from these enterprises (Tsui 1993; Hare 1994, Rozelle 1994). However, these observations raise the question of whether this growing inequality is due to everyone becoming better off at differing rates, or whether immiseration is occurring at the bottom of the income distribution.

This paper contributes a new dimension to the literature on interregional and intersectoral income distribution in China by focusing on the provision of social services by rural government as a measure of inequality in income and consumption, and as an index of the declining capacity of government to effect equalisation across regions. In the pre-reform period, the fiscal system had played an important redistributive role in the Chinese economy, extracting large surpluses from the rich provinces and making large transfers to poor regions (Lardy 1978). In the transition period both the willingness and ability to effect equalisation have weakened, and all administrative units have moved toward a higher degree of self-financing (Wong 1991,1992; Wong et al. 1995). This trend means that disparities in revenue collection translate more directly into disparities in per capita expenditure and provision of public services across administrative units in China today.

This paper draws on a study for the Asian Development Bank (ADB) on financing local government in China that focused on the

Table 1   Selected economic indicators for Shandong, Guizhou, and Hebei, 1993

	Shandong	Guizhou	Hebei	China
Gross domestic product (% sectoral share)				
Total	100	100	100	100
Agriculture	21	32	18	21
Industry	49	37	50	52
Services	30	31	32	27
Gross domestic product (% growth rate)				
Total	18	10	18	13
Agriculture	6	4	4	4
Industry	26	14	25	20
Services	17	13	17	9
Total revenue (billion yuan)	19.4	5.7	14.6	508.8
Total expenditure (billion yuan)	18.8	6.7	14.4	528.7
Population (million)	86.4	34.1	63.3	1,185.2
Per capita GDP (yuan)	3,222	1,034	2,682	2,648
Per capita revenue (yuan)	225	166	231	429
Per capita expenditure (yuan)	218	198	227	446

Sources: State Statistical Bureau 1995:34–5, State Statistical Bureau 1994:32, 59; Guizhou Statistical Bureau 1994:91; Shandong Statistical Bureau 1994:115–16; and Hebei Statistical Bureau 1994:498–9.

distribution of fiscal resources to identify the locus and size of fiscal gaps at the sub-provincial levels (Wong et al. 1997). Analysis was based on fieldwork conducted, during the autumns of 1993 and 1994, in a sample of subprovincial units that consists of counties and cities in three provinces: a dynamic coastal province (Shandong), a middle-income inland province (Hebei), and a poor inland province (Guizhou). The economic indicators for the three provinces are shown in Table 1.

While the ADB study was concerned primarily with the vertical and horizontal distribution of budgetary revenues and expenditures in China to assess the equity and efficiency of the fiscal system, much effort was also put into collecting and analysing data on the provision of social services. This was because we had anticipated substantial difficulty in collecting accurate information about off-budget resources (in the form of 'extra-budgetary revenues' and 'self-raised funds') and their importance in financing local government, and the focus on service provision would provide a critical check on the true fiscal capacity of local governments. Moreover, it is the efficient and equitable supply of services to residents that is the end goal of local public finance. The study found that disparities in per capita availability of selected key services, especially education and health care, are quite large across provinces. Within provinces, we also found large disparities between the urban and rural sectors, and, within each sector, between large and small cities, and across rural counties and townships.

In this paper, we present some of the results of the ADB study on growing regional disparities in service provision in the rural sector.[1] The availability of social services is an important indicator for income differentials not only because the levels of social service provision directly affect standards of living, but also because their trends are harbingers of the likely future growth path for the regions. If the experience of the high performance Asian economies is applicable to China, then one could expect that regions with higher expenditures in human resources are likely to enjoy higher growth rates in the future (World Bank 1993).

The paper first assesses disparities in rural service provision by examining the magnitude of regional disparities in service provision and attempts to discern the trend in disparities in Section II. Section III assesses the vertical distribution of revenues and expenditures in the Chinese economy. Section IV examines differences in revenue capacity across regions and the weakening of equalisation. Section V concludes with a discussion of needed reforms in the fiscal system.

II. Regional Disparities in Rural Service Provision

As the transition has progressed, disparities in public service provision have become visible across regions at multiple levels (province, county, and township). Stark contrasts in the quantity and quality of service provision are emerging between coastal provinces, such as Shandong, and inland provinces, such as Guizhou. The wide gap in the delivery of services is particularly apparent for education and public health, two major human development services traditionally provided by the government in China. Private provision of these services is just beginning to emerge in the transition period; however, the availability of these services is still largely determined by government provision. Moreover, the low income levels and scattered population of poor regions make these areas less likely to attract market supply of these services and more dependent on government intervention. An examination of a number of education and health status indicators reveals the disparity in the level and quality of service provision across regions. In addition, we compare the levels of provision with targets enunciated in state policy to show that not only is Guizhou lagging far behind Shandong, but that it is falling far short of national goals set by the national government.

Table 2   Distribution of students by level of school in counties, 1986 and 1993

	Regular senior high schools (%)	Regular junior high schools (%)	Primary schools (%)
1993			
National	3.0	23.0	74.0
Shandong	3.0	27.2	69.8
Guizhou	1.8	15.6	82.6
1986			
National	3.3	21.8	74.8
Shandong	3.3	25.5	71.2
Guizhou	2.0	14.6	83.4

Source: State Statistical Bureau 1987:776 and 782; State Statistical Bureau 1994:580–87.

Education

The Chinese government officially recognised the importance of improving the quality of the labour force for China's modernisation and growth by passing a 9-year Compulsory Education Law in 1986. This law covers completion of basic education, defined as 6 years of primary school and 3 years of junior high school. Although the 9-year Compulsory Education Law was passed at the national level, with decentralised financing, its implementation is being determined at the local levels. Provinces have set their own schedules for achieving 9 years of compulsory education. As expected, target dates vary, with more developed areas having earlier targets. For example, Shandong anticipates implementing compulsory education throughout the province by 1997, while Guizhou's goal for the year 2000 is 80 per cent of children completing primary school and 60 per cent of primary school graduates continuing on to junior high school.

Shandong is well on the way to achieving its target; in 1993, 83 per cent of primary school graduates continued on to junior high school. In contrast, only 42 per cent of primary school graduates in Guizhou continued on to junior high school. In fact, one-third of Guizhou's counties have not yet attained universal provision of primary schooling.

The regional disparity in the provision of education services is also seen in the distribution of students by level of education, shown in Table 2. Nationally, 1.4 per cent of all students attending school are enrolled in tertiary schools, 29.8 per cent in secondary schools, and 68.8 per cent in primary schools. Shandong has a comparable distribution with 1.2, 34.0, and 64.8 per cent of students enrolled in tertiary, secondary, and primary schools, respectively. Guizhou, on the other hand, has a much larger share of students at the primary level (79.1 per cent) and only 0.5 per cent receiving tertiary education. The distribution of rural students (within counties) across regular primary and secondary schools shows 3 per cent in Shandong attending senior high school but only 1.8 per cent in Guizhou. Rural students in Guizhou are more concentrated at the primary school level (83 per cent) as compared to Shandong (70 per cent). Only 36 per cent of graduates from rural primary schools in Guizhou continue on to junior high school. These distributions of students across levels of schooling are consistent with the more widespread implementation of compulsory education in Shandong than in Guizhou. This gap has persisted since the mid 1980s.

Table 3   **Rural illiteracy rates, 1982 and 1990** (per cent)

	1990 (age 15 and older)	1982 (age 12 and older)
National	26	38
Shandong	26	39
Guizhou	41	50

Source: Population Census Office 1985:368–69;1993:38–9.

A second education goal articulated by the government is the elimination of illiteracy among the young and middle-aged population. According to the 1990 population census, there were 59m illiterate young and middle-aged people, representing about 10 per cent of this group's total population. Again, there is wide regional variation in attaining this goal. The 11 most developed provinces and municipalities, including Shandong which was at 11 per cent in 1990, expect to reduce illiteracy to below 5 per cent by 1996. Six of the least developed provinces, including Guizhou which had a 29 per cent illiteracy rate among the target population in 1990, are hoping to reduce illiteracy to below 15 per cent by the end of the century. For the rural population aged 15 and over, the illiteracy rate in Guizhou (41 per cent) far exceeds that of Shandong (26 per cent), according to the 1990 population census (Table 3). Shandong has been more successful at reducing illiteracy in rural areas than Guizhou in the 1980s, with the gap between the two provinces widening. The difficulty in reducing the illiteracy rate in Guizhou is compounded by low current attendance rates. In Guizhou only 42 per cent of students are able to complete primary school within 6 years of first enrolment, well below the national average of 64 per cent. The low in-time completion rate is attributable to high failure and drop-out rates. Over 8 per cent of primary school students fail each year in Guizhou as compared to only 2.5 per cent of Shandong primary students

(Table 4). Guizhou also has a higher failure rate at the junior high school level and higher drop-out rates at both levels of schooling than Shandong.

In terms of the quality of education services provided, there also are substantial disparities between Guizhou and Shandong. Only 22 per cent of junior high school students in Guizhou pass national subject standards as compared to 76 per cent in Shandong. The gap between the two provinces is similarly wide for primary school students, with 38 per cent passing subject standards in Guizhou and 89 per cent passing in Shandong (Table 4). The regional contrast is apparent in the quality of teachers, as measured by academic credentials, as well. For example, throughout Penglai county in Shandong 90 per cent of all primary school teachers are qualified, while in Puding county in Guizhou the qualification rate for primary school teachers is only 59 per cent.

Another important component of the quality of education is school facilities and equipment. National campaigns to improve the physical infrastructure of education have served to reduce, and in more developed areas eliminate, the problem of dilapidated and dangerous school buildings. Dilapidated school buildings are now concentrated in the poorest areas of China. For Guizhou the problem remains serious in 28 out of the 75 counties (including county-level cities). In particular, 26 per cent of the school space in Puding county is still classified as dilapidated

Table 4   **Educational attendance indicators for Shandong and Guizhou, 1992** (per cent)

	Shandong	Guizhou
Junior middle school students passing standards for all classes	5.9	1.8
Primary school students passing standards for all subjects	89.0	38.3
Primary school drop-out rate	1.3	7.1
Primary school student failure rate	2.5	8.0
Junior middle school drop-out rate	2.1	3.6
Junior middle school student failure rate	0.4	2.9

Notes: The drop-out rate refers to students who dropped out and did not return to school for the remainder of the school year. These students may return to school in subsequent years. The failure rate refers to students who were not promoted to the next higher grade at the end of the school year.
Source: State Education Commission 1993:72–3.

and dangerous. Visits to several schools with no electricity, open window spaces, and holes in the floor, walls, and ceiling confirmed the extent of the problem.

In spite of national and provincial standards regarding the required facilities and equipment for each level of school, actual school conditions vary tremendously in China. At one extreme are the teaching points, which are one-room school houses with a single teacher, usually with no more than a junior high school education, instructing all children within walking distance. These schools, commonly found in Guizhou and other poor regions, often have insufficient desks and stools for all students and are considered fortunate if they possess a blackboard. At the other extreme is the quality of education imparted by the school systems in China's wealthiest rural areas, such as the Pearl River Delta across from Hong Kong and Penglai county. Primary and secondary schools in these areas contain libraries, science laboratories, and music rooms, and even computer laboratories are increasingly common.

Because the majority of government financing for education comes from the lowest levels, the provision of education services also

varies across counties within a province and, in some cases, across townships within a county. In Shandong, education is the most advanced in counties along the coast (including Penglai) and slightly less advanced in the middle of the province (including Qufu), while the few remaining counties experiencing difficulty in implementing compulsory education are to be found in the mountainous western portion of the province. West (1995) also found substantial variation in the provision of education across three counties in Guangdong, one of China's wealthiest provinces.

A comparison of the central junior high school in two townships in Zunyi county provides an illustration of the variation across townships. In Shiban township, the central junior high school is an old two-storey structure badly in need of repair. The school has no library or science laboratory and consists only of classrooms. Two rooms on the second floor are designated as housing for teachers. In Longkeng township the central junior high school is in better shape physically, with separate rooms for a library and school office. Housing for teachers is more extensive and spacious. The explanation offered by local officials for the disparity in schools is that there are no TVEs in Shiban, while there are 762 in Longkeng with a per capita output value of 2,200 yuan in 1993. With a stronger tax base and source of extrabudgetary funds, Longkeng is able to deliver better services than another township within the same county.

Health

The central government, through the Ministry of Public Health, initiates programs and sets targets for the delivery of health care to the population. National statistics and information gathered in Shandong and Guizhou indicate unevenness in the achievement of targets set by the Ministry of Public Health and, consequently, unevenness in the quality of health care services provided to rural residents throughout China.

The Ministry of Public Health has set a number of targets for the year 2000, including the establishment of a health care unit with part-time trained medical personnel in every village, a goal first announced in the mid 1960s. Nationally, 89 per cent of all villages have achieved this goal; however, it is evident that villages without a health care facility are concentrated in provinces such as Guizhou. In Guizhou only 60 per cent of all villages have a health station, while 97 per cent of villages in Shandong have such a facility. Within Guizhou, variation in health facilities is seen across counties, owing to the dependence on local financing. For example, 79 per cent of villages in Zunyi have managed to establish a health station, while only 9 per cent of villages in Puding offer this level of service. Disparities in the provision of public health are reflected in the variation across provinces in the number of hospital beds and doctors per 1,000 population (Table 5). Shandong residents have better access to health care with more beds and doctors per capita. While Guizhou has fewer beds and doctors than Shandong and the national average, these indicators do not fully reflect the differences in the level and quality of health care services provided. In coastal provinces, ultrasound machines, which are used as a general diagnostic and monitoring tool, are commonplace in township health centres. In Shandong, 90 per cent of all townships have one and even some village health stations have ultrasound machines and X-ray machines. In contrast, township health centres in Guizhou are more likely to rely on a stethoscope, blood pressure cuff, and thermometer as the instruments for providing medical care. Furthermore, one-third of the space occupied by township health centres in Guizhou

Table 5   **Province level indicators of health outcome and service provision, 1990 and 1993**

Indicator	Mean	Standard deviation	Shandong	Guizhou
Infant mortality rate, males, 1990 (per 1,000 births)	34.4	22.4	14.2	60.7
Infant mortality rate, females, 1990 (per 1,000 births)	36.3	20.9	18.0	65.6
Life expectancy at birth, males, 1990	67.4	3.2	69.5	64.3
Life expectancy at birth, females, 1990	70.5	3.8	73.0	66.0
Hospital beds per 1,000 population, 1993	2.79	1.08	2.05	1.56
Doctors per 1,000 population, 1993	1.92	0.93	1.28	1.14

Note: The mean is the unweighted average of 30 provinces.
Sources: Population Census Office 1993:38–9; Lu et al. 1994; Ministry of Public Health 1994:30.

is considered dilapidated and dangerous. Another indicator of the differences in care provided is the common use of disposable needles in township and village-level health care facilities in Penglai but their absence in both Zunyi and Puding.

In Penglai 89 per cent of babies were delivered at a county or township hospital, a major factor in Penglai's relatively low infant and maternal mortality rates of 13.7/1,000 and 2/10,000, respectively. In remote and poor areas, delivery in hospitals and the use of modern birth methods is not as widespread. In Zunyi less than half of all births take place in a township or county hospital, while in Puding, because township hospitals are so poorly equipped and the county hospital is too distant and costly, most births occur at home. Consequently, infant mortality rates in Guizhou are nearly twice the national average and more than triple the rate for Shandong (Table 5). The lower supply of health care in areas such as Guizhou also contributes to another unfavourable health outcome: lower life expectancy. Females in Shandong have a life expectancy that is 7 years longer than for females in Guizhou (Table 5).

Nationally, there are 1.4 beds per 1,000 population in rural areas. Qufu and Penglai counties in Shandong report 1.6–2 beds per 1,000 population, twice the level found in Zunyi and Puding in Guizhou (Table 6). In principle, rural residents have access to medical facilities in urban centres through a referral process. In practice, however, access to the major research and teaching hospitals is limited. During the period 1988–94, only 15 per cent of the inpatients at a major Shanghai hospital were from outside of Shanghai and some of them were probably residents of other cities (Hu 1995).

III. Intergovernmental Expenditure and Revenue Assignments

To understand the emergence and persistence of these large regional disparities in the provision of basic services, such as education and health care, we turn in this section to a brief explanation of the vertical distribution of revenues and expenditures among administrative levels in China to show that local governments are increasingly saddled with expenditure responsibilities that are often beyond their financing capabilities. As subventions from higher levels decline during the transition period, fiscal gaps are emerging, and local governments are forced to seek supplementary funding off budget. In the poor regions, however, access to off-budget resources is also limited, resulting in lower levels of services provided.

Intergovernmental expenditure assignments in China roughly follow international practice, with the central government responsible for expenditures related to national defence and external relations, and local governments responsible for day-to-day administration and

Table 6   **Rural health indicators, 1993**

	Beds (per 1,000 population)	Medical personnel (per 1,000 population)
National rural	1.4	2.0
Shandong rural	1.6–2.0	2.1–2.5
Guizhou rural	0.8–0.9	1.4

Sources: State Statistical Bureau 1994:59, 643; Wong et al. 1995.

service provisions (Shah 1991). Budgetary data show that the central government typically accounts for only about 10 per cent of total expenditures on 'culture, education, science, and health', the category that comprises 80–90 per cent of social expenditures in the Chinese budget (Wong et al. 1995b: Table 3.11). This means that education and health care are provided primarily by local governments. Further disaggregating among the four layers of 'local' government of province, city, country, and township, we find that rural governments at the county and township levels account for about 70 per cent of the local share of education and health expenditures, or more than 60 per cent of the total.

The trend has been toward shifting budgetary expenditures to the lower levels during the transition. Partly this is caused by the changing role of government. In the pre-reform centrally planned system, the central government financed the bulk of capital investments as a core part of its program of economic management. In the transition period, as investments have been shifted out of the budget on to enterprises and the banking sector, the central share of the budget has declined. Partly it is due to changes in the price structure—the costs of day-to-day administration and service provision have risen with wage increases, pushing up the expenditure

burdens of local governments. As a result, the central government share of budgetary expenditures has fallen from 54 per cent of the total in 1978 to less than 40 per cent in the 1990s (Wong et al. 1995b).

This trend is reflected also at the subnational levels, where the provincial share has fallen in favour of cities and counties. In Shandong it fell from 34 per cent in 1980 to 17 per cent in 1993, while the share of cities and prefectures rose from 16 per cent to 26 per cent during the same period, and the combined share of counties and townships rose from 50 per cent to 57 per cent. This shift to the subprovincial levels is driven by the same factors affecting the declining share of central expenditures relative to local: the transfer of investment finance out of the budget which reduced provincial outlays disportionately more than those of lower levels; the devolution of expenditure responsibilities for grain subsidies to the cities and counties; and the rising costs of providing government services.

In an earlier paper, Wong (1991) argued that within the formal budgetary sphere, changes introduced in the reform period have been much less favourable to local governments than commonly assumed. As local budgets shrank as a share of GDP, local governments were faced with expanded expenditure responsibilities,

Table 7   **Vertical distribution of revenues and expenditures, 1993**

	Own revenues	Expenditures	Net transfer (before revenue sharing)
Central	34	40	+6
Province	11	14	+3
(Urban) cities/prefectures	29	19	-10
(Rural) counties[a]	16	18	+2
(Rural) townships	11	8	-3

Note: [a] This category includes county-level cities, and therefore overstates the share of the rural sector.
Source: Wong et al. 1995.

Table 8   **Distribution of revenues and expenditures by administrative level, 1993** (per cent)

	PRC	Hebei[a]	Shandong	Guizhou
Revenues				
Province	16.7	9.3	8.2	7.0
Prefectures/cities	43.9	49.9	34.9	37.3
Counties	24.2	22.6	36.5	33.2
Townships	16.7	18.3	20.4	22.5
Expenditures				
Province	23.8	24.0	16.6	25.2
Prefectures/cities	31.7	32.1	28.1	23.4
Counties	30.2	33.5	38.2	34.8
Townships	12.7	10.4	17.1	16.6

Note: [a]1992 figures.
Source: Ministry of Finance and fieldwork data.

many stemming from obligations imposed by national policy, including grain price subsidies and mandated wage increases for civil servants. The result is that local governments at all levels are revenue-starved, but especially the lower levels. This can be seen in the vertical distribution of revenues in Table 7.

The distribution of expenditures by administrative level is shown in Table 8 for the fieldwork provinces. At each level, resources available to finance expenditures are equal to own revenues plus net transfers from the other levels. Data in Table 8 show that within the local fiscal hierarchy, the province and county levels spend a greater share of revenues than they collect, while the inverse is true for prefectures/cities and townships. This vertical imbalance reflects the tax system's reliance on industry and commerce

Table 9   **Variation in per-capita revenues by administrative level, early 1990s**

Administrative level	Maximum (yuan)	Minimum (yuan)	Mean (yuan)	Standard deviation (yuan)	Coefficient of variation
Province (1991)	1,431.9	28.3	266.3	269.9	1.01
Province (excluding Tibet, 1991)	1,431.9	94.1	274.5	270.8	0.99
Province (excluding Beijing, Tianjin, Shanghai, and Tibet, 1991)	404.9	94.1	194.9	68.9	0.35
County (Shandong, 1991)	411.9	25.0	65.8	50.9	0.77
County (Guizhou, 1993)	285.7	25.8	67.4	40.7	0.60
Township (Puding, 1993)	36.6	10.2	16.7	8.2	0.49
Township (Zunyi, 1993)	127.10	20.2	52.4	26.0	0.50
Township (Penglai, 1993)	294.4	23.4	73.2	63.3	0.86

Note: County-level figures include only non-urban counties and exclude county-level cities.
Sources: State Statistical Bureau 1994; Shandong Statistical Bureau 1992, 1993; Guizhou Statistical Bureau 1994; finance bureaux in Puding, Zunyi, and Penglai; fieldwork data.

to generate the bulk of revenues—since industrial and commercial activities are concentrated in the cities (and increasingly in townships and villages), so are revenues. At the same time, it also highlights the dependence of the province and county on transfers from other levels.

As the fiscal system moved toward self-financing, fiscal pressures intensified for these two levels, and especially for the county level, whose expenditure burdens have generally increased through the transition process. Moreover, the shift to household farming and the disbanding of agricultural collectives in the early 1980s meant that rural governments have had to find new ways to finance public services, such as education, health care, old age support, and welfare to poor families, that had been financed from the collective public accumulation funds. In other words, while the Chinese countryside had always been expected to provide for itself, the financing mechanisms that existed under collective agriculture are gone. With higher level governments themselves under severe fiscal strain and in no mood to start subsidising rural services, rural governments have to come up with new solutions on their own. Faced with no formal taxing authority, it is not surprising that they have resorted to imposing a variety of users' fees and charges that are the bane of rural livelihood in many regions.

IV. Regional Revenue Capacity and Equalisation

Previous studies have noted that differences in per capita budgetary revenues are unusually large across provinces in China (World Bank 1990; Wong et al. 1995). In 1991 the richest city of Shanghai had per capita revenues that were 15 times those of the poorest province of Anhui. If the three municipalities of Beijing, Tianjin, and Shanghai were also excluded from the sample (so that we are comparing only across 'true' provinces), the richest province, Liaoning, still had per capita revenues that were more than four times those of Anhui.

At the subprovincial levels, revenue differences are also very large. Table 9 shows the distribution of per capita revenues for the county and township levels from our fieldwork samples in Hebei, Shandong, and Guizhou provinces. At the county level, disparities in budgetary income are substantial, even within a single province. In Guizhou, per capita revenues varied from a high of 286 yuan in Guiding County to a low of only 26 yuan in Nayong County among the province's 69 non-urban counties in 1993, a ratio of 11:1 from richest to poorest. In Shandong Province, per capita revenues ranged from 412 yuan in Changdao County to 25 yuan in Guanxia County, a ratio of 16.5:1 from highest to lowest among the province's 74 non-urban counties in 1991. The range of revenue disparity is greatest at the lowest administrative levels. In 1993, the richest township in Penglai collected revenues of 294 yuan, compared to only 10 yuan in the poorest township in Puding, a ratio of 29:1 from highest to lowest.

Interregional disparities in per capita expenditures are somewhat smaller, but still quite substantial. Across provincial level units, in 1991 the highest to lowest per capita expenditure ranged from 758 yuan to 124 yuan, nearly 6:1. Excluding Beijing, Shanghai, and Tianjin the range was still 402 yuan to 124 yuan, more than 3:1. Comparing counties within Shandong Province, the range of variation was very large: the richest county spent 567 yuan, compared to less than 40 yuan in the poorest, or a ratio of nearly 15:1 (Table 10). For townships, the richest township in Penglai County (Shandong) spent 91 yuan per capita, compared to 34 yuan in the poorest township in Zunyi County (Guizhou).

In comparing Tables 9 and 10, it can be seen that both the range and dispersion are smaller for expenditures than for revenues, indicating that equalisation is effected through the fiscal system. However, the degree of equalisation is small, and the trend is toward a diminishing of equalisation. At the aggregate level, remittance rates for surplus provinces fell from 34.2 per cent to 18.1 per cent from 1985 to 1991 (Wong et al.

Table 10   Variation in per-capita expenditures by administrative level, early 1990s

Administrative level	Maximum (yuan)	Minimum (yuan)	Mean (yuan)	Standard deviation (yuan)	Coefficient of variation
Province (1991)	757.6	123.6	297.9	171.76	0.58
Province (excluding Tibet, 1991)	757.6	123.6	284.6	158.26	0.56
Province (excluding Beijing, Tianjin, Shanghai, and Tibet, 1991)	401.5	123.6	239.8	80.86	0.34
County (Shandong, 1991)	567.1	39.7	84.5	60.11	0.71
Township (Zunyi, 1993)	81.0	34.1	53.4	10.7	0.20
Township (Penglai, 1993)	91.3	42.5	67.8	12.59	0.19

Note: County-level figures include only non-urban counties and exclude county-level cities.
Sources: State Statistical Bureau 1994; Shandong Statistical Bureau 1992, 1993; finance bureaux in Zunyi and Penglai; fieldwork data.

1995:95). This pattern of declining transfers is borne out in all three fieldwork provinces and three of the four fieldwork counties in Shandong and Guizhou.

The effect of declining transfers on a poor county can be seen in the case of Guizhou Province, where subventions from the central government had financed nearly 60 per cent of total budgetary expenditures for the province in the early 1980s. By 1993 they financed less than 20 per cent. As its budget was squeezed, the province not only ended its own subsidies to the lower levels, but by the early 1990s was extracting a surplus from the counties to finance provincial government.

Decentralisation in the presence of large regional disparities tends to exacerbate regional differences (Prud'homme 1994). In China the extent of decentralisation is in fact much greater than indicated by the trends in budgetary data, because of the increasing reliance on off-budget funds to finance government.

Unfortunately, the level and distribution of off-budget funds are notoriously difficult to measure because reporting requirements are less stringent than for budgetary revenues, and because local governments have no incentive to

reveal the full extent of their control over resources. Our best estimate is that resources under the direct control of government and administrative agencies outside the budget may account for 6–7 per cent of GDP, adding about 50 per cent to the budget. In addition, funds under the control of local enterprises are often commandeered for local public finance, including bank loans (Wong et al. 1995; Wong 1997).

The importance of off-budget funds in financing government services and how their presence amplifies regional inequalities were starkly demonstrated by the comparison of service provisions in Shandong and Guizhou in Section II, which showed that Shandong provided much greater services of better quality even though its per capita fiscal expenditures are only about 10 per cent greater than that in Guizhou (Table 1). In-depth review of education and health financing in the ADB study found that off-budget funds are commonly used to supplement salaries of teachers and public health workers, to meet other recurrent expenditures for providing these services, and to provide matching funds that are often required for obtaining capital construction grants from higher level govern-ments. In Shandong extrabudgetary funds and 'self-raised funds' accounted for 42 per cent of the financing for education.

The capacity to raise funds locally to supplement budgetary expenditures is dependent on the vitality of the local economy, including agriculture and TVEs. Across rural China, communities have a very unequal ability to raise these funds. Outside of cities, the major 'tax base' for off-budget funds is TVEs, which are concentrated in coastal provinces and in rural areas adjacent to cities. In 1993, TVEs generated per capita profits of 10 yuan in Guizhou while in Shandong they generated 206 yuan. The uneven distribution of the TVE tax base contributes to differences in both budgetary and off-budget expenditures across rural areas. While rural local governments with developed TVEs may have benefited from fiscal decentralisation, many in poor regions with weak industrial bases are forced to cut back on basic services and/or resort to levying *ad hoc* fees and taxes on farm households.

V. Conclusion

This paper has provided evidence in terms of the disparities between Shandong and Guizhou in the basic services provided by local government and used it to confirm the view that fiscal decentralisation has contributed to very large and growing interregional inequalities in China. Regional disparities in the provision of these services not only directly affect the welfare and living standard of the populace, but also the lower investment in human resources in the poor provinces such as Guizhou is likely to doom their economies to a lower growth path unless corrective action is taken. The solution lies in extending fiscal reform to the lower tiers of government and rationalising intergovernmental expenditure assignments to provide a better match between revenues and expenditure responsibilities. To date, efforts at fiscal reform have focused primarily on central–provincial relations, leaving local budgets to the discretion

of provinces. Attention has also focused mostly on revenue divisions, leaving expenditures to adjust to the availability of funds. Under fiscal pressure, higher level governments have tended to devolve expenditures downwards while reducing transfers as they struggled to balance their own budgets. The result was that through the transition process, mismatches have emerged between revenue and expenditure assignments, with fiscal pressures mounting on local budgets (see also Wong 1991).

Indeed, the entire organisation of rural public finance is urgently in need of strengthening and rationalisation. The present conduct of rural public finance in China has not been fundamentally changed from that of the Maoist period, when, under policies calling for local self reliance, the countryside was expected to take care of itself and not impose financial burdens on the modern sector or government. Under the system of collectivised agriculture, all rural services (health, education, and social welfare) were funded from collective accumulation—that is, from an implicit tax on rural income. To provide supplementary funding, the government also allowed communes and brigades to run some light industries and exempted these rural enterprises from virtually all direct and indirect taxes (Wong 1988). Profits from these enterprises were expected to go to agricultural investment and supporting rural incomes.

This concept of rural public finance is no longer workable because conditions in the rural sector are so fundamentally different today. At present the fiscal system continues to treat the rural sector as a residual claimant of central resources, but this is inappropriate because of the sector's limited revenue capacity, and given the much more difficult tax environment faced by rural governments. With decollectivisation, rural household incomes are far more costly to monitor and tax. The profits of TVEs, the descendants of the former commune and brigade enterprises, no longer flow directly into collective coffers; now, most are privately owned and subject to indirect taxes shared with higher levels of government. The proliferating fees and levies represent township government attempts to capture revenues to finance rural government.

A fundamental reform of local public finance is long overdue. Some scholars have characterised the evolution of local finance as the outcome of reform thinking that has treated local governments much like enterprises in the process of decentralisation, with the same expectation that autonomy is bestowed in exchange for savings in state subsidies (Zhou and Yang 1992:52). This seems an apt description of the process whereby local governments are exhorted to reduce their dependence on budgetary transfers by expanding their tax bases, much as state-owned enterprises are urged to strive to 'turn losses into profits'. Unfortunately, this principle of self-financing for each administrative unit runs against the rationale for the efficient intergovernmental division of revenues and expenditures. It has also led to growing regional disparities through the past one-and-a-half decades, and these disparities are extremely large by international standards.

A fundamental reform of rural public finance must include a clarification of revenue division and tax assignments for different levels of government. While they represented a giant step forward in rationalising the fiscal system, reforms implemented in 1994 are very much incomplete because changes were specified only in the central–provincial division of taxes and revenues. As long as provinces remain as the sole arbiter for revenue assignments for subprovincial levels, the 1994 reform may be imperfectly transmitted downwards. To complete the reform of the fiscal system to suit the needs of a decentralised, market-oriented economy, measures must be introduced to ensure that appropriate revenue and expenditure assignments are extended to the lower levels of government. At the same time, a formal program of intergovernmental transfers must be established, targeted to achieve a few well-defined policy goals, such as poverty alleviation and the achievement of minimum standards in basic services (education, health, social security).

Finally, the present structure of off-budget fees and levies must be reformed, incorporating legitimate ones into the formal system of budgetary accounting. The existence of off-budget finance has substantially reduced both the equity and efficiency of the Chinese fiscal system. First, because off-budget revenues are often levied on the same tax base as budgetary taxes, their distribution is highly correlated with that of budgetary revenues—regions that are rich in budgetary revenues will also have large extrabudgetary resources, and regions that are poor in one will also be poor in the other. Second because off-budget funds are not subject to the sharing with higher levels of government, they are more unequally distributed than budgetary revenues. The growing reliance of the fiscal system on off-budget funding has amplified regional disparities in China. It also follows that the efficiency of tax collection and resource allocation is reduced by the multiple levies on the same tax base. Those fees and levies that are really taxes, that is, those that are not fees for a specific service, should be treated like any other taxes and included in the tax-sharing system. In contrast, genuine user fees should be retained by the local government to finance the services for which they are charged.

Appendix

Refer to original source for appendices.

Note

1. Views in this paper are solely those of the authors and do not necessarily reflect the official position of the Asian Development Bank.

References

Adelman, I., and Sunding, D., 1987.'Economic Policy and Income Distribution in China', *Journal of Comparative Economics*, 11:444–61.

Denny, D.L., 1991. 'Provincial Economic Differences Diminished in the Decade of reform', in *China's Economic Dilemmas in the 1990s: The Problems of Reform, Modernisation, and Interdependence*, Joint Economic Committee Congress of the United States, Washington, DC.

Guizhou Statistical Bureau , 1994. *Statistical Yearbook of Guizhou 1994*, China Statistical Publishing House, Beijing.

Hare, D., 1994. 'Rural Nonagricultural Activities and their Impact on the Distribution of Income: Evidence from Farm Households in Southern China', *China Economic Review*, 5(1):59–82.

Hebei Statistical Bureau, 1994. *Hebei jingji nianjian 1994* (Hebei Economic and Statistical Yearbook 1994), China Statistical Publishing House, Beijing.

Hu, J., 1995. 'The Imperative of Shanghai Hospitals Serving the Whole Country', *Shanghai Statistics*, 4, 27–8.

Khan, A.R., Griffin, K., Riskin, C. and Zhao, R., 1992. 'Household Income and its Distribution in China', *The China Quarterly*, 132(12):1029–61.

Lardy, N.R., 1978. *Economic Growth and Distribution in China*, New York, Cambridge University Press.

Lu, L., Hongsheng, H., and Ling, G., 1994. '1990 nian zhongguo fen sheng jianlue shengming biao'(Abridged life tables by provinces in China in 1990), *Renkou Yanjiu (Population Research)*, 3:52–9.

Ministry of Public Health, 1994. *Chinese Health Statistical Digest 1993*.

Population Census Office (ed.), 1985. *1982 Population Census of China*, China Statistical Publishing House, Beijing.

——, 1993. *Tabulation on the 1990 Population Census of the People's Republic of China*, China Statistical Publishing House, Beijing.

Prud'homme, R., 1994. 'On the Dangers of Decentralisation', World Bank Policy Research Working Paper, February, Washington.

Rozelle, S., 1994. 'Rural Industrialisation and Increasing Inequality: Emerging Patterns in China's Reform Economy', *Journal of Comparative Economics*, 19(3)62–91.

Shah, A., 1991.'Perspectives on Intergovemmental Fiscal Relations', World Bank Country Economics Department Working Paper No. 726, July.

Shandong Statistical Bureau, 1992. *Statistical Yearbook of Shandong 1992*, China, Statistical Publishing House, Beijing.

——, 1993. *Statistical Yearbook of Shandong 1993*, China Statistical Publishing House, Beijing.

——, 1994. *Statistical Yearbook of Shandong 1994*, China Statistical Publishing House, Beijing.

Sicular, T., 1991. 'China's Agricultural Policy During the Reform Period', in *China's Economic Dilemmas in the 1990s: The Problems of Reform, Modernisation and Interdependence*, Joint Economic Committee Congress of the United States, Washington, DC.

State Education Commission, 1993. *Report on the Development of Education Funds in China*, Tertiary Education Publishing House, Beijing.

State Statistical Bureau, 1987. *Statistical Yearbook of China 1987*, China Statistical Publishing House, Beijing.

——, 1994. *Statistical Yearbook of China 1994*, China Statistical Publishing House, Beijing.

——, 1995. *Statistical Yearbook of China 1995*, China Statistical Publishing House, Beijing.

Tsui, K.Y., 1991. 'China's Regional Inequality, 1952–1985', *Journal of Comparative Economics*, 15:1–21.

——, 1993. 'Decomposition of China's Regional Inequalities', *Journal of*

Comparative Economics, 17(3),600–27.

West, L.A., 1995. *Regional Economic Variation and Basic Education in Rural China*, Economic Development Institute of the World Bank, Washington, DC.

Wong, C.P.W., 1988. 'Interpreting Rural Industrial Growth in the Post-Mao Period', *Modern China*, 14(l):3–30, January.

——, 1991. 'Central-Local Relations in an Era of Fiscal Decline: The Paradox of Fiscal Decentralisation in Post-Mao China', *The China Quarterly*, 128, December.

——, 1992. 'Fiscal Reform and Local Industrialisation: The Problematic Sequencing of Reform in Post-Mao China', *Modern China*, 18(2):197–227, April.

—— (ed.), 1997. *Financing Local Government in the People's Republic of China*, Hong Kong, published by Oxford University Press for the Asian Development Bank.

——, Heady, C. and Woo, W.T., 1995. *Fiscal Management and Economic Reform in the People's Republic of China*, Hong Kong, published by Oxford University Press for the Asian Development Bank.

World Bank, 1985. *China: Long-Term Issues and Options*, Johns Hopkins University, Baltimore, MD.

——, 1990. *China: Revenue Mobilisation and Tax Policy*, Washington, DC.

——, 1993. *The East Asian Miracle: Economic Growth and Public Policy*, Oxford University Press, New York.

Yang, D.L., 1990. 'Patterns of China's Regional Development Strategy', *The China Quarterly*, 122, 23–57.

Zhou, X. and Yang, Z., 1992. *Zhongguo caishui tizhide wwntiyu chulu* (Issues and Solutions for China's Fiscal and Tax Systems), Tianjin's People's Press, Tianjin.

22 Wage Determination and Occupational Attainment in the Rural Industrial Sector of China

R.G. Gregory and Xin Meng

I. Introduction

As Eastern European countries struggle to transform their economies the process of moving successfully from a planned to a market economy has become a major challenge. In this paper we analyse some labour market aspects of a very successful reform process, the dismantling of centralised controls of the Chinese rural industrial sector. This economic history is particularly interesting because it demonstrates the considerable economic success that can be achieved by the combination of extensive product market liberalisation and minimal liberalisation of the labour market.[1]

Deregulation of the Chinese rural industrial sector began in the early 1980s when the central, provincial, and local governments of China first deregulated the market for most rural industrial products so that township and village enterprises (TVPs) could produce whatever they wished.[2] Prices could be set freely and products sold anywhere in China. This deregulation was also applied to material inputs.[3]

Capital and labour inputs were treated differently. Capital quotas were allocated and controlled by a process of overall allocation from the central government to each province and then by the provincial governments to each county. The counties then allocated capital quotas to the TVP firms. The TVP authorities, however, could use enterprise profits (after central and local taxes) to augment local capital requirements without approval of higher level authorities.

Central and provincial governments also withdrew from labour market regulation but three important controls were exercised by local government. First, labour inflows and outflows from the community were originally heavily regulated by the household registration system and then restricted by community authorities. Second, the *level* of employment for each firm owned by the community was usually determined by the community authority and not the firm's managers. Community authorities could effectively overman enterprises to absorb local labour or underman enterprises and leave workers in the fields. Third, community authorities

Reprinted with permission. R.G. Gregory and Xin Meng, 1995. 'Wage determination and occupational attainment in the rural industrial sector of China', *Journal of Comparative Economics*, 21:353–74 (with minor editing).

usually chose which workers would be assigned to particular firms. Each of these controls has gradually weakened but is still very strong. Labour is now marginally more mobile across geographic areas and firms increasingly more flexible in hiring labour.[4]

There was one important labour market reform, however, which was introduced early in the reform process. As a general rule, managers of each enterprise could determine the wage structure of the firm and who should be paid different amounts.[5] In 1978 the TVP wage system consisted largely of a mixed working-point system, adopted from agriculture, where payment points were related to gender and seniority. There was little attempt to relate wages directly to individual productivity or to use the wage structure to generate efficiency. Gradually the process moved toward a 'wage-link-up-with-profit' system whereby in addition to a wage workers received bonuses calculated from the overall performance of the firm.

The determinants and structure of the non-bonus component of earnings, however, is not well documented and unraveling some of the payment practices is an important contribution of this paper. For example, did the TVP sector generate a wage structure similar to that observed in firms in a western market economy, or did social, political, and other community objectives play an important part? Do variables, assumed to measure productivity in market economies, such as education and years of experience, influence individual wages in the TVP sector?[6]

II. Data and Results from a Basic Human Capital Model

The data were collected from a survey carried out jointly by the Institute of Economics of the Chinese Academy of Social Sciences and the World Bank in 1986–87.[7] The data are taken from one of the survey instruments—the Workers Survey Questionnaire—which was undertaken in 49 of the 121 sample firms from the TVP

sector.[8] There are 1174 observations on individual employees, but due to missing values the sample has been reduced to 1060 observations. In this study the analysis is confined to a sample of between 400 and 529 male workers, depending on the exact set of variables chosen for analysis. There are four counties in the sample: Wuxi county in Jiangsu province, Jieshou county in Anhui province, Shangrao county in Jiangxi province, and Nanhai county in Guangdong province.

These counties represent very different levels of economic development. When economic development is proceeding quickly from a low wage level, the variance of wages tends to increase across geographic areas and in China this phenomenon is exacerbated by strict control of labour mobility. In regions where demand for labour is high relative to supply, real and nominal wages have increased quickly and, where labour is in abundant supply, wages have increased more slowly.

There are, however, insufficient data observations to allow us to study each region separately[9] so the data have been combined and regional dummy variables added to each regression. The effect of regional differences on wage determination in the TVP sector is an important issue requiring separate study. In our sample, however, there is no simple relationship between per capita earnings in each region and the average level of education, firm tenure, or labour market experience. For example, Nanhai, with a per capita income level three times that of Jieshou, has a work force with 2 years less education and only 2 years more labour force experience.[10] The ranking of regional wage levels in our sample is in close accord with raw data of per capita income of rural population taken from the State Statistical Bureau.[11]

The survey collected the usual range of variables[12] used within a human capital wage equation and the regression model can be expressed as[13]

$$\ln(w) = a + b_1 S + b_2 OJ + b_3 OJ^2 + b_4 FT + b_5 FT^2 + b_6 RE + u, \qquad (1)$$

348

where w is daily wage; S is years of schooling; OJ is other job experience defined as total experience minus firm tenure; OJ^2 is other job experience squared; FT is firm-specific tenure; FT^2 is firm-specific tenure squared; and RE is a vector of regional dummies.

The sample size is quite small and very little is known about wage setting in the TVP sector. Consequently, we have adopted the methodology of reporting results for the data grouped together and then the sample is subdivided in various ways and findings are reported for each subdivision. As a result judgments as to the wage setting process change as each new regression on a different data subdivision provides new information.

The results for various specifications of Equation 1 are reported in Table 1.[14] The equations perform well. The adjusted R^2 is comparable with similar models applied to market economies but a significant proportion of the explanatory power is produced by regional dummy variables which indicate significant variations in the wage level across regions.

The results from the experience variables in Column 1 are in accord with the human capital model. The return to firm tenure is positive and significant—about 2.5 to 3 per cent per year over most of the first decade of work—and the usual inverted U-shaped relationship is evident. The return to other-job-experience is about the same. The source of the labour market experience seems not to matter and there seems to be no special advantage from firm-specific training.

In Column 2 other job experience is subdivided into other non-agricultural (ONAJ) and agricultural experience (AEXP).[15] In each instance the coefficients are statistically significant and the pattern is as expected. Within each experience category the return to experience is again about 2–3 per cent per annum during the early years.

There is no special advantage from accumulating experience in another firm relative to agricultural experience. The effects of agricultural and non-agricultural experience are

about the same and not statistically different from the effect of firm tenure. This result is surprising in that one should not expect a close relationship between wages in industrial firms and agricultural experience.

It is noticeable that the schooling coefficient is not statistically significant.[16] Given the emphasis that the development literature and some modern growth theories place on education as a force for economic development, this is an interesting result.[17] There may be a number of explanations for the insignificance of education. Many jobs are unskilled and perhaps education does not increase productivity. In addition, education may not be used as a screening device as the firm does not usually freely hire workers.[18] In this sample at least 40 per cent of workers were assigned to the firm by community authorities, often to achieve income distribution objectives across families.

Different occupational groups

The results listed in column 3 show that occupation has a major impact on wage and indicate that being a staff member increases the daily wage by 14 per cent, *ceteris paribus*. To pursue the role of education and experience in more depth the total male sample was subdivided into staff and workers.[19] The staff category includes shift leaders, operational personnel, technical personnel, ordinary staff, and middle level staff. The estimated equations are shown in Table 2.[20] Schooling remains an insignificant variable with a negative sign for staff and workers but the role of experience changes significantly across groups.[21,22]

Workers seem to gain significant wage increases as firm tenure lengthens but are not rewarded for agriculture experience. Experience at other firms contributes to wages. These results accord with our earlier conjectures as to the relationship between industrial wages and agricultural experience that might be expected in western economies.

For staff the link between wages and experience seems to work through other job

Table 1   Models of wage determination, China's TVP sector, 1985

	Models		
	1 ($n = 529$)	2 ($n = 457$)	3 ($n = 525$)
Constant	1.016 (10.69)	1.068 (9.89)	1.089 (11.44)
Schooling	0.011 (1.63)	0.007 (0.85)	-0.0002 (-0.003)
Other job experiences (OJ)			
OJ	0.029 (5.48)	(a)	0.027 (5.12)
OJ^2	-0.0006 (-3.83)	(a)	-0.006 (-3.89)
Firm tenure (FT)			
FT	0.028 (2.80)	0.032 (2.91)	0.021 (2.15)
FT^2	-0.0007 (1.93)	-0.0009 (-2.15)	-0.06 (-1.61)
Other non-agricultural experience (ONAJ)			
ONAJ	(a)	0.023 (3.76)	(a)
ONAJ^2	(a)	-0.0005 (-2.91)	(a)
Agricultural experience (AEXP)			
AEXP	(a)	0.025 (3.18)	(a)
AEXP^2	(a)	-0.0005 (-2.02)	(a)
Occupational dummy	(a)	(a)	0.144 (3.53)
County dummy			
Jieshou	-0.274 (-6.28)	-0.309 (6.36)	-0.265 (-6.16)
Shangrao	-0.441 (-8.19)	-0.495 (-8.77)	-0.427 (-7.72)
Nanhai	0.529 (7.70)	0.481 (6.61)	0.524 (7.54)
Breusch-Pagan χ^2	47.02 (8)	47.64 (10)	55.44 (9)
Adjusted R^2	0.34	0.34	0.37

Note: Technology statistics are presented in parentheses. OJ is other labour market experience, excluding firm tenure; (a) denotes variable not entered. Breusch-Pagan χ^2 tests for heteroscedasticity. The degrees of freedom for the χ^2 statistics are presented in parentheses.

experience, particularly agricultural experience, and *not* from an increase in firm-specific tenure. There are a number of possible interpretations of this result. The community authority normally assigned leaders of agricultural production teams or brigades to be management staff. The rank and starting wages of these leaders probably reflected the length of time they led the agricultural production team. Once in the firm pay increases might be related to firm performance and not tenure. In addition, the community often assigned to a new firm management or technical staff from an old firm. If the wage level depended on firm tenure, staff would be reluctant to move.[23] Finally, management skills learned in agriculture and other sectors might be easily transferred to a new enterprise in a way that workers' agricultural skills are not.

Piece and time-rate workers

The results to this point indicate that important variables that influence the relative wages of workers and staff are all variations of job experience. Since the education variables are not significant the question arises as to whether the wage equations capture productivity relationships or socially determined rules of payment. The form of payment adopted by the firm may throw some light on this question. Of the total sample, 40 per cent of employees are paid by piece-rate, which can be considered a direct measure of labour productivity.

The results for piece and time-rate employees are shown in Table 3.[24] Once again schooling is statistically insignificant for both groups, a result that holds no matter which specification of experience is adopted.[25] As piece-rate earnings may be regarded as a direct measure of productivity, it appears that the earlier conjecture, that education does not affect labour productivity in the TVP sector, may be correct.[26] On the assumption that piece-rate payment is a good measure of labour productivity the similarity of the coefficient pattern for the two groups suggests perhaps that time-rate employees are also paid according to their labour productivity

unless piece rates are set for each individual to vary by experience.

III. Institutional Change and the Role of Education

If there is rapid change the analysis of cross-sectional data may be misleading as an indication of the underlying economic structure. This might be particularly important because of the rapid growth and institutional change of the TVP sector. The year 1983 was a turning point for the TVP sector in terms of institutional change when *the production responsibility system* was introduced to most of the township or village-owned firms. The new system gave the enterprises more power over managerial decision-making, including a greater freedom in hiring labour.

In the worker's survey questionnaire workers were asked how they gained their jobs. There are roughly three groups: (i) assigned to the job by the local community authorities; (ii) found their job by own effort (through examination); and (iii) introduced to the job by relatives or friends. Although the data are drawn from a 1985 cross section it is still possible to comment on institutional transformation in the TVP labour market if we combine this information with individual's work tenure. Figure 1 shows the association between years of tenure and the proportion of employees assigned to jobs by local governments, and the proportion who obtained employment through their own effort. We refer to the two groups as non-market and market groups, respectively.[27] This a crude approximation but we think of those who find jobs by their own efforts as being more like western workers in that firms are choosing to hire them. Among people with tenure of 1 year, about 17 per cent were assigned to jobs, while among those with tenure of 8 years, about 70 per cent were assigned. The proportion of those who found employment through their own efforts is 48 per cent among the 1-year tenure group and 20 per cent among the 8-year tenure group. There is a third group who found jobs by being 'introduced by relatives

Table 2   **Wage determination by occupational groups[a]**

	Model 1		Model 2	
	Workers ($n = 271$)	Staff ($n = 262$)	Workers ($n = 230$)	Staff ($n = 230$)
Constant	0.967 (7.56)	1.466 (9.96)	1.012 (7.23)	1.494 (9.22)
Schooling	-0.009 (1.63)	0.009 (0.85)	-0.014 (-0.003)	-0.003
Other job experiences (OJ)				
OJ	0.015 (1.89)	0.031 (4.66)	(a)	(a)
OJ^2	-0.0002 (-0.77)	-0.0007 (-3.96)	(a)	(a)
Firm-specific tenure (FT)				
FT	0.049 (3.47)	0.0002 (0.02)	0.057 (3.86)	-0.002 (-0.13)
FT^2	-0.0017 (-2.91)	-0.0001 (0.23)	-0.02 (-3.39)	0.0002 (0.32)
Other non-agric. exp. (ONAJ)				
ONAJ	(a)	(a)	0.024 (2.82)	0.014 (1.66)
ONAJ^2	(a)	(a)	-0.0005 (-1.92)	-0.0004 (-1.20)
Agric. exp (AEXP)				
AEXP	(a)	(a)	0.012 (1.03)	0.026 (2.92)
AEXP^2	(a)	(a)	-0.0002 (-0.35)	-0.0007 (-2.36
County dummies				
Jieshou	-0.219 (-3.70)	-0.299 (-4.96)	-0.212 (-3.21)	-0.347 (-5.35)
Shangrao	-0.222 (-2.87)	-0.648 (-7.80)	-0.256 (-2.96)	0.694 (-8.07)
Nanhai	0.821 (8.22)	0.211 (2.93)	0.774 (7.35)	0.190 (2.44)
Breusch-Pagan χ^{2b}	36.31 (8)	7.05 (8)	29.96 (10)	9.21 (10)
Adjusted R^2	0.41	0.33	0.40	0.35

Note:
[a] For notes to table, see Table 1.
[b] The critical χ^2 value at the 5 per cent significance level for $n = 8$ is $\chi^2 = 15.51$: for $n = 10$, $\chi^2 = 18.31$.

Table 3   **Wage determination for piece and time-rate employees**[a]

| | Model 1 | | Model 2 | |
	Piece-rate ($n = 166$)	Time-rate ($n = 363$)	Piece-rate ($n = 147$)	Time-rate ($n = 310$)
Constant	1.041 (7.12)	1.011 (8.20)	1.038 (6.78)	1.012 (7.42)
Schooling	0.010 (0.91)	0.013 (1.54)	0.0094 (0.58)	0.010 (0.91)
Other job experiences (OJ)				
OJ	0.026 (2.53)	0.033 (5.38)		
OJ²	-0.0006 (-2.19)	-0.0006 (-3.65)		
Firm-specific tenure (FT)				
FT	0.045 (2.84)	0.019 (1.42)	0.05 (3.1)	-0.024 (1.56)
FT²	-0.0012 (-1.66)	-0.0004 (-0.89)	-0.001 (-2.0)	0.0006 (-1.19)
Other non-agri.exp. (ONAJ)				
ONAJ			0.026 (2.45)	0.025 (3.39)
OJAJ²			-0.001 (2.7)	-0.0005 (-2.50)
Agri.exp (AEXP)				
AEXP			0.031 (2.14)	0.027 (2.87)
AEXP²			-0.001 (-1.64)	-0.0006 (-1.83)
County dummies				
Jieshou	-0.339 (-5.01)	-0.261 (-4.60)	-0.356 (-5.30)	-0.287 (-4.60)
Shangrao	-0.381 (-5.10)	-0.591 (-8.18)	-0.441 (-5.40)	0.621 (-8.40)
Nanhai	0.524 (4.01)	0.521 (6.60)	0.448 (3.61)	0.471 (5.57)
Breusch-Pagan χ^{2b}	44.60 (8)	25.03 (8)	49.3 (10)	27.9 (10)
Adjusted R^2	0.36	0.34	0.36	0.34

Note:
[a] For notes to table, see Table 1.

[b] The critical χ^2 values for $n = 8$ and $n = 10$ at the 5 per cent significance level are the same as those shown for Table 2. In this table the standard errors in all four regressions are corrected for heteroscedasticity.

Figure 1   Institutional change of the TVP employment system

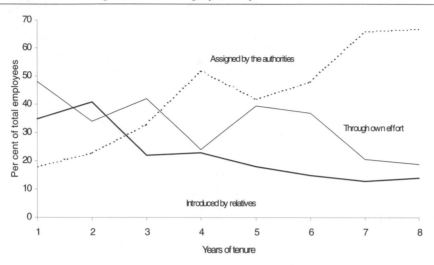

or friends.' It is not clear where this group belonged so they are excluded from the analysis.[28]

Table 4 lists the results from applying the basic human capital model to the market and non-market employees to see whether the TVP sector is moving toward a western-style wage determination process.[29] Other non-agricultural experience and agricultural experience impact in much the same way as in earlier results and exert a similar positive influence on earnings of each group. Earnings increase by approximately 3 to 4 per cent for each extra year of experience over the first 10 years. The effect of firm tenure, however, seems to be important only for the market group, that is, those who found their own jobs and who have been the predominant group among new hires. Once the non-market group is assigned to a firm, and earnings are set on the basis of previous experience, earnings do not seem to increase with further accumulation of experience as measured by firm tenure.

Most interestingly, from our viewpoint, is that education has a significantly different impact on wage determination for the market and non-market groups and for the first time is significant. Education delivers a positive rate of return to the market group of 4 per cent for an extra year of schooling.

To assess whether this education return is related to productivity we again have recourse to the method of payment data. We interact the piece rate dummy with other variables in Model 1 for both market and non-market groups[30] and the results suggest that the wage determination patterns for piece and time-rate groups are similar within both the market and the non-market groups. If piece-rate payment is a good measure of labour productivity, these results suggest that education has a significant impact on labour productivity for the piece-rate sample and, by inference, the education effect for the market non-piece-rate sample reflects the labour productivity effect. For the non-market group education is not related to productivity as measured by piece-rate earnings and not rewarded in the wage equation.

Why might there be such a difference in the role of education? Perhaps the underlying technological processes of work undertaken by each group are different. Workers involved with higher levels of technology need to be more educated compared with those who undertake

Table 4   **Wage determination for market and non-market oriented employees[a]**

	Model 1			Model 2		
	Market (n = 182)	Non market (n = 229)	Difference (n = 411)	Non market (n = 153)	Market (n = 206)	Difference (n = 359)
Constant	0.689 (4.24)	1.910 (8.90)	-0.603 (-2.69)	0.634 (3.23)	1.416 (9.15)	-0.782 (-3.13)
Schooling	0.039 (3.13)	-0.007 (0.68)	0.046 (2.80)	-0.041 (2.64)	-0.007 (0.61)	0.048 (2.46)
Other job experiences (OJ)						
OJ	0.038 (3.13)	0.029 (3.56)	0.009 (0.63)			
OJ²	-0.0007 (-1.79)	-0.0008 (-3.20)	0.0003 (0.08)			
Firm-specific tenure (FT)						
FT	0.039 (2.05)	0.007 (0.51)	0.031 (1.31)	-0.046 (2.04)	-0.005 (-0.29)	0.051 (1.83)
FT²	-0.0007 (-0.86)	-0.0003 (-0.47)	-0.0004 (-0.45)	-0.0008 (0.94)	0.0001 (0.17)	-0.0009 (-0.86)
Other non-agricultural experience (ONAJ)						
ONAJ				0.057 (3.47)	0.020 (1.62)	0.036 (1.76)
ONAJ²				-0.002 (-2.30)	-0.0009 (-1.59)	-0.0009 (-0.94)
Agricultural experience (AEXP)						
AEXP				0.029 (2.14)	0.022 (2.23)	0.006 (0.39)
AEXP²				-0.0003 (-0.63)	-0.0007 (-2.23)	0.0005 (0.89)
County dummy						
JS	-0.263 (-3.61)	-0.185 (-3.12)	-0.078 (-0.84)	-0.300 (-3.64)	-0.234 (-3.92)	-0.067 (-0.66)
SR	-0.382 (-3.12)	-0.496 (-6.97)	0.113 (-0.89)	-0.465 (-3.96)	-0.524 (-7.33)	0.059 (0.43)
NH	0.323 (2.78)	0.690 (6.72)	-0.368 (-2.28)	0.169 (1.27)	0.671 (6.35)	-0.503 (-2.96)
Breusch-Pagan χ^2	6.93 (8)	23.9 (8)	31.9 (10)	18.5 (10)	22.1 (10)	40.9 (21)
Adjusted R²	0.30	0.39	0.37	0.35	0.40	0.39

Note:
[a] The results listed in the Difference columns are the interaction terms between a dummy variable for the market and non-market groups and all other variables in a pooled data analysis.

simpler jobs. Perhaps the gradual liberalisation of the TVP labour market has allowed firms with more complicated technologies to freely hire employees according to their education level. Education therefore has a significant impact on labour productivity in these firms and productivity is rewarded. Firms in which the technology is relatively simple remain with the old job assignment system and education is not productivity enhancing. These firms probably pay employees according to labour productivity, which is related to experience but education does not contribute to output.

The market group comprises 40 per cent of the total sample and the return to education is quite low, perhaps 4–5 per cent. There is no evidence of a positive rate of return to education for the remaining proportion of the sample. Why then would a rural worker invest in further education? Does education play no labour market role for the non-market group?

IV. Education and Occupational Attainment

It is usual to explain an individual's occupational attainment as a function of the employers' willingness to hire that person (labour demand) and the individual's desire to work in a particular occupation (labour supply) (Brown et al. 1980). In the Chinese rural labour market it is not clear that this framework will apply. Demand and supply determinants may not be very important due to the scarcity of employment positions in the TVP sector (the positions are rationed and therefore individuals are not on the supply curve) and the widespread use of assignment by community authorities during most of the period (firms may not be on their demand curve).

To investigate occupational assignment we apply a multinomial logit model to explain the probability of individual i working in occupation j,

$$p_{ij} = prob(y_i = oc_j) = e^{x_i'\beta_k} / \sum_{k=1}^{J} e^{x_i'\beta_k},$$

$$i = 1, ..., N, j = 1, ..., J, \qquad (2)$$

where N is the sample size; J is the number of occupational groups; and x_i is a vector of exogenous variables affecting supply and demand factors.

This model enables us to judge whether education plays a significant role in occupational assignment. The independent variables used to estimate the occupational assignment equation include education, other job experience, firm tenure, and three regional dummies.

As a first step we analyse occupational attainment to the worker or staff category for the market (non-assigned) and non-market (assigned) groups. Then the staff group is further disaggregated into five categories (shift leaders, operational personnel, technical personnel, ordinary staff, and middle level staff).

The results of the binomial logit model for the total sample and for market and non-market groups separately are reported in Table 5. The workers group is used as a reference category. Each of the three human capital variables—education, other job experience, and firm tenure—are statistically significant determinants of occupational assignment for the total sample of employees and similar results are obtained for both the market and non-market oriented groups.

Occupational assignment in the TVP sector seems to operate in a similar way as in the west. People with more education, more experience, and a longer period of firm tenure are more likely to become senior staff. There is no obvious difference between the occupational assignment process in each sector. Market and non-market sectors seem to operate by the same rules. Finally, education is important for the occupational assignment of both groups even though it does not directly impact on the earnings of the non-market group.

Schooling and experience are not continuous variables. To measure the impact of change in each of the variables on the probability of becoming a staff member we calculate the effect of each additional year of education, firm tenure, and other job experience on the increase in the probability of being in the staff group[31] and list the results in Table 6.

These results show that each additional year of education increases the probability of being in the staff group by 12 per cent, which seems to be a large return in terms of status and position. Increases in firm tenure and other job experience are relatively unimportant.

The model of occupational attainment is generalised and applied to six levels of occupation: workers, shift leaders, operational personnel, technical personnel, ordinary staff, and middle level staff.[32] The results for the total sample and market and non-market groups confirm that the process of occupational attainment is similar in both sectors and education is a significant determinant of each group's occupational attainment and exhibits relatively high t values. By and large the results show that the higher the position the more important is the role that education plays.[33]

Table 5 **Binomial logit estimates of male occupational attainment** (0 = workers, 1 = staff)

Variables	Total sample	Market	Non-market
Constant	-5.359	-5.599	-5.125
	(-8.17)	(-5.26)	(-6.11)
EDU	0.470	0.503	0.43
	(8.29)	(5.58)	(5.94)
OJ	0.093	0.12	0.085
	(6.02)	(4.26)	(4.47)
FT	0.098	0.154	0.086
	(4.28)	(3.22)	(3.16)
JS	-0.288	-0.721	-0.697
	(-1.03)	(-1.77)	(-1.15)
SR	-0.166	-1.992	0.641
	(-0.45)	(-2.75)	(1.41)
NH	0.428	0.252	0.337
	(1.19)	(0.37)	(0.80)

Note: For total sample, n = 420, maximum likelihood is 231.05, χ^2 = 119.2, pseudo-R^2 = 0.205. For the market oriented group, n = 192, maximum likelihood is 96.06 χ^2 = 72.36, pseudo-R^2 = 0.274. For the non-market oriented group, n = 228, maximum likelihood is 132.32, χ^2 = 62.5, pseudo-R^2 = 0.19. The formula for the χ^2 measure is χ^2 = 2(ln L_r-ln L), where ln L_r and ln L are the log-likelihood at the maximised value with the constant term only and the log-likelihood at the maximised value with all regressors in the model, respectively (Greene 1990). The formula for the pseudo-R^2 measure is R^2 = 1-(lnL$_r$/ln L) (McFadden 1974).

Table 6 **Impact of additional year of education and experience on probability of being in the staff group**

	Mean probability	Add one more year	Increase in probability
Education	0.53	0.65	0.12
Firm tenure	0.53	0.56	0.03
Other-job-experience	0.53	0.56	0.03

The coefficients for the multinomial logit model are difficult to interpret but they suggest the following.[34] Education plays the most important role in determining whether a person can be a technical staff member. People with more education are more likely to be in a higher level of management. The longer the length of other job experience the more likely a person is to be a marketing staff member (operational personnel). Those with longer other job experience probably have more widespread business contacts, at least within the local area, which are very useful for marketing.

Since the results are similar for the market and non-market groups it might be concluded that the process of occupational assignment has not changed very much during economic reform. Since education affects the occupational assignment in a similar way in both sectors, but does not affect earnings in the non-market sector, there is a presumption that the TVP sector has used education as a screening device for occupational attainment in both market and non-market sectors.

For the market group therefore the effect of education seems consistent. More education brings more earnings and a higher occupational level. For the non-market group education brings no increase in earnings but a higher occupation. Thus the question becomes whether the impact of education on occupational attainment leads to higher earning by this route. To investigate the interaction between education, occupation, and earnings for the market and non-market groups separately we estimated Heckman's (1979) two-stage model with the correction for the endogeneity of occupational attainment. Thus we estimate a logit equation for occupational attainment and include the Mills ratio (λ) in the wage equation. The results suggest that for the market group the occupational level is significantly positively correlated with individual's wage level while for the non-market group the relationship is not statistically significant.

These results indicate that although education is used as a criterion for occupational attainment in the non-market group, a higher occupational level does not bring higher earnings. Hence, education has neither a direct nor an indirect (through occupation) effect on wage determination for the non-market group.

Why then did people invest in education when there appears to be no return in the non-market group? And furthermore, what is the motivation for people to seek promotion? Perhaps for non-wage benefits. Being a staff member means relief from heavy labour, the acquisition of status, and an enhanced ability to obtain employment for children and relatives. One question in the Questionnaire for Directors of TVP firms asks: 'How many of your family members are there in your firm?' The survey results show that on average directors have 2.65 family members employed in their own firm and if we consider that a director will have a business relationship with many other firms it might be possible to arrange a position for relatives in these other firms. The number of relatives employed in the TVP sector because of the Directors' status could be even larger.[35]

V. Concluding Remarks

Very little is known as to the details of the remarkably successful growth of TVP firms. This is particularly so with regard to the operation of their labour markets. We have begun to explore some of the features of this unique labour market with its emphasis on job security and job assignment by authorities outside the firm. Our emphasis has been on the wage-setting process, which, in general, has been under the control of the firm, and we have reached the following conclusions.

First, unlike most industrial and developing countries, educational background, on average, seems to play an insignificant role in individual wage determination. If, however, the 1985 sample of workers is divided into those assigned jobs and those who find jobs of their own accord then this latter and more recent group of workers seems to be earning a positive rate of return to education but the return seems to be very low.

Second, a number of different relationships between individual wages and the experience of the employees have been found. In general, wages increase with experience. The payment system, however, differs for staff and workers. For staff, experience in the firm seems less important than it is for workers. It seems as though payments to staff may be related to their position in earlier jobs in both the agricultural and TVP sectors. The system of staff payments seems to be a mixture of elements of the old agricultural leadership system, and how that relates to seniority positions in the TVP sector, and a new market-oriented payment system which relates management wages to skills teamed in previous non-agricultural jobs.

Third, for all workers, it seems that the wage determination pattern is productivity-related, as the wage determination pattern for time-rate workers is similar to that of piece-rate workers. This correlation holds both for those who were assigned jobs and those who found employment by their own efforts.

Fourth, except for the impact of education, the human capital model seems to work quite well for wage determination in the Chinese rural industrial sector.

Fifth, occupational attainment, unlike earnings, is consistently related to education levels, which suggests that the relationship between education and status and the non-wage benefits that status can deliver are particularly important. These relationships seem more stable than the wage determination process and do not differ between those assigned jobs and those who find employment by their own efforts.

To conclude, we have been working within data limitations but understanding the evolution of labour markets as they move from heavily regulated markets to those with greater degrees of freedom is important. We have been fortunate to gain access to a unique source of data for the Chinese TVP sector.

Acknowledgement

We thank Paul Miller for his valuable comments at various stages of this study.

Appendix

Refer to original source for appendices.

Notes

1. For a broader view of the process see McMillan and Naughton (1992).
2. The township was previously a commune and is now the lowest level of Chinese government hierarchy. The population of a typical township is 15,000 to 30,000.
3. A fuller discussion of the deregulation process can be found in Byrd and Lin (1990).
4. For detailed discussion of the characteristics of rural labour market in 1985 see Meng (1992).
5. In the 1985 data used in this study, 60 per cent of firms had decision-making power over wage determination.
6. Theoretical answers to these questions are not immediately obvious. For example, employment and dismissal were largely controlled by local community authorities and therefore the wage need not be used to attract employees or to encourage them to stay with the firm. Where there is no labour market mobility would efficiency wage theory with its emphasis on the threat of dismissal be at all relevant?
7. Xin Meng was employed by the Institute of Economics, Chinese Academy of Social Sciences and worked on the project. Most of the data have been brought to Australia.
8. The sample includes township and/or village-owned enterprises as well as a small number of privately owned enterprises. The extent of community (township or village) control varies by region and enterprise as does the level of economic development. A fuller discussion of the project can be found in Byrd and Lin (1990).
9. The number of observations are 235, 150, 88, and 58 for Wuxi, Jieshou, Nanhai, and Shangrao, respectively. When we subdivide the sample into piece and time-rate employees on staff and worker groups the sample is further reduced. Regression on the small samples for each region tended to be unsuccessful.
10. The means of each variable classified by region are presented in Table A of Appendix A.
11. In 1985, per capita income of the rural

population in Wuxi was 754 yuan. Nanhai was 36 per cent higher, Jieshou 60 per cent lower, and Shangrao 57 per cent lower (Svejnar and Woo 1990).

12. Statistical characteristics of the variables are shown in Appendix A. Most data are measured in the usual way but some variables require comment. For example, some of the work experience data are not directly available from the Workers Survey Questionnaire. Data exist for an individual's age, the length of employment in a given firm (firm-specific tenure), and the length of time spent working in non-agricultural jobs. Total experience variables are constructed by adopting Mincer's approach (Mincer 1974) which is to measure total experience, j, by $j = A - S - 7$, where A is age, S is the years of schooling, and 7 is the number of years before schooling begins. Agricultural work experience is obtained by subtracting total non-agricultural work experience, which is available in the survey, from total experience. Other non-agricultural experience (non-agricultural experience outside the current job) is obtained by subtracting firm-specific tenure from the total length of job experience in the non-agricultural sector. Negative values of other job experience, other non-agricultural experience, and agricultural experience are sometimes obtained. These observations are excluded from the regressions. An alternative procedure which involves setting negative values of experience equal to zero does not lead to any material changes in the results.

13. Some other variables which appeared to be important determinants of wage in a market economy such as number of children and marital status, were also included in the model. However, they do not appear to be significant in any of the model specifications.

14. A diagnostic test for the ordinary least-squares results usually reveals considerable heteroscedasticity. Where applicable White's consistent estimator of the covariance matrix is used (Greene 1990).

15. Most workers moved directly from agriculture to their current firm of employment. Managers and senior staff are often moved by the authorities to help set up new firms.

16. This result is consistent with that of Gelb (1990). It is also consistent with the belief of employees:

only about 2 per cent of employees in the sample believe that education is an important variable for wage determination (Meng 1992). Byron and Manaloto (1990), however, find a positive rate of return to education for urban workers.

17. The insignificance of the education variable does not seem to be a result of the way in which it is measured. Experimentation with a series of dummy variables for different levels of schooling did not make the education effect significant.

18. Education may be an important screening device at the university graduate level. For university graduates and above, there is a regulation that they should be assigned to jobs as technical or management staff and their wage level has to be higher than that of workers. This effect can be detected in Section IV when we develop a model to explain which workers become managers.

19. On average staff earn an additional 14 per cent, are 7 years older, and possess 1.7 additional years of education.

20. In Table 2, the results for the workers group (both model 1 and model 2) are corrected for heteroscedasticity (using White's consistent covariance matrix). There is no heteroscedasticity problem for the staff group. The results presented in the table for the staff group use the OLS covariance matrix.

21. A sample selectivity problem arises from separating the sample by an occupational variable. To correct for this bias, Heckman's (1979) two-stage estimation method is applied. This method involves including a correction factor (λ) in the wage equation. However, because the regressors in the wage equation are the same as in the selection criterion equation used to compute λ, there is a high degree of multicollinearity between λ and the regressors in the wage equation and it is impossible to obtain precise estimates. The general picture of wage determination for the two groups according to the selectivity correction estimation is similar to that of the OLS estimation. The OLS results are presented and discussed here.

22. F-tests are conducted to ascertain whether the structure of the wage determination process for workers and staff groups are the same. The null hypothesis that the underlying relationship is the same for both groups is rejected.

23. Support for this conjecture can be gained from the responses to the questions: 'Have you ever been a staff member in other TVP firms or township government before you came to this firm?' in the Director Survey Questionnaire. Some 64 per cent of the sampled firm directors gave a positive answer to this question.

24. To be a piece or time-rate worker is not a free choice. As labour mobility is restricted, a worker is paid piece or time-rates depending on the township or village in which the individual lives and the practice of the particular firm established there. As the form of payment is exogenous, there is no sample selectivity bias.

25. We do not distinguish between staff and workers because of the smallness of the sample.

26. F-tests indicate that the null hypothesis that the samples come from the same population cannot be rejected.

27. Market and non-market groups possess different characteristics. People in the market group earn about 20 per cent less than those in the non-market group (daily wage). They have about 1 year more schooling, 3.5 years less total experience, 2 years less firm tenure, and 1 year less agricultural experience. Apart from these, the distribution of the market group seems to concentrate on Jieshou county. About 48 per cent of the employees in the market group are from Jieshou county.

28. In a western labour market there is nothing unusual about finding a job by being 'introduced by relatives or friends' but in most developing regions of rural China, like Jieshou and Shangrao, positions in the TVP sector are very scarce and most workers would rather be employed by the TVP sector than stay in the fields. Only those whose relatives or friends have power (high position in the local government) would be able to be 'voluntarily' introduced into the TVP sector. In this instance this category would probably belong to the assigned non-market group. In some developed regions, like Nanhai and Wuxi, where positions in the TVP sector are not very scarce, it might be reasonable to treat this category as a component of a market-oriented recruitment system. However, even there the possibility of nepotism in appointment cannot be ruled out.

29. F-tests suggest that there is a statistically significant difference in the wage determination process between market and non-market groups. A binomial logit model is also estimated to clarify the determinants of an individual being in the market or non-market groups. Additional variables such as number of children and marital status are included in the regression. These variables, however, do not seem to be significant in determining whether an individual is likely to be in the market group or not. The results suggest that except for one of the regional dummy variables (Jieshou) and firm tenure other variables are not significant. This implies that being in the market or non-market group is not a free choice of the individual given the immobility of labour across regions. However, Heckman's (1979) two-stage estimation method is also applied to estimate wage equations for the market and non-market groups. The general picture of wage determination for the two groups according to the selectivity correction estimation is similar to that of OLS estimation. The OLS results are presented and discussed here.

30. The results are available upon request from the authors.

31. For the method of calculation see Layard et al. (1980.

32. Operational personnel are those who deal with marketing problems and technical personnel deal with technical problems. The other categories (shift leaders, ordinary staff, and middle level staff) are management staff.

33. The results are available upon request from the authors.

34. According to Greene (1990), the following relationship between relative probability and coefficients exists: Since

$$P_{ij} / P_{ik} = e^{x_i'(\beta_j - \beta_k)}, \therefore \ln(P_{ij} / P_{ik})$$

$$= X_j'(\beta_j - \beta_k), \therefore \partial \ln(P_{ij} / P_{ik}) / \partial X_i' = \beta_j - \beta_k..$$

Therefore, as X_i' increases, the likelihood that the individual is in occupation j rather than occupation k increases if $\beta_j > \beta_k$, and decreases if $\beta_j > \beta_k$. Thus, following Brown et al. (1980), by ranking the coefficients on a certain variable by magnitude, the relative impact of that variable on the probability of belonging in specific occupations can be identified.

35. Unfortunately this question was not asked of workers who did not have a relative who was a director and consequently we do not know whether 2.65 is a statistically significant different number from normal. However, if we consider the scarcity of employment opportunity in the TVP sector, it does seem a high number though.

References

Brown, Randall S., Moon, Marilyn, and Zoloth, Barbara S., 1980. 'Incorporating Occupational Attainment in Studies of Male/Female Earnings Differentials', *Journal of Human Resources*, 15(1):3–28.

Byrd, William A., and Lin, Qingsong, 1990. 'China's Rural Industry: an introduction', *China's Rural Industry*, 3–18, Oxford University Press, Oxford.

Byron, Raymond, P., and Manaloto, Evelyn Q., 1990. 'Return to Education in China', *Economic Development Cultural Change*, 38(4):783–96.

Chinese Rural Statistical Yearbook, various issues, Chinese Statistical Press, Beijing.

Chinese Statistical Yearbook, various issues, Chinese Statistical Press, Beijing.

Gelb, Alan, 1990. 'TVP Workers' Incomes, Incentives, and Attitudes', in William A. Byrd and Qingsong Lin (eds), *China's Rural Industry*, 280–98, Oxford University Press, Oxford.

Greene, William, H., 1990. *Econometric Analysis*, Macmillan, New York.

Heckman, James J., 1979. 'Sample Selection Bias as a Specification Error', *Econometrica*, 47(1):153–61.

Layard, R., Barton, M., and Zabalza, A., 1980. 'Married Women's Participation and Hours', *Economica*, 47(1):51–72.

McFadden, Daniel, 1974. 'The Measurement of Urban Travel Demand', *Journal of Public Economics*, 3(4):303–28.

McMillan, John, and Naughton, Barry, 1992. 'How to Reform a Planned Economy: Lessons from China', *Oxford Review of Economic Policy*, 8(1):130–43.

Meng, Xin, 1992. Individual Wage Determination in Township, Village and Private Enterprises in China, PhD dissertation, The Australian National University.

Mincer, Jacob, 1974. *Schooling, Experience and Earnings*, National Bureau of Economic Research, New York.

Svejnar, Jan, and Woo, Josephine, 1990. 'Development Patterns in Four Counties' in William A. Byrd and Qingsong Lin, Eds., *China's Rural Industry*, 63–84, Oxford University Press, Oxford.

23 Income and Inequality in China: composition, distribution and growth of household income, 1988 to 1995

Azizur Rahman Khan and Carl Riskin

The first comprehensive effort to estimate household income[1] and its distribution in China according to standard international definitions was made for the year 1988 by an international group of economists working with members of the host institution, the Economics Institute of the Chinese Academy of Social Sciences (CASS). The sample survey designed by this team produced estimates of household income that were substantially different from those of the State Statistical Bureau (SSB), based on its annual surveys, with different implications for both the average standard of living and the degree of inequality of income distribution. The study[2] found that per capita household income was both substantially higher and more unequally distributed than suggested by the SSB estimates. It also provided insights into sources of inequality in China that were unobtainable from the published official data on income and its distribution.

Given the success of the 1988 survey, it was felt that a repetition was essential in order to gauge the effects of the remarkable pace and changing character of China's recent economic growth upon personal income and its distribution—the principal determinants of the welfare of China's population. The incompleteness of the official data was an obstacle to monitoring these changes.

The survey was therefore repeated, using 1995 as the reference year. The research team took advantage of its previous experience to make numerous improvements in the survey instruments while trying to maintain comparability between the two studies despite changes in sample size and composition (see Table 1 and below) dictated by cost escalation.

Together, the surveys of 1988 and 1995 provide a better empirical foundation for the analysis of the nature, extent, evolution and sources of inequality in China as a whole than any other publicly available data.

There are still ambiguities and uncertainties regarding the completeness and statistical significance of some estimates, possible biases in the samples and other reasons for some of the differences between our results and official

Reprinted with permission. Extracted (with minor editing) from Azizur Rahman Khan and Carl Riskin, 1998. 'Income and Inequality in China: composition, distribution and growth of household income, 1988 to 1995', *The China Quarterly*, 154(June):221–53.

Table 1   A comparison of the surveys for 1988 and 1995

	1988	1995
Rural sample		
Number of households	10,258	7,998
Number of persons	51,352	34,739
Average household size	5.006	4.343
Number of provinces		
included in the survey	28	19
Provinces included in 1988		
but excluded in 1995	Heilongjiang, Inner Mongolia, Qinghai,	
	Ningxia, Guangxi, Fujian, Hainan, Tianjin, Shanghai	
Urban sample		
Number of households	9,009	6,931
Number of persons	31,827	21,694
Average household size	3.533	3.131
Number of provinces		
included in the survey	10	11
Provinces included in 1995		
but not in 1988	Sichuan	

estimates of the State Statistical Bureau. This paper does not pretend to resolve all of these issues, but merely reports some of the main results of the new urban and rural surveys and compares them with the results for 1988. That these results are of great intrinsic interest and occasionally quite unexpected strengthens the case for their early presentation. However, there is much room for further analysis of these rich data sets.

We begin by comparing the sizes and coverage of the survey samples used in 1988 and 1995 (Table 1). Both sets are sub-samples drawn from the national rural and urban household sample surveys conducted by the SSB. The main differences between the two years are the smaller sample sizes and the reduced number of rural provinces covered in 1995. In 1988 only two provinces—Tibet and Xinjiang—were excluded from the rural sample. Nine others were excluded in 1995 (see Table 1). Urban locations were selected to represent urban entities in different regions of China and cities and towns of different size. In 1995, one additional province, Sichuan, was added to 1988's sample.

Our rural sample was one-eighth of the SSB parent sample of 67,340 households in 1995. A larger sample size would have been desirable. Given the resources available, there was the usual trade-off between enlarging the sample size and incorporating the details required for comprehensive and accurate measurements. With regard to the reduction in the number of provinces, care was exercised in choosing which provinces would be excluded. They are uniformly spread among the provinces in terms of their ranking according to per capita rural income. The average rank of the excluded provinces for 1988 was 14.9 out of a total of 28 provinces. It is therefore reasonable to hope that the reduction in the number of provinces covered in the rural sample does not create a significant bias for the analysis of income in the country as a whole.[3] We derive some confidence in this regard from the fact that our survey reports a rural per capita household income according to the SSB definition that is virtually identical to the SSB's own estimate.[4]

Our urban sample in 1995 was one-fifth of the parent SSB sample of 36,370 households drawn nationally from 226 cities and counties. However, the restricted number of provinces covered by the urban sample is a source of concern, especially given the differentiation in urban economic activity in recent years. This should be kept in mind when considering the reported differences between our estimates and the SSB's. Moreover, for analysis of income within individual provinces, both urban and rural, the small sample sizes may cause undesirably high sampling error.

I. Definition of Income and its Components

The household is the basic unit of estimation. Household income includes the earnings of each individual member as well as the collective earnings of the household from its own enterprises, property and transfer. Each member of a household is assumed to have the same income, the per capita income of the household. This study does not attempt to examine issues of intra-household distribution.

Components of rural income

We have used the same definition of income as in 1988 except that, due to changes in economic and social policies and institutions, certain components of income have become extinct since then. For rural China the components of income are as follows:

1. Income from wages, pensions and other forms of labour compensation accruing to individual members of the household. In addition to cash earnings, all income in kind, valued at market prices, has been included.

2. Income, other than compensation for labour, accruing to individual household members from private, individual and joint venture enterprises, plus income from the collective welfare fund. This category is distinct from income accruing to enterprises owned by the household.[5]

3. Net income from farming. This includes the value of all output of farm, forest and fishery products, valued at market prices, whether sold or consumed by the household, and net of all costs of purchased inputs, including non-household labour.

4. Net income from non-farm household enterprises and subsidiary activities. This includes the output of all non-farm activities less the cost of purchased inputs including non household labour. For purposes of comparison with 1988 we have also estimated the gross value of consumption of farm products in 1995, although it is no longer a separate component of income according to the classification adopted in 1995.[6]

5. Income from property. This consists of interest on savings deposits and bonds, dividends, and rent on leased-out land, houses and other property.

6. Rental value of owned housing. Only the rental value of the owned part of the house occupied is included. As in 1988, it is assumed to be 8 per cent of the difference between the replacement value of the house and the debt on the house. Replacement value is estimated by applying the provincial average estimated market value per square metre of rural housing to the size of the house in square metres. Thus, our estimated inequality in the rental value of housing necessarily reflects the inequality in housing assets (which, for rural China, turns out to be quite small).

7. Net transfer from the state, local government and the remnants of the old collectives. This includes all welfare and relief payments and subsidies received by the household less all taxes and compulsory payments to the state and the collectives.

8. Other income. This residual category is dominated by remittances made by migrant members of the household working elsewhere and includes gifts received from private donors and

miscellaneous sources of income not classified elsewhere.

Components of urban income

The components of urban income are as follows:

1. Cash labour compensation from primary and secondary jobs of all working members of the household. This includes wages, bonuses, overtime payments, subsidies and any special cash payments. Wages are here defined to include allowances received while furloughed from shut-down enterprises, a growing phenomenon as the reform of state enterprises proceeds.

2. Income of retired members. This includes both pensions and income from post-retirement jobs.

3. Income from private and individual enterprises owned/operated by the household.

4. Income from property. This includes the same items as rural property income.

5. Housing subsidy in kind. This component consists of the difference between market rent (directly estimated by the head of each household surveyed) and the actual rent paid by all those who are occupying public housing.[7]

6. Other net subsidies. This includes all subsidies and payments in kind, other than housing subsidy, including in-kind compensation for labour. It also includes relief payments and hardship subsidies. All direct taxes and fees have been subtracted.

7. Rental value of owner-occupied housing. For households living in their own abodes the market rent (directly estimated by household heads) has been included. Estimated interest on housing debt has been subtracted from the estimated rental value of housing.

8. Other income. This consists of private transfers and other minor sources of income not classified under other headings.

Sources of urban income in 1995 are fewer than in 1988, because two components of the 1988 classification—income of non-working members and ration coupon subsidies—have been eliminated by institutional changes and the abolition of urban food rationing.

II. Rural Income and its Components: levels and changes

Table 2 summarises the level and composition of rural income in 1995, the composition of rural income in 1988 according to our survey and the real rates of growth between 1988 and 1995. The last are based on point comparisons, as are all subsequent estimates of change between the two years, and no inference should be drawn about what happened during the unobserved years in between.[8]

Household production activities (rows 3 and 4) remain the single largest source of rural income, but their share of total income fell sharply from 74 per cent in 1988 to 56 per cent in 1995. Income from farm production (row 3) accounts for the bulk of total income from household activities. This too, however, appears to have fallen as a proportion of total income between 1988 and 1995.[9]

Wages are the second largest component of rural income. Their share increased sharply, from about 9 per cent of the total in 1988 to over 22 per cent in 1995, accounting for more than three-quarters of the fall in the share of household production.

The next most important source of rural income after wages is rental value of owner-occupied housing. This increased moderately to about 10 per cent of total income. Income from enterprises consists overwhelmingly of individual entrepreneurial income,[10] which constituted around 6 per cent of total income in 1995. If this is combined with net income from household non-farm activities, the sum comes to about 16 per cent of total income, which is one way of assessing the relative importance of private

Table 2   **Per capita disposable rural income** (yuan per year)

Income and its sources	1995 Amount	1995 Per cent	1988 Per cent	Real growth rate
Total	2,308.63	100.00	100.00	4.71
1. Individual wages etc.	516.78	22.38	8.73	19.78
2. Receipts from enterprises, of which,	139.89	6.06	2.40	19.49
entrepreneurial income	137.36	5.95	n.a.	–
3. Net farm income	1,072.15	46.44 ⎱	74.21	0.62
4. Net income from household		⎰		
non-farm activities	224.08	9.71		
5. Income from property	9.98	0.43	0.17	19.41
6. Rental value of owned housing	267.93	11.61	9.67	7.48
7. Net transfer from state and collective	-10.99	-0.48	-1.90	-14.07
8. Other income (private transfer etc.)	88.81	3.85	6.71	-3.29
Memo item: gross value of self-consumption of food	659.37	28.56	41.13	-0.61

Note: Real growth rate is estimated by deflating the 1995 estimate by the overall rural CPI—not the price index of the component—and estimating the annual compound rate of growth between 1988 (for which the value from the 1988 survey is used) and 1995.

entrepreneurial activity in the rural economy.[11] The remaining sources of income are each very small. Property income, while increasing sharply between 1988 and 1995, still constituted less than half of 1 per cent of income in the latter year.[12] The rate of taxes (net of subsidies) on rural households (row 7) fell rather sharply although taxes still outweigh subsidies for an average rural household.

Real rates of growth have been estimated by deflating 1995 income and its components by the rural consumer price index (CPI) of the SSB— 220.09 (1988 = 100)[13]—although there is good reason to believe it understates the true increase in cost of living.[14]

Of the components of rural income, wages grew most quickly, closely followed by receipts from enterprises[15] and property income. Rental value of owner-occupied housing also had a much higher than average rate of growth. On the other hand, net income from household production activities grew very slowly, while gross value of self-consumption had a negative real growth

rate. Evidently, the commercialisation of the rural economy proceeded at a very brisk pace during this period, reducing (gross) subsistence production from over 40 per cent of income to under 30 per cent.

III. Urban Income and its Components: levels and changes

Table 3 summarises information about the level and composition of urban income in 1995, the composition of urban income according to the 1988 survey and the real growth rates between 1988 and 1995.

Cash wages are by far the largest component of urban income, contributing more than three-fifths of the total as compared to 44 per cent in 1988. Income of retired members is the distant runner-up, contributing just under 12 per cent, up from under 7 per cent in 1988.

Rental value of owner-occupied housing, the next largest component, has grown sharply, from less than 4 per cent of income in 1988 to more

Table 3   **Per capita disposable urban income** (yuan per year)

| | 1995 | | 1988 | Real growth |
	Amount	Per cent	Per cent	rate
Total	5,706.19	100.00	100.00	4.48
1. Cash income of working members				
(wages etc.)	3,497.77	61.30	44.42	17.32
2. Income of retired members				
(pensions etc.)	667.14	11.69	6.83	12.83
3. Private/individual enterprises	30.23	0.53	0.74	-0.31
4. Income from property	72.28	1.27	0.49	19.60
5. Housing subsidy in kind	555.66	9.74	18.14	-4.40
6. Other net subsidies	71.12	1.25	20.94	-69.82
7. Rental value of owner-occupied housing	650.12	11.39	3.90	21.78
8. Other income	161.87	2.84	4.53	-2.30

Note: Other net subsidies in 1988 include ration coupon subsidies which were abolished prior to 1995. Real growth rates, in per cent per year between 1988 and 1995, are estimated in the same way as for rural China.

than 11 per cent. Together with the subsidy on public housing it accounts for roughly the same proportion of income in 1995 (21 per cent) as in 1988 (22 per cent). Total 'expenditure' on housing requires the further addition of actual rent paid on rented accommodation, which was 0.7 per cent of income in 1988 and 2.8 per cent of income in 1995.[16] Thus the total cost of housing was marginally higher as a proportion of income in 1995 (23.8 per cent) than in 1988 (22.8 per cent).

However, the distribution of the housing cost burden changed dramatically. In 1988, 80 per cent of cost was borne by public subsidy, 17 per cent by owner-occupiers and only 3 per cent by renters. By 1995, the share of total expenditures borne by public subsidy had fallen by half, to 41 per cent; the share borne by owner-occupiers had almost trebled to 48 per cent; and renters' share had quadrupled to almost 12 per cent.

The sharp fall in housing subsidies was exceeded by that of non-housing subsidies, which dropped from 21 per cent of urban income in 1988 to a negligible 1.25 per cent in 1995. Income from property increased as a proportion of total income, while remaining a very small proportion of it.[17] The very low estimate of income from private and individual enterprises,

and its reported decrease since 1988, are contrary to much qualitative evidence and must be regarded with skepticism.[18] Other sources of income, mainly transfers, fell quite sharply as a proportion of income.

Growth rates of urban real income and its components have been estimated in the same way as those of rural real income—by deflating 1995 incomes by 227.9, the change in the urban CPI between 1988 and 1995. The highest annual rate of growth was in rental value of owned housing. This is due not only to increased rents, but more particularly to the pace of housing reform, which has strongly encouraged urban renters to purchase their own apartments. Our results suggest that this reform has made very substantial progress: in 1988 only 13.8 per cent of urban sample reported living in their own private housing, whereas in 1995 this proportion had risen to 41.7 per cent.

The second fastest growing component was property income which, however, still amounted to only a little more than 1 per cent of total income in 1995. Cash wages rose at an average rate of 17 per cent and earnings of retirees by almost 13 per cent. The growth of retirement income reflects the rapid ageing of the Chinese population. In

1988, only 8.4 per cent of the urban sample reported being retired, whereas by 1995 the retired fraction had grown to 13.7 per cent.

The remaining components of urban income had negative real rates of growth, the most remarkable decline occurring in net subsidies (subsidies less taxes) from the government which, as pointed out above, fell from over a fifth of total income to only 1 per cent.

IV. Comparison with Official Estimates

The differences between our definition of income and the one used by the SSB can only be gauged in broad terms and appear to have remained unchanged since 1988. The SSB excludes rental value of owner-occupied housing. Its coverage of income in kind and subsidies is less comprehensive than ours. It also appears to include fewer items of income from household production activities.

Some of the items excluded by official statistics have been changing rapidly as proportions of total income. This is particularly true for subsidies and income in kind in urban China, which together have fallen drastically

from 39 per cent of urban income in 1988 to only 11 per cent in 1995. Rental value of owner-occupied housing as a proportion of urban income has, on the other hand, increased sharply from 4 per cent in 1988 to more than 11 per cent in 1995. Together, these components excluded by the SSB have fallen sharply relative to urban income. This introduces a serious bias in official estimates of the *growth* of urban income as well as of the change in the urban/rural disparity over time.

Rural income

Our estimate of the real rate of increase in per capita rural income—4.71 per cent per year—is higher than the rate obtained from the official estimates (which, using the same deflator as above, turns out to be 4 per cent per year). Per capita rural income estimated from our survey was 46 per cent higher than the SSB estimate in 1995 (see Table 4) as compared to 39 per cent higher in 1988. The principal reason for the increasing divergence between the two estimates is that the SSB does not count rental value of owner-occupied housing, which grew rapidly.

Indeed, as in 1988, the SSB estimates of all the major components of rural income are below

Table 4   Comparison of SSB and survey estimates of rural income

Per capita net income of rural residents, 1995	SSB	Survey	Ratio: Survey/SSB
Total	1,578	2,309	1.46
Labour remuneration	354	517	1.46
Household business: farming, forestry, fishery, animal husbandry, etc.	937	1,072	1.14
Non-farm activity	188	224	1.19
Private transfer and property	98	99	1.01
Total of items included by the SSB	1,578	1,912	1.21
Items included by survey, excluded by the SSB (receipts from enterprises, rental value of owned housing, net transfer from state and collective)		397	

Source: SSB, *Statistical Yearbook of China* (Beijing: Statistical Publishers 1997:313 and Table 2).

Table 5   SSB estimates of urban income

Per capita net income of urban residents, 1995[21]	SSB	Survey	Ratio: Survey/SSB
Total	4,288	5,706	1.33
Wages	3,334	3,498	1.05
Individual enterprise/sidelines	91	30	0.33
Interest, dividends and rent	90	72	0.80
Re-employment of retirees	43	49	0.95
Pensions, transfers and 'special' income	740	780	1.15
Total of items included by SSB	4,288	4,429	1.03
Items included by survey, excluded by the SSB (housing subsidy in kind, rental value of owner-occupied housing, other net subsidies)		1,277	

Source: SSB, *Statistical Yearbook of China* (1997:294 and Table 3).

ours. The largest part of the difference between our estimates—37 per cent—is due to the rental value of owner-occupied housing. Their lower estimate of 'labourers' remuneration' (*laodongzhe shouru*)—354 yuan to our 517—is at first glance surprising, but this category is not as straightforward as it would seem. The SSB's figure for regular plus non-regular pay from the work unit is in fact only 10 yuan below ours. In addition to these wage items, however, we include several others that appear to have no other representation in the SSB accounts.[19]

Our estimate of income from household production is 15 per cent above the SSB counterpart. This is an average of a 14 per cent difference for farm-type income and a 19 per cent difference for non-farm income. Yet our *gross* income from total household production is only about 5 per cent higher, which suggests that part of the gap between our estimates may be due to a different way of accounting for production costs.[20]

Urban income

Per capita urban income according to our survey was 33 per cent higher than the official figure in 1995 (Table 5), as compared to 55 per cent higher in 1988. The reason for the diminishing difference

is the falling proportion of subsidies, which are excluded by the SSB but included by us, in urban income. In 1995, subsidies of all kinds account for 90 per cent of the difference between our estimates and those of SSB. The rest is accounted for by differences in the estimates of items included by both. The comparison points up our likely underestimation of income from individual and private enterprise, which is only one-third that of the SSB.

The real rate of growth of our estimates of urban income between 1988 and 1995 was only 4.48 per cent, slightly lower than the rate for rural income of 4.71 per cent, and much below the 6.74 per cent growth rate of the SSB estimate. By excluding from the definition of income those components that declined sharply as a proportion of total income, the official figures seriously overestimate the rate of urban income growth.

V. Some Implications of the Survey Findings on Composition of Income

The findings of the survey reported above have numerous implications for macroeconomic accounting which in turn have important implications for economic policies. This section highlights two of these issues in particular.

Level and growth of GNP

Available macroeconomic data do not permit a reconciliation of household income estimates with the estimates of GNP and other macroeconomic accounts. It is clear, however, that if our estimates of personal income are roughly correct, then the official national accounts are substantially understated. Our estimate of the weighted average per capita personal income in 1995 was 3,293.9 yuan or, for a population of 1,211.21 million, 3,989.6 billion yuan. The weighted average household saving rate was 17.25 per cent, yielding an estimated private consumption of 3,301.4 billion yuan—57.6 per cent of the GNP of 5,727.7 billion yuan reported by the SSB.[22] This compares with a private consumption-to-GNP ratio of 47 per cent in the official GNP accounts. If we substitute our estimate of private consumption for the one implied by the official ratio, then China's actual GNP would be 11.6 per cent higher than the official estimate. Moreover, the size of the different components of GNP would change as shown in Table 6.

China's investment rate would fall to a level that, while still high, is lower than in South-East Asian countries such as Thailand (43 per cent) and Malaysia (41 per cent), and closer to the rate in Indonesia (38 per cent), the Republic of Korea (37 per cent) and Hong Kong (35 per cent).[23] Also

the saving rate drops to a more plausible level, though still remaining about as high as in any Asian country.

The gap between GNP growth and personal income growth

According to the official estimates, per capita real GNP in China increased at an annual average rate of 8.07 per cent between 1988 and 1995.[24] The growth in real per capita household income, on the other hand, was only 4.71 per cent for rural China, 4.48 per cent for urban China and 5.05 per cent for China as a whole.[25] The big lag in the growth of personal income behind that of real GNP is consistent with the widespread suspicion that the official estimate of real GNP growth is exaggerated, in part because it is based on a price deflator thought to be too low.[26] Even if true, however, this could explain only a small part of the difference. That part of the gap in growth rates which is real implies that the non-household components of GNP must have been rising faster than GNP. That is, macroeconomic policies in China were redistributing incremental income in favour of accumulation, particularly business accumulation.[27]

The difference between the behaviour of personal income and that of GNP is a point rarely accorded the importance it deserves. For example, rapid growth is often counted upon to offset the adverse effects of widening inequality on the poverty rate. However, the relevant growth

---

Table 6   **Macroeconomic accounts** (per cent of GNP)

	Official estimates	Revised estimates
Private consumption	46	51.6
Government consumption	12	10.8
Savings	42	37.6
Investment	40	35.8
Exports	21	18.8
Imports	19	17.0

Note: 'Official estimates' are from SSB, *Statistical Yearbook of China* (1997:32). Revised estimates are obtained by dividing the official estimates by the ratio of revised GNP to official GNP (1.116).

rate is that of personal income, the variable in terms of which the poverty threshold is measured. Personal income has grown much more slowly than (measured) GDP, so a much smaller adverse change in distribution is required to affect the poor adversely.

VI. The Index of Inequality

As in the 1988 study, the index of inequality used in this paper is the Gini ratio of per capita household income. The main reasons for using it are its easy recognition value, the wide availability of estimates of this index both for China's past and for other countries with which comparisons might be intended, and its relative absence of disadvantages as an index of inequality. The value of the Gini ratio conveys an idea of the degree of inequality independent of the size of the sample on which the measurement is based, and avoids the need to make arbitrary welfare judgements. These attributes are not always satisfied by alternative measures of inequality.[28]

Apart from the disadvantage that it treats as equivalent changes due to a *given* amount of redistribution at *different* levels of income, the most serious disadvantage attributed to the Gini ratio is that it cannot be decomposed. There is no simple way of arriving at an estimate of the Gini ratio of the aggregate population from the Gini ratios of its constituent groups. Nor is there a way of aggregating the Gini ratios of different sources of income into the Gini ratio of total income. However, indirect decomposition of the Gini ratio into the contributions made by different sources of income is possible, an attribute of which this study makes extensive use. This attribute is owed to the following property of the Gini ratio.

$$G = \sum_i u_i C_i$$

where G = Gini ratio of total income; u_i = the ratio of the ith source of income to total income; and C_i = the so-called 'concentration'

ratio or 'pseudo-Gini' ratio for the ith source of income.

The concentration curve for a given source of income, for example, wages, shows the proportion of income from that source received by the lowest x per cent of *income* recipients. The concentration ratio is estimated from this concentration curve in exactly the same way that the Gini ratio is from the Lorenz curve, except that individuals are ranked in the former according to their per capita overall income rather than their per capita income from the particular source. For example, the high concentration ratio for rural wage income, 0.71 (see below), implies that wages are highly concentrated among richer individuals in the rural population, but not necessarily that wages are highly concentrated among wage earners, themselves.[29]

The contribution of a given source of income to overall inequality is the share of the Gini ratio accounted for by that source of income. This is designated q_i and depends both upon the distribution (concentration ratio) of that income source and upon its size relative to total income. Thus, $q_i = 100(u_i C_i)/G$. A component of income that has a q_i greater than its share of total income has a disequalising effect on overall income distribution in the sense that a rise in its share of total income will increase the Gini ratio.

VII. The Distribution of Rural Income

Table 7 shows the Gini ratios and concentration ratios for rural China for both 1988 and 1995.

Rural inequality and its sources in 1995

Table 7 shows a sharp rise in rural inequality between 1988 and 1995.[30] The Gini ratio of rural income distribution in 1995 (0.416) is at the high end of those observed in developing countries of Asia.[31]

The most important source of income inequality in rural China is income from wages. It accounts for 40 per cent of overall inequality in rural income distribution. Wage income is concentrated among the high income groups, the top two deciles of income recipients appropriating 78 per cent of all income from this source. This apparently counter-intuitive finding comes about because (1) the average wage was high relative to rural per capita income; (2) wage earners were still relatively few; and (3) these are probably concentrated in areas where incomes in general are higher.

The next most disequalising components of income are receipts from private and other enterprises, the bulk of which consist of entrepreneurial income, and property income, which remained a very small proportion of total income.[32] Income from non-farm household activities is also disequalising. These three income sources are all concentrated among higher income groups; almost 40 per cent of each of them goes to the top decile of the rural population.

The most disequalising effect on the distribution of rural income is from net transfer from the state and collectives—a negative source of income, signifying that on average rural households are subject to a positive rate of net 'taxation'. It has a negative concentration ratio

(-1.76), meaning that the burden of net taxes is more than fully borne by the lower income groups. The top two deciles are the only income groups which, on the average, receive positive net transfer from the state and collectives. This pattern is consistent with reports that in poorer localities, particularly those without prosperous township and village enterprises, local governments commonly impose various taxes and fees to support local services.[33]

All other sources of income have an equalising effect on distribution, that is, the poorer households' share of these sources of income is greater than their share of total income. Farm production activities are by far the most equalising source of income, its concentration ratio being the lowest of all components. Household farming activity, which provides 46.4 per cent of total income, contributes only 26.6 per cent to total inequality. Rental value of owned housing is also equalising, providing 11.6 per cent of income but only 9 per cent of total inequality.

The rich and the poor in rural China therefore have very different compositions of income. The

Table 7   Rural income inequality and its sources

	(1) Share of total income (per cent)		(2) Gini or concentration ratio		(3) Contribution of income component to overall inequality (per cent)	
	1988	1995	1988	1995	1988	1995
Total income	100.00	100.00	0.338	0.416	100.0	100.0
Wages	8.73	22.38	0.710	0.738	18.3	39.7
Receipts from private and other enterprises	2.40	6.06	0.487	0.543	3.6	7.9
Income from household prod. activities	74.21	56.15	0.282	0.281	61.8	37.9
Farm income	-	(46.44)	-	(0.238)	-	(26.6)
Income from non-farm activities	-	(9.71)	-	(0.484)	-	(11.3)
Property income	0.17	0.43	0.484	0.543	0.3	0.6
Rental value of owned housing	9.67	11.61	0.281	0.321	8.0	9.0
Net transfer from state and collectives	-1.90	-0.48	0.052	-1.759	-0.3	2.0
Miscellaneous income	6.71	3.85	0.418	0.337	8.3	3.1

Note: Column (1) is 100u. Column (2) is the index of inequality, that is, the Gini ratio for total income and the concentration ratios for income components. Column (3) is $100(u_i C_i)/G$.

principal sources of income for the rich are wage employment, non-farm entrepreneurship and transfers from the state and collectives. For the poor, the main sources of income are farming, rental value of owned housing and, to a lesser extent, private transfers. Net transfers to the state and collectives is a significant source of income erosion for poor households.

Change in income distribution between 1988 and 1995

The increase in rural inequality between 1988 and 1995 has been due mainly to a change in the *composition* of income—that is, a rise in the share of the more unequally distributed components—rather than an increase in inequality of distribution of the individual components.[34]

The single largest source of increased inequality in rural China was the very rapid rise in the share of wages in incremental rural income. The change in the concentration ratio of wages was very small indeed. The sharpest increase in the inequality of distribution of a component was in the case of net transfer from state and collectives. In 1988 net taxes were distributed more equally than income, signifying a regressive structure of net taxes. In 1995 such regression had become massive: the poorest decile's share of net taxes was 12 times its share of income, while the richest decile had a high *negative* rate of net taxes (net positive transfer from state and collective).

Rental value of owned housing was significantly less equalising in 1995 than in 1988. Rural housing assets were becoming concentrated in the hands of richer households. Concentration ratios also increased for wages and, more significantly, for property income and receipts from TVEs and other enterprises.

Household production activities, farm and non-farm enterprises together, were as equalising a source of income in 1995 as in 1988. One of the major explanations of rising inequality in rural China is the slow growth of farming as a source of rural income. The only component of income which became more equalising in 1995 than in

1988 was income of the miscellaneous 'other' category. Since this is dominated by private transfers, one is tempted to surmise that income remittances made by out-migrants mitigated rural inequality to a small extent.

VIII. The Distribution of Urban Income

Table 8 shows the indices of inequality for urban income and its sources in 1988 and 1995.

Urban inequality and its sources in 1995

Between 1988 and 1995 the Gini ratio of China's urban income distribution increased sharply, from 0.23 to 0.33. The increase in urban inequality was proportionately greater than the increase in rural inequality over the same period. Our estimate of urban inequality for 1995 is 18 per cent higher than that of the SSB (0.28).[35]

Of the eight sources of urban income identified in Table 8, four are disequalising in the sense that their concentration ratios are higher than the Gini ratio, that is, richer income groups appropriate higher proportions of income from these sources. Of these four, rental value of owned housing and housing subsidy have a quantitatively large effect on overall inequality. Together they account for 37 per cent of the urban Gini ratio although they contribute only 21 per cent of urban income.

Wages, the largest source of urban income, still exert an equalising effect in so far as their concentration ratio remains significantly lower than the Gini ratio. Except for the top two deciles, all other groups have higher shares of the total wage bill than of total income.

Unexpectedly, and unlike in rural China, reported income from privately and individually owned enterprises is strongly equalising, but this is an artifice of our failure to distinguish between two quite different kinds of private activity which are lumped together in this category: private entrepreneurship providing high incomes to relatively few households and rudimentary informal sector activities providing low incomes to many poor households. Moreover,

374

Table 8   Urban income inequality and its sources

	(1) Share of total income (per cent)		(2) Gini or concentration ratio		(3) Contribution of income component to overall inequality (per cent)	
	1988	1995	1988	1995	1988	1995
Total income	100.00	100.00	0.233	0.332	100.0	100.0
Cash income of working members	44.42	61.30	0.178	0.247	33.9	45.6
Cash income of retirees	6.83	11.69	0.335	0.316	9.8	11.1
Income from private/individual enterprises	0.74	0.53	0.413	0.042	1.3	0.1
Property income	0.49	1.27	0.437	0.484	0.9	1.9
Housing subsidy	18.14	9.74	0.311	0.516	24.2	15.1
Other net subsidies	20.94	1.25	0.188	0.296	16.9	1.1
Rental value of owned housing	3.90	11.39	0.338	0.639	5.7	21.9
Other (private transfer etc.)	4.53	2.84	0.383	0.371	7.4	3.2

Note: For further explanation of the columns see note to Table 7. For 1988, 'other net subsidies' include ration coupon subsidies (which ceased to exist in 1995) and 'other income' includes income of non-working members (which also ceased to exist in 1995).

there are too few observations of the former (private enterprise income alone) to say anything about its level or distribution.[30] The fact that the combined category has a bi-modal distribution in 1995, with high proportions of income appropriated by very low-income households and very high-income households but little of it going to the middle deciles, does suggest that there was a proliferation of informal sector activities between the two dates. The poorest decile in 1995 gets five times as high a share of this source as of total income. It is also clear that these activities are widespread not only among the floating migrants, who have not been captured by the survey, but also among registered urban residents.

Net subsidies, which are dominated by housing subsidies, have a fairly strongly disequalising effect on urban income distribution.

Change in income distribution between 1988 and 1995

Unlike the case for rural China, the increased inequality in urban China was due entirely to greater inequality of distribution of individual components of income. The change in the composition of income sources had no role in explaining rising urban inequality.

Of the eight sources of urban income, the distribution of five became more unequal between 1988 and 1995. There was little change in the distribution of two other components. The distribution of only one component—income from private and individual enterprises—improved sharply, and this result may well be spurious.

While still an equalising source of income, wages have become far less so in 1995 than in 1988. This was probably a desirable change; previously the wage spread was kept artificially low to the detriment of work incentives. Greater differentiation in wage structure may well enhance productive efficiency.

Unfortunately, there was no countervailing change in the distribution of net subsidies. Ideally one would want the redistributive effect of subsidies to bring down the overall Gini ratio, that is, their concentration ratios to be negative. Had the distribution of net subsidies been merely equal, that is, their concentration ratios been zero, the urban Gini ratio in 1995 would have been 0.278 despite all the disequalising change in the distribution of other sources. This would represent an egalitarian distribution of urban income by the standards of contemporary LDCs. Instead, however, urban subsidies became far more disequalising in 1995 than they were in 1988. This happened for a number of reasons. First, the most equalising component of urban subsidies in 1988—ration coupons—was abolished prior to 1995.[37] Second, while housing subsidies have been reduced to half their previous level as a proportion of urban household income, their distribution has become sharply more unequal. The top decile of the urban population appropriated 41 per cent of all housing subsidies in 1995 as compared to 28 per cent in 1988. The concentration ratio of housing subsidies increased by two-thirds.

Rental value of owned housing also became much more disequalising in 1995 than in 1988. Indeed, this was the most disequalising component of urban income in 1995. The privatisation of urban housing has clearly contributed to a sharp exacerbation of urban inequality. The richest 10 per cent of the urban population have been the major beneficiaries, garnering 60 per cent of privately-owned housing assets.

There is a caveat attached to the above two conclusions: estimates of both housing subsidies and rental value of owned housing depend upon respondents' estimates of the market rental value of their homes. Whether housing markets are sufficiently developed in urban China to permit accurate estimates is an open question. Subjective estimates might err considerably. For instance, our conclusions would be threatened if rental values were systematically overestimated, since this would raise the weight of their concentration ratios in the overall Gini ratio. If physical housing assets are concentrated among richer groups, then systematic exaggeration would also increase the concentration ratio of imputed rental income. We cannot think of any obvious reason why respondents would systematically exaggerate the rental value of their homes.

We do not give much credence to the dramatic increase in equality of distribution of income from individual and private enterprises between 1988 and 1995, for reasons already stated.[38] Property income doubled its still small contribution to the Gini ratio because it both grew larger as a source of income and became more unequally distributed.[39]

IX. The Overall Distribution of Income

The overall distribution of income was obtained by weighting the rural and urban samples of the 1995 survey so as to represent the relative shares of rural and urban population in 1995.[40] Table 9 shows the Gini ratios of income distribution for China as a whole and the concentration ratios of rural and urban income and their components for 1988 and 1995.

Overall inequality in China and its sources

Inequality between urban and rural China dominates inequality within both populations in 1995, as it did in 1988. That is, the Gini ratio for China as a whole is higher than it is for either rural or urban China. However, the dominance of urban/rural inequality was weaker in 1995: the overall Gini ratio was only 21 per cent higher than the average of rural and urban Ginis in 1995, whereas it was 34 per cent higher in 1988.

By the evidence of the Gini ratio, China was among the more unequal societies in developing Asia by the middle of the 1990s. The Gini ratio for China in 1995 (0.452) is higher than those for India, Pakistan and Indonesia and perhaps about the same as that for the Philippines.[41] It should also be noted that, while the estimated Gini ratio for China is 9 to 15 per cent higher than estimates reported by the World Bank (0.388 and 0.415),[42] it is very close to one estimated for 1994 by the Macroeconomics Institute of the State Planning Commission.[43]

The concentration ratios for rural income and most of its components are low, indicating that a redistribution in favour of the rural economy, other things remaining equal, would reduce inequality for China as a whole. The only component of rural income that is disequalising for China as a whole is wages. Indeed, rural income was somewhat less equalising in 1995 than it was in 1988, largely because the share of rural wages rose sharply.[44]

Even those other components of rural income that have a disequalising effect on *rural* income distribution have an equalising one on overall income distribution for China. A rise in their share of total income will make rural income distribution more unequal but, at the same time, will reduce inequality of income distribution for China as a whole. The concentration ratio for farm income is negative which indicates that it has an extremely high equalising effect on China's overall income distribution.

However, the negative concentration ratio for net transfer from the state and collectives to rural households has exactly the opposite meaning, viz. that net transfers have a highly disequalising effect on China's income distribution. The burden of net rural taxes is largely borne by households who are poor in the rural context and extremely poor in the context of China as a whole. Therefore, a reduction in net taxes on rural households would have a strongly equalising effect.

A rise in the share of urban income, coming from any of its components, will increase overall inequality for China, other things remaining unchanged. Even the most equalising of the urban components—income from individual and private enterprise, which has a strongly equalising effect on urban income distribution—is

Table 9   **Overall income inequality in China and its sources**

	(1) Share of total income (per cent)		(2) Gini or concentration ratio		(3) Contribution of income component to overall inequality (per cent)	
	1988	1995	1988	1995	1988	1995
Total income	100.00	100.00	0.382	0.452	100.0	100.0
Total rural income	(57.10)	(49.09)	0.116	0.192	(17.4)	(20.9)
Wages	4.99	10.71	0.528	0.567	6.9	13.4
Receipts from enterprises	1.37	2.94	0.279	0.301	1.0	2.0
Income from production activities	42.39	27.84	0.053	0.045	5.9	2.8
Farm income	-	(23.04)	-	-0.001	-	(-0.1)
Income from non-farm enterprises	-	(4.80)	-	0.266	-	(2.8)
Property income	0.10	0.22	0.272	0.327	0.1	0.2
Rental value of owned housing	5.52	5.74	0.067	0.090	1.0	1.1
Net transfer from state and collectives	-1.09	-0.26	-0.147	-1.924	0.4	1.1
Miscellaneous income	3.83	1.90	0.214	0.090	2.1	0.4
Total urban income	(42.90)	(50.89)	0.735	0.703	(82.5)	(79.1)
Cash income of working members	19.06	31.20	0.715	0.664	35.7	45.8
Cash income of retirees	2.93	5.95	0.773	0.698	5.9	9.2
Income from private/individual enterprises	0.32	0.27	0.836	0.516	0.7	0.3
Property income	0.21	0.64	0.810	0.776	0.4	1.1
Housing subsidy	7.78	4.96	0.761	0.789	15.5	8.7
Other net subsidies	8.99	0.63	0.719	0.687	16.9	1.0
Rental value of owned housing	1.67	5.80	0.767	0.840	3.4	10.8
Other (private transfer etc.)	1.94	1.44	0.785	0.719	4.0	2.3

Note: See note to Table 7 for further explanation of columns

disequalising for China as a whole. Although the recipients of income from this source are concentrated among the urban poor, they belong to relatively high income groups when the whole population is considered.

The two most disequalising sources of income for China are rental value of owned urban housing and urban housing subsidy

These were also the only components of urban income to become more disequalising between 1988 and 1995 (all other components, and urban income as a whole, were somewhat less disequalising in 1995). If the estimates are roughly accurate, then from the standpoint of income redistributive public policy nothing is more important than to re-evaluate the issue of urban housing reform. A less unequal access to housing assets and an abolition, or a drastic redirection, of urban housing subsidies should feature at the top of a public strategy for the reduction of inequality in China.

Urban subsidies are more disequalising in the context of China as a whole than in the context of urban China alone. Proportionately their contribution to urban inequality is only 50 per cent more than their share of urban income while their contribution to overall inequality is 75 per cent more than their share of overall household income.

Although urban wages are less disequalising a component of income than many others—and are an equalising source of income for urban China—they account for the single largest proportion of overall inequality in China, nearly 46 per cent. While urban wage workers are not among the highest income recipients within the towns and cities, they constitute a very high income group in the context of China as a whole.

X. Spatial Inequality

Urban/rural inequality

Official estimates show a sharp rise of 20 per cent in the urban/rural disparity in real per capita income between 1988 and 1995 (Table 10). The extent of this inequality in China has been greater than in most Asian LDCs,[45] and our 1988 survey indicated that the official statistics understated the extent of the urban/rural disparity. However, the 1995 survey shows the opposite: that official statistics overstate the urban/rural income gap, a result of exaggerating the rate of growth of urban income and understating that of rural income. In contrast, the survey yields a rate of growth in nominal urban income that is only slightly higher than that of nominal rural income. In real terms, the ratio of urban to rural per capita income actually declines modestly from 2.42 in 1988 to 2.38 in 1995.

The above conclusion should however be qualified. The urban–rural income disparity according to our definition was probably higher in 1994 than in 1995 (as is true for the SSB's ratio of urban to rural income, which peaked in 1994 at 2.87). The likelihood of such a decline is supported by the improvement in agriculture's terms of trade in 1995 and by the achievement that year of the highest rate of growth of agricultural production in a decade.[46]

Another qualification: as with the SSB estimates, income of rural–urban 'floating' migrants is not counted, except for the portion remitted to the rural household of record. This probably results in an overestimation of the urban–rural disparity.[47]

Inter-provincial inequality

Between 1988 and 1995, income inequality among China's provinces increased markedly. Table 11 shows the provincial range and coefficients of variation for variation for provinces *included in our 1995 survey*, according to the SSB and according to our survey.[48] While both sets of estimates indicate a sharp increase in the range of provincial incomes for rural China, the SSB estimate of this rise (51 per cent) is far lower than ours (70 per cent). For urban China there is no SSB range estimate for 1988; the SSB's estimate for 1995 is only three-quarters as great as ours.

The rural coefficient of variation of our survey is roughly the same as that of the SSB in 1998, but it too increases much faster than the SSB's. Our estimates of the coefficient of variation for both rural and urban incomes in 1995 are substantially higher than the official ones. Even according to the latter, however, it is clear that, while part of the sharp increase in absolute inter-regional inequality in incomes has been matched by increases in average income,[49] *relative* regional inequality has nevertheless also grown substantially.

Table 10   **Growth of urban and rural income**

	Survey estimates	SSB estimates
Growth in nominal income (per cent per year)		
Rural	17.20	16.40
Urban	17.52	20.07
Growth in real income (per cent per year)		
Rural	4.71	4.00
Urban	4.48	6.74
Growth of CPI (per cent per year)		
Rural	11.93	11.93
Urban	12.49	12.49
Urban per cap income as multiple of rural		
1988: nominal	2.42	2.19
1995: nominal	2.47	2.72
At 1988 cost of living	2.38	2.63

Note: Data for the survey estimates are from Tables 2 and 3. Data for the SSB estimates are from SSB, *Statistical Yearbooks of China* 1989 and 1996. Growth in CPI is based on the data given in text above.

Table 11   **Provincial distribution: ranges and coefficients of variation**

	Range				Coefficient of variation			
	Survey		SSB		Survey		SSB	
	1988	1995	1988	1995	1988	1995	1988	1995
Rural	2.69	4.60	2.42	3.66	0.33	0.55	0.35	0.41
Urban	2.19	2.93	-	2.25	0.37	0.46	-	0.30

Note: The sources of the SSB data for range estimates are SSB, *Statistical Yearbooks of China* 1989 and 1996. For 1988, estimates of urban income by province are not available from SSB sources. For both years, of the provinces included in the 1995 survey, the poorest rural province is Gansu and the richest is Beijing, while the poorest urban province is Shanxi and the richest Guangdong.

XI. Conclusion

Rather than attempt to provide a comprehensive summary of the many results presented above, we will conclude by reiterating a key issue raised by them: the need for public policies to take account of their distributional consequences.

Between 1988 and 1995 income inequality increased sharply in China, making it one of the more unequal of Asian developing countries. Inequality rose both in rural and urban areas, but the great urban–rural gap is still the dominant contributor to overall inequality. An increase in any category of rural income except wages would reduce overall inequality in China, *ceteris paribus*; an increase in any category of urban income would raise it.

While professing aversion to the threat of social and economic polarisation, China has encouraged or tolerated policies that contributed to the rapid growth of inequality. For example, instead of implementing compensatory measures to limit urban disparities as the wage spread necessarily grew wider, public policy has actually aggravated inequality by means of a highly disequalising system of net subsidies and by promoting housing reform that created an extremely skewed distribution of housing assets. The most important sources of urban inequality are rental value of owned housing and housing subsidy in kind. The highly disequalising distribution of these and other net subsidies to the urban population indicates a lack of focus of public policy on income distribution. If the basis for our housing subsidy estimates is sound, then more equal access to urban housing assets and either abolition or drastic redirection of urban housing subsidies would reduce the regressive nature of this policy.

In the countryside, similarly, the burden of net taxes and other transfers of income from households to the state and collectives is largely borne by households that are poor in the context of rural China and extremely poor in that of China as a whole. The regressive nature of rural fiscal policy hinders China's poverty alleviation effort and hastens income polarisation.

These results suggest that the rapidly widening inequality China has recently experienced was not all an inevitable result of the march toward a market economy, and that a more enlightened public policy could significantly ameliorate the polarising tendencies, while still reaping the rewards of greater efficiency and rapid growth.

Acknowledgements

We are greatly indebted to Professor Zhao Renwei of the Economics Institute, Chinese Academy of Social Sciences, whose leadership made possible the study on which this paper is based; and to Professor Li Shi, also of the Economics Institute, whose involvement in every phase of the project contributed immeasurably to its success. We thank Barry Naughton, Scott Rozelle, Terry Sicular, James Wen, and two anonymous referees for perceptive comments on an earlier draft of this paper. Acknowledgment is due to the Asian Development Bank and the Ford Foundation for their financial support of the project. Finally, we express appreciation for the co-operation of the State Statistical Bureau, which implemented the household income survey on the results of which this report is based.

Notes

1. Household income means the same thing as the more commonly used term personal income. The two terms are used interchangeably in this paper.
2. Main results were first published in A.R. Khan, K. Griffin, C. Riskin and Zhao Renwei, 'Household income and its distribution in China', *The China Quarterly*, No. 132 (December, 1992:1029–1061); a longer version appears as A.R. Khan, K. Griffin, C. Riskin and Zhao Renwei, 'Household income and its distribution in China', Chapter 1 of K. Griffin, and Zhao Renwei (eds), *The Distribution of Income in China*, (London: Macmillan, 1993).
3. A detailed discussion of the sampling methodology for 1988 can be found in Marc Eichen and Zhang Ming, 'The 1988 household

survey—data description and availability', in Griffin and Zhao (eds.), *Distribution of Income*. While selection of provinces for the 1995 survey changed as described in the text, selection of households proceeded as in 1988.

4. Our rural survey contained a question designed to elicit the household's net income as defined by the SSB. This was known because our sample was drawn from the SSB's larger sample. No similar question was included in the urban survey.

5. This somewhat incongruous combination was designed to maintain consistency with the 1988 survey. However, that survey under-counted non-wage income from enterprises. Therefore, the estimated increase from 1988 to 1995 is probably too high. This income item can be thought of as representing rural individual entrepreneurial income in 1995, since payments from the collective welfare fund comprised a very small part of it (averaging less than 2.5 yuan out of 140 yuan per capita).

6. In 1988, it was not possible to distinguish net farm income from net income of non-farm activities, since purchased inputs could not be differentiated by sector of use. Nor could they be differentiated by use between commercial and subsistence output, which led us to arbitrarily allocate them entirely to the former. Therefore, we ended up with net cash income from the sale of all farm and non-farm products, and gross value of consumption of farm products. Together these two items added up to the sum of net income from farming and non-farm activities.

7. It may be noted that in 1988 market rent was estimated indirectly, first, by indirectly estimating the replacement value of the house and, next, estimating market rent as 8 per cent of the replacement value. See Griffin and Zhao, *Distribution of Income*, Chapter 1. In the 1995 survey, respondents directly estimated the market rent of their abodes. This difference in estimation method should be kept in mind when assessing the differences in estimated housing subsidy between the two dates.

8. Thus, for example, our finding, reported later in this paper, that inequality increased between 1998 and 1995 does not imply that it rose steadily throughout that period. We suspect it

might in fact have peaked some time before 1995.

9. We did not have a separate estimate of net income from household farming for 1988 (see note 6). We had only the sum of the gross value of self-consumption of farm products and the net value of sale of farm products. Of these two, the first alone accounted for 41 per cent of rural income in 1988, strongly suggesting that total farm income as a proportion of total income was far above the 1995 ratio of 46 per cent.

10. 'Household member's net individual income from private, individual and/or jointly operated enterprises'.

11. 'Entrepreneurial income' differs from 'net income from household non-farm activities' in that the former arises from activity of individuals and the latter from household operations. While in practice the borderline may be somewhat blurred—for example, some respondents might regard a particular activity as individual, others as a family operation—we are confident that there is no overlap in the data from the two categories.

12. Reported property income is several times smaller than that implied by data on bank savings deposits and relevant interest rates (an observation we owe to an anonymous referee). Yet our estimate appears to be consistent with that of the SSB (which lumps property income from its household survey together with transfers; the combined estimate is virtually identical to ours. Whether or not the data on bank deposits from alternative sources shows that both the SSB and we have missed a part of this income is an issue on which we would like to reserve judgement, given the ambiguity of the evidence. For instance, it is apparently not uncommon for enterprises to place their funds in individual accounts, which bear higher interest rates. Nor is it certain that reported official interest rates are applicable to all deposits, especially those held by local savings institutions.

13. This is a Paasche index with 1985 as the base. The 'Rural CPI' for 1995 (220.09) is actually the value of the SSB's rural CPI for 1995 as a percentage of the same for 1988. The Paasche formula is known to understate the rate of increase in cost of living (see R.G.D. Allen, *Index*

Number, Theory and Practice, London: Macmillan, 1975). In this case, when neither of the two years compared is the index's base year, the use of the Paasche formula makes it impossible even to give a clear interpretation to the 'index' showing the change in CPI between 1988 and 1995.

14. For instance, the costs of a kilocalorie of food energy in both urban and rural areas increased at substantially higher rates than the official CPIs. If these are combined with the lowest of other available indices of price change for non-food goods, the resulting CPIs would be much higher than the official ones.

15. However, because non-wage income from enterprises was under-counted in 1988, growth of receipts from enterprises is very probably overstated.

16. The SSB estimates are 0.6 per cent of income in 1988 and 2.4 per cent in 1995, both somewhat below ours. This is surprising, since our estimates of income, the denominator, are substantially higher than the SSB's.

17. Urban property income may be under-reported. Our estimate is 80 per cent of the income from interest, dividends and rent as estimated by the SSB (see SSB, *Statistical Yearbook of China*, Beijing: Statistical Publishers, various years). We do not know how much of this difference is due to definition and classification of components and how much to possible bias in our sub-sample of the SSB parent sample. Both our estimate and the SSB's fall far short of an alternative estimate that could be derived from data on bank deposits and interest rates. The significance of this difference is unclear for reasons given above in note 12.

18. This item was probably substantially under-reported in both years. Moreover, there were too few non-zero observations for private enterprise income in 1995 to generate a statistically significant estimate for this item alone.

19. These include cash income from other jobs, unemployment benefits, income in kind, income received for being a village cadre and other cash income not from household activities. The statement that the SSB evidently excludes these items is based upon both the lack of any explicit mention of them in SSB, *Statistical Yearbook* (1997:313) and the close similarity between the

SSB's estimate for 'labourers' remuneration' and ours for regular plus non-regular wage income. We include pensions in wage-type income, whereas the SSB probably includes them in transfers. It is possible that some or all of our additional categories are indeed included in 'labourers' remuneration', in which case there is an inexplicably large gap between our respective estimates.

20. We asked for the total of all production costs, including labour costs, and subtracted them from gross revenues. Possibly, this resulted in under-enumeration of costs.

21. The SSB has two different concepts of urban income, 'per capita income' and 'per capita income available for living' (see SSB, *Statistical Yearbook of China* (Beijing: Statistical Publishers 1996), Table 9.5). From the meagre explanation of concepts provided by the SSB, it is impossible to know what the difference between them is. In a table of comparative urban and rural per capita incomes, the SSB shows the latter of the two urban measures along with 'per capita net income of rural households', suggesting that the two are comparable (SSB, *Statistical Yearbook of China* 1996: Table 9.4). After a careful comparison of components, we have decided that 'per capita income' is the relevant measure of income and this has been used throughout as representing the SSB estimate.

22. The saving rate for rural China was 17 per cent (on the basis of the data in SSB, *Statistical Yearbook of China* 1996:300) and for urban China 17.5 per cent (on the basis of the data in SSB, *Statistical Yearbook of China* 1996:284). Aggregate household incomes in urban and rural China are roughly equal, so that the weighted average saving rate is 17.25 per cent. GNP estimate is also from SSB, *Statistical Yearbook of China* (1996).

23. The estimates for these other Asian countries are from World Bank, *World Development Indicators 1997* (Washington, DC: The World Bank, 1997). There is, of course, the question of whether the rates elsewhere are accurately estimated.

24. This is based on the data in SSB, *Statistical Yearbook of China* (1996).

25. The annual growth rate in real per capita household income for China as a whole (the weighted average of rural and urban incomes) was higher than either the rural or the urban real income

growth because there was a rise in the weight of the urban population—the richer of the two income groups—between 1988 and 1995.

26. This point was called to our attention by Barry Naughton.

27. The share of government revenue in GNP *declined* sharply between 1988 and 1995: from 15.7 per cent to 10.9 per cent (SSB, *Statistical Yearbook of China* (1997)). Thus, if the shares of both the household and government sectors of the economy have decreased, then business sector income must have risen during the period in question.

28. Thus, the Theil Index, which, unlike the Gini ratio, can be decomposed, is sensitive to the sample size and is not amenable to intuitive interpretations such as one can make of the Gini ratio. The Atkinson Index is very sensitive to the subjective value of the inequality aversion parameter which is essentially arbitrary. Estimates of none of these other indices are nearly as widely available, for purposes of comparison, as the Gini ratio. For a comparison of different measures of inequality see Amartya Sen, *On Economic Inequality* (Oxford and New York: Oxford University Press, 1997).

29. See Khan, A. et al., 1998. 'Household income', *The China Quarterly*, June:221–53, for a more detailed discussion of Gini and concentration ratios.

30. Like other users of Gini ratios, we have not tried to measure their standard errors. We have adopted the convention of designating any change in Gini ratio of 10 per cent or greater as significant, but we cannot establish statistically the significance of a 10 per cent difference or, indeed, of a larger difference, for that matter. We believe the plausibility of individual estimates of increased inequality is enhanced by the broad range of such increases, and by the meagreness of examples of counter movements. Readers are of course free to arrive at their own judgements.

31. See Khan et al. 1998, 'Household income', *Distribution of Income*, for comparative data for other Asian countries.

32. If property income is underestimated (see note 12), then so is the Gini ratio, albeit by a small margin, because property income is such a highly disequalising source of income.

33. This pattern, and its exacerbation by fiscal decentralisation and government's declining share of GDP, is discussed in Christine Wong, C. Heady and L. West, *Financing Local Development in the People's Republic of China* (Oxford and New York: Oxford University Press, 1997). Its effect on health care is discussed in World Bank, *Financing Health Care* (Washington, DC: The World Bank, 1997).

34. Throughout this paper a change in the inequality of distribution of a component of income is measured by a change in its concentration ratio, not by a change in its Gini ratio.

35. See Guowuyuan yanjiushi ketizu (Study Group of State Planning Commission Research Office), 'Guanyu chengzhen jumin geren shouru chajude fenzi he jianyi' ('An analysis and proposal concerning income inequality among urban residents'), *Jingji yanjiu* (*Economic Research*), No. 8 (August 1997):3.

36. Despite the apparent equality of distribution of the combined category of private and individual enterprise income, we would conjecture that, if not underestimated, this category would be disequalising. This is because the chief source of underestimation is private enterprise income, which can be substantial and which accrues to very few individuals.

37. This paper does not take the position that ration coupons, with their allegedly adverse consequences for efficiency, should have been retained. The point is that they were not replaced by alternative measures to offset the adverse distributional consequences of their abolition.

38. See text above and note 18.

39. If property income is underestimated, as we suggested earlier it might be, then the Gini ratio is also slightly underestimated, since property income is such a disequalising source of income.

40. In 1995 rural China represented 71 per cent of the total population of China. The share of the rural population in the survey was just under 62 per cent. We therefore drew a 50 per cent random sample of rural households in the sample and added it to the sample. This raised the share of rural population in the survey to about 71 per cent.

41. International comparison of Gini ratios is subject to many problems. One has to be particularly careful about the variable for which

it is measured. The Gini ratio of the distribution of per capita expenditure is typically lower than the Gini ratio of the distribution of per capita income. The Gini ratio of per capita income distribution in Pakistan was 0.407 in 1990/91 (R. Amjad and A.R. Kemal, *Macro Economic Policies and their Impact on Poverty Alleviation in Pakistan* (Manila: ILO/South-East and Pacific Multidisciplinary Advisory Team, 1996)). The Gini ratio of expenditure distribution was 0.338 for India (1992) and 0.317 for Indonesia (1993) (World Bank, World Development Indicators). It seems implausible that the Gini ratios for income distribution in India and Indonesia would be so much higher than their Gini ratios for expenditure distribution as to be equal to China's Gini ratio. For the Philippines, the Gini ratio of distribution of expenditure was 0.43 (Arsenio Balisacan, What is the Real Story on Poverty in the Philippines? A Re-examination of Evidence and Policy, manuscript (Manila: School of Economics, University of the Philippines, 1996)).

42. See World Bank, *Sharing Rising Incomes: Disparities in China* (Washington, D.C.: The World Bank, 1997), for the first estimate, and World Bank, *World Development Indicators* for the second, both presumably based on official data and definitions.

43. Their estimated Gini for personal income for 1994 was 0.434, very close to our own estimate for 1995. Their estimate for rural income was 0.411, again close to our own; for urban income it was 0.377, well above our estimate (personal communication from State Planning Commission, Department of Social Development, November 1997).

44. Net taxes (negative net transfers), receipts from TVEs and other enterprises, property income and rental value of owned housing are other components of rural income that became more disequalising and thus contributed to the decline in the equalising character of rural income as a whole.

45. See Khan, A. et al., 1998. 'Household income', *Distribution of Income* for comparative evidence.

46. The index of terms of trade (the ratio of farm and sideline product price to rural retail price of industrial products) increased by 4.5 per cent. Gross value of agricultural production increased by 10.9 per cent. These data are from SSB, *Statistical Yearbook of China* (1996).

47. Assuming migrant income should be assigned to the urban category, its neglect almost certainly raises average urban income. If one thinks it belongs in rural income, its neglect probably lowers average rural income. In either case, the measured urban–rural gap is higher than it should be. We are indebted to an anonymous referee for raising the issue of treatment of migrant income.

48. The range is the ratio of the average per capita income of the richest province to that of the poorest. The coefficient of variation is the standard deviation of the distribution of provincial average per capita incomes divided by the mean provincial per capita income. It thus compares the absolute dispersion of the provincial average incomes with their mean, which has of course risen.

49. The standard deviation of rural provincial per capita income rises by 3.5 times while the mean doubles.

24 The Role of Foreign Trade and Investment in China's Economic Transformation

Nicholas R. Lardy

In the almost two decades since economic reform began in China the role of the foreign sector has burgeoned in ways that no one anticipated. The volume of foreign trade and the role of foreign capital are both far greater than could have been foreseen based on the modest Chinese economic reforms initiated in the late 1970s. By the mid 1990s China had become one of the world's largest trading nations, the recipient of more foreign direct investment than any other country in the world, the largest borrower from the World Bank, the largest recipient of official development assistance in the form of low-interest, long-term concessionary loans from industrialised countries, and, except for the Czech Republic, the only transition economy with ready access to international capital and equity markets.

This article attempts to analyse how important foreign trade and foreign capital have been to China's growth acceleration in the reform period and to identify those institutions and policies that have been most effective in this process. It then seeks to analyse the extent to which China's experience is relevant to other transition economies.

I. Foreign Capital

China has become a major participant in international capital markets. It has borrowed money from multilateral lending institutions such as the World Bank and the Asian Development Bank; from national development banks such as the Japanese Overseas Economic Co-operation Fund; from national export-import banks such as the United States Export Import Bank; and from commercial banks. In addition China has floated, both debt and equity issues on international capital markets. Finally, as noted above, China has become a major recipient of foreign direct investment. Indeed, in 1993 China was the site of more foreign direct investment than any other country.[1] In 1994 gross foreign direct investment inflows into China were exceeded only by those into the United States.

Foreign direct investment

Chinese data on foreign direct investment are given in Table 1. The data show it grew from modest amounts of a few hundred million dollars annually in the late 1970s and early 1980s to

Reprinted with permission. Nicholas R. Lardy, 1995. ' The role of foreign trade and investment in China's economic transformation', *China Quarterly*, 144(December):1065–82 (with minor editing).

almost four billion dollars annually in the late 1980s. Because many foreign invested projects were delayed in the aftermath of Tiananmen, actual investment showed no growth in 1990. However, beginning in 1991, China attracted greatly increased amounts of foreign direct investment. It more than doubled in both 1993 and 1994 and rose a further one-fifth in 1994 to reach almost $34 billion actual investment.

The dramatic increases in foreign direct investment in the first half of the 1990s appear to be caused by four factors. Firstly, the magnitude of aggregate foreign direct investment flowing to developing countries increased significantly in the 1990s. Average annual flows in 1990–93 were double those of 1987–89.[2]

Secondly, China's seeming political stability in the wake of Tiananmen, combined with the explosive growth of the domestic economy after 1992, led to a fundamental reassessment by foreign firms of China's economic and investment potential. China was deemed a less risky political and economic environment by risk assessment organisations such as the Economist Intelligence Unit.[3] Many multinationals decided that they could not afford not to invest in the world's fastest growing emerging market.

Thirdly, China systematically liberalised its foreign investment regime. Some of the special provisions to attract foreign direct investment, which in the late 1970s and early 1980s had only been available in the four special economic zones in South China, were made much more widely available. For example, special tax concessions, liberalised land leasing and other inducements were made available in a growing number of open coastal cities, economic development areas and high technology development zones, increasing the attractiveness of China as a site for foreign investment. China also opened up sectors such as retailing, power generation and port development that previously had been off limits for foreign investors.[4] Liberalisation of foreign participation in property development

---

Table 1   Foreign direct investment in China, 1979–94 (millions of US$)

Year	Contracted	Actual
1979–82 (cumulative)	6,999	1,767
1983	1,917	916
1984	2,875	1,419
1985	6,333	1,959
1986	3,330	2,244
1987	4,319	2,647
1988	6,191	3,739
1989	6,294	3,773
1990	6,987	3,755
1991	12,422	4,666
1992	58,736	11,292
1993	111,435	27,514
1994	81,406	33,787

Note: The data reported above are inclusive of foreign direct investment in equity joint ventures, contractual joint ventures, wholly foreign-owned enterprises and joint exploration as well as foreign investment in leasing, compensation trade, and processing and assembly.
Sources: Ministry of Foreign Trade and Economic Relations, *Zhonghua renmin gongheguo duiwai jingjimaoyibu xinwen gongbao (The Bulletin of the Ministry of Foreign Trade and Economic Relations of the People's Republic of China)*, No. 2 (25 April 1994):10, Xinhua News Service, 'Zhongguo qunian liyong waizi 337 yi duo meiyuan', ('Last year China's utilized foreign direct investment exceeded US$33.7 billion'), *Jinrong shibao (Banking Times)*, 26 January 1995:1.

in the early 1990s led to particularly significant foreign capital inflows directed toward the development of residential housing, retail complexes and other projects.

Fourthly, foreign direct investment flows increased in part because of the phenomenon of recycled capital of Chinese origin. In order to take advantage of the special tax and other incentives provided to foreign invested enterprises, Chinese firms moved money off-shore and then recycled it back into China disguised as 'foreign investment'. The World Bank guessed that these might comprise as much as 25 per cent of gross investment inflows in 1992.[5]

Foreign borrowing

China's second largest source of foreign capital, after foreign direct investment, has been borrowing. The cumulative amount of foreign borrowing from all sources is reflected in Table 2. The data show China's total external debt rising from well under $1 billion in 1978, as reform was just getting under way, to $93 billion by the end of 1994. To put these numbers in perspective, only Indonesia among low and lower-middle income economies has a larger outstanding debt. China's external debt is only modestly smaller than the two most heavily indebted upper-middle income economies, Mexico and Brazil.

However, China's debt burden remains modest. In part this is because its exports are so much larger, relative to its outstanding debt, than those of Brazil and Mexico, which the World Bank classifies as moderately and severely indebted, respectively.[6] For example, on average in 1991–93 China's total external debt relative to earnings from the export of goods and services was less than half that of Mexico and less than a third that of Brazil.[7]

In addition, a relatively large share of China's external debt is concessionary with grace periods of up to ten years before repayments of principal must begin and/or carrying below market interest rates. Even its non-concessionary debt carries favourable interest rates since China is

the only transition economy, except for the Czech Republic, that enjoys an investment grade rating on its sovereign debt, allowing it to sell its bonds internationally with a lower interest rate than the market would otherwise demand.[8]

These factors reduce China's debt service, including both amortisation and interest payments, below what it would otherwise be. For example, at year-end 1993, of China's total external debt of $83.6 billion, a little over $10 billion was owed to the World Bank and other multilateral lending agencies. A large share of this debt is to the World Bank's soft loan window, the International Development Association (IDA). Loans from IDA bear no interest at all and since 1989 even the initial commitment fee

Table 2   **China's external debt, 1978–94**

Year	Millions of US$
1978	623
1979	2,183
1980	4,504
1981	5,797
1982	8,358
1983	9,609
1984	12,082
1985	16,722
1986	23,746
1987	35,296
1988	42,362
1989	44,812
1990	52,554
1991	60,851
1992	69,321
1993	83,573
1994	92,806

Sources: World Bank, China: *Macroeconomic Stability in a Decentralised Economy* (Washington, DC: The World Bank, 1994:184). The People's Bank of China, *China Financial Outlook 1994* (Beijing: China Financial Publishing House, 1994:58). Xinhua News Agency, 'Woguo waizhai changzhailu he zhaiwulu diyu guoji gongren jingjie xian shuiping' ('China's external debt, debt service ratio, and debt-to-export ratio are lower than the international warning levels'), *Renmin ribao* (*People's Daily*), 21 July 1995:1.

borrowers were once charged has been eliminated.[9] Debt from official bilateral creditors stood at almost $23 billion. Thus borrowing from private creditors on commercial terms comprised only about three-fifths of China's total external debt.

Foreign equity investment

In addition to foreign direct investment and borrowing abroad, China has sold equities for hard currency on both domestic and international markets. The market for B shares in Chinese companies, which are priced in domestic currency but paid for in hard currencies, began in 1992. In that year the B shares of nine companies were listed on the Shanghai stock exchange. Thirteen companies were listed in 1993, with ten more in 1994. By the end of 1994 the B shares of 34 Chinese companies were traded on the Shanghai and Shenzhen stock markets.

Sales of Chinese companies on international markets began in the autumn of 1992 when China Brilliance Automotive was listed on the New York Stock Exchange.[10] At about the same time the Chinese Securities Regulatory Commission approved a plan to list nine Chinese state-owned companies on the Hong Kong Stock Exchange beginning in 1993. More issues were sold in New York in 1993 and 1994. Table 3 shows that the proceeds from the international sale of equities and debt instruments roughly doubled in 1993 compared to the previous year. Based on sales of bonds and equity on international markets to September 1994, proceeds in 1994 probably increased by about 25 per cent over 1993.

The data summarised above suggest that China was awash in foreign capital in the mid 1990s. In 1994 gross capital inflows exceeded $53 billion, including about $17 billion in borrowing from commercial banks, international organisations, bilateral development banks and international bond markets; $34 billion in foreign direct investment; and about $2.5 billion in equity investments. These numbers might suggest that China is heavily dependent on foreign capital to

Table 3	China's international equity and debt issues, 1991–94 (millions of US$)	
	Equity	Debt
1991	11	115
1992	1,049	1,289
1993	1,908	3,184
1994*	1,939	3,134

Notes: *to the end of September 1994.
The value of international equity issues is inclusive of listings of Chinese companies in New York and Hong Kong, the value of B share offerings in Shenzhen and Shanghai, and the value of so-called 'back door listings' in which China-backed companies obtain a listing on the Hong Kong Stock Exchange by purchasing a relatively dormant existing listed company. The company then injects assets financed by rights issues and placements. The best examples are CITIC Pacific, controlled by Beijing-based CITIC, and Guangdong Investment, controlled by the Guangdong provincial government.
Sources: International Monetary Fund, *International Capital Markets: Developments, Prospects, and Policy Issues* (Washington, DC: International Monetary Fund, 1994):127. World Bank, *World Debt Tables. External Finance for Developing Countries, 1994–95* (Washington, DC: The World Bank, 1994), Vol.1:103, 116–17.

finance investment and thus to generate the rapid economic growth of the 1990s. However, this conclusion would not be warranted. After taking into account outflows of Chinese capital and changes in holdings of foreign exchange, at least to the end of 1994 foreign capital appears to have been an insignificant source of investment in China.

A quick accounting explains the paradox. First, capital inflows may be used to finance a current account deficit (when imports of goods and services exceed exports of goods and services) or may added to the foreign exchange holdings of the government, enterprises or individuals. Secondly, capital inflows must be measured on a net basis, that is, outflows of capital must be taken into account.

The first adjustment is somewhat easier than the adjustment from gross to net. Official holdings of foreign exchange by the People's

Bank of China more than doubled in 1994, from $21.2 billion at year-end 1993 to $51.6 billion at year-end 1994.[11] In addition, individual holdings of foreign exchange in the Bank of China and other banks authorised to accept foreign exchange deposits, which since August 1992 have not been included in China's official foreign exchange holdings, grew by about $6 billion in 1994.[12] Retained foreign exchange earnings of the Bank of China and other financial institutions presumably also rose. Thus, holdings of foreign exchange appear to have increased by at least $36 billion in 1994.

The adjustment from gross to net capital flows is more difficult because of incomplete information. Outflows on the capital account include amortisation of previously contracted foreign debt, officially recorded foreign direct

investment abroad by Chinese companies and unrecorded capital outflows. Amortisation of existing debt was around $7.5 billion in 1994. Official Chinese balance of payments data, which are published with a considerable time lag, show that China's annual foreign direct investment abroad grew steadily from $20 million in 1982 to $913 million by 1991.[13] Most international observers put the actual amount considerably higher. China's foreign direct investment outflows in 1994 may have been about $5–10 billion. This would be roughly consistent with reports of the increases in the stock of Chinese foreign direct investment abroad. Chinese authorities placed cumulative Chinese investment in Hong Kong alone at $19.2 billion by the end of 1994, an amount that is far larger than could be accounted for by China's officially reported capital outflows.[14] Finally, the errors and omissions entry in the balance of payments, presumably largely reflecting unrecorded capital outflows, was $24.9 billion in 1992 and $20.9 billion in 1993.[15] Based on China's current account surplus of $7.7 billion in 1994, the estimated $36 billion increase in foreign exchange holdings, and other known or estimated components of the capital account, unrecorded capital outflows and the net capital inflow can be estimated at $7 to $12 billion and $28.7 billion, respectively.[16] Increases in holdings of foreign reserves more than absorbed net capital inflows. Thus, unless foreign direct investment outflows or unrecorded capital outflows have been overestimated there appears to have been no foreign contribution to capital formation in China in 1994.

Because of the many uncertainties surrounding entries in the capital account in China's balance of payments data, it is instructive to examine China's current account, that is, the balance on trade in goods and services. Ignoring for the moment changes in reserve holdings, any current account deficit (surplus) must be financed with a capital inflow (outflow). In short, net capital inflows must be used either to finance a current account deficit or be added to foreign exchange holdings. Thus, after adjusting for

Table 4	China's current account, 1978–94 (millions of US$)
1978	-932
1979	-2,489
1980	-3,281
1981	1,319
1982	5,748
1983	4,487
1984	2,509
1985	-11,810
1986	-7,334
1987	300
1988	-3,802
1989	-4,316
1990	11,997
1991	13,273
1992	6,401
1993	-11,609
1994	7,660

Sources: World Bank, China: *Macroeconomic Stability in a Decentralised Economy* (Washington, DC.: The World Bank, 1994:177). International Monetary Fund, *International Financial Statistics*, June 1995:166. Xinhua News Agency, 'Woguo qunian guoji shouzhi zhuangkuang haozhuan' ('China's balance of payments situation improved last year), *Renmin ribao*, 18 July 1995:1.

changes in holding of foreign reserves, China's net capital inflows over time can be measured by its cumulative current account deficit.

Two points emerge from an analysis of the data on China's current account deficit in Table 4. First, on a year-by-year basis China's current account position, whether deficit or surplus, has been relatively small. For example, even China's record current account surplus of about $13 billion in 1991 was only 3.7 per cent of GNP.[17] Moreover, the average current account deficit or surplus over the 12-year period was less than half that of 1991. Thus, China's average annual current account position has been quite modest.

More importantly, over time China's cumulative current account position is insignificant. From the beginning of 1982 to the end of 1993 it was actually a positive $5.846 billion. This does not mean that China experienced a net outflow of capital, for changes in China's foreign exchange reserves have been ignored.

Over the same period China's total foreign exchange reserves rose by $44.2 billion.[18] Thus China's cumulative capital inflow over the period is the difference between the increase in reserves and the current account surplus or about $38.4 billion. This is a very modest amount, regardless of one's view of the degree to which using the official exchange rate to convert yuan to dollars understates the size of China's real GNP. Even using the official exchange rate, which results in the lowest estimate of aggregate output, China's cumulative gross domestic product from 1982 to the end of 1993 was $4,100 billion. Thus cumulative net foreign capital inflows would amount to less than one per cent of cumulative output. Purchasing power parity estimates of Chinese output in 1990 place GDP at from 3.5 to 8 times the level calculated on the exchange rate.[19] If the same relationship holds over the entire period, China's cumulative net capital inflow over 12 years could have been as low as one-tenth of one per cent of Chinese GDP. In short, cumulative net foreign capital inflow relative to cumulative output of the Chinese economy over the 12 years was less than one per cent and may have been vanishingly small.

The same point is borne out by examining data on the relative importance of net foreign savings and gross national saving in financing gross domestic investment. Data for selective years are shown in Table 5. They show that the contribution of net foreign savings to gross domestic investment varies; in some years it is positive and in others negative. Thus, contrary to what one might believe from observing the flood of foreign capital flowing into China, on a net basis such inflows have not contributed to domestic capital formation in China.

Although foreign capital has not made a major impact on China's savings-investment balance, it has contributed significantly to the transfer to China of advanced technology and managerial practices in many industries; to the expansion of China's trade; and indirectly to the supply of foreign exchange.

Effect on foreign trade

The transforming effect of foreign investment on China's economy is revealed in Table 6, which

Table 5   **Investment and savings, selected years** (per cent gross domestic product)

	1980	1990	1991	1992	1993
Gross domestic investment	30	35	35	38	43
Gross national savings	28	38	39	39	40
Net foreign savings	2	-3	-4	-2	2

Source: World Bank, *China: Macroeconomic Stability in a Decentralised Economy*:8.

Table 6   **Exports of foreign invested enterprises, 1985–94**

Year	Millions of US$	Percentage of total exports
1985	320	1.1
1986	480	1.6
1987	1,200	3.0
1988	2,460	5.2
1989	4,920	8.3
1990	7,800	12.5
1991	12,100	16.8
1992	17,400	20.4
1993	25,240	27.5
1991	34,710	28.7

Note: Exports are inclusive of those produced by equity joint ventures, contractual joint ventures, and wholly foreign-owned firms.
Sources: Nicholas R. Lardy, 'Chinese foreign trade', *The China Quarterly*, No. 131 (September 1992:711). New China News Agency, 'Zhongguo duiwai maoyi zongjine qunian zengzhi 1957 yi meiyuan' ('China's foreign trade increases to reach $195.7 billion'), *Renmin ribao*, 10 January 1994. Li Ziaolei, 'Sanzi qiye waimao jinchukou zengjia' ('Foreign trade imports and exports of foreign invested enterprises increase'), *Renmin ribao*, 18 January 1995:1.

shows exports generated by foreign invested enterprises. The small amounts of foreign direct investment in the late 1970s and early 1980s initially made a negligible contribution to China's total exports. As late as 1985, six years after the passage of China's foreign investment law and five years after the establishment of special economic zones, the exports of foreign invested enterprises were only $320 million, barely over one per cent of China's total exports. From that modest base they expanded dramatically, reaching about $35 billion by 1994, almost 30 per cent of China's total exports.

Exports produced by foreign invested firms are predominantly products assembled from imported parts and components. In addition, many Chinese firms also produce processed exports using parts and components supplied by or purchased from foreign firms. Total processed exports grew to $57 billion in 1994, almost half of China's exports.[20] They comprised about 60 per cent of $100 billion in manufactured goods exports that year. In recent years about half of these exports have been produced by foreign-funded firms.

Effect on the supply of foreign exchange

Under the provisions of China's foreign exchange control system, foreign-funded enterprises have had full control of their foreign exchange earnings from exports throughout the reform period. Most importantly, a very large share of the exports of foreign-funded enterprises are processed products such as machinery, electronics and garments. Export earnings are largely used to pay for imported components and assemblies used in the production of these goods. For example, in 1994 foreign-funded firms exported $30.58 billion in processed products but imports of parts, components and the equipment needed to carry out the processing amounted to $28.09 billion.[21]

Despite their heavy expenditures on imported parts and components, foreign-funded firms generally have been net sellers of foreign exchange, first through informal markets and, since 1985, in the swap markets for foreign exchange. Their net sales of foreign exchange rose from $442 million in 1988 to more than $3 billion in 1994.[22]

Foreign trade

More outwardly oriented economies usually achieve higher rates of savings and investment, and greater efficiency in the use of investment resources, both of which contribute to higher rates of growth. Efficiency gains may accrue not only from economies of scale but, more importantly, from the stimulus that international competition provides for technical change and managerial efficiencies.[23] The World Bank in particular believes that success in the promotion of manufactured exports provides a powerful mechanism for technological upgrading and thus a source of rapid productivity growth in the high performing economies of East Asia.[24]

The pace of growth of Chinese exports shown in Table 7, particularly manufactured exports,

compares quite favourably with the countries the World Bank has identified as the high performing economies of East Asia. Not only have China's exports grown more rapidly than those of any other country, the commodity composition has shifted decisively toward manufactured goods. By 1994 China exported manufactured goods worth more than $100 billion and was probably the eighth largest such exporter in the world. At growth rates observed in recent years, by the year 2000 China's exports of manufactured goods will surpass those of the United Kingdom.

What is less clear is whether this growth has stimulated the postulated improvement in productivity in manufacturing that was characteristic of the other high performing economies in East Asia. If enhanced productivity had spread to the state-owned industrial sector,

Table 7   **Chinese exports, 1978–94**

Year	Exports Billions of $	Of which manufactured exports	
		Billions of $	% of total exports
1978	9.8	-	-
1979	13.7	-	-
1980	18.2	9,005	49.7
1981	22.0	11,756	53.4
1982	22.3	12,271	55.0
1983	22.2	12,606	56.7
1984	26.1	14,205	54.3
1985	27.4	13,522	49.4
1986	30.9	19,670	63.6
1987	39.4	26,206	66.5
1988	47.5	33,110	69.7
1989	52.5	37,460	71.3
1990	62.1	46,205	74.4
1991	71.8	55,698	77.5
1992	85.0	67,948	79.9
1993	91.8	75,090	81.8
1994	121.0	101,330	83.7

Note: Data for 1978 and 1979 were compiled by the Ministry of Foreign Economic Relations and Trade. A breakdown of manufactured goods for these years is not available since the Ministry combined data on exports of manufactures and mineral products in a single category.
Sources: State Statistical Bureau, *Zhongguo tongji nianjian 1993* (*Chinese Statistical Yearbook 1993*) (Beijing: State Statistical Publishing House, 1993:634). 'Wo waimao jinchukou zaichuang jiaji' ('China's foreign trade again achieves fine results'), *Renmin ribao*, 14 January 1995:1.

this presumably would be reflected in evidence of increasing ability to compete with foreign firms either in international or domestic markets.

As already suggested, the most impressive export performance in China has been by foreign-funded enterprises and Chinese firms engaged in export processing. For the most part the latter appear to be township and village enterprises rather than state-owned enterprises. Although exports of state-owned manufacturing firms have grown significantly, their contribution to export growth looks quite modest when measured against the share of manufactured goods that they produce. State-owned firms, which produced two-thirds of all manufactured goods in 1985, have contributed a rapidly declining share of annual incremental exports. In 1986 and 1987 they accounted for more than four-fifths of the growth of exports; in 1991–1992, when they still accounted for fully half of all manufactured goods production, their contribution was only a fifth.[25]

Foreign invested enterprises contribute such a small share of total manufactured goods output that they are not even listed as a separate category in the industrial output data published by the State Statistical Bureau in its annual *Statistical Yearbook of China*. The output of foreign-funded enterprises, along with that produced by firms with a variety of less important forms of ownership, is included in the category 'other' which expanded from about one per cent of output in 1985 to 7 per cent by 1992.[26] Yet the contribution of foreign-funded enterprises to annual incremental exports rose from 4 per cent in 1986 to an average of three-fifths in 1992–94. By 1994 foreign-funded enterprises accounted for 15 times more exports than would have been expected on the basis of their contribution to output.[27] In short, it is not easy to make the case that state-owned firms have become increasingly successful competitors in the international market.

What about in domestic markets? To what extent are state-owned manufacturing firms successfully competing with foreign firms in the Chinese market? A fully satisfactory answer to this question lies well beyond the scope of this article. However, some important evidence, such as the structure of tariff and non-tariff protection that insulates Chinese industry from international competition, does exist.

A World Bank study of China's trade regime showed that Chinese import tariffs in 1992 were relatively high by international standards, particularly for manufactured consumer goods.[28] In addition, China imposes a variety of non-tariff barriers including a mandatory import plan, canalisation of imports and import licensing. The sectors with the highest concentration of these non-tariff barriers are iron and steel products, textile yarns and machinery.[29]

An evaluation that takes into account the high degree of dispersion of China's nominal import tariff levels is even more revealing. Economists have long noted that if tariffs are below average on primary and intermediate goods then the effective rate of protection afforded to the final good will be substantially above the nominal tariff rate applied to that good. The World Bank's analysis of effective rates of protection showed that valued added at international prices was negative in 10 of 19 sectors examined, including petroleum refining, machinery, building materials, wood and pulp, food processing, textiles, apparel, paper, and miscellaneous manufactures. This means that under the assumptions of the model 'none of these activities would appear to be able to survive under full trade liberalisation.'[30] The study quickly adds that, because the analysis is based on quite aggregate categories, it would be incorrect to assume that the production of every good in each of these sectors would wither if subject to the full force of international competition. But the results are 'indicative of the highly distorted nature of the Chinese trade regime.'[31]

Moreover, even some major industries that have positive value added at international prices are heavily insulated from international competition. For example the chemical industry,

China's fourth largest, receives an effective rate of protection from imports of more than 110 per cent.[32] It is difficult to envisage that this industry has begun to feel the effects of international competition.

Chinese assessments of the challenge that would be presented by the reduction of tariff and non-tariff protection that presumably would accompany its participation in the General Agreement on Tariffs and Trade (GATT) generally confirms the analysis of the World Bank. An authoritative analysis of the State Planning Commission's Economic Research Institute reported that if China were to accede to the GATT, 'the branches of industry that would take the greatest pounding, in order, are the electronics industry (computers, video cameras, xerographic copiers, colour television tubes, cameras, and broadcast and communications equipment), motor vehicles and trucks, petroleum refining, numerically controlled machine tools, and instruments.'[33]

In short, the partial evidence that is available suggests that state-owned industries have not participated proportionately in the growth of China's exports. Since they are heavily insulated from international competition, they also appear ill-prepared to compete with foreign firms in China's domestic market. Thus if productivity has been rising in the state-owned sector in China, it would appear to be stimulated by processes that are quite different from those that were important in other high performing economies in East Asia.

II. China's Trade Reform Strategy in Comparative Perspective

Any comparative assessment of China's foreign trade and investment reform strategy needs to take into account two respects in which China differed fundamentally from many other transition economies. First, China was never a formal member of the Council of Mutual Economic Assistance (CMEA) and at the time economic reform began in China it had been trading predominantly with Western market economies for almost two decades. Thus it avoided the major disruption of trade associated with the collapse of intra-CMEA trade in the early 1990s, which followed the formal introduction of convertible currency settlements in world prices on 1 January 1991 and the decision to dissolve CMEA in June 1991.[34] In the case of Russia, exports to former CMEA countries fell by more than three-quarters between 1990 and 1992 and imports fell by five-sixths.[35] The collapse of intra-CMEA trade, in turn, was one of the most important factors leading to declining real output in Russia and Eastern Europe.

Second, China began its economic reform with virtually no external debt. It had imposed a policy of extreme financial self-reliance, right up until the time economic reform began. Its trade with the rest of the world was small and imports were all financed by export earnings. Thus China had not borrowed significant amounts on international markets.[36]

By contrast the former Soviet Union under Gorbachev between 1987 and 1991 had borrowed heavily from the West to finance its budget deficit. External debt shot up from $14.2 billion at the end of 1984 to $56.6 billion by the end of 1991.[37] However, this borrowing was utilised largely to finance current consumption rather than investment that would contribute to Soviet export earnings. As a result, as early as 1989 the USSR began to delay repayment of some external obligations. By the end of 1991, when Russia had become an independent sovereign entity, its unpaid international obligations were around $6 billion.[38] Although it was already in default on its debt, Russia assumed responsibility for almost all the debts of the former Soviet Union which, it was revealed in late 1994, meant year-end 1991 total external indebtedness was $103.9 billion. As a result of IMF and World Bank lending and modest amounts of official commodity credits from Western governments, by mid 1995 Russian external debt amounted to $130 billion.[39] Since this was more than twice the value of its exports outside the FSU, Russia sought to reach an agreement on rescheduling payments on outstanding debts from the Soviet era, which would presumably facilitate its return to international debt markets. In short, Russia was handicapped in its transition since its huge existing prior debt plus falling exports meant that debt rescheduling, if not default, was almost inevitable. That in turn deprived Russia of access to commercial credit in the early years of economic transition.

China's strategy of external reform was quite gradual. Key institutional reforms, such as ending the monopoly powers of state-owned trading companies, were phased in over more than a decade.[40] Even as late as 1993 only 839 Chinese manufacturing companies had been granted the right to trade directly in the international market.[41] By contrast in Russia all firms were given the right of direct international trade almost from the outset of reform in January 1992.[42] Similarly the process of convergence of Chinese domestic with international prices for traded goods lasted well into the 1990s whereas, with a few exceptions, prices were liberalised in Russia within a year or so of the break-up of the Soviet Union. The story is similar on import subsidies. As a percentage of gross domestic product they were initially much larger in Russia, but they were abolished in 1994. In China they persisted well beyond the first decade of reform.

China's comparatively gradualistic approach in the external sector was appropriate, given its initial economic conditions and the slow pace of reform in the domestic economy, particularly in the state-owned manufacturing sector. The immediate freeing of all prices in an environment in which state-owned enterprises were still not subject to hard budget constraints would have led, as it did in Russia, to skyrocketing prices for industrial goods. For the same reason moving rapidly to current account convertibility would have caused massive excessive devaluation of the renminbi. In short, application of the Russian model in China probably would have created severe macroeconomic imbalances.[43]

The challenge China faces now is to coordinate the further liberalisation of its trade regime, particularly reducing various barriers to imports, with the reform of the state-owned sector, especially in manufacturing. Subsidies to state-owned enterprises, increasingly in the form of bank loans that are not repaid, absorbed about 10 per cent of gross domestic product in 1993, 'an unsustainable structural situation' according to the World Bank.[44] Reform in the state-owned sector will require a substantial degree of industrial restructuring, a process that has been largely postponed.[45] Liberalisation of China's import regime, which would subject Chinese firms to increasing international competition, should be an important tool to facilitate industrial restructuring.

III. Conclusion

Despite the impressive expansion of exports, large inflows of foreign direct investment and access to international capital markets that is unparalleled among transition economies, it is still premature to judge that China's external sector reforms have been a stunning success in comparison with others. China has had rapid export growth, but this has depended to an unprecedented degree on foreign invested firms. There is nothing wrong with reliance on foreign-funded enterprises, per se. But, combined with the protection provided to state-owned industries, it has inhibited productivity growth, especially in intermediate input industries where prices are still above international levels.[46] Thus rapid export growth from foreign invested firms, a large share of which is export processing, has limited backward linkages and the domestic content of exports is very low. To some extent export industries appear to be enclaves and China's state-owned industries have under-participated in export growth by a wide margin. Over the longer term it will be difficult for China to sustain the growth of exports at a rate anywhere near that of the past decade unless there is widespread industrial restructuring.

395

China in recent years has attracted far more foreign direct investment than all the other transition economies combined. But, as already noted above, such investment in China is substantially overstated because of the recycling phenomenon. Moreover, the real difference that remains after correcting for this factor may reflect primarily the relatively early stage of the economic transitions of the former Soviet Union and Eastern Europe. As the data in Table 1 reflect, foreign direct investment in China in the first decade of reform was quite modest compared to the inflows recorded in the early 1990s. Foreign direct investment in the six countries of Eastern Europe was $2.4 billion, $3.3 billion and $5.0 billion in 1991–93, amounts that compare quite favourably with direct foreign investment in China at a comparable stage of its transition a decade earlier.[47]

Finally, China's better access to international capital markets was at least partially due to its lack of pre-reform borrowing. At the outset of their reforms Russia, Bulgaria and Poland struggled to generate trade surpluses in order to service debts accrued under old regimes. Ultimately they defaulted and so access to international capital markets was limited to debt restructurings, lending by international organisations and credits extended by Western governments to promote their own exports. By contrast China, with ready access to international borrowing, enjoyed the luxury of running relatively large trade deficits in the first three years of economic reform.[48]

Moreover, China's access to international capital has improved over time. The sale of equities on international markets, for example, did not start until 1992 and bond sales were relatively modest until the same year.[49] Again that suggests, as in the case of foreign direct investment, that the access to international capital markets of other transition economies may compare more favourably to China after their reforms are a decade and a half old.

Notes

1. World Bank, *World Debt Tables: External Finance for Developing Countries, 1994–95* (Washington, DC: The World Bank, 1994), (1):16.
2. *Ibid*:159.
3. On a scale in which 100 is the riskiest rating, China rated 15 in 1988, one of the EIU's lowest risk ratings. This jumped to 35 in 1989 but by 1992 had fallen back to 25. *The Economist*, 21 May 1994:120.
4. Nicholas, R. Lardy, *China in the World Economy* (Washington, DC: Institute for International Economics, 1994):63–71.
5. Peter Harrold and Rajiv Lall, *China. Reform and Development in 1992–93*, World Bank Discussion Paper No. 215 (Washington, DC: The World Bank, August 1993):24.
6. Severely indebted countries are those for which either the ratio of the present value of debt service to GNP exceeds 80 per cent or the ratio of the present value of debt service to exports of goods and sercices exceeds 220 per cent. For moderately indebted countries the ranges of the values of these variables is from 48 to 80 per cent and from 132 to 220 per cent respectively.
7. World Bank, *World Debt Tables 1994–95*(1):55–56.
8. Moody's rates China's long-term sovereign debt at A3 while Standard and Poor's gives a rating of BBB. Both are investment grade ratings. Other transition economies that have rated sovereign debt, but which have been assigned below investment grade ratings, are Hungary and Slovakia. *Transition* Vol. 5(9) (November–December) 1994:13. Both agencies initially assigned ratings to the Bank of China, the Industrial and Commercial Bank, the People's Construction Bank of China, the Bank of Communications, China International Trust and Investment Company (CITIC), and the Guangdong International Trust and Investment Company (GITIC) that were identical to those they gave to China's sovereign debt. However, in April 1995 Moody's downgraded the first four of these to Baa. Prior to that it had watchlisted CITIC for a potential downgrade. Although Baa is still an investment grade rating, the downgrade led the Bank of China to cancel a HK$5 billion floating rate certificate of deposit issue.

9. Technically the fee is still set annually by the Executive Directors of the World Bank. But it has been set at zero from fiscal year 1989 to fiscal year 1995.

10. Technically China Brilliance Automotive Holdings Limited is a Bermuda-based holding company, not a Chinese company. However, since the holding company's only asset is a 51 per cent ownership in the Shenyang Jinbei Passenger Vehicle Manufacturing Company, Ltd., for practical purposes it may be regarded as a Chinese company. The holding company was established in 1992, only a few months before the initial public offering of the stock of the New York Stock Exchange. According to some sources the Bermuda holding company was creatd simply to escape the approvals required by China's Securities Regulatory Commission for overseas listings of Chinese firms.

11. Zhu Baihua and Ou Yangwei, 'Zhongguo waihui chubei yu wubai yi meiyan' ('China's foreign exchange reserves exceed $US50 billion'), Renmin ribao (People's Daily), 28 January 1995:1.

12. Personal savings in foreign exchange denominated accounts amounted to some $20 billion at the end of 1994. 'BOC says $20b saved in foreign currency', China Daily, 11 January 1995:7.

13. State Statistical Bureau, 1979–91 Zhongguo duiwai jingji tongji daquan (1979–1991 China Foreign Economic Statistics) (Beijing: Chinese Statistical Publishing House, 1993):9–11.

14. New China News Agency, Hong Kong Branch quoted in Hong Kong Economic and Trade Office, Hong Kong Digest Issue No. 1/95:5–6.

15. World Bank, China: Macroeconomic Stability in a Decentralised Economy (Washington, DC:The World Bank, 1994):14.

16. Net capital inflow equals changes in reserves ($36.4 billion) minus current account surplus ($7.7 billion). Unrecorded capital outflows estimated from : gross capital inflow ($53.2 billion) minus gross capital outflow equals net capital inflow ($28.7 billion) where gross capital outflow is the sum of amortisation ($7.5 billion), Chinese foreign direct investment abroad ($5–10 billion) and unrecorded capital outflows.

17. World Bank, China: Macroeconomic Stability in a Decentralised Economy:14. Even this calculation,

since it utilises the official exchange rate to convert China's GNP in yuan into US dollars, overstates the magnitude of the surplus. Taking into account the real purchasing power of the Chinese currency, China's estimated GNP would be at least three times higher and the current account surplus as a percentage of GNP only one-third, or even less than the 3.7 per cent estimate.

18. Based on estimated total reserves of $49 billion at year-end 1993 and the official figure of $4.773 billion for year-end 1981. Chinese Finance and Banking Society, 1993 Zhongguo jinrong nianjian (Almanac of China's Finance and Banking 1993) (Beijing: Zhongguo jinrong nianjian bianjibu (Chinese Finance and Banking Compilation Department), 1993):368.

19. Lardy, China in the World Economy:15.

20. 'Wo jiagong maoyi jinchukou qunian tupo qianyi meiyuan' ('China's import and export processing trade broke through the level of US$100 billion last year'), Renmin ribao, 23 January 1995:1.

21. 'Processed goods lead exports to new high,' China Daily, 24 January 1995:5.

22. Nicholas R. Lardy, Foreign Trade and Economic Reform in China, 1978–1990 (New York. Cambridge University Press, 1992):61. Zhu Baihua, 'Wo waihui tizhi gaige qujian chengxiao' ('A preliminary view of the results of China's foreign exchange system reform'), Renmin ribao, 20 January 1995:1.

23. Gershon Feder, 'On exports and economic growth', Journal of Development Economics, No. 1–2 (1983):60–61.

24. World Bank, The East Asian Miracle: Economic Growth and Public Policy (Oxford University Press, Oxford, 1993):22–23.

25. Thomas G. Rawski, 'Export performance of China's state industries', unpublished manuscript, March 1994:Table 3.

26. State Statistical Bureau, Zhongguo tongji nianjian 1993 (Statistical Yearbook of China 1993) (Beijing: Chinese Statistical Publishing House, 1993):409. The note defining the scope of the category 'other' is at p. 471.

27. Based on the estimate that they account for 2 per cent of manufactured goods output.

28. World Bank, China: Foreign Trade Reform (Washington, DC: The World Bank, 1994):55–56.

29. *Ibid.*:67.
30. *Ibid.*:75.
31. *Ibid.*:75.
32. *Ibid.*:74.
33. State Planning Commission Economics Research Institute Task Force, 'Dui huifu guanmao zongxieding diwei hou de xiaoyi fenxi he duice' ('An effective analysis and counter-measures after China resumes its place in the General Agreement on Tariffs and Trade'), *Guoji maoyi* (International Trade), No. 2, 1993:10.
34. Harriet Matejka, 'Post-CMEA trade and payments arrangements in the East,' in Jozef M. van Brabant (ed.), *The New Eastern Europe and the World Economy* (Boulder, CO: Westview, 1993):63.
35. Anders Aslund, *How Russia Became a Market Economy* (Washington, DC: The Brookings Institution, 1995):46.
36. China's borrowing in the pre-reform period was limited to short-term trade financing.
37. Aslund, *How Russia Became a Market Economy*:49.
38. *Ibid.*:50.
39. John Thornhill and Andrew Fisher, 'Russia pleads for easier payment of Soviet debts', *The Financial Times*, 6 July 1995:2.
40. Lardy, *Foreign Trade and Economic Reform*:39–41.
41. 'The Ministry of Foreign Economic Relations and Trade quickens the approval of foreign trading rights of production enterprises', *Guoji shangbao* (*International Business*), 9 February 1993:1. At the end of 1992 China had 8.61 million industrial enterprises of which 1.03 million were state-owned.
42. Aslund, *How Russia Became a Market Economy*:147.
43. Ronald I. McKinnon, *The Order of Economic Liberalization: Financial Control in the Transition to a Market Economy* (Baltimore: The John Hopkins University Press, 1993):217–25.
44. Harry Broadman, *Meeting the Challenge of Chinese Enterprise Reform*, World Bank Discussion paper No. 283 (Washington, DC: The World Bank, 1995):15–16.
45. Nicholas, R. Lardy, 'Trade expansion and domestic structural adjustment in China, Japan, and the United States,' paper presented at the Trilateral Workshop, Beijing, October 1995.

46. World Bank, *China: Foreign Trade Reform*:77. Vinod Thomas, 'China: assuming its role in global trading,' unpublished manuscript, 1994:8. World Bank, *China Updating Economic Memorandum: Managing Rapid Growth and Transition* (Washington, DC: The World Bank, 1993):55.
47. Barry P. Bosworth and Gur Ofer, *Reforming Planned Economies in an Integrating World Economy* (Washington, DC: The Brookings Institution, 1995):140.
48. Lardy, *China in the World Economy*:30.
49. *Ibid.*:60–62.

25 Institutional Change, Trade Composition and Export Supply Potential in China

Ligang Song

The main objectives of this paper are to analyse the changing composition of China's trade within the context of the reform of the Chinese economy and to discuss its export supply potential with reference to the experience of other developing economies in Asia. The paper presents the following key arguments. First, the rapidly changing composition of trade in China during the past 15 years is the result of a convergence of its trade pattern toward market determined comparative advantage. Such convergence is primarily due to institutional reform, particularly trade system reform, aimed at introducing market mechanisms into economic and trading activities. Second, China's export supply potential will be very much determined by progress in further trade liberalisation that leads to a dynamic change of its comparative advantage. Progress may be examined in the context of the contribution of exports to economic growth in China and its economic integration into the world economy, namely, how the scale of China's expected future trade expansion will transform its stature in world trade.

I. Institutional Change, Trade Reform and Patterns of Trade

The arguments put forward in this paper are based on two fundamental considerations centering on the forces that influence China's comparative advantage in international trade: institutional change and trade liberalisation. Both have a strong impact on China's pattern of trade and therefore on China's rapid integration into the world economy. At the same time, the combination of the two makes China's case uniquely different from that of other developing countries that have been undergoing trade liberalisation.

International trade theory tells us that a country's relative factor endowment will strongly influence the focus of its comparative advantage in international trade. However, in an institutional setting such as a centrally planned economic system, a country's trade patterns could deviate from its market-determined comparative advantage (judging from its pattern of resource endowments). This is mainly because,

Reprinted with permission. Extracted (with minor editing) from Ligang Song, 1996. 'Institutional change, trade composition, and export supply potential in China', in Guitian and Mundell (eds), *Growth and Inflation in China*, International Monetary Fund, Washington, DC:190–225.

under that system, trade may be more consistent with serving a set of planned production and consumption (distribution) targets or development strategies (the heavy industry development strategy, for example) than with deliberately seeking gains from international trade by allowing market forces to allocate its resources.

The inability of a centrally planned economic system to take full advantage of international trade is due to institutional restrictions on economic activities, particularly on external economic activities, such as trade and capital flows. The key point is that when production and trade activities are subject to institutional controls or planning, there is not much incentive, from the point of view of enterprises and central planners, to reduce the costs incurred in production and trade activities. Therefore, there is no theoretical ground for seeking a country's comparative advantage in international trade on the basis of an efficient allocation of resources. The motive for trade, under these circumstances, is limited to filling the production gap that emerges under state planning.[1]

In theory, therefore, institutional changes that are accompanied by the introduction of market forces into the operation of the economy could alter the deviation between the pattern of trade and its resource supplies and make trade patterns conform more closely to the resource structure.

The speed and scale with which a country's pattern of trade conforms to the resource structure will inevitably be influenced by the degree of marketisation, which has been directly determined by the institutional changes implemented under various reform programs. In other words, there is a close link between the degree of marketisation and the degree of internationalisation of the economy. Internationalisation here refers to the degree to which a country participates in the world economy.

The increasing marketisation in China resulting from the reform program can be characterised as follows: an increasing share of goods and services transactions operates through the market (price signals increasingly direct the allocation of resources); there is a rapid reduction of state planning of both production and distribution; there is a diversification of the ownership structure in the overall economy, including private and foreign ownership; the way in which the Government adjusts and controls the economy (by resorting to macroeconomic control mechanisms suitable to a market economy) has changed; and laws and regulations compatible with a market economy have been introduced.

The progress of marketisation has fundamentally changed the attitude and behavior of enterprises and individuals. The incentive to make a profit has become a driving force in all kinds of business activities, including foreign trade. It is this fundamental change that provides a theoretical justification for the argument that the convergence between the pattern of trade and that of resources has taken place in China because of institutional changes.

Compared with trade reform in a market economy, changes in incentive brought about by institutional changes produced more immediate and profound changes in trading activities, which could partly explain why there was a sudden surge in exports and imports after China opened up its economy in the late 1970s and early 1980s. This incentive-enhancing effect, resulting from institutional changes, will exist during the entire transition period. Yet, the impact on economic activity will diminish along with the establishment of a new system. However, institutional change or the reform of the overall economic system is only one precondition for the convergence of China's patterns of trade and resource endowment. To enhance the realisation of this convergence, China must also formulate trade policy that addresses the incompatibility of its own trade system with the world standard on the one hand and that aims to improve efficiency in its production and trading activities on the other.

Unlike other developing countries that have undergone substantial changes by undertaking trade liberalisation, China is unique in the area of changing trade policies in the direction of market liberalisation. The central issue is the possible consequences of the interaction between institutional changes under the reform program and trade policy adjustments. These possible consequences may offer the Government a wide range of policy choices (subject to changing policy environments—for example, the changing conditions for removing export subsidies along with the adoption of new reform measures) in deciding its trade orientation. These choices, which may lead the country in different directions, may in turn strongly influence the pace of institutional change in China, patterns of trade, export supply potential, and general economic growth. In addition, they will also affect the welfare of the international community at large.

In choosing the pace of reform and trade liberalisation, the Government must treat the two issues, namely, institutional change and changes in trade policy, comprehensively and must handle them carefully by maintaining a balance between the domestic policy agenda and the external one. Although the two should in principle reinforce each other, in practice they may not because of some short-term conflicts emerging from the changes or because of the lag in the implementation of one or the other. One example is the attempt to increase the efficiency of the state-owned export sector, which might be hindered by difficulties in reforming the whole structure of the state sector.

Because the concept of comparative advantage is itself theoretically based on an essentially market-driven economy, further establishment and promotion of an integrated, open market system in China has become key to deepening the current reform of its trade system and to further realising China's international comparative advantage, which reflects a more efficient use of its resources.

In this sense, conformity of a country's comparative advantage to its pattern of resources could be used as a hypothetical measure of the extent to which domestic market distortions have been reduced. The implication is that the progress of China's trade expansion so far reflects only partial marketisation in China. The potential for further trade expansion along with the movement toward establishing a market system is enormous.

For an economy with a high degree of protection, relatively cheap labour or the abundance of other resources cannot automatically be translated into comparative advantage in the world market. Both institutional changes and trade policy reform with market orientation will be instrumental in the realisation of a country's true comparative advantage. In other words, the consequences of both institutional change and changes in trade policies would be better trade performance resulting from a more efficient use of a country's resources.[2]

A convergence of patterns of trade and resources in China has brought several immediate gains. The first one is a direct gain from trade owing to the changing composition of trade and the increasing market share of its products. The changing pattern of trade over time provides convincing support for this gain. The increasing share of foreign trade in total GDP and China's ever-increasing integration into the world economy are generally regarded as indications of the success of its policy to open up its economy.

The second gain is that increasing trade helps to ease the pressure of excess domestic demand generated by the rapid development of the economy. To a great extent, it cushions against inflationary pressures and thus helps to maintain the high economic growth rate and create favorable conditions for further reform. Without the realisation of China's comparative advantage on the world market, it would be impossible to maintain such a high level of imports to meet the ever-increasing domestic demand.

The third gain is that a convergence of patterns of trade and resource endowments has made China one of the most attractive places in the world for foreign direct investment, which in turn contributes significantly to trade expansion in China through the direct impact of investment on production and trade.

Some long-term gains are also associated with the convergence of patterns of trade and resource endowments. The first one is somewhat less obvious, but by no means less significant. It is a positive impact of trade activities (or externalities) on the process of reform, also called the 'indirect effects' of trade (Myint 1984:238). The effects are indirect because internationally accepted trading practices force enterprises in the export sector to compete in a competitive environment and consequently they have to change and adapt themselves just as firms in other countries do. Changes in the enterprise system are thereby enhanced, in particular those in the state sector in China. Consequently, substantial productivity gains can be obtained from such changes.[3]

The second one is the contribution of trade to economic growth, overall efficiency, and structural changes taking place in the economy.[4] 'Export-oriented policies lead to better growth performance than policies favoring import substitution. This result is said to obtain because export-oriented policies, which provide similar incentives to sales in domestic and in foreign markets, lead to resource allocation according to comparative advantage, allow for greater capacity utilisation, permit the exploitation of economies of scale, generate technological improvements in response to competition abroad, and, in labour-surplus countries, contribute to increased employment' (Balassa 1978:181).

Specialisation for the export market also helps ease the pressure resulting from structural problems. For example, capital is relatively scarce in China, but capital in many industries is very much underutilised. Resource allocation based on comparative advantage will change industrial structures toward optimality.

The relationships between factor endowments and trade patterns change over time in a dynamic fashion, supporting the hypothesis of shifting comparative advantage, which says that shifts take place as endowments change. These shifts, subject to market restraint, create a substantial export supply potential. The implication for China of shifting comparative advantage will be discussed in the context of trade and endowment structure in East Asian economies.

The forces that advocate change through altering trading practices have contributed positively to institutional reform in general and to reform of the trade system in particular over the entire history of economic reform. This has happened largely because of changes in the perceptions of the authorities over the role of foreign trade; they have realised the gains to be made from actively pursuing China's comparative advantage on the world market. As a result, further institutional reform and reform of the trade system and associated changes in trade policy have ranked high on the national reform agenda.

If the institutional framework continues to adjust and adapt in the direction of a market system and if policy, particularly trade policy, is becoming more rules based, there will be further dynamic changes in trade composition, and the gains from international trade will continue to benefit the Chinese economy.

II. Convergence of the Patterns of Trade and Resources

This section provides empirical evidence of the convergence between the patterns of trade and resources in China since the reform began in the late 1970s and then discusses the gains made from the rapid development of trade and economic integration with the world economy.

Studies show that the international distribution in China's resources changed substantially between the 1960s and the late 1980s.[5] The impact of changes in resource supplies on trade patterns of China's manufactured products can be seen in its growth rate of exports in comparison with other Asian economies that have similar patterns of factor endowments, particularly with respect to labour and capital. Table 1 lists the average annual growth rates of

GDP, total exports, and exports of manufactures in a group of selected Asian economies and in the United States for two periods: 1970–80 and 1980–90. It shows that annual real growth rates of manufactured exports in other Asian economies were considerably higher than the growth rates of total exports throughout the two periods, providing evidence for the expansion of manufacturing sectors in these Asian economies. In the case of China, both growth rates were high during both periods with the growth rate of exports of manufactures also higher than that of its total exports.

Table 1 also indicates that the more advanced an economy becomes, the narrower the gap is between the growth rate of its total exports and that of its manufactured exports. Thus, the potential for revealing comparative advantage (gaining a larger market share) in manufactured products is relatively large for developing economies. Fulfilment of this potential and the

structural changes that accompany this process will have important implications for market and policy issues as these economies industrialise further.

Table 2 reports the results of changing patterns of China's exports and imports by groups of commodities, which indicate clearly that China's commodity compositions have changed dramatically since the beginning of the reform in the late 1970s.

Commodity shares represent exports of a particular group of commodities in total exports. In 1978, the predominant commodity shares were agriculture-intensive (36.1 per cent) and labour-intensive (31.1 per cent), followed by mineral-intensive and capital-intensive products. Total manufacture accounted for about half of China's total exports (49.3 per cent) at that time.

By 1993, China's commodity shares for exports had changed remarkably. While agri-

Table 1 **Annual real growth rates of GDP, total exports, and manufactured exports for selected Asia-Pacific economies** (per cent)

Country	GDP		Total exports		Exports of manufactures	
	1970–80	1980–90	1970–80	1980–90	1970–80	1980–90
Hong Kong	9.27	7.13	8.41	4.29	8.50	4.31
Indonesia	7.24	5.61	7.56	3.27	13.64	34.96
Japan	4.51	4.14	9.49	4.21	9.73	4.41
Korea	8.60	9.31	22.62	11.89	24.66	12.31
Malaysia	7.86	5.99	3.88	10.51	14.20	20.12
Philippines	5.86	1.60	5.79	3.66	23.90	9.15
Singapore	8.91	7.04	4.88	8.50	11.05	11.76
Taiwan Province of China	5.77	8.92	10.01	10.45	10.02	10.96
Thailand	6.69	7.82	10.78	13.65	25.59	23.46
United States	2.74	2.90	6.64	3.06	6.24	4.57
China		14.7		13.1		17.8

Notes: The growth rates of GDP are based on the constant price in the local currency; growth rates of total exports and exports of manufactures are obtained by adjusting total exports and exports of manufactures against the U.S.-dollar-based export price index (1987=100). Annual growth rates of both total exports and exports of manufactures are based on 1972–80 for the first period for Taiwan Province of China and on 1980–89 for the second period for Hong Kong.
Source: GDP and trade figures were obtained from World Bank, *World Debt Tables 1992*, Washington, DC.

culture and mineral-intensive products dropped, those for labour and capital-intensive products increased substantially. Total manufacture accounted for about 88 per cent of China's total exports.

Commodity shares for imports also show a pattern of rapid changes. The shares for both agriculture and mineral-intensive products declined, but the former dropped more substantially during the period. The import share for labour-intensive products increased first and

then declined from the peak year of 1990. In contrast, import shares for capital-intensive products increased rapidly. By 1993, 72.1 per cent of China's total imports were capital-intensive products, accounting for about 81.5 per cent of total imports of manufactures.

An increasing share of exports of labour-intensive products compared with a declining share of imports of the same products provides strong evidence that China is gaining comparative advantage on world markets in labour-intensive

Table 2   **Patterns of China's exports and imports by groups of commodities** (per cent)

	1978			1985		
Commodity Group	Commodity share	Market share	RCA[a]	Commodity share	Market share	RCA
Exports						
Agriculture-intensive	36.1	0.5	2.00	21.7	2.3	1.50
Mineral-intensive	17.1	0.5	0.70	28.8	1.9	1.30
Labour-intensive	31.1	2.2	2.94	35.5	5.2	3.30
Capital-intensive	15.2	0.2	0.32	12.9	0.4	0.26
Total manufacture[b]	49.3	0.6	0.80	50.4	1.2	0.78
Imports						
Agriculture-intensive	29.0	1.1	1.60	10.6	1.4	0.72
Mineral-intensive	7.0	0.2	0.29	5.1	0.4	0.21
Labour-intensive	4.2	0.3	0.42	9.7	1.8	0.94
Capital-intensive	59.0	0.9	1.27	73.3	2.9	1.49
Total manufacture	65.7	0.7	1.08	86.0	2.5	1.36
	1990			1993		
Exports						
Agriculture-intensive	12.4	2.4	0.93	9.2	3.0	0.71
Mineral-intensive	9.4	1.6	0.61	4.7	1.6	0.38
Labour-intensive	50.8	10.3	4.02	56.8	17.4	4.13
Capital-intensive	26.8	1.2	0.47	28.8	2.1	0.49
Total manufacture[b]	80.1	2.8	1.08	87.9	4.8	1.14
Imports						
Agriculture-intensive	16.2	1.6	1.20	10.7	1.7	0.61
Mineral-intensive	5.1	0.4	0.31	6.5	1.3	0.49
Labour-intensive	16.0	1.7	1.29	12.7	2.5	0.93
Capital-intensive	60.8	1.5	1.09	72.1	3.4	1.24
Total manufacture	82.1	1.5	1.13	88.5	3.2	1.16

[a] Revealed comparative advantage.
[b] Total manufacture includes both capital and labour-intensive products.
Source: International Economic Databank, The Australian National University, Canberra.

products. This can be demonstrated by looking at the changing market shares of these products.

Market shares denote shares of exports and imports of particular groups of commodities in world total export and import shares of the same groups of commodities. The results show that by 1993 China's share of exports of labour-intensive products accounted for 17.4 per cent in world total exports and that it imported only 2.5 per cent of these products from the world. China had a slightly higher market share of imports than of exports for capital-intensive products for the same year, and both shares increased very rapidly from a low base in 1978.

Indexes of revealed comparative advantage, which measure the ratios of commodity share of a country to the world average, summarise the changing patterns of trade in China. The results show that China is losing international comparative advantage in both agriculture and mineral-intensive products while it is gaining comparative advantage substantially in labour-intensive products during the same period. It is noted that China is also gaining a slight comparative advantage in capital-intensive products (Table 2).

Table 3 reports major commodities exported by China from 1965 to 1992 and lists commodities that rank high as China's major export items. The most remarkable change over the period is the export of clothing: it increased from 3.12 per cent in 1965 to 20.50 per cent in 1992, ranking as the

Table 3   **Ranking of China's exports by share** (per cent)

		1965			1992	
Rank	SITC[a]	Commodity	Share	SITC	Commodity	Share
1	65	Textile yarn, fabric	18.33	84	Clothing	20.50
2	04	Cereals and preparations	7.14	89	Misc. manufactured goods	15.79
3	05	Fruit and vegetables	5.74	72	Electrical machinery	11.12
4	22	Oil seeds, nuts, kernels	5.48	65	Textile yarn, fabric	7.75
5	29	Crude animal, vegetable matter	4.98	85	Footwear	6.74
6	26	Textile fibers	4.62	83	Travel goods, handbags	3.84
7	00	Live animals	4.27	71	Machinery, nonelectrical	3.29
8	67	Iron and steel	3.95	33	Petroleum and products	2.97
9	84	Clothing	3.12	86	Instruments, watches, clocks	2.56
10	89	Misc. manufactured goods	3.10	69	Metal manufactures	2.23
11	66	Nonmetal minerals	2.96	05	Fruit and vegetables	2.14
12	03	Fish and preparations	2.75	51	Chemical elements	1.68
13	07	Coffee, tea, cocoa, spices	2.56	66	Nonmetal minerals	1.64
14	68	Nonferrous metals	2.08	03	Fish and preparations	1.52
15	06	Sugar, honey	2.02	04	Cereals and preparations	1.15
16	01	Meat and preparations	1.94	67	Iron and steel	1.02
17	02	Dairy products and eggs	1.84	73	Transport equipment	1.00
18	21	Undressed hides, skins, furs	1.60	82	Furniture	0.98
19	64	Paper, paperboard	1.49	29	Crude animal, vegetable matter	0.87
20	69	Metal manufactures	1.48	26	Textile fibers	0.84
Total			81.45			89.63

[a] Standard International Trade Classification.
Source: International Economic Databank, The Australian National University, Canberra.

Table 4   **Ranking of China's imports by share** (per cent)

		1965			1992	
Rank	SITC[1]	Commodity	Share	SITC	Commodity	Share
1	04	Cereals and preparations	25.94	71	Machinery, nonelectrical	17.47
2	26	Textile fibers	12.83	72	Electrical machinery	12.34
3	71	Machinery, nonelectrical	7.71	65	Textile yarn, fabric	10.47
4	06	Sugar, honey	7.05	73	Transport equipment	9.16
5	67	Iron and steel	6.79	67	Iron and steel	5.52
6	51	Chemical elements	5.71	58	Plastic materials	5.35
7	56	Fertilisers	5.36	89	Misc. manufactured goods	3.93
8	23	Rubber, crude, synthetic	5.13	86	Instruments, watches, clocks	3.34
9	68	Nonferrous metals	4.81	33	Petroleum and products	2.82
10	65	Textile yarn, fabric	2.89	51	Chemical elements	2.35
11	72	Electrical machinery	2.63	26	Textile fibers	2.35
12	73	Transport equipment	1.99	68	Nonferrous metals	2.26
13	86	Instruments, watches, clocks	1.86	04	Cereals and preparations	2.10
14	59	Chemicals	1.16	64	Paper, paperboard	1.98
15	07	Coffee, tea, cocoa, spices	0.87	61	Leather, dressed fur	1.57
16	64	Paper, paperboard	0.84	56	Fertilisers	1.44
17	25	Pulp and waste paper	0.74	28	Metalliferous ores	1.37
18	58	Plastic materials	0.66	93	Special transactions	1.36
19	27	Crude fertiliser	0.65	63	Wood, cork manufacture	1.31
20	53	Dyes, tanning	0.64	69	Metal manufactures	1.22
Total			96.28			89.70

[1]Standard International Trade Classification.
Source: International Economic Databank, The Australian National University, Canberra.

top export item in that year. In comparison with the situation in 1965, several items, mainly agricultural products (such as cereals) and energy-related products (such as petroleum products) disappeared from the list of major export items in 1992 or dropped to a lower position. This evidence also supports the changing patterns of China's comparative advantage during the period.

Table 4 lists major commodities imported by China from 1965 to 1992, showing that the composition of China's imports changed substantially during the period. For example, cereal imports ranked at the top as a proportion of total imports in 1965 but were replaced by more value-added manufactured products such as machines

in 1992. Imports of other manufactured commodities, particularly those associated with transportation and communication such as motor vehicles, aircraft, and telecommunications equipment, also rose.

The figures reported in Tables 3 and 4 not only reflect the changing pattern of trade owing mainly to its convergence with the pattern of resources, but also indicate that China has indeed further integrated its economy with the rest of the world since the beginning of the reform. In other words, China has become more and more dependent on the world market.

Table 5 presents China's geographic trade structure and reveals how China's economy has been linked with the rest of the world. The figures

Table 5   China's geographic trade structure (per cent)

Partner	Export share					Import share					Total trade				
	1970	1980	1985	1990	1993	1970	1980	1985	1990	1993	1970	1980	1985	1990	1993
Newly industrialising economies (NIEs)	31.2	24.5	33.7	48.0	30.9	1.9	3.8	11.8	39.3	20.3	17.1	14.1	20.4	43.8	25.6
Hong Kong	24.6	22.4	26.2	42.9	24.2	0.5	2.9	11.2	24.6	11.5	13.1	12.5	17.1	34.1	17.6
Taiwan Province of China	...	...	...	1.2	1.1	...	...	...	12.8	0.1	...	...	...	6.8	0.7
Korea	...	...	...	0.7	3.1	...	...	...	0.4	5.9	...	...	...	0.6	4.5
ASEAN	5.7	4.0	2.7	2.9	2.7	1.2	2.3	2.1	3.7	3.7	3.5	3.2	2.3	3.2	3.2
Japan	13.4	20.7	22.3	14.6	17.3	32.4	26.1	35.7	12.9	25.6	22.5	23.4	30.5	13.8	21.4
East Asia	50.3	49.3	58.7	65.5	50.8	35.5	32.3	49.6	55.9	49.6	43.2	40.7	53.2	60.9	50.2
Australia	2.1	1.2	0.7	0.7	1.2	7.4	5.4	2.7	2.3	2.1	4.6	3.3	1.9	1.5	1.7
North America	1.1	5.8	9.4	9.1	19.9	7.7	23.5	14.9	13.7	13.2	4.3	14.7	12.8	11.3	16.5
New Zealand and other Pacific	0.5	0.3	0.2	0.1	0.2	0.5	0.9	0.4	0.2	0.4	0.4	0.6	0.3	0.2	0.3
Asia-Pacific	53.8	56.5	68.9	75.5	72.1	50.8	62.1	67.6	72.1	65.3	52.4	59.3	68.1	73.8	68.7
Western Europe	21.8	14.3	9.4	10.3	13.9	29.5	17.7	17.2	16.5	18.6	25.7	16.0	14.2	13.3	16.2
Rest of the world	24.4	29.3	21.7	14.2	14.1	19.2	20.2	15.2	11.4	16.1	21.9	24.7	17.7	12.8	15.1
World total	100.0	100.0	100.0	100.0	100.0	100.0	100.0	100.0	100.0	100.0	100.0	100.0	100.0	100.0	100.0

Source: International Economic Databank, The Australian National University, Canberra.

show that about half of China's imports, exports, and total trade are conducted with East Asian economies, including the Association of South East Asian Nations (ASEAN), and about 70 per cent of that trade is with Asia-Pacific economies. This clearly indicates that China has strong trade relationships with the Asia-Pacific economies.

The rapid increase in foreign trade and the deepened market integration of the Chinese economy with other countries have changed China's position in the world economy. Tables 6a and 6b show leading exporters, importers, and merchandise traders in 1980 and 1993. China ranked twenty-fifth, twenty-third, and twenty-fourth in terms of exports, imports, and total trade, respectively, in 1980. In 1993, these rankings were eleventh for exports, imports, and total trade.

A rapid expansion of trade requires that China continue to open its markets to products from its trading partners. This is because rapid expansion of trade also causes market saturation, which in turn will lead to severe structural adjustments in many countries of the world.

One solution to this mounting pressure on the world market is to gradually open up China's domestic market to imports. In fact, 'the continued growth of China's economy and trade in line with its comparative advantage would, of course, also create valuable opportunities for others' (Drysdale and Elek 1992:13).

As China's exports have gained international competitiveness, its imports have also increased. Table 7 reports China's share of total world imports of those commodities (averages for 1987–89 and 1990–92) that constitute major import items for China. Although imports of wheat accounted for only a small proportion of China's total imports, its share in total world imports was very high. Other commodities of great importance on the world import market are machinery for producing textiles and leather, woven textiles, and iron and steel products. There was a notable increase in the share of aircraft.

Increases in both its exports and imports have made China more dependent upon the world economy. Table 8 reports import and export dependence ratios of the Chinese economy from 1965 to 1993. Both ratios increased very rapidly, particularly after the reform started in the late 1970s. It is noted that, except for a few years during the mid 1980s, China's export dependence ratios are higher than its import dependence ratios, indicating the competitiveness of China's export products on the world market.

Table 9 provides further evidence of China's increasing dependence on the world market by presenting the shares of exports in production and of imports in the domestic consumption of textiles, clothing, and leather products. By 1991, China exported more than half of its production of textiles, clothing, and leather products, and imports of the same groups of products became increasingly important to China's domestic consumption.

The results in this section show that China's trade patterns have indeed conformed more closely to its resource structure, and there has been a dynamic change in China's comparative advantage (an increasing trend of exporting capital-intensive products) in recent years. This change has some implications for China's export supply potential.

III. China's Export Supply Potential

China's export supply potential will depend very much upon the following factors: the pace and measurement of further trade liberalisation, future trade orientation, changing patterns of dynamic comparative advantage—both internationally and domestically—and conditions on the world market.

The central issue is the pace and measurement of further trade liberalisation based on previous reforms. These issues are important in that the implementation of already formulated trade reform measures and the design of future reforms will continue to contribute to trade expansion in China. The problem, however, is that adjustment costs and subsequent changing policy environments will have some impact (both positive and negative) on policy implementation and the reform process. For example, further

Table 6a Leading exporters, importers, and merchandise traders, 1980

Country	Exports (billion US$)	Share (%)	Country	Imports (billion US$)	Share (%)	Country	Total trade (billion US$)	Share (%)
World	2,007.9	100.0	World	2,069.1	100.0	World	4,077.0	100.0
United States	220.8	11.0	United States	257.1	12.4	United States	477.9	11.7
Germany, fmr Fed. Rep.	192.9	9.6	Germany, fmr Fed. Rep.	188.0	9.1	Germany, fmr Fed. Rep.	380.9	9.3
Japan	130.4	6.5	Japan	141.3	6.8	Japan	271.7	6.7
France	116.0	5.8	France	134.9	6.5	France	250.9	6.2
United Kingdom	110.1	5.5	United Kingdom	115.7	5.6	United Kingdom	225.8	5.5
Saudi Arabia	103.4	5.2	Italy	99.5	4.8	Italy	177.2	4.4
Italy	77.7	3.9	Netherlands	78.1	3.8	Netherlands	152.0	3.7
Netherlands	73.9	3.7	Belgium-Luxembourg	71.8	3.5	Belgium-Luxembourg	136.5	3.4
Canada	67.8	3.4	Canada	67.1	3.2	Canada	134.8	3.3
Belgium-Luxembourg	64.7	3.2	USSR, former	45.8	2.2	Saudi Arabia	133.6	3.3
USSR, former	48.4	2.4	Switzerland	36.4	1.8	USSR, former	94.2	2.3
Iraq	31.3	1.6	Spain	34.1	1.7	Switzerland	66.0	1.6
Sweden	30.9	1.5	Sweden	33.4	1.6	Sweden	64.3	1.6
Switzerland	29.6	1.5	Saudi Arabia	30.2	1.5	Spain	54.8	1.3
Nigeria	26.2	1.3	Singapore	26.5	1.3	Singapore	46.9	1.2
Libya	22.4	1.1	Brazil	25.0	1.2	Brazil	45.1	1.1
Australia	22.0	1.1	Austria	24.4	1.2	Australia	44.3	1.1
Indonesia	22.0	1.1	Hong Kong	22.4	1.1	Iraq	43.8	1.1
United Arab Emirates	21.8	1.1	Australia	22.3	1.1	Austria	41.9	1.0
Kuwait	20.8	1.0	Korea	22.3	1.1	Hong Kong	41.7	1.0
Spain	20.7	1.0	Poland	21.2	1.0	Nigeria	40.7	1.0
Singapore	20.4	1.0	Taiwan Province of China	20.2	1.0	Taiwan Province of China	40.0	1.0
Brazil	20.1	1.0	China	19.8	1.0	Korea	39.8	1.0
Taiwan Province of China	19.9	1.0	Mexico	19.5	0.9	China	39.3	1.0
China	19.5	1.0	Denmark	19.4	0.9	Poland	38.6	1.0
Hong Kong	19.3	1.0	Norway	16.9	0.8	Denmark	36.4	0.9

Source: International Economic Databank, Australian National University, Canberra.

409

Table 6b Leading exporters, importers, and merchandise traders, 1993

Country	Exports (billion US$)	Share (%)	Country	Imports (billion US$)	Share (%)	Country	Total trade (billion US$)	Share (%)
World	3,710.1	100.0	World	3,887.4	100.0	World	7,597.5	100.0
United States	461.6	12.4	United States	597.1	15.4	United States	1,058.7	13.9
Germany, fmr Fed. Rep.	366.2	9.9	Germany, fmr Fed. Rep.	328.7	8.5	Germany, fmr Fed. Rep.	694.9	9.2
Japan	362.2	9.8	Japan	240.0	6.2	Japan	602.2	7.9
France	207.9	5.6	United Kingdom	205.1	5.3	France	407.8	5.4
United Kingdom	180.4	4.9	France	199.9	5.1	United Kingdom	385.5	5.1
Italy	164.3	4.4	Canada	148.0	3.8	Italy	310.2	4.1
Canada	141.6	3.8	Italy	145.9	3.8	Canada	289.7	3.8
Hong Kong	133.4	3.6	Hong Kong	144.8	3.7	Hong Kong	278.2	3.7
Netherlands	114.5	3.1	Netherlands	132.9	3.4	Netherlands	247.5	3.3
Belgium-Luxembourg	97.3	2.6	Belgium-Luxembourg	125.4	3.2	Belgium-Luxembourg	222.8	2.9
China	91.3	2.5	China	91.1	2.3	China	182.4	2.4
Taiwan Province of China	88.1	2.4	Korea	84.7	2.2	Taiwan Province of China	166.3	2.2
Korea	75.1	2.0	Spain	82.2	2.1	Korea	159.8	2.1
Singapore	71.3	1.9	Singapore	81.2	2.1	Singapore	152.5	2.0
Switzerland	63.3	1.7	Taiwan Province of China	78.2	2.0	Spain	145.0	1.9
Spain	62.8	1.7	Mexico	65.2	1.7	Switzerland	124.1	1.6
Sweden	49.4	1.3	Switzerland	60.8	1.6	Mexico	112.2	1.5
Saudi Arabia	48.0	1.3	Austria	48.7	1.3	Sweden	91.7	1.2
Malaysia (IMF data)	47.5	1.3	Australia	46.6	1.2	Malaysia (IMF data)	89.5	1.2
Mexico	47.0	1.3	Thailand	45.4	1.2	Australia	89.3	1.2
Australia	42.8	1.2	Sweden	42.3	1.1	Austria	88.6	1.2

Source: International Economic Databank, The Australian National University, Canberra.

Table 7 **China's share of selected major imports in world trade** (per cent)

SITC[a]	Commodity	1987–89	1990–92
041	Wheat, unmilled	13.15	12.31
512	Organic chemicals	2.10	2.02
581	Plastic materials	4.19	3.69
651	Textile yarn and thread	2.42	3.48
653	Woven textiles, noncotton	3.16	5.32
674	Iron, steel, plate, sheet	8.06	4.26
714	Office machines	0.74	0.67
717	Textile, leather, machinery	8.03	8.94
718	Machinery for special industries	2.76	2.95
719	Machinery, nonelectrical	3.73	3.31
722	Electric power machines	1.91	2.11
724	Telecommunications equipment	3.31	2.82
729	Electrical machinery	1.84	1.81
732	Motor vehicles	1.38	1.43
734	Aircraft	1.66	2.14

[a] Standard International Trade Classification
Source: International Economic Databank, The Australian National University, Canberra.

trade liberalisation, particularly in reforming the import system, will lead to greater structural adjustments in industries with a high level of protection and a low level of efficiency. This problem has been complicated by China's difficulties in reforming its enterprise system. In that sense, the pace of trade liberalisation will be very much determined by the pace of reform of the enterprise system, particularly the state sector.

One policy suggestion is to let the export sector have a more positive effect on the industrial sector by implementing trade liberalisation faster than the overall reform of the enterprise system. This move will enhance the entire reform process in China and will eventually boost further trade liberalisation. Therefore, the move helps to create an environment in which economic reform programs and reform of the trade system reinforce each other in order to overcome the constraints on further trade liberalisation. The importance of this kind of positive effect (externalities) from the export sector and a strong demonstration effect through more frequent international

transactions cannot be underestimated.

When adopting reform measures for further trade liberalisation, the Government should also consider the balance between trade liberalisation and exchange rate policy. The issue is important because implementing different policies may lead to conflicting results in obtaining gains from trade.[6] In future liberalisation attempts, 'exchange rate policies and anti-inflation programs should be better designed so that they do not lead to overvalued exchange rates and loss of export competitiveness'. In other words, 'trade liberalisation must also be accompanied by a competitive exchange rate' (Congdon 1990:241).

Based on the discussion in the section on institutional change, trade reform, and trade patterns, one important consideration for the Government in adopting reform measures is to rely mainly on incentive policies or schemes that work through the market mechanism. This is consistent with the argument of market-driven conformity between patterns of trade and resources.

Second, the issue of future trade orientation is related to the question of whether it is preferable for a large developing country like China, which has a huge domestic market, to rely heavily on an export-oriented development strategy.[7] It can be argued that China is far from realising its full potential for developing its external economy and will continue to gain from deepening the international integration of its economy for many years to come.[8]

Third, relationships between factor endowments and trade patterns change over time in a dynamic fashion. These changes, subject to market restraint, create substantial export supply potential. The implication for China of shifting comparative advantage can be discussed in the context of trade and endowment structure in East Asian economies. The structure of factor endowments in East Asian economies has two notable characteristics. One is that rapid increases in capital accumulation were observed in these economies from the 1960s to the 1980s. Average annual growth rates of capital stock from 1965 to 1988 in a group of selected Asian economies were much higher than the world average in terms of capital per worker (6.8 per cent compared with 3.1 per cent). As a result, the capital per worker ranking of most of these economies rose substantially during this period.

The other characteristic is that the average annual growth rates for skilled labour in these economies during the period were almost the same as world average annual growth rates in terms of the share of skilled labour in total labour (3.6 per cent compared with 3 per cent). As a result, with respect to skilled labour as a percentage of total labour, the ranking of about half of the Asian economies in 1998 had worsened compared with 1965, while the remaining economies had increased their ranking only slightly. (China, Hong Kong, and Taiwan Province of China were the exceptions.) These data may indicate that these economies were on average doing a better job of accumulating physical capital than of producing highly skilled labour from 1965 to 1988 (Song 1993).

How have the resource patterns described above affected the development of trade,

Table 8   **Import and export dependence ratios**

Year	Imports	Exports	GDP	Import dependence ratio (per cent)	Export dependence ratio (per cent)
	(billion US dollars)				
1965	1.39	1.64	168.00	0.82	0.98
1966	1.51	1.91	192.25	0.79	0.99
1967	1.50	1.80	180.04	0.83	1.00
1968	1.30	1.66	171.39	0.76	0.97
1969	1.39	1.82	195.74	0.71	0.93
1970	1.67	1.77	233.11	0.71	0.76
1971	1.64	2.09	251.34	0.65	0.83
1972	2.11	2.70	283.38	0.75	0.95
1973	3.87	4.45	346.97	1.12	1.28
1974	5.91	5.73	356.47	1.66	1.61
1975	5.96	6.30	400.66	1.49	1.57
1976	4.68	6.56	372.12	1.26	1.76
1977	5.56	7.17	423.57	1.31	1.69
1978	8.77	9.12	482.72	1.82	1.89
1979	12.60	12.54	574.02	2.19	2.19
1980	17.07	17.48	655.47	2.60	2.67
1981	16.35	20.66	626.98	2.61	3.30
1982	14.69	20.66	657.44	2.23	3.14
1983	16.42	20.95	738.41	2.22	2.84
1984	22.80	24.87	830.45	2.75	2.99
1985	35.62	27.93	977.81	3.64	2.86
1986	33.68	32.59	943.12	3.57	3.46
1987	36.62	43.16	851.46	4.30	5.07
1988	48.26	56.09	972.89	4.96	5.77
1989	48.95	69.67	1,099.39	4.45	6.34
1990	45.92	84.16	1,156.31	3.97	7.28
1991	58.64	106.09	1,197.87	4.90	8.86
1992	76.80	129.25	1,265.19	6.07	10.22
1993	97.71	146.40	1,372.73	7.12	10.67

Source: International Economic Databank, The Australian National University, Canberra.

Table 9 **Trade dependence of China's textile, clothing, and leather industries** (per cent)

Year	Export/Production	Import/Consumption
1980	11.1	3.0
1985	19.7	6.7
1990	48.8	16.8
1991	62.4	26.5

Note: Trade dependence is based on International Standard Industrial Classification (ISIC) 32 (textile, clothing, and leather industries) because production data are not available for ISIC 322.
Source: International Economic Databank, The Australian National University, Canberra.

particularly in manufactured products, in these economies? The question can be approached using the three propositions most commonly put forward with respect to shifts in comparative advantage. These propositions are based on changes in commonly used but broadly defined capital-labour ratios as indicators of changes in resource supplies [9]

The first proposition is that an increase in the ratio of capital to labour will lead to an increase in the size of the manufacturing sector as a proportion of the total economy. The second proposition is that a further increase in this ratio will enhance production of more capital-intensive products within the manufacturing sector. The third proposition is that an increase in the ratio of skilled labour to workers, together with an increase in the capital-labour ratio, will be conducive to more sophisticated manufacturing production with greater value added.

In a dynamic context, these three propositions can be considered as three stages of structural change in the development process (overlapping between stages may exist), and they can thus be used to examine trade development in these Asian economies based on the characteristics of their resource patterns.

Rapid increases in capital-labour ratios from the 1960s to the 1980s led to a continuous expansion of the manufacturing sectors of these

Asian economies. In most cases, expansion took place in sectors where labour-intensive manufactured goods were being produced, partly because 'the process of capital accumulation and rising per capita incomes forces changes in the industrial composition of manufacturing activity through its effect on the wage level' (Garnaut and Anderson 1980:386).

Over time, as the per worker endowment of capital increases, the comparative advantage within the manufacturing sector will shift towards more capital-intensive activities (Anderson and Smith 1981:296).

All except Japan ranked low in terms of capital per worker in 1965. In 1974, Korea and Taiwan Province of China had improved their rankings of capital per worker, and by 1980, both had become net exporters of capital-intensive manufactured products. Taiwan Province of China's progress was even more obvious in 1988, by which time it had become a net exporter of labour-intensive, capital-intensive manufactured products and machinery after rapidly improving its capital per worker ranking (Song 1993:Ch. 3).

The third proposition is that, within its manufacturing sector, a country tends to specialise in the production and export of more sophisticated manufactured products with high value added, such as machinery and chemicals, and that this is mainly attributable to an increase in the country's skilled labour endowment together with an increase in its capital-labour ratio. This proposition in the context of East Asian economies also has important implications for China's export supply potential.

Relatively high growth rates in physical capital and semiskilled rather than skilled labour indicate that much of the change in trade structure (reflected in rapid increases in labour-intensive and capital-intensive manufactured products) in these economies during the period under study was driven by the accumulation of physical capital and semiskilled labour. This suggests there is a huge potential these economies can realise by increasing skilled labour as physical capital increases.

Table 10 presents manufactured commodity shares for the Asia-Pacific economies. These figures show that China almost doubled its manufactured commodity share from 1965 to 1992. The estimated share in 1992 was still lower than that of Hong Kong, Japan, Korea, and Taiwan Province of China but was much higher than that of many economies in the region and also above the average for the countries of the Asia-Pacific Economic Cooperation (APEC).

Further industrialisation requires the continual injection of large quantities of capital into an economy. Thus, capital flows on a larger scale and in various forms can be anticipated within the Asian economies. A combination of highly skilled labour and physical capital will definitely lead to production of highly sophisticated products. This in turn will generate demand for a highly skilled labour force along the path of further industrialisation in these Asian economies.

If the issues of market competition, enhancing international and regional capital flows, and facilitating the movement of skilled labour in the region are resolved, shifts in comparative advantage in the Asian region can be facilitated in such a way that its resources are used most efficiently. A natural consequence of this would be that the degree of integration in the region would increase.

In addition, the accumulation of human capital in these economies lagged behind the accumulation of physical capital during the period under study. Therefore, there is a huge potential for the East Asian economies to gain

Table 10   **Manufactured commodity shares of total exports** (per cent)

Country	1965	1970	1980	1990	1992
APEC countries[a]	55.30	63.80	64.40	78.32	80.70
Australia	14.55	18.87	26.26	36.15	35.51
Brunei Darussalam	0.02	0.07	0.01	13.57	11.25
Canada	36.68	51.21	48.48	63.65	64.18
Chile	4.12	4.44	9.70	12.64	15.24
China (estimated)	45.79	45.07	48.72	80.01	85.42
China (official)	...	...	...	73.46	79.25
Hong Kong	93.56	95.91	96.51	95.80	95.29
Indonesia	3.70	1.41	2.43	35.46	47.53
Japan	91.14	93.29	95.74	97.44	97.53
Korea	59.43	76.57	89.91	93.58	92.89
Malaysia	6.04	7.40	19.04	54.16	64.96
Mexico	16.42	32.53	28.08	43.51	52.43
New Zealand	5.42	11.00	20.18	24.93	26.54
Papua New Guinea	9.57	4.77	3.32	11.16	12.03
Philippines	5.66	7.60	36.83	68.80	72.96
Singapore	34.20	30.50	53.95	72.80	78.04
Taiwan Province of China	41.47	76.10	87.92	92.65	91.94
Thailand	3.05	8.01	28.08	64.32	67.92
United States	65.41	70.15	67.79	78.14	80.45

[a] Asia-Pacific Economic Cooperation.
Source: International Economic Databank, The Australian National University, Canberra.

more competitive edge by producing more sophisticated manufactured products through greater investment in human capital development through education, training, and diffusion of knowledge and technological know-how. A more efficient use of their labour force, particularly the skilled labour force, through better management and encouragement of labour flows will also help these economies gain more competitive edge.

These changes, based on the shift of comparative advantage in an international context, are particularly relevant for China. As a latecomer and one of the world's most rapidly developing economies, China is accumulating both physical capital and human capital on a large scale, which provide great opportunities for China to increase its export supplies not only of labour-intensive but also of capital-intensive products on the world market.

However, market issues remain. As Rana (1990:244) says, 'shifts in comparative advantage are...not smooth and could involve considerable frictions in adjustment'. Market constraints on the development process have been aggravated by structural adjustment in industrial countries and could lead to a resurgence of trade protectionism. Any such movement would undoubtedly affect the development process. As economies become more integrated, the sustained growth of the world economy depends very much upon whether countries can properly settle this market issue.

China's economic reform in general and the changes in trade policy in particular since the beginning of the reform process in the late 1970s have made China's patterns of trade conform more closely and dynamically to its patterns of resource endowment. The challenge is, however, that, owing to the size of China's economy and the increasing scale of its foreign trade, both China and its trading partners have to cope with China's dynamic realisation of its comparative advantage. The issue of China's membership in the recently formed World Trade Organization (WTO) becomes important in this context.

In a domestic context, endowment structure and wide regional differences in terms of level of development provide China with much leeway to expand its trade activities. There exists a ladder of comparative advantage owing to these regional and structural differences within China, which leads to a shift of comparative advantage domestically. The shift can be expected to last for quite a long time because of wide regional differences in terms of endowment structure and level of development. When shifts of comparative advantage take place domestically, they demonstrate different patterns of comparative advantage within a single economy and therefore indicate a wide scope for developing trade. This will overcome the economy's growth limits as set out in the traditional theory of comparative advantage.

The size of an economy makes a considerable difference in terms of domestic shifts of comparative advantage, because large countries tend to have different factor endowments and levels of development across regions. There are also some benefits in these shifts of comparative advantage within a country. For example, domestic trade barriers are relatively easier to overcome than those between countries.

One challenge posed by the large size of an economy, however, is that domestic shifts of comparative advantage like those in the international setting require a well-developed domestic market. In other words, shifts in comparative advantage are contingent on a market foundation for defining the relationship between patterns of trade and resource endowment. In this sense, the current market reform in China will enhance both types of shifts of comparative advantage, widening the scope for trade development in China. Domestic shifts in comparative advantage will not compromise China's external trade as long as such shifts do not lead to an expansion of import-competing industries relative to the country's export sector.

IV. Concluding Remarks

China has handled the sequencing and timing of its reform program well. The whole reform process is heading in the right direction, namely, toward gradual trade liberalisation and reform of the economic system. Market-oriented institutional change raises the degree of marketisation of the economy; marketisation causes a convergence of the pattern of trade and resource endowment, thereby generating trade expansion. In the transition economy, market-isation has differential effects on the export sector and nonexport sectors (owing to a quicker response in the export sector to the changing incentive scheme resulting from market-oriented reform measures), causing export expansion to contribute more to general economic growth. A dynamic shift of comparative advantage both internationally and domestically raises China's prospects for further increasing its export supplies and enhancing the contribution of export expansion to economic growth in China. This historical process started in the late 1970s, and its potential will continue to be realised for many years to come.

Future studies could focus on a more detailed analysis of policy-induced structural changes that lead to trade expansion and on theoretical explanations for, and the character of, shifts in comparative advantage in a domestic setting.

Notes

1. Howe and Walker (1989) conducted a documentary survey based on 'The Role of China's Import Trade During the First Five-Year Plan' by Lu Shiguang and Huang Junting, in which the roles of importing and exporting in state planning under a centrally planned economy system, with a particular emphasis on their role in overall and sectoral balances, were discussed.
2. A typical example of the impact of marketisation on economic and trading activities is the development of township and village enterprises (TVEs) in China. Subject to competition from both inside and outside, the expansion of TVEs has been accompanied by the development of both the product and the factor market within the traditional sector of the economy. As a result, the shares of TVEs in both GDP and exports have increased rapidly. For example, exports from TVEs increased from $8 billion in 1988 to $40 billion in 1994, which accounts for about one-third of China's total exports (*People's Daily*, overseas edition, May 6, 1995). This example illustrates that the direct gains from trade obtainable by bringing underutilised resources from the subsistence sector into export production offer a more convincing explanation of their growth than the conventional gains in terms of an increase in the static allocative efficiency of the 'given' and fully employed resources (Myint 1984:235).
3. However, these indirect effects are not theoretically demonstrable in the same way as the direct static gains from trade and are not conducive to accurate measurement. But they are based on widely acceptable general presumptions that are, at least in principle, capable of empirical verification (Myint 1984:238).
4. A positive statistical association between the expansion of exports and the growth of national incomes among the developing countries does not tell us much about causal relationships (Myint 1984:223). However, when the relationship between export growth and economic growth is examined in the context of institutional changes for a transition economy, which can be treated as a third factor, it is likely that exports will have some positive impact on economic growth because the export sector has to respond more quickly to market pressure, leading generally to a higher growth rate than the one for the overall economy.
5. Table 3.16 in Song (1993) provides world resource shares in selected countries. It shows that China's share of capital, skilled labour, and semiskilled labour increased dramatically, while its share of unskilled labour and arable land decreased. Zhang (1993) also provides evidence of changing resource patterns in China.
6. Sodersten and Reed use Chile as an example of a country in which 'a determined program of trade liberalisation yielded dramatic gains, but

where the gains were largely lost by an inappropriate exchange rate policy' (1994:415).

7. See Lau (1994) for further discussion of this issue.

8. This viewpoint is supported by the evidence of the changing comparative advantage reported in the section on the convergence of trade and resource patterns.

9. See Song (1993) for a more detailed discussion.

References

Anderson, Kym, and Ben Smith, 1981, 'Changing Economic Relations between the Asian ADCs and Resource-Exporting Advanced Countries of the Pacific Basin,' in *Trade and Growth of the Advanced Developing Countries in the Pacific Basin*, ed. by W. Hong and L. Krause (Seoul: Korea Development Institute).

Balassa, B., 1978, 'Exports and Economic Growth,' *Journal of Development Economics*, Vol. 5 (June), pp. 181–89.

Congdon, T., 1990, 'Export Promotion and Trade Liberalization in Latin America,' in C. Milner (ed.), *Export Promotion Strategies: Theory and Evidence from Developing Countries*, (New York: Harvester Wheatsheaf).

Drysdale, Peter, and Andrew Elek, 1992, 'China and the International Trade System,' *Pacific Economic Papers*, No. 214 (December).

Garnaut, Ross, and Kym Anderson, 1980, 'ASEAN Export Specialization and the Evolution of Comparative Advantage in the Western Pacific Region,' in *ASEAN in a Changing Pacific and World Economy*, ed. by Ross Garnaut (Canberra: Australian National University Press).

Howe, Christopher, and Kenneth R. Walker, 1989, *The Foundations of the Chinese Planned Economy: A Documentary Survey, 1953–65* (Basingstoke, Hants: Macmillan).

Lau, Lawrence J., 1994, 'The Chinese Economy in the Twenty-First Century,' paper presented at the International Conference on the Market Economy and China, Beijing, September 18–22.

Li, G., 1992, 'GATT and Foreign Trade System Reform in China,' *International Trade* (Beijing), Vol. 9, pp. 31–36.

Martin, Will, 1990, 'Two-Tier Pricing in China's Foreign Exchange Market' (unpublished; Canberra: National Centre for Development Studies, Australian National University).

Myint, Hla, 1984, 'Exports and Economic Development of Less Developed Countries,' in *Agricultural Development in the Third World*, ed. by C. Eicher and J. Staatz (Baltimore: Johns Hopkins University Press).

Rana, Pradumna B., 1990, 'Shifting Comparative Advantage Among Asian and Pacific Countries,' *International Trade Journal*, Vol. 4, pp. 243–58.

Sodersten, Bo, and Geoffrey Reed, 1994, *International Economics* (New York: St. Martin's Press, 3rd ed.).

Song, Ligang, 1993, *Sources of International Comparative Advantage: Further Evidence* (Ph.D. dissertation; Canberra: Australian National University).

Wu, Yi, 1992, 'Foreign Trade System Reform Enhances Trade Expansion,' *International Trade* (Beijing), Vol. 7, pp. 4–7.

Zhang, Xiaoguang, 1993, *China's Trade Patterns and International Comparative Advantage* (Ph.D. dissertation; Canberra: Australian National University).

26 China's WTO Membership: what's at stake?

Yongzheng Yang

I. Introduction

It is nearly ten years since China launched its campaign to enter the GATT/WTO. Although significant progress has been made, there are still key issues dividing China and its major developed economy trading partners. The sticking point is whether China should join the WTO as a developing or developed economy. China insists that its low per capita income warrants developing economy status, while developed economies, especially the United States, argue that China's huge size means that it is not an ordinary developing economy, and that it should take the responsibility of a developed economy in its commitments to trade liberalisation. The impasse on this issue has stalled membership negotiations in the WTO.

This paper addresses the key issues of market access in the negotiations. In particular, it examines the implications of different rates of tariff reductions by China both for itself and its major trading partners. To put market access in the broader context of China's WTO accession, the following section outlines the disagreements between China and its major trading partners regarding the terms of accession.

II. The Stumbling Blocks

The terms under which China enters the WTO are important not only for itself, but also for other prospective WTO members, especially the transitional economies of the Former Soviet Union and Vietnam, as these terms would set precedents for them. It is therefore useful to highlight the major disagreements on these terms as it will provide not only a background to subsequent analysis but also a guide to potential issues confronting other transitional economies. Quantitative assessments of some of these issues in Section V may also serve as a useful pointer to the consequences of trade reform for these transitional economies.

Developing versus developed economy commitments

Under various WTO agreements, developing economies are subject to less stringent rules and disciplines in their trade policies. They have also pledged less significant tariff reductions than developed economies and are given longer time periods for implementing their commitments in the Uruguay Round. Thus, whether China is treated as a developing or a developed economy

Reprinted with permission. Yongzheng Yang, 1996. 'China's WTO membership: what's at stake?', *World Economy*, 19(6):661–82 (with minor editing).

has major implications for its liberalisation commitments. For example, if admitted as a developing economy, China would be able to impose quantitative restrictions on trade in the case of severe current account imbalances and to maintain high protection for its 'infant' industries (GATT Articles XII and XVIII). Under the Uruguay Round Agreement on Agriculture, developing economy status would allow China to reduce its agricultural protection by only two-thirds of developed economy commitments and to be given an implementation period of ten years, instead of the six years for developed economies. China would also face the less strict rules regarding input and export subsidies and greater latitude in the application of sanitary and phytosanitary measures for developing economies. Similarly, under the General Agreement on Trade in Services (GATS), China would have to open fewer services sectors than developed economies. All these options would, of course, be proscribed if China is admitted as a developed economy.

China is concerned that if it liberalises as a developed economy it may not be able to manage the structural change arising from trade reform. It intends to pursue trade reform gradually in keeping pace with its overall economic reform to avoid major upheavals and market disruptions. The Chinese Government is already facing the daunting task of reforming its inefficient state enterprises. Rising unemployment resulting from the reform has increased the fear of social unrest, an anathema to the Government since the Tiananmen Square incident in 1989.

WTO members have two major concerns. One is to maintain and increase access to China's rapidly growing domestic markets. Developed economy status for China in the WTO would ensure substantial liberalisation in China. The second concern is that China's exports of manufactures may disrupt markets in developed economies. Since the 1970s, China's exports of labour-intensive manufactures have grown very rapidly. If that trend continues, China's market penetration may exert further pressure on structural adjustment and affect employment in developed economies.

Safeguards

To minimise the potential disruption to their domestic markets, some developed economies have insisted that a special safeguard provision be included in China's Protocol of Accession. This provision would enable importing economies to impose discriminatory measures against Chinese exports on the basis of market disruption or a modified version of 'serious' injury, which would be less stringent than the current GATT provisions (Article XIX). In addition, proposals by the United States and the EU for such a special safeguard provision also contain a mechanism for third countries to have recourse to such measures on the basis that the imposition of restrictions by other countries has resulted in a diversion of China's exports to their markets. China has opposed this special safeguard mechanism, fearing that its most dynamic exports, such as textiles and clothing, would be restricted by discriminatory measures. China is also concerned that the United States may invoke the non-application clause of the WTO Agreement (Article XIII), thus perpetuating the diplomatic tension associated with annual renewals of its most favoured nation (MFN) status in the US market.

Anti-dumping and countervailing

China's fear of discrimination is compounded by the rapidly increasing anti-dumping actions against it by the EU and the United States. In the past, the existence and margins of dumping have been determined mostly using third country or reference prices, which can be substantially different from China's actual domestic costs. China has opposed such practices in its accession negotiations, while some of its trading partners want to maintain them. China has also strongly opposed quantitative restrictions by the EU on a range of Chinese products such as toys, footwear, ceramics and porcelain.

Subsidies to state enterprises in the past have made China vulnerable to countervailing charges against it. With the abolition of explicit export subsidies in 1994, the grounds on which some countervailing duties are levied have disappeared, but the continued bailout of loss-making state enterprises by the Government remains a concern for China's trading partners.

Industrial tariffs

As a rule, China has offered to bind all its tariffs to 35 per cent upon accession and promised further reductions to 30 per cent afterwards. There are, however, many exceptions. China's main trading partners demand that China reduce its overall tariff level to less than ten per cent and participate in the Uruguay Round zero-for-zero tariff reductions and tariff harmonisation agreed by the Quad economies (The United States, Canada, the EU and Japan). Sectors included in the zero-for-zero tariff reductions are pharmaceuticals, construction equipment, medical equipment, steel, furniture, beer, agricultural equipment and distilled equipment, and steel. Tariff harmonisation (at 6.5 per cent or lower) was agreed on chemicals only. China maintains that these tariff reductions and harmonisation have been proposed for developed economies and that it does not have to join the initiative as some developing economies have.

Non-tariff barriers and industrial policy

China has offered to remove most of its non-tariff barriers in six years, but insisted on maintaining quotas on about 100 HS (Harmonised Commodity Description and Coding System Nomenclature) categories, which mainly consist of machinery and electronic equipment. The central issue is China's industrial policy towards its automobile industry. The Chinese authorities are concerned that this infant industry may never become competitive if strong foreign competition is allowed before it matures. China therefore intends to maintain high tariffs and a number of quotas on the automobile industry by invoking GATT Article XVIII. China's trading partners have demanded substantial reductions in the tariff rates and a timetable for the elimination of the quotas.

Agriculture

China intends to introduce tariff quotas on several agricultural commodities including wheat, barley, wool and several other commodities. It also wants to maintain state monopoly over key agricultural imports. Major agricultural exporting economies, including the United States and Australia, oppose tariff quotas and want the state's monopoly to be removed. China's desire for agricultural protection stems from its food self-sufficiency policy—a remnant of the Cold War era, when China was afraid of a Western blockade of food supplies. More recently, as the income gap between rural and urban populations widens, trade policy has been advocated to achieve greater income equality.

Intellectual property rights

Protection of intellectual property rights has been a contentious issue in bilateral trade talks between China and the United States. China has been urged to improve its law enforcement and apply the provisions of the Agreement on Trade-Related Aspects of Intellectual Property Rights, including Trade in Counterfeit Goods (TRIPS) as a developed economy. This means a one year period of transition for appliance, instead of five years for developing economies. China and the United States signed a bilateral agreement on the protection of intellectual property rights in early 1995. This, however, has not resolved the dispute over the issue. The United States has since accused China of failing to enforce the agreement, while China has asserted that it has achieved substantial progress in the protection of intellectual property rights and that the United States has not fulfilled its commitments to the enforcement of the agreement. Although the two countries have averted costly trade sanctions against each other in the last two years, the dispute is likely to continue given China's difficulties in law enforcement.

Trade regime

There are concerns among China's trading partners over the transparency of China's foreign trade regime. China insists that import and export quotas should not be published because of commercial confidentiality, while its trading partners demand that they be made public. They also demand to be given opportunities to comment on drafts of China's trade laws and regulations. China opposes this on grounds that foreign involvement in the legislative process infringes upon its sovereignty.

There are also disagreements on trading rights for both domestic and foreign enterprises. While China wants to control the types of enterprises which may engage in domestic and foreign trade, its trading partners demand that foreign enterprises be allowed into the trading sector. State monopoly, designated trading, and limitations on the number of enterprises and the scope of business are considered to be major obstacles to access to China's expanding trading sector.

Foreign exchange control is another area of concern for China's trading partners. Although significant progress has been made in liberalising the foreign exchange market, exchange control is still being used to influence the level and composition of imports. China wants to retain this policy to a certain degree, but its trading partners demand that all exchange control be removed.

Other disagreements

In the service sector, developed economies demand that China open its markets for domestic distribution, telecommunications, air transport, banking and insurance. China has also been asked to extend national treatment to foreign goods, services and investment. Of particular concern are the existing local content requirements and foreign exchange balance for foreign investment, both of which are inconsistent with GATT 1994 Article III and the Uruguay Round Agreement on Trade-Related Investment Measures (TRIMS).

III. China's Trade in Global Perspective

The potential benefits from China's trade liberalisation depend on the size of its economy. Equally, the potential pressure that China can exert on structural adjustment in developed economies also depends on its economic power. Controversy over defining the size of the Chinese economy has not helped China's WTO membership negotiations as the importance of China in the world market is often exaggerated and hence the stakes are raised in negotiations.

There is general consensus that exchange rate based approaches to the estimation of gross domestic product (GDP) substantially underestimate China's real income. Some estimates based on purchasing power parity (PPP) put China's GDP at several times the exchange rate based estimates (Ren and Chen 1995; IMF 1993; World Bank 1993a, Garnaut and Ma 1992, and Summers and Heston 1991). According to IMF and World Bank estimates, China is already the third largest economy in the world, after the United States and Japan. However, China's trade potential and its market power in the world economy depend on which components of the exchange rate based GDP are underestimated.

Several factors contribute to biases in exchange rate based estimates. If the domestic currency renminbi is undervalued, it will lead to underestimation of China's GDP when converted into its US dollar equivalent. There is, however, no evidence that the renminbi has been undervalued in recent years (Sun 1992). The second factor is price control and barriers to trade. For a number of primary commodities—such as petroleum, coal and grain—domestic prices have been well below international prices until very recently because of price ceilings and export restrictions. On the other hand, the prices of many manufactured products—for example, chemical fibres, automobiles and electricals—have been well above international prices. On balance, however, exchange rate based approaches may underestimate China's tradable sector. For example, Garnaut and Ma (1992) estimated that the value-added of a dozen or so major sectors would exceed the official World Bank GDP estimate—which is exchange rate based—for China in 1992 (US$371 per capita). The third, and perhaps most important factor contributing to the downward bias in China's exchange rate based GDP is the low prices of non-tradable services (Ren and Chen 1995). Normally, PPP estimates do not alter the size of the tradable sector in the economy to the same extent as they do the non-tradable sector.

The ultimate factor determining China's importance in the world market is its current trade volumes and potential. Publicity of China's trade performance and its concentration on exports of consumer manufactures (which are visible in retail markets) may have created a myth about China's potential in foreign trade. China is the eleventh largest trading economy in the world, and its exports were valued at US$92 billion in 1993 (UN COMTRADE statistics, obtained from the International Economic Databank, The Australian National University). This is only a little over one-fifth of US exports, or one-quarter of Japan's, and only about ten per cent larger than the exports of Taiwan or Korea.

While China's exports are not as significant as some perceive, their rate of growth has given reason to expect that China could soon dominate world markets for many products. Between 1978 and 1993. China's exports increased at 16.3 per cent per annum in real terms[1]—about four times the world average. Historically, only the newly industrialising economies (NIEs) in East Asia achieved such rapid growth in their early stage of industrialisation. Extrapolating this historical growth rate, by 2005 China's exports will be 80 per cent of the United States, and by 2015, more than twice as large as the United States. Such

extrapolation appeals to alarmists, but it makes little sense. China's export growth has already slowed in the last few years. If the 1987–93 growth rate is used for extrapolation, China's exports by 2005 would still be about 37 per cent of the United States level, and by 2015 about 59 per cent. China's annual export growth in the period 1987–93 was 13.1 per cent, higher than that achieved by the NIEs over the period 1965–93 (12.1 per cent per annum). This may serve as a guide for China's potential long-term growth rate.

There are strong reasons to believe that China will not be able to repeat the growth rate of the past reforming 15 years. First, China started from a relatively small export volume in 1978, when the value of China's exports was similar to that of Finland. As exports increase, the growth rate is likely to slow down. Second, there were many one-off factors that influenced China's past performance. Economic reforms led to substantial reductions in trade barriers. Rapid inflows of foreign investment also stimulated trade. While such factors will continue to influence trade growth, their effect will diminish over time. Finally, China's trade to GDP ratio is comparable to economies of similar size after the under-estimation of its real GDP is taken into account (Garnaut and Huang 1995). There is no reason to believe that China's trade-GDP ratio can be much higher than that of similar sized economies. Thus, even with rapid growth of the economy, export growth will most likely slow down.

In the long run, China's export growth is likely to be accompanied by a commensurate growth in imports if it continues to liberalise its trade. It makes little sense for a capital-scarce economy like China to run a large, continuous trade surplus. This will provide greater opportunities for exports from developed economies. After all, China's growth is not a zero-sum game. There is little doubt that developed economies have benefited from China's growth in the past, and will continue to do so. In fact, over the past 18 years since the reform, China's imports have grown at a similar rate to exports, and there has been no persistent trade surplus.

IV. Market Penetration

While the lack of understanding of China's trade volume may have caused concerns over the potential disruptive effect of China's economic growth on developed economies, its high border protection often leads to the perception that the Chinese economy is very much closed. Table 1 presents market penetration ratios[2] in six market groups. Among developed economies, North America and the EU have similar penetration ratios, while Japan has a lower ratio. Surprisingly, China has a higher penetration ratio than the developed markets. China's penetration ratio is biased upward because of the underestimation of China's gross output, but this would occur largely in the service and some primary sectors, where prices are lower in China than in developed economies. Penetration ratios for tradable industries are high and concentrated in

Table 1   Market penetration ratios, 1992 (per cent)

Commodity		North America	EU	Japan	China	Other Asia	Rest of the world
1	Paddy rice	1	10	0	0	0	0
2	Wheat	1	1	23	16	44	28
3	Other grain	1	2	33	0	33	9
4	Non-grain crops	14	21	15	2	18	9
5	Wool	57	66	100	78	85	20
6	Other livestock	2	1	4	0	11	2
7	Forestry	1	7	17	4	13	4
8	Fisheries	59	20	27	3	18	5
9	Coal	3	12	45	1	29	13
10	Oil	27	84	74	21	66	28
11	Gas	7	76	42	14	44	17
12	Other minerals	25	5	33	22	47	23
13	Processed rice	12	5	0	0	2	3
14	Meat products	4	2	16	1	7	5
15	Milk products	1	1	3	9	27	13
16	Other food products	5	5	3	6	13	10
17	Beverages and tobacco	6	4	5	1	15	6
18	Textiles	12	8	7	15	37	15
19	Clothing	32	32	14	10	53	20
20	Leather	63	23	29	27	59	25
21	Lumber	13	10	9	12	24	14
22	Pulp and pear	5	10	2	11	23	12
23	Petroleum and coal	3	3	7	9	20	7
24	Chemicals, rubber and plastics	18	11	6	18	36	21
25	Non-metallic minerals	9	3	2	2	18	9
26	Primary ferrous metals	10	29	4	16	28	17
27	Non-ferrous metals	18	32	13	23	52	18
28	Fabricated metal products	8	6	2	8	28	15
29	Transport equipment	28	14	9	63	52	42
30	Machinery and equipment	31	25	6	29	69	39
31	Other manufacturers	46	48	15	37	75	33
32	Services	1	3	2	1	6	4
33	All commodities	7	7	5	9	25	11

Source: GTAP database, version 2.

Table 2   **Bilateral market penetration ratios, 1992** (per cent)

Exporter	China	North America	EU	Japan	Asia	Rest of the world
China	0.0	0.3	0.2	0.3	2.9	0.2
North America	1.4	1.8	1.6	1.3	4.2	2.1
EU	1.0	1.1	0.0	0.7	3.0	4.8
Japan	1.4	1.1	0.7	0.0	5.8	0.9
Other Asia	3.7	1.0	0.8	1.1	5.8	0.9
Rest of the World	1.2	1.5	3.7	1.4	3.5	2.5
World	8.7	6.7	6.8	4.7	25.3	11.3

Source: GTAP database, version 2.

heavy industry. Furthermore, penetration ratios for heavy industry may be understated because of high protection (see Table 3 in the following section).[3] In developed economies, penetration ratios also vary between industries. Labour-intensive industries show the highest penetration ratios.

In terms of bilateral trade, North America captures 1.4 per cent of the Chinese market, whereas China takes only 0.3 per cent of the US market (Table 2)[4]. In fact, China's share in all three developed markets are no greater than 0.3 per cent, and developed economies' market shares in China are all above one per cent. China's share in the developed markets is less than one-third that of other Asian economies combined, or of Japan. Of course, penetration ratios vary substantially across industries. Leather, clothing, textiles and other labour-intensive products such as toys have much higher penetration ratios. But even for individual industries, China's exports are generally much smaller than those of the NIEs combined. It will be a long time before China can surpass the NIEs.

Developed economy markets are indeed important to China. Forty-six per cent of China's total exports were destined for these markets in 1992. The United States alone absorbed 20 per cent of China's total exports. In contrast, China

is not a particularly large market for the developed economies. In 1992, China accounted for two per cent of total US and EU exports and three per cent of Japanese exports. One may argue that these small shares are precisely due to China's high protection and that once the Chinese economy opens further, these shares will increase. Assuming that with continued trade liberalisation China's total exports/imports increase to 37 per cent of US exports by 2005, as extrapolated earlier using the average 1987–1993 growth rate (13.1 per cent per year in real terms), China would account for 4.6 per cent of total US exports in 2005, assuming it maintains its market share and its exports grow at the rate of 1987–93. China is still not a huge market for the United States.

This analysis suggests that the gain to developed economies from China's trade liberalisation will be limited. The expected small gain for developed economies through trade liberalisation by China, however, does not support the argument that China should be admitted to the WTO at the expense of GATT principles. It does suggest that resources invested by some developed economies in negotiating China's WTO membership are disproportionate to the expected benefits. Similarly, the overall impact of China's export expansion on developed economies will not be particularly large simply because China is a moderate player in world markets.

V. Trade Protection and Reform

China's trade policy has undergone substantial changes since the late 1970s when economic reform began. The process of reform has been a gradual one, in line with the pace of its overall economic reform. This gradualist approach is also reflected in China's demand for a relatively long transition period in its accession negotiations. It is therefore important to put the negotiations in the broader context of China's economic reforms. Understanding of current trade restrictions will also help interpret simulation results in the following section.

In pre-reform China, foreign trade was part of central planning and monopolised by a dozen state foreign trade corporations. There were also trade taxes and numerous quantitative restrictions. Foreign exchange was tightly controlled as part of trade planning. As economic reform proceeded, central planning was weakened and trade was increasingly controlled by border taxes and quantitative restrictions.

Over time, quantitative restrictions are being replaced by trade taxes. Many exports of primary products are taxed. The rationale for export taxes is to take advantage of the optimum export taxes that China seems to enjoy in certain products—for example, food exports to Hong Kong and exports of mineral products, such as tungsten. Some manufactured products, particularly semi-processed products (yarns and fabrics), are also subject to export taxes. Export restrictions are also used to stabilise domestic prices, such was the case with the curb on the export of corn in 1994 and 1995.

At the beginning of 1991, export subsidies were removed, state monopoly was reduced, and exporting enterprises became accountable for their profits and losses. At the end of 1992, China published a revised list of products subject to export quotas and licensing (*International Business*, 29 January 1992; *People's Daily*, Overseas Edition, 31 January 1992). In the revised list, the number of products subject to export licensing and quotas was reduced by more than 50 per cent. The share of products subject to licensing in total exports fell from 66 per cent to 31 per cent, and control of licensing and quotas was further decentralised.

Quantitative restrictions and tariffs on imports have been reduced. In 1991, tariffs were reduced for 225 commodities (*People's Daily*, Overseas Edition, 31 January 1992), and in 1992 they were further cut for 3,371 items, leading to a reduction of the average tariff level by 7.3 per cent. At the same time, regulatory tariffs which were introduced in 1985 were abolished. The list of products for import substitution was abolished, and the number of commodities under import licensing was reduced by more than 50 per cent from the 1986 level. To increase the transparency of the trade system, a number of internal policy documents concerning imports were published for the first time. By 1 July, 1995, only 15 machinery and electronic products were still subject to quotas, and only 15 categories of so-called general commodities were still controlled by licensing and quotas (for details see *China Securities*, 1 August 1995:1). These changes represent important liberalisation as compared to the mid 1980s situation, when most commodities were regulated by quotas and licensing.

Despite the reforms, tariff levels remain high in China (see Table 3). The structure of tariffs is typical of the protection pattern in most developing economies. Tariff levels tend to increase with the degree of processing. Manufactured products tend to be more protected than primary products (World Bank 1988; Zhang 1993). Among agricultural products, while rice (including processed rice) and wheat are subject to insignificant tariffs, other sectors have a tariff rate higher than ten per cent. Tariffs on non-grain crops, livestock, fisheries and processed food (except for processed rice) are quite high. Among industrial products, tariffs range from three per cent for oil to 97 per cent for beverages and tobacco. Clothing, textiles and other manufactures are among the most protected.

Leaving aside quantitative restrictions the actual effect of China's tariffs may not be as large as suggested by their statutory levels because of the 'water' in the tariffs. In 1984, tariff rebates were introduced, and with the abolition of export subsidies in 1991, rebates on indirect and value added taxes were also introduced (Sun 1992). In 1986, actual collections of tariff revenues were only ten per cent of import values (World Bank 1993b:60), and in 1992, the rate dropped to less than four per cent (*People's Daily*, Overseas Edition, 9 January, 1993). Smuggling is only partly responsible for the low revenue collections (World Bank 1993b).

Table 3   **Tariffs and their equivalents, 1992** (per cent)

Commodity	Value-added as per cent of GDP	Imports as per cent of total	Import tariffs
1 Paddy rice	5.0	0.0	0.0
2 Wheat	1.7	2.2	0.0
3 Other grain	5.6	0.2	10.1
4 Non-grain crops	11.3	1.2	24.2
5 Wool	0.0	0.7	15.0
6 Other livestock	6.8	0.3	34.7
7 Forestry	2.0	0.6	10.1
8 Fisheries	1.7	0.3	36.0
9 Coal	1.8	0.1	15.0
10 Oil	1.6	1.8	3.0
11 Gas	0.1	0.1	16.8
12 Other minerals	0.6	1.6	17.1
13 Processed rice	0.5	0.1	0.0
14 Meat products	0.3	0.1	45.4
15 Milk products	0.0	0.1	35.5
16 Other food products	0.7	1.9	29.4
17 Beverages and tobacco	1.7	0.3	96.8
18 Textiles	2.8	10.0	64.2
19 Clothing	1.7	0.6	94.7
20 Leather	1.1	1.8	42.1
21 Lumber	0.6	1.1	26.9
22 Pulp and paper	1.2	2.6	26.6
23 Petroleum and coal	0.8	1.5	12.7
24 Chemicals. rubber & plastics	3.6	14.2	18.3
25 Non-metallic metals	2.3	0.5	43.5
26 Primary ferrous metals	1.5	5.1	13.7
27 Non-ferrous metals	0.3	2.3	11.6
28 Fabricated metal products	1.1	1.4	40.5
29 Transport equipment	0.6	10.9	37.5
30 Machinery and equipment	5.4	30.4	29.9
31 Other manufactures	1.3	2.2	83.8
32 Services	34.2	4.0	2.2
33 All commodities	100.0	100.0	30.4[a]

Note: [a]import-weighted average.
Source: GTAP database, version 2.

At the APEC meeting in Osaka in November 1995, China announced that it would reduce its tariff levels by at least 30 per cent in 1996 as part of its commitment to the APEC trade liberalisation process. This will bring down the average tariff level from 36 per cent to 23 per cent. Quantitative restrictions on imports will be removed from 170 items, or 30 per cent of all items subject to quotas. In addition, China intends to further reduce its average tariff to about 15 per cent by 1997.

Trade liberalisation is part of China's on-going reform process which is aimed at transforming the entire economy into a fully fledged market economy. At the beginning of 1994, the government unified the multiple exchange rates and formed a single exchange rate. As a result, partial foreign exchange retention which was introduced in the early 1980s was abolished, and the foreign exchange certificate which had been in circulation in parallel with renminbi was taken out of circulation. It has been announced that renminbi will become convertible for current account transactions by the end of 1996 and be made fully convertible towards the year 2000. In April 1994, a primitive inter-bank foreign exchange market was established, parallel to foreign exchange swap markets. A fully operational inter-bank foreign exchange market is expected to be in place in 1996.

In 1994, multiple corporate tax rates for domestic firms were replaced by a single unified rate. Tax privileges for the special economic zones will be phased out in the near future. The services sector is gradually being opened for foreign investment. Foreign investment is allowed in retailing and real estate industries, but insurance and financial services still remain largely closed to foreign enterprises. Branches of some foreign banks are open in major cities, but they are restricted to foreign exchange business and to certain geographical locations. Telecommunications, transport and aviation industries have received some foreign investment, but foreign enterprises have not been allowed to operate on their own.

VI. The Impact of China's Trade Liberalisation

In this section, we examine the impact of China's trade liberalisation on both itself and its trading partners using a 32x6 version[5] (32 commodities by six regions) of the GTAP model.[6] The focus will be on the structural adjustment and welfare effects. China has indicated that it will continue to pursue trade reform whether or not it is admitted to the WTO. It is assumed in this analysis that China's reform will be carried out as part of the Uruguay Round trade liberalisation. The reform will therefore have its full effect by the year 2005, when the Uruguay Round trade liberalisation is completed. To look at the impact of trade reform in the year 2005, the world economy is projected to 2005. This provides a benchmark (baseline) against which the effect of trade reform is measured. All subsequent experiments are comparative-static in the year 2005. The projection essentially involves the forecast of the cumulation of primary factors, technological change, and the growth of quotas under the Multifibre Arrangement (MFA) over the period 1992–2005. Alternatively, real GDP growth and primary factor accumulation could be forecast and technological change deduced. The latter approach is followed in this study.

The projections for the world economy over the period 1992–2005 are based on projections of GDP growth and primary factor uses by Hertel et al. (1995) and the World Bank (1994a and 1994b) (see Table 4). For the growth of MFA quotas, projections are based on the estimates in Hertel et al. (1995) and UNCTAD (1995). These growth rates include both quota growth stipulated in bilateral MFA agreements and growth acceleration under the Uruguay Round Agreement on Textiles and Clothing.

As only economy-wide GDP forecasts are available, technological change only at the economy level can be deduced in the simulation. It should be noted, however, that GDP does not grow at the same rate across sectors in the simulation, even though only the economy-wide

GDP growth rate is projected. Because of variations in factor intensity among sectors, different rates of factor cumulation mean that GDP growth differs among sectors. In addition, consumer preferences are non-homothetic, so the growth of demand for various products differs as income rises.

For the comparative static experiments, the estimates of tariff cuts and agricultural liberalisation are based on GATT (1993 and 1994) and UNCTAD (1995). For developed economies, domestic support for agriculture is reduced by 20 per cent, and export subsidies and tariffs (including equivalent quantitative restrictions) by 36 per cent. Tariffs on textiles and clothing are reduced by 18 per cent in North America, 16 per cent in the EU (15 per cent for imports from developing economies), and 33 per cent in Japan. For developing economies, domestic support for agriculture is cut by 15 per cent, export subsidies by 24 per cent, and tariffs by 26 per cent. Tariff reductions in developing economies are generally two-thirds that of developed economy liberalisation. The MFA is eliminated completely by reducing its export tax equivalents to zero.

Three comparative static scenarios on China's trade reform are examined. In the first (reference) scenario, China is treated as a developing economy in terms of trade liberalisation, and in the second scenario, China is assumed to be a developed economy, as described above. It is assumed that the only difference between these two scenarios is the extent of liberalisation to be implemented by the year 2005. In the third scenario, China undertakes to cut its tariffs to a maximum of ten per cent on top of the developing economy liberalisation.[7] This leads to not only a deeper tariff cut for most products but also to a reduction in the variation of tariff rates.

The results show that the impact of trade liberalisation on output is significant (see Table 5). Whether China undertakes to liberalise as a developing or developed economy makes only limited difference. The similarity in the results for the two scenarios result from the moderate (one-third) difference in the depth of trade reform. In addition, tariff cuts are proportionate in the two scenarios and hence lead to similar changes in relative prices. Because of fixed endowment supplies, which determine the level of aggregate value added, the two scenarios produce similar changes in sectoral output.

In both scenarios, despite declines in the output of 'other' grains, wool, forestry and fisheries, total agricultural output increases by about one per cent due to increases in the output of rice, wheat, non-grain crops and other livestock products. Only if China undertakes to cut its tariffs to a maximum of ten per cent does overall agricultural output decline moderately.

Mining industries contract as a result of trade liberalisation, and contraction increases slightly with the depth of liberalisation. The fall in output results primarily from the increased cost of capital. Because mineral industries are much more capital intensive than other industries, they

Table 4   **Projections of cumulative growth of macroeconomic variables, 1992–2005** (per cent)

	Population	Labour	Capital	Real GDP
China	18	16	216	203
North America	12	13	43	41
EU	2	2	19	33
Japan	4	-2	52	39
Other Asia	24	31	132	118
ROW	32	35	50	68

Source: Hertel, Martin, Yanagishma and Dimaranan (1995).

Table 5   **Effects of trade liberalisation on sectoral value added in China, 2005** (percentage change)

		As a developing economy	As a developed economy	Tariff cut and leveling
1	Paddy rice	1	0	-3
2	Wheat	2	2	1
3	Other grain	-2	-2	-6
4	Non-grain crops	1	0	-9
5	Wool	-14	-16	-8
6	Other livestock	7	7	4
7	Forestry	-9	-10	-11
8	Fisheries	-11	-14	-29
9	Coal	-7	-7	-5
10	Oil	-13	-12	-19
11	Gas	-11	-12	-10
12	Other minerals	-19	-21	-22
13	Processed rice	0	0	-2
14	Meat products	-1	-1	2
15	Milk products	-4	-6	-15
16	Other food products	-8	-10	-15
17	Beverages and tobacco	-4	-6	-51
18	Textiles	35	37	4
19	Clothing	246	253	335
20	Leather	-36	-32	-3
21	Lumber	-13	-14	-14
22	Pulp and paper	-6	-7	-9
23	Petroleum and coal	-6	-6	-6
24	Chemicals, rubber & plastics	-7	-8	-5
25	Non-metallic metals	-5	-6	-8
26	Primary ferrous metals	-15	-16	-9
27	Non-ferrous metals	-21	-21	-18
28	Fabricated metal products	-10	-10	-13
29	Transport equipment	-21	-15	27
30	Machinery and equipment	-22	-23	-24
31	Other manufactures	-7	-3	31
32	Services	0	0	1

Source: Simulations of the GTAP model.

are hit the hardest by the rising cost of capital. The increase in capital costs results from imperfect capital mobility and the expansion of global production.

In the manufacturing sector, textiles and clothing are the only expanding industries. These two industries are among the largest in China's manufacturing sector and their expansion is the main contributor to the increase in real GDP. MFA restrictions on China are among the most severe.

Clothing output increases strongly when the MFA is abolished. This is consistent with some early studies (Trela and Whalley 1990; and Yang 1994). An upward bias may be imparted to this estimate as a result of the aggregation of all the other MFA-restricted developing economies. While clothing output expands mainly because of export expansion, textile output increases to meet domestic demand by the expanding clothing industry.

Trade liberalisation exerts most pressure on heavy industry. The output of metal products, transport equipment, and machinery and equipment falls by ten to 20 per cent. Interestingly, the extent of contraction does not increase with the depth of tariff cut. In fact, for transport equipment, the adverse impact declines considerably if China liberalises as a developed rather than a developing economy. Furthermore, the industry expands substantially if all tariffs are cut to a maximum of ten per cent. This paradoxical result arises from cost reductions in intermediate inputs to the industry when high tariffs on other manufacturing sectors are reduced. There may also be a bias in this result due to the high degree of aggregation in this industry. For example, the average tariff rate for transport equipment presented in Table 3 does not reveal the high tariff on motor vehicles. Had the industry been disaggregated, motor vehicle production would probably decline, while the production of other products would increase even more.[8]

The same aggregation bias may also exist for the chemicals industry. The average tariff for this industry is among the lowest and this leads to a moderate contraction of its output following trade liberalisation. Some products within the industry face much higher tariffs and a breakdown of the industry may well result in greater falls in the output of some sub-industries (for example, chemical fibres).

The macroeconomic effects of trade liberalisation are substantial (see Table 6). In the reference scenario, China's real GDP increases by four per cent and real wages rise by two per cent. Measured in terms of equivalent variations however, the gain is smaller—only 1.6 per cent of 2005 national income. This results from a considerable deterioration in China's terms of trade. Both exports and imports increase, but the latter increases more than the former. Despite this, China's trade balance improves due to a substantial surplus in the projected base year (2005).

The macroeconomic impact differs only marginally if China is treated as a developed economy. In general, deeper (proportional) tariff cuts result in greater economic gains despite a greater adverse effect on the terms of trade. However, deeper tariff cuts do lead to a smaller improvement in the trade balance as imports increase further.

The effect of trade liberalisation is much more beneficial when all tariffs are reduced to a

Table 6   **Macroeconomic effects of trade liberalisation on China, 2005** (percentage change or US$ billion)

	As a developing economy	As a developed economy	Tariff cut and leveling
Expenditure-based real GDP	4.0	4.4	7.7
GDP price	-0.6	-1.3	-6.1
Real wage	2.2	2.8	8.0
Consumer price index	3.0	2.2	-2.3
Equivalent variation (EV) (US$ billion)	18.0	19.1	27.4
EV as per cent of income	1.6	1.7	2.4
Government revenue	5.1	3.6	-8.3
Export volumes	29.8	35.4	81.2
Import volumes	35.9	45.5	119.1
Terms of trade	-5.9	-6.4	-10.2
Trade balance (US$ billion)	9.2	8.8	4.8

Source: Simulations of the GTAP model.

Table 7 **Macroeconomic effects of China's non-participation in the Uruguay Round compared with participation as a developing economy, 2005** (percentage difference)

	China	North America	EU	Japan	Other Asia	Rest of the world
Real GDP	-4.1	0.0	0.0	0.0	0.6	0.1
EV (US$ billion)	-23.9	-12.5	-10.5	-1.3	8.9	3.6
Export volumes	-30.3	-0.6	-0.7	0.2	3.7	1.0
Import volumes	-38.0	-2.1	-1.8	-0.7	3.0	0.6
Trade balance (US$ billion)	-11.3	0.9	2.4	3.2	2.8	2.0
Terms of trade	5.0	-1.0	-0.5	-0.1	-0.3	-0.1

Source: Simulations of the GTAP model.

maximum of ten per cent. Real GDP growth nearly doubles relative to the reference scenario, while the real wage increase is nearly four time as large. This sharp increase in real wages results from a six per cent decline in the consumer price index. Welfare as measured by equivalent variation does not improve to the same extent because of a further deterioration of the terms of trade. Both exports and imports increase, but the trade surplus is further reduced compared to the developed economy scenario.

The much larger gains from tariff cuts and leveling suggest that China's tariff structure is very distortionary and has led to major economic losses. As discussed earlier (see Table 5), this approach to tariff cuts leads to little, if any, additional adjustment pressure on most domestic industries, notwithstanding the aggregation bias discussed previously.

What will be the consequence if China does not participate in the Uruguay Round trade liberalisation, as either a developing or developed economy? In the fourth scenario, China is assumed not to participate in the Uruguay Round trade liberalisation and hence continues to face MFA quotas while they are removed for other developing economies. It is assumed, however, that China continues to enjoy most-favoured-nation (MFN) tariff reductions from its trading partners, as it has in the past. This scenario is hypothetical but realistic, and could

result from changes in domestic political balance or as a backlash from China's failure to join the WTO in the near future. In this circumstance, the process of economic reform is likely to continue, but the timing of trade reform may be extended if domestic political forces react to WTO exclusion.

If China fails to participate in the Uruguay Round liberalisation, while everyone else liberalises, it may lose as much as US$6 billion (measured by equivalent variation) compared with a situation of Uruguay Round trade liberalisation. This results largely from increased competition from other developing economies in the world textile and clothing markets. China would lose even more if the outcome of this scenario is compared with the result of China's participation in the Uruguay Round reform, even if it liberalises only as a developing economy (see Table 7). It makes a US$24 billion difference (scenario 4 minus scenario 1) whether China participates in the Round or not, of which 62 per cent is attributable to the MFA. The difference would be larger if compared with the scenarios of deeper trade liberalisation.

China's trading partners also lose from China's non-participation in the Uruguay Round liberalisation. North America and the European Union would lose the most. This is because the abolition of the MFA is one of the most important reforms in the Uruguay Round package. By continuing to discriminate against China, consumers in North America and the European Union would continue to pay higher prices for Chinese textiles and clothing than they otherwise would. China's high market shares in these two commodities mean that MFA reform is far from complete without including China.

This suggests that a large part of the welfare gains to North America and the European Union from China's participation in the Uruguay Round comes from their own reform, that is the abolition of the MFA. Table 8 reports the results of three scenarios of unilateral trade liberalisation by China using the same baseline as in the first four scenarios. China's tariff cuts do contribute to the welfare gains for North America and the European Union, but their effects are not nearly as large as their own trade reforms. China's tariff cuts to the extent of developing economy liberalisation would benefit North America by only US$0.3 billion, the European Union by US$1.2 billion and Japan by US$0.6 billion. This implies that out of the US$12.5 billion gain to the United States from China's participation in

the Uruguay Round reform as a developing economy, a little over two per cent comes from China's tariff cuts, and the rest is from the abolition of the MFA. For the EU and Japan, the share is 12 per cent and 42 per cent, respectively. It is the Asian developing economies that benefit most from China's reform (US$2.6 billion) because of their more extensive trade with China. Of course, as the extent of China's reform increases, the benefits to its trading partners increase, but they are still smaller than the effect of the MFA reform.

Developed economies hope that tariff reductions in China will reduce their trade deficits with China. Indeed, this is one of the objectives of bilateral trade talks on the part of the United States. Simulation results in Table 8, however, do not support this. In fact, developed economies' trade balances will deteriorate marginally as China liberalises. This is consistent with the view that huge US trade deficits result largely from its own macroeconomic policies, including exchange rate policy, rather than other countries' trade policies (Krugman 1991).

Table 8   **The impact of China's trade liberalisation on its own and other economies, 2005** (percentage change and US$ billion)

	China	North America	EU	Japan	Other Asia	Rest of the world
China as a developing economy						
Real GDP	1.1	0.0	0.0	0.0	0.0	0.0
EV (US$ billion)	8.4	0.3	1.2	0.6	2.6	0.4
Trade balance (US$ billion)	1.6	-0.2	-0.7	-0.8	0.6	-0.4
China as a developed economy						
Real GDP	1.5	0.0	0.0	0.0	0.0	0.0
EV (US$ billion)	9.8	0.6	2.1	0.8	3.5	0.5
Trade balance ($US billion)	1.4	-0.2	-0.8	-0.9	0.8	-0.4
Tariff cut and leveling						
Real GDP	4.2	0.0	0.0	0.0	0.0	0.0
EV (US$ billion)	27.4	6.0	6.5	1.3	14.5	0.3
Trade balance (US$ billion)	1.4	-0.6	-1.6	-1.8	3.3	-0.9

Source: Simulations of the GTAP model.

VII. Policy Implications

Simulation results in the previous section suggest that China is perhaps too anxious about the adjustment cost of trade liberalisation. It is inevitable that some of its inefficient industries will contract, especially heavy industry, but economic efficiency improves in the long run. A considerable part of the adjustment may have already been accomplished due to widespread tariff rebates and exemptions, which have rendered effective protection for many sectors low. As for agriculture, trade liberalisation would probably lead to a slight output expansion whether China liberalises as a developing or developed economy. Only when it undertakes to cut its tariffs to a maximum of ten per cent does agricultural output decline moderately.

Tariff cuts reduce output prices, but they also reduce the cost of intermediate inputs. Hence, some protected industries may not suffer as much as indicated by the high levels of tariff protection they currently receive. China's distorting tariff structure makes it difficult to forecast which industries will be most affected by trade reform without taking into account inter-sectoral effects, but it also means that there is much to gain from reducing variations in tariff levels.

China's concern over the potentially adverse balance of payments effects of trade liberalisation is unfounded. As mentioned earlier, economic theory suggests that external imbalances are mostly caused by failures in macroeconomic policies. Where imbalances do occur, macro-economic policy should be the preferred instrument, not trade policy. The simulations here suggest that China's balance of trade, which is the bulk of its current account balance, will improve if China liberalises. This assumes prudent macroeconomic policies maintaining stability in the lead up to trade liberalisation. This would make it unnecessary to invoke the balance of payments provisions under the GATT Articles XII and XVIII:B. Relinquishing this option would encourage discipline in macroeconomic management.

Just as China is pessimistic about the impact of trade liberalisation on its domestic economy, so are developed economies regarding the potential impact of China's exports on their economies. China is still a moderate player in the world market despite rapid growth in the last one and a half decades. With that growth expected to slow, it will be many years before the adjustment pressure created by China's export growth matches that of Japan or the NIEs. For the same reason, China's trade liberalisation will not benefit its trading partners as much as their own reforms. While overall welfare benefits for developed economies from China's liberal-isation are non-negligible, their trade deficits with China may worsen slightly because China may become more competitive with trade reform. Liberalisation in services is likely to improve developed economies' trade balances with China, but this will happen only if China participates as a WTO member in multilateral trade liberalisation. China has been reluctant to liberalise its services sector because it lacks competitiveness.

Both China and its trading partners will benefit from China's participation in the Uruguay Round trade liberalisation, whether it is treated as a developing or developed economy. In contrast, both China and developed economies would lose from China's exclusion, especially if MFA quotas were maintained. This highlights the importance of non-discriminatory conditions on WTO accession not only for China but also for other transitional economies. It is therefore in the interest of the world trading system that China and other transitional economies resist policies which discriminate against them.

The most effective way to secure the benefits of China's trade liberalisation would be an early entry to the WTO. For this to happen, China should set a concrete timetable for further comprehensive and substantial trade liberalis-ation, building on the commitments it made at the APEC Summit in Osaka in 1995. For developed economies, the abundance of discriminatory policies and a reasonable transitional period for

China could be used as tools of compromise for gradual, but substantive reform according to the timetable. Negotiations on China's WTO accession should therefore concentrate on liberalisation schedules for individual sectors rather than on the contentious, and often politically charged, issue of whether China should be admitted as a developing or developed economy.

Notes

1. Nominal exports deflated by the price of US imports.
2. Defined as imports divided by apparent consumption (production plus imports), multiplied by 100.
3. This is because in calculating the penetration ratios exports were valued at FOB prices whereas output was valued at domestic market prices which includes the price-raising effect of trade protection.
4. Re-exports via Hong Kong have been taken into account in these shares after deduction of value added in Hong Kong. This applies to the remainder of this section. See Gehlhar et al. (1997) for details of how Hong Kong re-exports are distributed among final destinations in the GTAP database.
5. See Table 1 for the commodity and regional details.
6. The GTAP model was developed at the Global Trade Analysis Project led by Thomas Hertel of Purdue University. Interested readers are referred to Hertel (1997) for more details of the model.
7. This formula of tariff cut is referred to as 'tariff cut and leveling' in the following.
8. Further aggregation is impossible in the current GTAP database. This also applies to the chemicals industry to be discussed in the following paragraph.

References

Garnaut, R. and Huang, Y., 1995. *China's Trade Reform and Transition: Opportunities and Challenges for OECD Countries*, Report prepared for the Trade Directorate, OECD, Paris.

—— and Ma, G., 1992. *China's Grain Economy*, Australian Government Publishing Services, Canberra.

GATT, 1993. *An Analysis of the Proposed Uruguay Round Agreement, with Particular Emphasis on Aspects of Interest to Developing Economies*, 29 November, GATT, Geneva,

——, 1994. *News of the Uruguay Round of Multilateral Trade Negotiations*, April, GATT, Geneva.

Gehlhar, M., Gray, D., Hertel, T., Huff, K., Ianchovichna, E., McDonald, B., McDougall, R., Tsigas, M.E. and Wigle, R., 1997. 'Overview of the GTAP Data Base', in T. Hertel (ed.), *Global Trade Analysis Using the GTAP Model*, Cambridge University Press, Cambridge.

Hertel, T. (ed.), 1997. *Global Trade Analysis Using the GTAP Model*, Cambridge University Press, Cambridge.

——, Martin, W., Yanagishma, K. and Dimaranan, B., 1995. 'Liberalising Manufactures Trade in a Changing World Economy', in W. Martin and L.A. Winters (eds), *The Uruguay Round and the Developing Economies*, World Bank Discussion Paper No. 307, World Bank, Washington, DC.

IMF, 1993. *Staff Studies for the World Economic Outlook*, IMF, Washington, DC.

Krugman. P.R., 1991. 'Has the Adjustment Process Worked?' in F. Bergsten (ed.), *International Adjustment and Financing: The lessons of 1985–1991*, Institute for International Economics, Washington. DC.

Ren, R. and Chen, K., 1995. 'An Expenditure-based Bilateral Comparison of Gross

Domestic Product between China and the United States', Policy Research Working Paper, World Bank, Washington DC.

Summers, R. and Heston, A., 1991. 'The Penn World Trade Table (Mark 5): An Expanded Set of International Comparisons, 1950–1988', *The Quarterly Journal of Economics*, 106(2):327–68.

Sun, F., 1992. 'The Role of Foreign Exchange Policy in China: A Historical Perspective', PhD dissertation, School of Economic and Financial Studies, Macquarie University, Sydney.

Trela, I. and Whalley, J., 1990. 'Global Effects of Developed Country Trade Restrictions on Textiles and Apparel', *Economic Journal*, 100:1190–205.

UNCTAD, 1995. *An Analysis of Trading Opportunities Resulting from the Uruguay Round in Selected Sectors: Agriculture, Textiles and Clothing, and Other Industrial products*, UNCTAD, Geneva.

World Bank, 1988. *China External Trade and Capital*, World Bank, Washington, DC.

——, 1993a. *World Development Report*, Oxford University Press, New York.

——, 1993b. *China: Foreign Trade Reform: Meeting the Challenge of the 1990s*, World Bank, Washington, DC.

——, 1994a. *World Development Report*, Oxford University Press, New York.

——, 1994b. *Global Economic Prospects and the Developing Countries*, World Bank, Washington, DC.

Yang, Y., 1994. 'The Impact of MFA Phasing out on World Clothing and Textile Markets', *Journal of Development Studies*, 30(4):892–915.

Zhang, X.G., 1993. China's Trade Pattern and International Comparative Advantage, PhD dissertation, National Centre for Development Studies, The Australian National University, Canberra.

27 China's Integration into the World Economy

Ross Garnaut and Yiping Huang

China has roughly quadrupled its annual output of goods and services since 1978. Real growth has averaged 9 per cent, and foreign trade has grown substantially more rapidly (Figure 1). The accommodation of sustained, rapid, internationally oriented growth in China is one of the greatest challenges facing the world economy over the next decade. Success will increase the gains from trade, while failure will lead to corrosion of the open international system.

China's rapid trade growth has been concentrated disproportionately in a narrow range of commodities. This is mostly a source of gain for China's international partners, except for those highly competitive with China. The main cost of China's growth to outsiders is adjustment. Viewed analytically, the adjustment challenge to the international community over the next one or two decades is of modest scale despite China's size.

A danger however is that the size and political weight of China will lead to perceptions of competition with an emerging China in the zero-sum context that is common in security but alien to economic analysis. This could interact with resistance to adjustment to weaken international rules as they apply to China. The international response to China's trade reform and rapid growth will determine the extent to which China sustains its trade expansion.

I. Aggregate Impact of China's Growth

China's economic size is not captured by the standard official national accounts data. The World Bank recorded China's per capita income in 1992 at US$371. This number is widely recognised as underestimated (Summers and Heston 1991; Perkins 1992; Garnaut and Ma 1993a). Comparisons of consumption patterns of food, durable appliances, steel, energy and natural fibre in China and other East Asian economies suggest that an accurate figure would be achieved by adjusting the Chinese official income level for 1990 upwards by a factor of three (Garnaut and Ma 1993a). Adjusted data suggest that China's per capita income in 1993 was about US$1,300. China is already a middle-income economy, the fourth largest after the United States, Japan and Germany.

Rapid internationally oriented growth is easier to sustain than to initiate. China shares with its Northeast Asian neighbours many characteristics that are important to their success: unusually high rates of saving and investment; strong emphasis on education; community support for the growth objective; acceptance of structural change and social transformation associated with growth; policies allowing access to international investment, technology and ideas about economic organisation; and policies

Figure 1   **Gross domestic product and trade growth rates, 1978 to 1994** (per cent)

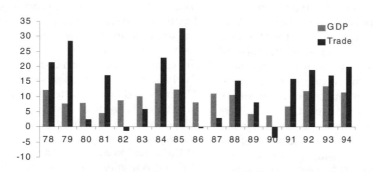

Notes: Trade includes exports and imports of commodities and non-factor services. Growth rates of both trade and GDP are calculated from their values at constant prices in yuan.
Sources: International Economic Databank, The Australian National University, Canberra; State Statistics Bureau, various issues. *China Statistical Yearbook*, China Statistics Press, Beijing; Asia Pacific Economics Group, 1994. *Asia-Pacific Insights 1994*, The Australian National University, Canberra.

supporting the rapid growth in foreign trade along the lines of comparative advantage (Garnaut 1989; World Bank 1993).

In comparison with its East Asian neighbours, China has the advantage of being a latecomer. East Asian rapid economic growth is a process of catching up with the technological and economic organisational frontiers of the world economy. In East Asia, it is an advantage to pursue an internationally oriented growth strategy when one has dynamic, outward-looking and economically substantial neighbours.

There are some particular disadvantages in China's legacy of central planning. The transfer of political power is more problematic and associated with the risk of political instability. In our view, however, while these disadvantages could have unexpected and damaging effects at times of stress and change, it is not likely that any of them will greatly influence the powerful trends of the past 15 years.

One important challenge for China is the containment of inflation and management of a smooth transition of the macroeconomic system (Lau 1993; Lin, Cai and Li 1994). The biggest

danger to continued success is that the Chinese leadership will make prosaic errors, that requires a response too big to manage (Garnaut 1992).

We expect China's growth to continue to be highly variable but to maintain the reform years average for the foreseeable future. If China grows at an annual rate of 8.5 per cent and the rest of the world at 4 per cent (unrealistically high for industrial economies), by the year 2000 China's GDP will be about midway between Germany and Japan. It will represent 11 per cent of world GDP.[1] This proportion will be something of a lower limit in circumstances where there is no major social and political fracture in China (the more likely case).

Total trade has grown faster than GDP in the reform period, at an average rate of 13 per cent in 1978–93 (Figure 1). The share of exports in GDP rose from 3 per cent in 1978 to 5.6 per cent in 1992. China's share of world merchandise exports rose from less than 1 per cent in 1978 to 2.4 per cent in 1993. China's current export–GDP ratio is much lower than other East Asian developing economies, and even lower than larger economies such as the United States.

There is a question about whether Chinese trade will continue to grow more rapidly than output. China's size and diversity of resource endowments, and the separation of a vast inland population from opportunities for low-cost participation in an international division of labour suggest that China's trade share of output will remain below other economies. The large difference between resource endowments in China and the rest of the world, the relatively low transactions cost of trade within an extensive Chinese community, the concentration of the most rapid growth in coastal regions, and the high cost of internal trade and specialisation suggest that foreign trade shares will be high. The reduction of high official barriers to international trade will raise trade shares. The reduction of high barriers to internal trade will have opposite effect—although less so in the context of increasing specialisation in production and intra-industry trade.

Lau (1993) predicts that the relative importance of internal trade will increase and the export ratio will fall because the world economy will not be able to adjust to continued rapid increases in Chinese exports. Lau's view implies a break from past relationships between trade and growth during the reform era, and from the pattern in other East Asian developing economies. Our own assessment is that within an effective, rules-based international trading system and with continued trade liberalisation, China's foreign trade will continue to grow more rapidly than output. There is currently powerful momentum in trade growth but eventually the Lau factor will take the edge off it.

If China's exports expand at reform period rates, its share of goods and non-factor services in world trade will rise from about 1.7 per cent in 1990 to 6.6 per cent in 2010 (Table 1). On balance, this seems a reasonable prospect—higher growth rates of exports are a possibility.

China's economy is considerably larger than Japan's three decades ago or the newly industrialising economies two decades ago. But the world economy is now two or three times as large and considerably more integrated across international borders. China's production is likely to remain less export-oriented than Japan's and the newly industrialising economies. On the assumption that China's exports will continue to grow at the rate of the reform era, the projected increase in China's trade share in the 1990s is less than Japan's share in the 1960s. The projected increase after 2000 is less than that of the newly industrialising economies in the 1980s (Table 1). Not only is world output and trade much larger now, but a substantial part of the adjustment can be carried by other East Asian economies which are more flexible than industrial economies.

The growth of Japanese trade in the 1960s and the newly industrialising economies in the 1970s was accompanied by the proliferation of exceptions to liberal international trading rules—voluntary export constraints (including the Multifibre Arrangement) and other 'grey area measures' were among the reasons why a multilateral negotiation in the form of the Uruguay Round was necessary by the 1980s. It would be

Table 1   **East Asian economies' share in world merchandise trade, 1960 to 2010** (per cent)

	Japan	NIEs	Japan	China and NIEs
1960	3.3	0.8	4.1	0.5
1965	4.8	1.0	5.8	0.8
1970	6.3	2.1	8.4	0.6
1975	6.5	2.6	9.1	0.7
1980	6.5	3.8	10.3	1.0
1985	9.3	6.0	15.3	1.4
1990	8.0	7.7	15.7	1.7
1993	9.5	9.9	19.3	2.4
1994	9.1	7.6	16.7	2.6
2000				3.6[a]
2010				6.6[a]

Note: [a] Based on growth rates in the reform period.
Source: International Economic Databank, The Australian National University, Canberra.

unfortunate for the international system if the rise in Chinese output and trade was accompanied by a similar proliferation of exceptions.

The impact of China's growth on the rest of the world will be lessened by the fact that its imports will expand as well. From 1978 to 1993, while China's exports and real GDP grew at 14 and 9 per cent, respectively, imports grew at an annual rate of 12 per cent. While there are large short-term fluctuations in China's current account and net exports, there is no general tendency towards surplus (Figure 1). This is not very different from Japan in the 1960s and the newly industrialising economies in the 1970s—tensions associated with large current account surpluses came later.

One advantage for the world economy in accommodating new participants now, is the increased number of internationally oriented economies sharing the adjustment burden and gains from trade. China has emerged as an important trading partner with Russia since the collapse of socialism.

The instability in China's trade balance is a potential source of adjustment problems for the rest of the world, especially if contraction of

economic activity and net imports coincides with recession in the rest of the world. There has been a fortuitous correlation between the Chinese and international business cycles over the past decade. The fortunate timing of the Chinese boom in the early 1990s helped to maintain growth in other East Asian developing economies through the OECD recession.

The inverse relationship between the Chinese and international cycles may not continue. The possibility that future periods of sharp increases in Chinese net exports might coincide with international recession, adds to the importance of domestic reforms to promote stability in the Chinese macroeconomic system (Garnaut and Ma 1993b).

II. Sectoral Effects

Viewed as an integrated unified economy, China has a relative abundance of labour and relative scarcity of natural resources (Garnaut and Anderson 1980; Garnaut 1989). This is especially true for the coastal provinces involved in

Table 2   **China's exports and imports by commodities, 1978 to 1993** (per cent)

	1978	1980	1985	1990	1993	Comparator world share 1993
Exports						
Agriculture-intensive	36.1	26.3	21.7	12.5	9.5	13.0
Capital-intensive	15.2	15.6	12.8	26.7	28.8	58.4
Labour-intensive	31.1	30.2	35.4	50.9	56.4	13.9
Textile and clothing	23.1	22.4	26.4	28.8	27.6	7.1
Mineral-intensive	17.0	27.3	28.8	9.4	4.8	12.2
Imports						
Agriculture-intensive	29.0	33.8	10.8	16.3	8.9	13.1
Capital-intensive	59.0	52.8	73.3	60.5	70.5	57.6
Labour-intensive	4.2	8.1	9.7	16.0	12.2	13.5
Textile and clothing	2.2	4.8	6.3	12.1	9.4	7.1
Mineral-intensive	7.0	4.2	5.1	5.1	6.9	13.6

Source: International Economic Databank, The Australian National University, Canberra.

international trade and experiencing the most rapid growth. These provinces, with up to 400 million people are about as densely populated as parts of island and peninsula Northeast Asia—Japan, Taiwan and the Republic of Korea—that experienced sustained rapid growth in the postwar periods. China's trade specialisation in the early stages of rapid, internationally oriented growth has followed these economies closely, with strong and increasing focus on labour-intensive exports, and imports of capital goods and a range of natural resource-based products. The concentration of Chinese exports and imports in a narrow range of commodities could exacerbate adjustment problems in industrial economies with labour-intensive import-competing industries and in competing labour-abundant developing economies.

Expansion of labour-intensive manufactured exports

China's foreign trade structure has moved more closely with its relative resource endowment in recent years (Table 2). Before reform, China's exports were dominated by agriculture-intensive products, whose share has fallen rapidly since 1978. The share of mineral-intensive products has fallen sharply since the mid 1980s, while the share of labour-intensive manufactured goods rose rapidly, in 1993 reaching 56 per cent, or four times the share of labour-intensive manufacturers in world trade. Textile and clothing alone accounted for an extraordinary 28 per cent of Chinese exports in 1993, or almost six times their share of total world trade, despite severe restrictions on Chinese exports to North America and Western Europe through the Multifibre Arrangement.

Table 3 **Shares of developing economies and China in world and OECD imports of manufactured products, 1992** (per cent)

	Australia & New Zealand	North America	European Community	Japan	OECD	World
Chemicals						
Developing economies	14.6	20.0	5.9	20.9	10.8	14.0
China	3.5	1.6	0.9	5.2	1.6	1.9
Machines						
Developing economies	17.1	24.3	6.9	21.6	13.3	13.6
China	0.6	1.0	0.3	1.0	0.5	0.8
Transport equipment						
Developing economies	3.5	8.7	2.5	4.6	4.8	6.4
China	0.4	0.2	0.1	0.4	0.2	0.3
Clothing						
Developing economies	77.4	91.1	43.2	81.1	62.6	61.5
China	48.6	16.6	6.7	43.4	14.0	18.4
Textile						
Developing economies	51.1	49.4	17.2	67.3	26.9	42.4
China	9.7	9.9	2.3	25.5	5.3	8.4
Total manufactures						
Developing economies	21.1	32.4	10.3	39.3	18.9	21.0
China	4.2	5.1	1.5	9.8	3.1	3.9
Share of manufactured imports (GDP)						
Developing economies	2.1	2.4	1.6	1.2	1.8	2.1
China	0.3	0.3	0.2	0.2	0.2	0.3

Source: International Economic Databank, The Australian National University, Canberra; World Bank, 1993. *China Foreign Trade Reform: meeting the challenge of the 1990s*, Report 11568–CHA, World Bank, Washington DC.

Figure 2   **Share of labour-intensive goods in total exports, world and East Asian economies, 1965 to 1992** (per cent)

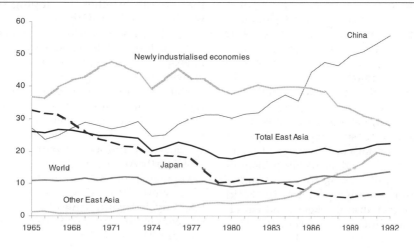

Source: International Economic Databank, The Australian National University, Canberra

Figure 3   **Changing shares of East Asian economies in world total labour-intensive manufactured exports, 1965 to 1992** (per cent)

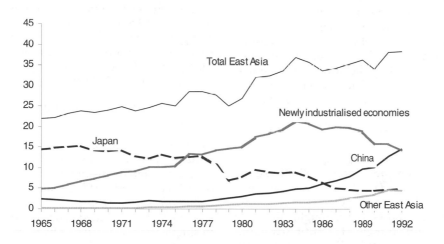

Source: International Economic Databank, The Australian National University, Canberra.

By 1992, China supplied about 2.3 per cent of world merchandise exports. China's position in world markets was larger only in a limited range of labour-intensive products, notably clothing (18 per cent) and textiles (8 per cent) (Table 3). The concentration of China's exports in a relatively narrow range of labour-intensive exports is more marked than the newly industrialising economies taken together at similar stages of development (Figure 2).

The world adjustment to expansion of Chinese labour-intensive exports has been facilitated by rapid falls in the shares of Japan (especially up to 1986) and the newly industrialising economies (after 1983). By 1992, China's share of labour-intensive products in world exports was higher than the newly industrialising economies, but at 15 per cent still well below the peak of the mid 1980s. The increase in China's share coincided with the rapid increase of Southeast Asia's role in world trade (Figure 3). East Asia's total share of world exports of labour-intensive products has hardly risen at all since 1984, while rising Chinese and ASEAN (other than Singapore) shares have been balanced by declines in Japan and the newly industrialising economies.

There is now some anxiety in lower-income Southeast Asian economies in the early stage of internationally oriented growth that continued rapid expansion of Chinese labour-intensive exports will crowd out their own opportunities. Certainly, the competition is severe, especially in textile and clothing where it will intensify in North America with the removal of the Multifibre Arrangement constraints on Chinese export expansion.

If Chinese and world exports of labour-intensive manufactured goods continue to grow at their 1980s rates (23 and 9 per cent, respectively), by 2000 China would account for 34 per cent of world exports. This is roughly the same as Japan and the newly industrialising economies combined in the mid 1980s, and would be achieved when exports from Japan and the newly industrialising economies fall to low levels (Figure 3). Nevertheless, China's exports of labour-intensive goods would grow so rapidly that growth in other developing economies would be limited. Otherwise the increased competitiveness of developing economies would need to force an increased role for labour-intensive products in world trade, with exports growing more rapidly than consumption. This would continue the observed pattern since rapid export-oriented industrialisation emerged in China and the lower-income economies of Southeast Asia in the first half of the 1980s (Figure 3).

Shares of European Community, Japanese and North American clothing imports from developing economies in total consumption in 1988 were 19.1, 27.9 and 13.1 per cent, respectively (World Bank 1993). The respective shares of imports from China were 1.6, 3 and 3.4 per cent. The World Bank projects future shares on the assumptions that China's exports continue to grow at about 15 per cent per annum, other developing economies at Korea's growth rate between 1980 and 1990, and that apparent consumption of clothing continues to expand at the rate of the past decade. The Bank projected shares of clothing imports from developing economies and China in 1988 at 23.5 per cent and 1.9 per cent for the European Community, 34.3 per cent and 3.8 per cent for North America and 16.1 per cent and 4.2 per cent for Japan. China's shares of exports to developing economies grew through 1988–92 at a rate well in excess of World Bank projections (Table 2).

Changing comparative advantage and economic diversity

Chinese export expansion at this rate would reduce opportunities for other relatively labour-abundant economies—Indonesia, India, Bangladesh, Vietnam and the Philippines for example—embarking on export-oriented industrialisation strategies, if it remained concentrated strongly in simple products. But is it likely to remain so concentrated?

With a per capita income slightly above US$1,000 China is not an integrated economy.

Rather, it is a set of provincial and regional economies, with widely differing resource endowments and comparative advantages and separated by high resistance to trade and factor flows.

The regional diversity of China's resource endowments and a history of heavy public investment relevant to comparative advantage in more sophisticated production, will tend to support early diversification of exports out of simple, labour-intensive products.

The dynamic Southeast coastal economies—from Hainan and Guangdong to Shanghai and Jiangsu—with a population over 300 million, have per capita incomes well within the range of middle-income economies. The richer and more dynamic parts of this region are already experiencing labour shortages, rising labour costs and pressure to transform production and exports into more sophisticated and capital-intensive activities. Over the next decade, many of the opportunities for sale of labour-intensive products from lower-income inland economies—with per capita incomes closer to Indonesia and India—will come from the provision of labour-intensive economies to dynamic coastal products undergoing structural change. Coastal regions will upgrade specialisation to more sophisticated versions of old products and to more capital-intensive processes, goods and services. Parts of coastal China will support industrialisation of inland China through structural change in trade and production in much the same way as structural transformation of the newly industrialising economies supported export-oriented growth in China in the 1980s.

The share of capital-intensive goods in China's total exports started to rise after the mid-1980s—more rapidly than the share of labour-intensive goods. At the disaggregated commodity level, exports of some capital-intensive goods experienced dramatic expansion both in relative (to total exports) and absolute terms in the 1980s. China is quickly accumulating the physical and human capital needed to produce capital-intensive products at internationally competitive costs when its average per capita income is still

low. One explanation is that some parts of China are already relatively capital-abundant. Another is that some 'capital-intensive' goods are produced more labour intensively in China. Another important factor is that in the 30 years of central planning, there was huge investment in capital and technology-intensive industries—the source of comparative advantage at the margin in producing some capital and technology-intensive manufactured goods.

For these reasons, some technology-intensive manufactured goods may become important in China's export pattern while labour-intensive exports remain absolutely large. More generally, China's comparative advantage will shift from labour-intensive industry to capital and technology-intensive industries as physical and human capital accumulate and labour costs rise, as illustrated by the experiences of Japan and the newly industrialising economies.

Evolving from labour-intensive to capital and technology-intensive manufacturing will be facilitated by China's historical investment in human capital relevant to technologically sophisticated industry. This will accelerate the emergence of new export sectors and smooth the path of structural change as labour-intensive industries lose competitiveness.

The special features of China, including its size and diversity, will cause capital-intensification to take an unusual form. As it will take several more decades of rapid growth for labour to become scarce and expensive, China will remain a competitive supplier of labour-intensive products for a longer period of internationally oriented growth than other East Asian economies. It will quickly lose competitiveness in the simplest, labour-intensive products as growth-enhancing reforms in lower-income economies become effective. At the same time, China will emerge as an important supplier of more sophisticated products.

The evolution of the age structure of China's population in future decades will also contribute to the process of changing comparative advantage, especially when compared to other large Asian countries such as India and Indonesia.

The Chinese population is relatively young, with the share of young workers (aged 15 to 39 years) in the labour force at 60 per cent (Table 4). This is similar to India (61 per cent) and Indonesia (62 per cent). The share of aged population (above 60 years) in China (9 per cent) is only slightly higher than that of India (8 per cent) and Indonesia (6 per cent).

Ageing will soon become an important demographic phenomenon in China because of rising life expectancy and the controlled birth rate. By 2000, the share of aged population will rise to 12 per cent, much higher than that of India and Indonesia. The age dependency ratio in China will remain almost the same mainly due to low fertility, while age dependency in India and Indonesia will fall significantly.

Young workers' share in total labour force participation will fall in all three economies, but most dramatically in China (from 60 per cent in 1990 to 45 per cent in 2010) (Table 4). The absolute number of people under 10 years is already much lower in China than in India, and this will be reflected in much faster and absolutely larger growth in the Indian labour force over the next two decades.

Compared to other populous Asian developing countries, China will lose its comparative advantages in labour-intensive manufacturing more rapidly due to reduced proportion, and pending absolute decline in numbers, of young unskilled workers. The result is likely to be a more diverse export pattern relatively early in the growth process, with more of China's exports focused on the deeper world markets for more technologically sophisticated products. Opportunities will expand for Chinese participation in intra-industry trade in manufactured goods, easing the problems of competition for other low-income economies and adjustment in OECD countries.

Developing economies will benefit from opportunities to expand exports to China itself. China's growth will deepen world markets for a range of manufactured commodities in which some developing economies have emerged as competitive exporters. In the larger world market associated with the emergence of China, there will be more opportunities for gains from trade through specialisation in production. This will place a premium on flexibility and capacity to transform production through rapid expansion

Table 4   **Demographic indicators, China, India and Indonesia, 1990 and 2010 (per cent)**

	Young workers[a] share in total labour force	Share of aged population[b]	Age dependency ratio[c]
China			
1990	60.3	9.0	0.5
2010	44.6	11.8	0.5
India			
1990	61.4	8.0	0.8
2010	57.4	8.4	0.6
Indonesia			
1990	62.1	6.3	0.7
2010	55.1	8.9	0.6

Notes: [a] aged 15 to 39 years.
[b] aged over 60 years
[c] population aged under 15 and over 60 years to those aged 15 to 60 years.
Source: World Bank, 1990. *World Population Projections, 1989–90*, World Bank, Washington, DC.

of activities that have proven their international competitiveness.

Fluctuations in individual commodity markets

China's trade liberalisation, economic expansion or structural change have the capacity to affect prices on world markets. Internationally oriented growth in China has depressed, to some extent, the terms of trade of competing developing economies. In addition, fluctuations in Chinese imports and exports of particular commodities can lead to instability in world prices.

Chinese policy seeks self-sufficiency in cotton producing. But China also actively participates in the international market because there are changes in domestic demand and supply. In some years, for example, between 1986 and 1988, China exported about 500–750 thousand tonnes of cotton a year to the world market, while in other years, for example, in 1980 and 1981, it imported about 80 thousand tonnes a year. World cotton prices tended to be low when China's net imports were low (or net exports were high), and high when China's net imports were high.

China is the world's largest producer and consumer of many commodities, and fluctuations in Chinese supply or demand have a substantial effect on world markets. These effects have been exacerbated by policy instability in China in the partially reformed economy of the past 15 years, especially in relation to industrial inputs. Fluctuations in Chinese supply and demand have their greatest impact on commodities whose international markets are separated from major domestic markets by quantitative controls, so that the international market is simply a residual market, potentially highly volatile in response to relatively small fluctuations in net exports from a major economy.

The impact of Chinese net exports fluctuations on world market prices has already been a source of international concern. The expansion of Chinese wool imports in the mid-1980s followed by sudden a contraction in 1989 and 1990, provides an example with relevance to Australia. If there are no demands for restrictions on Chinese participation in international markets, China and its trading

---

Figure 4   China's net imports of cotton and world cotton prices, 1972 to 1992 (tonnes, USc/lb)

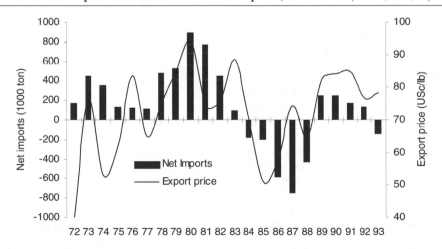

Sources: International Economic Databank, The Australian National University, Canberra; Australian Bureau for Agricultural Research Economics, 1992. *Commodity Statistical Bulletin*, ABARE, Canberra.

445

partners would be wise to implement cost-effective means of minimising such effects.

One is the general internationalisation of markets with the removal of quantitative restrictions on trade, whether imposed in China or abroad. This will have the effect of extending the market to cover more world production and trade, and reducing the impact of fluctuations on China's net exports. A larger and more diverse world market will be a more stable world market.

A second is to remove arbitrary changes in policy that introduce artificial fluctuations in supply and demand for particular products in China. Instability in markets for commodities in which China is a major player adds to the reasons for giving priority to reform designed to reduce macroeconomic instability within China.

III. Whose Adjustment?

Adjustment to China's exports

There has been some discussion in industrial economies in recent years of the effects of rapid trade expansion with labour-abundant China on industrial economies' employment levels and wage rates that are consistent with full employment (Forsyth 1993; Krugman and Lawrence 1993; McDougall and Tyers 1993). In reality, expansion of trade with China in industrial economies has been less rapid and has forced less adjustment compared to East Asia.

Chinese export expansion has required more adjustment in East Asian economies for three reasons. First, these economies maintain relatively open economies for manufactured goods, including labour-intensive products, so that changes in international markets are quickly transmitted. Second, East Asian economies are separated from China by relatively low resistance to trade on account of proximity and a range of factors affecting transaction costs. Third, some of these economies, especially Hong Kong, Korea and Taiwan, have large sectors which are directly competitive with emerging sectors of the Chinese economy. Their existing labour-intensive industries have been affected by China's rising market share.

The world's most dramatic example of structural adjustment associated with the expansion of trade with China is in Hong Kong. Only a decade ago, Hong Kong was strongly specialised in the export of labour-intensive manufactured goods. It had a large manufacturing sector, employing about 1.1 million people. Increased confidence in Hong Kong–China economic relations following China's commitment to economic reform and the Sino–British agreement of 1984 led to the rapid transfer of virtually all of the labour-intensive end of Hong Kong manufacturing into China. The main exception was part of the textiles and clothing

Table 5 **Destination of exports and source of imports, 1980 to 1993,** (US$ million, per cent)

	1980	1985	1990	1993
Exports total value ($ billion)	19.5	27.3	63.2	91.3
Per cent share				
NIEs	24.6	33.7	38.6	39.8
Other East Asia	4.0	2.7	2.9	2.4
Japan	20.7	22.3	14.2	13.6
American OECD	5.7	9.4	9.1	17.6
Oceanic OECD	1.3	0.8	0.8	1.2
European OECD	12.2	8.4	9.5	11.3
Former Soviet Union	1.2	3.8	3.2	3.0
Rest of the World	30.3	18.9	21.7	11.1
Imports total value ($ billion)	19.8	42.5	59.2	104.1
Per cent share				
NIEs	26.5	27.4	49.4	41.5
Other East Asia	2.3	2.1	3.7	3.7
Japan	26.1	35.7	12.9	19.2
American OECD	23.4	14.9	13.6	13.1
Oceanic OECD	6.2	3.0	2.5	2.4
European OECD	14.2	14.5	14.2	13.7
Former Soviet Union	1.3	2.4	3.7	6.4
Rest of the World	22.6	15.6	23.6	11.5

Sources: International Economic Databank, The Australian National University, Canberra; Asia Pacific Economics Group, 1994. *Asia-Pacific Insights 1994*, National Centre for Development Studies, The Australian National University, Canberra.

industry, locked into Hong Kong by country quotas within the Multifibre Arrangement. Employment in manufacturing had fallen to less than half a million by mid-1994. But far from the dismal outcomes for labour in the high-income economy predicted by the factor price equalisation theorem, full employment was maintained right through this massive adjustment and real wages rose dramatically.

Beyond Hong Kong, the most intense trade and rapid expansion of trade with China has been with other neighbouring Northeast Asian economies, then with the wider Asia-Pacific region including American OECD countries (Table 7). China is trading most intensively with Japan and the newly industrialising economies while its trade intensity with the American OECD increased significantly (Table 6).

In the main labour-intensive commodities neighbouring East Asian economies have borne most of the adjustment to China's emergence as a major trading economy. China's share of other East Asian imports is around four times larger than other OECD markets (excluding Japan) for labour-intensive goods (Figure 5). The difference is greatest with textiles and clothing, due in large

part to the artificial constraints of the Multifibre Arrangement in North America and Western Europe.

In 1992 China accounted for over 40 per cent of clothing imports into OECD countries that do not participate as importers in the Multifibre Arrangement (Australia, New Zealand and Japan), but only 17 per cent in North America and 7 per cent in the European Community. North American imports of manufactured goods from China represent a higher proportion of GDP than do Japan's, and yet Japanese imports of textiles and clothing from China are a substantially higher proportion of GDP than North America's. The increase in net imports from China during 1986–92, in nominal terms, represented only 2.2 per cent of peak annual production in European OECD and 2.7 per cent in American OECD (Table 7). It was much higher in the Western Pacific: 4.2 per cent in Japan; 5.9 per cent in Oceanic OECD; 10.6 per cent in Singapore; and 46.2 per cent in Hong Kong.

There will be some more 'catching up' in the North Atlantic economies' adjustment to China's trade expansion with the dismantling of the Multifibre Arrangement as the Uruguay Round is implemented. These are the economies that have felt most threatened by Chinese trade expansion, and the changes associated with the removal of the Multifibre Arrangement will exacerbate perceptions of an adjustment problem in the North Atlantic and will strengthen pressures for safeguards to constrain China's export growth.

Adjustment to China's imports

Alongside China's dramatic export expansion, its imports increased at a similar pace. Capital-intensive manufactured commodities accounted for around 60 per cent of China's imports during the reform period. At the same time, volumes of capital, labour and mineral-intensive imports also increased significantly. Total Chinese imports have increased eight-fold since 1978, the greater part of the increase being a consequence of unilateral trade liberalisation within the

---

Table 6   **Intensities in China's export trade, 1980 to 1993[a]**

	1980	1985	1990	1993
NIEs	5.5	6.0	5.0	3.9
Other East Asia	2.0	1.4	1.0	0.7
Japan	2.9	3.3	2.2	2.7
American OECD	0.4	0.4	0.5	1.0
Oceanic OECD	0.9	0.5	0.5	0.9
European OECD	0.3	0.2	0.2	0.4
Former Soviet Union	0.5	1.4	1.9	n.a.
Rest of the World	1.0	0.7	0.6	0.5

Note: [a] Trade intensities are calculated according to a formula given in Drysdale and Garnaut (1982). Intensity of trade measures the ratio of the economy's share in China's total exports, relative to its share in world imports.
Source: International Economic Databank, The Australian National University, Canberra.

Table 7 **Adjustments in OECD production and trade in manufacturing and textile and clothing, 1986 to 1992** (US$ billion)

	1986	1988	1990	1991	1992	1986–92
American OECD						
Production	133.1	154.5	157.3	155.4	164.0	
Exports	5.1	7.9	10.4	11.8	13.3	
Imports	31.4	38.2	43.2	44.1	50.8	
Exports to China	0.1	0.1	0.1	0.1	-	
Imports from China	2.6	3.1	4.8	5.3	7.0	
Increase in net imports from China						4.4
Increase as share in peak production (per cent)						2.7
Oceanic OECD						
Production	6.6	9.3	9.5	9.3	n.a.	
Exports	1.4	2.1	1.7	1.8	2.1	
Imports	2.2	2.8	3.0	3.1	3.3	
Exports to China	-	-	-	-	-	
Imports from China	0.2	0.4	0.4	0.6	0.7	
Increase in net imports from China						0.6
Increase share in peak production (per cent)						5.9
European OECD						
Production	129.5	162.2	187.7	184.7	n.a.	
Exports	51.3	67.0	86.1	85.5	91.1	
Imports	54.4	75.1	97.1	102.2	107.5	
Exports to China	-	0.1	0.1	0.1	0.1	
Imports from China	1.2	2.2	3.5	5.1	5.4	
Increase in net imports from China						4.1
Increase as share in peak production (per cent)						2.2
Japan						
Production	74.9	101.0	90.6	106.3	111.3	
Exports	6.3	6.2	6.4	7.1	7.7	
Imports	6.1	12.9	15.2	16.1	17.7	
Exports to China	0.3	0.4	0.5	0.7	1.0	
Imports from China	1.3	2.8	3.7	4.8	6.7	
Increase in net imports from China						4.7
Increase as share in peak production (per cent)						4.2
Hong Kong						
Production	11.5	14.2	16.6	17.0	19.1	
Exports	8.4	11.0	11.7	12.3	12.5	
Imports	8.7	13.5	18.9	22.9	26.6	
Exports to China	0.6	0.9	1.1	1.3	1.4	
Imports from China	4.4	6.9	9.9	12.3	14.0	
Increase in net imports from China						8.8
Increase as share in peak production (per cent)						46.2
Singapore						
Production	0.7	1.1	1.2	1.3	1.6	
Exports	1.2	2.0	2.6	3.0	3.1	
Imports	1.5	2.3	3.0	3.3	3.5	
Exports to China	0.0	0.0	0.0	0.0	0.0	
Imports from China	0.1	0.2	0.2	0.3	0.3	
Increase in net import from China						0.2
Increase as share in peak production (per cent)						10.6

Source: International Economic Databank, The Australian National University, Canberra.

Figure 5   **China's shares in world total and labour-intensive manufactured exports, 1978 to 1993** (per cent)

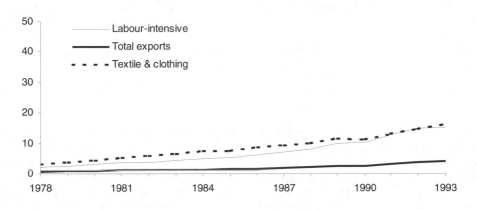

Sources: International Economic Databank, The Australian National University, Canberra; Asia Pacific Economics Group, 1994. *Asia Pacific Insights 1994*, National Centre for Development Studies, The Australian National University, Canberra.

reforms themselves. Chinese imports were estimated to be 92 per cent, or $US36 billion, higher in 1992 than they would have been in the absence of economic and trade reforms in the preceding decade (Drysdale and Song 1994). This represents an opportunity for other economies to raise incomes and high-income employment through structural reorientation.

The biggest expansion in exports to China has occurred in neighbouring East Asian economies. Hong Kong has respecialised, particularly into the export of high-value services and high-value components of manufactured goods, notably for export to China. This radical restructuring was associated with high prosperity. In 1994, Hong Kong's per capita income exceeded Britain and Australia for the first time. Of China's total imports, newly industrialising economies accounted for 27 per cent in 1980 and 42 per cent in 1993. The relative importance of Japan, Australasia and North America in China's imports declined during the reform period, while that of Western Europe remained steady. All these economies, however, experienced increased volumes of exports to China.

China's capital-intensive imports, including machinery and high value manufactured goods, increased proportionately more than total imports. These are the core areas of OECD countries' export specialisation, where the recent and prospective gains from Chinese trade expansion are most obvious.

Grain and steel imports are significant indicators of the transition in China's attitude to international trade. In the Maoist period, self-sufficiency in grain and steel was a key policy objective. During the reform period, China started to use the international market to meet the rapidly growing demand at a lower cost than could be achieved at the margin domestically. As a result, net imports of these products rose significantly. The change in China's attitude to international trade was encouraged by the successful expansion of labour-intensive manu-factured exports. Further significant increase in imports of these and other products would yield large gains for China and its trading partners.

Whether or not these possibilities materialise largely depends on China's commitment to further reform and on the international environment.

Machinery. China's capital-intensive imports increased from US$12 billion in 1980 to US$70 billion in 1993. Imports of non-electrical machinery increased from US$0.5 billion in 1978 to US$13.5 billion in 1992. It is expected that capital-intensive goods will continue to dominate China's imports in the next decade or so. Although China will gradually accumulate capital and skill and gain some competitiveness in producing capital-intensive goods, a productive international division of labour will remain within the category of capital-intensive manufactured goods between China and newly industrialising economies and OECD countries. While the newly industrialising economies are currently supplying capital-intensive goods to China and other ASEAN economies, they themselves still import large amounts of more sophisticated and capital-intensive goods from Japan, the United States and other OECD countries.

During 1978–93, China contributed 8 per cent of the increase in European OECD's exports beyond the European Community of non-electrical machinery and 6 per cent of Japan's increase in non-electrical machinery exports (Table 8). During 1978–93, the OECD's inter-regional exports of non-electrical machinery grew between 7 and 12 per cent per annum, and exports to China grew between 16 and 25 per cent per annum.

High-value services and manufactured components. China's demand for high-value services and manufactured components has grown rapidly with the upgrading of industry. Again, Hong Kong has quickly become one of the major exporters of these high-value products to China. The stake is also high for other newly industrialising economies and most OECD countries.

China's trade relations with the other East Asian economies and OECD countries will experience some structural change within the next two decades. Currently, a large part of China's trade with OECD countries is inter-

---

Figure 6 **Imports of non-electric machinery, 1970 to 1992** (per cent, US$ billion)

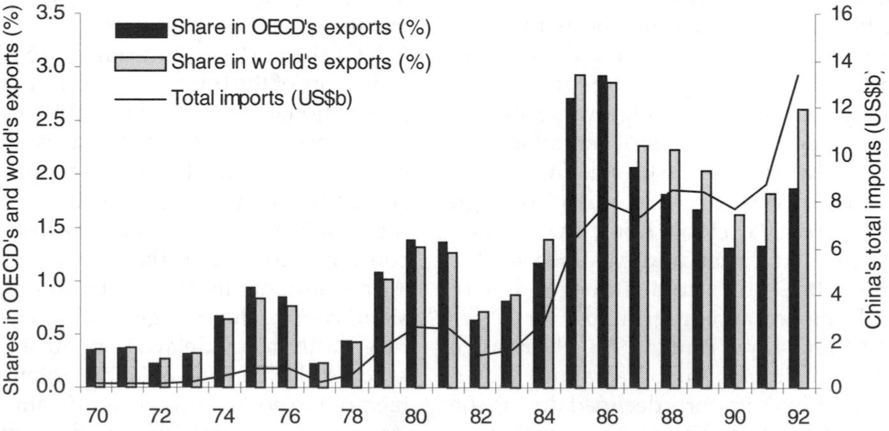

Source: International Economic Databank, The Australian National University, Canberra.

Table 8   China's share in OECD countries' inter-regional exports, 1978 to 1993 (US$million[a])

	Inter-regional exports to China		Inter-regional total		China's share in total export increase (per cent)
	1978	1993	1978	1993	
Non-electrical machinery					
Japan	261.5	4,547.8	14,257.2	82,639.7	6.3
Oceanic OECD	0.2	2.2	294.5	1,553.0	0.2
European OECD	201.0	5,639.7	42,379.2	111,202.3	7.9
American OECD	73.9	1,942.1	21,147.3	67,659.4	4.0
Electrical machinery					
Japan	77.8	2,598.2	13,820.0	72,760.0	4.3
Oceanic OECD	0.0	2.3	103.4	590.1	0.5
European OECD	69.3	1,389.4	19,051.0	55,545.3	3.6
American OECD	18.6	1,271.3	11,019.0	47,703.6	3.4

Note: [a] China's share of the increase in constant dollars or real terms is substantially higher.
Source: International Economic Databank, The Australian National University, Canberra.

industry trade—its imports are concentrated in capital and agricultural-intensive goods and its exports concentrated in labour-intensive goods. Intra-industry trade, although still accounting for a very small proportion, has been increasing (Table 9). The fact that China–OECD trade will be increasingly intra-industry, indicates lower adjustment costs associated with trade expansion.

While China may gradually export more and more capital and technology-intensive goods, its demand for high-value and sophisticated service and manufactured parts will also grow strongly. China is likely to export increasing values of capital-intensive goods to other labour-abundant economies, and engage in intra-industry trade in a wide range of manufactured goods while exporting predominantly low-value manu-factured goods to more industrial economies.

Grain. Chinese economic growth has been associated with rapid increases in demand for grain. Until the mid 1980s, this was partly due to direct human consumption. Since then, it has mainly been feed grain to meet the rapidly increasing demand for higher-value foods, such as meat, eggs, dairy products and alcoholic beverages (Garnaut and Ma 1992). Demand for grain can be expected to continue to expand strongly with incomes over the next two decades.

China is not particularly well endowed with agricultural land. Its per capita arable land area, at 0.08 hectare, is much lower than the world average (Garnaut, Ma and Huang, Chapter 2). China is already the world's largest producer and consumer of grain. Its grain yields are high by international standards. There is not a lot of scope for rapidly increasing yield, and still less for increasing sown areas, unless domestic prices are lifted well above world prices.

Despite the commitment to grain self-sufficiency, the incentive structure in the centrally planned system was strongly biased against agriculture. In the early years of reform, there was a strong supply response to new institutional arrangements (the 'household responsibility system') and higher producer prices. Up to 1984, grain production surged ahead of rapidly rising domestic demand. Since then, although grain prices have increased considerably and producer subsidy equivalents raised to about zero (Garnaut, Ma and Huang,

1994), output has increased below the rate of China's population increase.

China has already shifted from being a small net exporter of grain in the 1970s and 1980s to a substantial net importer (China imported a large amount of grain in 1994 and barred exports late in the year). Under free trade, China would emerge as the largest net importer of grain, transforming conditions in international grain markets and providing a substantially easier transition for many economies to the new international trade rules. Garnaut and Ma (1992) estimate net imports under free trade at 25–70 million tonnes in 2000, depending on the rate of Chinese income growth. The upper end of this range would represent almost half of current total world trade in grain. Huang (1995) estimates net imports at 30–60 million tonnes in 2000.

The Chinese choice will be affected considerably by perceptions of the reliability of international exchange of access for its exports, and of world markets in the supply of food. A choice in favour of international integration would require a high degree of confidence in China's place in the international trading system.

Table 9   **Indices of China's intra-industry trade with OECD countries, 1970, 1980 and 1992** (per cent)

	1970	1980	1992
Japan	5.6	10.5	22.2
Mexico	..	..	7.0
Canada	0.2	2.0	16.5
United States	..	9.0	12.5
Australia	1.7	2.4	10.7
New Zealand	..	5.6	3.5
EEC (12)	1.1	11.6	18.7

Source: International Economic Databank, The Australian National University, Canberra; Drysdale, P. and Garnaut, R., 1993. 'The Pacific: an application of a general theory of economic integration', in C.F. Bergsten and M. Norland, (eds), *Pacific Dynamism and the International Economic System*, Institute for International Economics, Washington DC.

Iron and steel. Steel, like grain, was a focus of concern for high production and self-sufficiency. Also like grain, steel's demand increases strongly with income growth in China (Feng 1994). Total consumption of steel increased by a similar proportion to income, from 24 million tonnes in 1978 to about 95 million tonnes in 1993. It is likely that steel demand will continue to expand at or near the rate of income growth, roughly doubling each decade. While Chinese production will continue to expand rapidly, it cannot expand continuously at this rate.

China does not have particularly strong comparative advantage in steel production. It is a capital-scarce economy and steel production (especially in the early stages) is capital-intensive—steel requirements in an increasingly sophisticated economy require technologies and skills that are expensive in China, Chinese steel-making raw materials tend to be of low quality and the limited availability of deepwater port capacity raises the cost of imported materials, and the environmental costs of emissions from early stage processing of iron are especially high in crowded coastal China. Chinese steel production had more or less kept pace with consumption in the era of central planning, with imports ranging up to 2–3 million tonnes per annum. In the reform era, iron and steel production lagged behind domestic demand. The loosening of the requirements of self-sufficiency saw China emerge as a major importer of steel-making materials, especially iron ore, semiprocessed iron, scrap and steel. Finished steel imports grew in years of strong domestic demand.

Chinese imports of steel in the reform period fluctuated wildly reflecting domestic demand fluctuations through the business cycle as well as uneven application of controls on trade and state enterprises. Net imports of finished steel rose to 7–8 million tonnes in the early years of reform, and then to almost 20 million tonnes in the mid 1980s. In response to the austerity program and growth recession, they fell nearly to zero in 1990 and 1991. As economic growth accelerated, imports of finished steel surged to about 30 million tonnes in 1993. The government sought to limit steel imports to 10 million tonnes in 1994 through the application of controls, but early estimates suggest a figure of around 20 million tonnes in that year.

Under an open and liberal international trading system, China is likely to emerge as a large net importer of finished steel—consistently the largest in the world by a wide margin. China would also emerge as a large importer of steel-making materials and as a participant in intra-industry iron and steel trade. Chinese confidence in the international steel economy to deliver markets for expansion of products in which it has comparative advantage, will affect its acceptance of integration into the system.

Historically OECD countries, especially Japan, Oceanic and European OECD, dominated China's imports of iron ore, iron and steel (Table 10). Australia, for instance, has provided most of China's imports of iron ore. Similarly, Japan and European OECD supplied 90 per cent of China's total imports of iron and steel. China's source of iron and steel imports have been somewhat diversified during the reform period. Nonetheless, European OECD and Japan still

accounted for more than half of China's imports of iron and steel in 1993.

IV. Implications for the World Economy

Opportunities for OECD

The emerging Chinese economy and its trade liberalisation provide OECD countries with great economic opportunities as well as some challenges. There is significant complementarity between China and OECD countries (Table 11). China's exports have been increasingly concentrated in labour-intensive manufactured goods, while most OECD countries do not have comparative advantage in the production of labour-intensive goods. Some of the countries' exports are concentrated in agriculture or mineral-intensive goods, while others' exports, are concentrated in capital-intensive goods.

The strong complementarity is already reflected in the trade pattern. While China's exports to OECD countries were dominated by labour-intensive goods, its imports from OECD countries were dominated by capital and agricultural-intensive goods. This pattern of

Table 10 **Imports of iron and steel from OECD countries, 1980 to 1993** (US$ million, per cent)

	80	85	88	90	93
Iron ore imports (US$ million)	81.1	156.8	103.6	153.2	202.9
per cent share					
Oceanic OECD	88.6	79.5	53.2	67.1	0.2
Iron and steel imports (US$ million)	2076.8	5677.5	4063.0	2045.6	8407.0
per cent share					
Oceanic OECD	5.7	1.7	0.1	0.4	0.0
European OECD	16.2	20.2	12.3	14.5	16.2
Japan	66.0	56.2	60.9	51.8	35.0
American OECD	4.3	0.2	1.5	2.0	0.9

Source: International Economic Databank, The Australian National University, Canberra.

Table 11   Indices of Chinese and OECD export specialisation[a], 1978, 1985 and 1992

		Agricultural-intensive	Capital-intensive	Labour-intensive	Mineral-intensive
China	1978	2.04	0.32	2.94	0.73
	1985	1.49	0.26	3.32	1.25
	1992	0.80	0.47	4.07	0.45
Australia	1992	2.21	0.26	0.17	2.79
Canada	1992	1.42	0.94	0.29	1.41
EEC	1992	1.02	1.11	0.94	0.57
Japan	1992	0.09	1.52	0.50	0.16
New Zealand	1992	5.15	0.32	0.32	0.57
United States	1992	1.15	1.19	0.51	0.41

Note: [a]Export specialisation index is calculated by dividing the share of a group of commodities in the economy's total exports by its corresponding share for the world.
Source: International Economic Databank, The Australian National University, Canberra.

trade will probably continue for a long time. In particular, China will increasingly rely on mineral and agricultural-intensive imports from OECD countries, capital-intensive imports will continue to expand strongly. In fact, the share of China's mineral-intensive imports in its total imports from OECD countries surged from around 5 per cent in the 1980s to 15 per cent in 1992.

China's labour-intensive manufactured exports to OECD countries are expected to expand continuously, which may require some domestic adjustments in OECD countries. But these adjustments will be moderate, especially in comparison with the adjustments that have already occurred in other East Asian economies. First, labour-intensive manufacturing sectors usually only account for small shares in OECD economies. Second, there is no evidence of a relationship between trade expansion of labour-intensive manufactured goods and domestic labour markets within OECD countries. Third, as other East Asian economies' labour-intensive manufactured exports are declining, part of China's expansion is only a replacement of their

exports and should not have overall effects on importing economies.

In terms of future development, the biggest opportunity arises from the improved specialisation of production and the increased gains from trade. Rapid growth and trade expansion in China has made labour-intensive manufactured goods available to OECD countries at cheap prices, and has subsequently raised living standards. It has enabled most OECD countries to become more specialised in production of resource, capital and technology-intensive goods and to more fully exploit their comparative advantages. At the aggregate level, China's total imports increased from US$7.2 billion in 1978 to US$58.4 billion in 1993, recording an average real growth rate of 14 per cent per annum.

The critical factor determining the extent of China's integration into the international trading system, is Chinese and international confidence in the rules governing integration. In the reform period China has moved a long way from the commitment to self-sufficiency, but it is still a big step for China to accept the trade and structural implications of free trade. China will not take that step if it lacks confidence in its opportunities to expand exports in line with comparative advantage or in the international capacity to expand its supplies of goods and services in which China lacks comparative advantage. The accommodation of China's internationally oriented growth in a period of disillusionment with the liberal multilateral system in the North Atlantic and tension in United States' trade relations with East Asia further complicates the issues.

Tensions in United States–Japan trade relations in the late 1980s and early 1990s were overlaid by perceptions that in the aftermath of the Cold War, economic rivalry between Japan and the United States would have political significance. Japan was identified by some scholars in the United States as having characteristics that made it a poor citizen of the world economy: a chronic surplus in current payments, low intra-industry trade, low shares of manufactured goods in total imports, and low levels of inward direct foreign investment. Trade with China will become just as contentious. The adjustment challenge will be as large, the overlay of political rivalry will be just as great as awareness grows of China's real economic size and given China's political self-confidence and ambitions for military modernisation. Intra-industry trade is larger and increasing more rapidly, the current account and net exports have fluctuated around zero, manufactured goods dominate imports and direct foreign investment is now being committed at a rate that has no precedent in East Asia or the developing world. This will not protect China from criticism: the political economy of trade policy and protectionism places modest value on logical consistency. The differences between China and Japan on these and other points of public concern, however, will make it less likely that tensions in US relations with Japan and China will be less tractable by their merging into a general 'East Asian' problem.

V. China's World Trade Organization Accession

Early Chinese membership of the World Trade Organization (WTO) is crucial. As a WTO member, there would be less chance of vested interests gathering around restrictive trade policies. There is much more at stake in the broad principles of Chinese participation in the international system and in its membership of the WTO, than in any details of the rules or timing of their application.

One key issue in the negotiation of China's membership is whether it should join the WTO as a developing or industrial economy. According to WTO rules, industrial economies are exempt from some of the trade disciplines. As a low-income economy, the member can maintain some quantitative restrictions. One important difference is that the Uruguay Round settlement would require China to implement the rules on intellectual property rights within one year if it joins the WTO as an industrial economy. Given the current legal system on intellectual property rights, China feels that it requires a longer period of time. Another difference also related to the Uruguay Round settlement is that industrial economies are required to reduce their domestic agricultural support by 36 per cent within six years, while developing economies are only required to reduce it by 24 per cent.

No developing economies would contribute to China's welfare, if the alternative were prompt accession to the industrial economy rules. What rate of progress towards industrial economy rules is feasible given China's stage of institutional development and its commitment to, and success with, a gradual approach to reform and internationalisation? It would be a first-best outcome for both parties if China met all requirements for an industrial member when it joins the WTO. Another option would be to grant China WTO conditional membership on a clear timetable for future reform. This is a much better choice than simply leaving China out of the international trading system.

A realistic solution would be for China to join the WTO as a developing economy, considering its current income level and institutional framework, and unilaterally commit itself to further reforms within a finite period. Commitment to move towards an industrial economy in the short term for some commodities would help China's acceptance in the international community. The recently concluded Uruguay Round trade negotiations provide a favourable environment for China to deliver further reforms. First, the phasing out of the MFA will support faster growth of China's textile and clothing exports to the North American and Western European markets. Second, the world economy will start agricultural reform, reversing the trend in the 1980s. This will have some positive effects on China's agricultural policy choices—one of the key issues in the membership negotiation. Moreover, the expected rises in international agricultural prices following the implementation of the settlements may raise China's confidence in the internationalisation of its agricultural sector as the adjustment costs are expected to be low. The significance of Uruguay Round negotiations go beyond issues in specific sectors. Phasing out of the MFA, for instance, will help China's overall trade reform. As confidence in its export exchange earnings rises, China will find it easier to abolish some of its own restrictions on trade which have been motivated by anxiety about access to foreign exchange.

Asia-Pacific Economic Cooperation

China's most intense and largest economic relations are with its East Asian and Asia-Pacific neighbours. It is important that there be a secure framework for open trade relations between these economies. Thus, Asia-Pacific Economic Cooperation (APEC) is significant to economic reform and internationalisation in China.

It has made substantial progress in a program of trade and investment facilitation—essentially co-operation between Asia-Pacific governments to reduce transactions costs in intra-regional trade and investment. Some areas of trade facilitation, notably disputes settlement, have been agreed in principle without practical progress having been made. This area of APEC has considerable momentum and will be helpful to China's integration into the world economy.

Heads of government of the 18 APEC members agreed in November 1994, to achieve free trade in the region by 2010 for industrial members and 2020 for developing members. Interestingly, in the context of the debate over WTO membership, China was accepted as a developing economy. There was no agreement on the shape of 'free trade in the region'— whether it will involve at least an element of discrimination against outsiders, in which case a comprehensive agreement is required under Article 24 of the GATT/WTO; or whether progress will occur through movement towards free trade in each economy on a multilateral basis. Progress is unlikely in the foreseeable future if the demanding prior requirements of Article 24 must be met. If there is an understanding that progress will be made towards free trade in the region on a non-discriminatory basis, the November 1994 agreement will be helpful in building a secure framework for China's reform and internationalisation.

The challenge

If the rest of the world supports China's entry into the world trading system, the widening of the international market will increase potential gains from specialisation and trade, will increase stability in international prices for some commodities, and will increase the importance of flexibility in other developing economies seeking internationally oriented growth.

The main downside for the international system will materialise if the rest of the world baulks at the adjustment task and seeks to manage closely the scale and content of interaction with China. Such response would lead to the decline of Chinese confidence in integration into the world economy. Political

456

competition would overlay trade relations between China and the largest external economies, especially the United States. The end point would be retreat from the rule-based system, with consequences for internationally oriented growth in China, East Asia and beyond.

Note

1. An average annual growth rate of 8.5 per cent for real GDP is the same as 7.2 per cent for real per capita income growth which is assumed in other studies (such as Garnaut and Ma 1992).

References

Asia Pacific Economics Group, 1994. *Asia Pacific Insights, 1994*, National Centre for Development Studies, The Australian National University, Canberra.

Australian Bureau for Agricultural and Research Economics, 1992. *Commodity Statistical Bulletin*, ABARE, Canberra.

Drysdale, P. and Garnaut, R., 1982. 'Trade intensities and the analysis of bilateral trade flows in a many-country world', *Hitotsubashi Journal of Economics*, 22(2):62–84.

——, 1993. 'The Pacific: an application of a general theory of economic integration', in C.F. Bergsten and M. Norland, (eds), *Pacific Dynamism and the International Economic System*, Institute for International Economics, Washington, DC.

Drysdale, P. and Song, L., 1994. China's trade policy agenda in the 90s, paper presented to China and East Asian Trade Policy workshop, The Australian National University, Canberra, 1–2 September.

Feng, L., 1994. Changing comparative advantage and the restructuring of the international steel industry, PhD dissertation, The Australian National University, Canberra.

Forsyth, P., 1993. Trade patterns and labour demand: international influences on wages and unemployment in Australia', paper presented to Unemployment: causes, costs and solutions conference, The Australian National University and Department of Employment, Education and Training, Canberra, 16–17 February.

Garnaut, R., 1989. *Australia and Northeast Asian Ascendancy*, Australian Government Publishing Service, Canberra.

Garnaut, Ross (ed.), 1992. *Economic Reform and Internationalisation*, Allen and Unwin, Sydney.

Garnaut, R. and Anderson, K., 1980. 'ASEAN export specialisation and the evolution of comparative advantage in the western Pacific region', in R. Garnaut (ed.), *ASEAN in a Changing Pacific and World Economy*, Australian National University Press, Canberra.

Garnaut, R. and Ma, G., 1992. *Grain in China*, Australian Government Publishing Service, Canberra.

——, 1993a. 'How rich is China: evidence from the food economy', *Australian Journal of Chinese Affairs*, (30):121–46.

——, 1993b. 'Economic growth and stability in China', *Journal of Asian Economics*, 4(1):5–24.

Garnaut, Ross, Ma, Guonan and Huang, Yiping, 1994. 'How rich is China? Further evidences from energy, fibre and steel consumption', mimeo, The Australian National University, Canberra.

Huang, Y., 1995. *The Chinese Grains and Oilseeds Sectors: a review of major changes underway*, OECD, Paris.

International Economic Databank, The Australian National University, Canberra.

Krugman, P.R. and Lawrence, R.Z., 1993. *Trade, Jobs, and Wages*, NBER Working Papers 4478, NBER.

Lau, Lawrence, 1993. 'Macroeconomic prospects of China', Seminar paper presented at the Research School of Pacific and Asian Studies, The Australian National University, Canberra.

Lin, J., Cai, F. and Li, Z., 1994. *China's Economic Reforms: pointers for other economies in transition?*, Policy Research Working Paper 1310, The World Bank, Washington, DC.

McDougall, R. and Tyers, R., 1993. Developing country expansion and factor markets in industrial countries, paper presented at International Agricultural Trade Research Consortium Annual Meeting, San Diego, 12–14 December.

Perkins, Dwight H., 1992. 'Price reforms vs. enterprise autonomy: which should have priority?', in US Congress Joint Economic Committee, *China's Economic Dilemmas in the 1990s: The problems of reforms, modernization, and interdependence*, Studies on Contemporary China, Sharpe, New York and London:160–66.

State Statistical Bureau, various issues. *China Statistical Yearbook*, China Statistical Press, Beijing.

Summers, R. and Heston, C., 1991. 'The Penn world table (mark 5): an expanded set of international comparison, 1950–1988', *Quarterly Journal of Economics*, 106(2):327–68.

Yang, Y., 1994. 'Trade liberalisation with externalities: a general equilibrium assessment of the Uruguay Round', paper presented to the Challenges and Opportunities for East Asian Trade workshop, The Australian National University, Canberra, 13–14 July 1994.

World Bank, 1990. *World Population Projections, 1989–90*, World Bank, Washington, DC.

World Bank, 1993. *China Foreign Trade Reform: meeting the challenge of the 1990s*, Report 11568–CHA, World Bank, Washington, DC.

458

28 How to Reform a Planned Economy: lessons from China

John McMillan and Barry Naughton[1]

I. Introduction

The countries of Eastern Europe and the former Soviet Union have been flooded with advice from the West on how to liberalise their planned economies. This advice is, unfortunately, offered in an empirical vacuum: no one knows how these economies will react to the proposed liberalisation measures. There exists, however, a neglected source of information. China offers a long time-series of data—over a decade's worth—on the effects of reforms on a planned economy. China's reforms were gradual, but their cumulative effect has been large; and they have been remarkably successful. China's experiments provide some practical lessons on what kinds of reforms can work elsewhere. The dominant school of thought among economists favours the 'big bang' policy of reforming quickly and according to a comprehensive plan. Partial reforms, in this view, are useless: they will be negated by the remnants of the planning system. The proponents of big bang reform have been influential, with Poland, Czechoslovakia, and Russia announcing plans for a rapid transition to capitalism.

China's reforms, by contrast, were not conceived as a grand plan; rather they have consisted of small, step-by-step changes. No ultimate goals were announced, nor any timetable for the transition. Some of the changes were initiated spontaneously at ground level and only later ratified by government regulation. The reforms have proceeded by trial and error, with frequent mid-course corrections and reversals of policy; the reformers were probing into the unknown. China has muddled through.[2] We shall therefore characterise China's approach (in keeping with the natural-science phraseology of 'big bang') as evolutionary reform.

Evolutionary reform is not intrinsically superior to big bang reform: it is obviously desirable to create an efficient, market-based economy as quickly as possible. But, as is becoming increasingly clear, any reform process will be protracted. All the institutions of the planned economy were developed as component parts of that system; they are mutually consistent, but incompatible with a true market economy. The price, fiscal, monetary, ownership, and legal systems must all be changed. A big bang transition can indeed cause the interconnected socialist system to collapse. But there is more to moving to a market economy than just removing government controls. New institutions must be

Reprinted with permission. John McMillan and Barry Naughton, 1992. 'How to reform a planned economy: lessons from China', *Oxford Review of Economic Policy*, 8(1): 130–43 (with minor editing).

created. Some government direction of the process of building the institutions of the market economy is needed. But, as we shall argue, this is a highly complex and unpredictable process, and so it is only in a limited way susceptible to planning and control.

China's example shows that there are specific characteristics of the centrally planned system that can be used to initiate a step-by-step reform process. Once a crack is opened in the monolith that is the centrally planned economy, cumulative forces take over and prise the crack open even more widely. The crack, in the case of China, was the elimination of the state monopoly over industry, which began a process of change that became irreversible. This process is compatible with vigorous economic growth, so a reform-oriented government gains time and resources to build the new institutions required to run the market economy.

What are the lessons from China? While the exact sequence of events in China cannot and should not be replicated elsewhere, the key features of China's reforms can be adopted in other countries. China's reform success can be seen with hindsight to have resulted from, first, massive entry of non-state firms; second, a dramatic increase in competition, both among state firms and between state firms and non-state firms; and, third, improvements in the performance of state owned firms resulting from state-imposed market-like incentives. The process in turn drove a realignment of prices, which caused an erosion in governmental resources and a shift of economic power towards households. China shows the potency of the fundamental market forces of entry and competition. China's example does not, however, justify *laissez-faire*: the state must monitor firms during the transition.

II. China's Reforms have been Successful

China is a counter-example to the claim, often made by the proponents of big bang, that gradual reform must fail. Conventional wisdom notwithstanding, China's economic reforms have indeed been successful. This economic success is in glaring contrast to the deplorable lack of progress in political freedoms; China has had *perestroika* without *glasnost*.

Real per capita GNP grew 7.2 per cent annually from 1978 to 1990. Growth was particularly rapid between 1982 and 1988, averaging 9.7 per cent per capita over six years, among the best in the world, before slowing sharply in 1988–90 with the political crisis around Tiananmen. Vigorous growth did, however, resume in 1991. The increasing efficiency of China's industry is indicated by its success in selling in competitive world markets: exports grew in real terms at over 10 per cent per year between 1978 and 1990; the ratio of exports to GNP had risen to 17 per cent by 1990 (compare this to Japan's 9 per cent). While growth of national income should not be the only criterion for evaluating the success of economic policies, it is the first and most important indicator of success. An economic system—especially in a poor country—must be judged by its performance in providing increased levels of goods to its citizens, and this can be roughly measured by the growth of GNP per capita.[3] By the simple criterion of making ordinary people better off (or, more accurately, less badly off), China has been spectacularly successful.

In many obvious cases, specific aspects of the Chinese reforms were misconceived or self-defeating. Thus, we are far from arguing that Chinese reforms were anything close to optimal. But it is precisely China's success in the face of initial poverty and repeated policy mistakes that makes its reform process interesting. It appears that the Chinese approach to reform has been quite robust, capable of producing good results in spite of large deviations from best practice. This is particularly significant as it becomes increasingly clear that all reform processes will be protracted and marked by significant policy errors and backtracking.

460

In some respects, Eastern Europe and the former Soviet Union face a more difficult transition than China. Macroeconomic imbalances have been more severe in Eastern Europe than in China, creating an urgent need for anti-inflationary policies. The need for macro-economic stabilisation complicates the reform transition, requiring some big bang policies, at least in the macroeconomic sphere. China made great gains, as will be seen, through agricultural reforms; there is less scope for such gains in the more industrialised countries of Eastern Europe. In other respects, however, China has had the bigger impediments to transition. Education levels are much lower in China than in Eastern Europe. To the extent that institution-building is a crucial component of the reform process, China, like any developing country, faces greater challenges than the relatively wealthy countries of Eastern Europe. The rapid political change in Eastern Europe means that those countries have largely discarded political constraints to the reform process, while China continues to labour under the dead hand of a repressive and ideologically rigid group of Communist Party elders. How, if at all, the choice of reform policy—big bang versus evolutionary—is constrained by the form of government—authoritarian versus democratic—is a topic on which there are many strong opinions but few hard facts. Country-to-country differences such as these limit the transferability of any lessons from China. But China offers one of the few sources, as yet, of empirical information on the long-term effects of reforms on a planned economy. For a reformer, some data must be better than none.

III. Privatisation is not Crucial; Competition is

Many Western economists maintain that reform necessitates the rapid transfer of state-owned firms to private ownership; there are lengthy debates about the best way to achieve this (for example, Blanchard et. al. 1991; Lipton and Sachs 1990; Sinn 1991). China's experience suggests that privatisation is a red herring. Rapid privatisation need not be the centrepiece of a reform policy. Scarce resources of economic and administrative expertise might better be directed into thinking about other problems. We see three reasons to delay privatisation.

Entrepreneurs set up new firms

Investment in new firms by profit-seeking entrepreneurs is the most potent force to be harnessed by reformers. China's most dynamic sector, particularly since 1984, has been non-state-owned industrial firms. These firms, mostly located in rural areas, have a range of formal organisational structures; but they are primarily profit-seeking firms (Byrd and Lin 1990). The non-state sector has grown since 1978 at an annual rate of 17.6 per cent, such that in 1990 it accounted for a striking 45 per cent of total industrial output. While the output of state-owned firms has also grown in absolute terms (7.6 per cent annually from 1978 to 1990), it has shrunk dramatically relative to the non-state sector: state-owned firms accounted for only 55 per cent of industrial output in 1990, down from 78 per cent in 1978. China is growing out of the plan (Naughton 1992a). Over time, the issue of how and when to privatise China's state-owned firms is becoming less important, as the state-owned firms weigh less and less heavily in the overall economy.

The scope for new entry in socialist economies is particularly great because of two fundamental characteristics of those economies. First, the size distribution of industrial enterprises is highly skewed towards large firms. In economies such as the Soviet Union or Czechoslovakia, there were virtually no small industrial firms. While China was known for the large number of 'small' firms in its pre-reform system, even these were relatively large, typically having over fifty employees. Rapid growth has occurred in 'micro-enterprises', those with less than fifty employees. The size distribution of

461

industrial firms in market economies, developed and developing, is quite consistent: small firms typically account for around 25–30 per cent of industrial employment.[4] There are numerous niches in both modern and developing economies that are best filled by small firms. Since those niches are empty in socialist economies, the potential rewards to entrepreneurs who arrive first are quite large, ensuring rapid entry and at the same time, holding the promise of efficiency gains for the economy as a whole.

Second, the price system of socialist economies is skewed in a fashion that raises profitability in manufacturing. Socialist governments maintain high prices for manufactured goods (except for a small number of items judged to be necessities). The purpose is to concentrate taxable revenues in the large-scale, state-dominated manufacturing sector. This means that once barriers to entry are lowered, new entrants will be able to reap high profits in the initial phase. This effect is magnified by the presence of shortages of certain essential goods and services. Rural enterprises in China in 1978, before reforms, were earning an average rate of profit on capital of 32 per cent. This very high profitability was not the result of superb efficiency on the part of these firms, but rather of the fact that they were able to share in a part of the monopoly profits created by state pricing policy. As entry has proceeded and the rural industrial sector has grown explosively, profitability has declined steadily, falling to below 10 per cent of capital.

Lenin understood that the state's monopoly on production was essential for the survival of the planning system: he wrote 'small production engenders capitalism and the bourgeoisie continuously, daily, hourly, spontaneously, and on a mass scale' (Lenin 1968:284). Lenin foresaw what China illustrates, the corrosive effect of the entry of non-state firms, 'the decisive thing is the organisation of the strictest and country-wide accounting and control of production and distribution of goods' (Lenin 1968:252).[5]

The entry of new firms in China illustrates the vitality of market forces. Despite impressive impediments—little law of contract, weak property rights, underdeveloped capital markets—when the restrictions on the activities of non-state firms were loosened, a huge amount of entrepreneurial investment occurred, such that by 1990 non-state firms were producing almost a half of industrial output. Because of the pre-existing distortions both in the size structure of industry and in industrial prices, the economic forces that propel entry are particularly strong. Entry looks to be a fringe phenomenon in the early stages of reform; but in fact it attacks the heart of the planning system.

State-owned firms' performance can be improved

While shrinking relative to the rest of the economy, China's state-owned industry has itself achieved respectable productivity gains. This has been the result of liberalisation measures that fall far short of privatisation. China's state-owned firms are notoriously inefficient; press reports commonly describe them as 'dinosaurs' and 'terminally ill'. But recent empirical studies show they are significantly less inefficient than they used to be.

China's state-owned firms have been commercialised: they have been given some market or market-like incentives. State-owned enterprises are now allowed to keep some fraction of their profits, where before all profits had to be remitted to the state; enterprises now sell and buy in free markets, rather than selling and procuring everything at state-controlled prices; managers' pay is based on firm performance; and production decisions have been shifted from the state to the firm.

This commercialisation has resulted in improved productivity. Under the system of enterprise contracting, state firms are required to deliver a certain fixed amount of profit to the government, and are allowed to retain a substantial fraction of any profits they generate beyond this fixed amount; many firms now keep as much as 100 per cent of residual profits.

The data show that, when firms' autonomy increased (in either of two senses: the firm's profit retention rate was increased, or the responsibility for deciding output levels was shifted down from the state to the firm), managers responded by strengthening the discipline imposed on workers: they increased the proportion of the workers' income paid in the form of bonuses; and they increased the fraction of workers whom, since they were on fixed-term contracts, it was in principle possible to dismiss. The new incentives were effective: productivity increased significantly following the strengthening of worker incentives. Also, the extra autonomy was followed by an increase in productive investment by the state-owned firms (Groves et al. 1992a).

Managers of state-owned firms are now paid according to their firms' performance: the data show a strong link between a firm's sales and its top manager's pay, and a weaker link between profits and pay. As well as these direct monetary incentives, managers can be demoted for sub-par performance by their firms, and promoted for unusually good performance. The data show that the careers of the managers of China's state-owned firms are in fact affected by how well or badly their firms do, so the prospect of promotion or demotion does work as an incentive (Groves et al. 1992b).

Instead of auctioning off firms, the Chinese government has begun auctioning off top management jobs. Potential managers (including, often, the incumbent manager) vie for the right to be manager by submitting bids— promises of how the firm will perform in the future. This process has revealed information about the potential capabilities of both the firms and the potential managers. As a result, it has put better people in top managerial positions than the old system, under which mangers were simply appointed by government bureaucrats (Byrd 1991; Groves et al. 1992b).

Firms in capitalist economies face discipline from their product markets (Schumpeter 1950:7). In order to survive, a firm must produce at a high enough quality and low enough price to persuade customers to buy from it rather than its competitors. As a result of both the entry of non-state firms and the fact that state firms have begun to sell on free markets, China's state-owned firms now face active product-market competition. This market-based discipline has given the state-owned firms additional incentives to improve their productivity.

Output per worker in state-owned industry rose 52 per cent (in constant prices) during the reform years 1980 to 1989.[6] China proves, then, that it is possible for state-owned firms to be induced to improve their productivity by measures that fall short of privatisation.

The state-owned sector acts as safety net

The transition process in Eastern Europe has imposed large costs on workers, as inefficient state-owned firms suddenly exposed to competition have been forced to lay off workers and national income has plummeted. China, by contrast, has managed its reform with little overt unemployment. There has been a lot of disguised unemployment, as firms maintain bloated labour forces. If these firms had been privatised, many workers would probably have been dismissed. State-owned firms, even if they face increased competition, can avoid laying off workers by relying on government subsidies, as China's state-owned firms have in fact done. Conceivably the inefficiencies this causes have been justified by their cushioning effects, spreading the costs of transition among the population. Workers in state-run firms undoubtedly have low productivity. However, unless there are alternative high-productivity occupations available for them, it is unclear that the economy benefits from dismissing such workers, particularly if society must then support them through a new safety net. The creation of such a safety net is costly in terms of scarce administrative and economic expertise. By keeping firms in state hands, such measures may be delayed until several years into the reform process. This was the case in China, where by the late 1980s rudimentary unemployment compensation measures were in place and gradual workforce rationalisation had begun.

State-owned firms produce goods that are of notoriously low quality. For the delayed-privatisation policy to work, consumers must want to purchase these firms' outputs; this implies some degree of protection from imports. Thus this approach requires that any reduction in pre-existing barriers to international trade proceed no faster than the international liberalisation. This occurred in China, and could occur in other liberalising countries. It was not possible, however, when the former East Germany became part of the united Germany: East German firms immediately had to compete with West German firms.

IV. The State must Monitor Firms during the Transition

Financial markets in modern market economies impose a variety of disciplines on firms, prodding managers to ensure firms operate efficiently. In the United States and the United Kingdom managers know that poor performance is likely to cost them their jobs: they will be dismissed by the board of directors; or their firm will be taken over and a new managerial team installed; or the firm will fall into bankruptcy, with blame attached to the manager. Further incentives come from the fact that their pay is linked to the firm's stockmarket performance. (Anecdotal evidence sometimes raises doubts about whether US managers do face genuine incentives; but the data show that they do. A correlation, small but statistically significant, exists between poor firm performance and the manager's loss of job; and a correlation, also small but statistically significant, exists between a firm's stockmarket value and its top manager's pay, see Jensen and Murphy 1990). In Japan and Germany the source of managers' incentives is different but the incentives are not weaker: banks with large stakes in the firm, both as creditors and as equity holders, monitor the managers' decisions (Hoshi et al. 1991).

An economy in the process of transition lacks financial markets. Fully operating financial markets will take years to develop (Tirole 1991). In the transforming economy, therefore, the usual capitalist managerial disciplines are absent. The only available substitute is the state. Government officials in a reforming economy must oversee the managers of state-owned firms, as they did when the economy was centrally planned. The incentives of the monitors thus become important (especially since, in the planned economy, government supervision used to produce grossly inefficient firms). Is it in the interest of officials in the reforming economy to maintain the right sort of supervision? Can the bureaucracy be relied on to induce managers to make their firms efficient?

China shows that officials' oversight of managers can generate managerial incentives that, while undoubtedly far from perfect, work in the right direction. State-imposed incentives have replaced state-imposed controls; and, as noted, these incentives have dramatically improved state firms' productivity. What induced China's bureaucrats to regulate for firm efficiency? The increased competition squeezed state-owned firms' profits; this meant that state firms' remittances to the government fell. State firms were the main source of government revenue (as we discuss below). To slow the drop in government revenue, the state was impelled in the mid-to-late 1980s to spur the state firms to become more profitable. Firms had been given some profit incentives at the beginning of the 1980s. But during the late 1980s, driven by their need for revenue, state officials increasingly made profit remittances the primary obligation of firms.

Financial discipline was tightened, so that firms faced greater financial risk but also steeper compensation schedules and stronger incentives. The need for increased financial discipline was created by the increased product-market discipline that resulted from entry and competition; financial discipline then reinforced the effects of the product-market discipline.

'Spontaneous privatisation' is a problem that has arisen in Eastern Europe and the Soviet Union: with the breakdown of centralised control, some managers have extracted value from the firms for their own benefit (Johnson 1991). Preventing such plundering is an additional reason why state oversight of state-owned firms must continue during the transition. China's reforms replaced direct controls on firms with incentives. This relaxation of oversight resulted, as noted, in the firms' increasing their productivity; but much of this increase in productivity stayed within the firm. When a firm was granted increased autonomy, the incomes of managers and workers rose significantly, as did the firms' welfare funds. Despite the improved productivity, the amount of profits remitted to the state fell and the subsidies given to the firms by the state rose following the increases in autonomy. Perhaps this is evidence of some plundering; but it was not simply a transfer from the state to the employees of state firms, because other effects worked in the same direction. First, the lower profits were at least, in part attributable to the increased competition that the firms were facing as a result of the reforms; and second, the increase in employees' pay reflected the improvements in productivity that followed these forms. Evidence that autonomy did not lead to severe plundering comes from the fact that state-owned firms significantly increased their productive investments following increases in their autonomy (Groves et al. 1992a).

V. Price Reform can be Done Gradually

One of the most discussed distortions in planned economies is the irrationality of prices: prices bear little relation to either production costs or demand, resulting in a severe misallocation of resources.

China is often criticised for having neglected to reform its price system. This criticism is misplaced. Prices have been reformed: not by grand policy, but by stealth.

China did not undertake comprehensive price reform. But gradual marketisation accompanied by sustained entry of new producers caused a realignment of prices. Before the reforms, state-owned enterprises were required to sell all their output to the state at state-fixed prices. Under the reforms, these firms have been allowed to sell some of their output on free markets: in 1989, on average 38 per cent of a state-owned firm's outputs were directly sold on markets, and for some state firms, market sales were 100 per cent of output. Similarly, an increasingly large fraction of state firms' inputs have been purchased on free markets, rather than being allocated by the state: in 1989, on average 56 per cent of a state-owned firm's inputs were procured through market purchases, and for some state firms, 100 per cent of inputs were market-procured.[7] There is a dual price system, with the market price usually being substantially above the official price. From the viewpoint of economic incentives the key point is that, at the margin, decisions are made in the face of market prices. The fact that the price received from the state is less than the price received from the market merely means that the firm is paying a lump-sum tax. For a firm's decisions on how much to produce, what inputs to use, and what kind of investment to undertake, the state-imposed output quota is irrelevant, as long as that quota is smaller than total output. What matters for such decisions is the price that will be received for any extra output, which is the free-market price (Byrd 1987).

Evidence that most industries' prices have been effectively reformed comes from data on profit rates. With the erratic pricing of the centrally planned economy, prices bear little relation to costs. In 1980 this was the case: profit rates in industry ranged from 7 per cent to 98 per cent. By 1989 prices had become more uniformly related to costs: in most industries profit rates were between 8 per cent and 23 per cent (Naughton 1992b). Further evidence on China's progressive marketisation comes from calculation of marginal products. In a textbook-perfect market economy, the free operation of the price system would ensure that the marginal product of labour became the same in all firms; and similarly for the marginal product of capital. Wide variations among marginal products indicate, on the other hand, that the economy is using its valuable resources of labour and capital inefficiently. Recent research finds that the variation in marginal products of both capital and labour has shrunk as China's reforms have progressed (Jefferson and Xu 1991; Jefferson et al. 1992).

Dual pricing forced state-owned firms to compete, both with other state-owned firms and with non-state firms. In order to sell on free markets, state-owned firms had to please their customers; they were forced to produce to a higher quality than when they had the government as guaranteed buyer.

The dual-price system is, of course, not ideal. It has enabled illicit profits to be made by obtaining goods at planned prices and selling them at market prices. Buying low and selling high is a normal market activity; but the dual-price system has meant that certain well-connected people can buy at artificially low prices. Anger at such corrupt practices, was one of the sparks that ignited Tiananmen. Dual pricing is a temporary expedient to smooth the reform process, and it should be replaced by full market pricing as soon as is feasible. This should have occurred in China (as is obvious with the benefit of hindsight) by the late 1980s.[8]

VI. Agriculture Booms with Reform

Agriculture was the first area in which China implemented reforms. The commune system was replaced by the 'household responsibility system'. Under the commune system, peasants were organised into production teams. Each team member was assigned work points, which attempted to measure both how many hours and how effectively he or she had worked. Income depended on the number of work points accumulated. Income was not perfectly related to effort, however, because it was impossible to observe how conscientiously each individual worked: this would have required each peasant to be continually monitored. Moreover, there was a tendency to spread the commune's earnings across the individual commune members: those with larger families were given more income, regardless of effort. Thus the link between individual effort and reward was weak. Under the responsibility system, in contrast, each peasant family is given a long-term lease of a plot of land. The household must deliver a certain quota of produce to the government each year, and may keep anything it produces beyond that quota. The household members consume it themselves, sell it to the government, or sell it in the newly instituted rural markets. With the exception of the special case of grain, they may decide for themselves what crops to sow and what animals to raise.

In 1978 and 1979 the government increased the prices paid for agricultural outputs, while leaving the structure of the commune system unchanged. Then, from 1980 to 1984, the commune system was gradually replaced by the responsibility system. The results were clear. Agricultural output increased by 67 per cent between 1978 and 1985. In part this was caused by an increase in inputs. But mainly it was due to the strengthened incentives: productivity (measured as the amount of output for a given amount of inputs) increased by nearly 50 per cent, compared with no increase in productivity over the previous two and a half decades (Lin 1992; McMillan et al. 1989). Over the second half of the decade, agricultural growth was slower but still respectable, averaging 4.5 per cent annually. While land remains state-owned, each peasant family essentially has its own plot of land, and sells any output in excess of the fixed state quota on free markets. A household's income therefore depends on that household's efforts; this linking of effort and rewards has resulted in spectacular increased in the production of food.

466

The increase in agricultural productivity in turn spurred the growth of rural industry, by generating a pool of savings and excess labour (Byrd and Lin 1990; Jefferson et al. 1992). Beginning from a small base, rural industry was allowed to grow with few of the restrictions that hobbled state-run industry. Rural industry expanded rapidly. The entry of these profit-seeking firms provided, as we have argued, the main ingredient in China's transition. Thus the transformation of agriculture was crucial to the overall success of the reforms.

VII. Reform Entails Redesigning the Tax System

Centrally planned economies do not have regularised taxation systems. Instead, taxation is implicit in government control of the price system. As a result, price reform in the absence of fiscal restructuring causes an erosion in government revenues; rapid price reform, by itself, entails rapid fiscal collapse. Some contraction in the government's financial resources is, of course, highly desirable. But in the centrally planned economy the government's fiscal revenues include virtually all of national saving. Rapid fiscal collapse thus implies a collapse in national saving and investment; and what economist would advise a country undertaking a difficult restructuring process to begin by reducing investment to zero? By contrast, the Chinese experience shows that gradual marketisation can steadily undermine the government's fiscal resources without leading to total collapse. This provides time for the government to build a modern taxation system. It also provides a favourable environment for the growth of private saving and the financial intermediaries that channel such saving into productive investment.

Instead of clearly codified tax systems, socialist economies rely on governmental control of the price system to concentrate revenues in a relatively small number of state-run industrial firms. The government then relies on a variety of formal and informal means to draw industrial surpluses into the state budget. In China in 1978, industrial enterprises turned over an enormous 25 per cent of GNP to the budgetary authorities in the form of both profits and taxes. Such revenue deliveries were not explicitly regulated by tax codes, but rather reflected the state's roles as both taxation authority and owner of the bulk of industrial firms. The fiscal system was implicit (McKinnon 1991; Naughton 1992b). In 1980 state-firm profits and taxes accounted for 85 per cent of China's fiscal revenues.

The well-known distortions in the socialist price system are not random. They systematically increase profitability in manufacturing, while maintaining profitability low in a range of agricultural and extractive industries. Moreover, accounting procedures in manufacturing systematically understate capital costs (both depreciation and interest rates are low), also creating a large (and illusory) volume of profits. Finally, wage payments are low, because a portion of worker income is provided by the state in the form of subsidies. Thus, manufacturing costs are severely understated—materials, capital, and labour are all undervalued—and manufacturing paper profits correspondingly high.

Big bang price liberalisation will cause a rapid decline in the relative price of manufactures, and a collapse in fiscal revenues. Since the fiscal system is only implicit in government control of the price system, abandonment of that control will result in fiscal collapse. Implementing an effective big bang conversion is made substantially more difficult because a newly designed fiscal system must be implemented simultaneously with price liberalisation. Moreover, the existing distortions in the price system imply that state industrial enterprises are highly liquid in the initial phases of reform. This liquidity provides firms with resources to deflect stabilisation measures, permitting them, for instance, to increase worker non-wage incomes and maintain their own investment programs. This was quite apparent during the Polish stabilisation in 1990.

By contrast, with evolutionary reform this problem is less pressing. On the one hand, entry-driven marketisation will gradually push price relationships towards something closer to relative scarcities. State-run industry will be placed under continuous cost pressure as it struggles to meet new competition for underpriced inputs and in output markets. Such pressure is all to the good, as it makes it easier to monitor state enterprise performance. On the other hand, the government can stretch scarce administrative resources by successively implementing reforms that make enterprise accounting more realistic. Capital costs can be increased by raising depreciation charges and interest rates. Such a process can greatly reduce the massive uncertainty which is recognised as a major difficulty of the transition (Tirole 1991). Constant pressure on inefficient state firms will be the greatest challenge they face, instead of high and non-stationary uncertainty. Fiscal pressure will also be expressed as steady erosion of fiscal revenues, rather than sudden collapse. This is also preferable, since it provides greater scope both for reduction in expenditures, and for gradual creation of an explicit taxation system as a substitute for the former implicit revenue system.

The development of a modern tax system for China has undoubtedly proceeded more slowly than would be desirable. But fiscal authorities now operate a rudimentary value-added tax (with rebates for exporters), urban land-use fees, and a system of social security contributions; meanwhile, taxes collected on international trade and petty commerce have increased substantially. These are not trivial accomplishments for a developing country.

VII. Monetary Policy must Accommodate Rising Demand for Money

As the government surrenders its control over saving and investment flows, households and private businesses must assume the dominant role in accumulating saving and channelling it into productive investment. This calls for dramatic changes in household behaviour, but the Chinese experience shows that these changes will be forthcoming if appropriate economic policies are followed. An increasing role for households in saving and investment generally leads to an increased demand for money balances. Monetisation (or re-monetisation) occurs, and monetary policy must accommodate a sustained increase in money demand.

In the pre-reform economy, household choice is severely restricted. Money incomes are low and a substantial share of total income is received in non-monetary form as subsidies or benefits over which households have little discretion. As a result, money demand is limited and households hold relatively small amounts of both currency and savings deposits. Money holdings are lower in a socialist economy than in a market economy at a comparable level of development, for an obvious reason: money's value as a bearer of options is greatly restricted under traditional socialism; since money's value is less, households naturally hold less of it.[9]

When reform begins, the range of options open to households expands enormously. On the consumption side, they have access to expensive consumption goods that require preparatory saving. On the production side, households become business units, and their demand for monetary assets for both consumption and investment increases. In China, the most striking transformation was the rapid creation of over 200 million family (farm) businesses that replaced a few hundred thousand collectives. Demand for money increased rapidly. Narrow money increased from 6 per cent of GNP in 1978 to 15 per cent in 1988, then stabilised. Broad money increased much more rapidly.

Reformers must accommodate this increased demand for money; otherwise, an unplanned macroeconomic tightness could suffocate the microeconomic reforms at birth. Generally, the Chinese succeeded in accommodating a money demand curve that was steadily shifting upwards. While there were periods of macroeconomic imbalance and even an incipient inflationary crisis in 1988, overall this monetisation was accomplished fairly smoothly. Between 1980 and 1991, the consumer price index increased at an average annual rate of 7 per cent, not a high inflation rate by comparative standards.

In a big bang transition, it is much more difficult to cope with large and unpredictable shifts in the money demand schedule. This is a variation on the standard problem of stabilisation: in inflationary economies, households reduce their holdings of currency that is depreciating in value. Credible stabilisation will cause money demand schedules to shift upward, but a stabilisation is unlikely to be credible if it permits rapid growth of the money supply. In the short run, the only feasible intersection of money supply and demand may be at ruinously high interest rates. This dilemma appears to be unavoidable in countries where macroeconomic imbalances have already reached critical levels (including Poland at the end of 1989). But in countries where macroeconomic problems are not at critical levels, the argument is strong for gradual accommodation of increasing money demand, side-stepping the traditional dilemma of stabilisation.

A contrast with the Chinese experience is provided by the Czech stabilisation of 1991. There was broad agreement that macroeconomic imbalances and monetary overhang in Czechoslovakia were modest. But Czech policymakers believed that they must clearly transform a sellers' market into a buyers' market in order to signal to state enterprises the need to orient themselves to market competition. A zero monetary growth target was set for 1991, and adhered to at the beginning of the year. But since Czech households were beginning to respond to new economic opportunities, money demand schedules shifted upward. The result was a sharp decline in GNP, and a rapid proliferation of inter-enterprise debts, frustrating an intended tight credit policy. Czech policy was excessively rigid, not taking into account the changed behaviour of households and enterprises who would demand more money. The difficulty of managing monetary policy is, therefore, another argument against attempting to achieve an over-rapid transition.

IX. The Paradox of Big Bang Reform

The paradox of big bang reform is that the impediments to planning a comprehensive reform strategy are similar to the impediments to planning the economy.[10] Central planning fails because it attempts to control the uncontrollable. The planner needs an impossibly large amount of information; the well-known inefficiencies of socialist economies are, in essence, due to decision makers' lack of some crucial information. The market system, once it is in place, works because it does not require knowledge to be concentrated in one place: a vast amount of information about how to produce things and what things people want to buy is summarised by prices. The problem confronting designers of a big bang reform is similar in nature if not in degree to the problem facing the planner of an economy.

The planner of big bang reforms, like the central planner, needs to know a lot. The reformer must decide in what sequence prices are to be freed, enterprises privatised, trade barriers removed, and the financial system revamped. The reformer must decide how to assign ownership rights for state enterprises; whether to institute a Japanese/German-style or a US/British-style financial system; how to design a law of exchange; what kinds of taxation to introduce; and so on. Such choices must also be made, of course, under evolutionary reform. But it is easier to make such decisions piecemeal than all at once. By a process of institutional atonement, a gradual convergence to the set of institutions consistent with the available resources and suitable to the economy's needs is allowed to occur. As Robert Solow said, 'There is not some glorious theoretical synthesis of capitalism that you can write down in a book and follow. You have to grope your way.'[11]

A market is not an abstraction in which a demand curve spontaneously intersects a supply curve. A market is an institution, which needs rules and customs in order to work. Given the disparate goals of the market participants and the uneven distribution of information among them, the rules of exchange must be craftily structured for a market to operate smoothly (Wilson 1987). In practice the rules and customs differ widely from market to market. In a transition economy, these rules and customs must either be designed or evolve. The liberalisation process of the other China, Taiwan, is instructive here. Reflecting on his experience as Taiwan's Minister of Economic Affairs and of Finance during the 1960s and 1970s, K.T. Li said: 'A free market is not a given in the social calculus. It must be constructed, slowly, through a process of changes in policy focus' (Li 1988:104). Muddling through is a way of economising on the information needed by the reformers: by trial and error, information is accumulated through the reform process; and since each step is small, errors are not costly.

Lacking clear objectives and having weak administrative capabilities, China began its reforms by permitting entry of non-state firms and state firms to sell outside the plan. Markets then spread, gradually revealing, and putting increasing pressure on, inadequate institutional arrangements. The limited administrative resources were then devoted to 'putting out fires', as the progressive marketisation undermined the privileged position of the state enterprises and put pressure on the fiscal and banking systems. The pace of marketisation was largely driven not by bureaucratic decisions but by the decisions of individual households on saving and entry into new fields of productive endeavour.

X. The Coherence of Evolutionary Reform

China's jumble of ad hoc reforms can be seen, with hindsight, to have added up to a coherent package. Ironically, certain key features of the old planning system eased the beginning of the reforms; and other key features of the planning system gave the reform process the momentum that made it self-sustaining.

State control of the price system ensured high profitability of manufacturing at the start of the reforms. This high profitability induced rapid entry of new firms once restrictions on non-state firms were removed. The profits earned elicited high levels of household saving, generating still more investment by non-state firms. Entry in turn subjected state enterprises to market discipline and reduced state-sector profitability. As a result, the government faced erosion of its revenue base. In an attempt to slow this erosion, the state intensified its monitoring of state firms, and increasingly provided them with incentive systems based on profitability. State firms responded by increasing their efficiency (which was abysmal to begin with), providing the economy with enough stability to encourage further growth, both inside and outside the state sector, while also providing essential producer goods. Faced with the erosion of its traditional sources of revenue, the state also sought to strengthen newly developing financial systems—the banking system and embryonic capital markets—in order to transfer private saving to productive uses.

Reform proceeds by a series of feedback loops: reform begets further reform. A microeconomic reform (resulting in competition for state firms) creates a macroeconomic problem (a squeeze on government revenue) which impels further microeconomic reforms (increasingly profit-oriented regulation of state firms). This positive feedback presupposes a series of constructive policy responses from government leaders; reform will not proceed without appropriate state action. But the

470

dynamics of the process create opportunities for pro-reform leaders to push the reforms forward.[12]

Gradualist reforms, it is sometimes said, will fail because they are not sustainable. A variant of this argument says that only a totalitarian government is strong enough to maintain its course of gradual change. Credibility ceases to be an issue, however, once evolutionary reform is properly understood. The government must only maintain its commitment to allow entry and competition. Beyond that commitment, there is only trial and error; no further promises are being made. Rather, the government is driven by its own need for revenue to create new fiscal institutions, and impelled by its need for popular support to create additional institutions to foster economic growth. Surely, the new democracies of Eastern Europe are at least as capable of sustaining this approach as is the Chinese democracy.

XI. Conclusion

We have given a rosy view of China. Even putting aside the primary issue of the lack of political liberties, there is much that is wrong with the Chinese economy: the financial system misdirects funds, with state banks being unable to refuse loans to state enterprises, however unproductive, and non-state firms having restricted access to credit; agricultural production is distorted by the continuing state regulation of grain output; government policy keeps urban incomes artificially high and rural incomes artificially low; labour markets are inadequate or non-existent; the lack of basic laws of exchange and contract is a hindrance to both state and non-state firms; and property rights are ill-defined. China's reforms have probably been too gradual: it could be argued, without contradicting our case against hasty privatisation, that the reforms had progressed far enough by the late 1980s that privatisation of state-owned firms, development of a stock market, and full market pricing should have begun. But, in order to derive lessons from

China's experience, we have focused on what has worked.

Competition is crucial. This Schumpeterian point is the main lesson from China. Competition, notably absent in the socialist planned economies, disciplines firms to operate efficiently. Competition in China was generated by the massive entry of non-state firms. Competition was intensified by having state firms sell on free markets against other producers.

China provides a case for evolutionary reform. China's experience does not prove big bang reforms cannot work: that would require examination of countries in which sudden, comprehensive reform was tried. (Though a recent remark by Polish President Lech Walesa is apposite: 'We listened to the West, and we made too big a leap.')[13] China's experience does not even conclusively establish that evolutionary reform does work, for China is still far short of an efficiently operating economy. But China's reforms have met with measurable success: entry of entrepreneurial firms has generated vigorous growth, so much so that by 1990 non-state firms were producing almost a half of industrial output; state-owned firms have become more productive; agricultural output has soared; the price system has been effectively realigned; the fiscal and monetary systems have been changed in ways that reinforce the shift to a market economy; and, as the bottom line, living standards have risen for all.

Notes

1. We thank William Byrd, Stanley Fischer, Peter Gourevitch, Gary Jefferson, Miles Kahler, Michael Rothschild, and Jeffrey Sachs for comments, and the Ford Foundation for research support.
2. In 'The Science of "Muddling Through"' (1959), Lindblom argued that incremental policymaking—muddling through—works better than grand planning, because the huge amount of information needed to make a comprehensive policy is never fully available;

people can agree about a small policy change even if they disagree about ultimate goals; and a comprehensive policy rests heavily on the theory it is built on.

3. GNP data must be treated with some caution. China specialists believe that, because of measurement problems, the official data slightly overstate the true growth rate. The improvement in Chinese living standards is somewhat greater than growth rates indicate, on the other hand, in that the range of available goods and household choice has also expanded dramatically. The standard of living in 1978 was lower than the GNP figures indicate, because many goods were subject to rationing and could not be purchased freely. By 1990, however, virtually all goods were available at market prices (though some rationing persists as a means to distribute subsidies to privileged urban dwellers). There seems to have been little increase in inequality over the decade, so the increases in GNP have been broadly shared.

4. In the United States in 1984, for example, firms with fewer than 100 employees accounted for 39 per cent of all jobs (Brock and Evans 1989:8).

5. Kornai (1990:35–6) describes the vigorous entry of private firms in Hungary; he says, 'the development of the private sector is the most important achievement of the reform process so far'.

6. Production-function estimates (by Chen et al. 1988; Gordon and Li 1989; and Jefferson, Rawski and Zheng 1992) find significant improvements in state-owned firms' productivity.

7. The input and output of market ratios are calculated from a Chinese Academy of Social Sciences survey.

8. Dual pricing pre-empted a difficulty that has been identified as a pitfall of partial reform. If the state-owned firms had remained rigidly planned, then they would have been at a competitive disadvantage *vis-à-vis* the non-state firms, in that the non-state firms would have been able to bid inputs away from the state-owned firms (Murphy, Shleifer, and Vishny 1991). Allowing the state-owned firms to sell some of their outputs and buy some of their inputs on free markets prevented such a misallocation of inputs in China.

9. This does not contradict the popular wisdom of 'currency overhang', which says that, in planned economies, people hold more money than they need for their transactions. Under socialist conditions, there could be currency overhang relative to the low money demand; but then, as the economy becomes marketised the demand for money could increase by more than enough to cancel out the currency overhang.

10. This point was made in the mid 1980s by some young economists at the Institute of Economics, Chinese Academy of Social Sciences, including Hua Sheng and Zhang Xuejun.

11. *New York Times*, 29 September 1991:E1.

12. This is consistent with Hirschman's view of economic development as a process of unbalanced growth; of 'development as a chain of disequilibria'. Hirschman argued that imbalances can be useful in inducing not only market reactions but also appropriate government actions, 'since the desire for political survival is at least as strong a motive force as the desire to realise a profit' (Hirschman 1958:4).

13. *New York Times*, 25 October 1991:C4. Walesa said this 22 months after the enactment of big bang reforms intended rapidly to transform Poland into a market economy by extensive privatisation and institutional reform. At the time of Walesa's remark, the reforms had achieved some successes, but unemployment was over 10 per cent and rising, and national income had plummeted (although Berg and Sachs (1991) give some evidence that the costs of Poland's big bang have been overestimated).

References

Berg, A. and Sachs, J., 1991. 'Structural Adjustment and International Trade in Eastern Europe: The Case of Poland', mimeo, Harvard University.

Blanchard, O., Dornbusch, R., Krugman, P., Layard, R. and Summers, L., 1991. *Reform in Eastern Europe*, Cambridge, MIT Press.

Brock, W. A. and Evans, D.S., 1989. 'Small Business Economics', *Small Business Economics*, 1:7–20.

Byrd, W.A., 1987. 'The Impact of the Two-Tier Plan/Market System in Chinese Industry', *Journal of Comparative Economics*, 11:295–308.

——, 1991. 'Contractual Responsibility Systems in Chinese State-Owned Industry', *Advances in Chinese Industrial Studies*, 2:7–35.

——, and Lin, Q. (eds.), 1990. *China's Rural Industry*, Oxford, Oxford University Press.

Chen, K., Jefferson, G., Rawski, T., Wang, H., and Zheng, Y., 1988. 'Productivity Change in Chinese Industry':1953–1985', *Journal of Comparative Economics*, 12:570–91.

Gordon, R., and Li, W., 1989. 'The Change in Productivity of Chinese State Enterprises, 1983 1987: Preliminary Results', mimeo, University of Michigan.

Groves, T., Hong, Y., McMillan, J., and Naughton, B., 1992a. 'Autonomy and Incentives in Chinese State Enterprises', mimeo, UCSD.

——, 1992b. 'China's Managerial Labour Market', mimeo, UCSD.

Hirschman, A.O., 1958. *The Strategy of Economic Development*, New Haven, Yale University Press.

Hoshi, T., Kashyap, A., and Scharfstein, D., 1991. 'Corporate Structure, Liquidity, and Investment: Evidence from Japanese Industrial Groups', *Quarterly Journal of Economics*, 106, 33–60.

Jefferson, G.H., Chen, K., and Singh, I., 1992. 'Lessons from China's Economic Reform', *Journal of Comparative Economics*, 16(2):201–25.

——, Rawski, T., and Zheng, Y., 1992. 'Growth, Efficiency and Convergence in China's State and Collective Industry', *Economic Development and Cultural Change*, 40(2):239–66.

——, and Xu, W., 1991. 'The Impact of Reform on Socialist Enterprises in Transition: Structure, Conduct, and Performance in Chinese Industry', *Journal of Comparative Economics*, 15:45–64.

Jensen, M.C., and Murphy, K.J., 1990. 'Performance Pay and Top-Management Incentives', *Journal of Political Economy*, 98:225–64.

Johnson, S., 1991. 'Spontaneous Privatization in the Soviet Union: How, Why, and for Whom?', mimeo, Duke University.

Kornai, J., 1990. *The Road to a Free Economy*, New York, Norton.

Lenin, V.I., 1968. *Lenin on Politics and Revolution*, ed. by J.E. O'Connor, New York, Pegasus.

Li, K.T., 1988. *The Evolution of Policy behind Taiwan's Development Success*, New Haven, Yale University Press.

Lin, Y., 1992. 'Rural Reforms and Agricultural Growth in China', *American Economic Review*, 82(1):34 51.

Lindbolm, C.E., 1959. 'The Science of "Muddling Through"', *Public Administration Review*, 19, 79–88.

Lipton, D., and Sachs, J. 1990, 'Privatization in Eastern Europe: The Case of Poland', *Brook-ings Paper on Economic Activity*, 2:293–333.

McKinnon, R., 1991. 'Financial Control in the Transition from Classical Socialism to a Market Economy', *Journal of Economic Perspectives*, 5:107–22.

McMillan, J., Whalley, J., and Zhu, L., 1989. 'The Impact of China's Economic Reforms on Agricultural Productivity Growth', *Journal of Political Economy*, 97:781–807.

Murphy, K.M., Shleifer, A., and Vishny, R.W., 1991. 'The Transition to a Market Economy: Pitfalls of Partial Reform', mimeo, University of Chicago.

Naughton, B., 1992a. 'Growing out of the Plan: Chinese Economic Reform, 1978 90', mimeo.

——, 1992b. 'Implication of the State Monopoly over Industry and Its Relaxation', *Modern China*, 18.

Schumpeter, J.A., 1950. *Capitalism, Socialism and Democracy*, 3rd edn, New York, Harper.

Sinn, H-W., 1991, 'Privatization in East Germany', mimeo, University of Munich.

Tirole, J., 1991. Privatization in Eastern Europe: Incentives and the Economics of Transition', in O.J. Blanchard and S.S. Fischer (eds.), *NBER Macroeconomics Annual 1991*, Cambridge, Massachusetts, MIT Press.

Wilson, R., 1987. 'Game-Theoretic Analyses of Trading Process', in T. Bewley (ed.), *Advances in Economic Theory*, Cambridge, Cambridge University Press.

29 Structural Factors in China's Economic Reform

Jeffrey Sachs and Wing Thye Woo

The divergent reform experiences of Eastern Europe, the Former Soviet Union, and China raise important questions about the strategy of economic transition. China has grown rapidly since market reforms began in 1978, while Eastern Europe and the Former Soviet Union (EEFSU) have faced continued economic turmoil and significant declines in output. The reasons for these divergent trends have been heatedly debated.[1]

The Chinese experience is variously held to demonstrate the merit of 'gradualism' compared with 'shock therapy' (McMillan and Naughton 1992) or the superiority of 'experimentation' to 'top-down reform'; the fallacy of the 'orthodox' view that rapid stabilisation, liberalisation, and privatisation are keys to successful reform;[2] the wisdom of beginning reform in agriculture before reform of industry; and the advantage of economic reform prior to political reform rather than vice versa.

All these explanations miss the principal point. It was neither gradualism nor experimentation, but rather China's economic structure, that proved so felicitous to reform.[3] The reform experience elsewhere in East Asia reinforces this

conclusion.[4] China began reform as a peasant agricultural society, EEFSU as urban and over industrialised. China faced the classic problem of normal economic development, the transfer of workers from low-productivity agriculture to higher-productivity industry.[5] In EEFSU, the problem is structural adjustment: cutting employment in inefficient and subsidised industry to allow new jobs in efficient industry and services. For many reasons, normal economic development is easier than structural adjustment, both politically and economically (see also Fischer 1993a, 1993b).

Policy differences also mattered, but not in the ways usually assumed. China's structural policies (enterprise reform, trade liberalisation, price reform) were not unusual; Eastern Europe's post-1989 reforms did as much or more to stimulate exports and new enterprises. The main policy differences have been macroeconomic. China was more cautious than Russia and many other EEFSU countries in monetary policy. Although China is now experiencing inflationary pressures, its monetary policy was never as reckless as that in the Soviet Union in 1989–91 or in Russia in 1992.

Reprinted with permission. Extracted from Jeffrey Sachs and Wing Thye Woo, 1994. 'Structural factors in China's economic reforms', *Economic Policy: A European Forum*, 9(18):101–45 (with minor editing).

Broadly speaking, normal economic development is usually Pareto-improving: all major groups can benefit from the flow of workers from agriculture to industry, especially if the new industry is export-oriented and labour-intensive, as in East Asia. Structural adjustment, however, is likely to be conflictual. Workers in the declining sectors fight to maintain their previous status and living standards. Crucially, China's agricultural workers had nothing to lose, indeed much to gain, from the dismantling of socialism, while much of the industrial and even agricultural workforce in EEFSU has plausible fears that dismantling the old system could leave them worse off, at least in the short term.

The economic structure in EEFSU has three interrelated flaws not present in China. First, industry is overbuilt: too much heavy industry, too little light industry, consumer goods and services. Second, virtually all workers before 1992 were in jobs heavily subsidised by the state, seriously impeding structural change. Third, virtually the entire EEFSU population was covered by an extensive social welfare system, with many of the benefits linked to the place of employment. The EEFSU population is therefore used to economic security: job tenure, pension benefits, guaranteed income, health and housing. Even though such guarantees are beyond the financial capacity of the state, they remain a potent rallying cry for much of society.

China is very different. In Gershchenkron's famous phrase, it had the 'advantages of backwardness'. Even though the agricultural commune system was brutally regimental before 1978, it did not suffer the rigidities of heavy subsidies, soft budget constraints, and guaranteed employment of state industry. When the communes were dismantled, nearly three-fourths of Chinese workers found themselves outside the socialised economy and subject to hard budget constraints with little social protection. This spurred enormous flows of workers out of subsistence agriculture into new sectors of the economy, including township and village enterprises (TVEs) and new labour-

intensive manufacturing exporters set up in coastal regions. The latter used offshore Chinese capital, technology and management.

China's strategy involved a 'two-track approach': continued state control of state enterprises while permitting growth of a new non-state sector largely outside the state control. Although some countries in EEFSU tried a similar course during the 1980s, their two-track approach failed. Chinese peasants left farms to joint the non-state sector; industrial workers in EEFSU did not leave the state sector in sufficient numbers until industrial subsidies were cut sharply. In the meantime, the liberalisation of the economy in both cases contributed to macro-economic instability, which got out of hand in most of EEFSU, because of egregious monetary mismanagement. The turn to a 'big bang' in EEFSU came in the wake of the failures of the two-track approach and in response to growing macroeconomic destabilisation (see Berliner 1993; Brada 1993; Sachs 1993).

I. The Economic Structure of China and EEFSU

In this section we identify the basic structural characteristics that underlie the success of the two-track approach in China and its failure in the EEFSU.

Structural differences between China and EEFSU

The preponderance of peasant agriculture in China. China and EEFSU began reforms at very different stages of economic development, China as a peasant society (not unlike Russia in 1910 in the share of labour in agriculture), EEFSU as overwhelmingly urban and industrial. Under central planning the Soviet Union developed a considerable division of labour, but one that was inefficient and difficult to reorient. Since pre-reform rural China had much less division of labour, creating a market-based division of labour was much easier.

In 1978 China had 71 per cent of the labour force in agriculture, only 15 per cent in industry, just half of which was in state-owned enterprises (the rest being in urban or rural collectives, and rural individual enterprises). In Russia, by contrast, only 14 per cent of the labour force was in agriculture, but 32 per cent in industry.[6]

There was also a big difference in the gap between urban and rural living standards in China and EEFSU. China's peasants were living near subsistence levels in 1978, far below the levels of the non-agricultural sectors: rural real consumption averaged around one-third of that in cities.[7] In the Soviet Union in 1990 agricultural workers on the state farms and collective farms had incomes only 15 per cent below those of urban workers. Even these smaller differentials probably overstate the actual differences in living standards, since measured agricultural compensation excludes income from private plots, and since the cost of living is lower in the rural areas (Nove, 1986). The wider income spread in China probably reflects three things: a vast supply of surplus labour in the Chinese countryside at the start of the reforms, held in place by restrictions of migration and on starting non-agricultural enterprises; prior elimination of most of the Soviet Union's earlier peasant labour force by

industrialisation or violent deaths during twentieth century upheavals of war, revolution and collectivisation; and large subsidies to Soviet agriculture in contrast to heavy taxation of Chinese agriculture.

The rural sector in China enjoyed a one-time jump in productivity after 1978 as the chaos of the Cultural Revolution faded and private agriculture was re-established. For rice output per hectare, during 1952–57 (before the period of the Great Leap Forward), productivity grew at 2.3 per cent a year. During the Cultural Revolution, productivity growth fell to 1.1 per cent because of political turmoil and the pursuit of radical commune policies. Post-1978 liberalisation allowed a rebound of productivity during 1979–84 as it caught up with the past trend.[8] Since 1984 productivity growth has stagnated, averaging a mere 0.7 per cent a year during 1985–91. In Russia productivity growth in agriculture has been low but not held back by specific events. Improvement in Russian agricultural productivity will require more than 'bouncing back' to a previous trend.

State-sector employment. The Chinese state enterprise sector is small, employing just 18 per cent of the workforce (Table 1). Urban collectives, typically attached to state enterprises, employ another 5 per cent of the labour force. Rural

Table 1 **Distribution of employment by type of organisation** (per cent of total employment)

	China			Russia	
	1978	1984	1991	1985	1991
State enterprise	18.6	17.9	18.3	93.1	86.1
Collective agriculture	72.0	67.0	63.9	6.0	5.3
Urban collective	5.1	6.7	6.2	n.a.	n.a.
Industrial TVEs	4.3	7.6	10.0	n.a.	n.a.
Private and other	0.0	0.8	1.6	0.9	8.6

Notes: For China, all agricultural activities and non-industrial TVEs are put in the 'collective agriculture' category. For Russia, state enterprises include leased state enterprises as well as traditional (pre 1985) consumer cooperatives (mainly in retail distribution). Post-1985 cooperatives are counted in 'private and other'. For Russia, collective agriculture is *kolkhoz* employment. As described in the text, the organisation of the *kolkhoz* sector is virtually indistinguishable from the state-farm sector (*sokhoz*).
Source: *China Statistical Yearbook 1992.*

communes, with over 70 per cent of the labour force in 1978, were not state enterprises and were subject to a hard budget constraint. In Russia 93 per cent of the labour force in 1985 was in state and municipal enterprises and organisations (including state farms) with soft budget constraints,[9] and a further 6 per cent in collective farms and consumer cooperatives that, in organisation and financial dependence on the state, differ little from their state-owned counterparts. Individual and private enterprises employed only 1 per cent of the labour force in 1985.

Social welfare system. Some observers claim that East Asian two-track reforms offer a 'kinder, gentler' path than the 'big bang' approach in parts of post-1989 EEFSU. In fact, China's two-track approach also includes a two-track social policy: extensive protection for urban workers but virtually no social guarantees for rural workers. EEFSU social protections are deemed to be universal, and the commitments are often very generous, at least on paper.

China's structural change is probably accelerated by the absence of social guarantees in the countryside: rural workers flood into the cities in search of jobs at extremely low pay, and are absorbed by the burgeoning export and construction sectors. Yet true social conditions in China are often hidden from view. Unemployment is not counted in the countryside, and is vastly undercounted among the estimated 50 million 'floating population' of Chinese workers in urban areas without residence permits.[10]

Ahmad and Hussain (1989) and World Bank (1990) offer detailed accounts of Chinese social security programs. There are four broad categories of social security: labour insurance (*laodong baoxian*); occupational and communal provisions (*shehui fuli*); social relief (*shehui jiuji*) and disaster relief (*ziran zaihai juiji*); and public provision of health care. Direct budgetary expenditures by the central government on these items is minuscule; most coverage is provided through enterprise funds or local governments. Moreover, the coverage is almost entirely for urban workers. Labour insurance, for example, includes disability, maternity and sickness benefits, and old age pensions. In the 1980s, the coverage was fairly steady, around 23 per cent of the labour force, essentially the state-enterprise employees. Rural workers were not included. This is why the aggregate expenditure on social security benefits in 1991 came to only 5.5 per cent of GDP.

Social relief directed at the countryside mainly covers the elderly who lack direct family support. In 1986 an estimated 6.4 per cent of the rural population was covered by social relief, a mere 16.4 per cent of those deemed to be below the rural poverty threshold. Public provision of health care is also mainly limited to other cities. An earlier rudimentary rural health insurance system was largely dismantled after 1978, and just 5 per cent of villages were covered by rural health insurance in 1985 compared with 80 per cent in 1979.[11]

The penetration of central planning in China. Economic planning was far more deeply entrenched in EEFSU than in China. The specificity of state planning was far greater in the EEFSU, where it had been carried out for decades, than in China. Qian and Xu (1993) note that around 25 million commodities entered the Soviet economic plans; in China only around 1,200 commodities were included. Regional governments were given greater autonomy in China than in the EEFSU, especially during the Cultural Revolution. Fairbank (1992) notes that: 'Local governments were given autonomy to set up small-scale rural industries outside of central planning. In 1965 there had been under the control of central ministries a total of 10,533 nonmilitary enterprises that produced 47 per cent of state-run industrial output. By 1971 these had been reduced to 142 factories that produced only 8 per cent of the output'.

Wong (1986) gives a striking example of the increased local role: 'even in the strategic iron and steel industry, local investment accounted for 52 per cent of the total during the Fourth Five

Year Plan (1981–75) compared with only 8 per cent during the First Five Year Plan'. In addition to increased oversight of existing state enterprises, local governments were given much wider freedom to establish small-scale enterprises, leading to the rapid growth of the TVE sector even before 1978.

Political conditions on the eve of reform.[12] China began reform after more than a decade of tumult and stagnant (or falling) living standards in the countryside. The Cultural Revolution had directly undermined the control of the party apparatus. Fairbank (1992) reports that 60 per cent of party officials were purged during this period. Local and regional autonomy rose markedly in the chaos. The Cultural Revolution also contributed directly to rural impoverishment and a growing disparity between urban and rural incomes. In 1966 urban consumption was 2.3 times higher than rural consumption; by 1978 it was 2.9 times higher. Peasants, seething with discontent, were eager to reclaim their property rights. Not only did they receive few financial transfers from the state, they were heavily taxed through the administratively-set rural-urban terms of trade. Chen and Hu (1993) cite an estimate that in 1978 agricultural prices were set on average 33 per cent below equilibrium levels but industrial prices 20 per cent above equilibrium levels. The peasants had no financial attachment to the commune system.

Structural linkages to international markets. Since so much of successful reform involves export promotion and attraction of foreign capital, structural differences in this regard also affect reform prospects. On the whole, the Eastern European countries should be better placed than either the former Soviet Union or China to reintegrate into world markets, given their small size and easy proximity to EC markets. Nonetheless, China has obviously received a vast boost from the offshore Chinese economy of Southeast Asia, which has supplied knowhow, management, financial and physical

capital, and trade infrastructure, for China's coastal regions. By 1989 Hong Kong accounted for over 60 per cent of cumulated foreign investment in China (Chen et al. 1991). Moreover, roughly 70 per cent of China's overall trade leaves through Hong Kong. China's coastal regions have outstripped interior regions in economic growth in the last 15 years.

II. Implications of the Differing Economic Structures

The basic difference between Chinese and EEFSU reform is that in China, 80 per cent of the labour force was outside the deeply conservative state sector at the start of the reforms, whereas in EEFSU the state sector covered virtually the entire population, even in agriculture. This had several implications. First, the two-track approach could work effectively in China where the state sector was sufficiently small, but could not work effectively in EEFSU. The non-state sector in China could draw upon a vast rural hinterland, as well as offshore capital and management expertise. Second, restructuring in EEFSU requires a sharp cutback in existing subsidies, provoking political conflict. Third, the sense of entitlement (for example, expectation of a guaranteed income with social protection) is much more extensive among EEFSU workers than among Chinese peasant workers. The result is greater immobility, higher registered unemployment, and significant expressions of social grievance.

Even when non-state activities are permitted alongside state enterprises, and even when non-state activities are much more productive than state-sector activities, it is hard to induce flows of workers, capital and productive inputs from the state sector to the non-state sector. As long as the subsidies to the state sector are large enough to offset the productivity differences between the state and non-state sectors, resources will remain in the state sector rather than flow voluntarily to the non-state sector.

In the Appendix we outline a formal model to make the point. There are three sectors: subsistence agriculture, state industry, and non-state industry. Productivity is lowest in the first, moderate in the second, and highest in the third. The state sector is heavily subsidised, however, so that workers earn far more than their marginal product. The subsidies to the state sector are paid for by all workers through explicit and implicit taxes (such as inflation). Initially, the more efficient non-state sector is suppressed by law. Then liberalisation takes place, so that workers may voluntarily leave their jobs to move to the new sector.

Subsistence agricultural workers happily move, since wages in the new sector are higher than in subsistence agriculture. State-sector workers, however, will prefer to remain in the state enterprises, even though their productivity would be higher in the new firms, if the subsidy to state-enterprise workers is greater than the difference in productivity in the two sectors. This analysis suggests that in China, the non-state sector can grow rapidly, relying on the flow of labour from agriculture. In EEFSU, the non-state sector will not develop. The two-track approach is not enough.

Subsidisation of the state sector stops not only the flow of workers but also of capital and other inputs. For example, in pre-1989 Poland struggling private-sector construction firms had trouble buying bricks, since the output of bricks was automatically flowing to the state enterprises. Of course bricks were available in the black market at prices far higher than official prices, but the price differential rendered the private-sector work unprofitable. Lack of access to financial capital by non-state firms was even more notorious. Thus, although the model in the Appendix focuses on labour mobility between sectors, the analysis is at least as relevant to intersectoral mobility of other production inputs.

Our model stresses that the subsidies must be paid for through some form of taxation, such as inflation. Thus, the net benefits of the subsidies to state workers are much smaller than the gross benefits. Suppose all workers are initially in the state sector (largely true in pre-reform EEFSU). The subsidy per worker must be paid for by a tax per worker that averages the same amount. The net subsidy is zero. Nonetheless, the presence of the subsidy will still stop the flow of workers to the non-state sector, as long as a non-state sector worker would have to continue paying the tax to cover the subsidy of the state workers, as for example if subsidies were financed by inflation or universal personal income tax.

III. Adjustment under Gradual Reform

Both China and EEFSU attempted gradual reform in the 1980s, with vastly different results. We now draw the links between the structural differences and differences in economic performance.

China's reforms were undertaken in three main stages after Deng's political ascendancy in 1978. The first phase, 1979–82, focussed mainly on rural liberalisation. The 'personal responsibility system' allowed farm households to lease land from the state and sell their output on a two-track basis: a fixed quota at state-set prices to official procurement agencies and the remaining output at freely determined prices in agricultural markets. State procurement prices were also raised to ease the financial strain on an impoverished rural sector whose real consumption had been stagnant for more than a decade. Township and village governments were increasingly allowed to establish TVEs for the production and sale of industrial goods outside the central plan. While TVEs had been allowed throughout the communist period, it was after 1978 that they were given the most dramatic encouragement.

The second phase of reform opened the economy to international trade and capital (see Lardy 1992). Market opening began around 1979, with the devaluation of the highly overvalued exchange rate and establishment of a retention system for foreign exchange for exporting firms.

Trade liberalisation proceeded gradually throughout the 1980s: further devaluations of the exchange rate, increased rights of exporting firms to hold foreign exchange, creation of special economic zones in the coastal regions, increased scope for foreign direct investment, and finally the establishment of a rudimentary foreign exchange market (in so-called swap centers) at the end of the 1980s.

The third phase of reform involved urban industry, and began around 1984, with the unveiling of the 'Provisional Regulations on the Expansion of Self-Management Powers in State Enterprises'. These reforms aimed to establish greater autonomy for industrial enterprises, including increased freedom to set contract prices, and choose inputs and outputs. Managers and workers received extra incentives by having their pay more tightly linked to enterprise performance. The system of profit remittance was replaced by an income tax (*ligaishui*). State enterprises were set into a two-tier framework conceptually akin to that of household farmers: the enterprise had to deliver a portion of its output to the state on the quota basis, while the rest could be sold in an increasingly free market. Other kinds of property ownership (urban and rural collectives, private joint venture) were liberalised too. From 1987 the 'contract responsibility system' (*chengbao*) was introduced, allowing enterprises to make quasi-contracts with the state to deliver a negotiated amount of taxes. Income in excess of the negotiated tax payment reverted to the enterprise for reinvestment and compensation of workers and management.

These reforms were granted in several senses. First, they extended over more than a decade, and indeed are still proceeding. Second, they were not conceived as an integrated strategy to create a market economy, much less a capitalist economy. Only at the CCP Congress in 1992 was there a formal endorsement of the market economy, albeit a 'socialist market economy'. Third, for over a decade there was no attempt to curtail the state enterprise sector, either financially (reduced subsidisation) or through privatisation. Large state enterprises remain subject to a central plan, though one that applied to an ever-shrinking proportion of national output.

At the same time, some reforms have been breathtakingly rapid. The rural reforms ending the commune system that covered hundreds of million of peasant farmers essentially took place in the three years 1979–81. Notably, the impetus for reform came both from below and from above (Zweig 1989). In the late 1970s, individual regions began reverting to 'team accounting' rather than 'brigade accounting' (moving the locus of responsibility closer to the household level), and to increased reliance on private plots. Deng Ziaoping halted radical collectivisation: the Communist Party adopted his programme entitled 'The New Sixty Articles' in 1978. The rise in centrally-mandated procurement prices in 1979–80 raised peasant income and also fuelled pressures to reverse collectivisation. By 1981 there was a massive, almost spontaneous, dismantling of collective property in agriculture. In 1983, the People's Communes were formally eliminated, and the individual household was established as the basis of agricultural production.

Turning to the results of reform, we note that most of China's rapid growth came in two areas: rural regions where non-state enterprises at the township and village level flourished, and in the coastal areas where market opening led to an export boom and later to a massive inflow of foreign direct investment. Areas heavily involved in state industry fared much less well, even though initially they were often the richest regions.

Table 2 shows these patterns in the structure and performance of 11 characteristic regions. The two regions of traditional heavy industry, Liaoning and Heilongjiang, are on the Russian border and were favoured by the Soviet economic advisors in the early 1950s who came to China to implement the Stalinist strategy of heavy industrialisation. The coastal regions, Jiangzu, Zhejiang, and Guangdong, were favoured in the 1980s with special economic zones linking them to Hong Kong. The inland regions are overwhelming agricultural, with more than 80 per cent of their population in agriculture in 1990. The two province-status cities, Beijing and Shanghai, have a high proportion of state-owned, heavy industry. We see that the coastal regions started out with a more felicitous industrial structure than either Manchuria, the inland regions, or the independent cities: less reliance on heavy industry and on state-owned enterprises, and a higher proportion of output from small, rural industries outside of the national plan.

Coastal regions boomed, traditional areas of heavy industry grew more slowly than the national average, and agricultural regions lay in the middle. We offer a 'Russification' hypothesis.

preceding industrialisation (along Soviet lines) was a hindrance, not a help, to economic growth in the 1980s. The main sources of growth were the non-state industries; TVEs in rural areas, private firms and joint ventures in urban areas, particularly along the coast. Table 3 reports that during 1980–91, gross industrial output grew by 13 per cent a year (8 per cent in the state sector, 14 per cent in the urban collective-individual sector, and 25 per cent in the rural collective-individual sector). The share of gross industrial output originating in SOEs fell from 78 per cent in 1978 to 53 per cent in 1991.

The small role played by import-substituting industrialisation is consistent with the experience of East Asia more broadly. Throughout East Asia, rapid growth was spurred by labour-intensive export-oriented manufactures, developed independently of the heavy industry that had been fostered by import-substitution policies.

Table 2   Economic growth and production structure in selected Chinese provinces

| | % output growth | Per capita regional incomes as % of national average | | % of gross industrial output produced by | | | | | |
| | | | | SOEs | | heavy industry | | rural industry | |
	1983–91	1984	1990	1982	1991	1982	1991	1985	1991
National	100	100	100	78	53	50	51	18	29
Industrial northeast									
Liaoning	80	177	158	80	60	65	69	12	22
Heilongjiang	57	147	129	84	81	66	68	6	9
Coastal									
Jiangsu	124	128	134	61	33	41	47	38	46
Zhejiang	165	127	136	58	29	36	35	37	48
Guandong	157	118	146	67	39	35	34	19	26
Inland									
Henan	88	73	70	82	53	47	55	16	33
Sichuan	83	73	72	80	62	50	54	15	25
Guizhou	83	59	51	86	76	60	58	12	14
Gansu	111	75	75	94	78	77	73	6	13
Province-cities									
Beijing	89	304	284	81	60	54	56	13	23
Shanghai	80	518	383	87	65	44	50	10	20
11 above provinces		71		50	46	50	20	30	

Source: *China Statistical Yearbook*, various issues.

Table 3   Industrial production by type of organisation, China, 1980–91

| | Output (trillions of 1980 yuan) | | | | |
	1980	1984	1988	1991	average annual real growth (%), 1980–91
SOEs	392	513	772	890	7.8
Collectives	121	226	560	789	18.6
Individuals	0	2	68	126	91.4
Other	2	9	44	129	43.7
Total	515	749	1,444	1,934	12.8
Collectives and individuals					
urban	67	112	221	268	13.5
rural	54	116	407	647	25.3

Notes: Industrial output of rural-based collectives and individuals computed from industrial output reported in rural total outputs in *1992 CSY*. From matching employment data in *1991 CSY*, we conclude that 'other forms of ownership' are urban-based enterprises. In 1978–83, employment in industrial enterprises below the village level were put under agriculture. Rural industrial employment from *CSY*. The reader should be warned that output figures in Table 9.56 in *CSY* are in constant prices but with different base years for different years.
Source: *China Statistical Yearbook (CSY).*

Workers in the new export-oriented firms came from agriculture not from heavy industrial enterprises. Riedel (1993) confirms that in the export-oriented industrialisation in Taiwan, Thailand, and China; know-how, material inputs, and even capital were found abroad more than at home. Furthermore, those who went to work in labour-intensive manufacturing (disproportionately women) in all three countries were recruited for the most part from the rural sector, not the existing industrial workforce. And those who started up the small-scale manufacturing activities, which in both Hong Kong and Taiwan account for the bulk of manufacturing output, often had no previous managerial or entrepreneurial experience at all.

Importantly, the state-owned enterprise sector did not actually shrink. Employment in the new non-state sector came entirely from agriculture. Total employment in SOEs actually rose from 74.5 million in 1978 to 106.6 million in 1991. Even the proportion of the total labour force in SOEs has remained unchanged at 18 per cent. The proportion of the labour force in farming fell from 71 per cent in 1978 to 56 per cent in 1991, matched by a sharp rise of employment in rural enterprises (so-called township and village enterprises, or TVEs).

The results of attempts to reform the state sector have been disappointing, a point acknowledged by the Chinese leadership itself. This sector in China has continued to perform poorly. It is heavily loss-making;[13] lagging in total factor productivity (TFP) growth; dependent on state subsidies; and apparently suffused with economic corruption. China has grown rapidly only because state industrial enterprises account for less than 15 per cent of total employment, and a steadily diminishing share of GNP.

Several recent studies of the Chinese experience have confirmed the poor performance of the state sector, at least relative to the non-state sector. Xiao (1991a, b) demonstrates that productivity growth was significantly higher in the non-state than state sector. Calculating total factor productivity for 29 provinces, he finds a strong correlation between the level of TFP and the proportion of the economy in the non-state sector. The coastal regions Guangdong, Jiangsu, and Zhejiang have non-state shares of industrial output of 50.6 per cent, 63.4 per cent, and 66.7 per cent respectively, compared with a national average of 40.3 per cent. These regions had total factor productivity levels that, respectively, were 26 per cent, 23 per cent, and 39 per cent above the national average. The industrialised Manchurian provinces, Liaoning and Heilongjiang, had non-state shares in industry of 36.0 per cent and 19.4 per cent, below the national average. Total factor productivity levels were 1 per cent and 16 per cent below the national average.

While almost all observers agree that the state sector lags behind the non-state sector in productivity and financial performance (for example, Lardy 1989), some have declared its performance to be adequate and to have improved after the reforms of the mid 1980s (Jefferson et al. 1992; McMillan and Naughton 1992; Rawski 1993). Rawski's (1993) criterion for 'success' of SOE reforms is rather weak; it merely stresses that SOEs have become subject to market forces and that the managers have begun to respond to these forces. Even Rawski acknowledges that 'the experience of China as well as of other socialist and non-socialist states demonstrates that, in comparison with feasible private alternatives, state enterprises often perform dismally in terms of productivity, cost control, technical development, customer satisfaction, and even (though not in China) output growth'.

Jefferson, Rawski, and Zheng (JRZ) argue that productivity performance in the SOE sector has improved since the enterprise reforms have been implemented, but they too find that productivity growth was faster in collective enterprises (urban collectives and TVEs) than in state-owned industry. However, JRZ's estimates of total factor productivity growth for the SOEs are likely to be biased upward. Woo et al (1993) show that JRZ's use of an implausible price deflator for intermediate inputs accentuates the exaggeration of value added that is introduced by the official real gross output data, which is well-known to be inflated.[14]

The debate over technical efficiency has also diverted attention from other areas of SOE failure: heavy financial burdens on the banking system and the budget of loss-making enterprises; the unworkability of bankruptcy mechanisms; the 'investment hunger' of state enterprises, leading to a proliferation of poor projects; and the high level of corruption and politicisation of the enterprises. These phenomena relate to the absence of bankruptcy, the low risk attached to making bad investments, and the incentives for managers and workers to strip the state enterprise income and assets to their personal benefit (for example, by distributing profits in the form of higher compensation), given the fact that nobody is in place to defend the interests of the enterprise capital. One strong symptom of this is the tendency of the SOEs to distribute higher earnings in the form of fringe benefits (see Xiao 1991c; Hussain and Stern 1991; Fan and Woo 1992; and the report of the China Economic System Reform Research Institute in Reynolds, 1987).

IV. Monetary Management in China and EEFSU

Economic structure is only part of the explanation for the differing performance in China and EEFSU. While reform was inevitably harder in EEFSU, there have been serious self-inflicted wounds in macroeconomic management in several countries in the region, particularly in Russia. China too has faced serious macroeconomic imbalances but has tended to manage them more appropriately and with better results.

Macroeconomic instability plagues virtually all countries in transition from central planning (see McKinnon 1993a). Socialist economies relied overwhelmingly on the collection of revenues from state enterprises. State prices were set as markups on costs in part to assure a surplus for budgetary purposes. Economic reforms tend to undermine revenue collection for two main reasons: state enterprise profits fall as increased competition erodes profit margins and as managers allow workers to capture a larger proportion of enterprise revenues in compensation; and tax collection from the new non-state firms lags behind the flow of resources to the non-state sector, largely because of administrative difficulties.

Table 4 shows the sharp fall in government revenues experienced by China and EEFSU since the early 1980s. Revenue shortfalls lead to increased budget deficits and macroeconomic instability unless compensated by cuts in expenditures or by non-inflationary borrowing. If borrowing is used, there is a risk that a short period of borrowing will be followed by an even greater burst of inflation.

The Chinese government also ran large deficits during the latter half of the 1980s, partly hidden from the budgetary accounts in the form of credits from the central bank to the enterprise sector. We have already noted that the loss-making state enterprise sector imposed a heavy fiscal burden. As shown in Table 5, direct fiscal support came in two forms, price subsidies and enterprise-loss subsidies. In total, these amounted to around 5 per cent of GNP. In addition, the central bank issued credits to the banking system (seigniorage not used for

Table 4 **Decline in fiscal revenues of economies in transition** (fiscal revenues as per cent of GDP)

	China	USSR	Poland	Hungary
1978	34.8	47.1		
1984	26.5	49.6		
1987	22.8	52.8	34.3	59.1
1990	19.9	47.2	32.5	57.4
1991	18.4	35.1	22.8	52.4

Notes: For China, official revenues are corrected by subtracting government borrowing and adding subsidies that were reported as negative revenues. For Poland, starting in 1992, local government budgets are removed from the national budget. In 1991, local government revenues and expenditures amounted to 3.5 per cent of GDP.
Source: *China Statistical Yearbook 1992*; USSR: Alexashenko (1992); Poland: De Crombrugghe and Lipton (1994); Hungary: *IMF data.*

Table 5 **Subsidies and central bank credits to SOEs in China** (per cent of GDP)

	price subsidies	+	enterprise loss subsidies	=	total subsidies	+	central bank credits to banks	=	Total
1978	0.3		3.2		3.5				
1984	3.1		2.9		6.0				
1988	2.2		3.2		5.4		2.6		8.0
1989	2.3		3.7		6.1		2.6		8.7
1990	2.1		3.3		5.4		3.8		9.2
1991	1.9		2.6		4.5		3.4		7.8

Note: To calculate the total resource flow to state-owned enterprise, we assume that half the new central bank credits not financing the central budget deficit are used for financing of state-owned enterprises.
Source: *China Financial Statistics, 1950–1991*; *China Statistical Yearbook 1992*; *Almanac of China's Finance and Banking 1991*; *Annual Report 1991 of The People's Bank of China.*

budgetary finance) of about 6 per cent of GNP. Since a third of SOEs were running open losses and another third were running hidden losses, we estimate that half of the new (nonbudget-related) seigniorage was enterprise loss subsidies. Adding these two forms of support for state enterprises, total fiscal and monetary support came to about 8 per cent of GNP.[15]

China managed these large deficits without an explosive inflation, principally because Chinese households substantially increased their real money balances during the 1980s: seigniorage was collected without inflation. While the ratio of money to GNP collapsed in Russia, it rose sharply in China (Table 6). The Chinese government reaped approximately 8 per cent of GDP in seigniorage each year in the early 1990s, in effect financing the budget deficit and substantial needs of loss-making enterprises through money creation but without inflation.

There are two interrelated phenomena at work: very high saving rates, and a high marginal propensity to hold wealth in the form of bank deposits. The Chinese government maintained positive real interest rates on household bank balances through most of the period (except 1988, when inflation started to accelerate). Overall Chinese saving rates have been extraordinarily high, more than 30 per cent of GNP in the 1980s rising to nearly 40 per cent in the early 1990s. Much of household saving was held as money balances in the state banking system.

V. Some Implications for Further Reforms

Our analysis has helped to expose the limitations of reform to date in China. China was able to avoid the difficult choices of state-enterprise restructuring during the past decade, but that luxury may be disappearing for both macro-economic and microeconomic reasons. On the macroeconomic side, the burdens of the inefficient state enterprise sector have remained large despite the overall rapid growth of the economy. Losses in the state sector amount to about 8 per cent of GNP, when hidden subsidies in the form of state credits are added to overt budgetary subsidies. Until now, China has been able to pay for these losses through extensive seigniorage, as households accumulated remarkably large money balances in the state banking system. This option may be over, as households now seek to hold more of their portfolios in non-monetary assets, an option increasingly available in the liberalised economy. If the demand for real balances peaks, as seems likely, or even starts to decline, urgent budgetary adjustments will become necessary, and state enterprise reform will take centre stage.

Microeconomic problems are also exposing the reforms to new dangers. A major problem is the significant widening of the income gap between urban and rural workers in recent years after the spurt of higher agricultural productivity

Table 6	**Money M2** (per cent of GDP)					
	1979	1985	1989	1990	1991	1992
China	37.5	60.8	74.6	86.5	97.8	106.1
Russia				67.7	59.8	16.6

Note: Russian 1992 data is for June 1992.
Source: *China Statistical Yearbook 1992; Almanac of China's Finance and Banking 1991; Annual Report 1991 of The People's Bank of China, Russian Economic Trends, 1991, 1992.*

after 1978 came to an end in 1985. The widening of the gap has been exacerbated by continued restrictions on migration from the countryside, special privileges granted to non-agricultural regions (for example, foreign-exchange retention rights of non-state enterprises in the coastal areas), the increased ability of capital to flow from poor agricultural regions to wealthy coastal regions, and the falling relative prices of foodstuffs in recent years. While it is hard to judge, absolute living standards in the countryside may actually have declined in the past couple of years.[16] In 1993 there was a surge of rural protest against the prevailing economic conditions.

Conditions in the TVEs and state industries show the limitations of China's muddled property rights. Privatisation of large state-owned enterprises is coming to the fore in view of the continued failures of SOE reform in the past 10 years. The continued losses of SOEs despite rapid economic growth in 1992–93 is the clearest sign that SOE problems are chronic, not cyclical. The larger TVEs are outgrowing their peculiar and ill-defined collective ownership structure. There are widespread attempts to re-register TVEs as joint-stock companies to give an adequate long-term basis for growth. According to widespread reports, official and unofficial, corruption is rampant, in significant part because of the lack of clarity in ownership rights. 'Spontaneous privatisation', in which managers redefine part of state property as their own, has reached alarming proportions (Yang 1993).[17]

The TVEs in southern Jiangsu which received wide attention in the 1980s for being successful despite being tightly controlled by the local authorities are now facing financial difficulties. 'Ambiguous property relationship' has been identified as the source of their poor performance, and the authorities have been leasing and selling deficit-ridden TVEs by auction since mid 1992.[18]

The largest reform challenges in Russia and China, however, will almost surely be political: how to establish stable, legitimate political systems in vast countries undergoing rapid change. Both countries face the profound task of defining relations between a weakening central government and strengthening regional governments, which threaten to undermine even basic fiscal stability at the center. China's long-term political crisis is likely to be more grave than Russia's. Russia seems fitfully to be on the path to democratic government, though of course the ultimate success of multiparty democracy is still in question. In authoritarian China, struggling with rapid change, macroeconomic tensions, and widening income disparities by regions and sector, the path to long-term political stability seems even less clear.

Appendix: Intersectoral mobility and the political economy of subsidies

There are three sectors of the economy: peasant agriculture (subscript a), state-owned industry (s), and the non-state sector (n). For simplicity imagine that output Q in each sector is produced just with labour L, though the analysis applies equally to problems of intersectoral mobility of other factors as well. Thus

$$Q_i = \theta_i L_i \quad i = a, s, n \quad \text{(A.1)}$$

where θ_i is the marginal product of labour in sector i. Assume $\theta_a < \theta_s < \theta_n$. For simplicity ignore the demand side, by assuming that relative prices are fixed (for example, at world levels), and by choice of units we set $p_a = p_s = p_n = 1$. The labour force L is divided among the three sectors

$$L = L_a + L_s + L_n \quad \text{(A.2)}$$

and $\lambda_i = L_i/L$ is the proportion of labour in each sector. Prior to reform the non-state sector is repressed ($\lambda_n = 0$). In China, λ_s was initially 0.2, in EEFSU it was 0.8. In the short run, labour markets are segmented; labour flows gradually between sectors in response to post-tax wage differentials and capacity constraints in each sector.

State enterprises are highly favoured by subsidies, directed credits, centralised investments, and priority access to underpriced (and therefore scarce) inputs; the 'soft budget constraint' that allows state-owned enterprises to pay wages far in excess of productivity and to maintain employment despite a shortfall in demand for the enterprise's output. In China, the system of privileged employment in the state sector is dubbed the 'iron rice bowl'. We assume that subsidisation is equivalent to an employment subsidy σ. State enterprises pay a gross wage $\theta_s + \sigma$. These high-paying jobs are rationed, with the limit determined by the amount of capital in the state enterprise sector (not explicitly shown). Therefore, we consider cases where λ_s can fall but cannot rise.

The total subsidy $S = \sigma L_s$ must be paid by society. We assume a specific tax levied on all workers at rate τ such that $\tau L = S$. Hence $\tau = \sigma \lambda_s$. After-tax wages in the non-state and agricultural sectors are given by $\theta_i - \tau$ where $i = n, a$. Workers in all sectors bear the cost of the soft budget constraint in the state-owned industry. In most economies in transition, at least part of the tax has been implicit: industrial subsidies are frequently financed by inflationary central bank credits to industry, and indirectly by central bank credits to the government to cover budgetary subsidies to industry.

Social welfare is maximised when all workers shift to the non-state sector, where productivity is highest. However, if the subsidy σ exceeds the productivity differential $(\theta_n - \theta_s)$, then after-tax wages w are given by

$$w_s = \theta_s + \sigma - \tau > w_n = \theta_n - \tau > w_a = \theta_a - \tau \quad (A.3)$$

After-tax wages are highest in state-owned industry, whose workers will not wish to move to new private firms. Since employment is limited by available capacity, peasant cultivators will wish to move to the state sector but no such jobs will be available; however peasants will still wish to move into jobs in the new private sector now that intersectoral mobility has been legalised.

When the state sector is large, as in EEFSU, it is likely that $(\theta_n - \theta_s)/(1 - \lambda_s) > \sigma$, so that

$$\theta_n > \theta_s + \sigma(1 - \lambda_s) > \theta_n - \sigma \lambda_s \quad (A.4)$$

When (A.4) holds, workers will not voluntarily leave the state sector while the subsidy remains, but will be made better off by a complete cancellation of the tax-subsidy scheme combined with a transfer to a job in the non-state sector. However, the initial subsidy to state-sector employment might be so high that the first inequality in (A.4) does not hold. Then state-enterprise workers will oppose an elimination of the tax-subsidy scheme even if it is combined with a transfer to a more productive job in the non-state sector. Such is certainly the case with the subsidies received by the senior communist *nomenklatura*, many of whom therefore remain implacable foes of subsidy cutbacks.

Suppose the subsidy-tax scheme is abolished and that (A.4) holds, but that the flow of labour among sectors takes time. Before labour starts to move between sectors, workers initially in agriculture and non-state sectors will benefit, while state-sector workers suffer because the taxes had been paid by all and the benefits had been reaped only by state workers. As workers move to the non-state sector, they end up with a real wage above that in the pre-reform period, while workers remaining behind in the state sector continue to lag behind their pre-reform real wage, at least initially.

Can workers that remain be made better off by a cut in their subsidy? Yes, if the tax cut that corresponds to the subsidy cut is enough to compensate them, as, for example, if the subsidy cut is partial rather than complete and enough workers flow from the state sector to the non-state sector as a result of the subsidy cut. Consider an initial situation with parameters σ, τ, λ_s. The wage level net of taxes and subsidies is $\theta_s + \sigma - \tau$, or $\theta_s + (1 - \lambda_s)$ since $\tau = \lambda_s \sigma$. Now cut σ to a level $\sigma^* < \sigma$ so that the inequality in the first part of (A.3) is reversed. Workers start to exit the state sector. If $(\theta_n - \theta_s) > \sigma^* > \sigma(1 - \lambda_s)$, there exists a value λ_s^* such that if the share of state employment falls below λ_s^*, then

$$\theta_s + \sigma^* - \tau^* = \theta_s + (1 - \lambda_s^*)\sigma^*$$

$$> \theta_s + (1 - \lambda_s)\sigma = \theta_s + \sigma - g \qquad (A.5)$$

When (A.5) holds, the post-tax wage of workers remaining in the state sector will be higher than before the cut in subsidies.

Taxes that finance subsidies can be so distortionary that workers that remain in the state sector might benefit even from a complete cut in subsidies. For example, if subsidisation is financed by an inflation tax, the damage from high inflation could undermine productivity in the economy so much that even immobile state sector workers benefit from a complete elimination of subsidies combined with an end to inflation.

Notes

1. Singh (1991) asks whether these differences reflect 'a professional schizophrenia on socialist reform'. See Perkins (1992) for a review of Chinese reforms.
2. Singh (1991) argues that China's success raises many challenges to the orthodox views: reforms were partial, incremental, and often experimental; caused no initial downturn; made no use of large scale privatisation; avoided declining incomes and high unemployment; targeted agriculture first; reformed prices and trade controls only gradually; maintained exchange controls; and adopted active industrial policy.
3. In our view, China's gradualism in embracing private ownership and market reforms reflected not an economic judgement on the most effective strategy for the transition, but rather the continuing ideological commitments of China's Communist Party. Xiao (1991d) notes the strong link between non-state ownership and productivity growth across different regions of China. Gradualism also reflected political paralysis caused by disagreements between conservative and pragmatic reformers (see Woo 1993).
4. A clear example is Vietnam, whose gradual reform during 1985–88 failed to address serious macroeconomic imbalances. Output and trade stagnated as inflation took off (Drabek 1990). In 1989 Vietnam adopted a 'big bang', liberalising prices, devaluing 450 per cent to unify the exchange market, sharply tightening credit, and returning collective farms to families with long leases. Growth accelerated, inflation ended, agricultural productivity soared, and small enterprises proliferated outside the state sector (Leipziger 1992; Dollar 1993). Unlike EEFSU, output did not fall after the big bang. As in China, Vietnam enjoyed surplus agricultural labour that flowed to jobs in the new sector. This flow was accelerated not by the gradualism of reform but the adoption of strong market-oriented reforms.
5. Chen and Hu (1993) discuss surplus labour more fully. The *China Daily* (4 June 1993) reported 'At present there are still 130 million surplus farm labourers in the countryside [out of an agricultural labour force of 342 million], according to the Ministry of Agriculture.
6. We emphasise the distribution of labour rather than of capital or output because we focus on the political economy of reform. The focus of labour, not output, also sidesteps problems in interpreting highly distorted prices and hence output values during the period before liberalising.
7. The urban–rural gap was sustained by the household registration system. Until free markets became widespread after 1980, ration coupons for food were dispensed at an individual's permitted place of residency, namely the place of birth. During 1960–80 travel restrictions on the purchase of train tickets further segmented rural and urban labour markets.
8. Similar surges in rice productivity took place in Taiwan after World War II and the Communist Revolution, and in Indonesia after 1966.
9. Distinguishing state from non-state is difficult in both China and Russia. For Russia we treat 'enterprises leased from the state' as state enterprises since the absence of clear ownership allows perverse incentives (for example, asset stripping) to survive. For China we treat township and village enterprises (TVEs) as non-state: although collective organisations, they

operate with a hard budget constraint. This latter classification is standard among Chinese scholars and makes sense here since the hardness of the budget constraint is the chief concern.

10. World Bank (1992).

11. Data in this paragraph from Ahmad and Hussain (1989). The delivery of social services to the poor areas has not improved with the reforms (see for example, World Bank 1992).

12. In a perceptive article before the Soviet collapse, Aslund (1989) stressed the differing political conditions in China and the Soviet Union, especially the absence in the latter of any sense of imminent crisis as a spur for fundamental reforms.

13. Gao Shogquan, Deputy Director of the State System Reform Committee of the State Council (the Cabinet) reported that in the early 1990s one-third of SOEs were explicitly losing money, and another third were making losses that were hidden by creative accounting (Keynote Speech, Conference of Chinese Economic Association of the UK 1992). *China Daily* (26 January 1993) also reported that only one-third of SOEs were profitable in 1992.

14. There is no satisfactory official deflator for intermediate inputs. JRZ construct an index, but it implies that the value added deflator for industrial output fell in the 1980s despite high inflation rates observed throughout the decade. Woo et al. (1993) point out that the official method of calculating real value added produces two opposite biases: overcounting gross output and overcounting intermediate output. They argue that, given the existence of the first bias, JRZ's over-correction of the second bias therefore greatly overstates the growth of real value added in industrial SOEs, giving too optimistic a picture of their productivity growth.

15. Data on enterprise losses and subsidies are incomplete and hard to reconcile. Summing enterprise losses across provinces in 1991 yielded 78 billion yuan, yet a national total of 93 billion yuan is also given. It has been claimed, wrongly, the most subsidies went to the energy sector. In 1990 energy did receive 75 per cent of the loss subsidies to industrial SOEs, but the latter received only 12 per cent of the loss subsidies to all SOEs.

16. Conditions in the countryside vary widely. There is insufficient data on local taxation and other transfers to enable a precise picture to be constructed.

17. This includes money laundering (for example, through Hong Kong); the use of state funds to invest in private firms, in return for which the state manager receives privileged access to shares in the private enterprise; and leasing of SOE facilities to a private firm controlled by the manager.

18. See *China Daily* (2 June 1993; 15 December 1993).

References

Ahmad, E. and Hussain, A., 1989. 'Social Security in China: A Historical Perspective', Development Economic Research Programme, LSE, China Programme No. 4.

Alexashenko, S., 1992. 'The Collapse of the Soviet Fiscal System: What Should Be Done?', mimeo.

Aslund, A., 1989. 'Soviet and Chinese Reforms—Why They Must Be Different', *The World Today*, November.

Berg. A., 1993. 'Radical Transformation of a Socialist Economy: Poland, 1989–91', PhD dissertation, Massachusetts Institute of Technology.

—— and Sachs, J., 1992. 'Structural Adjustment and International Trade in Eastern Europe: the Case of Poland', *Economic Policy*.

Berliner, J., 1993. 'Perestroika and the Chinese Model, Brandeis University, mimeo.

Boone, P., 1992. 'Why Prices Rose So Much: Collapsing Monetary Bubbles in Socialist Transforming Economies', Harvard Institute for International Development, mimeo.

Boycko, M., Shleifer, A. and Vishny, R., 1993. 'Privatising Russia', *Brookings Papers on Economic Activity*.

Brada, J., 1993. 'The Transformation from Communism to Capitalism: How Far? How Fast?', *Post-Soviet Affairs*.

Chen, E., Wong, T., and Wong, P.W., 1991. 'South China Economic Zone: Its Development and Prospect', mimeo.

Chen, J. and Hu, B., 1993. 'China's rural Industrial Development and Surplus Labor Transfer', paper presented at the National Workshop on Rural Industrialisation in Post-Reform China, Beijing.

De Crombrugghe, A. and Lipton, D., 1994. 'The Government Budget and the Transformation of Poland', in J. Sachs, O. Blanchard and K. Froot (eds.), *NBER Conference on Transition in Eastern Europe*, University of Chicago Press, Chicago.

Dollar, D., 1993. 'Macroeconomic Management and the Transition to the Market in Vietnam', presented at the Conference on Transition of Centrally Planned Economies in Pacific Asia, Asia Foundation, San Francisco.

Drabek, Z., 1990. 'A Case Study of a Gradual Approach to Economic Reform: The Vietnam Experience of 1985–98', World Bank Report No. 1 DP74.

Fairbank, J., 1992. *China: A New History*, Harvard University Press, Cambridge, Massachusetts.

Fan, G. and Woo, W.T., 1992. 'Decentralised Socialism and Macroeconomic Stability: Lessons from China', Economic Department Working Paper No. 411, University of California at Davis.

Fischer, S., 1993a. 'Socialist Economic Reform: Lessons of the First Three Years', *American Economic Review*, Papers and Proceedings.

——, 1993b. 'Economic Performance in the FSU, Mid-1993', Aspen Institute, unpublished.

Graham, C., 1992. 'The Political Economy of Safety Nets During Market Transition: The Case of Poland', Brookings Institute.

Hofman, B., 1993. 'Seigniorage and Inflation Tax in China', World Bank, mimeo.

Hussain, A. and Stern, N., 1991. 'Effective Demand, Enterprise Reforms and Public Finance in China', *Economic Policy*.

IMF, 1992. *Economic Review: Russian Federation*.

Jefferson, G., Rawski, T. and Zheng, Y., 1992. 'Growth, Efficiency, and Convergence in China's State and Collective Industry', *Economic Development and Cultural Change*.

Kornai, J., 1986. 'The Hungarian Reform Process: Visions, Hopes and Reality', *Journal of Economic Literature*, 24(4):1687–737.

——, 1992. *The Socialist System*, Princeton University Press, Princeton.

Lardy, N., 1989. 'Technical Change and Economic Reform in China: A Tale of Two Sectors', mimeo.

——, 1992. *Foreign Trade and Economic Reform in China, 1978–1990*, Cambridge University Press, Cambridge.

Leipziger, D., 1992. 'Awakening the Market: Vietnam's Economic Transition', World Bank Development Paper No 157.

Lipton, D. and Sachs, J., 1992. 'Prospects for Russia's Economic Reforms', *Brookings Papers on Economic Activity*, 0(2):213-65.

McKinnon, R., 1993a. 'Gradual versus Rapid Liberalisation in Socialist Economies: Financial Policies and Macroeconomic Stability in China and Russia Compared', presented at the World Bank Conference on Development Economies.

——, 1993b. 'Financial Growth and Macroeconomic Stability in China 1978–92: Implications for Russia and Eastern Europe', presented to the conference on Transition of the Centrally Planned Economies in Pacific Asia, Asia Foundation, San Francisco.

McMillan, J. and Naughton, B., 1992. 'How to Reform a Planned Economy: Lessons from China', *Oxford Review of Economic Policy*.

Nove, A., 1986. *The Soviet Economic System*, Winchester, Unwin Hyman, MA.

Perkins, D., 1992. 'China's "Gradual" Approach to Market Reforms', mimeo.

Qian, Y. and Xu, C., 1993. 'Why China's Economic Reforms Differ: The MacKillop-Form Hierarchy and Entry/Expansion of the Non-State Sector', presented at the Conference on Transition of Centrally Planned Economies in Pacific Asia, Asia Foundation, San Francisco.

Rajewski, Z., 1993. 'National Income', in L. Ziekowski (ed.), *Results of the Polish Economic transformation*, GUS/Polish Academy of Science, Warsaw.

Rawski, T., 1993. 'Progress without Privatisation: the Reform of China's State Industries', mimeo.

Reynolds, B. (ed.), 1987. *Reform in China: Challenges and Choices*, Report of the Chinese Economic System Reform Research Institute, M.E. Sharpe, New York.

Riedel, J., 1993. 'Vietnam: On the Trail of the Tigers', *The World Economy*, 16(4):401–22.

Rostowski, J., 1993. 'The Implications of Very Rapid Private Sector Growth in Poland', University College, London, mimeo.

Sachs, J., 1993. *Poland's Jump to the Market Economy*, MIT Press, Cambridge, Massachusetts.

Singh, I., 1991. 'China and Central and Eastern Europe: Is there a Professional Schizophrenia on Socialist Reform?', Socialist Economics Reform Unit, Research Paper No. 17, World Bank, Washington, DC.

Winiecki, J., 1993. 'Knowledge of Soviet-Type Economy and "Heterodox" Stabilisation-Based Outcomes in Eastern Europe', *Weltwirtschaftliches Archiv*, 129(2):384–410.

Wong, C., 1986. 'Ownership and Control in Chinese Industry: The Maoist Legacy and Prospects for the 1980s', in *China's Economy Looks Towards the Year 2000*, Joint Economic Committee, US Congress, Washington, DC.

Woo, W.T., 1993. 'The Art of Reforming Centrally-Planned Economies: Comparing China, Poland, and Russia', mimeo, University of California, Davis.

——, Hai, W., Jin, Y. and Fan, G., 1993. 'How Successful has Chinese Enterprise Reform Been? Pitfalls in Opposite Biases and Focus', University of California, Davis, mimeo.

World Bank, 1990. *China: Reforming Social Security in a Socialist Economy*, World Bank, Washington, DC.

——, 1992. *China: Strategies for Reducing Poverty in the 1990s*, World Bank, Washington, DC.

Xiao, G., 1991a. 'Property Rights Arrangements and Industrial Productivity in China', Socialist Economies Reform Unit, World Bank.

——, 1991b. 'The Economic Role of Chinese Central and Local Governments: Challenges and Opportunities from the State and Non-State Industrial Enterprises', Socialist Economies Reform Unit, World Bank, Washington, DC.

——, 1991c. 'Managerial Autonomy, Fringe Benefits, and Ownership Structure—A Comparative Study of Chinese State and Collective Enterprises', Socialist Economies Reform Unit, World Bank, Washington, DC.

——, 1991d. 'What is Special About China's Economic Reform?', Socialist Economies Reform Unit, World Bank, Washington, DC.

Yang, X., 1993. 'Report on Conference on China's Reforms, Hainan Island, China', Monash University, Melbourne, mimeo.

Zweig, D., 1989. *Agrarian Radicalism in China, 1968–1981*, Harvard University Press, Cambridge, Massachusetts.

30 Challenges of China's Economic System for Economic Theory

Gregory C. Chow

The challenges of the market economy in China for economic theory touch on four topics: private versus public ownership of assets, Western legal systems versus Eastern semiformal legal systems, individualism versus the collective good, and multiparty versus one-party political systems. I came in contact with these issues while advising the government of Taiwan in the 1960s and 1970s, and the government of mainland China in the 1980s and 1990s (see Chow 1994:Ch. 4–5). Others have studied these issues as scholars, including Patrick Bolton (1990), Bolton and Philippe Aghion (1992), Masahiko Aoki and Hyung-Ki Kim (1995), and Oliver Hart (1995).

I. Private versus Public Ownership

China is an interesting experimental station for both public and private enterprises, as state-owned enterprises coexist with collectively owned enterprises (many by township and villages) and private enterprises (owned individually, by foreign corporations, or jointly with foreign corporations). Some state-owned enterprises, especially those having joint ventures with foreign corporations, appear to be efficient, as they are financially independent and are making large profits. Many collectively owned township and village enterprises are successful in increasing output and making profits. The successful experience of the township and village enterprises in China is sufficient to challenge the dogma that only private enterprises in a capitalist economy can be efficient.

Most assets in China are publicly owned, by the central government, by provincial and local governments, and by villages as collectives. Incentive systems have been adopted to make the management of these assets efficient. The most prevalent is leasing, known as the 'responsibility system'. Notable examples are leasing of land by the village to farm households and the leasing of enterprises of all kinds by different levels of government. The terms of the lease include fixed rents and forms of profit-sharing. In all cases there is a positive relation between profits of the enterprise and the economic benefits of the management and workers. Providing incentives for the management of publicly owned assets is a key to China's success.

In a private communication, Milton Friedman questioned the above statement; 'Most

Reprinted with permission. Gregory C. Chow, 1997. 'Challenges of China's economic system for economic theory', *American Economic Review*, 87(2):321–27 (with minor editing).

assets in China are publicly owned'. Two kinds of 'assets' need to be distinguished. Land as an asset is publicly owned. The enterprise managed by a farm household using the land is privately owned. This private enterprise leases a piece of publicly owned land to produce and make profits, as in a capitalist society, but the government or village authority owns the piece of land under a Chinese socialist system. Publicly owned assets consist mainly of land, state enterprises, and township and village enterprises. The government can lease a state enterprise to a manager who operates it for profit. The advantages and disadvantages for the manager to own rather than to rent the enterprise from the government are discussed in Hart (1995).

In addition to managing existing assets, government units at different levels have created new enterprises. Even universities as public institutions have created and own enterprises, some selling research and consulting services, and others selling products produced in factories run by faculty members.

An example of this outside China is Ex Libris, a library software firm owned by Hebrew University in Jerusalem. Ownership by a public institution in China confers advantages to the enterprise, including the institution's reputation, personnel, and physical assets, which the enterprise can share. Possible disadvantages of public ownership might be the social costs associated with monopoly power. However, publicly owned enterprises in China are subject to competition from other public enterprises and from private enterprises as well.

Theories to explain the efficiency of Chinese state enterprises are found in Theodore Groves et al. (1994, 1995), who appeal to the improved incentives provided for the management and workers of these enterprises. Operating losses in state enterprises may be the result of antiquated capital, slow adaptation of management to a new market environment, or the government's responsibility to provide employment to workers, and not of state-ownership per se. Causes of losses in Chinese state enterprises are studied by Athar Hussain and Juzhong Zhuang (1996).

Theories to explain the efficiency of township and village enterprises are found in Martin L. Weitzman and Chenggang Xu (1994), C. Chang and Y. Wang (1994), Jiahua Che (1996), and David D. Li (1996). Weitzman and Xu (1994) appeal to the cooperative nature of Chinese culture, Chang and Wang (1994) and Li (1996) to the economic power of local governments or their officials, and Che (1996) to the creditworthiness of local governments. Weitzman and Xu (1994) and Li (1996) allow for ownership right being vague, an issue related to the subject of Section II. A related subject is corruption, as studied by Susanto Basu and Li (1996). Rewards to government officials could provide incentives not only to promote economic reform, as discussed in Roger H. Gordon and Li (1995), but also to facilitate enterprise operations.

Once the ownership of an enterprise is separated from its management, as in a modern corporation, the incentive of the management to pursue profits for the owners becomes problematic. Corporate governance issues in the context of public enterprises are important topics for research. Some important issues concerning publicly versus privately owned enterprises are treated in Aoki and Kim (1995) and in Hart (1995). The latter provides a useful discussion of 'Firms, Contracts and Financial Structure' and notes two features of an economic relationship (Hart 1995:3): 'The first is that contracts are incomplete. The second is that, because of this, the ex post allocation of power (or control) matters. Here power refers roughly to the position of each party if the other party does not perform (for example, if the other party behaves opportunistically).' Hart's theories are relevant for the topic of Section II on modern legal system versus the informal Chinese system in terms of solving the ex post allocation of power and for explaining the possible advantages of the township and village enterprises. These advantages stem from the local government's power to enforce contracts and from the credibility of such a 'public' enterprise in raising funds as compared with an entirely private enterprise.

II. Modern Legal System

A modern legal system as practised in a Western developed economy is sometimes considered essential for the proper functioning of a market economy. The non-Western legal system in China is considered deficient by Western investors and economists. Although it might be called a 'semilegal system', it is definitely a legal system, as law has been practised in China for several thousand years. However, this system is different from legal systems in the West. One major difference is that under Chinese law a contract is enforced partly by an informal social relationship known as *guanxi*. *Guanxi* plays an important role in ensuring that a contract is honoured.

First, there is a question as to whether all contracts should be strictly enforced. An economic answer is that, given an objective function, there is some optimum degree for enforcing contracts to balance the costs and benefits. A formal model to determine the optimum degree would be useful. Second, granted that it is advantageous to have a certain contract enforced, there is the question of enforcement through legal means versus enforcement through *guanxi*. *Guanxi* is a network of human relationships which sets the rules of behaviour among the parties concerned. When applied to two individuals engaging in certain business dealings it is like a handshake accompanied by a verbal or written agreement for each party to do something in the future contingent on the occurrence of certain events. The events might involve the sale of certain merchandise for profit. The agreement stipulates how profits should be shared. The judicial system need not be relied upon to enforce such an agreement. The high cost of enforcement under the American legal system suggests that perhaps there is some advantage in enforcement partly by an informal network. Third, given the fact that not all contingencies can be anticipated and written down explicitly, how complete should a contract be? In areas where the contract is vague, should disputes be settled by legal means or by informal relations?

What explains the appearance of the semi-legal system (with the other half being supplied by the informal network) in China and some other Asian countries and the modern legal system that appeared in the West after the Industrial Revolution? What are the circumstances that make the informal system work? The Chinese government has been trying to modernise its legal system to make it resemble that of a Western country, partly for the convenience of Western investors and partly to enable Chinese producers and traders to enter the world market. This does not necessarily mean that the current legal system works poorly for China's internal economic development. At least the system is not so bad that it hindered the rapid economic growth that has taken place since 1978.

It would be interesting to study the economics of *guanxi* (see Janet Tai Landa and Jing Lu 1997). *Guanxi* is a form of human capital. Having *guanxi* is like having knowledge of which friend would be helpful when needed, having a reputation similar to that conveyed by a college degree, and having a good credit rating. Developing *guanxi* is accumulating human capital just like getting a college degree or promoting a reputable brand name. The service from this form of human capital can supplement legal enforcement of contracts by social pressure. A formal model should explain the relative roles of legal enforcement of contracts and the enforcement through *guanxi*, and the optimum combination of the two in a society.

People in China are sometimes considered insufficiently law-abiding, as in the case of violation of intellectual property rights. The optimum level of enforcement of patent rights in any economy is an interesting question. On the one hand, patent enforcement helps encourage technological innovations. But as a monopoly right, a patent discourages innovations which might infringe upon this right and makes the invented products more expensive to consumers. Opinions on the economic effects of patents differ. For example, the view of Almarin Phillips (1996:302) is 'that a weakening of the patent rights of large corporations…would do little to hinder the 'Progress of Science and useful Arts' and, in some market situations, would be instrumental to these ends'. Patents have been invented partly to service the economic interests of industrial monopolies at the expense of the common people. For example, patent protection for American pharmaceutical companies might have harmful effects in restricting the sales of drugs which cannot be offset by the benefits in encouraging the development of new drugs.

Less than strict enforcement of a law can sometimes be beneficial. Consider a law to make abortion illegal in the United States. Its rationale is to protect the lives of unborn babies, but this law is in conflict with the mothers' right to choose. A solution is to enforce the law less than strictly according to particular circumstances. Such a law would discourage unwanted pregnancy, but if unwanted pregnancy does occur, the right of the woman could be respected. As a second example, birth control by contraceptives was illegal in Massachusetts, but doctors made diaphragms available by placing them on a table and allowing patients to help themselves. The trouble with strict enforcement of a law is that it imposes uniform treatment on all persons, even those who hold different opinions as a matter of their freedom. Less than strict enforcement allows the coexistence of opposite viewpoints in a society. Both Catholics who opposed birth control and other citizens who favoured birth control benefited from a less-than-strict enforcement of the law in Massachusetts. Two other examples of laws for which selective enforcement may be beneficial are the law prohibiting suicide and the legalisation of the death penalty. In the case of the death penalty, the governor is given the authority to make an exception to strict enforcement. Economists need to re-examine the relationship between the Western legal system and the effective functioning of a market economy. What features of the Western legal system are essential, and under what circumstances?

It is said that China is ruled by people and not by law. This statement does not necessarily imply that the Chinese system is bad. A State Department official having had dealings with the Chinese once remarked to me that 'After signing a contract, the Chinese often regard the provisions in the contract as a starting point for further negotiations'. Referring to a personal contractual experience, Hart (1995:2) remarks 'In fact, the contract is best seen as providing a suitable backdrop or starting point in the United States for such renegotiations rather than specifying the final outcome'. A formal legal system does not necessarily solve the problems which the institution of informal personal relationships may be able to solve.

III. Individual versus Collective Welfare

Individualism is an ideal in a Western market economy, as expounded by F.A. Hayek (1949). This ideal is not generally accepted in Asian countries. Individual rights may be in conflict with the common good. Economists have learned that under appropriate conditions the pursuit of individual self-interest in the marketplace can lead to efficient social output, an ideal well articulated by the Chinese historian Sima Wian (see Young 1996). In Asian societies, the common good is often considered to be more important than individual rights. Not only is individual freedom restricted, but members of a society are educated to serve the society. The society is more than a collection of individuals. Hence the welfare of the society is more than the sum of the welfares of its individual members. People in many developing countries are striving for nationalism and may consider the common good and national unity more important than individual rights.

The practice of human rights differs among countries. People in Western societies consider human rights to be violated in Singapore. China does not practise the same kind of human rights as the United States. With the consent of many, and perhaps a majority, of its citizens, the Chinese government considers a high degree of individual freedom and the practise of American-style human rights to be harmful to the common good of the country. Among other things, it makes the enforcement of law and order more difficult. Market economies have functioned with a limited amount of political freedom in mainland China, Taiwan, Singapore, and South Korea.

The welfare economics for a market economy that emphasises the common good deserve further study. Much has been written about the welfare state in which the government provides consumption goods or redistributes income to individual citizens. The pros and cons of welfare programs have been extensively discussed. An important research topic is the modeling of government provision of education for the common good, and not simply for the private needs of individual citizens as in the case of many welfare programs. Three key questions are raised in welfare economics. First, how is a welfare function defined for an individual citizen or family, for a collection of citizens, and for a political organisation? Second, how are the welfare functions of different economic and political entities in the society formed? Third, by what process do the welfare objectives of these entities affect the economic outcome in the society? When the collective good is emphasised, answers to these questions may be different from those given under an individualistic society.

Consider the determination of the education levels of the citizens for example. For a purely individualistic society, the welfare function of each citizen or family might be assumed to have its own level of education as the only argument, and the welfare function of the government may be assumed to be an aggregation of the individual welfare functions obtained by some weighting scheme. When collectivism is emphasised, the education levels of other citizens and perhaps some aggregates of these levels also enter the welfare function of each citizen. Furthermore, the welfare function of the government may depend not only on the individual welfare functions, but on some measure of collective education. In

addition, traditional welfare economics takes welfare functions as given. A collective society tends to motivate its citizens to serve the common good. The formation of welfare functions has to be explained. An American president may choose to motivate citizens to achieve a higher level of education as a national purpose. In a society emphasising the collective good, government leadership is stronger, and its effects require more careful study. Finally, the process by which a given set of individual and government welfare functions affects the economic outcomes may differ according to the degree of individualism versus collectivism in the society. In the next section, possible differences in this process due to the institution of a one-party versus a two-party political system will be discussed.

IV. Multiparty versus One-party Systems

What is the relationship between a multiparty political system and a market economy? The answer is not simple. A one-party political system is consistent with a market economy, as evident from the institutions in mainland China, Taiwan (until recently), South Korea, and Singapore, all of which practise a one-party system. Although Japan had a multiparty system, the country was ruled by the Liberal Democratic Party from 1958 to 1994. A multi-party democratic system is also not required for the practice of human rights. Human rights have been practised in Hong Kong under British rule, but there has not been a democracy, because government officials have not been elected by the Hong Kong people until very recently, and then only to a very limited extent. Democracy in the sense of a government of the people, for the people, and by the people can be practised under a one-party rule. Sun Yat-sen tried to form a democratic government in China under the leadership of the Nationalist party and later asked the Communist Party to joint when Soviet help was needed.

The study of the relationship between an economic system and the associated political system is an interesting topic. The development of Western countries, along with the increase in economic power of a large segment of the population, gradually led to democratic government, as the rich citizens demanded more rights to govern their own destiny. As the Chinese people become richer and more educated, they will demand more political rights from the government. Under a one-party system, political representation of the people in China through elected members of the People's Congress has been strengthened in the past decade. What forms of political institutions are likely to emerge from the current practice of a market economy in China?

Several topics concerning the relationship between a democratic government and economic behaviour can be mentioned. In macroeconomics, the outcomes of elections and business cycles are interrelated, one affecting the other, as studied by Ray C. Fair (1988) and others. In political economy, Avinash Dixit and John Londregan (1996) have provided a model for the determination of the income transfers to each group of voters under a two-party system. The social-welfare-function for each voter or party is a (voter or party-specific) weighted average of the economy's deadweight loss and the population variance of consumption. A voter in each group maximises her objective function, which is a (group-specific) weighted average of the consumption level of the group and the individual's own social welfare. Each political party maximises its objective function, which is a (party-specific) weighted average of its vote share and its social-welfare function by choosing an income-transfer strategy that will produce a particular vector of final consumptions for all groups. The final consumption vector is determined in a Nash equilibrium as each party maximises its objective taking the other party's strategy as given. How is income redistribution determined under a one-party political system

in which elected representatives in a congress can enact laws on tax and transfers? Possibly the above model may be relevant if the party proposes two candidates who behave like the two parties in the model. Alternatively, one may model the economy as if the government maximises an objective function while each group of voters can propose a final consumption schedule, as in Gene M. Grossman and Elhanan Helpman (1994), or simply vote yes or no to a government strategy, as in Grossman and Helpman (1995). The government's objective function can be similar to the objective function of the party, as in Dixit and Londregan (1996), or may include political contributions as in Grossman and Helpman (1994). There are other possibilities, depending on institutional realities.

What are the effects of democratic politics on economic growth? Some citizens in Hong Kong are concerned that introducing democratic politics might affect the current flat tax system which provides incentives for entrepreneurship. Some economists in Taiwan have stated that the recent introduction of a multiparty system has made rational government economic decision-making difficult and thus hinders economic growth. What is the statistical relationship between the rate of growth of different countries and the number of political parties or the practice of democracy? Can economic analysis shed light on this question?

In this paper I have stated a number of questions worthy of further economic research. These questions have been stimulated by the reality of recent economic developments in China. China's economic institutions are evolving, but some features may be long-lasting, and the existing institutions provide ample challenges for research. In further economics textbooks, China, Russia, and Eastern European countries will appear more frequently in the index. The American economics profession is in the process of internationalisation, as is the American economy itself.

References

Aoki, Masahiko and Kim, Hyung-ki., 1995. *Corporate Governance in Transitional Economics: Insider control and the role of banks*, World Bank, Washington, DC.

Basu, Susanto and Li, David D., 1996. 'Corruption and Reform', Mimeo, University of Michigan.

Bolton, Patrick, 1990. 'Renegotiations and the Dynamics of Contract Design', *European Economic Review*, May, 34(23):303–10.

—— and Aghion, P., 1992. 'An Incomplete Contracts Approach to Financial Contracting', *Review of Economic Studies*, July, 59(3):473–94, represented in Michael J. Brennan, ed., 1996. *The Theory of Corporate Finance*, Elgar, Cheltenham, UK:381-402.

Chang, C. and Wang, Y., 1994. 'The Nature of the Township—Village Enterprises', *Journal of Comparative Economics*, December, 19(3):434–52.

Che, Jiahua, 1996. 'Township Village Enterprises: An Organizational Approach in Investment Finance', Mimeo, University of Notre Dame.

Chow, Gregory C., 1994. *Understanding China's Economy*, World Scientific Publishing, Singapore.

Dixit, Avinash and Londregan, John, 1996. 'Ideology, tactics, and Efficiency in redistributive Politics', Mimeo, Princeton University.

Fair, Ray C., 1988. 'The Effect of Economic Event on Votes for President: 1984 Update', *Political Behaviour*, Summer, 10(2):1668–79.

Gordon, Roger H. and Li, David, 1995. 'Government Incentives and Policies During the Transition in China and Eastern Europe', Mimeo, University of Michigan.

Grossman, Gene M. and Helpman, Elhanan, 1994. 'Protection for Sale', *American Economic Review*, September, 85(4):833–50.

——, 1995. 'The Politics of Free Trade Agreements', *American Economic Review*, September, 85(4):667–90.

Groves, Theodore, Hong, Yongmiao, McMillan, John and Naughton, Barry, 1994. 'Autonomy and Incentives in Chinese State Enterprises', *Quarterly Journal of Economics*, February, 109(1):183–209.

——, 1995. 'China Evolving Managerial Labor Market', *Journal of Political Economy*, August, 103(4):873–92.

Hart, Oliver, 1995. *Firms, Contracts and Financial Structure*, Oxford University Press, Oxford.

Hayek, F.A., 1949. *Individualism and Economic Order*, University of Chicago Press, Chicago.

Hussain, Athar and Zhuang, Juzhong, 1996. 'Pattern and Causes of Loss-Making in Chinese State Enterprises', Working Paper, Economic and Social Research Council, London School of Economics.

Landa, Janet Tai and Lu, Jing, 1997. 'The Economics of Connections (*Guanxi*) in China's Emerging Markets', Unpublished manuscript, York University (presented at the Allied Social Science Associations meeting, New Orleans, LA).

Li, David D., 1996. 'Ambiguous Property Rights in Transitional Economics: The Case of the Chinese Non-state Sector', *Journal of Comparative Economics*, August, 23(1):1–19.

Phillips, Almarin, 1966. 'Patents, Potential Compensation, and Technical Progress', *American Economic Review*, May (papers and proceedings), 66(2):301–10.

Weitzman, Martin I., and Xu, Chenggang, 1994. 'Chinese Township-Village Enterprises as Vaguely Defined Cooperatives', *Journal of Comparative Economics*, April, 18(2)121–45.

Young, Leslie, 1996. 'The Tao of Markets: Sima Qian and the Invisible Hand', *Pacific Economic Review*, September, 1(2):137–46.

Index